Spreadsheet Modeling
And
Decision Analysis

Cliff T. Ragsdale

THOMSON ™

Australia · Canada · Mexico · Singapore · Spain · United Kingdom · United States

Spreadsheet Modeling and Decision Analysis
Cliff T. Ragsdale

Executive Editors:
Michele Baird, Maureen Staudt &
Michael Stranz

Project Development Manager:
Linda de Stefano

Marketing Coordinators:
Lindsay Annett and Sara Mercurio

Production/Manufacturing
Supervisor:
Donna M. Brown

Pre-Media Services Supervisor:
Dan Plofchan

Rights and Permissions Specialists:
Kalina Hintz and Bahman Naraghi

Cover Image
Getty Images*

The Adaptable Courseware Program consists of products and additions to existing Thomson products that are produced from camera-ready copy. Peer review, class testing, and accuracy are primarily the responsibility of the author(s).

ISBN-13: 978-0-324-43515-6
ISBN-10: 0-324-43515-0

International Divisions List

Asia (Including India):
Thomson Learning
(a division of Thomson Asia Pte Ltd)
5 Shenton Way #01-01
UIC Building
Singapore 068808
Tel: (65) 6410-1200
Fax: (65) 6410-1208

Australia/New Zealand:
Thomson Learning Australia
102 Dodds Street
Southbank, Victoria 3006
Australia

Tel 34 (0)91 446-3350

Latin America:
Thomson Learning
Seneca 53
Colonia Polano
11560 Mexico, D.F., Mexico
Tel (525) 281-2906
Fax (525) 281-2656

Canada:
Thomson Nelson
1120 Birchmount Road
Toronto, Ontario
Canada M1K 5G4
Tel (416) 752-9100
Fax (416) 752-8102
Fax 34 (0)91 445-6218

UK/Europe/Middle East/Africa:
Thomson Learning
High Holborn House
50-51 Bedford Row
London, WC1R 4LS
United Kingdom
Tel 44 (020) 7067-2500
Fax 44 (020) 7067-2600

Spain (Includes Portugal):
Thomson Paraninfo
Calle Magallanes 25
28015 Madrid
España

TABLE OF CONTENTS

Chapter 1

Introduction to Modeling and Decision Analysis

1.0 Introduction

This book is titled *Spreadsheet Modeling and Decision Analysis: A Practical Introduction to Management Science*, so let's begin by discussing exactly what this title means. By the very nature of life, all of us must continually make decisions that we hope will solve problems and lead to increased opportunities for ourselves or the organizations for which we work. But making good decisions is rarely an easy task. The problems faced by decision makers in today's competitive, fast-paced business environment are often extremely complex and can be addressed by numerous possible courses of action. Evaluating these alternatives and choosing the best course of action represents the essence of decision analysis.

During the past decade, millions of business people discovered that one of the most effective ways to analyze and evaluate decision alternatives involves using electronic spreadsheets to build computer models of the decision problems they face. A computer model is a set of mathematical relationships and logical assumptions implemented in a computer as a representation of some real-world decision problem or phenomenon. Today, electronic spreadsheets provide the most convenient and useful way for business people to implement and analyze computer models. Indeed, most business people probably would rate the electronic spreadsheet as their most important analytical tool apart from their brain! Using a spreadsheet model (a computer model implemented via a spreadsheet), a business person can analyze decision alternatives before having to choose a specific plan for implementation.

This book introduces you to a variety of techniques from the field of management science that can be applied in spreadsheet models to assist in the decision-analysis process. For our purposes, we will define management science as a field of study that uses computers, statistics, and mathematics to solve business problems. It involves applying the methods and tools of science to management and decision making. It is the science of making better decisions. Management science is also sometimes referred to as operations research or decision science. See Figure 1.1 for a summary of how management science has been applied successfully in several real-world situations.

In the not too distant past, management science was a highly specialized field that generally could be practiced only by those who had access to mainframe computers and who possessed an advanced knowledge of mathematics and computer programming languages. However, the proliferation of powerful personal computers (PCs) and the development of easy-to-use electronic spreadsheets have made the tools of management science far more practical and available to a much larger audience. Virtually

FIGURE 1.1

Examples of successful management science applications

Home Runs in Management Science

Over the past decade, scores of operations research and management science projects saved companies millions of dollars. Each year, the Institute For Operations Research and the Management Sciences (INFORMS) sponsors the Franz Edelman Awards competition to recognize some of the most outstanding OR/MS projects during the past year. Here are some of the "home runs" from the 2004 Edelman Awards (described in *Interfaces*, Vol. 31, No. 1, January–February, 2005).

- At the turn of the century, **Motorola** faced a crisis due to economic conditions in its marketplaces; the company needed to reduce costs dramatically and quickly. A natural target was its purchases of goods and services, as these expenses account for more than half of Motorola's costs. Motorola decided to create an Internet-based system to conduct multi-step negotiations and auctions for supplier negotiation. The system can handle complex bids and constraints, such as bundled bids, volume-based discounts, and capacity limits. In addition, it can optimize multi-product, multi-vendor awards subject to these constraints and nonlinear price schedules. **Benefits:** In 2003, Motorola used this system to source 56 percent of its total spending, with 600 users and a total savings exceeding $600 million.

- **Waste Management** is the leading company in North America in the waste-collection industry. The company has a fleet of over 26,000 vehicles for collecting waste from nearly 20 million residential customers, plus another two million commercial customers. To improve trash collection and make its operations more efficient, Waste Management implemented a vehicle-routing application to optimize its collection routes. **Benefits:** The successful deployment of this system brought benefits including the elimination of nearly 1,000 routes within one year of implementation and an estimated annual savings of $44 million.

- Hong Kong has the world's busiest port. Its largest terminal operator, **Hong Kong International Terminals** (HIT), has the busiest container terminal in the world serving over 125 ships per week, with 10 berths at which container ships dock, and 122 yard cranes to move containers around the 227 acres of storage yard. Thousands of trucks move containers into and out of the storage yard each day. HIT implemented a decision-support system (with several embedded decision models and algorithms) to guide its operational decisions concerning the number and deployment of trucks for moving containers, the assignment of yard cranes, and the storage locations for containers. **Benefits:** The cumulative effect of this system has led to a 35 percent reduction in container handling costs, a 50 percent increase in throughput, and a 30 percent improvement in vessel turnaround time.

- The **John Deere Company** sells lawn equipment, residential and commercial mowers, and utility tractors through a network of 2,500 dealers, supported by five Deere warehouses. Each dealer stocks about 100 products, leading to approximately 250,000 product-stocking locations. Furthermore, demand is quite seasonal and stochastic. Deere implemented a system designed to optimize large-scale multi-echelon, non-stationary stochastic inventory systems. Deere runs the system each week to obtain recommended stocking levels for each product for each stocking location for each week over a 26-week planning horizon. **Benefits:** The impact of the application has been remarkable, leading to an inventory reduction of nearly one billion dollars and improving customer-service levels.

everyone who uses a spreadsheet today for model building and decision making is a practitioner of management science—whether they realize it or not.

1.1 The Modeling Approach to Decision Making

The idea of using models in problem solving and decision analysis is really not new, and certainly is not tied to the use of computers. At some point, all of us have used a modeling approach to make a decision. For example, if you ever have moved into a dormitory, apartment, or house, you undoubtedly faced a decision about how to arrange the furniture in your new dwelling. There probably were several different arrangements to consider. One arrangement might give you the most open space but require that you build a loft. Another might give you less space but allow you to avoid the hassle and expense of building a loft. To analyze these different arrangements and make a decision, you did not build the loft. You more likely built a mental model of the two arrangements, picturing what each looked like in your mind's eye. Thus, a simple mental model is sometimes all that is required to analyze a problem and make a decision.

For more complex decision problems, a mental model might be impossible or insufficient, and other types of models might be required. For example, a set of drawings or blueprints for a house or building provides a visual model of the real-world structure. These drawings help illustrate how the various parts of the structure will fit together when it is completed. A road map is another type of visual model because it assists a driver in analyzing the various routes from one location to another.

You probably also have seen car commercials on television showing automotive engineers using physical models or scale models to study the aerodynamics of various car designs, to find the shape that creates the least wind resistance and maximizes fuel economy. Similarly, aeronautical engineers use scale models of airplanes to study the flight characteristics of various fuselage and wing designs. And civil engineers might use scale models of buildings and bridges to study the strengths of different construction techniques.

Another common type of model is a mathematical model, which uses mathematical relationships to describe or represent an object or decision problem. Throughout this book we will study how various mathematical models can be implemented and analyzed on computers using spreadsheet software. But before we move to an in-depth discussion of spreadsheet models, let's look at some of the more general characteristics and benefits of modeling.

1.2 Characteristics and Benefits of Modeling

Although this book focuses on mathematical models implemented in computers via spreadsheets, the examples of non-mathematical models given earlier are worth discussing a bit more because they help illustrate several important characteristics and benefits of modeling in general. First, the models mentioned earlier are usually simplified versions of the object or decision problem they represent. To study the aerodynamics of a car design, we do not need to build the entire car complete with engine and stereo. Such components have little or no effect on aerodynamics. So, although a model is often a simplified representation of reality, the model is useful as long as it is valid. A valid model is one that accurately represents the relevant characteristics of the object or decision problem being studied.

Second, it is often less expensive to analyze decision problems using a model. This is especially easy to understand with respect to scale models of big-ticket items such as cars and planes. Besides the lower financial cost of building a model, the analysis of a model can help avoid costly mistakes that might result from poor decision making. For example, it is far less costly to discover a flawed wing design using a scale model of an aircraft than after the crash of a fully loaded jetliner.

Frank Brock, former executive vice president of the Brock Candy Company, related the following story about blueprints his company prepared for a new production facility. After months of careful design work he proudly showed the plans to several of his production workers. When he asked for their comments, one worker responded, "It's a fine looking building, Mr. Brock, but that sugar valve looks like it's about twenty feet away from the steam valve." "What's wrong with that?" asked Brock. "Well, nothing," said the worker, "except that I have to have my hands on both valves at the same time!"[1] Needless to say, it was far less expensive to discover and correct this "little" problem using a visual model before pouring the concrete and laying the pipes as originally planned.

Third, models often deliver needed information on a more timely basis. Again, it is relatively easy to see that scale models of cars or airplanes can be created and analyzed more quickly than their real-world counterparts. Timeliness is also an issue when vital data will not become available until later. In these cases, we might create a model to help predict the missing data to assist in current decision making.

Fourth, models are frequently helpful in examining things that would be impossible to do in reality. For example, human models (crash dummies) are used in crash tests to see what might happen to an actual person if a car were to hit a brick wall at a high speed. Likewise, models of DNA can be used to visualize how molecules fit together. Both of these are difficult, if not impossible, to do without the use of models.

Finally, and probably most important, models allow us to gain insight and understanding about the object or decision problem under investigation. The ultimate purpose of using models is to improve decision making. As you will see, the process of building a model can shed important light and understanding on a problem. In some cases, a decision might be made while building the model as a previously misunderstood element of the problem is discovered or eliminated. In other cases, a careful analysis of a completed model might be required to "get a handle" on a problem and gain the insights needed to make a decision. In any event, the insight gained from the modeling process ultimately leads to better decision making.

1.3 Mathematical Models

As mentioned earlier, the modeling techniques in this book differ quite a bit from scale models of cars and planes, or visual models of production plants. The models we will build use mathematics to describe a decision problem. We use the term "mathematics" in its broadest sense, encompassing not only the most familiar elements of math, such as algebra, but also the related topic of logic.

---

[1] Colson, Charles and Jack Eckerd, *Why America Doesn't Work* (Denver, Colorado: Word Publishing, 1991), 146–147.

Now, let's consider a simple example of a mathematical model:

$$\text{PROFIT} = \text{REVENUE} - \text{EXPENSES} \qquad \textbf{1.1}$$

Equation 1.1 describes a simple relationship between revenue, expenses, and profit. It is a mathematical relationship that describes the operation of determining profit—or a mathematical model of profit. Of course, not all models are this simple, but taken piece by piece, the models we will discuss are not much more complex than this one.

Frequently, mathematical models describe functional relationships. For example, the mathematical model in equation 1.1 describes a functional relationship between revenue, expenses, and profit. Using the symbols of mathematics, this functional relationship is represented as:

$$\text{PROFIT} = f(\text{REVENUE, EXPENSES}) \qquad \textbf{1.2}$$

In words, the previous expression means "profit is a function of revenue and expenses." We also could say that profit *depends* on (or is *dependent* on) revenue and expenses. Thus, the term PROFIT in equation 1.2 represents a dependent variable, whereas REVENUE and EXPENSES are independent variables. Frequently, compact symbols (such as A, B, and C) are used to represent variables in an equation such as 1.2. For instance, if we let Y, X_1, and X_2 represent PROFIT, REVENUE, and EXPENSES, respectively, we could rewrite equation 1.2 as follows:

$$Y = f(X_1, X_2) \qquad \textbf{1.3}$$

The notation $f(\cdot)$ represents the function that defines the relationship between the dependent variable Y and the independent variables X_1 and X_2. In the case of determining PROFIT from REVENUE and EXPENSES, the mathematical form of the function $f(\cdot)$ is quite simple: $f(X_1, X_2) = X_1 - X_2$. However, in many other situations we will model, the form of $f(\cdot)$ is quite complex and might involve many independent variables. But regardless of the complexity of $f(\cdot)$ or the number of independent variables involved, many of the decision problems encountered in business can be represented by models that assume the general form,

$$Y = f(X_1, X_2, \ldots, X_k) \qquad \textbf{1.4}$$

In equation 1.4, the dependent variable Y represents some bottom-line performance measure of the problem we are modeling. The terms $X_1, X_2, \ldots, X_k$ represent the different independent variables that play some role or have some effect in determining the value of Y. Again, $f(\cdot)$ is the function (possibly quite complex) that specifies or describes the relationship between the dependent and independent variables.

The relationship expressed in equation 1.4 is very similar to what occurs in most spreadsheet models. Consider a simple spreadsheet model to calculate the monthly payment for a car loan, as shown in Figure 1.2.

The spreadsheet in Figure 1.2 contains a variety of input cells (for example, purchase price, down payment, trade-in, term of loan, annual interest rate) that correspond conceptually to the independent variables $X_1, X_2, \ldots, X_k$ in equation 1.4. Similarly, a variety of mathematical operations are performed using these input cells in a manner analogous to the function $f(\cdot)$ in equation 1.4. The results of these mathematical operations determine the value of some output cell in the spreadsheet (for example, monthly payment) that corresponds to the dependent variable Y in equation 1.4. Thus, there is a direct correspondence between equation 1.4 and the spreadsheet in Figure 1.2. This type of correspondence exists for most of the spreadsheet models in this book.

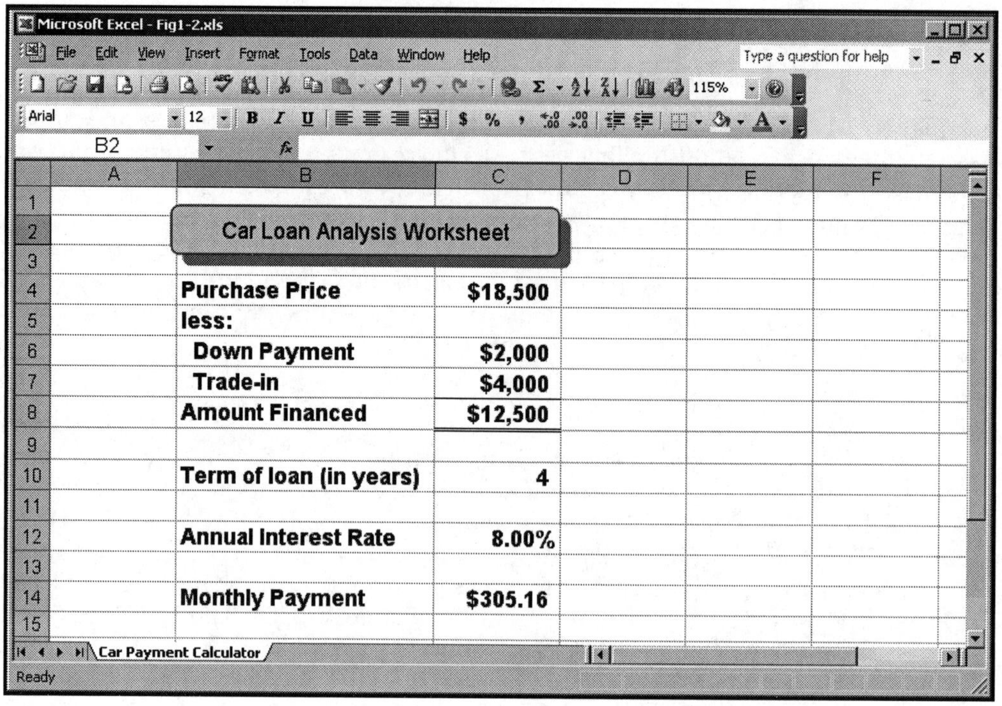

FIGURE 1.2

Example of a simple spreadsheet model

1.4 Categories of Mathematical Models

Not only does equation 1.4 describe the major elements of mathematical or spreadsheet models, but it also provides a convenient means for comparing and contrasting the three categories of modeling techniques presented in this book—Prescriptive Models, Predictive Models, and Descriptive Models. Figure 1.3 summarizes the characteristics and techniques associated with each of these categories.

In some situations, a manager might face a decision problem involving a very precise, well-defined functional relationship $f(\cdot)$ between the independent variables $X_1, X_2, \ldots, X_k$ and the dependent variable Y. If the values for the independent variables are under

FIGURE 1.3

Categories and characteristics of management science modeling techniques

	Model Characteristics		
Category	Form of $f(\cdot)$	Values of Independent Variables	Management Science Techniques
Prescriptive Models	known, well-defined	known or under decision maker's control	Linear Programming, Networks, Integer Programming, CPM, Goal Programming, EOQ, Nonlinear Programming
Predictive Models	unknown, ill-defined	known or under decision maker's control	Regression Analysis, Time Series Analysis, Discriminant Analysis
Descriptive Models	known, well-defined	unknown or uncertain	Simulation, Queuing, PERT, Inventory Models

the decision maker's control, the decision problem in these types of situations boils down to determining the values of the independent variables $X_1, X_2, \ldots, X_k$ that produce the best possible value for the dependent variable Y. These types of models are called Prescriptive Models because their solutions tell the decision maker what actions to take. For example, you might be interested in determining how a given sum of money should be allocated to different investments (represented by the independent variables) to maximize the return on a portfolio without exceeding a certain level of risk.

A second category of decision problems is one in which the objective is to predict or estimate what value the dependent variable Y will take on when the independent variables $X_1, X_2, \ldots, X_k$ take on specific values. If the function $f(\cdot)$ relating the dependent and independent variables is known, this is a very simple task—simply enter the specified values for $X_1, X_2, \ldots, X_k$ into the function $f(\cdot)$ and compute Y. In some cases, however, the functional form of $f(\cdot)$ might be unknown and must be estimated for the decision maker to make predictions about the dependent variable Y. These types of models are called Predictive Models. For example, a real estate appraiser might know that the value of a commercial property (Y) is influenced by its total square footage (X_1) and age (X_2), among other things. However, the functional relationship $f(\cdot)$ that relates these variables to one another might be unknown. By analyzing the relationship between the selling price, total square footage, and age of other commercial properties, the appraiser might be able to identify a function $f(\cdot)$ that relates these two variables in a reasonably accurate manner.

The third category of models you are likely to encounter in the business world is called Descriptive Models. In these situations, a manager might face a decision problem that has a very precise, well-defined functional relationship $f(\cdot)$ between the independent variables $X_1, X_2, \ldots, X_k$ and the dependent variable Y. However, there might be great uncertainty as to the exact values that will be assumed by one or more of the independent variables $X_1, X_2, \ldots, X_k$. In these types of problems, the objective is to describe the outcome or behavior of a given operation or system. For example, suppose a company is building a new manufacturing facility and has several choices about the type of machines to put in the new plant, and also various options for arranging the machines. Management might be interested in studying how the various plant configurations would affect on-time shipments of orders (Y), given the uncertain number of orders that might be received (X_1) and the uncertain due dates (X_2) that might be required by these orders.

1.5 The Problem-Solving Process

Throughout our discussion, we have said that the ultimate goal in building models is to help managers make decisions that solve problems. The modeling techniques we will study represent a small but important part of the total problem-solving process. To become an effective modeler, it is important to understand how modeling fits into the entire problem-solving process.

Because a model can be used to represent a decision problem or phenomenon, we might be able to create a visual model of the phenomenon that occurs when people solve problems—what we call the problem-solving process. Although a variety of models could be equally valid, the one in Figure 1.4 summarizes the key elements of the problem-solving process and is sufficient for our purposes.

The first step of the problem-solving process, identifying the problem, is also the most important. If we do not identify the correct problem, all the work that follows will amount to nothing more than wasted effort, time, and money. Unfortunately, identifying

FIGURE 1.4

A visual model of the problem-solving process

the problem to solve is often not as easy as it seems. We know that a problem exists when there is a gap or disparity between the present situation and some desired state of affairs. However, we usually are not faced with a neat, well-defined problem. Instead, we often find ourselves facing a "mess"![2] Identifying the real problem involves gathering a lot of information and talking with many people to increase our understanding of the mess. We must then sift through all this information and try to identify the root problem or problems causing the mess. Thus, identifying the real problem (and not just the symptoms of the problem) requires insight, some imagination, time, and a good bit of detective work.

The end result of the problem-identification step is a well-defined statement of the problem. Simply defining a problem well will often make it much easier to solve. Having identified the problem, we turn our attention to creating or formulating a model of the problem. Depending on the nature of the problem, we might use a mental model, a visual model, a scale model, or a mathematical model. Although this book focuses on mathematical models, this does not mean that mathematical models are always applicable or best. In most situations, the best model is the simplest model that accurately reflects the relevant characteristic or essence of the problem being studied.

We will discuss several different management science modeling techniques in this book. It is important that you not develop too strong a preference for any one technique. Some people have a tendency to want to formulate every problem they face as a model that can be solved by their favorite management science technique. This simply will not work.

As indicated in Figure 1.3, there are fundamental differences in the types of problems a manager might face. Sometimes, the values of the independent variables affecting a problem are under the manager's control; sometimes they are not. Sometimes, the form of the functional relationship $f(\cdot)$ relating the dependent and independent variables is well-defined, and sometimes it is not. These fundamental characteristics of the problem should guide your selection of an appropriate management science modeling technique. Your goal at the model-formulation stage is to select a modeling technique that fits your problem, rather than trying to fit your problem into the required format of a pre-selected modeling technique.

After you select an appropriate representation or formulation of your problem, the next step is to implement this formulation as a spreadsheet model. We will not dwell on the implementation process now because that is the focus of the remainder of this book. After you verify that your spreadsheet model has been implemented accurately, the next step in the problem-solving process is to use the model to analyze the problem it represents. The main focus of this step is to generate and evaluate alternatives that might lead to a solution. This often involves playing out a number of scenarios or asking several "What if?" questions. Spreadsheets are particularly helpful in analyzing mathematical models in this manner. In a well-designed spreadsheet model, it should be fairly simple to change some of the assumptions in the model to see what might happen in different

---

[2] This characterization is borrowed from Chapter 5, James R. Evans, *Creative Thinking in the Decision and Management Sciences* (Cincinnati, Ohio: South-Western Publishing, 1991), 89–115.

situations. As we proceed, we will highlight some techniques for designing spreadsheet models that facilitate this type of "what if?" analysis. "What if?" analysis is also very appropriate and useful when working with nonmathematical models.

The end result of analyzing a model does not always provide a solution to the actual problem being studied. As we analyze a model by asking various "What if?" questions, it is important to test the feasibility and quality of each potential solution. The blueprints that Frank Brock showed to his production employees represented the end result of his analysis of the problem he faced. He wisely tested the feasibility and quality of this alternative before implementing it, and discovered an important flaw in his plans. Thus, the testing process can give important new insights into the nature of a problem. The testing process is also important because it provides the opportunity to double-check the validity of the model. At times, we might discover an alternative that appears to be too good to be true. This could lead us to find that some important assumption has been left out of the model. Testing the results of the model against known results (and simple common sense) helps ensure the structural integrity and validity of the model. After analyzing the model, we might discover that we need to go back and modify the model.

The last step of the problem-solving process, implementation, is often the most difficult. By their very nature, solutions to problems involve people and change. For better or for worse, most people resist change. However, there are ways to minimize the seemingly inevitable resistance to change. For example, it is wise, if possible, to involve anyone who will be affected by the decision in all steps of the problem-solving process. This not only helps develop a sense of ownership and understanding of the ultimate solution, but it also can be the source of important information throughout the problem-solving process. As the Brock Candy story illustrates, even if it is impossible to include those affected by the solution in all steps, their input should be solicited and considered before a solution is accepted for implementation. Resistance to change and new systems also can be eased by creating flexible, user-friendly interfaces for the mathematical models that often are developed in the problem-solving process.

Throughout this book, we focus mostly on the model formulation, implementation, analysis, and testing steps of the problem-solving process, summarized in Figure 1.4. Again, this does not imply that these steps are more important than the others. If we do not identify the correct problem, the best we can hope for from our modeling effort is "the right answer to the wrong question," which does not solve the real problem. Similarly, even if we do identify the problem correctly and design a model that leads to a perfect solution, if we cannot implement the solution, then we still have not solved the problem. Developing the interpersonal and investigative skills required to work with people in defining the problem and implementing the solution are as important as the mathematical modeling skills you will develop by working through this book.

1.6 Anchoring and Framing Effects

At this point, some of you reading this book are probably thinking it is better to rely on subjective judgment and intuition rather than models when making decisions. Indeed, most nontrivial decision problems involve some issues that are difficult or impossible to structure and analyze in the form of a mathematical model. These unstructurable aspects of a decision problem might require the use of judgment and intuition. However, it is important to realize that human cognition is often flawed and can lead to incorrect judgments and irrational decisions. Errors in human judgment often arise because of what psychologists term anchoring and framing effects associated with decision problems.

Anchoring effects arise when a seemingly trivial factor serves as a starting point (or anchor) for estimations in a decision-making problem. Decision makers adjust their estimates from this anchor but nevertheless remain too close to the anchor and usually under-adjust. In a classic psychological study on this issue, one group of subjects were asked to individually estimate the value of $1 \times 2 \times 3 \times 4 \times 5 \times 6 \times 7 \times 8$ (without using a calculator). Another group of subjects were each asked to estimate the value of $8 \times 7 \times 6 \times 5 \times 4 \times 3 \times 2 \times 1$. The researchers hypothesized that the first number presented (or perhaps the product of the first three or four numbers) would serve as a mental anchor. The results supported the hypothesis. The median estimate of subjects shown the numbers in ascending sequence ($1 \times 2 \times 3 \ldots$) was 512, whereas the median estimate of subjects shown the sequence in descending order ($8 \times 7 \times 6 \ldots$) was 2,250. Of course, the order of multiplication for these numbers is irrelevant and the product of both series is the same: 40,320.

Framing effects refer to how a decision maker views or perceives the alternatives in a decision problem—often involving a win/loss perspective. The way a problem is framed often influences the choices made by a decision maker and can lead to irrational behavior. For example, suppose you have just been given $1,000 but must choose one of the following alternatives: (A_1) Receive an additional $500 with certainty, or ($B_1$) Flip a fair coin and receive an additional $1,000 if heads occurs or $0 additional is tails occurs. Here, alternative A_1 is a "sure win" and is the alternative most people prefer. Now suppose you have been given $2,000 and must choose one of the following alternatives: (A_2) Give back $500 immediately, or ($B_2$) Flip a fair coin and give back $0 if heads occurs or $1,000 if tails occurs. When the problem is framed this way, alternative A_2 is a "sure loss" and many people who previously preferred alternative A_1 now opt for alternative B_2 (because it holds a chance of avoiding a loss). However, Figure 1.5 shows a single decision tree for these two scenarios making it clear that, in both cases, the "A" alternative guarantees a total payoff of $1,500, whereas the "B" alternative offers a 50% chance of a $2,000 total payoff and a 50% chance of a $1,000 total payoff. (Decision trees will be covered in greater detail in a later chapter.) A purely rational decision maker should focus on the consequences of his or her choices and consistently select the same alternative, regardless of how the problem is framed.

Whether we want to admit it or not, we are all prone to make errors in estimation due to anchoring effects and may exhibit irrationality in decision making due to framing effects. As a result, it is best to use computer models to do what they are best at (i.e., modeling structurable portions of a decision problem) and let the human brain do what it is best at (i.e., dealing with the unstructurable portion of a decision problem).

FIGURE 1.5

Decision tree for framing effects

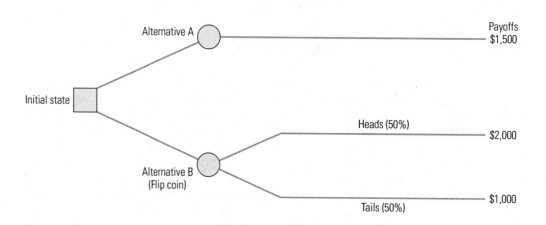

1.7 Good Decisions vs. Good Outcomes

The goal of the modeling approach to problem solving is to help individuals make good decisions. But good decisions do not always result in good outcomes. For example, suppose the weather report on the evening news predicts a warm, dry, sunny day tomorrow. When you get up and look out the window tomorrow morning, suppose there is not a cloud in sight. If you decide to leave your umbrella at home and subsequently get soaked in an unexpected afternoon thundershower, did you make a bad decision? Certainly not. Unforeseeable circumstances beyond your control caused you to experience a bad outcome, but it would be unfair to say that you made a bad decision. Good decisions sometimes result in bad outcomes. See Figure 1.6 for the story of another good decision having a bad outcome.

The modeling techniques presented in this book can help you make good decisions, but cannot guarantee that good outcomes will always occur as a result of those decisions. Even when a good decision is made, luck often plays a role in determining whether a good or bad outcome occurs. However, using a structured, modeling approach to decision making should produce good outcomes more frequently than making decisions in a more haphazard manner.

1.8 Summary

This book introduces you to a variety of techniques from the field of management science that can be applied in spreadsheet models to assist in decision analysis and problem solving. This chapter discussed how spreadsheet models of decision problems can be used to analyze the consequences of possible courses of action before a particular alternative is selected for implementation. It described how models of decision problems differ in several important characteristics and how you should select a modeling technique that is most appropriate for the type of problem being faced. Finally, it discussed how spreadsheet modeling and analysis fit into the problem-solving process.

FIGURE 1.6

A good decision with a bad outcome

Andre-Francois Raffray thought he had a great deal in 1965 when he agreed to pay a 90-year-old woman named Jeanne Calment $500 a month until she died to acquire her grand apartment in Arles, northwest of Marseilles in the south of France—a town Vincent Van Gogh once roamed. Buying apartments "for life" is common in France. The elderly owner gets to enjoy a monthly income from the buyer who gambles on getting a real estate bargain—betting the owner doesn't live too long. Upon the owner's death, the buyer inherits the apartment regardless of how much was paid. But in December of 1995, Raffray died at age 77, having paid more than $180,000 for an apartment he never got to live in.

On the same day, Calment, then the world's oldest living person at 120, dined on foie gras, duck thighs, cheese, and chocolate cake at her nursing home near the sought-after apartment. And she does not need to worry about losing her $500 monthly income. Although the amount Raffray already paid is twice the apartment's current market value, his widow is obligated to keep sending the monthly check to Calment. If Calment also outlives her, then the Raffray children will have to pay. "In life, one sometimes makes bad deals," said Calment of the outcome of Raffray's decision. (Source: *The Savannah Morning News*, 12/29/95.)

1.9 References

Edwards, J., P. Finlay, and J. Wilson. "The role of the OR specialist in 'do it yourself' spreadsheet development." *European Journal of Operational Research*, vol. 127, no. 1, 2000.

Forgione, G. "Corporate MS Activities: An Update." *Interfaces*, vol. 13, no. 1, 1983.

Hall, R. "What's So Scientific about MS/OR?" *Interfaces*, vol. 15, 1985.

Hastie, R. and R. M. Dawes. *Rational Choice in an Uncertain World*, Sage Publications, 2001.

Schrage, M. *Serious Play*, Harvard Business School Press, 2000.

Sonntag, C. and Grossman, T. "End-User Modeling Improves R&D Management at AgrEvo Canada, Inc." *Interfaces*, vol. 29, no. 5, 1999.

THE WORLD OF MANAGEMENT SCIENCE

"Business Analysts Trained in Management Science Can Be a Secret Weapon in a CIO's Quest for Bottom-Line Results."

Efficiency nuts. These are the people you see at cocktail parties explaining how the host could disperse that crowd around the popular shrimp dip if he would divide it into three bowls and place them around the room. As she draws the improved traffic flow on a paper napkin, you notice that her favorite word is "optimize"—a tell-tale sign that she has studied the field of "operations research" or "management science" (also known as OR/MS).

OR/MS professionals are driven to solve logistics problems. This trait might not make them the most popular people at parties, but it is exactly what today's information systems (IS) departments need to deliver more business value. Experts say that smart IS executives will learn to exploit the talents of these mathematical wizards in their quest to boost a company's bottom line.

According to Ron J. Ponder, chief information officer (CIO) at Sprint Corp. in Kansas City, Mo., and former CIO at Federal Express Corp., "If IS departments had more participation from operations research analysts, they would be building much better, richer IS solutions." As someone who has a Ph.D. in operations research and who built the renowned package-tracking systems at Federal Express, Ponder is a true believer in OR/MS. Ponder and others say analysts trained in OR/MS can turn ordinary information systems into money-saving, decision-support systems, and are ideally suited to be members of the business process reengineering team. "I've always had an operations research department reporting to me, and it's been invaluable. Now I'm building one at Sprint," says Ponder.

The Beginnings

OR/MS got its start in World War II, when the military had to make important decisions about allocating scarce resources to various military operations. One of the first business applications for computers in the 1950s was to solve operations research problems for the petroleum industry. A technique called linear programming was used to figure out how to blend gasoline for the right flash point, viscosity, and octane in the most economical way. Since then, OR/MS has spread throughout business and government, from designing efficient drive-thru window operations for Burger King Corp. to creating ultrasophisticated computerized stock trading systems.

A classic OR/MS example is the crew scheduling problem faced by all major airlines. How do you plan the itineraries of 8,000 pilots and 17,000 flight attendants when there is an astronomical number of combinations of planes, crews, and cities? The OR/MS analysts at United Airlines came up with a scheduling system called Paragon that attempts to minimize the amount of paid time that crews spend waiting for flights. Their model factors in constraints such as labor agreement provisions and Federal Aviation Administration regulations, and is projected to save the airline at least $1 million a year.

OR/MS and IS

Somewhere in the 1970s, the OR/MS and IS disciplines went in separate directions. "The IS profession has had less and less contact with the operations research folks . . . and IS lost a powerful intellectual driver," says Peter G. W. Keen, executive director of the International Center for Information Technologies in Washington, D.C. However, many feel that now is an ideal time for the two disciplines to rebuild some bridges.

Today's OR/MS professionals are involved in a variety of IS-related fields, including inventory management, electronic data interchange, supply chain management, IT security, computer-integrated manufacturing, network management, and practical applications of artificial intelligence. Furthermore, each side needs something the other side has: OR/MS analysts need corporate data to plug into their models, and the IS folks need to plug the OR/MS models into their strategic information systems. At the same time, CIOs need intelligent applications that enhance the bottom line and make them heroes with the chief executive officer.

OR/MS analysts can develop a model of how a business process works now and simulate how it could work more efficiently in the future. Therefore, it makes sense to have an OR/MS analyst on the interdisciplinary team that tackles business process reengineering projects. In essence, OR/MS professionals add more value to the IS infrastructure by building "tools that really help decision makers analyze complex situations," says Andrew B. Whinston, director of the Center for Information Systems Management at the University of Texas at Austin.

Although IS departments typically believe their job is done if they deliver accurate and timely information, Thomas M. Cook, president of American Airlines Decision Technologies, Inc. says that adding OR/MS skills to the team can produce intelligent systems that actually recommend solutions to business problems. One of the big success stories at Cook's operations research shop is a "yield management" system that decides how much to overbook and how to set prices for each seat so that a plane is filled up and profits are maximized. The yield management system deals with more than 250 decision variables and accounts for a significant amount of American Airlines' revenue.

Where to Start

So how can the CIO start down the road toward collaboration with OR/MS analysts? If the company already has a group of OR/MS professionals, the IS department can draw on their expertise as internal consultants. Otherwise, the CIO can simply hire a few OR/MS wizards, throw a problem at them, and see what happens. The payback may come surprisingly quickly. As one former OR/MS professional put it: "If I couldn't save my employer the equivalent of my own salary in the first month of the year, then I wouldn't feel like I was doing my job."

Adapted from: Mitch Betts, "Efficiency Einsteins," *ComputerWorld*, March 22, 1993, p. 64.

Questions and Problems

1. What is meant by the term decision analysis?
2. Define the term computer model.
3. What is the difference between a spreadsheet model and a computer model?
4. Define the term management science.
5. What is the relationship between management science and spreadsheet modeling?
6. What kinds of spreadsheet applications would not be considered management science?
7. In what ways do spreadsheet models facilitate the decision-making process?
8. What are the benefits of using a modeling approach to decision making?
9. What is a dependent variable?
10. What is an independent variable?
11. Can a model have more than one dependent variable?
12. Can a decision problem have more than one dependent variable?
13. In what ways are prescriptive models different from descriptive models?
14. In what ways are prescriptive models different from predictive models?
15. In what ways are descriptive models different from predictive models?
16. How would you define the words description, prediction, and prescription? Carefully consider what is unique about the meaning of each word.
17. Identify one or more mental models you have used. Can any of them be expressed mathematically? If so, identify the dependent and independent variables in your model.
18. Consider the spreadsheet model shown in Figure 1.2. Is this model descriptive, predictive, or prescriptive in nature, or does it not fall into any of these categories?
19. What are the steps in the problem-solving process?
20. Which step in the problem-solving process do you think is most important? Why?
21. Must a model accurately represent every detail of a decision situation to be useful? Why or why not?
22. If you were presented with several different models of a given decision problem, which would you be most inclined to use? Why?
23. Describe an example in which business or political organizations may use anchoring effects to influence decision making.
24. Describe an example in which business or political organizations may use framing effects to influence decision making.
25. Suppose sharks have been spotted along the beach where you are vacationing with a friend. You and your friend have been informed of the shark sightings and are aware of the damage a shark attack can inflict on human flesh. You both decide (individually) to go swimming anyway. You are promptly attacked by a shark while your friend has a nice time body surfing in the waves. Did you make a good or bad decision? Did your friend make a good or bad decision? Explain your answer.
26. Describe an example in which a well-known business, political, or military leader made a good decision that resulted in a bad outcome, or a bad decision that resulted in a good outcome.

CASE 1.1   Patrick's Paradox

Patrick's luck had changed overnight—but not his skill at mathematical reasoning. The day after graduating from college he used the $20 that his grandmother had given him as a graduation gift to buy a lottery ticket. He knew that his chances of winning the lottery were extremely low and it probably was not a good way to spend this money. But he also remembered from the class he took in management science that bad decisions sometimes result in good outcomes. So he said to himself, "What the heck? Maybe this bad decision will be the one with a good outcome." And with that thought, he bought his lottery ticket.

The next day Patrick pulled the crumpled lottery ticket out of the back pocket of his blue jeans and tried to compare his numbers to the winning numbers printed in the paper. When his eyes finally came into focus on the numbers they also just about popped out of his head. He had a winning ticket! In the ensuing days he learned that his share of the jackpot would give him a lump sum payout of about $500,000 after taxes. He knew what he was going to do with part of the money: buy a new car, pay off his college loans, and send his grandmother on an all-expenses-paid trip to Hawaii. But he also knew that he couldn't continue to hope for good outcomes to arise from more bad decisions. So he decided to take half of his winnings and invest it for his retirement.

A few days later, Patrick was sitting around with two of his fraternity buddies, Josh and Peyton, trying to figure out how much money his new retirement fund might be worth in 30 years. They were all business majors in college and remembered from their finance class that if you invest p dollars for n year at an annual interest rate of i percent then in n years you would have $p(1 + i)^n$ dollars. So they figure that if Patrick invested $250,000 for 30 years in an investment with a 10% annual return then in 30 years he would have $4,362,351 (that is, $250,000(1 + 0.10)^{30}$).

But after thinking about it a little more, they all agreed that it would be unlikely for Patrick to find an investment that would produce a return of exactly 10% each and every year for the next 30 years. If any of this money is invested in stocks then some years the return might be higher than 10% and some years it would probably be lower. So to help account for the potential variability in the investment returns Patrick and his friends came up with a plan; they would assume he could find an investment that would produce an annual return of 17.5% seventy percent of the time and a return (or actually a loss) of −7.5% thirty percent of the time. Such an investment should produce an average annual return of $0.7(17.5\%) + 0.3(−7.5\%) = 10\%$. Josh felt certain that this meant Patrick could still expect his $250,000 investment to grow to $4,362,351 in 30 years (because $250,000(1 + 0.10)^{30} = \$4,362,351$).

After sitting quietly and thinking about it for a while, Peyton said that he thought Josh was wrong. The way Peyton looked at it, Patrick should see a 17.5% return in 70% of the 30 years (or $0.7(30) = 21$ years) and a −7.5% return in 30% of the 30 years (or $0.3(30) = 9$ years). So, according to Peyton, that would mean Patrick should have $250,000(1 + 0.175)^{21}(1 − 0.075)^9 = \$3,664,467$ after 30 years. But that's $697,884 less than what Josh says Patrick should have.

After listening to Peyton's argument, Josh said he thought Peyton was wrong because his calculation assumes that the "good" return of 17.5% would occur in each of the first 21 years and the "bad" return of −7.5% would occur in each of the last 9 years. But Peyton countered this argument by saying that the order of good and bad returns does not matter. The commutative law of arithmetic says that when you add or multiply numbers, the order doesn't matter (that is, $X + Y = Y + X$ and $X \times Y = Y \times X$). So Peyton says that because Patrick can expect 21 "good" returns and 9 "bad" returns and it doesn't matter in what order they occur, then the expected outcome of the investment should be $3,664,467 after 30 years.

Patrick is now really confused. Both of his friends' arguments seem to make perfect sense logically—but they lead to such different answers, and they can't both be right. What really worries Patrick is that he is starting his new job as a business analyst in a couple of weeks. And if he can't reason his way to the right answer in a relatively simple problem like this, what is he going to do when he encounters the more difficult problems awaiting him the business world? Now he really wishes he had paid more attention in his management sciences class.

So what do you think? Who is right, Josh or Peyton? And more important, why?

Chapter 2

Introduction to Optimization and Linear Programming

2.0 Introduction

Our world is filled with limited resources. The amount of oil we can pump out of the earth is limited. The amount of land available for garbage dumps and hazardous waste is limited and, in many areas, diminishing rapidly. On a more personal level, each of us has a limited amount of time in which to accomplish or enjoy the activities we schedule each day. Most of us have a limited amount of money to spend while pursuing these activities. Businesses also have limited resources. A manufacturing organization employs a limited number of workers. A restaurant has a limited amount of space available for seating.

Deciding how best to use the limited resources available to an individual or a business is a universal problem. In today's competitive business environment, it is increasingly important to make sure that a company's limited resources are used in the most efficient manner possible. Typically, this involves determining how to allocate the resources in such a way as to maximize profits or minimize costs. Mathematical programming (MP) is a field of management science that finds the optimal, or most efficient, way of using limited resources to achieve the objectives of an individual or a business. For this reason, mathematical programming often is referred to as optimization.

2.1 Applications of Mathematical Optimization

To help you understand the purpose of optimization and the types of problems for which it can be used, let's consider several examples of decision-making situations in which MP techniques have been applied.

Determining Product Mix. Most manufacturing companies can make a variety of products. However, each product usually requires different amounts of raw materials and labor. Similarly, the amount of profit generated by the products varies. The manager of such a company must decide how many of each product to produce to maximize profits or to satisfy demand at minimum cost.

Manufacturing. Printed circuit boards, like those used in most computers, often have hundreds or thousands of holes drilled in them to accommodate the different electrical components that must be plugged into them. To manufacture these boards, a computer-controlled drilling machine must be programmed to drill in a given location, then move the drill bit to the next location and drill again. This process is repeated hundreds or thousands of times to complete all the holes on a circuit board. Manufacturers of these boards would benefit from determining the drilling order that minimizes the total distance the drill bit must be moved.

Routing and Logistics. Many retail companies have warehouses around the country that are responsible for keeping stores supplied with merchandise to sell. The amount of merchandise available at the warehouses and the amount needed at each store tends to fluctuate, as does the cost of shipping or delivering merchandise from the warehouses to the retail locations. Large amounts of money can be saved by determining the least costly method of transferring merchandise from the warehouses to the stores.

Financial Planning. The federal government requires individuals to begin withdrawing money from individual retirement accounts (IRAs) and other tax-sheltered retirement programs no later than age 70.5. There are various rules that must be followed to avoid paying penalty taxes on these withdrawals. Most individuals want to withdraw their money in a manner that minimizes the amount of taxes they must pay while still obeying the tax laws.

Optimization Is Everywhere

Going to Disney World this summer? Optimization will be your ubiquitous companion, scheduling the crews and planes, pricing the airline tickets and hotel rooms, even helping to set capacities on the theme park rides. If you use Orbitz to book your flights, an optimization engine sifts through millions of options to find the cheapest fares. If you get directions to your hotel from MapQuest, another optimization engine figures out the most direct route. If you ship souvenirs home, an optimization engine tells UPS which truck to put the packages on, exactly where on the truck the packages should go to make them fastest to load and unload, and what route the driver should follow to make his deliveries most efficiently.

(Adapted from: V. Postrel, "Operation Everything," *The Boston Globe*, June 27, 2004.)

2.2 Characteristics of Optimization Problems

These examples represent just a few areas in which MP has been used successfully. We will consider many other examples throughout this book. However, these examples give you some idea of the issues involved in optimization. For instance, each example involves one or more *decisions* that must be made: How many of each product should be produced? Which hole should be drilled next? How much of each product should be shipped from each warehouse to the various retail locations? How much money should an individual withdraw each year from various retirement accounts?

Also, in each example, restrictions, or *constraints*, are likely to be placed on the alternatives available to the decision maker. In the first example, when determining the number of products to manufacture, a production manager probably is faced with a limited amount of raw materials and a limited amount of labor. In the second example, the drill never should return to a position where a hole has already been drilled. In the third example, there is a physical limitation on the amount of merchandise a truck can carry from one warehouse to the stores on its route. In the fourth example, laws determine the minimum and maximum amounts that can be withdrawn from retirement accounts without incurring a penalty. There might be many other constraints for these examples. Indeed, it is not unusual for real-world optimization problems to have hundreds or thousands of constraints.

A final common element in each of the examples is the existence of some goal or *objective* that the decision maker considers when deciding which course of action is best. In the first example, the production manager can decide to produce several different product mixes given the available resources, but the manager probably will choose the mix of products that maximizes profits. In the second example, a large number of possible drilling patterns can be used, but the ideal pattern probably will involve moving the drill bit the shortest total distance. In the third example, there are numerous ways merchandise can be shipped from the warehouses to supply the stores, but the company probably will want to identify the routing that minimizes the total transportation cost. Finally, in the fourth example, individuals can withdraw money from their retirement accounts in many ways without violating the tax laws, but they probably want to find the method that minimizes their tax liability.

2.3 Expressing Optimization Problems Mathematically

From the preceding discussion, we know that optimization problems involve three elements: decisions, constraints, and an objective. If we intend to build a mathematical model of an optimization problem, we will need mathematical terms or symbols to represent each of these three elements.

2.3.1 DECISIONS

The decisions in an optimization problem often are represented in a mathematical model by the symbols $X_1, X_2, \ldots, X_n$. We will refer to $X_1, X_2, \ldots, X_n$ as the decision variables (or simply the variables) in the model. These variables might represent the quantities of different products the production manager can choose to produce. They might represent the amount of different pieces of merchandise to ship from a warehouse to a certain store. They might represent the amount of money to be withdrawn from different retirement accounts.

The exact symbols used to represent the decision variables are not particularly important. You could use $Z_1, Z_2, \ldots, Z_n$ or symbols like Dog, Cat, and Monkey to represent the decision variables in the model. The choice of which symbols to use is largely a matter of personal preference and might vary from one problem to the next.

2.3.2 CONSTRAINTS

The constraints in an optimization problem can be represented in a mathematical model in several ways. Three general ways of expressing the possible constraint relationships in an optimization problem are:

A "less than or equal to" constraint: $f(X_1, X_2, \ldots, X_n) \leq b$

A "greater than or equal to" constraint: $f(X_1, X_2, \ldots, X_n) \geq b$

An "equal to" constraint: $f(X_1, X_2, \ldots, X_n) = b$

In each case, the constraint is some function of the decision variables that must be less than or equal to, greater than or equal to, or equal to some specific value (represented above by the letter b). We will refer to $f(X_1, X_2, \ldots, X_n)$ as the left-hand-side (LHS) of the constraint and to b as the right-hand-side (RHS) value of the constraint.

For example, we might use a "less than or equal to" constraint to ensure that the total labor used in producing a given number of products does not exceed the amount of available labor. We might use a "greater than or equal to" constraint to ensure that the total amount of money withdrawn from a person's retirement accounts is at least the minimum amount required by the IRS. You can use any number of these constraints to represent a given optimization problem depending on the requirements of the situation.

2.3.3 OBJECTIVE

The objective in an optimization problem is represented mathematically by an objective function in the general format:

$$\text{MAX (or MIN):} \quad f(X_1, X_2, \ldots, X_n)$$

The objective function identifies some function of the decision variables that the decision maker wants to either MAXimize or MINimize. In our earlier examples, this function might be used to describe the total profit associated with a product mix, the total distance the drill bit must be moved, the total cost of transporting merchandise, or a retiree's total tax liability.

The mathematical formulation of an optimization problem can be described in the general format:

$$\text{MAX (or MIN):} \quad f_0(X_1, X_2, \ldots, X_n) \qquad \textbf{2.1}$$
$$\text{Subject to:} \quad f_1(X_1, X_2, \ldots, X_n) \leq b_1 \qquad \textbf{2.2}$$
$$\vdots$$
$$f_k(X_1, X_2, \ldots, X_n) \geq b_k \qquad \textbf{2.3}$$
$$\vdots$$
$$f_m(X_1, X_2, \ldots, X_n) = b_m \qquad \textbf{2.4}$$

This representation identifies the objective function (equation 2.1) that will be maximized (or minimized) and the constraints that must be satisfied (equations 2.2 through 2.4). Subscripts added to the f and b in each equation emphasize that the functions describing the objective and constraints can all be different. The goal in optimization is to find the values of the decision variables that maximize (or minimize) the objective function without violating any of the constraints.

2.4 Mathematical Programming Techniques

Our general representation of an MP model is just that—general. You can use many kinds of functions to represent the objective function and the constraints in an MP model. Of course, you always should use functions that accurately describe the objective and constraints of the problem you are trying to solve. Sometimes, the functions in a model are linear in nature (that is, they form straight lines or flat surfaces); other times, they are nonlinear (that is, they form curved lines or curved surfaces). Sometimes, the optimal values of the decision variables in a model must take on integer values (whole numbers); other times, the decision variables can assume fractional values.

Given the diversity of MP problems that can be encountered, many techniques have been developed to solve different types of MP problems. In the next several chapters, we will look at these MP techniques and develop an understanding of how they differ and when each should be used. We will begin by examining a technique called linear programming (LP), which involves creating and solving optimization problems with linear objective functions and linear constraints. LP is a very powerful tool that can be applied in many business situations. It also forms a basis for several other techniques discussed later and is, therefore, a good starting point for our investigation into the field of optimization.

2.5 An Example LP Problem

We will begin our study of LP by considering a simple example. You should not interpret this to mean that LP cannot solve more complex or realistic problems. LP has been used to solve extremely complicated problems, saving companies millions of dollars. However, jumping directly into one of these complicated problems would be like starting a marathon without ever having gone out for a jog—you would get winded and could be left behind very quickly. So we'll start with something simple.

Blue Ridge Hot Tubs manufactures and sells two models of hot tubs: the Aqua-Spa and the Hydro-Lux. Howie Jones, the owner and manager of the company, needs to decide how many of each type of hot tub to produce during his next production cycle. Howie buys prefabricated fiberglass hot tub shells from a local supplier and adds the pump and tubing to the shells to create his hot tubs. (This supplier has the capacity to deliver as many hot tub shells as Howie needs.) Howie installs the same type of pump into both hot tubs. He will have only 200 pumps available during his next production cycle. From a manufacturing standpoint, the main difference between the two models of hot tubs is the amount of tubing and labor required. Each Aqua-Spa requires 9 hours of labor and 12 feet of tubing. Each Hydro-Lux requires 6 hours of labor and 16 feet of tubing. Howie expects to have 1,566 production labor hours and 2,880 feet of tubing available during the next production cycle. Howie earns a profit of $350 on each Aqua-Spa he sells and $300 on each Hydro-Lux he sells. He is confident that he can sell all the hot tubs he produces. The question is, how many Aqua-Spas and Hydro-Luxes should Howie produce if he wants to maximize his profits during the next production cycle?

2.6 Formulating LP Models

The process of taking a practical problem—such as determining how many Aqua-Spas and Hydro-Luxes Howie should produce—and expressing it algebraically in the form of an LP model is known as formulating the model. Throughout the next several chapters, you will see that formulating an LP model is as much an art as a science.

2.6.1 STEPS IN FORMULATING AN LP MODEL

There are some general steps you can follow to help make sure your formulation of a particular problem is accurate. We will walk through these steps using the hot tub example.

1. **Understand the problem.** This step appears to be so obvious that it hardly seems worth mentioning. However, many people have a tendency to jump into a problem and start writing the objective function and constraints before they really understand the problem. If you do not fully understand the problem you face, it is unlikely that your formulation of the problem will be correct.

   The problem in our example is fairly easy to understand: How many Aqua-Spas and Hydro-Luxes should Howie produce to maximize his profit, while using no more than 200 pumps, 1,566 labor hours, and 2,880 feet of tubing?

2. **Identify the decision variables.** After you are sure you understand the problem, you need to identify the decision variables. That is, what are the fundamental decisions that must be made to solve the problem? The answers to this question often will help you identify appropriate decision variables for your model. Identifying the decision variables means determining what the symbols $X_1, X_2, \ldots, X_n$ represent in your model.

   In our example, the fundamental decision Howie faces is this: How many Aqua-Spas and Hydro-Luxes should be produced? In this problem, we will let X_1 represent the number of Aqua-Spas to produce and X_2 represent the number of Hydro-Luxes to produce.

3. **State the objective function as a linear combination of the decision variables.** After determining the decision variables you will use, the next step is to create the objective function for the model. This function expresses the mathematical relationship between the decision variables in the model to be maximized or minimized.

   In our example, Howie earns a profit of $350 on each Aqua-Spa ($X_1$) he sells and $300 on each Hydro-Lux ($X_2$) he sells. Thus, Howie's objective of maximizing the profit he earns is stated mathematically as:

   $$\text{MAX:} \quad 350X_1 + 300X_2$$

   For whatever values might be assigned to X_1 and X_2, the previous function calculates the associated total profit that Howie would earn. Obviously, Howie wants to maximize this value.

4. **State the constraints as linear combinations of the decision variables.** As mentioned earlier, there are usually some limitations on the values that can be assumed by the decision variables in an LP model. These restrictions must be identified and stated in the form of constraints.

   In our example, Howie faces three major constraints. Because only 200 pumps are available and each hot tub requires one pump, Howie cannot produce more than a total of 200 hot tubs. This restriction is stated mathematically as:

   $$1X_1 + 1X_2 \leq 200$$

   This constraint indicates that each unit of X_1 produced (that is, each Aqua-Spa built) will use one of the 200 pumps available—as will each unit of X_2 produced (that is, each Hydro-Lux built). The total number of pumps used (represented by $1X_1 + 1X_2$) must be less than or equal to 200.

   Another restriction Howie faces is that he has only 1,566 labor hours available during the next production cycle. Because each Aqua-Spa he builds (each unit of X_1) requires 9 labor hours and each Hydro-Lux (each unit of X_2) requires 6 labor hours, the constraint on the number of labor hours is stated as:

   $$9X_1 + 6X_2 \leq 1,566$$

The total number of labor hours used (represented by $9X_1 + 6X_2$) must be less than or equal to the total labor hours available, which is 1,566.

The final constraint specifies that only 2,880 feet of tubing is available for the next production cycle. Each Aqua-Spa produced (each unit of X_1) requires 12 feet of tubing, and each Hydro-Lux produced (each unit of X_2) requires 16 feet of tubing. The following constraint is necessary to ensure that Howie's production plan does not use more tubing than is available:

$$12X_1 + 16X_2 \leq 2,880$$

The total number of feet of tubing used (represented by $12X_1 + 16X_2$) must be less than or equal to the total number of feet of tubing available, which is 2,880.

5. **Identify any upper or lower bounds on the decision variables.** Often, simple upper or lower bounds apply to the decision variables. You can view upper and lower bounds as additional constraints in the problem.

In our example, there are simple lower bounds of zero on the variables X_1 and X_2 because it is impossible to produce a negative number of hot tubs. Therefore, the following two constraints also apply to this problem:

$$X_1 \geq 0$$
$$X_2 \geq 0$$

Constraints like these are often referred to as nonnegativity conditions and are quite common in LP problems.

2.7 Summary of the LP Model for the Example Problem

The complete LP model for Howie's decision problem can be stated as:

MAX:	$350X_1 + 300X_2$	**2.5**
Subject to:	$1X_1 + 1X_2 \leq 200$	**2.6**
	$9X_1 + 6X_2 \leq 1,566$	**2.7**
	$12X_1 + 16X_2 \leq 2,880$	**2.8**
	$1X_1 \geq 0$	**2.9**
	$1X_2 \geq 0$	**2.10**

In this model, the decision variables X_1 and X_2 represent the number of Aqua-Spas and Hydro-Luxes to produce, respectively. Our goal is to determine the values for X_1 and X_2 that maximize the objective in equation 2.5 while simultaneously satisfying all the constraints in equations 2.6 through 2.10.

2.8 The General Form of an LP Model

The technique of linear programming is so named because the MP problems to which it applies are linear in nature. That is, it must be possible to express all the functions in an

LP model as some weighted sum (or linear combination) of the decision variables. So, an LP model takes on the general form:

$$\text{MAX (or MIN):} \quad c_1X_1 + c_2X_2 + \cdots + c_nX_n \qquad \textbf{2.11}$$

$$\text{Subject to:} \quad a_{11}X_1 + a_{12}X_2 + \cdots + a_{1n}X_n \leq b_1 \qquad \textbf{2.12}$$

$$\vdots$$

$$a_{k1}X_1 + a_{k2}X_2 + \cdots + a_{kn}X_n \geq b_k \qquad \textbf{2.13}$$

$$\vdots$$

$$a_{m1}X_1 + a_{m2}X_2 + \cdots + a_{mn}X_n = b_m \qquad \textbf{2.14}$$

Up to this point, we have suggested that the constraints in an LP model represent some type of limited resource. Although this is frequently the case, in later chapters you will see examples of LP models in which the constraints represent things other than limited resources. The important point here is that *any* problem that can be formulated in the above fashion is an LP problem.

The symbols $c_1, c_2, \ldots, c_n$ in equation 2.11 are called objective function coefficients and might represent the marginal profits (or costs) associated with the decision variables $X_1, X_2, \ldots, X_n$, respectively. The symbol a_{ij} found throughout equations 2.12 through 2.14 represents the numeric coefficient in the ith constraint for variable X_j. The objective function and constraints of an LP problem represent different weighted sums of the decision variables. The b_i symbols in the constraints, once again, represent values that the corresponding linear combination of the decision variables must be less than or equal to, greater than or equal to, or equal to.

You should now see a direct connection between the LP model we formulated for Blue Ridge Hot Tubs in equations 2.5 through 2.10 and the general definition of an LP model given in equations 2.11 through 2.14. In particular, note that the various symbols used in equations 2.11 through 2.14 to represent numeric constants (that is, the c_j, a_{ij}, and b_i) were replaced by actual numeric values in equations 2.5 through 2.10. Also, note that our formulation of the LP model for Blue Ridge Hot Tubs did not require the use of "equal to" constraints. Different problems require different types of constraints, and you should use whatever types of constraints are necessary for the problem at hand.

2.9 Solving LP Problems: An Intuitive Approach

After an LP model has been formulated, our interest naturally turns to solving it. But before we actually solve our example problem for Blue Ridge Hot Tubs, what do you think is the optimal solution to the problem? Just by looking at the model, what values for X_1 and X_2 do you think would give Howie the largest profit?

Following one line of reasoning, it might seem that Howie should produce as many units of X_1 (Aqua-Spas) as possible because each of these generates a profit of $350, whereas each unit of X_2 (Hydro-Luxes) generates a profit of only $300. But what is the maximum number of Aqua-Spas that Howie could produce?

Howie can produce the maximum number of units of X_1 by making no units of X_2 and devoting all his resources to the production of X_1. Suppose we let $X_2 = 0$ in the model in equations 2.5 through 2.10 to indicate that no Hydro-Luxes will be produced.

What then is the largest possible value of X_1? If $X_2 = 0$, then the inequality in equation 2.6 tells us:

$$X_1 \leq 200 \qquad \qquad \textbf{2.15}$$

So we know that X_1 cannot be any greater than 200 if $X_2 = 0$. However, we also have to consider the constraints in equations 2.7 and 2.8. If $X_2 = 0$, then the inequality in equation 2.7 reduces to:

$$9X_1 \leq 1{,}566 \qquad \qquad \textbf{2.16}$$

If we divide both sides of this inequality by 9, we find that the previous constraint is equivalent to:

$$X_1 \leq 174 \qquad \qquad \textbf{2.17}$$

Now consider the constraint in equation 2.8. If $X_2 = 0$, then the inequality in equation 2.8 reduces to:

$$12X_1 \leq 2{,}880 \qquad \qquad \textbf{2.18}$$

Again, if we divide both sides of this inequality by 12, we find that the previous constraint is equivalent to:

$$X_1 \leq 240 \qquad \qquad \textbf{2.19}$$

So, if $X_2 = 0$, the three constraints in our model imposing upper limits on the value of X_1 reduce to the values shown in equations 2.15, 2.17, and 2.19. The most restrictive of these constraints is equation 2.17. Therefore, the maximum number of units of X_1 that can be produced is 174. In other words, 174 is the largest value X_1 can take on and still satisfy all the constraints in the model.

If Howie builds 174 units of X_1 (Aqua-Spas) and 0 units of X_2 (Hydro-Luxes), he will have used all of the labor that is available for production ($9X_1 = 1{,}566$ if $X_1 = 174$). However, he will have 26 pumps remaining ($200 - X_1 = 26$ if $X_1 = 174$) and 792 feet of tubing remaining ($2{,}880 - 12X_1 = 792$ if $X_1 = 174$). Also, notice that the objective function value (or total profit) associated with this solution is:

$$\$350X_1 + \$300X_2 = \$350 \times 174 + \$300 \times 0 = \$60{,}900$$

From this analysis, we see that the solution $X_1 = 174$, $X_2 = 0$ is a *feasible solution* to the problem because it satisfies all the constraints of the model. But is it the *optimal solution*? In other words, is there any other possible set of values for X_1 and X_2 that also satisfies all the constraints *and* results in a higher objective function value? As you will see, the intuitive approach to solving LP problems that we have taken here cannot be trusted because there actually is a *better* solution to Howie's problem.

2.10 Solving LP Problems: A Graphical Approach

The constraints of an LP model define the set of feasible solutions—or the feasible region—for the problem. The difficulty in LP is determining which point or points in the feasible region correspond to the best possible value of the objective function. For simple problems with only two decision variables, it is fairly easy to sketch the feasible region for the LP model and locate the optimal feasible point graphically. Because the graphical approach can be used only if there are two decision variables, it has limited practical use. However, it is an extremely good way to develop a basic understanding of the strategy involved in solving LP problems. Therefore, we will use the graphical approach to solve the simple problem faced by Blue Ridge Hot Tubs. Chapter 3 shows how to solve this and other LP problems using a spreadsheet.

To solve an LP problem graphically, first you must plot the constraints for the problem and identify its feasible region. This is done by plotting the *boundary lines* of the constraints and identifying the points that will satisfy all the constraints. So, how do we do this for our example problem (repeated below)?

$$\text{MAX:} \qquad 350X_1 + 300X_2 \qquad\qquad\qquad \textbf{2.20}$$
$$\text{Subject to:} \qquad 1X_1 + 1X_2 \leq 200 \qquad\qquad \textbf{2.21}$$
$$9X_1 + 6X_2 \leq 1{,}566 \qquad\qquad \textbf{2.22}$$
$$12X_1 + 16X_2 \leq 2{,}880 \qquad\qquad \textbf{2.23}$$
$$1X_1 \qquad\quad \geq 0 \qquad\qquad\qquad \textbf{2.24}$$
$$1X_2 \geq 0 \qquad\qquad\qquad \textbf{2.25}$$

2.10.1 PLOTTING THE FIRST CONSTRAINT

The boundary of the first constraint in our model, which specifies that no more than 200 pumps can be used, is represented by the straight line defined by the equation:

$$X_1 + X_2 = 200 \qquad\qquad\qquad \textbf{2.26}$$

If we can find any two points on this line, the entire line can be plotted easily by drawing a straight line through these points. If $X_2 = 0$, we can see from equation 2.26 that $X_1 = 200$. Thus, the point $(X_1, X_2) = (200, 0)$ must fall on this line. If we let $X_1 = 0$, from equation 2.26, it is easy to see that $X_2 = 200$. So, the point $(X_1, X_2) = (0, 200)$ also must fall on this line. These two points are plotted on the graph in Figure 2.1 and connected to form the straight line representing equation 2.26.

Note that the graph of the line associated with equation 2.26 actually extends beyond the X_1 and X_2 axes shown in Figure 2.1. However, we can disregard the points beyond these axes because the values assumed by X_1 and X_2 cannot be negative (because we also have the constraints given by $X_1 \geq 0$ and $X_2 \geq 0$).

The line connecting the points (0, 200) and (200, 0) in Figure 2.1 identifies the points (X_1, X_2) that satisfy the equality $X_1 + X_2 = 200$. But recall that the first constraint in the LP model is the inequality $X_1 + X_2 \leq 200$. Thus, after plotting the boundary line of a constraint, we must determine which area on the graph corresponds to feasible solutions for the original constraint. This can be done easily by picking an arbitrary point on either side of (*i.e.*, not on) the boundary line and checking whether it satisfies the original constraint. For example, the point $(X_1, X_2) = (0, 0)$ is not on the boundary line of the first constraint and also satisfies the first constraint. Therefore, the area of the graph on the same side of the boundary line as the point (0, 0) corresponds to the feasible solutions of our first constraint. This area of feasible solutions is shaded in Figure 2.1.

2.10.2 PLOTTING THE SECOND CONSTRAINT

Some of the feasible solutions to one constraint in an LP model usually will not satisfy one or more of the other constraints in the model. For example, the point $(X_1, X_2) = (200, 0)$ satisfies the first constraint in our model, but it does not satisfy the second constraint, which requires that no more than 1,566 labor hours be used (because $9 \times 200 + 6 \times 0 = 1{,}800$). So, what values for X_1 and X_2 will satisfy both of these

FIGURE 2.1

Graphical representation of the pump constraint

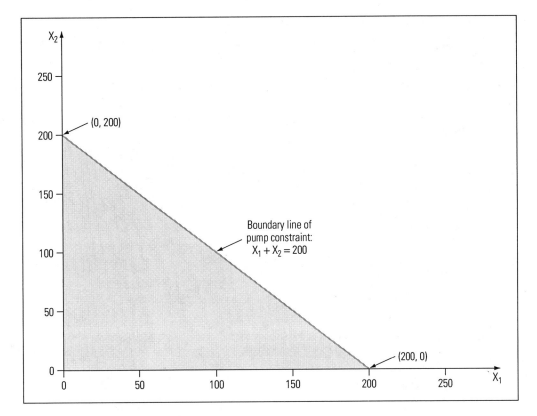

constraints simultaneously? To answer this question, we also need to plot the second constraint on the graph. This is done in the same manner as before—by locating two points on the boundary line of the constraint and connecting these points with a straight line.

The boundary line for the second constraint in our model is given by:

$$9X_1 + 6X_2 = 1{,}566 \qquad \textbf{2.27}$$

If $X_1 = 0$ in equation 2.27, then $X_2 = 1{,}566/6 = 261$. So, the point (0, 261) must fall on the line defined by equation 2.27. Similarly, if $X_2 = 0$ in equation 2.27, then $X_1 = 1{,}566/9 = 174$. So, the point (174, 0) also must fall on this line. These two points are plotted on the graph and connected with a straight line representing equation 2.27, as shown in Figure 2.2.

The line drawn in Figure 2.2 representing equation 2.27 is the boundary line for our second constraint. To determine the area on the graph that corresponds to feasible solutions to the second constraint, we again need to test a point on either side of this line to see if it is feasible. The point $(X_1, X_2) = (0, 0)$ satisfies $9X_1 + 6X_2 \leq 1{,}566$. Therefore, all points on the same side of the boundary line satisfy this constraint.

2.10.3 PLOTTING THE THIRD CONSTRAINT

To find the set of values for X_1 and X_2 that satisfies all the constraints in the model, we need to plot the third constraint. This constraint requires that no more than 2,880 feet of tubing be used in producing the hot tubs. Again, we will find two points on the graph that fall on the boundary line for this constraint and connect them with a straight line.

FIGURE 2.2

Graphical representation of the pump and labor constraints

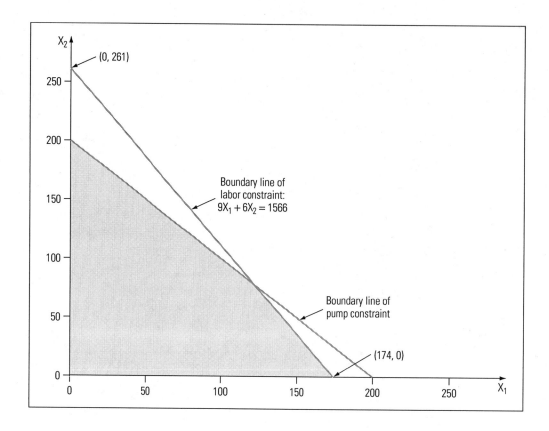

The boundary line for the third constraint in our model is:

$$12X_1 + 16X_2 = 2,880 \qquad \textbf{2.28}$$

If $X_1 = 0$ in equation 2.28, then $X_2 = 2,880/16 = 180$. So, the point (0, 180) must fall on the line defined by equation 2.28. Similarly, if $X_2 = 0$ in equation 2.28, then $X_1 = 2,880/12 = 240$. So, the point (240, 0) also must fall on this line. These two points are plotted on the graph and connected with a straight line representing equation 2.28, as shown in Figure 2.3.

Again, the line drawn in Figure 2.3 representing equation 2.28 is the boundary line for our third constraint. To determine the area on the graph that corresponds to feasible solutions to this constraint, we need to test a point on either side of this line to see if it is feasible. The point $(X_1, X_2) = (0, 0)$ satisfies $12X_1 + 16X_2 \leq 2,880$. Therefore, all points on the same side of the boundary line satisfy this constraint.

2.10.4 THE FEASIBLE REGION

It is now easy to see which points satisfy all the constraints in our model. These points correspond to the shaded area in Figure 2.3, labeled "Feasible Region." The feasible region is the set of points or values that the decision variables can assume and simultaneously satisfy all the constraints in the problem. Take a moment now to carefully compare the graphs in Figures 2.1, 2.2, and 2.3. In particular, notice that when we added the second constraint in Figure 2.2, some of the feasible solutions associated with the first constraint were eliminated because these solutions did not satisfy the second constraint. Similarly, when we added the third constraint in Figure 2.3, another portion of the feasible solutions for the first constraint was eliminated.

FIGURE 2.3

Graphical representation of the feasible region

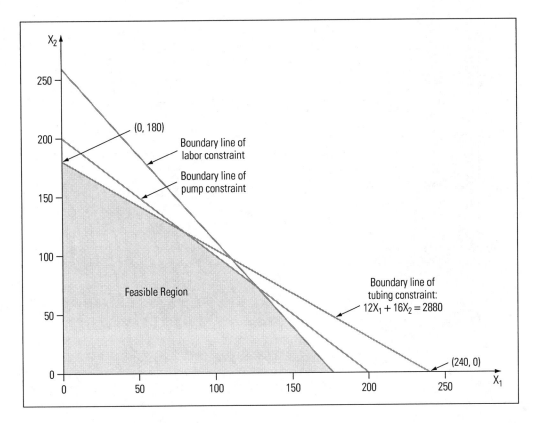

2.10.5 PLOTTING THE OBJECTIVE FUNCTION

Now that we have isolated the set of feasible solutions to our LP problem, we need to determine which of these solutions is best. That is, we must determine which point in the feasible region will maximize the value of the objective function in our model. At first glance, it might seem that trying to locate this point is like searching for a needle in a haystack. After all, as shown by the shaded region in Figure 2.3, there are an *infinite* number of feasible solutions to this problem. Fortunately, it is easy to eliminate most of the feasible solutions in an LP problem from consideration. It can be shown that if an LP problem has an optimal solution with a finite objective function value, this solution always will occur at a point in the feasible region where two or more of the boundary lines of the constraints intersect. These points of intersection are sometimes called corner points or extreme points of the feasible region.

To see why the finite optimal solution to an LP problem occurs at an extreme point of the feasible region, consider the relationship between the objective function and the feasible region of our example LP model. Suppose we are interested in finding the values of X_1 and X_2 associated with a given level of profit, such as $35,000. Then, mathematically, we are interested in finding the points (X_1, X_2) for which our objective function equals $35,000, or where:

$$\$350X_1 + \$300X_2 = \$35{,}000 \qquad \textbf{2.29}$$

This equation defines a straight line, which we can plot on our graph. Specifically, if $X_1 = 0$ then, from equation 2.29, $X_2 = 116.67$. Similarly, if $X_2 = 0$ in equation 2.29, then $X_1 = 100$. So, the points $(X_1, X_2) = (0, 116.67)$ and $(X_1, X_2) = (100, 0)$ both fall on the line defining a profit level of $35,000. (Note that all the points on this line produce a profit level of $35,000.) This line is shown in Figure 2.4.

FIGURE 2.4

Graph showing values of X_1 and X_2 that produce an objective function value of $35,000

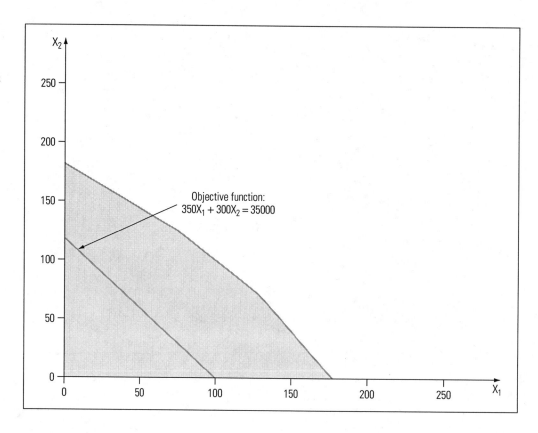

Now, suppose we are interested in finding the values of X_1 and X_2 that produce some higher level of profit, such as $52,500. Then, mathematically, we are interested in finding the points (X_1, X_2) for which our objective function equals $52,500, or where:

$$\$350X_1 + \$300X_2 = \$52,500 \qquad \textbf{2.30}$$

This equation also defines a straight line, which we could plot on our graph. If we do this, we'll find that the points $(X_1, X_2) = (0, 175)$ and $(X_1, X_2) = (150, 0)$ both fall on this line, as shown in Figure 2.5.

2.10.6 FINDING THE OPTIMAL SOLUTION USING LEVEL CURVES

The lines in Figure 2.5 representing the two objective function values are sometimes referred to as level curves because they represent different levels or values of the objective. Note that the two level curves in Figure 2.5 are *parallel* to one another. If we repeat this process of drawing lines associated with larger and larger values of our objective function, we will continue to observe a series of parallel lines shifting away from the origin—that is, away from the point (0, 0). The very last level curve we can draw that still intersects the feasible region will determine the maximum profit we can achieve. This point of intersection, shown in Figure 2.6, represents the optimal feasible solution to the problem.

As shown in Figure 2.6, the optimal solution to our example problem occurs at the point where the largest possible level curve intersects the feasible region at a single point. This is the feasible point that produces the largest profit for Blue Ridge Hot Tubs. But how do we figure out exactly what point this is and how much profit it provides?

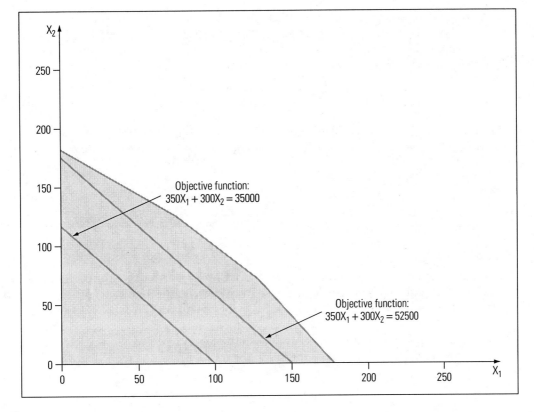

FIGURE 2.5

Parallel level curves for two different objective function values

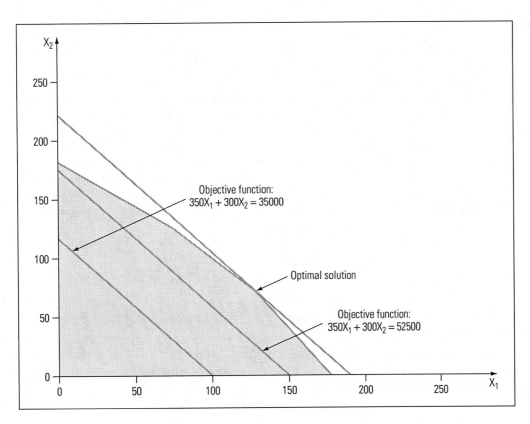

FIGURE 2.6

Graph showing optimal solution where the level curve is tangent to the feasible region

If you compare Figure 2.6 to Figure 2.3, you see that the optimal solution occurs where the boundary lines of the pump and labor constraints intersect (or are equal). Thus, the optimal solution is defined by the point (X_1, X_2) that simultaneously satisfies equations 2.26 and 2.27, which are repeated below:

$$X_1 + X_2 = 200$$
$$9X_1 + 6X_2 = 1,566$$

From the first equation, we easily conclude that $X_2 = 200 - X_1$. If we substitute this definition of X_2 into the second equation we obtain:

$$9X_1 + 6(200 - X_1) = 1,566$$

Using simple algebra, we can solve this equation to find that $X_1 = 122$. And because $X_2 = 200 - X_1$, we can conclude that $X_2 = 78$. Therefore, we have determined that the optimal solution to our example problem occurs at the point $(X_1, X_2) = (122, 78)$. This point satisfies all the constraints in our model and corresponds to the point in Figure 2.6 identified as the optimal solution.

The total profit associated with this solution is found by substituting the optimal values of $X_1 = 122$ and $X_2 = 78$ into the objective function. Thus, Blue Ridge Hot Tubs can realize a profit of $66,100 if it produces 122 Aqua-Spas and 78 Hydro-Luxes ($350 × 122 + $300 × 78 = $66,100). Any other production plan results in a lower total profit. In particular, note that the solution we found earlier using the intuitive approach (which produced a total profit of $60,900) is inferior to the optimal solution identified here.

2.10.7 FINDING THE OPTIMAL SOLUTION BY ENUMERATING THE CORNER POINTS

Earlier, we indicated that if an LP problem has a finite optimal solution, this solution always will occur at some corner point of the feasible region. So, another way of solving an LP problem is to identify all the corner points, or extreme points, of the feasible region and calculate the value of the objective function at each of these points. The corner point with the largest objective function value is the optimal solution to the problem.

This approach is illustrated in Figure 2.7, where the X_1 and X_2 coordinates for each of the extreme points are identified along with the associated objective function values. As expected, this analysis also indicates that the point $(X_1, X_2) = (122, 78)$ is optimal.

Enumerating the corner points to identify the optimal solution is often more difficult than the level curve approach because it requires that you identify the coordinates for *all* the extreme points of the feasible region. If there are many intersecting constraints, the number of extreme points can become rather large, making this procedure very tedious. Also, a special condition exists for which this procedure will not work. This condition, known as an unbounded solution, is described shortly.

2.10.8 SUMMARY OF GRAPHICAL SOLUTION TO LP PROBLEMS

To summarize this section, a two-variable LP problem is solved graphically by performing these steps:

1. Plot the boundary line of each constraint in the model.
2. Identify the feasible region, that is, the set of points on the graph that simultaneously satisfies all the constraints.

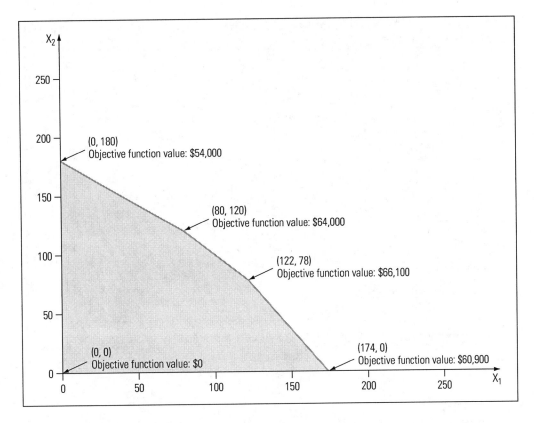

3. Locate the optimal solution by one of the following methods:
   a. Plot one or more level curves for the objective function and determine the direction in which parallel shifts in this line produce improved objective function values. Shift the level curve in a parallel manner in the improving direction until it intersects the feasible region at a single point. Then find the coordinates for this point. This is the optimal solution.
   b. Identify the coordinates of all the extreme points of the feasible region and calculate the objective function values associated with each point. If the feasible region is bounded, the point with the best objective function value is the optimal solution.

2.10.9 UNDERSTANDING HOW THINGS CHANGE

It is important to realize that if changes occur in any of the coefficients in the objective function or constraints of this problem, then the level curve, feasible region, and optimal solution to this problem also might change. To be an effective LP modeler, it is important for you to develop some intuition about how changes in various coefficients in the model will affect the solution to the problem. We will study this in greater detail in Chapter 4 when discussing sensitivity analysis. However, the spreadsheet shown in Figure 2.8 (and in the file named Fig2-8.xls on your data disk) allows you to change any of the coefficients in this problem and, instantly, see its effect. You are encouraged to experiment with this file to make sure that you understand the relationships between various model coefficients and their impact on this LP problem. (Case 2-1 at the end of this chapter asks some specific questions that can be answered using the spreadsheet shown in Figure 2.8.)

FIGURE 2.8

Interactive spreadsheet for the Blue Ridge Hot Tubs LP problem

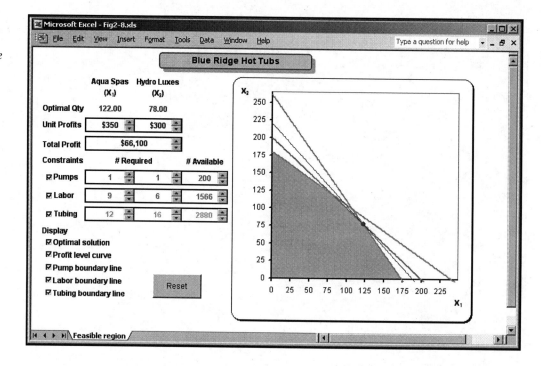

2.11 Special Conditions in LP Models

Several special conditions can arise in LP modeling: *alternate optimal solutions, redundant constraints, unbounded solutions,* and *infeasibility.* The first two conditions do not prevent you from solving an LP model and are not really problems—they are just anomalies that sometimes occur. On the other hand, the last two conditions represent real problems that prevent us from solving an LP model.

2.11.1 ALTERNATE OPTIMAL SOLUTIONS

Some LP models can have more than one optimal solution, or alternate optimal solutions. That is, there can be more than one feasible point that maximizes (or minimizes) the value of the objective function.

For example, suppose Howie can increase the price of Aqua-Spas to the point at which each unit sold generates a profit of $450 rather than $350. The revised LP model for this problem is:

$$
\begin{aligned}
\text{MAX:} \quad & 450X_1 + 300X_2 \\
\text{Subject to:} \quad & 1X_1 + 1X_2 \leq 200 \\
& 9X_1 + 6X_2 \leq 1{,}566 \\
& 12X_1 + 16X_2 \leq 2{,}880 \\
& 1X_1 \quad\quad\quad \geq 0 \\
& \quad\quad 1X_2 \geq 0
\end{aligned}
$$

Because none of the constraints changed, the feasible region for this model is the same as for the earlier example. The only difference in this model is the objective function. Therefore, the level curves for the objective function are different from what we observed earlier. Several level curves for this model are plotted with its feasible region in Figure 2.9.

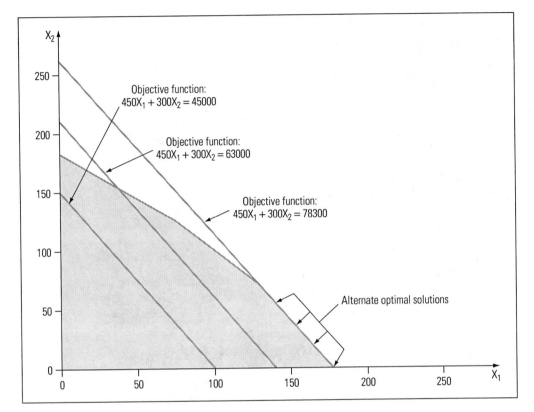

Notice that the final level curve in Figure 2.9 intersects the feasible region along an *edge* of the feasible region rather than at a single point. All the points on the line segment joining the corner point at (122, 78) to the corner point at (174, 0) produce the same optimal objective function value of $78,300 for this problem. Thus, all these points are alternate optimal solutions to the problem. If we used a computer to solve this problem, it would identify only one of the corner points of this edge as the optimal solution.

The fact that alternate optimal solutions sometimes occur is really not a problem because this anomaly does not prevent us from finding an optimal solution to the problem. In fact, in Chapter 7, "Goal Programming and Multiple Objective Optimization," you will see that alternate optimal solutions are sometimes very desirable.

2.11.2 REDUNDANT CONSTRAINTS

Redundant constraints present another special condition that sometimes occurs in an LP model. A redundant constraint is a constraint that plays no role in determining the feasible region of the problem. For example, in the hot tub example, suppose that 225 hot tub pumps are available instead of 200. The earlier LP model can be modified as follows to reflect this change:

$$
\begin{array}{lrcrcl}
\text{MAX:} & 350X_1 & + & 300X_2 & & \\
\text{Subject to:} & 1X_1 & + & 1X_2 & \leq & 225 \\
& 9X_1 & + & 6X_2 & \leq & 1{,}566 \\
& 12X_1 & + & 16X_2 & \leq & 2{,}880 \\
& 1X_1 & & & \geq & 0 \\
& & & 1X_2 & \geq & 0
\end{array}
$$

FIGURE 2.10

Example of a redundant constraint

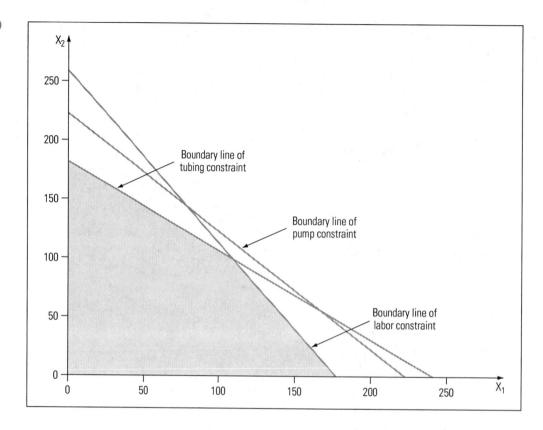

This model is identical to the original model we formulated for this problem *except* for the new upper limit on the first constraint (representing the number of pumps that can be used). The constraints and feasible region for this revised model are shown in Figure 2.10.

Notice that the pump constraint in this model no longer plays any role in defining the feasible region of the problem. That is, as long as the tubing constraint and labor constraints are satisfied (which is always the case for any feasible solution), then the pump constraint will also be satisfied. Therefore, we can remove the pump constraint from the model without changing the feasible region of the problem—the constraint is simply redundant.

The fact that the pump constraint does not play a role in defining the feasible region in Figure 2.10 implies that there will always be an excess number of pumps available. Because none of the feasible solutions identified in Figure 2.10 fall on the boundary line of the pump constraint, this constraint will always be satisfied as a strict inequality $(1X_1 + 1X_2 < 225)$ and never as a strict equality $(1X_1 + 1X_2 = 225)$.

Again, redundant constraints are not really a problem. They do not prevent us (or the computer) from finding the optimal solution to an LP problem. However, they do represent "excess baggage" for the computer; so if you know that a constraint is redundant, eliminating it saves the computer this excess work. On the other hand, if the model you are working with will be modified and used repeatedly, it might be best to leave any redundant constraints in the model because they might not be redundant in the future. For example, from Figure 2.3, we know that if the availability of pumps is returned to 200, then the pump constraint again plays an important role in defining the feasible region (and optimal solution) of the problem.

2.11.3 UNBOUNDED SOLUTIONS

When attempting to solve some LP problems, you might encounter situations in which the objective function can be made infinitely large (in the case of a maximization problem) or infinitely small (in the case of a minimization problem). As an example, consider this LP problem:

$$
\begin{aligned}
\text{MAX:} \qquad & X_1 + X_2 \\
\text{Subject to:} \qquad & X_1 + X_2 \geq 400 \\
& -X_1 + 2X_2 \leq 400 \\
& X_1 \qquad\quad \geq 0 \\
& \qquad\quad X_2 \geq 0
\end{aligned}
$$

The feasible region and some level curves for this problem are shown in Figure 2.11. From this graph, you can see that as the level curves shift farther and farther away from the origin, the objective function increases. Because the feasible region is not bounded in this direction, you can continue shifting the level curve by an infinite amount and make the objective function infinitely large.

Although it is not unusual to encounter an unbounded solution when solving an LP model, such a solution indicates that there is something wrong with the formulation—for example, one or more constraints were omitted from the formulation, or a "less than" constraint was entered erroneously as a "greater than" constraint.

While describing how to find the optimal solution to an LP model by enumerating corner points, we noted that this procedure will not always work if the feasible region for the problem is unbounded. Figure 2.11 provides an example of such a situation. The only extreme points for the feasible region in Figure 2.11 occur at the points (400, 0) and

FIGURE 2.11

Example of an LP problem with an unbounded solution

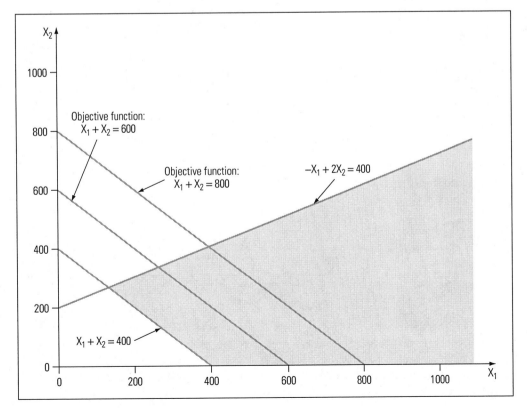

(133.$\overline{3}$, 266.$\overline{6}$). The objective function value at both of these points (and at any point on the line segment joining them) is 400. By enumerating the extreme points for this problem, we might erroneously conclude that alternate optimal solutions to this problem exist that produce an optimal objective function value of 400. This is true if the problem involved *minimizing* the objective function. However, the goal here is to *maximize* the objective function value, which, as we have seen, can be done without limit. So, when trying to solve an LP problem by enumerating the extreme points of an unbounded feasible region, you also must check whether or not the objective function is unbounded.

2.11.4 INFEASIBILITY

An LP problem is infeasible if there is no way to satisfy all the constraints in the problem simultaneously. As an example, consider the LP model:

$$\text{MAX:} \quad X_1 + X_2$$
$$\text{Subject to:} \quad X_1 + X_2 \leq 150$$
$$X_1 + X_2 \geq 200$$
$$X_1 \geq 0$$
$$X_2 \geq 0$$

The feasible solutions for the first two constraints in this model are shown in Figure 2.12. Notice that the feasible solutions to the first constraint fall on the left side of its boundary line, whereas the feasible solutions to the second constraint fall on the right side of its boundary line. Therefore, no possible values for X_1 and X_2 exist that satisfy both constraints in the model simultaneously. In such a case, there are no feasible solutions to the problem.

FIGURE 2.12

Example of an LP problem with no feasible solution

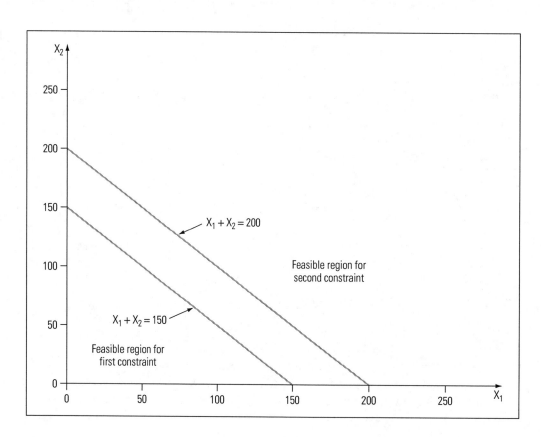

Infeasibility can occur in LP problems, perhaps because of an error in the formulation of the model—such as unintentionally making a "less than or equal to" constraint a "greater than or equal to" constraint. Or there just might not be a way to satisfy all the constraints in the model. In this case, constraints would have to be eliminated or loosened to obtain a feasible region (and feasible solution) for the problem.

Loosening constraints involves increasing the upper limits (or reducing the lower limits) to expand the range of feasible solutions. For example, if we loosen the first constraint in the previous model by changing the upper limit from 150 to 250, there is a feasible region for the problem. Of course, loosening constraints should not be done arbitrarily. In a real model, the value 150 would represent some actual characteristic of the decision problem (such as the number of pumps available to make hot tubs). We obviously cannot change this value to 250 unless it is appropriate to do so—that is, unless we know another 100 pumps can be obtained.

2.12 Summary

This chapter provided an introduction to an area of management science known as mathematical programming (MP), or optimization. Optimization covers a broad range of problems that share a common goal—determining the values for the decision variables in a problem that will maximize (or minimize) some objective function while satisfying various constraints. Constraints impose restrictions on the values that can be assumed by the decision variables and define the set of feasible options (or the feasible region) for the problem.

Linear programming (LP) problems represent a special category of MP problems in which the objective function and all the constraints can be expressed as linear combinations of the decision variables. Simple, two-variable LP problems can be solved graphically by identifying the feasible region and plotting level curves for the objective function. An optimal solution to an LP problem always occurs at a corner point of its feasible region (unless the objective function is unbounded).

Some anomalies can occur in optimization problems; these include alternate optimal solutions, redundant constraints, unbounded solutions, and infeasibility.

2.13 References

Bazaraa, M. and J. Jarvis. *Linear Programming and Network Flows*. New York: Wiley, 1990.

Dantzig, G. *Linear Programming and Extensions*. Princeton, NJ: Princeton University Press, 1963.

Eppen, G., F. Gould, and C. Schmidt, *Introduction to Management Science*. Englewood Cliffs, NJ: Prentice Hall, 1993.

Shogan, A. *Management Science*. Englewood Cliffs, NJ: Prentice Hall, 1988.

Winston, W. *Operations Research: Applications and Algorithms*. Belmont, CA: Duxbury Press, 1997.

Questions and Problems

1. An LP model can have more than one optimal solution. Is it possible for an LP model to have exactly two optimal solutions? Why or why not?
2. In the solution to the Blue Ridge Hot Tubs problem, the optimal values for X_1 and X_2 turned out to be integers (whole numbers). Is this a general property of the solutions to LP problems? In other words, will the solution to an LP problem always consist of integers? Why or why not?

3. To determine the feasible region associated with "less than or equal to" constraints or "greater than or equal to" constraints, we graphed these constraints as if they were "equal to" constraints. Why is this possible?

4. Are the following objective functions for an LP model equivalent? That is, if they are both used, one at a time, to solve a problem with exactly the same constraints, will the optimal values for X_1 and X_2 be the same in both cases? Why or why not?

$$\begin{aligned} \text{MAX:} & \quad 2X_1 + 3X_2 \\ \text{MIN:} & \quad -2X_1 - 3X_2 \end{aligned}$$

5. Which of the following constraints are not linear or cannot be included as a constraint in a linear programming problem?
   a. $2X_1 + X_2 - 3X_3 \geq 50$
   b. $2X_1 + \sqrt{X_2} \geq 60$
   c. $4X_1 - \frac{1}{3}X_2 = 75$
   d. $\dfrac{3X_1 + 2X_2 - 3X_3}{X_1 + X_2 + X_3} \leq 0.9$
   e. $3X_1^2 + 7X_2 \leq 45$

6. Solve the following LP problem graphically by enumerating the corner points.

$$\begin{aligned} \text{MAX:} & \quad 3X_1 + 4X_2 \\ \text{Subject to:} & \quad X_1 \qquad\quad \leq 12 \\ & \qquad\quad X_2 \leq 10 \\ & \quad 4X_1 + 6X_2 \leq 72 \\ & \qquad X_1, X_2 \geq 0 \end{aligned}$$

7. Solve the following LP problem graphically using level curves.

$$\begin{aligned} \text{MIN:} & \quad 2X_1 + 3X_2 \\ \text{Subject to:} & \quad 2X_1 + 1X_2 \geq 3 \\ & \quad 4X_1 + 5X_2 \geq 20 \\ & \quad 2X_1 + 8X_2 \geq 16 \\ & \quad 5X_1 + 6X_2 \leq 60 \\ & \qquad X_1, X_2 \geq 0 \end{aligned}$$

8. Solve the following LP problem graphically using level curves.

$$\begin{aligned} \text{MAX:} & \quad 2X_1 + 5X_2 \\ \text{Subject to:} & \quad 6X_1 + 5X_2 \leq 60 \\ & \quad 2X_1 + 3X_2 \leq 24 \\ & \quad 3X_1 + 6X_2 \leq 48 \\ & \qquad X_1, X_2 \geq 0 \end{aligned}$$

9. Solve the following LP problem graphically by enumerating the corner points.

$$\begin{aligned} \text{MIN:} & \quad 5X_1 + 20X_2 \\ \text{Subject to:} & \quad X_1 + X_2 \geq 12 \\ & \quad 2X_1 + 5X_2 \geq 40 \\ & \quad X_1 + X_2 \leq 15 \\ & \qquad X_1, X_2 \geq 0 \end{aligned}$$

10. Consider the following LP problem.

$$\text{MAX:} \quad 3X_1 + 2X_2$$
$$\text{Subject to:} \quad 3X_1 + 3X_2 \leq 300$$
$$6X_1 + 3X_2 \leq 480$$
$$3X_1 + 3X_2 \leq 480$$
$$X_1, X_2 \geq 0$$

a. Sketch the feasible region for this model.
b. What is the optimal solution?
c. Identify any redundant constraints in this model.

11. Solve the following LP problem graphically by enumerating the corner points.

$$\text{MAX:} \quad 10X_1 + 12X_2$$
$$\text{Subject to:} \quad 8X_1 + 6X_2 \leq 98$$
$$6X_1 + 8X_2 \leq 98$$
$$X_1 + X_2 \geq 14$$
$$X_1, X_2 \geq 0$$

12. Solve the following LP problem using level curves.

$$\text{MAX:} \quad 4X_1 + 5X_2$$
$$\text{Subject to:} \quad 2X_1 + 3X_2 \leq 120$$
$$4X_1 + 3X_2 \leq 140$$
$$X_1 + X_2 \geq 80$$
$$X_1, X_2 \geq 0$$

13. The marketing manager for Mountain Mist soda needs to decide how many TV spots and magazine ads to run during the next quarter. Each TV spot costs $5,000 and is expected to increase sales by 300,000 cans. Each magazine ad costs $2,000 and is expected to increase sales by 500,000 cans. A total of $100,000 may be spent on TV and magazine ads; however, Mountain Mist wants to spend no more than $70,000 on TV spots and no more than $50,000 on magazine ads. Mountain Mist earns a profit of $0.05 on each can it sells.
a. Formulate an LP model for this problem.
b. Sketch the feasible region for this model.
c. Find the optimal solution to the problem using level curves.

14. Blacktop Refining extracts minerals from ore mined at two different sites in Montana. Each ton of ore type 1 contains 20% copper, 20% zinc and 15% magnesium. Each ton of ore type 2 contains 30% copper, 25% zinc and 10% magnesium. Ore type 1 costs $90 per ton and ore type 2 costs $120 per ton. Blacktop would like to buy enough ore to extract at least 8 tons of copper, 6 tons of zinc, and 5 tons of magnesium in the least costly manner.
a. Formulate an LP model for this problem.
b. Sketch the feasible region for this problem.
c. Find the optimal solution.

15. The Electrotech Corporation manufactures two industrial-sized electrical devices: generators and alternators. Both of these products require wiring and testing during the assembly process. Each generator requires 2 hours of wiring and 1 hour of testing and can be sold for a $250 profit. Each alternator requires 3 hours of wiring and 2 hours of testing and can be sold for a $150 profit. There are 260 hours of wiring

time and 140 hours of testing time available in the next production period and Electrotech wants to maximize profit.
   a. Formulate an LP model for this problem.
   b. Sketch the feasible region for this problem.
   c. Determine the optimal solution to this problem using level curves.
16. Refer to the previous question. Suppose that Electrotech's management decides that they need to make at least 20 generators and at least 20 alternators.
   a. Reformulate your LP model to account for this change.
   b. Sketch the feasible region for this problem.
   c. Determine the optimal solution to this problem by enumerating the corner points.
   d. Suppose that Electrotech can acquire additional wiring time at a very favorable cost. Should it do so? Why or why not?
17. Bill's Grill is a popular college restaurant that is famous for its hamburgers. The owner of the restaurant, Bill, mixes fresh ground beef and pork with a secret ingredient to make delicious quarter-pound hamburgers that are advertised as having no more than 25% fat. Bill can buy beef containing 80% meat and 20% fat at $0.85 per pound. He can buy pork containing 70% meat and 30% fat at $0.65 per pound. Bill wants to determine the minimum cost way to blend the beef and pork to make hamburgers that have no more than 25% fat.
   a. Formulate an LP model for this problem. (*Hint*: The decision variables for this problem represent the percentage of beef and the percentage of pork to combine.)
   b. Sketch the feasible region for this problem.
   c. Determine the optimal solution to this problem by enumerating the corner points.
18. Zippy motorcycle manufacturing produces two popular pocket bikes (miniature motorcycles with 49cc engines): the Razor and the Zoomer. In the coming week, the manufacturer wants to produce a total of up to 700 bikes and wants to ensure that the number of Razors produced does not exceed the number of Zoomers by more than 300. Each Razor produced and sold results in a profit of $70, and each Zoomer results in a profit of $40. The bikes are identical mechanically and differ only in the appearance of the polymer-based trim around the fuel tank and seat. Each Razor's trim requires 2 pounds of polymer and 3 hours of production time, and each Zoomer requires 1 pound of polymer and 4 hours of production time. Assume that 900 pounds of polymer and 2400 labor hours are available for production of these items in the coming week.
   a. Formulate an LP model for this problem.
   b. Sketch the feasible region for this problem.
   c. What is the optimal solution?
19. The Quality Desk Company makes two types of computer desks from laminated particle board. The Presidential model requires 30 square feet of particle board, 1 keyboard sliding mechanism, and 5 hours of labor to fabricate. It sells for $149. The Senator model requires 24 square feet of particle board, 1 keyboard sliding mechanism, and 3 hours of labor to fabricate. It sells for $135. In the coming week, the company can buy up to 15,000 square feet of particle board at $1.35 per square foot and up to 600 keyboard sliding mechanisms at a cost of $4.75 each. The company views manufacturing labor as a fixed cost and has 3000 labor hours available in the coming week for the fabrication of these desks.
   a. Formulate an LP model for this problem.
   b. Sketch the feasible region for this problem.
   c. What is the optimal solution?
20. A farmer in Georgia has a 100-acre farm on which to plant watermelons and cantaloupes. Every acre planted with watermelons requires 50 gallons of water per day and must be prepared for planting with 20 pounds of fertilizer. Every acre planted

with cantaloupes requires 75 gallons of water per day and must be prepared for planting with 15 pounds of fertilizer. The farmer estimates that it will take 2 hours of labor to harvest each acre planted with watermelons and 2.5 hours to harvest each acre planted with cantaloupes. He believes that watermelons will sell for about $3 each, and cantaloupes will sell for about $1 each. Every acre planted with watermelons is expected to yield 90 salable units. Every acre planted with cantaloupes is expected to yield 300 salable units. The farmer can pump about 6,000 gallons of water per day for irrigation purposes from a shallow well. He can buy as much fertilizer as he needs at a cost of $10 per 50-pound bag. Finally, the farmer can hire laborers to harvest the fields at a rate of $5 per hour. If the farmer sells all the watermelons and cantaloupes he produces, how many acres of each crop should the farmer plant to maximize profits?

    a. Formulate an LP model for this problem.

    b. Sketch the feasible region for this model.

    c. Find the optimal solution to the problem using level curves.

21. Sanderson Manufacturing produces ornate, decorative wood frame doors and windows. Each item produced goes through 3 manufacturing processes: cutting, sanding, and finishing. Each door produced requires 1 hour in cutting, 30 minutes in sanding, and 30 minutes in finishing. Each window requires 30 minutes in cutting, 45 minutes in sanding, and 1 hour in finishing. In the coming week Sanderson has 40 hours of cutting capacity available, 40 hours of sanding capacity, and 60 hours of finishing capacity. Assume that all doors produced can be sold for a profit of $500 and all windows can be sold for a profit of $400.

    a. Formulate an LP model for this problem.

    b. Sketch the feasible region.

    c. What is the optimal solution?

22. PC-Express is a computer retail store that sells two kinds of microcomputers: desktops and laptops. The company earns $600 on each desktop computer it sells and $900 on each laptop. The microcomputers PC-Express sells are manufactured by another company. This manufacturer has a special order to fill for another customer and cannot ship more than 80 desktop computers and 75 laptops to PC-Express next month. The employees at PC-Express must spend about 2 hours installing software and checking each desktop computer they sell. They spend roughly 3 hours to complete this process for laptop computers. They expect to have about 300 hours available for this purpose during the next month. The store's management is fairly certain that they can sell all the computers they order, but are unsure how many desktops and laptops they should order to maximize profits.

    a. Formulate an LP model for this problem.

    b. Sketch the feasible region for this model.

    c. Find the optimal solution to the problem by enumerating the corner points.

23. American Auto is evaluating their marketing plan for the sedans, SUVs, and trucks they produce. A TV ad featuring this SUV has been developed. The company estimates that each showing of this commercial will cost $500,000 and increase sales of SUVs by 3%, but reduce sales of trucks by 1%, and have no effect of the sales of sedans. The company also has a print ad campaign developed that it can run in various nationally distributed magazines at a cost of $750,000 per title. It is estimated that each magazine title the ad runs in will increase the sales of sedans, SUVs, and trucks by 2%, 1%, and 4%, respectively. The company desires to increase sales of sedans, SUVs, and trucks by at least 3%, 14%, and 4%, respectively, in the least costly manner.

    a. Formulate an LP model for this problem.

    b. Sketch the feasible region.

    c. What is the optimal solution?

For the Lines They Are A-Changin' (with apologies to Bob Dylan)

The owner of Blue Ridge Hot Tubs, Howie Jones, has asked for your assistance in analyzing how the feasible region and solution to his production problem might change in response to changes in various parameters in the LP model. He is hoping that this might further his understanding of LP and how the constraints, objective function, and optimal solution interrelate. To assist in this process, he asked a consulting firm to develop the spreadsheet shown earlier in Figure 2.8 (and the file Fig. 2-8.xls on your data disk) that dynamically updates the feasible region and optimal solution and the various parameters in the model change. Unfortunately, Howie has not had much time to play around with this spreadsheet, so he has left it in your hands and asked you to use it to answer the following questions. (Click the Reset button in file Fig. 2-8.xls before answering each of the following questions.)

a. In the optimal solution to this problem, how many pumps, hours of labor, and feet of tubing are being used?

b. If the company could increase the number of pumps available, should they? Why or why not? And if so, what is the maximum number of additional pumps that they should consider acquiring, and by how much would this increase profit?

c. If the company could acquire more labor hours, should they? Why or why not? If so, how much additional labor should they consider acquiring and by how much would this increase profit?

d. If the company could acquire more tubing, should they? Why or why not? If so, how additional tubing should they consider acquiring and how much would this increase profit?

e. By how much would profit increase if the company could reduce the labor required to produce Aqua-Spas from 9 to 8 hours? And from 8 to 7 hours? And from 7 to 6 hours?

f. By how much would profit increase if the company could reduce the labor required to produce Hydro-Luxes from 6 to 5 hours? And from 5 to 4 hours? And from 4 to 3 hours?

g. By how much would profit increase if the company could reduce the amount of tubing required to produce Aqua-Spas from 12 to 11 feet? And from 11 to 10 feet? And from 10 to 9 feet?

h. By how much would profit increase if the company could reduce the amount of tubing required to produce Hydro-Luxes from 16 to 15 feet? And from 15 to 14 feet? And from 14 to 13 feet?

i. By how much would the unit profit on Aqua-Spas have to change before the optimal product mix changes?

j. By how much would the unit profit on Hydro-Luxes have to change before the optimal product mix changes?

Chapter 3

Modeling and Solving
LP Problems in a Spreadsheet

3.0 Introduction

Chapter 2 discussed how to formulate linear programming (LP) problems and how to solve simple, two-variable LP problems graphically. As you might expect, very few real-world LP problems involve only two decision variables. So, the graphical solution approach is of limited value in solving LP problems. However, the discussion of two-variable problems provides a basis for understanding the issues involved in all LP problems and the general strategies for solving them.

For example, every solvable LP problem has a feasible region, and an optimal solution to the problem can be found at some extreme point of this region (assuming the problem is not unbounded). This is true of all LP problems regardless of the number of decision variables. Although it is fairly easy to graph the feasible region for a two-variable LP problem, it is difficult to visualize or graph the feasible region of an LP problem with three variables because such a graph is three-dimensional. If there are more than three variables, it is virtually impossible to visualize or graph the feasible region for an LP problem because such a graph involves more than three dimensions.

Fortunately, several mathematical techniques exist to solve LP problems involving almost any number of variables without visualizing or graphing their feasible regions. These techniques are now built into spreadsheet packages in a way that makes solving LP problems a fairly simple task. So, using the appropriate computer software, you can solve almost any LP problem easily. The main challenge is ensuring that you formulate the LP problem correctly and communicate this formulation to the computer accurately. This chapter shows you how to do this using spreadsheets.

3.1 Spreadsheet Solvers

Excel, Quattro Pro, and Lotus 1-2-3 all come with built-in spreadsheet optimization tools called solvers. Their inclusion in these applications demonstrates the importance of LP (and optimization in general). This book uses Excel to illustrate how spreadsheet solvers can solve optimization problems. However, the same concepts and techniques presented here apply to other spreadsheet packages, although certain details of implementation may differ.

You can also solve optimization problems without using a spreadsheet by using a specialized mathematical programming package. A partial list of these packages includes: LINDO, MPSX, CPLEX, and MathPro. Typically, these packages are used by researchers and businesses interested in solving extremely large problems that do not fit conveniently in a spreadsheet.

The Spreadsheet Solver Company

Frontline Systems, Inc. created the solvers in Microsoft Excel, Lotus 1-2-3, and Corel Quattro Pro. Frontline markets enhanced versions of these spreadsheet solvers that offer greater capacity, faster speed, and several ease-of-use features. You can find out more about Frontline Systems and their products by visiting their Web site at http://www.solver.com.

3.2 Solving LP Problems in a Spreadsheet

We will demonstrate the mechanics of using the Solver in Excel by solving the problem faced by Howie Jones, described in Chapter 2. Recall that Howie owns and operates Blue Ridge Hot Tubs, a company that sells two models of hot tubs: the Aqua-Spa and the Hydro-Lux. Howie purchases prefabricated fiberglass hot tub shells and installs a common water pump and the appropriate amount of tubing into each hot tub. Every Aqua-Spa requires 9 hours of labor and 12 feet of tubing; every Hydro-Lux requires 6 hours of labor and 16 feet of tubing. Demand for these products is such that each Aqua-Spa produced can be sold to generate a profit of $350, and each Hydro-Lux produced can be sold to generate a profit of $300. The company expects to have 200 pumps, 1,566 hours of labor, and 2,880 feet of tubing available during the next production cycle. The problem is to determine the optimal number of Aqua-Spas and Hydro-Luxes to produce to maximize profits.

Chapter 2 developed the following LP formulation for the problem Howie faces. In this model, X_1 represents the number of Aqua-Spas to be produced, and X_2 represents the number of Hydro-Luxes to be produced.

$$
\begin{aligned}
\text{MAX:} \quad & 350X_1 + 300X_2 && \text{\} profit} \\
\text{Subject to:} \quad & 1X_1 + 1X_2 \leq 200 && \text{\} pump constraint} \\
& 9X_1 + 6X_2 \leq 1{,}566 && \text{\} labor constraint} \\
& 12X_1 + 16X_2 \leq 2{,}880 && \text{\} tubing constraint} \\
& 1X_1 \qquad\quad \geq 0 && \text{\} simple lower bound} \\
& \qquad 1X_2 \geq 0 && \text{\} simple lower bound}
\end{aligned}
$$

So, how do you solve this problem in a spreadsheet? First, you must implement, or build, this model in the spreadsheet.

3.3 The Steps in Implementing an LP Model in a Spreadsheet

The following four steps summarize what must be done to implement any LP problem in a spreadsheet.

1. **Organize the data for the model on the spreadsheet.** The data for the model consist of the coefficients in the objective function, the various coefficients in the

constraints, and the right-hand-side (RHS) values for the constraints. There is usually more than one way to organize the data for a particular problem on a spreadsheet, but you should keep in mind some general guidelines. First, the goal is to organize the data so their purpose and meaning are as clear as possible. Think of your spreadsheet as a management report that needs to communicate clearly the important factors of the problem being solved. To this end, you should spend some time organizing the data for the problem in your mind's eye—visualizing how the data can be laid out logically—before you start typing values in the spreadsheet. Descriptive labels should be placed in the spreadsheet to clearly identify the various data elements. Often, row and column structures of the data in the model can be used in the spreadsheet to facilitate model implementation. (Note that some or all of the coefficients and values for an LP model might be calculated from other data, often referred to as the primary data. It is best to maintain primary data in the spreadsheet and use appropriate formulas to calculate the coefficients and values that are needed for the LP formulation. Then, if the primary data change, appropriate changes will be made automatically in the coefficients for the LP model.)

2. **Reserve separate cells in the spreadsheet to represent each decision variable in the algebraic model.** Although you can use any empty cells in a spreadsheet to represent the decision variables, it is usually best to arrange the cells representing the decision variables in a way that parallels the structure of the data. This is often helpful in setting up formulas for the objective function and constraints. When possible, it is also a good idea to keep the cells representing decision variables in the same area of the spreadsheet. In addition, you should use descriptive labels to clearly identify the meaning of these cells.

3. **Create a formula in a cell in the spreadsheet that corresponds to the objective function in the algebraic model.** The spreadsheet formula corresponding to the objective function is created by referring to the data cells where the objective function coefficients have been entered (or calculated) and to the corresponding cells representing the decision variables.

4. **For each constraint, create a formula in a separate cell in the spreadsheet that corresponds to the left-hand-side (LHS) of the constraint.** The formula corresponding to the LHS of each constraint is created by referring to the data cells where the coefficients for these constraints have been entered (or calculated) and to the appropriate decision variable cells. Many of the constraint formulas have a similar structure. Thus, when possible, you should create constraint formulas that can be copied to implement other constraint formulas. This not only reduces the effort required to implement a model, but also helps avoid hard-to-detect typing errors.

Although each of the previous steps must be performed to implement an LP model in a spreadsheet, they do not have to be performed in the order indicated. It is usually wise to perform step 1 first, followed by step 2. But the order in which steps 3 and 4 are performed often varies from problem to problem.

Also, it is often wise to use shading, background colors, and/or borders to identify the cells representing decision variables, constraints, and the objective function in a model. This allows the user of a spreadsheet to distinguish more readily between cells representing raw data (that can be changed) and other elements of the model. We have more to say about how to design and implement effective spreadsheet models for LP problems. But first, let's see how to use the previous steps to implement a spreadsheet model using our example problem.

3.4 A Spreadsheet Model for the Blue Ridge Hot Tubs Problem

One possible spreadsheet representation for our example problem is given in Figure 3.1 (and in the file named Fig3-1.xls on your data disk). Let's walk through the creation of this model step-by-step so you can see how it relates to the algebraic formulation of the model.

A Note About Macros

In most of the spreadsheet examples accompanying this book, you can click on the blue title bars at the top of the spreadsheet to toggle on and off a note that provides additional documentation about the spreadsheet model. This documentation feature is enabled through the use of macros. Because macros pose a risk for spreading software viruses, when you open these files, Excel might warn you that the file contains a macro and, depending on your security settings, might even disable the macros from running. All the files accompanying this book were thoroughly scanned for viruses. When using these files, we recommend that you use Excel's medium macro security setting (click Tools, Macro, Security, Medium). If you then open a file containing macros, Excel will ask you if you want to enable or disable the macros. You must click the Enable Macros option to make use of the macro features in the spreadsheet files accompanying this book.

FIGURE 3.1

A spreadsheet model for the Blue Ridge Hot Tub production problem

X_1

X_2

Objective Function =
$B6 \times B5 + C6 \times C5$

LHS of 1st constraint =
$B9 \times B5 + C9 \times C5$

LHS of 2nd constraint =
$B10 \times B5 + C10 \times C5$

LHS of 3rd constraint =
$B11 \times B5 + C11 \times C5$

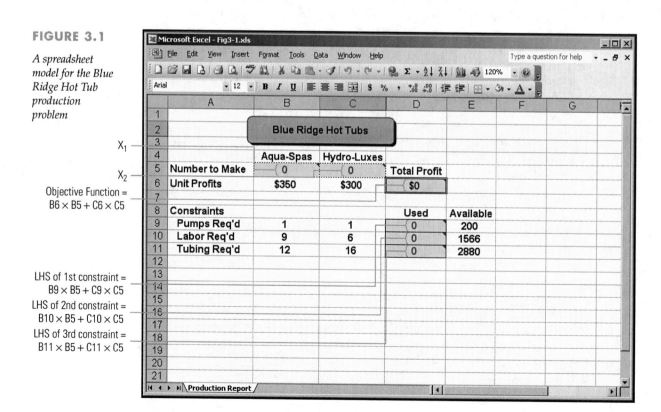

3.4.1 ORGANIZING THE DATA

One of the first steps in building any spreadsheet model for an LP problem is to organize the data for the model on the spreadsheet. In Figure 3.1, we enter the data for the unit profits for Aqua-Spas and Hydro-Luxes in cells B6 and C6, respectively. Next, we enter the number of pumps, labor hours, and feet of tubing required to produce each type of hot tub, in cells B9 through C11. The values in cells B9 and C9 indicate that one pump is required to produce each type of hot tub. The values in cells B10 and C10 show that each Aqua-Spa produced requires 9 hours of labor, and each Hydro-Lux requires 6 hours. Cells B11 and C11 indicate that each Aqua-Spa produced requires 12 feet of tubing, and each Hydro-Lux requires 16 feet. The available number of pumps, labor hours, and feet of tubing are entered in cells E9 through E11. Notice that appropriate labels also are entered to identify all the data elements for the problem.

3.4.2 REPRESENTING THE DECISION VARIABLES

As indicated in Figure 3.1, cells B5 and C5 represent the decision variables X_1 and X_2 in our algebraic model. These cells are shaded and outlined with dashed borders to distinguish them visually from other elements of the model. Values of zero were placed in cells B5 and C5 because we do not know how many Aqua-Spas and Hydro-Luxes should be produced. Shortly, we will use Solver to determine the optimal values for these cells. Figure 3.2 summarizes the relationship between the decision variables in the algebraic model and the corresponding cells in the spreadsheet.

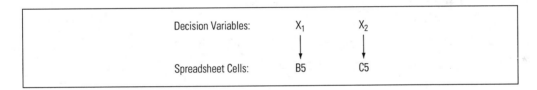

FIGURE 3.2

Summary of the relationship between the decision variables and corresponding spreadsheet cells

3.4.3 REPRESENTING THE OBJECTIVE FUNCTION

The next step in implementing our LP problem is to create a formula in a cell of the spreadsheet to represent the objective function. We can accomplish this in many ways. Because the objective function is $350X_1 + 300X_2$, you might be tempted to enter the formula =350*B5+300*C5 in the spreadsheet. However, if you wanted to change the coefficients in the objective function, you would have to go back and edit this formula to reflect the changes. Because the objective function coefficients are entered in cells B6 and C6, a better way of implementing the objective function is to refer to the values in cells B6 and C6 rather than entering numeric constants in the formula. The formula for the objective function is entered in cell D6 as:

Formula for cell D6:   =B6*B5+C6*C5

As shown in Figure 3.1, cell D6 initially returns the value 0 because cells B5 and C5 both contain zeros. Figure 3.3 summarizes the relationship between the algebraic objective function and the formula entered in cell D6. By implementing the objective function in this manner, if the profits earned on the hot tubs ever change, the spreadsheet model can be changed easily and the problem can be re-solved to determine the effect of this change on the optimal solution. Note that cell D6 has been shaded and outlined with a double border to distinguish it from other elements of the model.

FIGURE 3.3

Summary of the relationship between the decision variables and corresponding spreadsheet cells

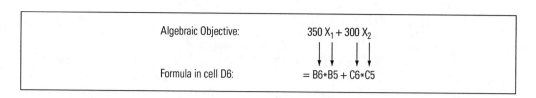

3.4.4 REPRESENTING THE CONSTRAINTS

The next step in building the spreadsheet model involves implementing the constraints of the LP model. Earlier we said that for each constraint in the algebraic model, you must create a formula in a cell of the spreadsheet that corresponds to the LHS of the constraint. The LHS of each constraint in our model is:

LHS of the pump constraint

$1X_1 + 1X_2 \leq 200$

LHS of the labor constraint

$9X_1 + 6X_2 \leq 1,566$

LHS of the tubing constraint

$12X_1 + 16X_2 \leq 2,880$

We need to set up three cells in the spreadsheet to represent the LHS formulas of the three constraints. Again, we do this by referring to the data cells containing the coefficients for these constraints and to the cells representing the decision variables. The LHS of the first constraint is entered in cell D9 as:

Formula for cell D9:   =B9*B5+C9*C5

Similarly, the LHS of the second and third constraints are entered in cells D10 and D11 as:

Formula for cell D10:   =B10*B5+C10*C5
Formula for cell D11:   =B11*B5+C11*C5

These formulas calculate the number of pumps, hours of labor, and feet of tubing required to manufacture the number of hot tubs represented in cells B5 and C5. Note that cells D9 through D11 were shaded and outlined with solid borders to distinguish them from the other elements of the model.

Figure 3.4 summarizes the relationship between the LHS formulas of the constraints in the algebraic formulation of our model and their spreadsheet representations.

We know that Blue Ridge Hot Tubs has 200 pumps, 1,566 labor hours, and 2,880 feet of tubing available during its next production run. In our algebraic formulation of the LP model, these values represent the RHS values for the three constraints. Therefore, we entered the available number of pumps, hours of labor, and feet of tubing in cells E9, E10, and E11, respectively. These terms indicate the upper limits on the values that cells D9, D10, and D11 can assume.

3.4.5 REPRESENTING THE BOUNDS ON THE DECISION VARIABLES

Now, what about the simple lower bounds on our decision variables represented by $X_1 \geq 0$ and $X_2 \geq 0$? These conditions are quite common in LP problems and are referred

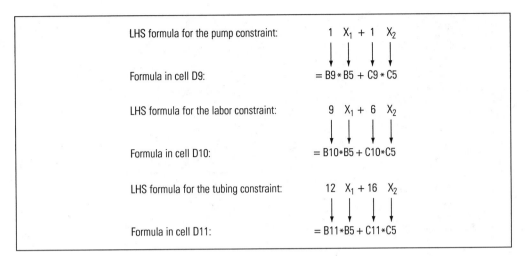

FIGURE 3.4

Summary of the relationship between the LHS formulas of the constraints and their spreadsheet representations

to as nonnegativity conditions because they indicate that the decision variables can assume only nonnegative values. These conditions might seem like constraints and can, in fact, be implemented like the other constraints. However, Solver allows you to specify simple upper and lower bounds for the decision variables by referring directly to the cells representing the decision variables. Thus, at this point, we have taken no specific action to implement these bounds in our spreadsheet.

3.5 How Solver Views the Model

After implementing our model in the spreadsheet, we can use Solver to find the optimal solution to the problem. But first, we need to define the following three components of our spreadsheet model for Solver:

1. **Set (or Target) cell.** The cell in the spreadsheet that represents the *objective function* in the model (and whether its value should be maximized or minimized).
2. **Variable (or Changing) cells.** The cells in the spreadsheet that represent the *decision variables* in the model.
3. **Constraint cells.** The cells in the spreadsheet that represent the *LHS formulas* of the constraints in the model (and any upper and lower bounds that apply to these formulas).

These components correspond directly to the cells in the spreadsheet that we established when implementing the LP model. For example, in the spreadsheet for our example problem, the set (or target) cell is represented by cell D6, the variable (or changing) cells are represented by cells B5 and C5, and the constraint cells are represented by cells D9, D10, and D11. Figure 3.5 shows these relationships. Figure 3.5 also shows a cell note documenting the purpose of cell D6. Cell notes can be a very effective way of describing details about the purpose or meaning of various cells in a model.

By comparing Figure 3.1 with Figure 3.5, you can see the direct connection between the way we formulate LP models algebraically and how Solver views the spreadsheet implementation of the model. The decision variables in the algebraic model correspond to the variable (or changing) cells for Solver. The LHS formulas for the different

FIGURE 3.5

*Summary of
Solver's view of
the model*

Variable (or Changing)
Cells

Set (or Target) Cell

Constraint Cells

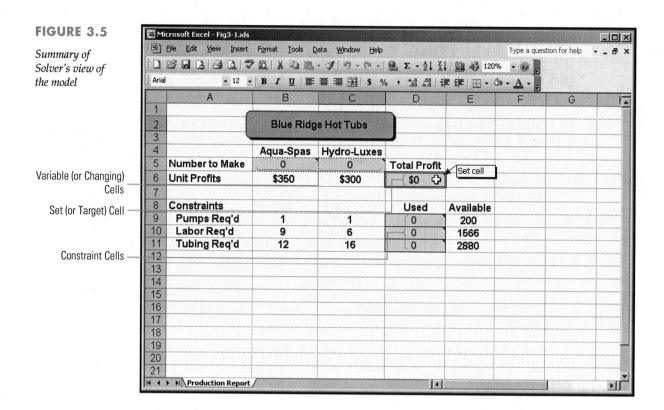

constraints in the algebraic model correspond to the constraint cells for Solver. Finally, the objective function in the algebraic model corresponds to the set (or target) cell for Solver. So, although the terminology Solver uses to describe spreadsheet LP models is somewhat different from the terminology we use to describe LP models algebraically, the concepts are the same. Figure 3.6 summarizes these differences in terminology.

Note that some versions of Solver refer to the cells containing the objective function as the "target" cell, whereas other versions of Solver refer to it simply as the "set" cell. Similarly, some versions of Solver refer to the cells representing the decision variables as "changing" cells, whereas other versions refer to them as "variable" cells. As a result, we may use the terms "target" cell and "set" cell interchangeably in this book to refer to the cell containing the objective function. Similarly, we may use the terms "changing" cells and "variable" cells interchangeably to refer to cells representing decision variables.

FIGURE 3.6

*Summary of
Solver terminology*

Terms used to describe LP models algebraically	Corresponding terms used by solver to describe spreadsheet LP models
objective function	set (or target) cell
decision variables	variable (or changing) cells
LHS formulas of constraints	constraint cells

A Note About Creating Cell Comments...

It is easy to create cell comments like the one shown for cell D6 in Figure 3.5. To create a comment for a cell:

1. Click the cell to select it.
2. Choose the Comment command on the Insert menu (or press the Shift key and function key F2 simultaneously).
3. Type the comment for the cell, and then select another cell.

The display of cell comments can be turned on or off as follows:

1. Choose the Options command on the Tools menu.
2. Select the appropriate option in the Comments section on the View tab.
3. Click the OK button.

To copy a cell comment from one cell to a series of other cells:

1. Click the cell containing the comment you want to copy.
2. Choose the Copy command on the Edit menu (or press the Ctrl and C keys simultaneously).
3. Select the cells you want to copy the comment to.
4. Select the Paste Special command on the Edit menu (or click the right mouse button and select Paste Special).
5. Select the Comments option button.
6. Click the OK button.

Installing Premium Solver for Education

This book comes with Premium Solver for Education—an upgraded version of the standard Solver that ships with Excel. If you have not already done so, install Premium Solver for Education now by running the program called PremSolv.exe found on the CD-ROM that accompanies this book. To do this, use Windows Explorer to locate the file named PremSolv.exe and then double-click the file name. (If you are running Excel in a networked environment, consult with your network administrator.) Although most of the examples in this book also work with the standard Solver that comes with Excel, Premium Solver for Education includes several helpful features that are discussed throughout this book.

3.6 Using Solver

After implementing an LP model in a spreadsheet, we still need to solve the model. To do this, we must first indicate to Solver which cells in the spreadsheet represent the objective function, the decision variables, and the constraints. To invoke Solver in Excel,

FIGURE 3.7

Command for invoking Solver

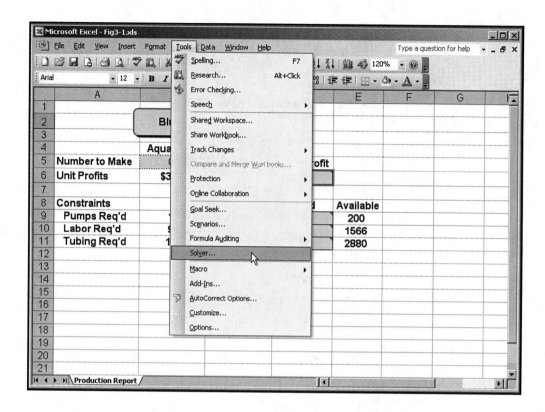

choose the Solver command from the Tools menu, as shown in Figure 3.7. This should display one of the Solver Parameters dialog boxes shown in Figure 3.8.

If the Solver Parameters dialog box on your computer looks like the first box in Figure 3.8, click the Premium button. (If the Solver Parameters dialog box on your computer looks like the first box in Figure 3.8 but does not have a Premium button, refer to the previous instruction box titled "Installing Premium Solver for Education.") The second Solver Parameters dialog box, shown in Figure 3.8, displays the user interface for Premium Solver for Education that is used throughout this book.

Premium Solver for Education provides three different algorithms for solving optimization problems: Standard GRG Nonlinear, Standard Simplex LP, and Standard Evolutionary. If the problem you are trying to solve is an LP problem (that is, an optimization problem with a linear objective function and linear constraints), Solver can use a special algorithm known as the *simplex method* to solve the problem. The simplex method provides an efficient way of solving LP problems and, therefore, requires less solution time. Furthermore, using the simplex method allows for expanded sensitivity information about the solution obtained. (Chapter 4 discusses this in detail.) In any event, when using Solver to solve an LP problem, it is a good idea to select the Standard Simplex LP option, as indicated in Figure 3.8.

3.6.1 DEFINING THE SET (OR TARGET) CELL

In the Solver Parameters dialog box, specify the location of the cell that represents the objective function by entering it in the Set Cell box, as shown in Figure 3.9.

Notice that cell D6 contains a formula representing the objective function for our problem and that we instructed Solver to try to maximize this value, as specified by the Max button. Select the Min button when you want Solver to find a solution that minimizes the value of the objective. The Value button may be used to find a solution for which the objective function takes on a specific value.

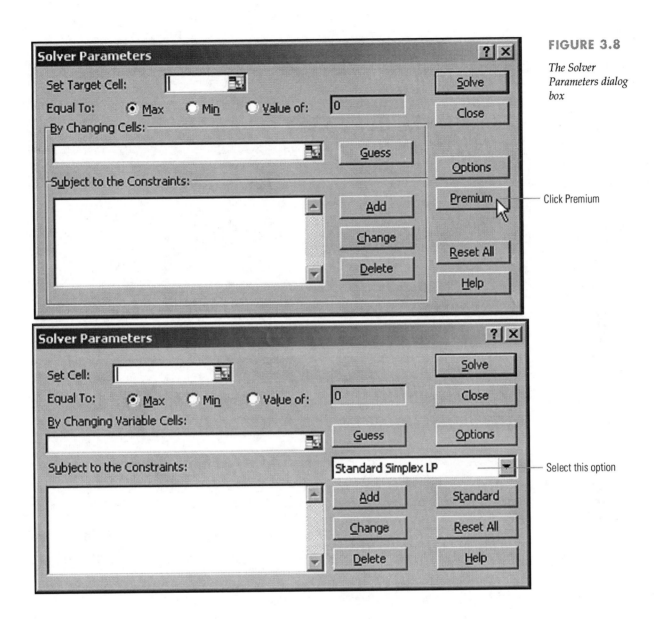

Click Premium

Select this option

FIGURE 3.8

The Solver Parameters dialog box

Guess What?

The Guess button in the Solver Parameters dialog box instructs Solver to make an educated guess regarding which cells in the spreadsheet represent decision variables. If you click this button, Solver displays all the cells upon which the value of the set (or target) cell depends. In some cases, these are only the variable cells. In other cases, these are the variable cells plus some additional cells that you will have to edit out of the variable cells box before continuing. In general, it is probably a good idea for you to enter the variable cells manually by clicking on the appropriate cells in your spreadsheet. But if you use the Guess button, remember that you will often need to remove some of the cells it identifies as variable cells.

FIGURE 3.9

*Specifying the set
(or target) cell*

Indicate Set Cell

Select Max

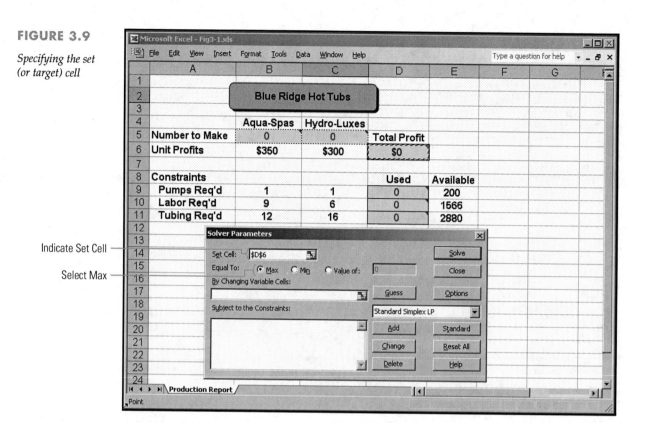

3.6.2 DEFINING THE VARIABLE CELLS

To solve our LP problem, we also need to indicate which cells represent the decision variables in the model. Again, Solver refers to these cells as variable cells. The variable cells for our example problem are specified as shown in Figure 3.10.

Cells B5 and C5 represent the decision variables for the model. Solver will determine the optimal values for these cells. If the decision variables were not in a contiguous range, we would have to list the individual decision variable cells separated by commas in the By Changing Variable Cells box. Whenever possible, it is best to use contiguous cells to represent the decision variables.

3.6.3 DEFINING THE CONSTRAINT CELLS

Next, we must define the constraint cells in the spreadsheet and the restrictions that apply to these cells. As mentioned earlier, the constraint cells are the cells in which we implemented the LHS formulas for each constraint in our model. To define the constraint cells, click the Add button shown in Figure 3.10, and then complete the Add Constraint dialog box shown in Figure 3.11. In the Add Constraint dialog box, click the Add button again to define additional constraints. Click the OK button when you have finished defining constraints.

Cells D9 through D11 represent constraint cells whose values must be less than or equal to the values in cells E9 through E11, respectively. If the constraint cells were not in contiguous cells in the spreadsheet, we would have to define the constraint cells repeatedly. As with the variable cells, it usually is best to choose contiguous cells in your spreadsheet to implement the LHS formulas of the constraints in a model.

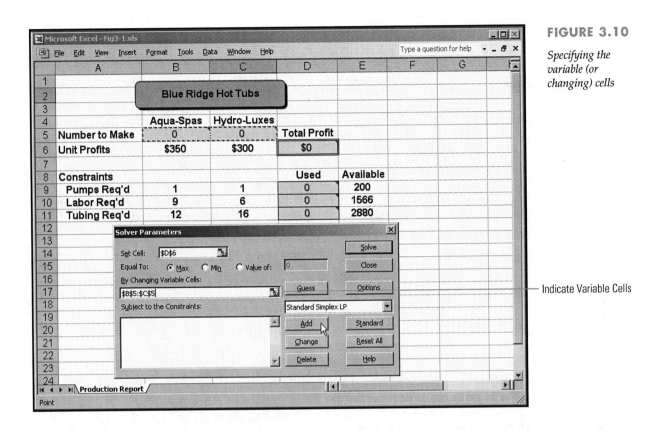

FIGURE 3.10

Specifying the variable (or changing) cells

Indicate Variable Cells

FIGURE 3.11

Specifying the constraint cells

Indicate RHS Formula Cells

Indicate LHS Formula Cells

If you want to define more than one constraint at the same time, as in Figure 3.11, all the constraint cells you select must be the same type (that is, they must all be $\leq$, $\geq$, or $=$). Therefore, it is a good idea to keep constraints of a given type grouped in contiguous cells so that you can select them at the same time. For example, in our case, the three constraint cells we selected are all "less than or equal to" ($\leq$) constraints. However, this consideration should not take precedence over setting up the spreadsheet in the way that communicates its purpose most clearly.

3.6.4 DEFINING THE NONNEGATIVITY CONDITIONS

One final specification we need to make for our model is that the decision variables must be greater than or equal to zero. As mentioned earlier, we can impose these conditions as constraints by placing appropriate restrictions on the values that can be assigned to the cells representing the decision variables (in this case, cells B5 and C5). To do this, we simply add another set of constraints to the model, as shown in Figure 3.12.

Figure 3.12 indicates that cells B5 and C5, which represent the decision variables in our model, must be greater than or equal to zero. Notice that the RHS value of this constraint is a numeric constant that is entered manually. The same type of constraints also could be used if we placed some strictly positive lower bounds on these variables (for example, if we wanted to produce at least 10 Aqua-Spas and at least 10 Hydro-Luxes). However, in that case, it probably would be best to place the minimum required production amounts on the spreadsheet so that these restrictions are displayed clearly. We can then refer to those cells in the spreadsheet when specifying the RHS values for these constraints.

FIGURE 3.12

Adding the nonnegativity conditions for the problem

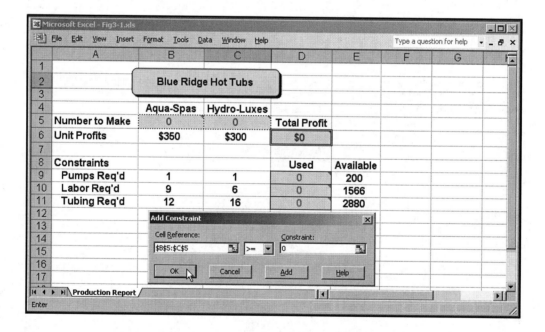

Important Software Note

There is another way to impose nonnegativity conditions—just check the Assume Non-Negative check box in the Solver Options dialog box (shown in Figure 3.14.) Checking this box tells Solver to assume that all the variables (or variable cells) in your model that have not been assigned explicit lower bounds should have lower bounds of zero.

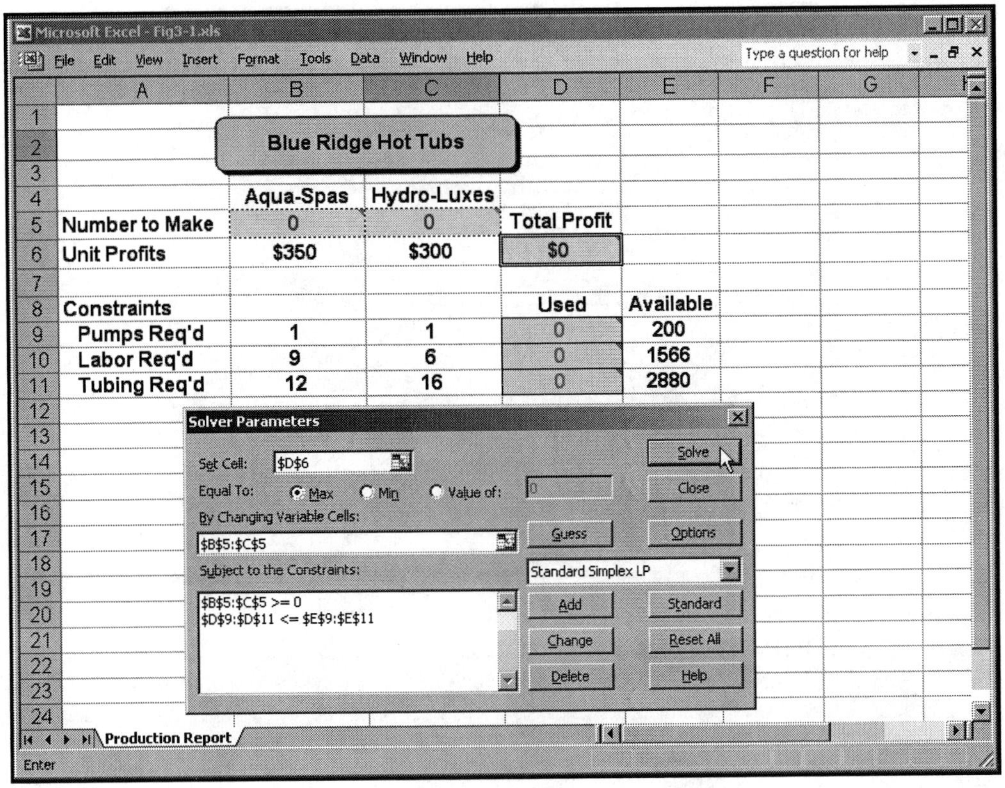

FIGURE 3.13

Summary of how Solver views the model

3.6.5 REVIEWING THE MODEL

After specifying all the constraints for our model, the final Solver Parameters dialog box appears, as shown in Figure 3.13. This dialog box provides a summary of how Solver views our model. It is a good idea to review this information before solving the model to make sure that you entered all the parameters accurately, and to correct any errors before proceeding.

3.6.6 OPTIONS

Solver provides several options that affect how it solves a problem. These options are available in the Solver Options dialog box, which you display by clicking the Options button in the Solver Parameters dialog box. Figure 3.14 shows the Solver Options dialog box for the Standard Simplex LP solution algorithm. We will discuss the meanings of several of these options as we proceed. You also can find out more about these options by clicking the Help button in the Solver Options dialog box.

3.6.7 SOLVING THE MODEL

After entering all the appropriate parameters and choosing any necessary options for our model, the next step is to solve the problem. Click the Solve button in the Solver Parameters dialog box to solve the problem. When Solver finds the optimal solution, it displays the Solver Results dialog box shown in Figure 3.15. If the values on your screen do not match those in Figure 3.15, click the Restore Original Values option button, click OK, and try again.

This dialog box provides options for keeping the solution found by Solver or restoring the spreadsheet to its original condition. Most often, you will want to keep Solver's solution unless there is an obvious problem with it. Notice that the Solver Results dialog

FIGURE 3.14

*The Solver
Options dialog box*

FIGURE 3.14

*The Solver
Options dialog box*

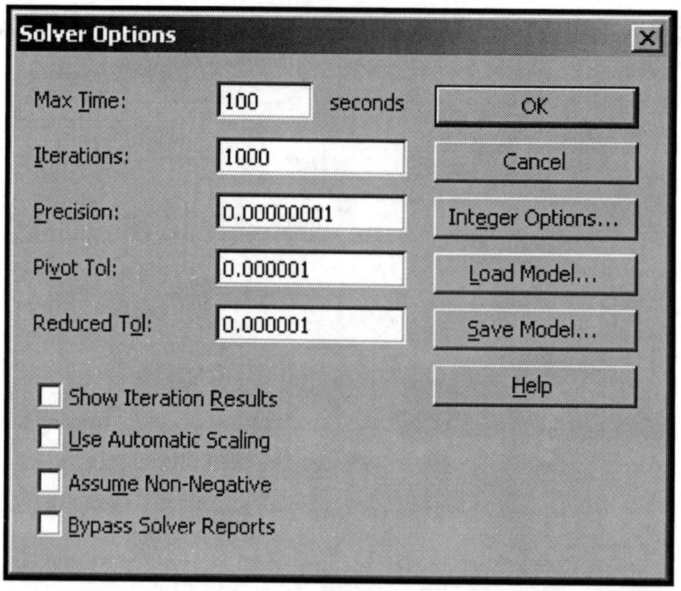

FIGURE 3.15

*Optimal solution
for the Blue Ridge
Hot Tubs problem*

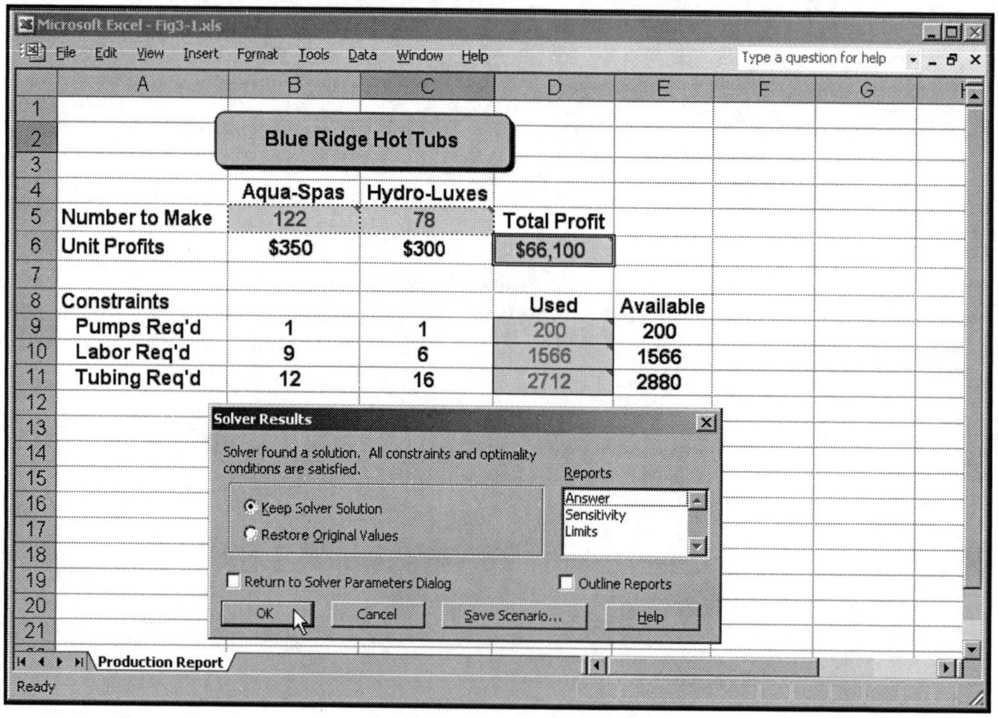

box also provides options for generating Answer, Sensitivity, and Limits reports. Chapter 4 discusses these options.

As shown in Figure 3.15, Solver determined that the optimal value for cell B5 is 122 and the optimal value for cell C5 is 78. These values correspond to the optimal values for X_1 and X_2 that we determined graphically in Chapter 2. The value of the set cell (D6) now indicates that if Blue Ridge Hot Tubs produces and sells 122 Aqua-Spas and 78 Hydro-Luxes, the company will earn a profit of $66,100. Cells D9, D10, and D11 indicate that this solution uses all the 200 available pumps, all the 1,566 available labor hours, and 2,712 of the 2,880 feet of available tubing.

3.7 Goals and Guidelines for Spreadsheet Design

Now that you have a basic idea of how Solver works and how to set up an LP model in a spreadsheet, we'll walk through several more examples of formulating LP models and solving them with Solver. These problems highlight the wide variety of business problems in which LP can be applied and also will show you some helpful "tricks of the trade" that should help you solve the problems at the end of this chapter. When you work through the end-of-the-chapter problems, you will better appreciate how much thought is required to find a good way to implement a given model.

As we proceed, keep in mind that you can set up these problems more than one way. Creating spreadsheet models that communicate their purpose effectively is very much an art—or at least an acquired skill. Spreadsheets are inherently free-form and impose no particular structure on the way we model problems. As a result, there is no one "right" way to model a problem in a spreadsheet; however some ways certainly are better (or more logical) than others. To achieve the end result of a logical spreadsheet design, your modeling efforts should be directed toward the following goals:

- **Communication.** A spreadsheet's primary business purpose is that of communicating information to managers. As such, the primary design objective in most spreadsheet modeling tasks is to communicate the relevant aspects of the problem at hand in as clear and intuitively appealing a manner as possible.
- **Reliability.** The output that a spreadsheet generates should be correct and consistent. This has an obvious impact on the degree of confidence a manager places in the results of the modeling effort.
- **Auditability.** A manager should be able to retrace the steps followed to generate the different outputs from the model, to understand the model and to verify results. Models that are set up in an intuitively appealing, logical layout tend to be the most auditable.
- **Modifiability.** The data and assumptions upon which we build spreadsheet models can change frequently. A well-designed spreadsheet should be easy to change or enhance to meet changing user requirements.

In most cases, the spreadsheet design that communicates its purpose most clearly also will be the most reliable, auditable, and modifiable design. As you consider different ways of implementing a spreadsheet model for a particular problem, consider how well the modeling alternatives compare in terms of these goals. Some practical suggestions and guidelines for creating effective spreadsheet models are given in Figure 3.16.

FIGURE 3.16

Guidelines for effective spreadsheet design

Spreadsheet Design Guidelines

- **Organize the data, then build the model around the data.** After the data is arranged in a visually appealing manner, logical locations for decision variables, constraints, and the objective function tend to naturally suggest themselves. This also tends to enhance the reliability, auditability, and maintainability of the model.
- **Do not embed numeric constants in formulas.** Numeric constants should be placed in individual cells and labeled appropriately. This enhances the reliability and modifiability of the model.
- **Things which are logically related (for example, LHS and RHS of constraints) should be arranged in close physical proximity to one another and in the same columnar or row orientation.** This enhances reliability and auditability of the model.

(Continued)

- **A design that results in formulas that can be copied is probably better than one that does not.** A model with formulas that can copied to complete a series of calculations in a range is less prone to error (more reliable) and tends to be more understandable (auditable). Once users understand the first formula in a range, they understand all the formulas in a range.
- **Column or row totals should be in close proximity to the columns or rows being totaled.** Spreadsheet users often expect numbers at the end of a column or row to represent a total or some other summary measure involving the data in the column or row. Numbers at the ends of columns or rows that do not represent totals can be misinterpreted easily (reducing auditability).
- **The English-reading human eye scans left to right, top to bottom.** This fact should be considered and reflected in the spreadsheet design to enhance the auditability of the model.
- **Use color, shading, borders, and protection to distinguish changeable parameters from other elements of the model.** This enhances the reliability and modifiability of the model.
- **Use text boxes and cell comments to document various elements of the model.** These devices can be used to provide greater detail about a model or particular cells in a model than labels on a spreadsheet might allow.

Spreadsheet-Based LP Solvers Create New Applications for Linear Programming

In 1987, *The Wall Street Journal* reported on an exciting new trend in business—the availability of solvers for personal computers that allowed many businesses to transfer LP models from mainframe computers. Newfoundland Energy Ltd., for example, had evaluated its mix of crude oils to purchase with LP on a mainframe for 25 years. Since it began using a personal computer for this application, the company has saved thousands of dollars per year in mainframe access time charges.

The expansion of access to LP also spawned new applications. Therese Fitzpatrick, a nursing administrator at Grant Hospital in Chicago, used spreadsheet optimization to create a staff scheduling model that was projected to save the hospital $80,000 per month in overtime and temporary hiring costs. The task of scheduling 300 nurses so that those with appropriate skills were in the right place at the right time required 20 hours per month. The LP model enabled Therese to do the job in four hours, even with such complicating factors as leaves, vacations, and variations in staffing requirements at different times and days of the week.

Hawley Fuel Corp., a New York wholesaler of coal, found that it could minimize its cost of purchases while still meeting customers' requirements for sulfur and ash content by optimizing a spreadsheet LP model. Charles Howard of Victoria, British Columbia, developed an LP model to increase electricity generation from a dam just by opening and closing the outlet valves at the right time.

(Source: Bulkely, William M., "The Right Mix: New Software Makes the Choice Much Easier," *The Wall Street Journal*, March 27, 1987, p. 17.)

3.8 Make vs. Buy Decisions

As mentioned at the beginning of Chapter 2, LP is particularly well-suited to problems where scarce or limited resources must be allocated or used in an optimal manner. Numerous examples of these types of problems occur in manufacturing organizations. For example, LP might be used to determine how the various components of a job should be assigned to multipurpose machines to minimize the time it takes to complete the job. As another example, a company might receive an order for several items that it cannot fill entirely with its own production capacity. In such a case, the company must determine which items to produce and which items to subcontract (or buy) from an outside supplier. The following is an example of this type of make vs. buy decision.

The Electro-Poly Corporation is the world's leading manufacturer of slip rings. A slip ring is an electrical coupling device that allows current to pass through a spinning or rotating connection—such as a gun turret on a ship, aircraft, or tank. The company recently received a $750,000 order for various quantities of three types of slip rings. Each slip ring requires a certain amount of time to wire and harness. The following table summarizes the requirements for the three models of slip rings.

	Model 1	Model 2	Model 3
Number Ordered	3,000	2,000	900
Hours of Wiring Required per Unit	2	1.5	3
Hours of Harnessing Required per Unit	1	2	1

Unfortunately, Electro-Poly does not have enough wiring and harnessing capacity to fill the order by its due date. The company has only 10,000 hours of wiring capacity and 5,000 hours of harnessing capacity available to devote to this order. However, the company can subcontract any portion of this order to one of its competitors. The unit costs of producing each model in-house and buying the finished products from a competitor are summarized below.

	Model 1	Model 2	Model 3
Cost to Make	$50	$83	$130
Cost to Buy	$61	$97	$145

Electro-Poly wants to determine the number of slip rings to make and the number to buy to fill the customer order at the least possible cost.

3.8.1 DEFINING THE DECISION VARIABLES

To solve the Electro-Poly problem, we need six decision variables to represent the alternatives under consideration. The six variables are:

M_1 = number of model 1 slip rings to make in-house

M_2 = number of model 2 slip rings to make in-house

M_3 = number of model 3 slip rings to make in-house

B_1 = number of model 1 slip rings to buy from competitor

B_2 = number of model 2 slip rings to buy from competitor

B_3 = number of model 3 slip rings to buy from competitor

As mentioned in Chapter 2, we do not have to use the symbols X_1, X_2, . . ., X_n for the decision variables. If other symbols better clarify the model, you are certainly free to use them. In this case, the symbols M_i and B_i help distinguish the **Make** in-house variables from the **Buy** from competitor variables.

3.8.2 DEFINING THE OBJECTIVE FUNCTION

The objective in this problem is to minimize the total cost of filling the order. Recall that each model 1 slip ring made in-house (each unit of M_1) costs $50; each model 2 slip ring made in-house (each unit of M_2) costs $83; and each model 3 slip ring (each unit of M_3) costs $130. Each model 1 slip ring bought from the competitor (each unit of B_1) costs $61; each model 2 slip ring bought from the competitor (each unit of B_2) costs $97; and each model 3 slip ring bought from the competitor (each unit of B_3) costs $145. Thus, the objective is stated mathematically as:

$$\text{MIN:} \quad 50M_1 + 83M_2 + 130M_3 + 61B_1 + 97B_2 + 145B_3$$

3.8.3 DEFINING THE CONSTRAINTS

Several constraints affect this problem. Two constraints are needed to ensure that the number of slip rings made in-house does not exceed the available capacity for wiring and harnessing. These constraints are stated as:

$$2M_1 + 1.5M_2 + 3M_3 \leq 10{,}000 \quad \} \text{ wiring constraint}$$
$$1M_1 + 2M_2 + 1M_3 \leq 5{,}000 \quad \} \text{ harnessing constraint}$$

Three additional constraints ensure that 3,000 model 1 slip rings, 2,000 model 2 slip rings, and 900 model 3 slip rings are available to fill the order. These constraints are stated as:

$$M_1 + B_1 = 3{,}000 \quad \} \text{ demand for model 1}$$
$$M_2 + B_2 = 2{,}000 \quad \} \text{ demand for model 2}$$
$$M_3 + B_3 = 900 \quad \} \text{ demand for model 3}$$

Finally, because none of the variables in the model can assume a value of less than zero, we also need the following nonnegativity condition:

$$M_1, M_2, M_3, B_1, B_2, B_3 \geq 0$$

3.8.4 IMPLEMENTING THE MODEL

The LP model for Electro-Poly's make vs. buy problem is summarized as:

MIN: $50M_1 + 83M_2 + 130M_3 + 61B_1 + 97B_2 + 145B_3$ } total cost

Subject to:

$$M_1 + B_1 = 3{,}000 \quad \} \text{ demand for model 1}$$
$$M_2 + B_2 = 2{,}000 \quad \} \text{ demand for model 2}$$
$$M_3 + B_3 = 900 \quad \} \text{ demand for model 3}$$
$$2M_1 + 1.5M_2 + 3M_3 \leq 10{,}000 \quad \} \text{ wiring constraint}$$
$$1M_1 + 2M_2 + 1M_3 \leq 5{,}000 \quad \} \text{ harnessing constraint}$$
$$M_1, M_2, M_3, B_1, B_2, B_3 \geq 0 \quad \} \text{ nonnegativity condition}$$

The data for this model are implemented in the spreadsheet shown in Figure 3.17 (and in the file Fig3-17.xls on your data disk). The coefficients that appear in the objective function are entered in the range B10 through D11. The coefficients for the LHS

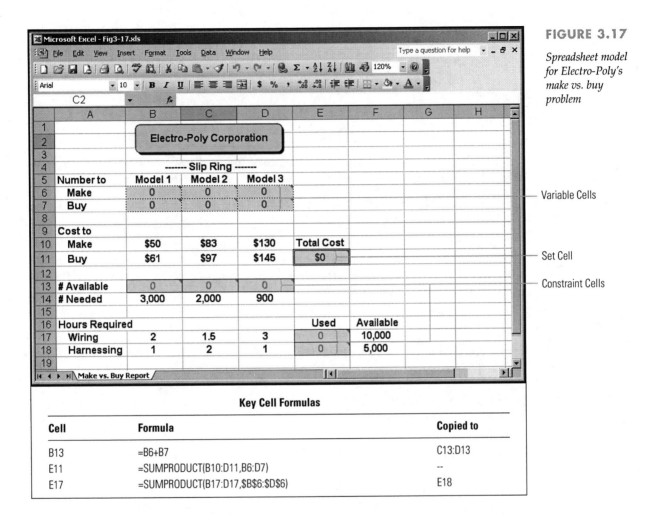

FIGURE 3.17

Spreadsheet model for Electro-Poly's make vs. buy problem

— Variable Cells

— Set Cell

— Constraint Cells

Key Cell Formulas

Cell	Formula	Copied to
B13	=B6+B7	C13:D13
E11	=SUMPRODUCT(B10:D11,B6:D7)	--
E17	=SUMPRODUCT(B17:D17,$B$6:$D$6)	E18

formulas for the wiring and harnessing constraints are entered in cells B17 through D18, and the corresponding RHS values are entered in cells F17 and F18. Because the LHS formulas for the demand constraints involve simply summing the decision variables, we do not need to list the coefficients for these constraints in the spreadsheet. The RHS values for the demand constraints are entered in cells B14 through D14.

Cells B6 through D7 are reserved to represent the six variables in our algebraic model. So, the objective function could be entered in cell E11 as:

Formula for cell E11: $=B10*B6+C10*C6+D10*D6+B11*B7+C11*C7+D11*D7$

In this formula, the values in the range B6 through D7 are multiplied by the corresponding values in the range B10 through D11; these individual products are then added together. Therefore, the formula is simply the sum of a collection of products—or a *sum of products*. It turns out that this formula can be implemented in an equivalent (and easier) way as:

Equivalent formula for cell E11: $=SUMPRODUCT(B10:D11,B6:D7)$

The preceding formula takes the values in the range B10 through D11, multiplies them by the corresponding values in the range B6 through D7, and adds (or sums) these products. The SUMPRODUCT( ) function greatly simplifies the implementation of many formulas required in optimization problems and will be used extensively throughout this book.

Because the LHS of the demand constraint for model 1 slip rings involves adding variables M_1 and B_1, this constraint is implemented in cell B13 by adding the two cells in the spreadsheet that correspond to these variables—cells B6 and B7:

Formula for cell B13:   =B6+B7

(Copy to C13 through D13.)

The formula in cell B13 is then copied to cells C13 and D13 to implement the LHS formulas for the constraints for model 2 and model 3 slip rings.

The coefficients for the wiring and harnessing constraints are entered in cells B17 through D18. The LHS formula for the wiring constraint is implemented in cell E17 as:

Formula for cell E17:   =SUMPRODUCT(B17:D17,$B$6:$D$6)

(Copy to cell E18.)

This formula is then copied to cell E18 to implement the LHS formula for the harnessing constraint. (In the preceding formula, the dollar signs denote absolute cell references. An absolute cell reference will not change if the formula containing the reference is copied to another location.)

3.8.5 SOLVING THE MODEL

To solve this model, we need to specify the set cell, variable cells, and constraint cells identified in Figure 3.17, just as we did earlier in the Blue Ridge Hot Tubs example. Figure 3.18 shows the Solver parameters required to solve Electro-Poly's make vs. buy problem.

After we click the Solve button in the Solver Parameters dialog box, Solver finds the optimal solution shown in Figure 3.19.

3.8.6 ANALYZING THE SOLUTION

The optimal solution shown in Figure 3.19 indicates that Electro-Poly should make (in-house) 3,000 model 1 slip rings, 550 model 2 slip rings, and 900 model 3 slip rings (that is, $M_1 = 3,000$, $M_2 = 550$, $M_3 = 900$). Additionally, it should buy 1,450 model 2 slip rings from its competitor (that is, $B_1 = 0$, $B_2 = 1,450$, $B_3 = 0$). This solution allows Electro-Poly

FIGURE 3.18

Solver parameters for the make vs. buy problem

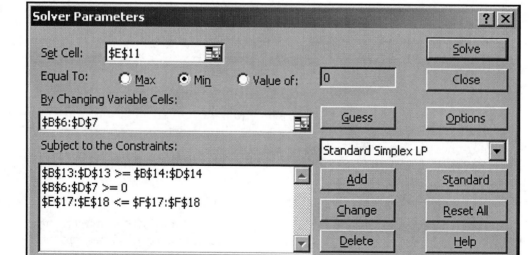

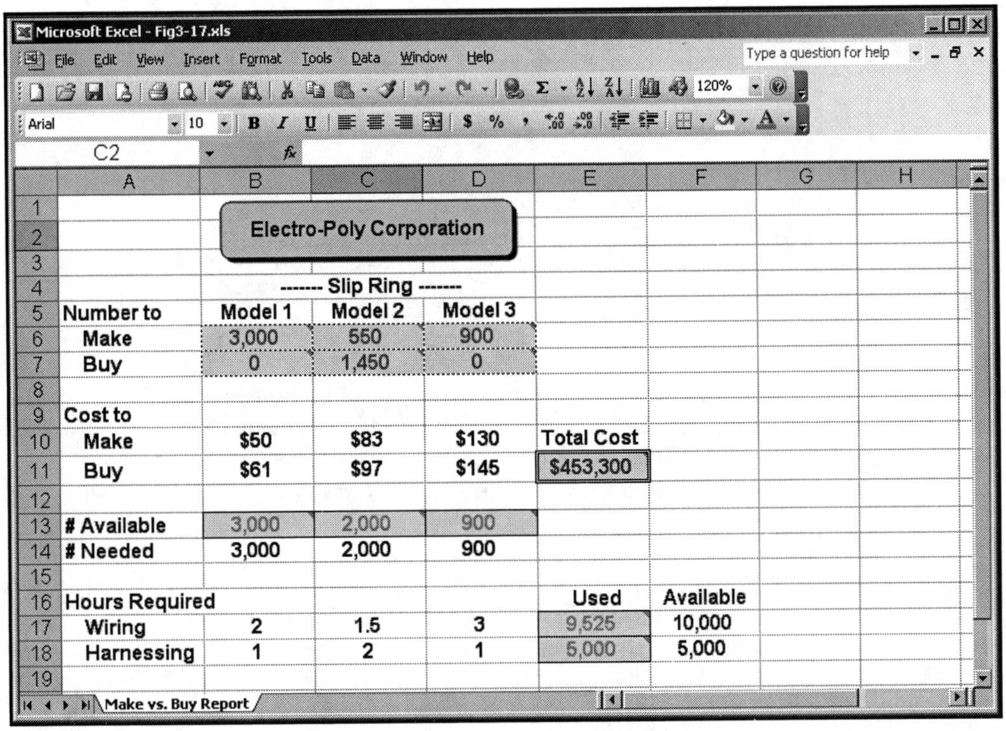

Microsoft Excel - Fig3-17.xls

	A	B	C	D	E	F
2		Electro-Poly Corporation				
4		------- Slip Ring -------				
5	Number to	Model 1	Model 2	Model 3		
6	Make	3,000	550	900		
7	Buy	0	1,450	0		
9	Cost to					
10	Make	$50	$83	$130	Total Cost	
11	Buy	$61	$97	$145	$453,300	
13	# Available	3,000	2,000	900		
14	# Needed	3,000	2,000	900		
16	Hours Required				Used	Available
17	Wiring	2	1.5	3	9,525	10,000
18	Harnessing	1	2	1	5,000	5,000

Make vs. Buy Report

FIGURE 3.19

Optimal solution to Electro-Poly's make vs. buy problem

to fill the customer order at a minimum cost of $453,300. This solution uses 9,525 of the 10,000 hours of available wiring capacity and all 5,000 hours of the harnessing capacity.

At first glance, this solution might seem a bit surprising. Electro-Poly has to pay $97 for each model 2 slip ring that it purchases from its competitor. This represents a $14 premium over its in-house cost of $83. On the other hand, Electro-Poly has to pay a premium of $11 over its in-house cost to purchase model 1 slip rings from its competitor. It seems as if the optimal solution would be to purchase model 1 slip rings from its competitor rather than model 2 slip rings because the additional cost premium for model 1 slip rings is smaller. However, this argument fails to consider the fact that each model 2 slip ring produced in-house uses twice as much of the company's harnessing capacity as does each model 1 slip ring. Making more model 2 slip rings in-house would deplete the company's harnessing capacity more quickly, and would require buying an excessive number of model 1 slip rings from the competitor. Fortunately, the LP technique automatically considers such trade-offs in determining the optimal solution to the problem.

3.9 An Investment Problem

There are numerous problems in the area of finance to which we can apply various optimization techniques. These problems often involve attempting to maximize the return on an investment while meeting certain cash flow requirements and risk constraints. Alternatively, we might want to minimize the risk on an investment while maintaining a certain level of return. We'll consider one such problem here and discuss several other financial engineering problems throughout this text.

Brian Givens is a financial analyst for Retirement Planning Services, Inc. who specializes in designing retirement income portfolios for retirees using corporate bonds. He has just completed a consultation with a client who expects to have

$750,000 in liquid assets to invest when she retires next month. Brian and his client agreed to consider upcoming bond issues from the following six companies:

Company	Return	Years to Maturity	Rating
Acme Chemical	8.65%	11	1-Excellent
DynaStar	9.50%	10	3-Good
Eagle Vision	10.00%	6	4-Fair
MicroModeling	8.75%	10	1-Excellent
OptiPro	9.25%	7	3-Good
Sabre Systems	9.00%	13	2-Very Good

The column labeled "Return" in this table represents the expected annual yield on each bond, the column labeled "Years to Maturity" indicates the length of time over which the bonds will be payable, and the column labeled "Rating" indicates an independent underwriter's assessment of the quality or risk associated with each issue.

Brian believes that all of the companies are relatively safe investments. However, to protect his client's income, Brian and his client agreed that no more than 25% of her money should be invested in any one investment and at least half of her money should be invested in long-term bonds that mature in ten or more years. Also, even though DynaStar, Eagle Vision, and OptiPro offer the highest returns, it was agreed that no more than 35% of the money should be invested in these bonds because they also represent the highest risks (i.e., they were rated lower than "very good").

Brian needs to determine how to allocate his client's investments to maximize her income while meeting their agreed-upon investment restrictions.

3.9.1 DEFINING THE DECISION VARIABLES

In this problem, Brian must decide how much money to invest in each type of bond. Because there are six different investment alternatives, we need the following six decision variables:

$$X_1 = \text{amount of money to invest in Acme Chemical}$$
$$X_2 = \text{amount of money to invest in DynaStar}$$
$$X_3 = \text{amount of money to invest in Eagle Vision}$$
$$X_4 = \text{amount of money to invest in MicroModeling}$$
$$X_5 = \text{amount of money to invest in OptiPro}$$
$$X_6 = \text{amount of money to invest in Sabre Systems}$$

3.9.2 DEFINING THE OBJECTIVE FUNCTION

The objective in this problem is to maximize the investment income for Brian's client. Because each dollar invested in Acme Chemical (X_1) earns 8.65% annually, each dollar invested in DynaStar (X_2) earns 9.50%, and so on, the objective function for the problem is expressed as:

MAX: $.0865X_1 + .095X_2 + .10X_3 + .0875X_4 + .0925X_5 + .09X_6$ } total annual return

3.9.3 DEFINING THE CONSTRAINTS

Again, there are several constraints that apply to this problem. First, we must ensure that exactly $750,000 is invested. This is accomplished by the following constraint:

$$X_1 + X_2 + X_3 + X_4 + X_5 + X_6 = 750{,}000$$

Next, we must ensure that no more than 25% of the total is invested in any one investment. Twenty-five percent of $750,000 is $187,500. Therefore, Brian can put no more than $187,500 into any one investment. The following constraints enforce this restriction:

$$X_1 \le 187{,}500$$
$$X_2 \le 187{,}500$$
$$X_3 \le 187{,}500$$
$$X_4 \le 187{,}500$$
$$X_5 \le 187{,}500$$
$$X_6 \le 187{,}500$$

Because the bonds for Eagle Vision (X_3) and OptiPro (X_5) are the only ones that mature in fewer than 10 years, the following constraint ensures that at least half the money ($375,000) is placed in investments maturing in ten or more years:

$$X_1 + X_2 + X_4 + X_6 \ge 375{,}000$$

Similarly, the following constraint ensures that no more than 35% of the money ($262,500) is placed in the bonds for DynaStar (X_2), Eagle Vision (X_3), and OptiPro (X_5):

$$X_2 + X_3 + X_5 \le 262{,}500$$

Finally, because none of the variables in the model can assume a value of less than zero, we also need the following nonnegativity condition:

$$X_1, X_2, X_3, X_4, X_5, X_6 \ge 0$$

3.9.4 IMPLEMENTING THE MODEL

The LP model for the Retirement Planning Services, Inc. investment problem is summarized as:

MAX: $.0865X_1 + .095X_2 + .10X_3 + .0875X_4 + .0925X_5 + .09X_6$ } total annual return

Subject to:

$X_1 \le 187{,}500$	} 25% restriction per investment
$X_2 \le 187{,}500$	} 25% restriction per investment
$X_3 \le 187{,}500$	} 25% restriction per investment
$X_4 \le 187{,}500$	} 25% restriction per investment
$X_5 \le 187{,}500$	} 25% restriction per investment
$X_6 \le 187{,}500$	} 25% restriction per investment
$X_1 + X_2 + X_3 + X_4 + X_5 + X_6 = 750{,}000$	} total amount invested
$X_1 + X_2 + X_4 + X_6 \ge 375{,}000$	} long-term investment
$X_2 + X_3 + X_5 \le 262{,}500$	} higher-risk investment
$X_1, X_2, X_3, X_4, X_5, X_6 \ge 0$	} nonnegativity conditions

FIGURE 3.20

Spreadsheet model for Retirement Planning Services, Inc. bond selection problem

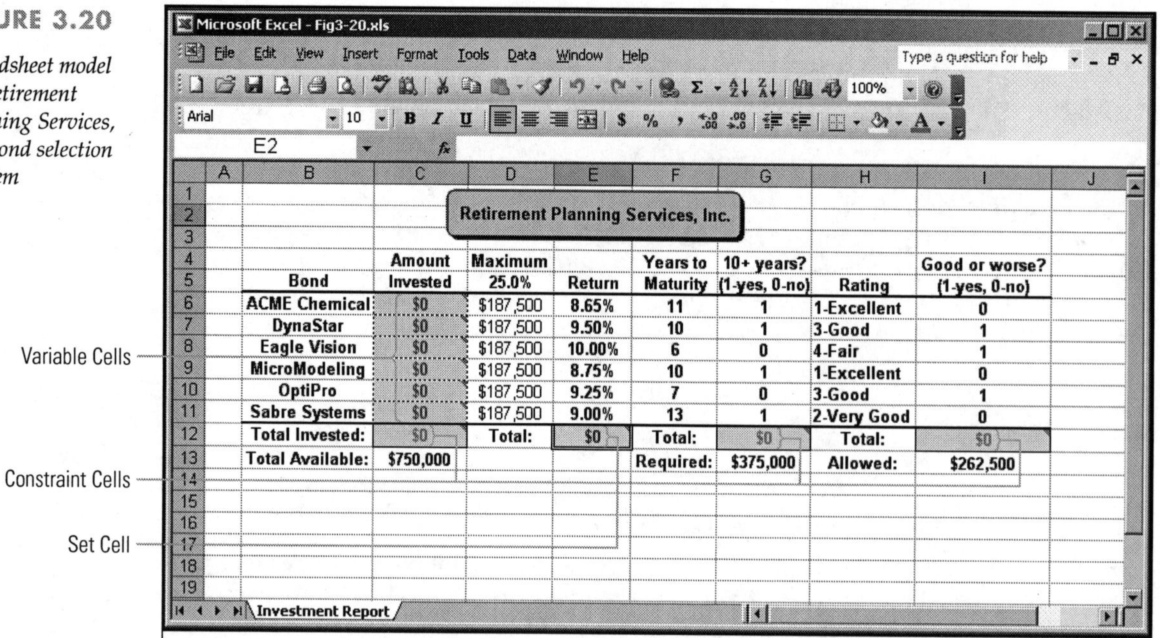

Variable Cells

Constraint Cells

Set Cell

Key Cell Formulas

Cell	Formula	Copied to
C12	=SUM(C6:C11)	--
E12	=SUMPRODUCT(E6:E11,$C$6:$C$11)	G12 and I12

A convenient way of implementing this model is shown in Figure 3.20 (file Fig3-20.xls on your data disk). Each row in this spreadsheet corresponds to one of the investment alternatives. Cells C6 through C11 correspond to the decision variables for the problem ($X_1, \ldots, X_6$). The maximum value that each of these cells can take on is listed in cells D6 through D11. These values correspond to the RHS values for the first six constraints. The sum of cells C6 through C11 is computed in cell C12 as follows, and will be restricted to equal the value shown in cell C13:

Formula for cell C12: =SUM(C6:C11)

The annual returns for each investment are listed in cells E6 through E11. The objective function is then implemented conveniently in cell E12 as follows:

Formula for cell E12: =SUMPRODUCT(E6:E11,$C$6:$C$11)

The values in cells G6 through G11 indicate which of these rows correspond to "long-term" investments. Note that the use of ones and zeros in this column makes it convenient to compute the sum of the cells C6, C7, C9, and C11 (representing $X_1, X_2, X_4,$ and X_6) representing the LHS of the "long-term" investment constraint. This is done in cell G12 as follows:

Formula for cell G12: =SUMPRODUCT(G6:G11,$C$6:$C$11)

Similarly, the zeros and ones in cells I6 through I11 indicate the higher-risk investments and allow us to implement the LHS of the "higher-risk investment" constraint as follows:

Formula for cell I12: =SUMPRODUCT(I6:I11,$C$6:$C$11)

Note that the use of zeros and ones in columns G and I to compute the sums of selected decision variables is a very useful modeling technique that makes it easy for the user to change the variables being included in the sums. Also note that the formula for the objective in cell E12 could be copied to cells G12 and I12 to implement LHS formulas for these constraint cells.

3.9.5 SOLVING THE MODEL

To solve this model, we need to specify the set cell, variable cells, and constraint cells identified in Figure 3.20. Figure 3.21 shows the Solver parameters required to solve this problem. After we click the Solve button in the Solver Parameters dialog box, Solver finds the optimal solution shown in Figure 3.22.

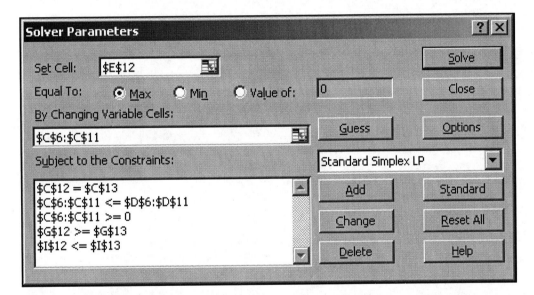

FIGURE 3.21

Solver parameters for the bond selection problem

Bond	Amount Invested	Maximum 25.0%	Return	Years to Maturity	10+ years? (1-yes, 0-no)	Rating	Good or worse? (1-yes, 0-no)
ACME Chemical	$112,500	$187,500	8.65%	11	1	1-Excellent	0
DynaStar	$75,000	$187,500	9.50%	10	1	3-Good	1
Eagle Vision	$187,500	$187,500	10.00%	6	0	4-Fair	1
MicroModeling	$187,500	$187,500	8.75%	10	1	1-Excellent	0
OptiPro	$0	$187,500	9.25%	7	0	3-Good	1
Sabre Systems	$187,500	$187,500	9.00%	13	1	2-Very Good	0
Total Invested:	$750,000	Total:	$68,888	Total:	$562,500	Total:	$262,500
Total Available:	$750,000			Required:	$375,000	Allowed:	$262,500

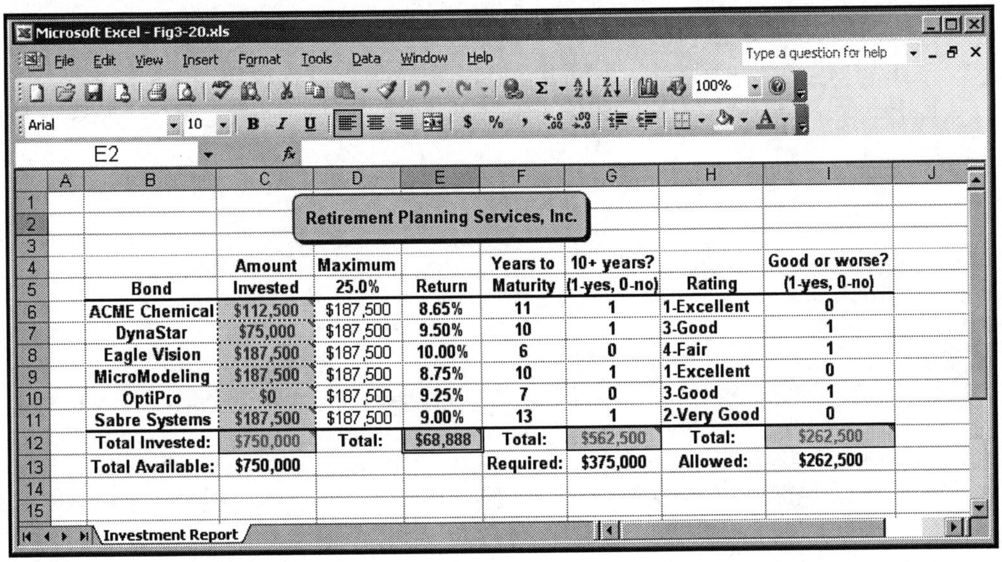

FIGURE 3.22

Optimal solution to the bond selection problem

3.9.6 ANALYZING THE SOLUTION

The solution shown in Figure 3.22 indicates that the optimal investment plan places $112,500 in Acme Chemical (X_1), $75,000 in DynaStar ($X_2$), $187,500 in Eagle Vision (X_3), $187,500 in MicroModeling (X_4), $0 in OptiPro ($X_5$), and $187,500 in Sabre Systems (X_6). It is interesting to note that more money is being invested in Acme Chemical than DynaStar and OptiPro even though the return on Acme Chemical is lower than on the returns for DynaStar and OptiPro. This is because DynaStar and OptiPro are both "higher-risk" investments and the 35% limit on "higher-risk" investments is a binding constraint (or is met as a strict equality in the optimal solution). Thus, the optimal solution could be improved if we could put more than 35% of the money into the higher-risk investments.

3.10 A Transportation Problem

Many transportation and logistics problems businesses face fall into a category of problems known as network flow problems. We will consider one such example here and study this area in more detail in Chapter 5.

Tropicsun is a leading grower and distributor of fresh citrus products with three large citrus groves scattered around central Florida in the cities of Mt. Dora, Eustis, and Clermont. Tropicsun currently has 275,000 bushels of citrus at the grove in Mt. Dora, 400,000 bushels at the grove in Eustis, and 300,000 bushels at the grove in Clermont. Tropicsun has citrus processing plants in Ocala, Orlando, and Leesburg with processing capacities to handle 200,000, 600,000, and 225,000 bushels, respectively. Tropicsun contracts with a local trucking company to transport its fruit from the groves to the processing plants. The trucking company charges a flat rate for every mile that each bushel of fruit must be transported. Each mile a bushel of fruit travels is known as a bushel-mile. The following table summarizes the distances (in miles) between the groves and processing plants:

	Distances (in miles) Between Groves and Plants		
Grove	Ocala	Orlando	Leesburg
Mt. Dora	21	50	40
Eustis	35	30	22
Clermont	55	20	25

Tropicsun wants to determine how many bushels to ship from each grove to each processing plant to minimize the total number of bushel-miles the fruit must be shipped.

3.10.1 DEFINING THE DECISION VARIABLES

In this situation, the problem is to determine how many bushels of fruit should be shipped from each grove to each processing plant. The problem is summarized graphically in Figure 3.23.

The circles (or nodes) in Figure 3.23 correspond to the different groves and processing plants in the problem. Note that a number has been assigned to each node. The arrows (or arcs) connecting the various groves and processing plants represent different shipping routes. The decision problem faced by Tropicsun is to determine how many bushels of fruit to ship on each of these routes. Thus, one decision variable is associated with each of the arcs in Figure 3.23. We can define these variables in general as:

X_{ij} = number of bushels to ship from node i to node j

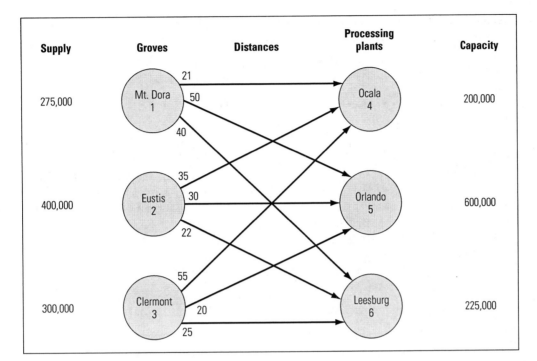

FIGURE 3.23

Diagram for the Tropicsun transportation problem

Specifically, the nine decision variables are:

X_{14} = number of bushels to ship from Mt. Dora (node 1) to Ocala (node 4)

X_{15} = number of bushels to ship from Mt. Dora (node 1) to Orlando (node 5)

X_{16} = number of bushels to ship from Mt. Dora (node 1) to Leesburg (node 6)

X_{24} = number of bushels to ship from Eustis (node 2) to Ocala (node 4)

X_{25} = number of bushels to ship from Eustis (node 2) to Orlando (node 5)

X_{26} = number of bushels to ship from Eustis (node 2) to Leesburg (node 6)

X_{34} = number of bushels to ship from Clermont (node 3) to Ocala (node 4)

X_{35} = number of bushels to ship from Clermont (node 3) to Orlando (node 5)

X_{36} = number of bushels to ship from Clermont (node 3) to Leesburg (node 6)

3.10.2 DEFINING THE OBJECTIVE FUNCTION

The goal in this problem is to determine how many bushels to ship from each grove to each processing plant while minimizing the total distance (or total number of bushel-miles) the fruit must travel. The objective function for this problem is represented by:

MIN: $21X_{14} + 50X_{15} + 40X_{16} + 35X_{24} + 30X_{25} + 22X_{26} + 55X_{34} + 20X_{35} + 25X_{36}$

The term $21X_{14}$ in this function reflects the fact that each bushel shipped from Mt. Dora (node 1) to Ocala (node 4) must travel 21 miles. The remaining terms in the function express similar relationships for the other shipping routes.

3.10.3 DEFINING THE CONSTRAINTS

Two physical constraints apply to this problem. First, there is a limit on the amount of fruit that can be shipped to each processing plant. Tropicsun can ship no more than

200,000, 600,000, and 225,000 bushels to Ocala, Orlando, and Leesburg, respectively. These restrictions are reflected by the following constraints:

$$X_{14} + X_{24} + X_{34} \leq 200{,}000 \quad \} \text{ capacity restriction for Ocala}$$
$$X_{15} + X_{25} + X_{35} \leq 600{,}000 \quad \} \text{ capacity restriction for Orlando}$$
$$X_{16} + X_{26} + X_{36} \leq 225{,}000 \quad \} \text{ capacity restriction for Leesburg}$$

The first constraint indicates that the total bushels shipped to Ocala (node 4) from Mt. Dora (node 1), Eustis (node 2), and Clermont (node 3) must be less than or equal to Ocala's capacity of 200,000 bushels. The other two constraints have similar interpretations for Orlando and Leesburg. Notice that the total processing capacity at the plants (1,025,000 bushels) exceeds the total supply of fruit at the groves (975,000 bushels). Therefore, these constraints are "less than or equal to" constraints because not all the available capacity will be used.

The second set of constraints ensures that the supply of fruit at each grove is shipped to a processing plant. That is, all of the 275,000, 400,000, and 300,000 bushels at Mt. Dora, Eustis, and Clermont, respectively, must be processed somewhere. This is accomplished by the following constraints:

$$X_{14} + X_{15} + X_{16} = 275{,}000 \quad \} \text{ supply available at Mt. Dora}$$
$$X_{24} + X_{25} + X_{26} = 400{,}000 \quad \} \text{ supply available at Eustis}$$
$$X_{34} + X_{35} + X_{36} = 300{,}000 \quad \} \text{ supply available at Clermont}$$

The first constraint indicates that the total amount shipped from Mt. Dora (node 1) to the plants in Ocala (node 4), Orlando (node 5), and Leesburg (node 6) must equal the total amount available at Mt. Dora. This constraint indicates that all the fruit available at Mt. Dora must be shipped somewhere. The other two constraints play similar roles for Eustis and Clermont.

3.10.4 IMPLEMENTING THE MODEL

The LP model for Tropicsun's fruit transportation problem is summarized as:

MIN:
$$\left. \begin{array}{l} 21X_{14} + 50X_{15} + 40X_{16} + \\ 35X_{24} + 30X_{25} + 22X_{26} + \\ 55X_{34} + 20X_{35} + 25X_{36} \end{array} \right\} \begin{array}{l} \text{total distance fruit is shipped} \\ \text{(in bushel-miles)} \end{array}$$

Subject to:
$$X_{14} + X_{24} + X_{34} \leq 200{,}000 \quad \} \text{ capacity restriction for Ocala}$$
$$X_{15} + X_{25} + X_{35} \leq 600{,}000 \quad \} \text{ capacity restriction for Orlando}$$
$$X_{16} + X_{26} + X_{36} \leq 225{,}000 \quad \} \text{ capacity restriction for Leesburg}$$
$$X_{14} + X_{15} + X_{16} = 275{,}000 \quad \} \text{ supply available at Mt. Dora}$$
$$X_{24} + X_{25} + X_{26} = 400{,}000 \quad \} \text{ supply available at Eustis}$$
$$X_{34} + X_{35} + X_{36} = 300{,}000 \quad \} \text{ supply available at Clermont}$$
$$X_{ij} \geq 0, \text{ for all } i \text{ and } j \quad \} \text{ nonnegativity conditions}$$

The last constraint, as in previous models, indicates that all the decision variables must be nonnegative.

A convenient way to implement this model is shown in Figure 3.24 (and in the file Fig3-24.xls on your data disk). In this spreadsheet, the distances between each grove and plant are summarized in a tabular format in cells C7 through E9. Cells C14 through E16 are reserved for representing the number of bushels of fruit to ship from each grove to each processing plant. Notice that these nine cells correspond directly to the nine decision variables in the algebraic formulation of the model.

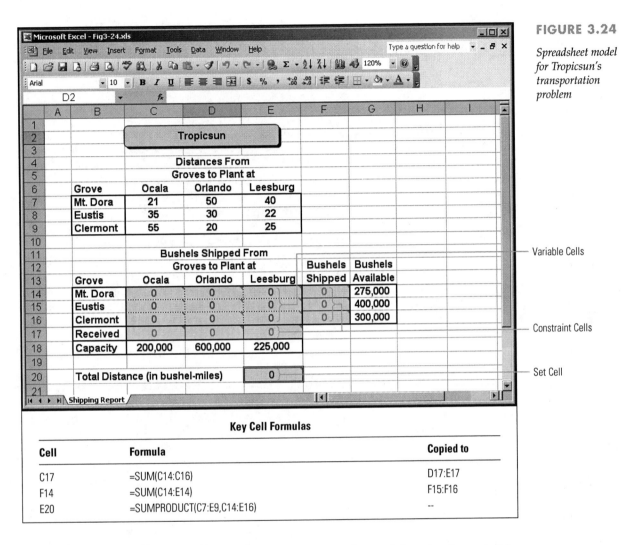

FIGURE 3.24

*Spreadsheet model
for Tropicsun's
transportation
problem*

Key Cell Formulas

Cell	Formula	Copied to
C17	=SUM(C14:C16)	D17:E17
F14	=SUM(C14:E14)	F15:F16
E20	=SUMPRODUCT(C7:E9,C14:E16)	--

The LHS formulas for the three capacity constraints in the model are implemented in cells C17, D17, and E17 in the spreadsheet. To do this, the following formula is entered in cell C17 and copied to cells D17 and E17:

Formula for cell C17:   =SUM(C14:C16)

(Copy to D17 and E17.)

These cells represent the total bushels of fruit being shipped to the plants in Ocala, Orlando, and Leesburg, respectively. Cells C18 through E18 contain the RHS values for these constraint cells.

The LHS formulas for the three supply constraints in the model are implemented in cells F14, F15, and F16 as:

Formula for cell F14:   =SUM(C14:E14)

(Copy to F15 and F16.)

These cells represent the total bushels of fruit being shipped from the groves at Mt. Dora, Eustis, and Clermont, respectively. Cells G14 through G16 contain the RHS values for these constraint cells.

Finally, the objective function for this model is entered in cell E20 as:

Formula for cell E20:   =SUMPRODUCT(C7:E9,C14:E16)

The SUMPRODUCT( ) function multiplies each element in the range C7 through E9 by the corresponding element in the range C14 through E16 and then sums the individual products.

3.10.5 HEURISTIC SOLUTION FOR THE MODEL

To appreciate what Solver is accomplishing, let's consider how we might try to solve this problem manually using a heuristic. A heuristic is a rule of thumb for making decisions that might work well in some instances, but is not guaranteed to produce optimal solutions or decisions. One heuristic we can apply to solve Tropicsun's problem is to always ship as much as possible along the next available path with the shortest distance (or least cost). Using this heuristic, we solve the problem as follows:

1. Because the shortest available path between any grove and processing plant is between Clermont and Orlando (20 miles), we first ship as much as possible through this route. The maximum we can ship through this route is the smaller of the supply at Clermont (300,000 bushels) or the capacity at Orlando (600,000 bushels). So we would ship 300,000 bushels from Clermont to Orlando. This depletes the supply at Clermont.
2. The next shortest available route occurs between Mt. Dora and Ocala (21 miles). The maximum we can ship through this route is the smaller of the supply at Mt. Dora (275,000 bushels) or the capacity at Ocala (200,000 bushels). So we would ship 200,000 bushels from Mt. Dora to Ocala. This depletes the capacity at Ocala.
3. The next shortest available route occurs between Eustis and Leesburg (22 miles). The maximum we can ship through this route is the smaller of the supply at Eustis (400,000 bushels) or the capacity at Leesburg (225,000 bushels). So we would ship 225,000 bushels from Eustis to Leesburg. This depletes the capacity at Leesburg.
4. The next shortest available route occurs between Eustis and Orlando (30 miles). The maximum we can ship through this route is the smaller of the remaining supply at Eustis (175,000 bushels) or the remaining capacity at Orlando (300,000 bushels). So we would ship 175,000 bushels from Eustis to Orlando. This depletes the supply at Eustis.
5. The only remaining route occurs between Mt. Dora and Orlando (because the processing capacities at Ocala and Leesburg have both been depleted). This distance is 50 miles. The maximum we can ship through this route is the smaller of the remaining supply at Mt. Dora (75,000 bushels) and the remaining capacity at Orlando (125,000 bushels). So we would ship the final 75,000 bushels at Mt. Dora to Orlando. This depletes the supply at Mt. Dora.

As shown in Figure 3.25, the solution identified with this heuristic involves shipping the fruit a total of 24,150,000 bushel-miles. All the bushels available at each grove have been shipped to the processing plants and none of the capacities at the processing plants have been exceeded. Therefore, this is a *feasible* solution to the problem. And the logic used to find this solution might lead us to believe it is a reasonably good solution—but is it the *optimal* solution? Is there no other feasible solution to this problem that can make the total distance the fruit has to travel less than 24,150,000 bushel-miles?

3.10.6 SOLVING THE MODEL

To find the optimal solution to this model, we must indicate to Solver the set cell, variable cells, and constraint cells identified in Figure 3.24. Figure 3.26 shows the Solver parameters required to solve this problem. The optimal solution is shown in Figure 3.27.

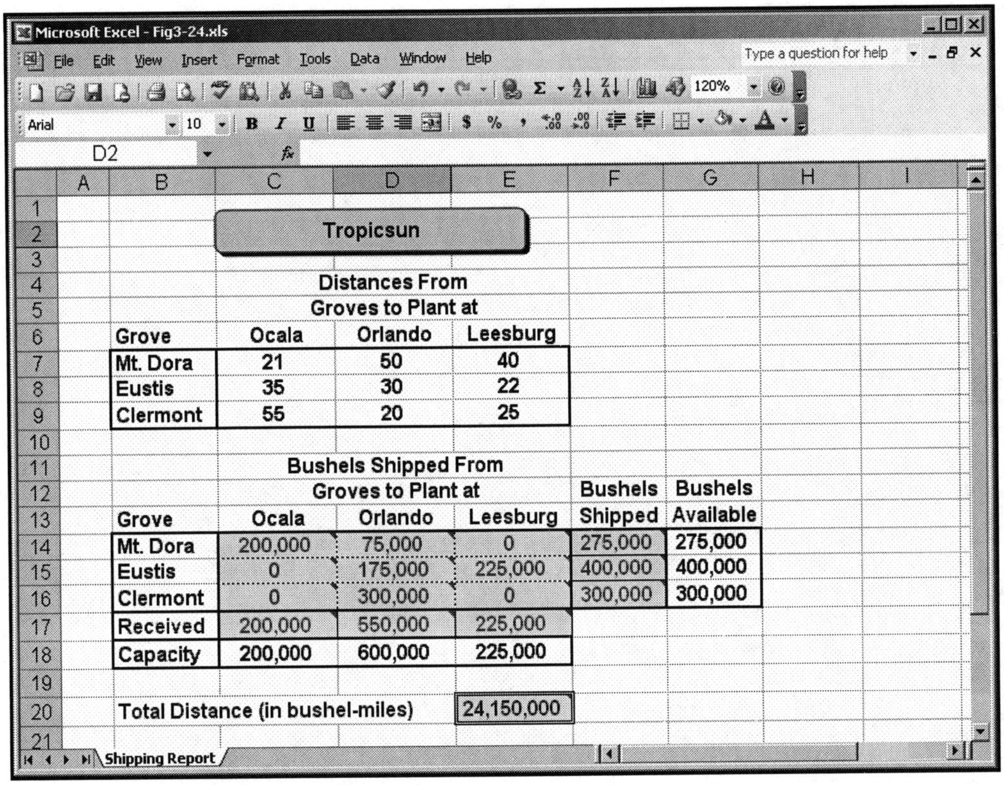

FIGURE 3.25

A heuristic solution to the transportation problem

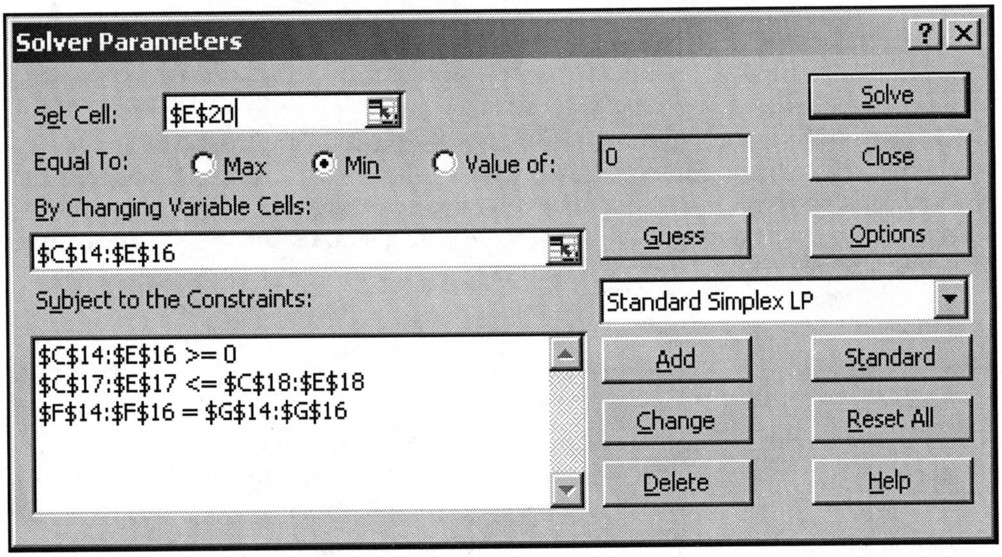

FIGURE 3.26

Solver parameters for the transportation problem

3.10.7 ANALYZING THE SOLUTION

The optimal solution in Figure 3.27 indicates that 200,000 bushels should be shipped from Mt. Dora to Ocala ($X_{14} = 200,000$) and 75,000 bushels should be shipped from Mt. Dora to Leesburg ($X_{16} = 75,000$). Of the 400,000 bushels available at the grove in Eustis, 250,000 bushels should be shipped to Orlando for processing ($X_{25} = 250,000$) and

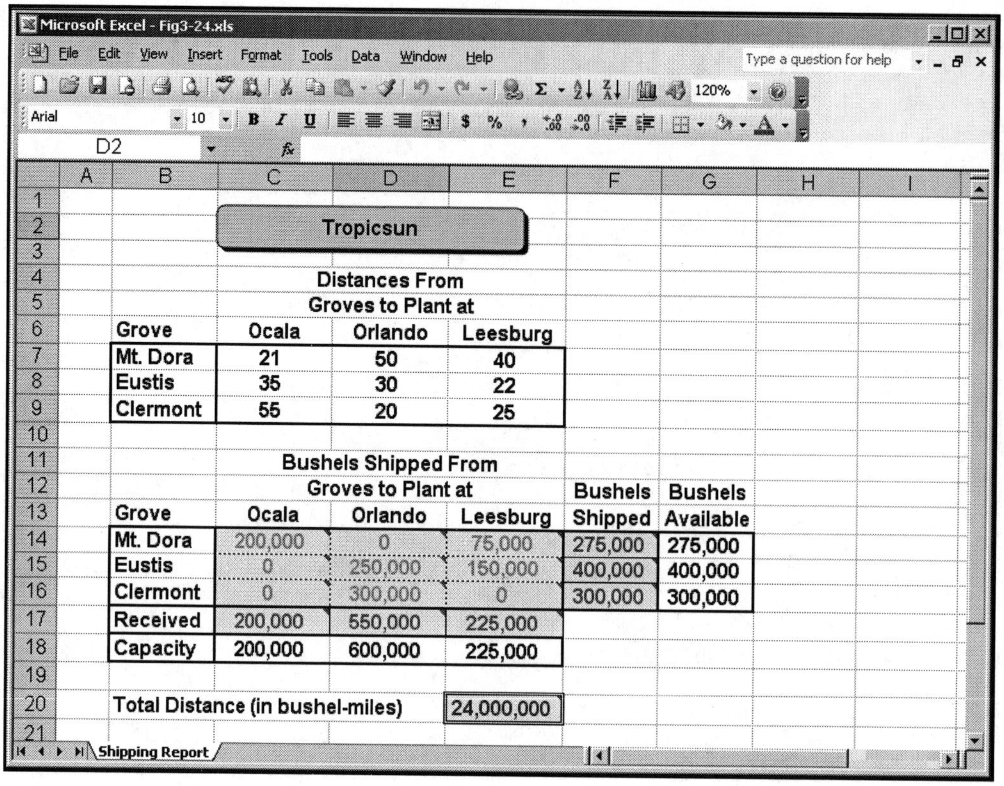

	Distances From Groves to Plant at		
Grove	Ocala	Orlando	Leesburg
Mt. Dora	21	50	40
Eustis	35	30	22
Clermont	55	20	25

	Bushels Shipped From Groves to Plant at				
Grove	Ocala	Orlando	Leesburg	Bushels Shipped	Bushels Available
Mt. Dora	200,000	0	75,000	275,000	275,000
Eustis	0	250,000	150,000	400,000	400,000
Clermont	0	300,000	0	300,000	300,000
Received	200,000	550,000	225,000		
Capacity	200,000	600,000	225,000		

Total Distance (in bushel-miles) 24,000,000

FIGURE 3.27

Optimal solution to Tropicsun's transportation problem

150,000 bushels should be shipped to Leesburg ($X_{26} = 150{,}000$). Finally, all 300,000 bushels available in Clermont should be shipped to Orlando ($X_{35} = 300{,}000$). None of the other possible shipping routes will be used.

The solution shown in Figure 3.27 satisfies all the constraints in the model and results in a minimum shipping distance of 24,000,000 bushel-miles, which is better than the heuristic solution identified earlier. Therefore, simple heuristics can solve LP problems sometimes, but as this example illustrates, there is no guarantee that a heuristic solution is the best possible solution.

3.11 A Blending Problem

Many business problems involve determining an optimal mix of ingredients. For example, major oil companies must determine the least costly mix of different crude oils and other chemicals to blend together to produce a certain grade of gasoline. Lawn care companies must determine the least costly mix of chemicals and other products to blend together to produce different types of fertilizer. The following is another example of a common blending problem faced in the U.S. agricultural industry, which annually produces goods valued at approximately $200 billion.

Agri-Pro is a company that sells agricultural products to farmers in several states. One service it provides to customers is custom feed mixing, whereby a farmer can order a specific amount of livestock feed and specify the amount of corn, grain, and minerals the feed should contain. This is an important service because the proper feed for various farm animals changes regularly depending on the weather, pasture conditions, and so on.

Agri-Pro stocks bulk amounts of four types of feeds that it can mix to meet a given customer's specifications. The following table summarizes the four feeds, their composition of corn, grain, and minerals, and the cost per pound for each type.

	Percent of Nutrient in			
Nutrient	Feed 1	Feed 2	Feed 3	Feed 4
Corn	30%	5%	20%	10%
Grain	10%	30%	15%	10%
Minerals	20%	20%	20%	30%
Cost per Pound	$0.25	$0.30	$0.32	$0.15

On average, U.S. citizens consume almost 70 pounds of poultry per year. To remain competitive, chicken growers must ensure that they feed the required nutrients to their flocks in the most cost-effective manner. Agri-Pro has just received an order from a local chicken farmer for 8,000 pounds of feed. The farmer wants this feed to contain at least 20% corn, 15% grain, and 15% minerals. What should Agri-Pro do to fill this order at minimum cost?

3.11.1 DEFINING THE DECISION VARIABLES

In this problem, Agri-Pro must determine how much of the various feeds to blend together to meet the customer's requirements at minimum cost. An algebraic formulation of this problem might use the following four decision variables:

$$X_1 = \text{pounds of feed 1 to use in the mix}$$
$$X_2 = \text{pounds of feed 2 to use in the mix}$$
$$X_3 = \text{pounds of feed 3 to use in the mix}$$
$$X_4 = \text{pounds of feed 4 to use in the mix}$$

3.11.2 DEFINING THE OBJECTIVE FUNCTION

The objective in this problem is to fill the customer's order at the lowest possible cost. Because each pound of feed 1, 2, 3, and 4 costs $0.25, $0.30, $0.32, and $0.15, respectively, the objective function is represented by:

$$\text{MIN:} \quad .25X_1 + .30X_2 + .32X_3 + .15X_4$$

3.11.3 DEFINING THE CONSTRAINTS

Four constraints must be met to fulfill the customer's requirements. First, the customer wants a total of 8,000 pounds of feed. This is expressed by the constraint:

$$X_1 + X_2 + X_3 + X_4 = 8,000$$

The customer also wants the order to consist of at least 20% corn. Because each pound of feed 1, 2, 3, and 4 consists of 30%, 5%, 20%, and 10% corn, respectively, the total amount of corn in the mix is represented by:

$$.30X_1 + .05X_2 + .20X_3 + .10X_4$$

To ensure that *corn* constitutes at least 20% of the 8,000 pounds of feed, we set up the following constraint:

$$\frac{.30X_1 + .05X_2 + .20X_3 + .10X_4}{8,000} \geq .20$$

Similarly, to ensure that *grain* constitutes at least 15% of the 8,000 pounds of feed, we use the constraint:

$$\frac{.10X_1 + .30X_2 + .15X_3 + .10X_4}{8,000} \geq .15$$

Finally, to ensure that *minerals* constitute at least 15% of the 8,000 pounds of feed, we use the constraint:

$$\frac{.20X_1 + .20X_2 + .20X_3 + .30X_4}{8,000} \geq .15$$

3.11.4 SOME OBSERVATIONS ABOUT CONSTRAINTS, REPORTING, AND SCALING

We need to make some important observations about the constraints for this model. First, these constraints look somewhat different from the usual linear sum of products. However, these constraints are equivalent to a sum of products. For example, the constraint for the required percentage of corn can be expressed as:

$$\frac{.30X_1 + .05X_2 + .20X_3 + .10X_4}{8000} \geq .20$$

or as:

$$\frac{.30X_1}{8,000} + \frac{5.0X_2}{8,000} + \frac{.20X_3}{8,000} + \frac{.10X_4}{8,000} \geq .20$$

or, if you multiply both sides of the inequality by 8,000, as:

$$.30X_1 + .05X_2 + .20X_3 + .10X_4 \geq 1,600$$

All these constraints define exactly the same set of feasible values for $X_1, \ldots, X_4$. Theoretically, we should be able to implement and use *any* of these constraints to solve the problem. However, we need to consider a number of practical issues in determining which form of the constraint to implement.

Notice that the LHS formulas for the first and second versions of the constraint represent the *proportion* of corn in the 8,000 pound order, whereas the LHS in the third version of the constraint represents the *total pounds* of corn in the 8,000 pound order. Because we must implement the LHS formula of one of these constraints in the spreadsheet, we need to decide which number to display in the spreadsheet—the *proportion* (or percentage) of corn in the order, or the *total pounds of corn* in the order. If we know one of these values, we can easily set up a formula to calculate the other value. But, when more than one way to implement a constraint exists (as is usually the case), we need to consider what the value of the LHS portion of the constraint means to the user of the spreadsheet so that the results of the model can be reported as clearly as possible.

Another issue to consider involves *scaling* the model so that it can be solved accurately. For example, suppose we decide to implement the LHS formula for the first or second version of the corn constraint given earlier so that the *proportion* of corn in the 8,000 pound feed order appears in the spreadsheet. The coefficients for the variables in these constraints are *very* small values. In either case, the coefficient for X_2 is 0.05/8,000 or 0.000006250.

As Solver tries to solve an LP problem, it must perform intermediate calculations that make the various coefficients in the model larger or smaller. As numbers become extremely large or small, computers often run into storage or representation problems that force them to use approximations of the actual numbers. This opens the door for problems to occur in the accuracy of the results and, in some cases, can prevent the computer from solving the problem at all. So, if some coefficients in the initial model are extremely large or extremely small, it is a good idea to rescale the problem so that all the coefficients are of similar magnitudes.

3.11.5 RESCALING THE MODEL

To illustrate how a problem is rescaled, consider the following equivalent formulation of the Agri-Pro problem:

$$X_1 = \text{amount of feed 1 } \textit{in thousands of pounds} \text{ to use in the mix}$$
$$X_2 = \text{amount of feed 2 } \textit{in thousands of pounds} \text{ to use in the mix}$$
$$X_3 = \text{amount of feed 3 } \textit{in thousands of pounds} \text{ to use in the mix}$$
$$X_4 = \text{amount of feed 4 } \textit{in thousands of pounds} \text{ to use in the mix}$$

The objective function and constraints are represented by:

MIN: $250X_1 + 300X_2 + 320X_3 + 150X_4$ } total cost

Subject to: $X_1 + X_2 + X_3 + X_4 = 8$ } pounds of feed required

$$\frac{.30X_1 + .05X_2 + .20X_3 + .10X_4}{8} \geq 0.20 \quad \text{\} min \% of corn required}$$

$$\frac{.10X_1 + .30X_2 + .15X_3 + .10X_4}{8} \geq 0.15 \quad \text{\} min \% of grain required}$$

$$\frac{.20X_1 + .20X_2 + .20X_3 + .30X_4}{8} \geq 0.15 \quad \text{\} min \% of minerals required}$$

$$X_1, X_2, X_3, X_4 \geq 0 \quad \text{\} nonnegativity conditions}$$

Each unit of X_1, X_2, X_3, and X_4 now represents 1,000 pounds of feed 1, 2, 3, and 4, respectively. So the objective now reflects the fact that each unit (or each 1,000 pounds) of X_1, X_2, X_3, and X_4 costs $250, $300, $320, and $150, respectively. The constraints have also been adjusted to reflect the fact that the variables now represent thousands of pounds of the different feeds. Notice that the smallest coefficient in the constraints is now $0.05/8 = 0.00625$ and the largest coefficient is 8 (that is, the RHS value for the first constraint). In our original formulation, the smallest coefficient was 0.00000625 and the largest coefficient was 8,000. By rescaling the problem, we dramatically reduced the range between the smallest and largest coefficients in the model.

Automatic Scaling

In solving some earlier problems in this chapter, you might have noticed that the Solver Options dialog box provides an option called Use Automatic Scaling (see Figure 3.14). If you select this option, Solver attempts to rescale the data automatically before solving the problem. Although this option is effective, you should not rely solely on it to solve all scaling problems that occur in your models.

The Assume Linear Model Option

When the Assume Linear Model option is selected, Solver conducts several internal tests to verify that the model is truly linear in the objective and constraints. If this option is selected and Solver's tests indicate that the model is not linear, a dialog box appears indicating that the conditions for linearity are not satisfied. The internal tests Solver applies are not always 100% accurate and sometimes indicate that the model is not linear when, in fact, it is. This often occurs when a model is poorly scaled. If you encounter this message and you are certain that your model is linear, re-solving the model might result in Solver identifying the optimal solution. If this does not work, try reformulating your model so that it is more evenly scaled.

3.11.6 IMPLEMENTING THE MODEL

One way to implement this model in a spreadsheet is shown in Figure 3.28 (and in the file Fig3-28.xls on your data disk). In this spreadsheet, cells B5 through E5 contain the costs of the different types of feeds. The percentage of the different nutrients found in each type of feed is listed in cells B10 through E12.

FIGURE 3.28

Spreadsheet model for Agri-Pro's blending problem

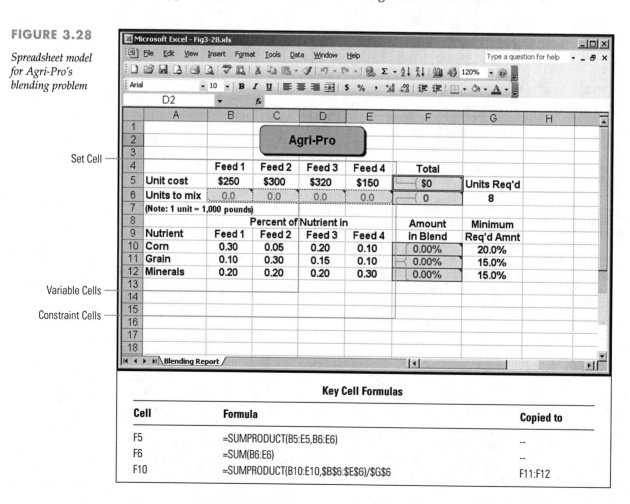

Cell	Formula	Copied to
F5	=SUMPRODUCT(B5:E5,B6:E6)	--
F6	=SUM(B6:E6)	--
F10	=SUMPRODUCT(B10:E10,$B$6:$E$6)/$G$6	F11:F12

Cell G6 contains the total amount of feed (in 1,000s of pounds) required for the order, and the minimum percentage of the three types of nutrients required by the customer order are entered in cells G10 through G12. Notice that the values in column G correspond to the RHS values for the various constraints in the model.

In this spreadsheet, cells B6, C6, D6, and E6 are reserved to represent the decision variables X_1, X_2, X_3, and X_4. These cells ultimately will indicate how much of each type of feed should be mixed together to fill the order. The objective function for the problem is implemented in cell F5 using the formula:

Formula for cell F5:   =SUMPRODUCT(B5:E5,B6:E6)

The LHS formula for the first constraint involves calculating the sum of the decision variables. This relationship is implemented in cell F6 as:

Formula for cell F6:   =SUM(B6:E6)

The RHS for this constraint is in cell G6. The LHS formulas for the other three constraints are implemented in cells F10, F11, and F12. Specifically, the LHS formula for the second constraint (representing the proportion of corn in the mix) is implemented in cell F10 as:

Formula for cell F10:   =SUMPRODUCT(B10:E10,$B$6:$E$6)/$G$6
(Copy to F11 through F12.)

This formula is then copied to cells F11 and F12 to implement the LHS formulas for the remaining two constraints. Again, cells G10 through G12 contain the RHS values for these constraints.

Notice that this model is implemented in a user-friendly way. Each constraint cell has a logical interpretation that communicates important information. For any given values for the variable cells (B6 through E6) totaling 8,000, the constraint cells (F10 through F12) indicate the *actual* percentage of corn, grain, and minerals in the mix.

3.11.7 SOLVING THE MODEL

Figure 3.29 shows the Solver parameters required to solve this problem. The optimal solution is shown in Figure 3.30.

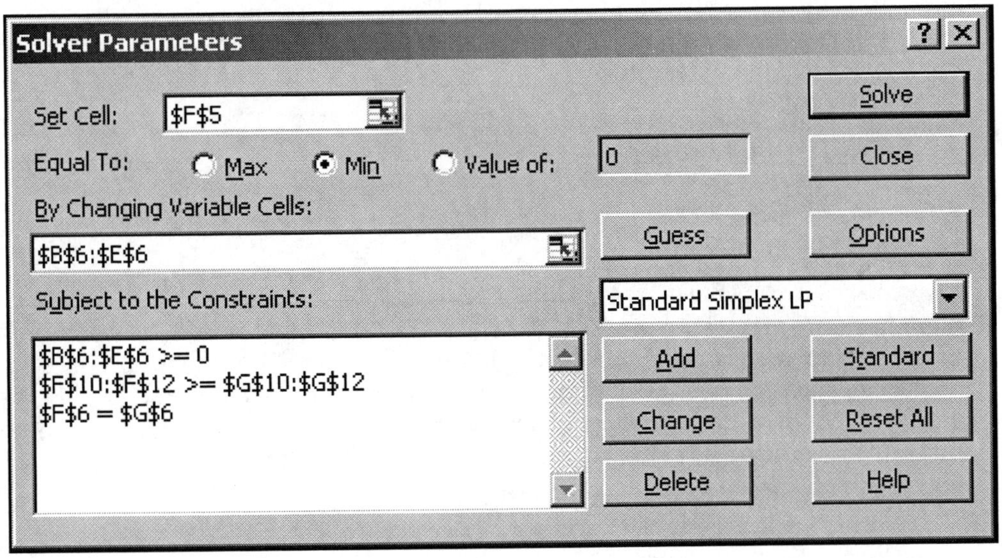

FIGURE 3.29

Solver parameters for the blending problem

FIGURE 3.30

Optimal solution to Agri-Pro's blending problem

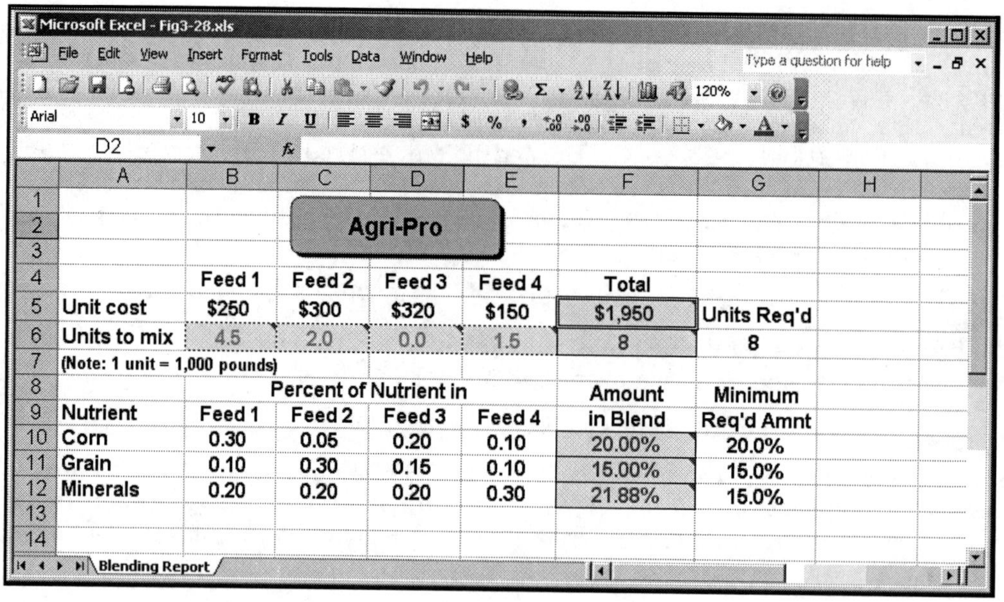

	A	B	C	D	E	F	G
4		Feed 1	Feed 2	Feed 3	Feed 4	Total	
5	Unit cost	$250	$300	$320	$150	$1,950	Units Req'd
6	Units to mix	4.5	2.0	0.0	1.5	8	8
7	(Note: 1 unit = 1,000 pounds)						
8			Percent of Nutrient in			Amount	Minimum
9	Nutrient	Feed 1	Feed 2	Feed 3	Feed 4	in Blend	Req'd Amnt
10	Corn	0.30	0.05	0.20	0.10	20.00%	20.0%
11	Grain	0.10	0.30	0.15	0.10	15.00%	15.0%
12	Minerals	0.20	0.20	0.20	0.30	21.88%	15.0%

3.11.8 ANALYZING THE SOLUTION

The optimal solution shown in Figure 3.30 indicates that the 8,000 pound feed order is produced at the lowest possible cost by mixing 4,500 pounds of feed 1 ($X_1 = 4.5$) with 2,000 pounds of feed 2 ($X_2 = 2$) and 1,500 pounds of feed 4 ($X_4 = 1.5$). Cell F6 indicates this produces exactly 8,000 pounds of feed. Furthermore, cells F10 through F12 indicate this mix contains 20% corn, 15% grain, and 21.88% minerals. The total cost of producing this mix is $1,950, as indicated by cell F5.

Have You Seen LP at Your Grocery Store?

The next time you are at your local grocery store, make a special trip down the aisle where the pet food is located. On the back of just about any bag of dog or cat food, you should see the following sort of label (taken directly from the author's dog's favorite brand of food):

This product contains:

- At least 21% crude protein
- At least 8% crude fat
- At most 4.5% crude fiber
- At most 12% moisture

In making such statements, the manufacturer guarantees that these nutritional requirements are met by the product. Various ingredients (such as corn, soybeans, meat and bone meal, animal fat, wheat, and rice) are blended to make the product. Most companies are interested in determining the blend of ingredients that satisfies these requirements in the least costly way. Not surprisingly, almost all of the major pet food manufacturing companies use LP extensively in their production process to solve this type of blending problem.

3.12 A Production and Inventory Planning Problem

One of the most fundamental problems facing manufacturing companies is that of planning their production and inventory levels. This process considers demand forecasts and resource constraints for the next several time periods and determines production and inventory levels for each of these time periods so as to meet the anticipated demand in the most economical way. As the following example illustrates, the multiperiod nature of these problems can be handled very conveniently in a spreadsheet to greatly simplify the production planning process.

> The Upton Corporation manufactures heavy-duty air compressors for the home and light industrial markets. Upton is presently trying to plan its production and inventory levels for the next six months. Because of seasonal fluctuations in utility and raw material costs, the per unit cost of producing air compressors varies from month to month—as does the demand for air compressors. Production capacity also varies from month to month due to differences in the number of working days, vacations, and scheduled maintenance and training. The following table summarizes the monthly production costs, demands, and production capacity Upton's management expects to face over the next six months.

| | **Month** | | | | | |
	1	**2**	**3**	**4**	**5**	**6**
Unit Production Cost	$ 240	$ 250	$ 265	$ 285	$ 280	$ 260
Units Demanded	1,000	4,500	6,000	5,500	3,500	4,000
Maximum Production	4,000	3,500	4,000	4,500	4,000	3,500

> Given the size of Upton's warehouse, a maximum of 6,000 units can be held in inventory at the end of any month. The owner of the company likes to keep at least 1,500 units in inventory as safety stock to meet unexpected demand contingencies. To maintain a stable workforce, the company wants to produce no less than one half of its maximum production capacity each month. Upton's controller estimates that the cost of carrying a unit in any given month is approximately equal to 1.5% of the unit production cost in the same month. Upton estimates the number of units carried in inventory each month by averaging the beginning and ending inventory for each month.
>
> There are 2,750 units currently in inventory. Upton wants to identify the production and inventory plan for the next six months that will meet the expected demand each month while minimizing production and inventory costs.

3.12.1 DEFINING THE DECISION VARIABLES

The basic decision Upton's management team faces is how many units to manufacture in each of the next six months. We will represent these decision variables as follows:

$$P_1 = \text{number of units to produce in month 1}$$
$$P_2 = \text{number of units to produce in month 2}$$
$$P_3 = \text{number of units to produce in month 3}$$
$$P_4 = \text{number of units to produce in month 4}$$
$$P_5 = \text{number of units to produce in month 5}$$
$$P_6 = \text{number of units to produce in month 6}$$

3.12.2 DEFINING THE OBJECTIVE FUNCTION

The objective in this problem is to minimize the total production and inventory costs. The total production cost is computed easily as:

$$\text{Production Cost} = 240P_1 + 250P_2 + 265P_3 + 285P_4 + 280P_5 + 260P_6$$

The inventory cost is a bit more tricky to compute. The cost of holding a unit in inventory each month is 1.5% of the production cost in the same month. So, the unit inventory cost is \$3.60 in month 1 (i.e., 1.5% × \$240 = \$3.60), \$3.75 in month 2 (i.e., 1.5% × \$250 = \$3.75), and so on. The number of units held each month is to be computed as the average of the beginning and ending inventory for the month. Of course, the beginning inventory in any given month is equal to the ending inventory from the previous month. So if we let B_i represent the beginning inventory for month i, the total inventory cost is given by:

$$\text{Inventory Cost} = 3.6(B_1 + B_2)/2 + 3.75(B_2 + B_3)/2 + 3.98(B_3 + B_4)/2$$
$$+ 4.28(B_4 + B_5)/2 + 4.20(B_5 + B_6)/2 + 3.9(B_6 + B_7)/2$$

Note that the first term in the previous formula computes the inventory cost for month 1 using B_1 as the beginning inventory for month 1 and B_2 as the ending inventory for month 1. Thus, the objective function for this problem is given as:

$$\text{MIN:} \quad \left. \begin{array}{l} 240P_1 + 250P_2 + 265P_3 + 285P_4 + 280P_5 + 260P_6 \\ + 3.6(B_1 + B_2)/2 + 3.75(B_2 + B_3)/2 + 3.98(B_3 + B_4)/2 \\ + 4.28(B_4 + B_5)/2 + 4.20(B_5 + B_6)/2 + 3.9(B_6 + B_7)/2 \end{array} \right\} \text{total cost}$$

3.12.3 DEFINING THE CONSTRAINTS

There are two sets of constraints that apply to this problem. First, the number of units produced each month cannot exceed the maximum production levels stated in the problem. However, we also must make sure that the number of units produced each month is no less than one half of the maximum production capacity for the month. These conditions can be expressed concisely as follows:

$$2,000 \leq P_1 \leq 4,000 \quad \} \text{ production level for month 1}$$
$$1,750 \leq P_2 \leq 3,500 \quad \} \text{ production level for month 2}$$
$$2,000 \leq P_3 \leq 4,000 \quad \} \text{ production level for month 3}$$
$$2,250 \leq P_4 \leq 4,500 \quad \} \text{ production level for month 4}$$
$$2,000 \leq P_5 \leq 4,000 \quad \} \text{ production level for month 5}$$
$$1,750 \leq P_6 \leq 3,500 \quad \} \text{ production level for month 6}$$

These restrictions simply place the appropriate lower and upper limits on the values that each of the decision variables may assume. Similarly, we must ensure that the ending inventory each month falls between the minimum and maximum allowable inventory levels of 1,500 and 6,000, respectively. In general, the ending inventory for any month is computed as:

$$\text{Ending Inventory} = \text{Beginning Inventory} + \text{Units Produced} - \text{Units Sold}$$

Thus, the following restrictions indicate that the ending inventory in each of the next six months (after meeting the demand for the month) must fall between 1,500 and 6,000.

$$1,500 \le B_1 + P_1 - 1,000 \le 6,000 \quad \} \text{ending inventory for month 1}$$
$$1,500 \le B_2 + P_2 - 4,500 \le 6,000 \quad \} \text{ending inventory for month 2}$$
$$1,500 \le B_3 + P_3 - 6,000 \le 6,000 \quad \} \text{ending inventory for month 3}$$
$$1,500 \le B_4 + P_4 - 5,500 \le 6,000 \quad \} \text{ending inventory for month 4}$$
$$1,500 \le B_5 + P_5 - 3,500 \le 6,000 \quad \} \text{ending inventory for month 5}$$
$$1,500 \le B_6 + P_6 - 4,000 \le 6,000 \quad \} \text{ending inventory for month 6}$$

Finally, to ensure that the beginning balance in one month equals the ending balance from the previous month, we have the following additional restrictions:

$$B_2 = B_1 + P_1 - 1,000$$
$$B_3 = B_2 + P_2 - 4,500$$
$$B_4 = B_3 + P_3 - 6,000$$
$$B_5 = B_4 + P_4 - 5,500$$
$$B_6 = B_5 + P_5 - 3,500$$
$$B_7 = B_6 + P_6 - 4,000$$

3.12.4 IMPLEMENTING THE MODEL

The LP problem for Upton's production and inventory planning problem may be summarized as:

MIN: $240P_1 + 250P_2 + 265P_3 + 285P_4 + 280P_5 + 260P_6$
$+ 3.6(B_1 + B_2)/2 + 3.75(B_2 + B_3)/2 + 3.98(B_3 + B_4)/2$ $\Big\}$ total cost
$+ 4.28(B_4 + B_5)/2 + 4.20(B_5 + B_6)/2 + 3.9(B_6 + B_7)/2$

Subject to:
$$2,000 \le P_1 \le 4,000 \quad \} \text{production level for month 1}$$
$$1,750 \le P_2 \le 3,500 \quad \} \text{production level for month 2}$$
$$2,000 \le P_3 \le 4,000 \quad \} \text{production level for month 3}$$
$$2,250 \le P_4 \le 4,500 \quad \} \text{production level for month 4}$$
$$2,000 \le P_5 \le 4,000 \quad \} \text{production level for month 5}$$
$$1,750 \le P_6 \le 3,500 \quad \} \text{production level for month 6}$$
$$1,500 \le B_1 + P_1 - 1,000 \le 6,000 \quad \} \text{ending inventory for month 1}$$
$$1,500 \le B_2 + P_2 - 4,500 \le 6,000 \quad \} \text{ending inventory for month 2}$$
$$1,500 \le B_3 + P_3 - 6,000 \le 6,000 \quad \} \text{ending inventory for month 3}$$
$$1,500 \le B_4 + P_4 - 5,500 \le 6,000 \quad \} \text{ending inventory for month 4}$$
$$1,500 \le B_5 + P_5 - 3,500 \le 6,000 \quad \} \text{ending inventory for month 5}$$
$$1,500 \le B_6 + P_6 - 4,000 \le 6,000 \quad \} \text{ending inventory for month 6}$$

where:
$$B_2 = B_1 + P_1 - 1,000$$
$$B_3 = B_2 + P_2 - 4,500$$
$$B_4 = B_3 + P_3 - 6,000$$
$$B_5 = B_4 + P_4 - 5,500$$
$$B_6 = B_5 + P_5 - 3,500$$
$$B_7 = B_6 + P_6 - 4,000$$

FIGURE 3.31

Spreadsheet model for Upton's production problem

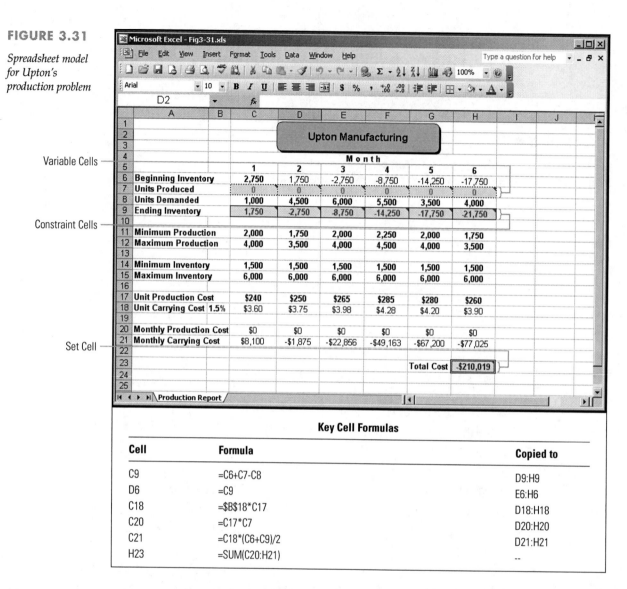

Cell	Formula	Copied to
C9	=C6+C7-C8	D9:H9
D6	=C9	E6:H6
C18	=$B$18*C17	D18:H18
C20	=C17*C7	D20:H20
C21	=C18*(C6+C9)/2	D21:H21
H23	=SUM(C20:H21)	--

A convenient way of implementing this model is shown in Figure 3.31 (and file Fig3-31.xls on your data disk). Cells C7 through H7 in this spreadsheet represent the number of air compressors to produce in each month and therefore correspond to the decision variables (P_1 through P_6) in our model. We will place appropriate upper and lower bounds on these cells to enforce the restrictions represented by the first six constraints in our model. The estimated demands for each time period are listed just below the decision variables in cells C8 through H8.

With the beginning inventory level of 2,750 entered in cell C6, the ending inventory for month 1 is computed in cell C9 as follows:

$$\text{Formula for cell C9:} \qquad =C6+C7-C8$$

(Copy to cells D9 through H9.)

This formula can be copied to cells D9 through H9 to compute the ending inventory levels for each of the remaining months. We will place appropriate lower and upper limits on these cells to enforce the restrictions indicated by the second set of six constraints in our model.

To ensure that the beginning inventory in month 2 equals the ending inventory from month 1, we place the following formula in cell D6:

Formula for cell D6:   =C9

(Copy to cells E6 through H6.)

This formula can be copied to cells E6 through H6 to ensure that the beginning inventory levels in each month equal the ending inventory levels from the previous month. It is important to note that because the beginning inventory levels can be calculated directly from the ending inventory levels, there is no need to specify these cells as constraint cells to Solver.

With the monthly unit production costs entered in cell C17 through H17, the monthly unit carrying costs are computed in cells C18 through H18 as follows:

Formula for cell C18:   =$B$18*C17

(Copy to cells D18 through H18.)

The total monthly production and inventory costs are then computed in rows 20 and 21 as follows:

Formula for cell C20:   =C17*C7

(Copy to cells D20 through H20.)

Formula for cell C21:   =C18*(C6 + C9)/2

(Copy to cells D21 through H21.)

Finally, the objective function representing the total production and inventory costs for the problem is implemented in cell H23 as follows:

Formula for cell H23:   =SUM(C20:H21)

3.12.5 SOLVING THE MODEL

Figure 3.32 shows the Solver parameters required to solve this problem. The optimal solution is shown in Figure 3.33.

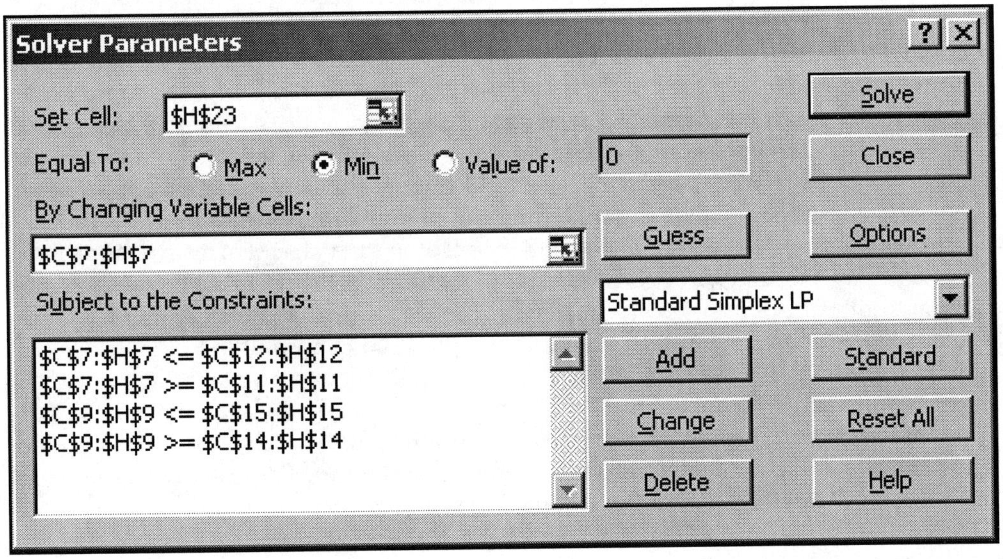

FIGURE 3.32

Solver parameters for the production problem

FIGURE 3.33

*Optimal solution
to Upton's
production problem*

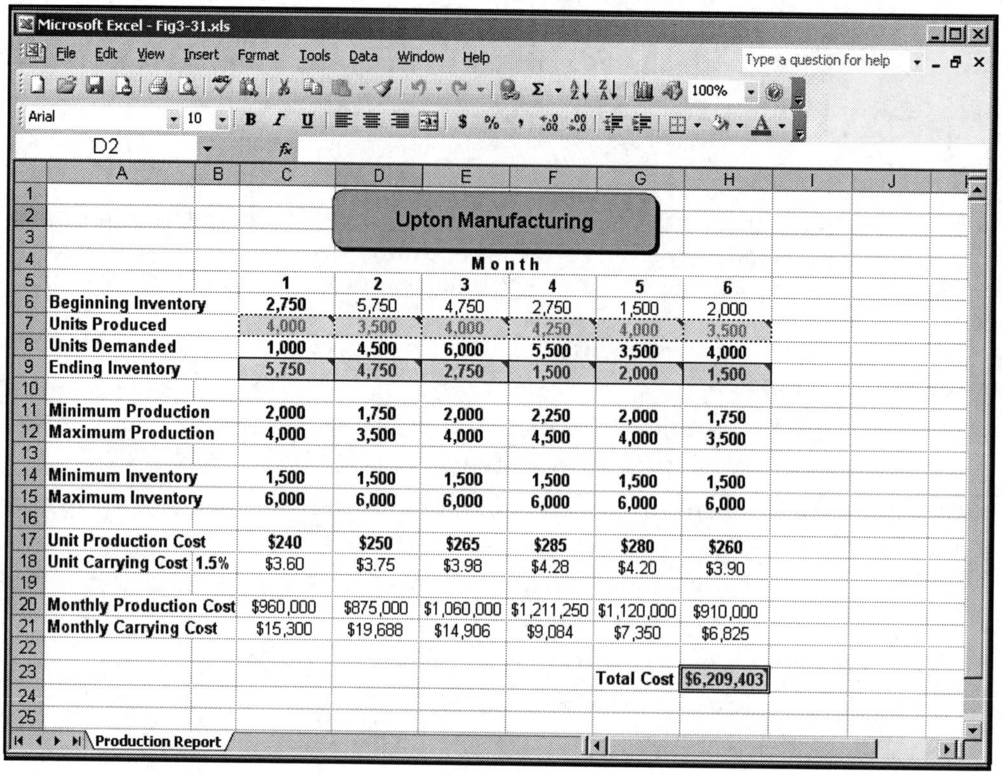

	A	B	C	D	E	F	G	H
1								
2				Upton Manufacturing				
3								
4					**Month**			
5			**1**	**2**	**3**	**4**	**5**	**6**
6	**Beginning Inventory**		2,750	5,750	4,750	2,750	1,500	2,000
7	**Units Produced**		4,000	3,500	4,000	4,250	4,000	3,500
8	**Units Demanded**		1,000	4,500	6,000	5,500	3,500	4,000
9	**Ending Inventory**		5,750	4,750	2,750	1,500	2,000	1,500
10								
11	**Minimum Production**		2,000	1,750	2,000	2,250	2,000	1,750
12	**Maximum Production**		4,000	3,500	4,000	4,500	4,000	3,500
13								
14	**Minimum Inventory**		1,500	1,500	1,500	1,500	1,500	1,500
15	**Maximum Inventory**		6,000	6,000	6,000	6,000	6,000	6,000
16								
17	**Unit Production Cost**		$240	$250	$265	$285	$280	$260
18	**Unit Carrying Cost**	1.5%	$3.60	$3.75	$3.98	$4.28	$4.20	$3.90
19								
20	**Monthly Production Cost**		$960,000	$875,000	$1,060,000	$1,211,250	$1,120,000	$910,000
21	**Monthly Carrying Cost**		$15,300	$19,688	$14,906	$9,084	$7,350	$6,825
22								
23							**Total Cost**	$6,209,403
24								
25								

3.12.6 ANALYZING THE SOLUTION

The optimal solution shown in Figure 3.33 indicates that Upton should produce 4,000 units in period 1, 3,500 units in period 2, 4,000 units in period 3, 4,250 units in period 4, 4,000 units in period 5, and 3,500 units in period 6. Although the demand for air compressors in month 1 can be met by the beginning inventory, production in month 1 is required to build inventory for future months in which demand exceeds the available production capacity. Notice that this production schedule calls for the company to operate at full production capacity in all months except month 4. Month 4 is expected to have the highest per unit production cost. Therefore, it is more economical to produce extra units in prior months and hold them in inventory for sale in month 4.

It is important to note that although the solution to this problem provides a production plan for the next six months, it does not bind Upton's management team to implement this particular solution throughout the next six months. At an operational level, the management team is most concerned with the decision that must be made now—namely, the number of units to schedule for production in month 1. At the end of month 1, Upton's management should update the inventory, demand, and cost estimates, and re-solve the model to identify the production plan for the next six months (presently months 2 through 7). At the end of month 2, this process should be repeated. Thus, multiperiod planning models such as this should be used repeatedly on a periodic basis as part of a rolling planning process.

3.13 A Multi-Period Cash Flow Problem

Numerous business problems involve decisions that have a ripple effect on future decisions. In the previous example, we saw how the manufacturing plans for one time period can affect the amount of resources available and the inventory carried in subsequent time periods. Similarly, many financial decisions involve multiple time periods because the amount of money invested or spent at one point in time directly affects the amount of money available in subsequent time periods. In these types of multi-period problems, it can be difficult to account for the consequences of a current decision on future time periods without an LP model. The formulation of such a model is illustrated next in an example from the world of finance.

> Taco-Viva is a small but growing restaurant chain specializing in Mexican fast food. The management of the company has decided to build a new location in Wilmington, North Carolina, and wants to establish a construction fund (or sinking fund) to pay for the new facility. Construction of the restaurant is expected to take six months and cost $800,000. Taco-Viva's contract with the construction company requires it to make payments of $250,000 at the end of the second and fourth months, and a final payment of $300,000 at the end of the sixth month when the restaurant is completed. The company can use four investment opportunities to establish the construction fund; these investments are summarized in the following table:

Investment	Available in Month	Months to Maturity	Yield at Maturity
A	1, 2, 3, 4, 5, 6	1	1.8%
B	1, 3, 5	2	3.5%
C	1, 4	3	5.8%
D	1	6	11.0%

> The table indicates that investment A will be available at the beginning of each of the next six months, and funds invested in this manner mature in one month with a yield of 1.8%. Funds can be placed in investment C only at the beginning of months 1 and/or 4, and mature at the end of three months with a yield of 5.8%.
>
> The management of Taco-Viva needs to determine the investment plan that allows them to meet the required schedule of payments while placing the least amount of money in the construction fund.

This is a multi-period problem because a six-month planning horizon must be considered. That is, Taco-Viva must plan which investment alternatives to use at various times during the next six months.

3.13.1 DEFINING THE DECISION VARIABLES

The basic decision faced by the management of Taco-Viva is how much money to place in each investment vehicle during each time period when the investment opportunities are available. To model this problem, we need different variables to represent each investment/time period combination. This can be done as:

$A_1, A_2, A_3, A_4, A_5, A_6 =$ the amount of money (in \$1,000s) placed in investment A at the beginning of months 1, 2, 3, 4, 5, and 6, respectively

$B_1, B_3, B_5 =$ the amount of money (in \$1,000s) placed in investment B at the beginning of months 1, 3, and 5, respectively

$C_1, C_4 =$ the amount of money (in \$1,000s) placed in investment C at the beginning of months 1 and 4, respectively

$D_1 =$ the amount of money (in \$1,000s) placed in investment D at the beginning of month 1

Notice that all variables are expressed in units of thousands of dollars to maintain a reasonable scale for this problem. So, keep in mind that when referring to the amount of money represented by our variables, we mean the amount in thousands of dollars.

3.13.2 DEFINING THE OBJECTIVE FUNCTION

Taco-Viva's management wants to minimize the amount of money it must place in the construction fund initially to cover the payments that will be due under the contract. At the beginning of month 1, the company wants to invest some amount of money that, along with its investment earnings, will cover the required payments without an additional infusion of cash from the company. Because A_1, B_1, C_1, and D_1 represent the initial amounts invested by the company in month 1, the objective function for the problem is:

MIN: $A_1 + B_1 + C_1 + D_1$ } total cash invested at the beginning of month 1

3.13.3 DEFINING THE CONSTRAINTS

To formulate the cash-flow constraints for this problem, it is important to clearly identify: (1) when the different investments can be made, (2) when the different investments will mature, and (3) how much money will be available when each investment matures. Figure 3.34 summarizes this information.

The negative values, represented by −1 in Figure 3.34, indicate when dollars can flow *into* each investment. The positive values indicate how much these same dollars will be worth when the investment matures, or when dollars flow *out* of each investment. The double-headed arrow symbols indicate time periods in which funds remain in a particular investment. For example, the third row of the table in Figure 3.34 indicates that every dollar placed in investment C at the beginning of month 1 will be worth \$1.058 when this investment matures three months later—at the *beginning* of month 4. (Note that the beginning of month 4 occurs at virtually the same instant as the *end* of month 3. Thus, there is no practical difference between the beginning of one time period and the end of the previous time period.)

Assuming that the company invests the amounts represented by A_1, B_1, C_1, and D_1 at the beginning of month 1, how much money would be available to reinvest or make the required payments at the beginning of months 2, 3, 4, 5, 6, and 7? The answer to this question allows us to generate the set of cash-flow constraints needed for this problem.

As indicated by the second column of Figure 3.34, the only funds maturing at the beginning of month 2 are those placed in investment A at the beginning of month 1 (A_1). The value of the funds maturing at the beginning of month 2 is \$1.018A_1. Because no payments are required at the beginning of month 2, all the maturing funds

FIGURE 3.34

Cash-flow summary table for Taco-Viva's investment opportunities

Investment	**Cash Inflow/Outflow at the Beginning of Month**						
	1	**2**	**3**	**4**	**5**	**6**	**7**
A_1	−1	1.018					
B_1	−1	←→	1.035				
C_1	−1	←→	←→	1.058			
D_1	−1	←→	←→	←→	←→	←→	1.11
A_2		−1	1.018				
A_3			−1	1.018			
B_3			−1	←→	1.035		
A_4				−1	1.018		
C_4				−1	←→	←→	1.058
A_5					−1	1.018	
B_5					−1	←→	1.035
A_6						−1	1.018
Req'd Payments (in $1,000s)	$0	$0	$250	$0	$250	$0	$300

must be reinvested. But the only new investment opportunity available at the beginning of month 2 is investment A (A_2). Thus, the amount of money placed in investment A at the beginning of month 2 must be $1.018A_1$. This is expressed by the constraint:

$$1.018A_1 = A_2 + 0 \qquad \} \text{ cash flow for month 2}$$

This constraint indicates that the total amount of money maturing at the beginning of month 2 ($1.018A_1$) must equal the amount of money reinvested at the beginning of month 2 (A_2) plus any payment due in month 2 ($0).

Now, consider the cash flows that will occur during month 3. At the beginning of month 3, any funds that were placed in investment B at the beginning of month 1 (B_1) will mature and be worth a total of $1.035B_1$. Similarly, any funds placed in investment A at the beginning of month 2 (A_2) will mature and be worth a total of $1.018A_2$. Because a payment of $250,000 is due at the beginning of month 3, we must ensure that the funds maturing at the beginning of month 3 are sufficient to cover this payment, and that any remaining funds are placed in the investment opportunities available at the beginning of month 3 (A_3 and B_3). This requirement can be stated algebraically as:

$$1.035B_1 + 1.018A_2 = A_3 + B_3 + 250 \qquad \} \text{ cash flow for month 3}$$

This constraint indicates that the total amount of money maturing at the beginning of month 3 ($1.035B_1 + 1.018A_2$) must equal the amount of money reinvested at the beginning of month 3 ($A_3 + B_3$) plus the payment due at the beginning of month 3 ($250,000).

The same logic we applied to generate the cash-flow constraints for months 2 and 3 also can be used to generate cash-flow constraints for the remaining months. Doing so produces a cash-flow constraint for each month that takes on the general form:

$$\begin{pmatrix} \text{Total \$ amount} \\ \text{maturing at the} \\ \text{beginning} \\ \text{of the month} \end{pmatrix} = \begin{pmatrix} \text{Total \$ amount} \\ \text{reinvested at the} \\ \text{beginning} \\ \text{of the month} \end{pmatrix} + \begin{pmatrix} \text{Payment} \\ \text{due at the} \\ \text{beginning} \\ \text{of the month} \end{pmatrix}$$

Using this general definition of the cash flow relationships, the constraints for the remaining months are represented by:

$$1.058C_1 + 1.018A_3 = A_4 + C_4 \qquad \} \text{ cash flow for month 4}$$
$$1.035B_3 + 1.018A_4 = A_5 + B_5 + 250 \qquad \} \text{ cash flow for month 5}$$
$$1.018A_5 = A_6 \qquad \} \text{ cash flow for month 6}$$
$$1.11D_1 + 1.058C_4 + 1.035B_5 + 1.018A_6 = 300 \qquad \} \text{ cash flow for month 7}$$

To implement these constraints in the spreadsheet, we must express them in a slightly different (but algebraically equivalent) manner. Specifically, to conform to our general definition of an equality constraint ($f(X_1, X_2, \ldots, X_n) = b$) we need to rewrite the cash-flow constraints so that all the *variables* in each constraint appear on the LHS of the equal sign, and a numeric constant appears on the RHS of the equal sign. This can be done as:

$$1.018A_1 - 1A_2 = 0 \qquad \} \text{ cash flow for month 2}$$
$$1.035B_1 + 1.018A_2 - 1A_3 - 1B_3 = 250 \qquad \} \text{ cash flow for month 3}$$
$$1.058C_1 + 1.018A_3 - 1A_4 - 1C_4 = 0 \qquad \} \text{ cash flow for month 4}$$
$$1.035B_3 + 1.018A_4 - 1A_5 - 1B_5 = 250 \qquad \} \text{ cash flow for month 5}$$
$$1.018A_5 - 1A_6 = 0 \qquad \} \text{ cash flow for month 6}$$
$$1.11D_1 + 1.058C_4 + 1.035B_5 + 1.018A_6 = 300 \qquad \} \text{ cash flow for month 7}$$

There are two important points to note about this alternate expression of the constraints. First, each constraint takes on the following general form, which is algebraically equivalent to our previous general definition for the cash-flow constraints:

$$\begin{pmatrix} \text{Total \$ amount} \\ \text{maturing at the} \\ \text{beginning} \\ \text{of the month} \end{pmatrix} - \begin{pmatrix} \text{Total \$ amount} \\ \text{reinvested at the} \\ \text{beginning} \\ \text{of the month} \end{pmatrix} = \begin{pmatrix} \text{Payment} \\ \text{due at the} \\ \text{beginning} \\ \text{of the month} \end{pmatrix}$$

Although the constraints look slightly different in this form, they enforce the same relationships among the variables as expressed by the earlier constraints.

Second, the LHS coefficients in the alternate expression of the constraints correspond directly to the values listed in the cash-flow summary table in Figure 3.34. That is, the coefficients in the constraint for month 2 correspond to the values in the column for month 2 in Figure 3.34; the coefficients for month 3 correspond to the values in the column for month 3, and so on. This relationship is true for all the constraints and will be very helpful in implementing this model in the spreadsheet.

3.13.4 IMPLEMENTING THE MODEL

The LP model for Taco-Viva's construction fund problem is summarized as:

MIN: $A_1 + B_1 + C_1 + D_1$ $\}$ cash invested at beginning of month 1

Subject to:

$$1.018A_1 - 1A_2 \qquad\qquad = \quad 0 \quad \} \text{ cash flow for month 2}$$
$$1.035B_1 + 1.018A_2 - 1A_3 - 1B_3 \qquad = 250 \quad \} \text{ cash flow for month 3}$$
$$1.058C_1 + 1.018A_3 - 1A_4 - 1C_4 \qquad = \quad 0 \quad \} \text{ cash flow for month 4}$$
$$1.035B_3 + 1.018A_4 - 1A_5 - 1B_5 \qquad = 250 \quad \} \text{ cash flow for month 5}$$
$$1.018A_5 - 1A_6 \qquad\qquad = \quad 0 \quad \} \text{ cash flow for month 6}$$
$$1.11D_1 + 1.058C_4 + 1.035B_5 + 1.018A_6 = 300 \quad \} \text{ cash flow for month 7}$$
$$A_i, B_i, C_i, D_i, \geq 0, \text{ for all } i \qquad\qquad \} \text{ nonnegativity conditions}$$

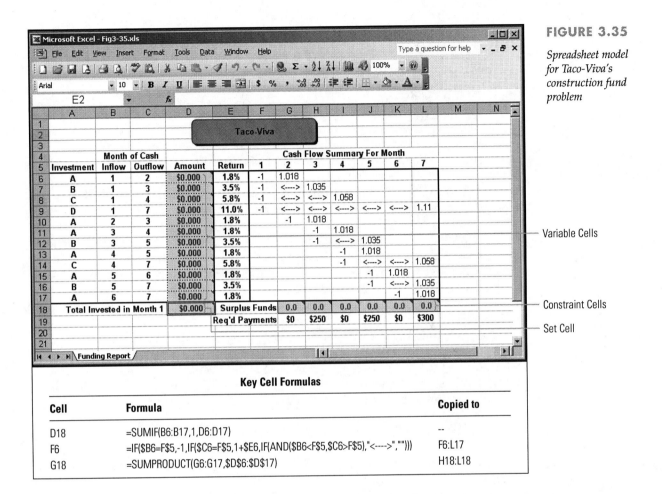

FIGURE 3.35

Spreadsheet model for Taco-Viva's construction fund problem

Key Cell Formulas

Cell	Formula	Copied to
D18	=SUMIF(B6:B17,1,D6:D17)	--
F6	=IF($B6=F$5,-1,IF($C6=F$5,1+$E6,IF(AND($B6<F$5,$C6>F$5),"<---->","")))	F6:L17
G18	=SUMPRODUCT(G6:G17,$D$6:$D$17)	H18:L18

One approach to implementing this model is shown in Figure 3.35 (and file Fig3-35.xls on your data disk). The first three columns of this spreadsheet summarize the different investment options that are available and the months in which money may flow into and out of these investments. Cells D6 through D17 represent the decision variables in our model and indicate the amount of money (in $1,000s) to be placed in each of the possible investments.

The objective function for this problem requires that we compute the total amount of money being invested in month 1. This was done in cell D18 as follows:

Formula for cell D18:   =SUMIF(B6:B17,1,D6:D17)

This SUMIF function compares the values in cells B6 through B17 to the value 1 (its second argument). If any of the values in B6 through B17 equal 1, it sums the corresponding values in cells D6 through D17. In this case, the values in cells B6 through B9 all equal 1; therefore, the function returns the sum of the values in cells D6 through D9. Note that although we could have implemented the objective using the formula SUM(D6:D9), the previous SUMIF formula makes for a more modifiable and reliable model. If any of the values in column B are changed to or from 1, the SUMIF function continues to represent the appropriate objective function, whereas the SUM function would not.

Our next job is to implement the cash inflow/outflow table described earlier in Figure 3.34. Recall that each row in Figure 3.34 corresponds to the cash flows associated with a particular investment alternative. This table can be implemented in our spreadsheet using the following formula:

Formula for cell F6: =IF($B6=F$5,-1,IF($C6=F$5,1+$E6,IF(AND($B6<F$5,$C6>F$5)," <--->","")))
(Copy to cells F6 through L17.)

This formula first checks to see if the "month of cash inflow" value in column B matches the month indicator value in row 5. If so, the formula returns the value -1. Otherwise, it goes on to check to see if the "month of cash outflow" value in column C matches the month indicator value in row 5. If so, the formula returns a value equal to 1 plus the return for the investment (from column E). If neither of the first two conditions are met, the formula next checks whether the current month indicator in row 5 is larger than the "month of cash inflow" value (column B) and smaller than the "month of cash outflow" value (column C). If so, the formula returns the characters "<--->" to indicate periods in which funds neither flow into or out of a particular investment. Finally, if none of the previous three conditions are met, the formula simply returns an empty (or null) string "". Although this formula looks a bit intimidating, it is simply a set of three nested IF functions. More important, it automatically updates the cash flow summary if any of the values in columns B, C, or E are changed, increasing the reliability and modifiability of the model.

Earlier, we noted that the values listed in columns 2 through 7 of the cash inflow/outflow table correspond directly to the coefficients appearing in the various cash-flow constraints. This property allows us to implement the cash-flow constraints in the spreadsheet conveniently. For example, the LHS formula for the cash-flow constraint for month 2 is implemented in cell G18 through the formula:

Formula in cell G18:   =SUMPRODUCT(G6:G17,$D$6:$D$17)
(Copy to H18 through L18.)

This formula multiplies each entry in the range G6 through G17 by the corresponding entry in the range D6 through D17 and then sums these individual products. This formula is copied to cells H18 through L18. (Notice that the SUMPRODUCT( ) formula treats cells containing labels and null strings as if they contained the value zero.) Take a moment now to verify that the formulas in cells G18 through L18 correspond to the LHS formulas of the cash-flow constraints in our model. Cells G19 through L19 list the RHS values for the cash-flow constraints.

3.13.5 SOLVING THE MODEL

To find the optimal solution to this model, we must indicate to Solver the set cell, variable cells, and constraint cells identified in Figure 3.35. Figure 3.36 shows the Solver parameters required to solve this model. The optimal solution is shown in Figure 3.37.

3.13.6 ANALYZING THE SOLUTION

The value of the set cell (D18) in Figure 3.37 indicates that a total of $741,363 must be invested to meet the payments on Taco-Viva's construction project. Cells D6 and D8 indicate that approximately $241,237 should be placed in investment A at the beginning of month 1 ($A_1 = 241.237$) and approximately $500,126 should be placed in investment C ($C_1 = 500.126$).

At the beginning of month 2, the funds placed in investment A at the beginning of month 1 will mature and will be worth $245,580 ($241,237 \times 1.018 = 245,580$). The value

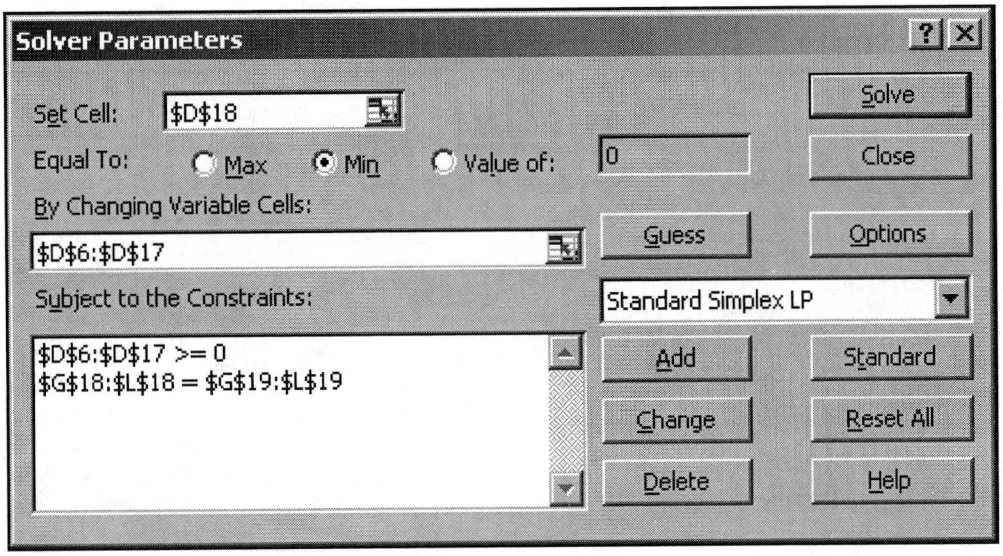

FIGURE 3.36

Solver parameters for the construction fund problem

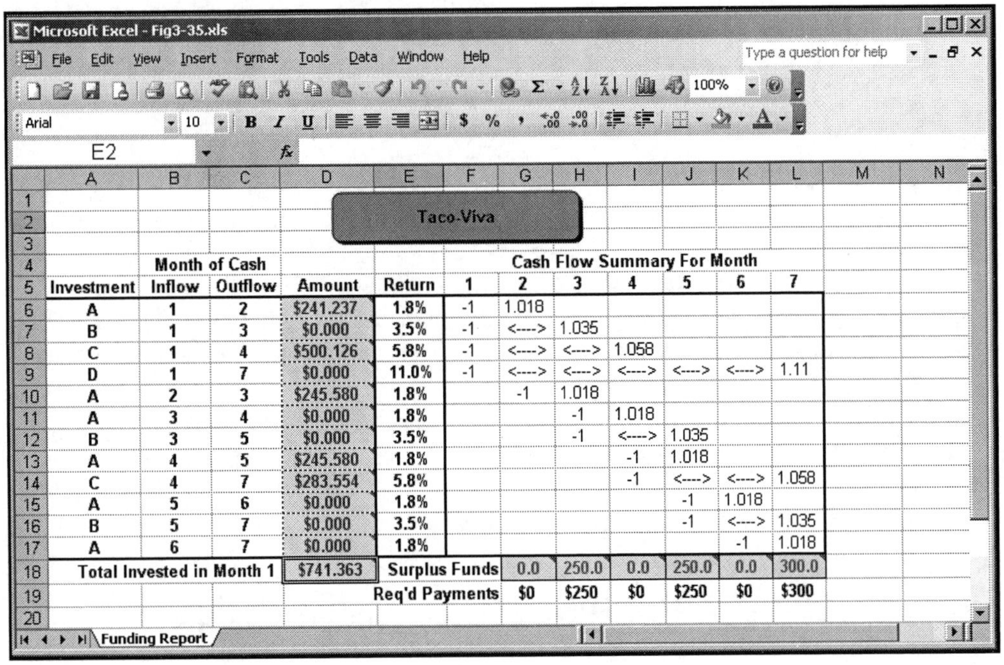

	Month of Cash				Cash Flow Summary For Month						
Investment	Inflow	Outflow	Amount	Return	1	2	3	4	5	6	7
A	1	2	$241.237	1.8%	-1	1.018					
B	1	3	$0.000	3.5%	-1	<---->	1.035				
C	1	4	$500.126	5.8%	-1	<---->	<---->	1.058			
D	1	7	$0.000	11.0%	-1	<---->	<---->	<---->	<---->	<---->	1.11
A	2	3	$245.580	1.8%		-1	1.018				
A	3	4	$0.000	1.8%			-1	1.018			
B	3	5	$0.000	3.5%			-1	<---->	1.035		
A	4	5	$245.580	1.8%				-1	1.018		
C	4	7	$283.554	5.8%				-1	<---->	<---->	1.058
A	5	6	$0.000	1.8%					-1	1.018	
B	5	7	$0.000	3.5%					-1	<---->	1.035
A	6	7	$0.000	1.8%						-1	1.018
Total Invested in Month 1			$741.363	Surplus Funds	0.0	250.0	0.0	250.0	0.0	300.0	
				Req'd Payments	$0	$250	$0	$250	$0	$300	

FIGURE 3.37

Optimal solution to Taco-Viva's construction fund problem

in cell D10 indicates that these funds should be placed back into investment A at the beginning of month 2 ($A_2 = 245.580$).

At the beginning of month 3, the first $250,000 payment is due. At that time, the funds placed in investment A at the beginning of month 2 will mature and will be worth $250,000 ($1.018 \times 245{,}580 = 250{,}000$) – allowing us to make this payment.

At the beginning of month 4, the funds placed in investment C at the beginning of month 1 will mature and will be worth $529,134. Our solution indicates that $245,580 of this amount should be placed in investment A ($A_4 = 245.580$) and that the rest should be reinvested in investment C ($C_4 = 283.554$).

If you trace through the cash flows for the remaining months, you will discover that our model is doing exactly what it was designed to do. The amount of money scheduled to mature at the beginning of each month is exactly equal to the amount of money scheduled to be reinvested after required payments are made. Thus, out of an infinite number of possible investment schedules, our LP model found the one schedule that requires the least amount of money up front.

3.13.7 MODIFYING THE TACO-VIVA PROBLEM TO ACCOUNT FOR RISK (OPTIONAL)

In investment problems like this, it is not uncommon for decision makers to place limits on the amount of risk they are willing to assume. For instance, suppose that the chief financial officer (CFO) for Taco-Viva assigned the following risk ratings to each of the possible investments on a scale from 1 to 10 (where 1 represents the least risk and 10 the greatest risk). We also will assume that the CFO wants to determine an investment plan where the weighted average risk level does not exceed 5.

Investment	Risk Rating
A	1
B	3
C	8
D	6

We will need to formulate an additional constraint for each time period to ensure that the weighted average risk level never exceeds 5. To see how this can be done, let's start with month 1.

In month 1, funds can be invested in A_1, B_1, C_1, and/or D_1, and each investment is associated with a different degree of risk. To calculate the weighted average risk during month 1, we must multiply the risk factors for each investment by the proportion of money in that investment. This is represented by:

$$\text{Weighted average risk in month 1} = \frac{1A_1 + 3B_1 + 8C_1 + 6D_1}{A_1 + B_1 + C_1 + D_1}$$

We can ensure that the weighted average risk in month 1 does not exceed the value 5 by including the following constraint in our LP model:

$$\frac{1A_1 + 3B_1 + 8C_1 + 6D_1}{A_1 + B_1 + C_1 + D_1} \leq 5 \quad \} \text{ risk constraint for month 1}$$

Now, consider month 2. According to the column for month 2 in our cash inflow/outflow table, the company can have funds invested in B_1, C_1, D_1, and/or A_2 during this month. Thus, the weighted average risk that occurs in month 2 is defined by:

$$\text{Weighted average risk in month 2} = \frac{3B_1 + 8C_1 + 6D_1 + 1A_2}{B_1 + C_1 + D_1 + A_2}$$

Again, the following constraint ensures that this quantity never exceeds 5:

$$\frac{3B_1 + 8C_1 + 6D_1 + 1A_2}{B_1 + C_1 + D_1 + A_2} \leq 5 \quad \} \text{ risk constraint for month 2}$$

The risk constraints for months 3 through 6 are generated in a similar manner, and appear as:

$$\frac{8C_1 + 6D_1 + 1A_3 + 3B_3}{C_1 + D_1 + A_3 + B_3} \le 5 \quad \} \text{ risk constraint for month 3}$$

$$\frac{6D_1 + 3B_3 + 1A_4 + 8C_4}{D_1 + B_3 + A_4 + C_4} \le 5 \quad \} \text{ risk constraint for month 4}$$

$$\frac{6D_1 + 8C_4 + 1A_5 + 3B_5}{D_1 + C_4 + A_5 + B_5} \le 5 \quad \} \text{ risk constraint for month 5}$$

$$\frac{6D_1 + 8C_4 + 3B_5 + 1A_6}{D_1 + C_4 + B_5 + A_6} \le 5 \quad \} \text{ risk constraint for month 6}$$

Although the risk constraints listed here have a very clear meaning, it is easier to implement these constraints in the spreadsheet if we state them in a different (but algebraically equivalent) manner. In particular, it is helpful to eliminate the fractions on the LHS of the inequalities by multiplying each constraint through by its denominator and re-collecting the variables on the LHS of the inequality. The following steps show how to rewrite the risk constraint for month 1:

1. Multiply both sides of the inequality by the denominator:

$$(A_1 + B_1 + C_1 + D_1) \frac{1A_1 + 3B_1 + 8C_1 + 6D_1}{A_1 + B_1 + C_1 + D_1} \le (A_1 + B_1 + C_1 + D_1)5$$

to obtain:

$$1A_1 + 3B_1 + 8C_1 + 6D_1 \le 5A_1 + 5B_1 + 5C_1 + 5D_1$$

2. Re-collect the variables on the LHS of the inequality sign:

$$(1 - 5)A_1 + (3 - 5)B_1 + (8 - 5)C_1 + (6 - 5)D_1 \le 0$$

to obtain:

$$-4A_1 - 2B_1 + 3C_1 + 1D_1 \le 0$$

Thus, the following two constraints are algebraically equivalent:

$$\frac{1A_1 + 3B_1 + 8C_1 + 6D_1}{A_1 + B_1 + C_1 + D_1} \le 5 \quad \} \text{ risk constraint for month 1}$$

$$-4A_1 - 2B_1 + 3C_1 + 1D_1 \le 0 \quad \} \text{ risk constraint for month 1}$$

The set of values for A_1, B_1, C_1, and D_1 that satisfies the first of these constraints also satisfies the second constraint (that is, these constraints have exactly the same set of feasible values). So, it does not matter which of these constraints we use to find the optimal solution to the problem.

The remaining risk constraints are simplified in the same way, producing the following constraints:

$-2B_1$	$+$	$3C_1$	$+$	$1D_1$	$-$	$4A_2$			$\le$	0	} risk constraint for month 2
		$3C_1$	$+$	$1D_1$	$-$	$4A_3$	$-$	$2B_3$	$\le$	0	} risk constraint for month 3
				$1D_1$	$-$	$2B_3$	$-$	$4A_4$	$+$	$3C_4$	$\le$	0	} risk constraint for month 4
				$1D_1$	$+$	$3C_4$	$-$	$4A_5$	$-$	$2B_5$	$\le$	0	} risk constraint for month 5
				$1D_1$	$+$	$3C_4$	$-$	$2B_5$	$-$	$4A_6$	$\le$	0	} risk constraint for month 6

Notice that the coefficient for each variable in these constraints is simply the risk factor for the particular investment minus the maximum allowable weighted average risk value of 5. That is, all A_i variables have coefficients of $1 - 5 = -4$; all B_i variables have coefficients of $3 - 5 = -2$; all C_i variables have coefficients of $8 - 5 = 3$; and all D_i variables have coefficients of $6 - 5 = 1$. This observation will help us implement these constraints efficiently.

3.13.8 IMPLEMENTING THE RISK CONSTRAINTS

Figure 3.38 (and file Fig3-38.xls on your data disk) shows a split screen that illustrates an easy way to implement the risk constraints for this model. Earlier we noted that the coefficient for each variable in each risk constraint is simply the risk factor for the particular investment minus the maximum allowable weighted average risk value. Thus, the strategy in Figure 3.38 is to generate these values in the appropriate columns and rows of the spreadsheet so that the SUMPRODUCT( ) function can implement the LHS formulas for the risk constraints.

Recall that the risk constraint for each month involves only the variables representing investments that actually held funds during that month. For any given month, the investments that actually held funds during that month have the value −1 or contain a text entry starting with the "<" symbol (the first character of the "<---->" entries) in the

FIGURE 3.38

Spreadsheet model for Taco-Viva's revised construction fund problem

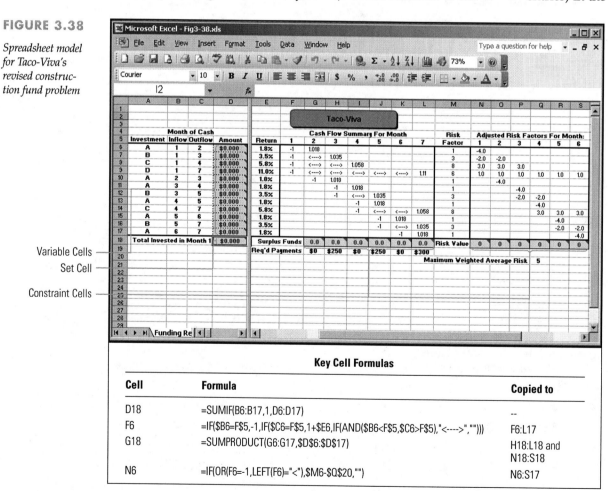

Variable Cells

Set Cell

Constraint Cells

Cell	Formula	Copied to
Key Cell Formulas		
D18	=SUMIF(B6:B17,1,D6:D17)	--
F6	=IF($B6=F$5,-1,IF($C6=F$5,1+$E6,IF(AND($B6<F$5,$C6>F$5),"<---->","")))	F6:L17
G18	=SUMPRODUCT(G6:G17,$D$6:$D$17)	H18:L18 and N18:S18
N6	=IF(OR(F6=-1,LEFT(F6)="<"),$M6-$Q$20,"")	N6:S17

corresponding column of the cash inflow/outflow summary table. For example, during month 2, funds can be invested in B_1, C_1, D_1, and/or A_2. The corresponding cells for month 2 in Figure 3.38 (cells G7, G8, G9, and G10, respectively) each contain either the value -1 or a text entry starting with the "<" symbol. Therefore, to generate the appropriate coefficients for the risk constraints, we can instruct the spreadsheet to scan the cash inflow/outflow summary for cells containing the value -1 or text entries starting with the "<" symbol, and return the correct risk constraint coefficients in the appropriate cells. To do this we enter the following formula in cell N6:

Formula in cell N6: =IF(OR(F6=-1,LEFT(F6)="<"),$M6-$Q$20,""))

(Copy to N6 through S17.)

To generate the appropriate value in cell N6, the previous formula checks if cell F6 is equal to -1 or contains a text entry that starts with the "<" symbol. If either of these conditions is true, the function takes the risk factor for the investment from cell M6 and subtracts the maximum allowable risk factor found in cell Q20; otherwise, the function returns a null string (with a value of zero). This formula is copied to the remaining cells in the range N6 through S17, as shown in Figure 3.38.

The values in cells N6 through S17 in Figure 3.38 correspond to the coefficients in the LHS formulas for each of the risk constraints formulated earlier. Thus, the LHS formula for the risk constraint for month 1 is implemented in cell N18 as:

Formula in cell N18: =SUMPRODUCT(N6:N17,$D$6:$D$17)

(Copy to O18 through S18.)

The LHS formulas for the remaining risk constraints are implemented by copying this formula to cells O18 through S18. We will tell Solver that these constraint cells must be less than or equal to zero.

3.13.9 SOLVING THE MODEL

To find the optimal solution to this model, we must communicate the appropriate information about the new risk constraints to Solver. Figure 3.39 shows the Solver parameters required to solve this model. The optimal solution is shown in Figure 3.40.

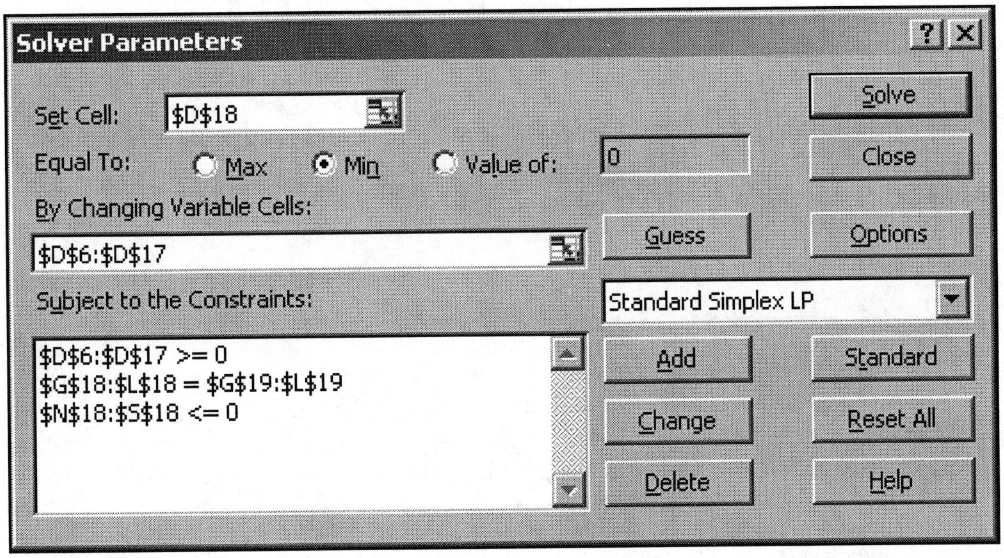

FIGURE 3.39

Solver parameters for the revised construction fund problem

FIGURE 3.40

Optimal solution to Taco-Viva's revised construction fund problem

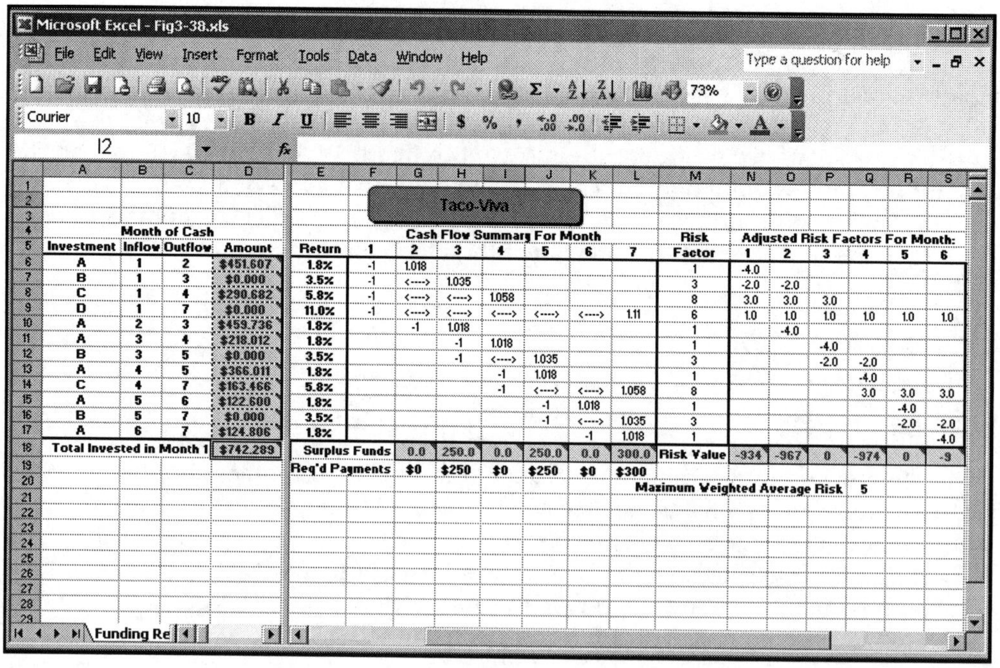

3.13.10 ANALYZING THE SOLUTION

The optimal solution to the revised Taco-Viva problem with risk constraints is quite different than the solution obtained earlier. In particular, the new solution requires that funds be placed in investment A in every time period. This is not too surprising given that investment A has the lowest risk rating. It may be somewhat surprising that of the remaining investments, B and D never are used. Although these investments have lower risk ratings than investment C, the combination of funds placed in investment A and C allows for the least amount of money to be invested in month 1 while meeting the scheduled payments and keeping the weighted average risk at or below the specified level.

3.14 Data Envelopment Analysis

Managers often are interested in determining how efficiently various units within a company operate. Similarly, investment analysts might be interested in comparing the efficiency of several competing companies within an industry. Data Envelopment Analysis (DEA) is an LP-based methodology for performing this type of analysis. DEA determines how efficiently an operating unit (or company) converts inputs to outputs when compared with other units. We will consider how DEA may be applied via the following example.

Mike Lister is a district manager for the Steak & Burger fast-food restaurant chain. The region Mike manages contains 12 company-owned units. Mike is in the process of evaluating the performance of these units during the past year to make recommendations on how much of an annual bonus to pay each unit's manager. He wants to base this decision, in part, on how efficiently each unit has been operated. Mike has collected the data shown in the following table on each of the 12 units. The outputs he has chosen include each unit's net profit (in $100,000s), average customer satisfaction rating, and average monthly cleanliness score. The inputs include total labor hours (in 100,000s) and total operating costs (in $1,000,000s). He wants to apply DEA to this data to determine an efficiency score of each unit.

	Outputs			Inputs	
Unit	Profit	Satisfaction	Cleanliness	Labor Hours	Operating Costs
1	5.98	7.7	92	4.74	6.75
2	7.18	9.7	99	6.38	7.42
3	4.97	9.3	98	5.04	6.35
4	5.32	7.7	87	3.61	6.34
5	3.39	7.8	94	3.45	4.43
6	4.95	7.9	88	5.25	6.31
7	2.89	8.6	90	2.36	3.23
8	6.40	9.1	100	7.09	8.69
9	6.01	7.3	89	6.49	7.28
10	6.94	8.8	89	7.36	9.07
11	5.86	8.2	93	5.46	6.69
12	8.35	9.6	97	6.58	8.75

3.14.1 DEFINING THE DECISION VARIABLES

Using DEA, the efficiency of an arbitrary unit i is defined as follows:

$$\text{Efficiency of unit } i = \frac{\text{Weighted sum of unit } i\text{'s outputs}}{\text{Weighted sum of unit } i\text{'s inputs}} = \frac{\sum\limits_{j=1}^{n_O} O_{ij} w_j}{\sum\limits_{j=1}^{n_I} I_{ij} v_j}$$

Here, O_{ij} represents the value of unit i on *output* j, I_{ij} represents the value of unit i on *input* j, w_j is a nonnegative weight assigned to output j, v_j is a nonnegative weight assigned to input j, n_O is the number of output variables, and n_I is the number of input variables. The problem in DEA is to determine values for the weights w_j and v_j. Thus, w_j and v_j represent the decision variables in a DEA problem.

3.14.2 DEFINING THE OBJECTIVE

A separate LP problem is solved for each unit in a DEA problem. However, for each unit the objective is the same: to maximize the weighted sum of that unit's outputs. For an arbitrary unit i, the objective is stated as:

$$\text{MAX: } \sum_{j=1}^{n_O} O_{ij} w_j$$

Thus, as each LP problem is solved, the unit under investigation is given the opportunity to select the best possible weights for itself (or the weights that maximize the weighted sum of its output), subject to the following constraints.

3.14.3 DEFINING THE CONSTRAINTS

It is impossible for any unit to be more than 100% efficient. So as each LP is solved, the unit under investigation cannot select weights for itself that would cause the efficiency for any unit (including itself) to be greater than 100%. Thus, for each individual unit, we require the weighted sum of the unit's outputs to be less than or equal to the weighted sum of its inputs (so the ratio of weighted outputs to weighted inputs does not exceed 100%).

$$\sum_{j=1}^{n_o} O_{kj}w_j \leq \sum_{j=1}^{n_I} I_{kj}v_j, \quad \text{for } k = 1 \text{ to the number of units}$$

or equivalently,

$$\sum_{j=1}^{n_o} O_{kj}w_j - \sum_{j=1}^{n_I} I_{kj}v_j \leq 0, \quad \text{for } k = 1 \text{ to the number of units}$$

To prevent unbounded solutions, we also require the sum of the weighted inputs for the unit under investigation (unit i) to equal one.

$$\sum_{j=1}^{n_I} I_{ij}v_j = 1$$

Because the sum of weighted inputs for the unit under investigation must equal one and its sum of the weighted outputs (being maximized) cannot exceed this value, the maximum efficiency score for the unit under investigation is also one (or 100%). Thus, units that are efficient will have a DEA efficiency score of 100%.

Important Point

When applying DEA, it is assumed that for output variables "more is better" (e.g., profit) and for input variables "less is better" (e.g., costs). Any output or input variables that do not naturally conform to these rules should be transformed before applying DEA. For example, the percentage of defective products produced is not a good choice for an output because fewer defects is actually a good thing. However, the percentage of nondefective products produced would be an acceptable choice for an output because "more is better" in that case.

3.14.4 IMPLEMENTING THE MODEL

To evaluate the efficiency of unit 1 in our example problem, we would solve the following LP problem,

MAX: $5.98w_1 + 7.7w_2 + 92w_3$ } weighted output for unit 1

Subject to: $5.98w_1 + 7.7w_2 + 92w_3 - 4.74v_1 - 6.75v_2 \leq 0$ } efficiency constraint for unit 1

$7.18w_1 + 9.7w_2 + 99w_3 - 6.38v_1 - 7.42v_2 \leq 0$ } efficiency constraint for unit 2

and so on to . . .

$8.35w_1 + 9.6w_2 + 97w_3 - 6.58v_1 - 8.75v_2 \leq 0$ } efficiency constraint for unit 12

$4.74v_1 + 6.75v_2 = 1$ } input constraint for unit 1

$w_1, w_2, w_3, v_1, v_2 \geq 0$ } nonnegativity conditions

A convenient way to implement this model is shown in Figure 3.41 (and in the file Fig3-41.xls on your data disk).

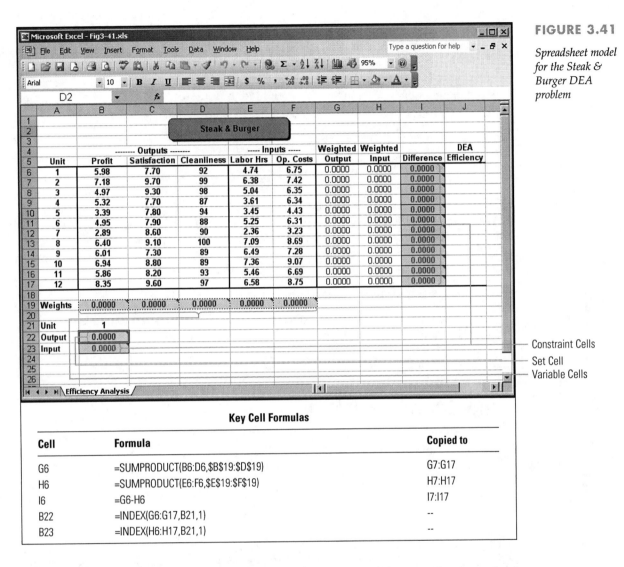

FIGURE 3.41

*Spreadsheet model
for the Steak &
Burger DEA
problem*

Key Cell Formulas

Cell	Formula	Copied to
G6	=SUMPRODUCT(B6:D6,$B$19:$D$19)	G7:G17
H6	=SUMPRODUCT(E6:F6,$E$19:$F$19)	H7:H17
I6	=G6-H6	I7:I17
B22	=INDEX(G6:G17,B21,1)	--
B23	=INDEX(H6:H17,B21,1)	--

In Figure 3.41, cells B19 through F19 are reserved to represent the weights for each of
the input and output variables. The weighted output for each unit is computed in column G as follows:

Formula for cell G6:   =SUMPRODUCT(B6:D6,$B$19:$D$19)
(Copy to G7 through G17.)

Similarly, the weighted input for each unit is computed in column H as:

Formula for cell H6:   =SUMPRODUCT(E6:F6,$E$19:$F$19)
(Copy to H7 through H17.)

The differences between the weighted outputs and weighted inputs are computed in
column I. We will instruct Solver to constrain these values to be less than or equal to 0.

Formula for cell I6:   =G6-H6
(Copy to I7 through I17.)

The weighted output for unit 1 (computed in cell G6) implements the appropriate
objective function and could be used as the set cell for Solver in this problem. Similarly,
the weighted input for unit 1 is computed in cell H6 and could be constrained to equal 1

(as specified by the input constraint for unit 1 above). However, because we need to solve a separate LP problem for each of the 12 units, it will be more convenient to handle the objective function and input constraint in a slightly different manner. To this end, we reserve cell B21 to indicate the unit number currently under investigation. Cell B22 contains a formula that returns the weighted output for this unit from the list of weighted outputs in column G.

Formula for cell B22:   =INDEX(G6:G17,B21,1)

In general, the function INDEX(*range,row number,column number*) returns the value in the specified *row number* and *column number* of the given *range*. Because cell B21 contains the number 1, the previous formula returns the value in the first row and first column of the range G6:G17—or the value in cell G6. Thus, as long as the value of cell B21 represents a valid unit number from 1 to 12, the value in cell B22 will represent the appropriate objective function for the DEA model for that unit. Similarly, the input constraint requiring the weighted inputs for the unit in question to equal 1 can be implemented in cell B23 as follows:

Formula for cell B23:   =INDEX(H6:H17,B21,1)

So, for whatever unit number is listed in cell B21, cell B22 represents the appropriate objective function to be maximized and cell B23 represents the weighted input that must be constrained to equal 1. This arrangement greatly simplifies the process of solving the required series of DEA models.

3.14.5 SOLVING THE MODEL

To solve this model, we specify the set cells, variable cells, and constraints specified in Figure 3.42. Note that exactly the same Solver settings would be used to find the optimal DEA weights for any other unit. The optimal solution for unit 1 is shown in Figure 3.43. Notice that unit 1 achieves an efficiency score of 0.9667 and therefore is slightly inefficient.

FIGURE 3.42

Solver parameters for the DEA problem

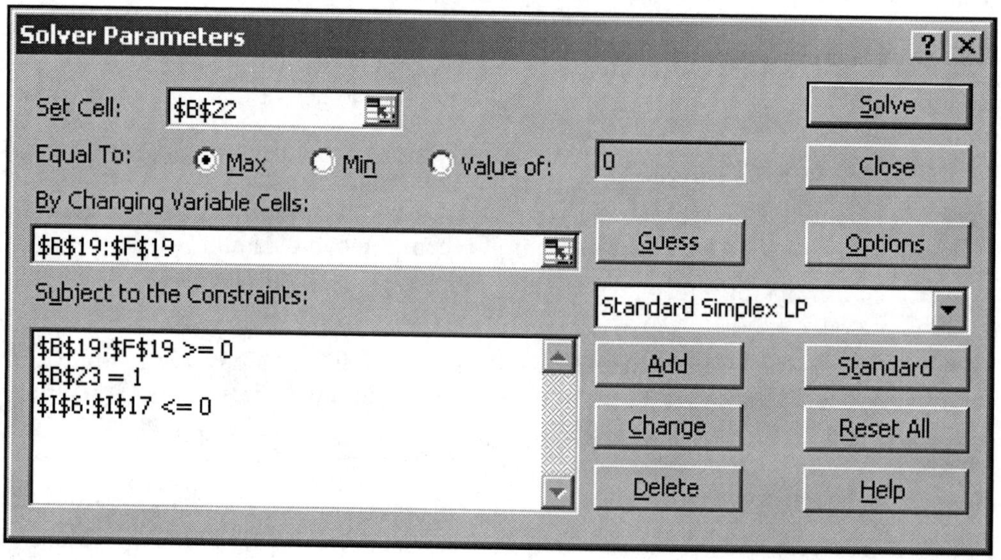

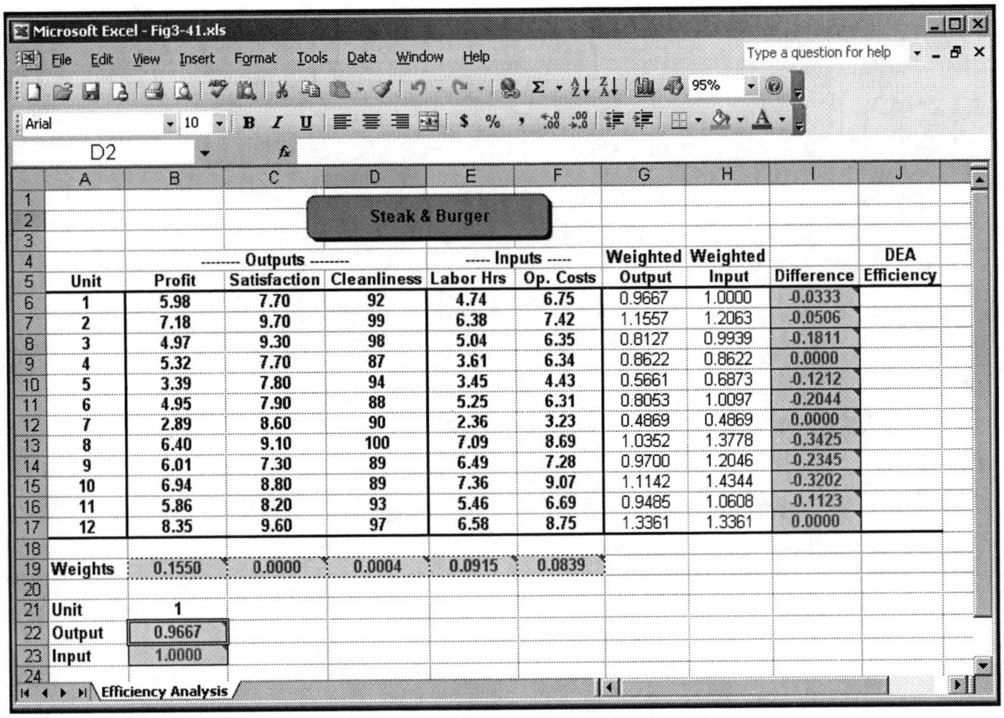

FIGURE 3.43

*Optimal DEA
solution for unit 1*

	A	B	C	D	E	F	G	H	I	J
1										
2			Steak & Burger							
3										
4			------- Outputs -------		----- Inputs -----		Weighted	Weighted		DEA
5	Unit	Profit	Satisfaction	Cleanliness	Labor Hrs	Op. Costs	Output	Input	Difference	Efficiency
6	1	5.98	7.70	92	4.74	6.75	0.9667	1.0000	-0.0333	
7	2	7.18	9.70	99	6.38	7.42	1.1557	1.2063	-0.0506	
8	3	4.97	9.30	98	5.04	6.35	0.8127	0.9939	-0.1811	
9	4	5.32	7.70	87	3.61	6.34	0.8622	0.8622	0.0000	
10	5	3.39	7.80	94	3.45	4.43	0.5661	0.6873	-0.1212	
11	6	4.95	7.90	88	5.25	6.31	0.8053	1.0097	-0.2044	
12	7	2.89	8.60	90	2.36	3.23	0.4869	0.4869	0.0000	
13	8	6.40	9.10	100	7.09	8.69	1.0352	1.3778	-0.3425	
14	9	6.01	7.30	89	6.49	7.28	0.9700	1.2046	-0.2345	
15	10	6.94	8.80	89	7.36	9.07	1.1142	1.4344	-0.3202	
16	11	5.86	8.20	93	5.46	6.69	0.9485	1.0608	-0.1123	
17	12	8.35	9.60	97	6.58	8.75	1.3361	1.3361	0.0000	
18										
19	Weights	0.1550	0.0000	0.0004	0.0915	0.0839				
20										
21	Unit	1								
22	Output	0.9667								
23	Input	1.0000								

To complete the analysis for the remaining units, Mike could change the value in cell B21 manually to 2, 3, . . ., 12 and use Solver to reoptimize the worksheet for each unit and record their efficiency scores in column J. However, if there were 120 units rather than 12, this manual approach would become quite cumbersome. Fortunately, it is easy to write a simple macro in Excel to carry out this process for us automatically with the click of a button. To do this, turn on the Control Toolbox command bar and place a command button on your worksheet (as shown in Figure 3.44) as follows:

1. Click View, Toolbars, Control Toolbox.
2. Click the Command Button icon on the Control Toolbox.
3. Click and drag on your worksheet to draw a command button.

Next, we need to change a few properties of our newly created command button. To do this,

1. Click the Command Button to make sure it is selected.
2. Click the Properties icon on the Control Toolbox.

These actions cause the Properties window shown in Figure 3.45 to appear. This window lists several properties (or attributes) of the command button that you can change to customize its appearance and behavior. For present purposes, change the command button's property values as follows,

Property	New Value
(Name)	DEA
Caption	Run DEA
TakeFocusOnClick	False

FIGURE 3.44

Using the Control Toolbox to create a command button

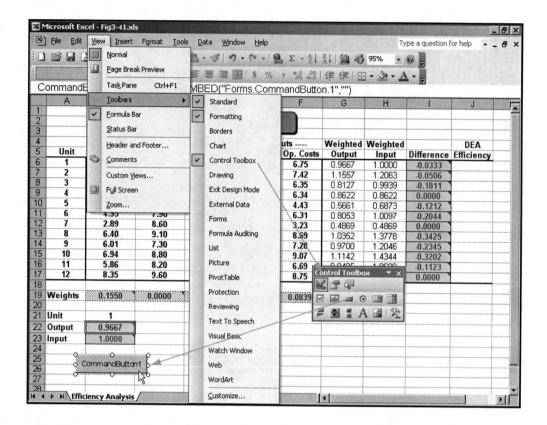

FIGURE 3.45

Adjusting the properties of the command button

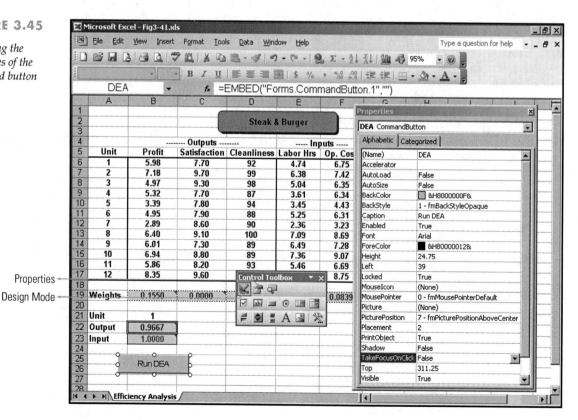

Important Software Note

When you place a command button on a worksheet, it is a good idea to set its "TakeFocusOnClick" property to False. This prevents the command button from receiving the focus when it is clicked. "Focus" refers to the object on the screen that is selected or has the computer's attention. An Excel macro cannot perform certain operations if a command button has the focus.

Next, double-click the command button. This should launch Excel's Visual Basic Editor and bring up the code window for the command button's click event. Initially, the click event will not have any commands in it. Insert the statements shown in Figure 3.46. These statements will be executed whenever the command button is clicked.

Software Tip

You can toggle back and forth easily between Excel and the Visual Basic Editor by pressing Alt+F11.

If you have any programming experience, you can probably follow the logic behind the programming code listed in Figure 3.46. In a nutshell, the For and Next statements define a loop of code that will be repeated 12 times. During the first execution of the loop, the variable "unit" will equal 1. During the second execution of the loop, the variable "unit" will equal 2, and so on. During each execution of the loop, the following operations take place:

Macro Statement	Purpose
RANGE("B21")=unit	Places the current value of "unit" (the number 1, 2, 3, . . ., or 12) into cell B21 on the worksheet.
SolverSolve UserFinish:=True	Tells Solver to solve the problem without displaying the usual Solver Results dialog box.
Range("J" & 5 + unit) = Range("B22")	Takes the optimal objective function value in cell B22 and places it in row "5 + unit" (that is, row 6, 7, . . ., or 17) in column J.

To call Solver from within a macro program, we must first set a reference to the Solver.xla file. You do this from within Excel's Visual Basic editor as follows,

1. Click Tools, References and check the box for solver.xla.
2. Click OK.

We can now test our command button to see if it works. To do this,

1. Close the Visual Basic editor window (or press Alt+F11).
2. Click the Exit Design Mode icon on the Control Toolbox.
3. Click the Run DEA command button.

FIGURE 3.46

VBA code for the command button's click event

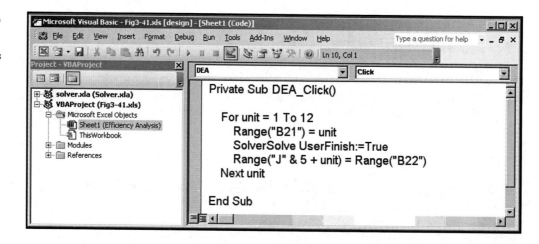

```
Private Sub DEA_Click()

    For unit = 1 To 12
        Range("B21") = unit
        SolverSolve UserFinish:=True
        Range("J" & 5 + unit) = Range("B22")
    Next unit

End Sub
```

If everything worked correctly, you should see the results shown in Figure 3.47 (or see the completed file Fig3-47.xls on your data disk).

Important Software Note

It is important to remember that command buttons and other controls become operational only after you exit design mode. If you close the Control Toolbox toolbar before clicking the Exit Design Mode icon, you will still be in design mode even after the Control Toolbox is gone, and your controls will not operate correctly.

FIGURE 3.47

DEA efficiency scores for all the units

		------- Outputs -------		----- Inputs -----		Weighted	Weighted		DEA
Unit	Profit	Satisfaction	Cleanliness	Labor Hrs	Op. Costs	Output	Input	Difference	Efficiency
1	5.98	7.70	92	4.74	6.75	0.7248	0.7639	-0.0392	0.9667
2	7.18	9.70	99	6.38	7.42	0.8658	0.8658	0.0000	1.0000
3	4.97	9.30	98	5.04	6.35	0.6106	0.7316	-0.1211	0.8345
4	5.32	7.70	87	3.61	6.34	0.6467	0.6988	-0.0521	1.0000
5	3.39	7.80	94	3.45	4.43	0.4268	0.5089	-0.0821	0.8426
6	4.95	7.90	88	5.25	6.31	0.6044	0.7324	-0.1280	0.8259
7	2.89	8.60	90	2.36	3.23	0.3676	0.3676	0.0000	1.0000
8	6.40	9.10	100	7.09	8.69	0.7762	1.0055	-0.2293	0.7720
9	6.01	7.30	89	6.49	7.28	0.7271	0.8546	-0.1275	0.8572
10	6.94	8.80	89	7.36	9.07	0.8343	1.0486	-0.2143	0.7958
11	5.86	8.20	93	5.46	6.69	0.7113	0.7741	-0.0628	0.9188
12	8.35	9.60	97	6.58	8.75	1.0000	1.0000	0.0000	1.0000

Weights	0.1153	0.0000	0.0004	0.0223	0.0975

Unit	12
Output	1.0000
Input	1.0000

Steak & Burger

Run DEA

Efficiency Analysis

3.14.6 ANALYZING THE SOLUTION

The solution shown in Figure 3.47 indicates that units 2, 4, 7, and 12 are operating at 100% efficiency (in the DEA sense), while the remaining units are operating less efficiently. Note that an efficiency rating of 100% does not necessarily mean that a unit is operating in the best possible way. It simply means that no linear combination of the other units in the study results in a composite unit that produces at least as much output using the same or less input. On the other hand, for units that are DEA *inefficient*, there exists a linear combination of efficient units that results in a composite unit that produces at least as much output using the same or less input than the inefficient unit. The idea in DEA is that an inefficient unit should be able to operate as efficiently as this hypothetical composite unit formed from a linear combination of the efficient units.

For instance, unit 1 has an efficiency score of 96.67% and is, therefore, somewhat inefficient. Figure 3.48 (in file Fig3-48.xls on your data disk) shows that a weighted average of 26.38% of unit 4, plus 28.15% of unit 7, plus 45.07% of unit 12 produces a hypothetical composite unit with outputs greater than or equal to those of unit 1 and requiring less input than unit 1. The assumption in DEA is that unit 1 should have been able to achieve this same level of performance.

For any inefficient unit, you can determine the linear combination of efficient units that results in a more efficient composite unit as follows:

1. Solve the DEA problem for the unit in question.
2. In the Solver Results dialog box, select the Sensitivity report option.

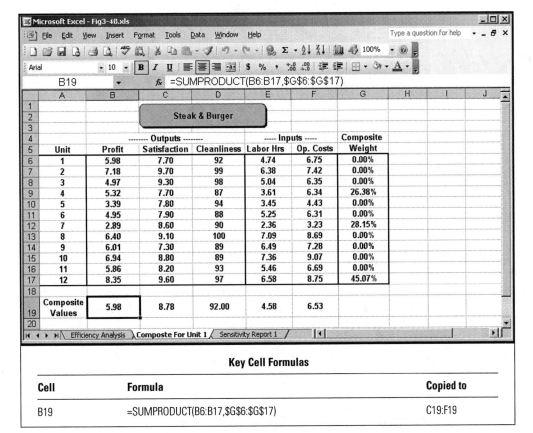

FIGURE 3.48

Example of a composite unit that is more efficient than unit 1

FIGURE 3.49

Sensitivity report for unit 1

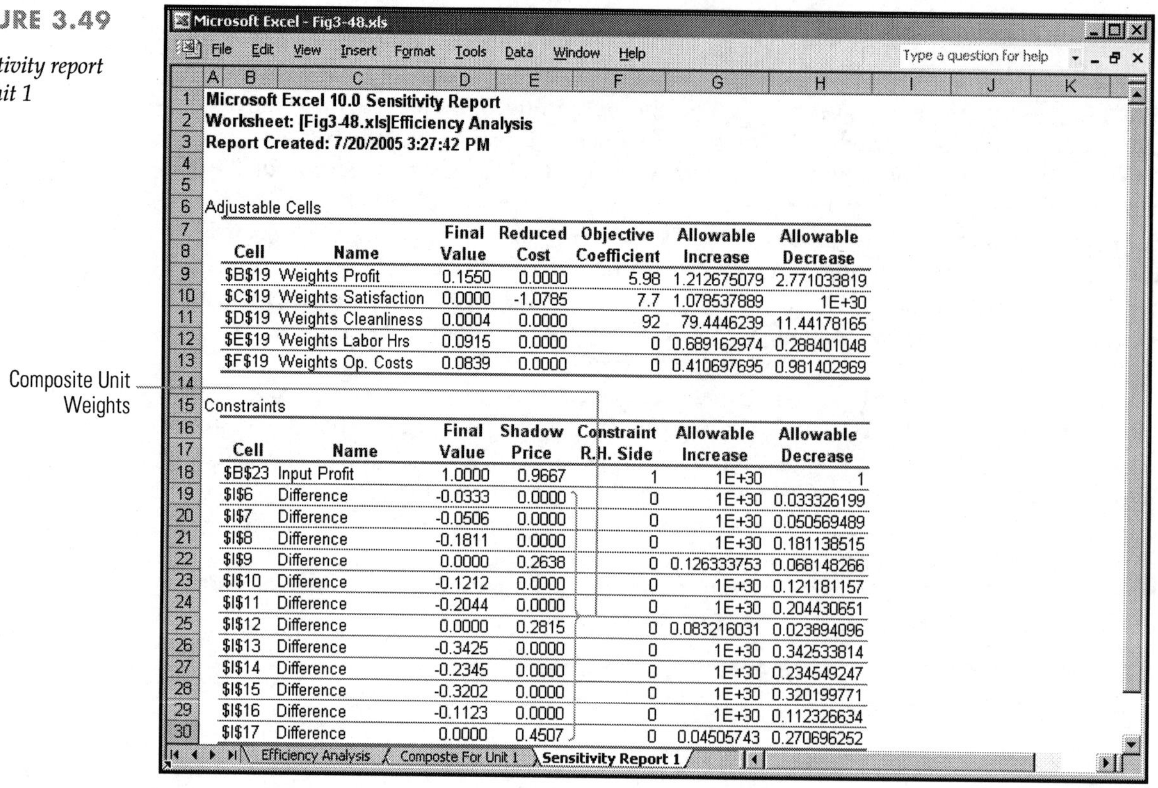

Composite Unit Weights

	Cell	Name	Final Value	Reduced Cost	Objective Coefficient	Allowable Increase	Allowable Decrease
		Adjustable Cells					
	$B$19	Weights Profit	0.1550	0.0000	5.98	1.212675079	2.771033819
	$C$19	Weights Satisfaction	0.0000	-1.0785	7.7	1.078537889	1E+30
	$D$19	Weights Cleanliness	0.0004	0.0000	92	79.4446239	11.44178165
	$E$19	Weights Labor Hrs	0.0915	0.0000	0	0.689162974	0.288401048
	$F$19	Weights Op. Costs	0.0839	0.0000	0	0.410697695	0.981402969

	Cell	Name	Final Value	Shadow Price	Constraint R.H. Side	Allowable Increase	Allowable Decrease
		Constraints					
	$B$23	Input Profit	1.0000	0.9667	1	1E+30	1
	$I$6	Difference	-0.0333	0.0000	0	1E+30	0.033326199
	$I$7	Difference	-0.0506	0.0000	0	1E+30	0.050569489
	$I$8	Difference	-0.1811	0.0000	0	1E+30	0.181138515
	$I$9	Difference	0.0000	0.2638	0	0.126333753	0.068148266
	$I$10	Difference	-0.1212	0.0000	0	1E+30	0.121181157
	$I$11	Difference	-0.2044	0.0000	0	1E+30	0.204430651
	$I$12	Difference	0.0000	0.2815	0	0.083216031	0.023894096
	$I$13	Difference	-0.3425	0.0000	0	1E+30	0.342533814
	$I$14	Difference	-0.2345	0.0000	0	1E+30	0.234549247
	$I$15	Difference	-0.3202	0.0000	0	1E+30	0.320199771
	$I$16	Difference	-0.1123	0.0000	0	1E+30	0.112326634
	$I$17	Difference	0.0000	0.4507	0	0.04505743	0.270696252

In the resulting sensitivity report, the absolute value of the Shadow Prices for the "Difference" constraints are the weights that should create a composite unit that is more efficient than the unit in question. The sensitivity report for unit 1 is shown in Figure 3.49.

Want To Know More?

To learn more about writing VBA macros in Excel, see *Excel 2003 Power Programming with VBA* by Wiley Publishing. To learn more about controlling Solver from within macros, click the Help button on the Solver Options dialog box (available in Premium Solver for Education).

3.15 Summary

This chapter described how to formulate an LP problem algebraically, implement it in a spreadsheet, and solve it using Solver. The decision variables in the algebraic formulation of a model correspond to the variable cells in the spreadsheet. The LHS formulas for each constraint in an LP model must be implemented in different cells in the spreadsheet. Also, a cell in the spreadsheet must represent the objective function in the LP model. Thus, there is a direct relationship between the various components of an algebraic formulation of an LP problem and its implementation in a spreadsheet.

There are many ways to implement a given LP problem in a spreadsheet. The process of building spreadsheet models is more an art than a science. A good spreadsheet implementation represents the problem in a way that clearly communicates its purpose, is reliable, auditable, and modifiable.

It is possible to use Excel's macro language (known as Visual Basic for Applications or VBA) to automate the process of solving LP models. This is particularly useful in problems in which an analyst might want to solve several related problems in succession.

3.16 References

Charnes, C., et al. *Data Envelopment Analysis: Theory, Methodology, and Application*, New York: Kluwer Academic Publishers, 1996.

Hilal, S., and W. Erickson. "Matching Supplies to Save Lives: Linear Programming the Production of Heart Valves." *Interfaces*, vol. 11, no. 6, 1981.

Lanzenauer, C., et al. "RRSP Flood: LP to the Rescue." *Interfaces*, vol. 17, no. 4, 1987.

McKay, A. "Linear Programming Applications on Microcomputers." *Journal of the Operational Research Society*, vol. 36, July 1985.

Roush, W., et al. "Using Chance-Constrained Programming for Animal Feed Formulation at Agway." *Interfaces*, vol. 24, no. 2, 1994.

Shogan, A. *Management Science*. Englewood Cliffs, NJ: Prentice Hall, 1988.

Subramanian, R., et al., "Coldstart: Fleet Assignment at Delta Airlines," *Interfaces*, vol. 24, no. 1, 1994.

Williams, H. *Model Building in Mathematical Programming*. New York: Wiley, 1990.

THE WORLD OF MANAGEMENT SCIENCE

Optimizing Production, Inventory, and Distribution at Kellogg

The Kellogg Company (http://www.kelloggs.com) is the largest cereal producer in the world and a leading producer of convenience foods. In 1999, Kellogg's worldwide sales totaled nearly $7 billion. Kellogg operates five plants in the United States and Canada and has seven core distribution centers and roughly fifteen co-packers that contract to produce or pack some of Kellogg's products. In the cereal business alone, Kellogg must coordinate the production of 80 products while inventorying and distributing over 600 stock keeping units with roughly 90 production lines and 180 packaging lines. Optimizing this many decision variables is obviously a daunting challenge.

Since 1990, Kellogg has been using a large-scale, multiperiod linear program, called the Kellogg Planning System (KPS), to guide production and distribution decisions. Most large companies like Kellogg employ some sort of enterprise resource planning (ERP). Kellogg's ERP systems is a largely custom, home-grown product, and KPS is a custom-developed tool to complement the ERP system.

An operational-level version of KPS is used at a weekly level of detail to help determine where products are produced and how finished products and in-process products are shipped between plants and distribution centers. A tactical-level version of KPS is used at a monthly level of detail to help establish plant budgets and make capacity and consolidation decisions. Kellogg attributes annual savings of $40–$45 million to the use of the KPS system.

Source: Brown, G., J. Keegan, B. Vigus, and K. Wood, "The Kellogg Company Optimizes Production, Inventory, and Distribution," *Interfaces*, Vol. 35, No. 6, 2001.

Questions and Problems

1. In creating the spreadsheet models for the problems in this chapter, cells in the spreadsheets had to be reserved to represent each of the decision variables in the algebraic models. We reserved these cells in the spreadsheets by entering values of zero in them. Why didn't we place some other value or formula in these cells? Would doing so have made any difference?

2. Four goals should be considered when trying to design an effective spreadsheet model: communication, reliability, auditability, and maintainability. We also noted that a spreadsheet design that results in formulas that can be copied is usually more effective than other designs. Briefly describe how using formulas that can be copied supports the four spreadsheet modeling goals.

3. Refer to question 13 at the end of Chapter 2. Implement a spreadsheet model for this problem and solve it using Solver.

4. Refer to question 14 at the end of Chapter 2. Implement a spreadsheet model for this problem and solve it using Solver.

5. Refer to question 17 at the end of Chapter 2. Implement a spreadsheet model for this problem and solve it using Solver.

6. Refer to question 18 at the end of Chapter 2. Implement a spreadsheet model for this problem and solve it using Solver.

7. Refer to question 19 at the end of Chapter 2. Implement a spreadsheet model for this problem and solve it using Solver.

8. Refer to question 20 at the end of Chapter 2. Implement a spreadsheet model for this problem and solve it using Solver.

9. Refer to question 21 at the end of Chapter 2. Implement a spreadsheet model for this problem and solve it using Solver.

10. Refer to question 22 at the end of Chapter 2. Implement a spreadsheet model for this problem and solve it using Solver.

11. Refer to question 23 at the end of Chapter 2. Implement a spreadsheet model for this problem and solve it using Solver.

12. A furniture manufacturer produces two types of tables (country and contemporary) using three types of machines. The time required to produce the tables on each machine is given in the following table.

Machine	Country	Contemporary	Total Machine Time Available per Week
Router	1.5	2.0	1,000
Sander	3.0	4.5	2,000
Polisher	2.5	1.5	1,500

Country tables sell for $350 and contemporary tables sell for $450. Management has determined that at least 20% of the tables made should be country and at least 30% should be contemporary. How many of each type of table should the company produce if it wants to maximize its revenue?

a. Formulate an LP model for this problem.

b. Create a spreadsheet model for this problem and solve it using Solver.

c. What is the optimal solution?

d. How will your spreadsheet model differ if there are 25 types of tables and 15 machine processes involved in manufacturing them?

13. Aire-Co produces home dehumidifiers at two different plants in Atlanta and Phoenix. The per unit cost of production in Atlanta and Phoenix is $400 and $360, respectively. Each plant can produce a maximum of 300 units per month. Inventory

holding costs are assessed at $30 per unit in beginning inventory each month. Aire-Co estimates the demand for its product to be 300, 400, and 500 units, respectively, over the next three months. Aire-Co wants to be able to meet this demand at minimum cost.

a. Formulate an LP model for this problem.
b. Implement your model in a spreadsheet and solve it.
c. What is the optimal solution?
d. How does the solution change if each plant is required to produce at least 50 units per month?
e. How does the solution change if each plant is required to produce at least 100 units per month?

14. The Molokai Nut Company (MNC) makes four different products from macadamia nuts grown in the Hawaiian Islands: chocolate-coated whole nuts (Whole), chocolate-coated nut clusters (Cluster), chocolate-coated nut crunch bars (Crunch), and plain roasted nuts (Roasted). The company is barely able to keep up with the increasing demand for these products. However, increasing raw material prices and foreign competition are forcing MNC to watch its margins to ensure that it is operating in the most efficient manner possible. To meet marketing demands for the coming week, MNC needs to produce at least 1,000 pounds of the Whole product, between 400 and 500 pounds of the Cluster product, no more than 150 pounds of the Crunch product, and no more than 200 pounds of Roasted product. Each pound of the Whole, Cluster, Crunch, and Roasted product contains, respectively, 60%, 40%, 20%, and 100% macadamia nuts, with the remaining weight made up of chocolate coating. The company has 1,100 pounds of nuts and 800 pounds of chocolate available for use in the next week. The various products are made using four different machines that hull the nuts, roast the nuts, coat the nuts in chocolate (if needed), and package the products. The following table summaries the time required by each product on each machine. Each machine has 60 hours of time available in the coming week.

Minutes Required per Pound

Machine	Whole	Cluster	Crunch	Roasted
Hulling	1.00	1.00	1.00	1.00
Roasting	2.00	1.50	1.00	1.75
Coating	1.00	0.70	0.20	0.00
Packaging	2.50	1.60	1.25	1.00

The selling price and variable cost associated with each pound of product is summarized below:

Per Pound Revenue and Costs

	Whole	Cluster	Crunch	Roasted
Selling Price	$5.00	$4.00	$3.20	$4.50
Variable Cost	$3.15	$2.60	$2.16	$3.10

a. Formulate an LP model for this problem.
b. Create a spreadsheet model for this problem and solve it using Solver.
c. What is the optimal solution?

15. A company is trying to determine how to allocate its $145,000 advertising budget for a new product. The company is considering newspaper ads and television commercials as its primary means for advertising. The following table summarizes the costs

of advertising in these different media and the number of new customers reached by increasing amounts of advertising.

Media & # of Ads	# of New Customers Reached	Cost per Ad
Newspaper: 1–10	900	$1,000
Newspaper: 11–20	700	$900
Newspaper: 21–30	400	$800
Television: 1–5	10,000	$12,000
Television: 6–10	7,500	$10,000
Television: 11–15	5,000	$8,000

For instance, each of the first ten ads the company places in newspapers will cost $1,000 and is expected to reach 900 new customers. Each of the next 10 newspaper ads will cost $900 and is expected to reach 700 new customers. Note that the number of new customers reached by increasing amounts of advertising decreases as the advertising saturates the market. Assume that the company will purchase no more than 30 newspaper ads and no more than 15 television ads.

a. Formulate an LP model for this problem to maximize the number of new customers reached by advertising.
b. Implement your model in a spreadsheet and solve it.
c. What is the optimal solution?
d. Suppose the number of new customers reached by 11–20 newspaper ads is 400 and the number of new customers reached by 21–30 newspaper ads is 700. Make these changes in your spreadsheet and reoptimize the problem. What is the new optimal solution? What (if anything) is wrong with this solution and why?

16. The Shop at Home Network sells various household goods during live television broadcasts. The company owns several warehouses to hold many of the goods it sells, but also leases extra warehouse space when needed. During the next five months the company expects that it will need to lease the following amounts of extra warehouse space:

Month	1	2	3	4	5
Square Feet Needed	20,000	30,000	40,000	35,000	50,000

At the beginning of any month the company can lease extra space for one or more months at the following costs:

Lease Term (months)	1	2	3	4	5
Cost per Sq. Ft. Leased	$55	$95	$130	$155	$185

So, for instance, at the start of month 1 the company can lease as much space as it wants for 4 months at a cost of $155 per square foot. Similarly, at the start of month 3 it can lease any amount of space for 2 months at a cost of $95 per square foot. The company wants to determine the least costly way of meeting its warehousing needs over the coming 5 months.

a. Formulate an LP model for this problem.
b. Create a spreadsheet model for this problem and solve it using Solver.
c. What is the optimal solution?
d. How much would it cost the company to meet its space needs if in each month it leases for one month exactly the amount of space required for the month?

17. A bank has $650,000 in assets to allocate among investments in bonds, home mortgages, car loans, and personal loans. Bonds are expected to produce a return of 10%, mortgages 8.5%, car loans 9.5%, and personal loans 12.5%. To make sure the portfolio is not too risky, the bank wants to restrict personal loans to no more than the 25% of the total portfolio. The bank also wants to ensure that more money is invested in mortgages than in personal loans. It also wants to invest more in bonds than personal loans.

   a. Formulate an LP model for this problem with the objective of maximizing the expected return on the portfolio.
   b. Implement your model in a spreadsheet and solve it.
   c. What it the optimal solution?

18. Valu-Com Electronics manufactures five different models of telecommunications interface cards for personal and laptop computers. As summarized in the following table, each of these devices requires differing amounts of printed circuit (PC) board, resistors, memory chips, and assembly.

Per Unit Requirements

	HyperLink	FastLink	SpeedLink	MicroLink	EtherLink
PC Board (square inches)	20	15	10	8	5
Resistors	28	24	18	12	16
Memory Chips	8	8	4	4	6
Assembly Labor (in hours)	0.75	0.6	0.5	0.65	1

The unit wholesale price and manufacturing cost for each model are as follows.

Per Unit Revenues and Costs

	HyperLink	FastLink	SpeedLink	MicroLink	EtherLink
Wholesale Price	$189	$149	$129	$169	$139
Manufacturing Cost	$136	$101	$ 96	$137	$101

   In their next production period, Valu-Com has 80,000 square inches of PC board, 100,000 resistors, 30,000 memory chips, and 5,000 hours of assembly time available. The company can sell all the product it can manufacture, but the marketing department wants to be sure that it produces at least 500 units of each product and at least twice as many FastLink cards as HyperLink cards while maximizing profit.

   a. Formulate an LP model for this problem.
   b. Create a spreadsheet model for this problem and solve it using Solver.
   c. What is the optimal solution?
   d. Could Valu-Com make more money if it schedules its assembly workers to work overtime?

19. A trust officer at the Blacksburg National Bank needs to determine how to invest $100,000 in the following collection of bonds to maximize the annual return.

Bond	Annual Return	Maturity	Risk	Tax-Free
A	9.5%	Long	High	Yes
B	8.0%	Short	Low	Yes
C	9.0%	Long	Low	No
D	9.0%	Long	High	Yes
E	9.0%	Short	High	No

The officer wants to invest at least 50% of the money in short-term issues and no more than 50% in high-risk issues. At least 30% of the funds should go into tax-free investments and at least 40% of the total annual return should be tax-free.

a. Formulate an LP model for this problem.

b. Create a spreadsheet model for this problem and solve it using Solver.

c. What is the optimal solution?

20. The Weedwacker Company manufactures two types of lawn trimmers: an electric model and a gas model. The company has contracted to supply a national discount retail chain with a total of 30,000 electric trimmers and 15,000 gas trimmers. However, Weedwacker's production capability is limited in three departments: production, assembly, and packaging. The following table summarizes the hours of processing time available and the processing time required by each department, for both types of trimmers:

	Hours Required per Trimmer		
	Electric	Gas	Hours Available
Production	0.20	0.40	10,000
Assembly	0.30	0.50	15,000
Packaging	0.10	0.10	5,000

The company makes its electric trimmer in-house for $55 and its gas trimmer for $85. Alternatively, it can buy electric and gas trimmers from another source for $67 and $95, respectively. How many gas and electric trimmers should Weedwacker make and how many should it buy from its competitor to fulfill its contract in the least costly manner?

a. Formulate an LP model for this problem.

b. Create a spreadsheet model for this problem and solve it using Solver.

c. What is the optimal solution?

21. A manufacturer of prefabricated homes has decided to subcontract four components of the homes. Several companies are interested in receiving this business, but none can handle more than one subcontract. The bids made by the companies for the various subcontracts are summarized in the following table.

**Bids by Companies
(in $1,000s) for Various Subcontracts**

	Company			
Component	A	B	C	D
1	185	225	193	207
2	200	190	175	225
3	330	320	315	300
4	375	389	425	445

Assuming that all the companies can perform each subcontract equally well, to which company should each subcontract be assigned if the home manufacturer wants to minimize payments to the subcontractors?

a. Formulate an LP model for this problem.

b. Create a spreadsheet model for this problem and solve it using Solver.

c. What is the optimal solution?

22. Tarmac Chemical Corporation produces a special chemical compound—called CHEMIX—that is used extensively in high school chemistry classes. This compound must contain at least 20% sulfur, at least 30% iron oxide, and at least 30% but no

more than 45% potassium. Tarmac's marketing department has estimated that it will need at least 600 pounds of this compound to meet the expected demand during the coming school session. Tarmac can buy three compounds to mix together to produce CHEMIX. The makeup of these compounds is shown in the following table.

Compound	Sulfur	Iron Oxide	Potassium
1	20%	60%	20%
2	40%	30%	30%
3	10%	40%	50%

Compounds 1, 2, and 3 cost $5.00, $5.25, and $5.50 per pound, respectively. Tarmac wants to use an LP model to determine the least costly way of producing enough CHEMIX to meet the demand expected for the coming year.
a. Formulate an LP model for this problem.
b. Create a spreadsheet model for this problem and solve it using Solver.
c. What is the optimal solution?

23. Holiday Fruit Company buys oranges and processes them into gift fruit baskets and fresh juice. The company grades the fruit it buys on a scale from 1 (lowest quality) to 5 (highest quality). The following table summarizes Holiday's current inventory of fruit.

Grade	Supply (1000s of lbs)
1	90
2	225
3	300
4	100
5	75

Each pound of oranges devoted to fruit baskets results in a marginal profit of $2.50, whereas each pound devoted to fresh juice results in a marginal profit of $1.75. Holiday wants the fruit in its baskets to have an average quality grade of at least 3.75 and its fresh juice to have a average quality grade of at least 2.50.
a. Formulate an optimization model for this problem.
b. Implement your model in a spreadsheet and solve it.
c. What it the optimal solution?

24. Riverside Oil Company in eastern Kentucky produces regular and supreme gasoline. Each barrel of regular sells for $21 and must have an octane rating of at least 90. Each barrel of supreme sells for $25 and must have an octane rating of at least 97. Each of these types of gasoline are manufactured by mixing different quantities of the following three inputs:

Input	Cost per Barrel	Octane Rating	Barrels Available (in 1000s)
1	$17.25	100	150
2	$15.75	87	350
3	$17.75	110	300

Riverside has orders for 300,000 barrels of regular and 450,000 barrels of supreme. How should the company allocate the available inputs to the production of regular and supreme gasoline if it wants to maximize profits?
a. Formulate an LP model for this problem.
b. Create a spreadsheet model for this problem and solve it using Solver.
c. What is the optimal solution?

25. Maintenance at a major theme park in central Florida is an ongoing process that occurs 24 hours a day. Because it is a long drive from most residential areas to the park, employees do not like to work shifts of fewer than eight hours. These 8-hour shifts start every four hours throughout the day. The number of maintenance workers needed at different times throughout the day varies. The following table summarizes the minimum number of employees needed in each 4-hour time period.

Time Period	Minimum Employees Needed
12 a.m. to 4 a.m.	90
4 a.m. to 8 a.m.	215
8 a.m. to 12 p.m.	250
12 p.m. to 4 p.m.	165
4 p.m. to 8 p.m.	300
8 p.m. to 12 a.m.	125

The maintenance supervisor wants to determine the minimum number of employees to schedule that meets the minimum staffing requirements.
   a. Formulate an LP model for this problem.
   b. Create a spreadsheet model for this problem and solve it using Solver.
   c. What is the optimal solution?

26. Radmore Memorial Hospital has a problem in its fluids analysis lab. The lab has available three machines that analyze various fluid samples. Recently, the demand for analyzing blood samples has increased so much that the lab director is having difficulty getting all the samples analyzed quickly enough and still completing the other fluid work that comes into the lab. The lab works with five types of blood specimens. Any machine can be used to process any of the specimens. However, the amount of time required by each machine varies depending on the type of specimen being analyzed. These times are summarized in the following table.

Required Specimen Processing Time in Minutes

	Specimen Type				
Machine	1	2	3	4	5
A	3	4	4	5	3
B	5	3	5	4	5
C	2	5	3	3	4

Each machine can be used a total of 8 hours a day. Blood samples collected on a given day arrive at the lab and are stored overnight and processed the next day. So, at the beginning of each day, the lab director must determine how to allocate the various samples to the machines for analysis. This morning, the lab has 80 type-1 specimens, 75 type-2 specimens, 80 type-3 specimens, 120 type-4 specimens, and 60 type-5 specimens awaiting processing. The lab director wants to know how many of each type of specimen should be analyzed on each machine to minimize the total time that the machines are devoted to analyzing blood samples.
   a. Formulate an LP model for this problem.
   b. Create a spreadsheet model for this problem and solve it using Solver.
   c. What is the optimal solution?
   d. How much processing time will be available on each machine if this solution is implemented?
   e. How would the model and solution change if the lab director wanted to balance the use of each machine so that each machine were used approximately the same amount of time?

27. Virginia Tech operates its own power generating plant. The electricity generated by this plant supplies power to the university and to local businesses and residences in the Blacksburg area. The plant burns three types of coal, which produce steam that drives the turbines that generate the electricity. The Environmental Protection Agency (EPA) requires that for each ton of coal burned, the emissions from the coal furnace smoke stacks contain no more than 2,500 parts per million (ppm) of sulfur and no more than 2.8 kilograms (kg) of coal dust. The following table summarizes the amounts of sulfur, coal dust, and steam that result from burning a ton of each type of coal.

Coal	Sulfur (in ppm)	Coal Dust (in kg)	Pounds of Steam Produced
1	1,100	1.7	24,000
2	3,500	3.2	36,000
3	1,300	2.4	28,000

The three types of coal can be mixed and burned in any combination. The resulting emission of sulfur or coal dust and the pounds of steam produced by any mixture are given as the weighted average of the values shown in the table for each type of coal. For example, if the coals are mixed to produce a blend that consists of 35% of coal 1, 40% of coal 2, and 25% of coal 3, the sulfur emission (in ppm) resulting from burning one ton of this blend is:

$$0.35 \times 1,100 + 0.40 \times 3,500 + 0.25 \times 1,300 = 2,110$$

The manager of this facility wants to determine the blend of coal that will produce the maximum pounds of steam per ton without violating the EPA requirements.

a. Formulate an LP model for this problem.
b. Create a spreadsheet model for this problem and solve it using Solver.
c. What is the optimal solution?
d. If the furnace can burn up to 30 tons of coal per hour, what is the maximum amount of steam that can be produced per hour?

28. Kentwood Electronics manufactures three components for stereo systems: CD players, tape decks, and stereo tuners. The wholesale price and manufacturing cost of each item are shown in the following table.

Component	Wholesale Price	Manufacturing Cost
CD Player	$150	$75
Tape Deck	$85	$35
Stereo Tuner	$70	$30

Each CD player produced requires 3 hours of assembly; each tape deck requires 2 hours of assembly; and each tuner requires 1 hour of assembly. The marketing department has indicated that it can sell no more than 150,000 CD players, 100,000 tape decks, and 90,000 stereo tuners. However, the demand is expected to be at least 50,000 units of each item, and Kentwood wants to meet this demand. If Kentwood has 400,000 hours of assembly time available, how many CD players, tape decks, and stereo tuners should it produce to maximize profits while meeting the minimum demand figures?

a. Formulate an LP model for this problem.
b. Create a spreadsheet model for this problem and solve it using Solver.
c. What is the optimal solution?

29. The Rent-A-Dent car rental company allows its customers to pick up a rental car at one location and return it to any of its locations. Currently, two locations (1 and 2) have 16 and 18 surplus cars, respectively, and four locations (3, 4, 5, and 6) each need 10 cars. The costs of getting the surplus cars from locations 1 and 2 to the other locations are summarized in the following table.

Costs of Transporting Cars Between Locations

	Location 3	Location 4	Location 5	Location 6
Location 1	$54	$17	$23	$30
Location 2	$24	$18	$19	$31

Because 34 surplus cars are available at locations 1 and 2, and 40 cars are needed at locations 3, 4, 5, and 6, some locations will not receive as many cars as they need. However, management wants to make sure that all the surplus cars are sent where they are needed, and that each location needing cars receives at least five.
   a. Formulate an LP model for this problem.
   b. Create a spreadsheet model for this problem and solve it using Solver.
   c. What is the optimal solution?

30. The Sentry Lock Corporation manufactures a popular commercial security lock at plants in Macon, Louisville, Detroit, and Phoenix. The per unit cost of production at each plant is $35.50, $37.50, $39.00, and $36.25, respectively, and the annual production capacity at each plant is 18,000, 15,000, 25,000, and 20,000, respectively. Sentry's locks are sold to retailers through wholesale distributors in seven cities across the United States. The unit cost of shipping from each plant to each distributor is summarized in the following table along with the forecasted demand from each distributor for the coming year.

Unit Shipping Cost to Distributor in

Plants	Tacoma	San Diego	Dallas	Denver	St. Louis	Tampa	Baltimore
Macon	$2.50	$2.75	$1.75	$2.00	$2.10	$1.80	$1.65
Louisville	$1.85	$1.90	$1.50	$1.60	$1.00	$1.90	$1.85
Detroit	$2.30	$2.25	$1.85	$1.25	$1.50	$2.25	$2.00
Phoenix	$1.90	$0.90	$1.60	$1.75	$2.00	$2.50	$2.65
Demand	8,500	14,500	13,500	12,600	18,000	15,000	9,000

Sentry wants to determine the least expensive way of manufacturing and shipping locks from their plants to the distributors. Because the total demand from distributors exceeds the total production capacity for all the plants, Sentry realizes it will not be able to satisfy all the demand for its product, but wants to make sure each distributor will have the opportunity to fill at least 80% of the orders they receive.
   a. Create a spreadsheet model for this problem and solve it.
   b. What is the optimal solution?

31. A paper recycling company converts newspaper, mixed paper, white office paper, and cardboard into pulp for newsprint, packaging paper, and print stock quality paper. The following table summarizes the yield for each kind of pulp recovered from each ton of recycled material.

Recycling Yield

	Newsprint	Packaging	Print Stock
Newspaper	85%	80%	—
Mixed Paper	90%	80%	70%
White Office Paper	90%	85%	80%
Cardboard	80%	70%	—

For instance, a ton of newspaper can be recycled using a technique that yields 0.85 tons of newsprint pulp. Alternatively, a ton of newspaper can be recycled using a technique that yields 0.80 tons of packaging paper. Similarly, a ton of cardboard can be recycled to yield 0.80 tons of newsprint or 0.70 tons of packaging paper pulp. Note that newspaper and cardboard cannot be converted to print stock pulp using the techniques available to the recycler.

The cost of processing each ton of raw material into the various types of pulp is summarized in the following table, along with the amount of each of the four raw materials that can be purchased and their costs.

	Processing Costs per Ton			Purchase Cost Per Ton	Tons Available
	Newsprint	Packaging	Print Stock		
Newspaper	$6.50	$11.00	—	$15	600
Mixed Paper	$9.75	$12.25	$9.50	$16	500
White Office Paper	$4.75	$7.75	$8.50	$19	300
Cardboard	$7.50	$8.50	—	$17	400

The recycler wants to determine the least costly way of producing 500 tons of newsprint pulp, 600 tons of packaging paper pulp, and 300 tons of print stock quality pulp.
a. Create a spreadsheet model for this problem and solve it.
b. What is the optimal solution?

32. A winery has the following capacity to produce an exclusive dinner wine at either of its two vineyards at the indicated costs:

Vineyard	Capacity	Cost per Bottle
1	3,500 bottles	$23
2	3,100 bottles	$25

Four Italian restaurants around the country are interested in purchasing this wine. Because the wine is exclusive, they all want to buy as much as they need but will take whatever they can get. The maximum amounts required by the restaurants and the prices they are willing to pay are summarized in the following table.

Restaurant	Maximum Demand	Price
1	1,800 bottles	$69
2	2,300 bottles	$67
3	1,250 bottles	$70
4	1,750 bottles	$66

The costs of shipping a bottle from the vineyards to the restaurants are summarized in the following table.

	Restaurant			
Vineyard	1	2	3	4
1	$7	$8	$13	$9
2	$12	$6	$8	$7

The winery needs to determine the production and shipping plan that allows it to maximize its profits on this wine.
a. Formulate an LP model for this problem.
b. Create a spreadsheet model for this problem and solve it using Solver.
c. What is the optimal solution?

33. The Pitts Barbecue Company makes three kinds of barbecue sauce: Extra Hot, Hot, and Mild. Pitts' vice president of marketing estimates that the company can sell 8,000 cases of its Extra Hot sauce plus 10 extra cases for every dollar it spends promoting this sauce; 10,000 cases of Hot sauce plus 8 extra cases for every dollar spent promoting this sauce; and 12,000 cases of its Mild sauce plus 5 extra cases for every dollar spent promoting this sauce. Although each barbecue sauce sells for $10 per case, the cost of producing the different types of sauce varies. It costs the company $6 to produce a case of Extra Hot sauce, $5.50 to produce a case of Hot sauce, and $5.25 to produce a case of Mild sauce. The president of the company wants to make sure the company manufactures at least the minimum amounts of each sauce that the marketing vice president thinks the company can sell. A budget of $25,000 total has been approved for promoting these items, of which at least $5,000 must be spent advertising each item. How many cases of each type of sauce should be made and how do you suggest that the company allocate the promotional budget if it wants to maximize profits?
    a. Formulate an LP model for this problem.
    b. Create a spreadsheet model for this problem and solve it using Solver.
    c. What is the optimal solution?
34. Acme Manufacturing makes a variety of household appliances at a single manufacturing facility. The expected demand for one of these appliances during the next four months is shown in the following table along with the expected production costs and the expected capacity for producing these items.

	Month			
	1	2	3	4
Demand	420	580	310	540
Production Cost	$49.00	$45.00	$46.00	$47.00
Production Capacity	500	520	450	550

Acme estimates that it costs $1.50 per month for each unit of this appliance carried in inventory (estimated by averaging the beginning and ending inventory levels each month). Currently, Acme has 120 units in inventory on hand for this product. To maintain a level workforce, the company wants to produce at least 400 units per month. It also wants to maintain a safety stock of at least 50 units per month. Acme wants to determine how many of each appliance to manufacture during each of the next four months to meet the expected demand at the lowest possible total cost.
    a. Formulate an LP model for this problem.
    b. Create a spreadsheet model for this problem and solve it using Solver.
    c. What is the optimal solution?
    d. How much money could Acme save if it were willing to drop the restriction about producing at least 400 units per month?
35. Paul Bergey is in charge of loading cargo ships for International Cargo Company (ICC) at the port in Newport News, Virginia. Paul is preparing a loading plan for an ICC freighter destined for Ghana. An agricultural commodities dealer wants to transport the following products aboard this ship.

Commodity	Amount Available (tons)	Volume per Ton (cubic feet)	Profit per Ton ($)
1	4,800	40	70
2	2,500	25	50
3	1,200	60	60
4	1,700	55	80

Paul can elect to load any and/or all of the available commodities. However, the ship has three cargo holds with the following capacity restrictions:

Cargo Hold	Weight Capacity (tons)	Volume Capacity (cubic feet)
Forward	3,000	145,000
Center	6,000	180,000
Rear	4,000	155,000

More than one type of commodity can be placed in the same cargo hold. However, because of balance considerations, the weight in the forward cargo hold must be within 10% of the weight in the rear cargo hold and the center cargo hold must be between 40% to 60% of the total weight on board.

  a. Formulate an LP model for this problem.
  b. Create a spreadsheet model for this problem and solve it using Solver.
  c. What is the optimal solution?

36. The Pelletier Corporation has just discovered that it will not have enough warehouse space for the next five months. The additional warehouse space requirements for this period are:

Month	1	2	3	4	5
Additional Space Needed (in 1000 sq ft)	25	10	20	10	5

To cover its space requirements, the firm plans to lease additional warehouse space on a short-term basis. Over the next five months, a local warehouse has agreed to lease Pelletier any amount of space for any number of months according to the following cost schedule.

Length of Lease (in months)	1	2	3	4	5
Cost per 1000 square feet	$300	$525	$775	$850	$975

This schedule of leasing options is available to Pelletier at the beginning of each of the next five months. For example, the company could elect to lease 5,000 square feet for 4 months beginning in month 1 (at a cost of $850 × 5) and lease 10,000 square feet for 2 months beginning in month 3 (at a cost of $525 × 10).

  a. Formulate an LP model for this problem.
  b. Create a spreadsheet model for this problem and solve it using Solver.
  c. What is the optimal solution?

37. Carter Enterprises is involved in the soybean business in South Carolina, Alabama, and Georgia. The president of the company, Earl Carter, goes to a commodity sale once a month where he buys and sells soybeans in bulk. Carter uses a local warehouse for storing his soybean inventory. This warehouse charges $10 per average ton of soybeans stored per month (based on the average of the beginning and ending inventory each month). The warehouse guarantees Carter the capacity to store up to 400 tons of soybeans at the end of each month. Carter has estimated what he believes the price per ton of soybeans will be during each of the next six months. These prices are summarized in the following table.

Month	1	2	3	4	5	6
Price per Ton	$135	$110	$150	$175	$130	$145

Assume that Carter currently has 70 tons of soybeans stored in the warehouse. How many tons of soybeans should Carter buy and sell during each of the next six months to maximize his profit trading soybeans?

a. Formulate an LP model for this problem.
b. Create a spreadsheet model for this problem and solve it using Solver.
c. What is the optimal solution?

38. Jack Potts recently won $1,000,000 in Las Vegas and is trying to determine how to invest his winnings. He has narrowed his decision down to five investments, which are summarized in the following table.

Summary of Cash Inflows and Outflows (at beginning of years)

	1	2	3	4
A	−1	0.50	0.80	
B		−1	⟷	1.25
C	−1	⟷	⟷	1.35
D			−1	1.13
E	−1	⟷	1.27	

If Jack invests $1 in investment A at the beginning of year 1, he will receive $0.50 at the beginning of year 2 and another $0.80 at the beginning of year 3. Alternatively, he can invest $1 in investment B at the beginning of year 2 and receive $1.25 at the beginning of year 4. Entries of "⟷" in the table indicate times when no cash inflows or outflows can occur. At the beginning of any year, Jack can place money in a money market account that is expected to yield 8% per year. He wants to keep at least $50,000 in the money market account at all times and doesn't want to place any more than $500,000 in any single investment. How would you advise Jack to invest his winnings if he wants to maximize the amount of money he'll have at the beginning of year 4?

a. Formulate an LP model for this problem.
b. Create a spreadsheet model for this problem and solve it using Solver.
c. What is the optimal solution?

39. Fred and Sally Merrit recently inherited a substantial amount of money from a deceased relative. They want to use part of this money to establish an account to pay for their daughter's college education. Their daughter, Lisa, will be starting college 5 years from now. The Merrits estimate that her first year college expenses will amount to $12,000 and increase $2,000 per year during each of the remaining three years of her education. The following investments are available to the Merrits:

Investment	Available	Matures	Return at Maturity
A	Every year	1 year	6%
B	1, 3, 5, 7	2 years	14%
C	1, 4	3 years	18%
D	1	7 years	65%

The Merrits want to determine an investment plan that will provide the necessary funds to cover Lisa's anticipated college expenses with the smallest initial investment.

a. Formulate an LP model for this problem.
b. Create a spreadsheet model for this problem and solve it using Solver.
c. What is the optimal solution?

40. Refer to the previous question. Suppose the investments available to the Merrits have the following levels of risk associated with them.

Investment	A	B	C	D
Risk Factor	1	3	6	8

If the Merrits want the weighted average risk level of their investments to not exceed 4, how much money will they need to set aside for Lisa's education and how should they invest it?

a. Formulate an LP model for this problem.
b. Create a spreadsheet model for this problem and solve it using Solver.
c. What is the optimal solution?

41. WinterWearhouse operates a clothing store specializing in ski apparel. Given the seasonal nature of its business, often there is somewhat of an imbalance between when bills must be paid for inventory purchased and when the goods actually are sold and cash is received. Over the next six months, the company expects cash receipts and requirements for bill paying as follows:

	Month					
	1	2	3	4	5	6
Cash Receipts	$100,000	$225,000	$275,000	$350,000	$475,000	$625,000
Bills Due	$400,000	$500,000	$600,000	$300,000	$200,000	$100,000

The company likes to maintain a cash balance of at least $20,000 and currently has $100,000 cash on hand. The company can borrow money from a local bank for the following term/rate structure: 1 month at 1%, 2 months at 1.75%, 3 months at 2.49%, 4 months at 3.22%, and 5 months at 3.94%. When needed, money is borrowed at the end of a month and repaid, with interest, at the end of the month in which the obligation is due. For instance, if the company borrows $10,000 for 2 months in month 3, it would have to pay back $10,175 at the end of month 5.

a. Create a spreadsheet model for this problem and solve it.
b. What is the optimal solution?
c. Suppose its bank limits WinterWearhouse to borrowing no more than $100,000 at each level in the term/rate structure. How would this restriction change the optimal solution?

42. The accounting firm of Coopers & Andersen is conducting a benchmarking survey to assess the satisfaction level of its clients versus clients served by competing accounting firms. The clients are divided into four groups:

Group 1: Large clients of Coopers & Andersen
Group 2: Small clients of Coopers & Andersen
Group 3: Large clients of other accounting firms
Group 4: Small clients of other accounting firms

A total of 4,000 companies are being surveyed either by telephone or via a two-way web-cam interview. The costs associated with surveying the different types of companies are summarized below:

	Survey Costs	
Group	Telephone	Webcam
1	$18	$40
2	$14	$35
3	$25	$60
4	$20	$45

Coopers & Andersen wants the survey to carry out the survey in the least costly way that meets the following conditions:

- At least 10% but not more than 50% of the total companies surveyed should come from each group.
- At least 50% of the companies surveyed should be clients of Coopers & Andersen.
- At least 25% of the surveys should be done via web cam.
- At least 50% of the large clients of Coopers & Anderson who are surveyed should be done via web cam.
- A maximum of 40% of those surveyed may be small companies.
- A maximum of 25% of the small companies surveyed should be done via web cam.

a. Formulate an LP model for this problem.
b. Create a spreadsheet model for this problem and solve it using Solver.
c. What is the optimal solution?

43. The chief financial officer for Eagle's Beach Wear and Gift Shop is planning for the company's cash flows for the next six months. The following table summarizes the expected accounts receivables and planned payments for each of these months (in $100,000s).

	January	February	March	April	May	June
Accounts Receivable Balances Due	1.50	1.00	1.40	2.30	2.00	1.00
Planned Payments (net of discounts)	1.80	1.60	2.20	1.20	0.80	1.20

The company currently has a beginning cash balance of $400,000 and desires to maintain a balance of at least $25,000 in cash at the end of each month. To accomplish this, the company has several ways of obtaining short-term funds:

1. *Delay Payments.* In any month, the company's suppliers permit it to delay any or all payments for one month. However, for this consideration, the company forfeits a 2% discount that normally applies when payments are made on time. (Loss of this 2% discount is, in effect, a financing cost.)
2. *Borrow Against Accounts Receivables.* In any month, the company's bank will loan it up to 75% of the accounts receivable balances due that month. These loans must be repaid in the following month and incur an interest charge of 1.5%.
3. *Short-Term Loan.* At the beginning of January, the company's bank will also give it a 6-month loan to be repaid in a lump sum at the end of June. Interest on this loan is 1% per month and is payable at the end of each month.

Assume the company earns 0.5% interest each month on cash held at the beginning of the month. Create a spreadsheet model that the company can use to determine the least costly cash management plan (*i.e.*, minimal net financing costs) for this 6-month period. What is the optimal solution?

44. The DotCom Corporation is implementing a pension plan for its employees. The company intends to start funding the plan with a deposit of $50,000 on January 1, 2008. It plans to invest an additional $12,000 one year later, and continue making additional investments (increasing by $2,000 per year) on January 1 of each year from 2010 through 2022. To fund these payments, the company plans to purchase a

number of bonds. Bond 1 costs $970 per unit and will pay a $65 coupon on January 1 of each year from 2009 through 2012 plus a final payment of $1065 on January 1, 2013. Bond 2 costs $980 and will pay a $73 coupon on January 1 of each year from 2009 through 2018 plus a final payment of $1073 on January 1, 2019. Bond 3 costs $1025 and will pay a $85 coupon on January 1 of each year from 2009 through 2021 plus a final payment of $1085 on January 1, 2022. The company's cash holdings earn an interest rate of 4.5%. Assume that the company wants to purchase bonds on January 1, 2008 and cannot buy them in fractional units. How much should the company invest in the various bonds and cash account to fund this plan through January 1, 2022 in the least costly way?

a. Create a spreadsheet model for this problem and solve it.
b. What is the optimal solution?

45. A natural gas trading company wants to develop an optimal trading plan for the next 10 days. The following table summarizes the estimated prices (per thousand cubic feet (cf)) at which the company can buy and sell natural gas during this time. The company may buy gas at the "Ask" price and sell gas at the "Bid" price.

Day	1	2	3	4	5	6	7	8	9	10
Bid	$3.06	$4.01	$6.03	$4.06	$4.01	$5.02	$5.10	$4.08	$3.01	$4.01
Ask	$3.22	$4.10	$6.13	$4.19	$4.05	$5.12	$5.28	$4.23	$3.15	$4.18

The company currently has 150,000 cf of gas in storage and has a maximum storage capacity of 500,000 cf. To maintain the required pressure in the gas transmission pipeline system, the company can inject no more than 200,000 cf into the storage facility each day and can extract no more than 180,000 cf per day. Assume that extractions occur in the morning and injections occur in the evening. The owner of the storage facility charges a storage fee of 5% of the market (bid) value of the average daily gas inventory. (The average daily inventory is computed as the average of each day's beginning and ending inventory.)

a. Create a spreadsheet model for this problem and solve it.
b. What is the optimal solution?
c. Assuming price forecasts for natural gas change on a daily basis, how would you suggest that the company in this problem actually use your model?

46. The Embassy Lodge hotel chain wants to compare its brand efficiency to that of its major competitors using DEA. Embassy collected the following data reported in industry trade publications. Embassy views customers' perceptions of satisfaction and value (scored from 0 to 100 where 100 is best) to be outputs produced as a function of the following inputs: price, convenience, room comfort, climate control, service, and food quality. (All inputs are expressed on scales where less is better.)

Brand	Satisfaction	Value	Price	Convenience	Room Comfort	Climate Control	Service	Food Quality
Embassy Lodge	85	82	70.00	2.3	1.8	2.7	1.5	3.3
Sheritown Inn	96	93	70.00	1.5	1.1	0.2	0.5	0.5
Hynton Hotel	78	87	75.00	2.2	2.4	2.6	2.5	3.2
Vacation Inn	87	88	75.00	1.8	1.6	1.5	1.8	2.3
Merrylot	89	94	80.00	0.5	1.4	0.4	0.9	2.6
FairPrice Inn	93	93	80.00	1.3	0.9	0.2	0.6	2.8
Nights Inn	92	91	85.00	1.4	1.3	0.6	1.4	2.1
Western Hotels	97	92	90.00	0.3	1.7	1.7	1.7	1.8

a. Compute the DEA efficiency for each brand.
b. Which brands are efficient?
c. Is Embassy Lodge efficient? If not, what input and output values should it aspire to, to become efficient?

47. Fidelity Savings & Loans (FS&L) operates several banking facilities throughout the Southeastern United States. The officers of FS&L want to analyze the efficiency of the various branch offices using DEA. The following data has been selected to represent appropriate input and output measures of each banking facility.

Branch	R.O.A.	New Loans	Satisfaction	Labor Hrs	Op. Costs
1	5.32	770	92	3.73	6.34
2	3.39	780	94	3.49	4.43
3	4.95	790	93	5.98	6.31
4	6.01	730	82	6.49	7.28
5	6.40	910	98	7.09	8.69
6	2.89	860	90	3.46	3.23
7	6.94	880	89	7.36	9.07
8	7.18	970	99	6.38	7.42
9	5.98	770	94	4.74	6.75
10	4.97	930	91	5.04	6.35

a. Identify the inputs and outputs for FS&L. Are they all measured on the appropriate scale for use with DEA?
b. Compute the DEA efficiency of each branch office.
c. Which offices are DEA efficient?
d. What input and output levels should branch 5 aspire to, to become efficient?

CASE 3.1 Putting the Link in the Supply Chain

Rick Eldridge is the new Vice President for operations at the The Golfer's Link (TGL), a company specializing in the production of quality, discount sets of golf clubs. Rick was hired primarily because of his expertise in supply chain management (SCM). SCM is the integrated planning and control of all resources in the logistics process from the acquisition of raw materials to the delivery of finished products to the end user. Because SCM seeks to optimize all activities in the supply chain including transactions between firms, Rick's first priority is ensuring that all aspects of production and distribution within TGF are operating optimally.

TGL produces three different lines of golf clubs for men, women, and junior golfers at manufacturing plants in Daytona Beach, FL, Memphis, TN, and Tempe, AZ. The plant in Tempe produces all three lines of clubs. The one in Daytona produces only the men's and women's lines, and the plant in Memphis produces only the women's and juniors' lines. Each line of clubs requires varying amounts of three raw materials that are sometimes in short supply: titanium, aluminum, and a distinctive rock maple wood that TGL uses in all of its drivers. The manufacturing process for each line of clubs at each plant is identical. Thus, the amount of each of these materials required in each set of the different lines of clubs is summarized below:

	Resources Required per Club Set (in lbs)		
	Men's	Women's	Juniors'
Titanium	2.9	2.7	2.5
Aluminum	4.5	4	5
Rock Maple	5.4	5	4.8

The estimated amount of each of these key resources available at each plant during the coming month is given as:

	Estimated Resource Availability (in lbs)		
	Daytona	Memphis	Tempe
Titanium	4500	8500	14500
Aluminum	6000	12000	19000
Rock Maple	9500	16000	18000

TGL's reputation for quality and affordability ensures that it can sell all the clubs it can make. The men's, women's, and juniors' lines generate wholesale revenues of $225, $195, and $165, respectively, regardless of where they are produced. Club sets are shipped from the production plants to distribution centers in Sacramento, CA, Denver, CO, and Pittsburgh, PA. Each month, the different distribution centers order the number of club sets in each of the three lines that they would like to receive. TGL's contract with this distributor requires filling at least 90% (but no more than 100%) of all distributor orders. Rick recently received the following distributor orders for the coming month:

	Number of Club Sets Ordered		
	Men's	Women's	Juniors'
Sacramento	700	900	900
Denver	550	1000	1500
Pittsburgh	900	1200	1100

The cost of shipping a set of clubs to each distribution point from each production facility is summarized in the following table. Note again that Daytona does not produce juniors' club sets and Memphis does not produce men's club sets.

	Shipping Costs							
	Men's		Women's			Juniors'		
To/From	Daytona	Tempe	Daytona	Memphis	Tempe	Memphis	Tempe
Sacramento	$51	$10	$49	$33	$9	$31	$8
Denver	$28	$43	$27	$22	$42	$21	$40
Pittsburgh	$36	$56	$34	$13	$54	$12	$52

Rick has asked you to determine an optimal production and shipping plan for the coming month.

a. Create a spreadsheet model for this problem and solve it. What is the optimal solution?
b. If Rick wanted to improve this solution, what additional resources would be needed and where would they be needed? Explain.
c. What would TGL's optimal profit be if they were not required to supply at least 90% of each distributor's order?
d. Suppose TGL's agreement included the option of paying a $10,000 penalty if they cannot supply at least 90% of each the distributor's order but instead supply at least 80% of each distributor's order. Comment on the pros and cons of TGL exercising this option.

Foreign Exchange Trading at Baldwin Enterprises

Baldwin Enterprises is a large manufacturing company with operations and sales divisions located in the United States and several other countries. The CFO of the organization, Wes Hamrick, is concerned about the amount of money Baldwin has been paying in transaction costs in the foreign exchange markets and has asked you to help optimize Baldwin's foreign exchange treasury functions.

With operations in several countries, Baldwin maintains cash assets in several different currencies: U.S. dollars (USD), the European Union's euro (EUR), Great Britain's pound (GBP), Hong Kong dollars (HKD), and Japanese yen (JPY). To meet the different cash flow requirements associated with its operations around the world, Baldwin often must move funds from one location (and currency) to another. For instance, to pay an unexpected maintenance expense at its facility in Japan, Baldwin might need to convert some of its holdings in U.S. dollars to Japanese yen.

The foreign exchange (FX) market is a network of financial institutions and brokers in which individuals, businesses, banks, and governments buy and sell the currencies of different countries. They do so to finance international trade, invest or do business abroad, or speculate on currency price changes. The FX market operates 24 hours a day and represents the largest and most liquid marketplace in the global economy. On average, the equivalent of about $1.5 trillion in different currencies is traded daily in the FX market around the world. The liquidity of the market provides businesses with access to international markets for goods and services by providing foreign currency necessary for transactions worldwide (see:http://www.ny.frb.org/fxc).

The FX market operates in much the same way as a stock or commodity market; there is a bid price and ask price for each commodity (or, in this case, currency). A bid price is the price at which the market is willing to buy a particular currency and the ask price is the price at which the market is willing to sell a currency. The ask prices are typically slightly higher than the bid prices for the same currency—representing the transaction cost or the profit earned by the organizations that keep the market liquid.

The following table summarizes the current FX rates for the currencies Baldwin currently holds. The entries in this table represent the conversion rates from the row currencies to the column currencies.

Convert/To	USD	EUR	GBP	HKD	JPY
USD	1	1.01864	0.6409	7.7985	118.55
EUR	0.9724	1	0.6295	7.6552	116.41
GBP	1.5593	1.5881	1	12.154	184.97
HKD	0.12812	0.1304	0.0821	1	15.1005
JPY	0.00843	0.00856	0.0054	0.0658	1

For example, the table indicates that one British pound (GBP) can be exchanged (or sold) for 1.5593 U.S. dollars (USD). Thus, $1.5593 is the bid price, in U.S. dollars, for one British pound. Alternatively, the table indicates one U.S. dollar (USD) can be exchanged (sold) for 0.6409 British pounds (GBP). So, it takes about 1.5603 U.S. dollars (or 1/0.6409) to buy one British pound (or the ask price, in U.S. dollars, for one British pound is roughly $1.5603).

Notice that if you took one British pound, converted it to 1.5593 U.S. dollars, and then converted those 1.5593 dollars back to British pounds, you would end up with only

0.999355 British pounds (i.e., $1 \times 1.5593 \times 0.6409 = 0.999355$). The money that you lose in this exchange is the transaction cost.

Baldwin's current portfolio of cash holdings includes 2 million USD, 5 million EUR, 1 million GBP, 3 million HKD, and 30 million JPY. This portfolio is equivalent to $9,058,710 USD under the current exchange rates (given above). Wes has asked you to design a currency trading plan that would increase Baldwin's euro and yen holdings to 8 million EUR and 54 JPY, respectively, while maintaining the equivalent of at least $250,000 USD in each currency. Baldwin measures transaction costs as the change in the USD equivalent value of the portfolio.

a. Create a spreadsheet model for this problem and solve it.
b. What is the optimal trading plan?
c. What is the optimal transaction cost (in equivalent USD)?
d. Suppose that another executive thinks that holding $250,000 USD in each currency is excessive and wants to lower the amount to $50,000 USD in each currency. Does this help to lower the transaction cost? Why or why not?
e. Suppose the exchange rate for converting USD to GBP increased from 0.6409 to 0.6414. What would happen to the optimal solution in this case?

The Wolverine Retirement Fund   CASE 3.3

Kelly Jones is a financial analyst for Wolverine Manufacturing, a company that produces engine bearings for the automotive industry. Wolverine is hammering out a new labor agreement with its unionized workforce. One of the major concerns of the labor union is the funding of Wolverine's retirement plan for their hourly employees. The union believes that the company has not been contributing enough money to this fund to cover the benefits it will need to pay to retiring employees. Because of this, the union wants the company to contribute approximately $1.5 million dollars in additional money to this fund over the next 20 years. These extra contributions would begin with an extra payment of $20,000 at the end of one year with annual payments increasing by 12.35% per year for the next 19 years.

The union has asked the company to set up a sinking fund to cover the extra annual payments to the retirement fund. Wolverine's Chief Financial Officer and the union's chief negotiator have agreed that AAA-rated bonds recently issued by three different companies may be used to establish this fund. The following table summarizes the provisions of these bonds.

Company	Maturity	Coupon Payment	Price	Par Value
AC&C	15 years	$80	$847.88	$1,000
IBN	10 years	$90	$938.55	$1,000
MicroHard	20 years	$85	$872.30	$1,000

According to this table, Wolverine may buy bonds issued by AC&C for $847.88 per bond. Each AC&C bond will pay the bondholder $80 per year for the next 15 years, plus an extra payment of $1,000 (the par value) in the fifteenth year. Similar interpretations apply to the information for the IBN and MicroHard bonds. A money market fund yielding 5% may be used to hold any coupon payments that are not needed to meet the company's required retirement fund payment in any given year.

Wolverine's CFO has asked Kelly to determine how much money the company would have to invest and which bonds the company should buy to meet the labor union's demands.

a. If you were Kelly, what would you tell the CFO?
b. Suppose that the union insists on including one of the following stipulations into the agreement:
   1. No more than half of the total number of bonds purchased may be purchased from a single company.
   2. At least 10% of the total number of bonds must be purchased from each of the companies.

Which stipulation should Wolverine agree to?

CASE 3.4   Saving the Manatees

"So how am I going to spend this money," thought Tom Wieboldt as he sat staring at the pictures and posters of manatees around his office. An avid environmentalist, Tom is the president of "Friends of the Manatees"—a nonprofit organization trying to help pass legislation to protect manatees.

Manatees are large, gray-brown aquatic mammals with bodies that taper to a flat, paddle-shaped tail. These gentle and slow-moving creatures grow to an average adult length of 10 feet and weigh an average of 1,000 pounds. Manatees are found in shallow, slow-moving rivers, estuaries, saltwater bays, canals, and coastal areas. In the United States, manatees are concentrated in Florida in the winter, but can be found in summer months as far west as Alabama and as far north as Virginia and the Carolinas. They have no natural enemies, but loss of habitat is the most serious threat facing manatees today. Most human-related manatee deaths occur from collisions with motor boats.

Tom's organization has been supporting a bill before the Florida legislature to restrict the use of motor boats in areas known to be inhabited by manatees. This bill is scheduled to come up for a vote in the legislature. Tom recently received a phone call from a national environmental protection organization indicating that it will donate $300,000 to Friends of the Manatees to help increase public awareness about the plight of the manatees, and to encourage voters to urge their representatives in the state legislature to vote for this bill. Tom intends to use this money to purchase various types of advertising media to "get the message out" during the four weeks immediately preceding the vote.

Tom is considering several different advertising alternatives: newspapers, TV, radio, billboards, and magazines. A marketing consultant provided Tom with the following data on the costs and effectiveness of the various types of media being considered.

Advertising Medium	Unit Cost	Unit Impact Rating
Half-page, Daily paper	$800	55
Full-page, Daily paper	$1,400	75
Half-page, Sunday paper	$1,200	65
Full-page, Sunday paper	$1,800	80
Daytime TV spot	$2,500	85
Evening TV spot	$3,500	100
Highway Billboards	$750	35
15-second Radio spot	$150	45
30-second Radio spot	$300	55
Half-page, magazine	$500	50
Full-page, magazine	$900	60

According to the marketing consultant, the most effective type of advertising for this type of problem would be short TV ads during the evening prime-time hours.

Thus, this type of advertising was given a "unit impact rating" of 100. The other types of advertising were then given unit impact ratings that reflect their expected effectiveness relative to an evening TV ad. For instance, a half-page magazine ad is expected to provide half the effectiveness of an evening TV ad and is therefore given an impact rating of 50.

Tom wants to allocate the $300,000 to these different advertising alternatives in a way that will maximize the impact achieved. However, he realizes that it is important to spread his message via several different advertising channels, as not everyone listens to the radio and not everyone watches TV in the evenings.

The two most widely read newspapers in the state of Florida are the *Orlando Sentinel* and the *Miami Herald*. During the four weeks before the vote, Tom wants to have half-page ads in the daily (Monday-Saturday) versions of each of these papers at least three times per week. He also wants to have one full-page ad in the daily version of each paper the week before the vote, and he is willing to run more full-page ads if this would be helpful. He also wants to run full-page ads in the Sunday editions of each paper the Sunday before the vote. Tom never wants to run a full-page and half-page ad in a paper on the same day. So the maximum number of full and half-page ads that can be run in the daily papers should be 48 (i.e., 4 weeks × 6 days per week × 2 papers = 48). Similarly, the maximum number of full and half-page ads that can be run in the Sunday papers is eight.

Tom wants to have at least one and no more than three daytime TV ads every day during the four-week period. He also wants to have at least one ad on TV every night but no more than two per night.

There are 10 billboard locations throughout the state that are available for use during the four weeks before the vote. Tom definitely wants to have at least one billboard in each of the cities of Orlando, Tampa, and Miami.

Tom believes that the ability to show pictures of the cute, pudgy, lovable manatees in the print media offers a distinct advantage over radio ads. However, the radio ads are relatively inexpensive and might reach some people that the other ads will not reach. Thus, Tom wants to have at least two 15-second and at least two 30-second ads on the radio each day. However, he wants to limit the number of radio ads to five 15-second ads and five 30-second ads per day.

There are three different weekly magazines in which Tom can run ads. Tom wants to run full-page ads in each of the magazines at some point during the four-week period. However, he never wants to run full- and half-page ads in the same magazine in a given week. Thus, the total number of full- and half-page magazine ads selected should not exceed 12 (i.e., 4 weeks × 3 magazines × 1 ad per magazine per week = 12 ads).

Although Tom has some ideas about the minimum and maximum number of ads to run in the various types of media, he's not sure how much money this will take. And if he can afford to meet all the minimums, he's really confused about the best way to spend the remaining funds. So again Tom asks himself, "How am I going to spend this money?"

a. Create a spreadsheet model for this problem and solve it. What is the optimal solution?

b. Of the constraints Tom placed on this problem, which are "binding" or preventing the objective function from being improved further?

c. Suppose Tom was willing to increase the allowable number of evening TV ads. How much would this improve the solution?

d. Suppose Tom was willing to double the allowable number of radio ads aired each day. How much would this improve the solution?

Chapter 4

Sensitivity Analysis and the Simplex Method

4.0 Introduction

In Chapters 2 and 3, we studied how to formulate and solve LP models for a variety of decision problems. However, formulating and solving an LP model does not necessarily mean that the original decision problem has been solved. Several questions often arise about the optimal solution to an LP model. In particular, we might be interested in how sensitive the optimal solution is to changes in various coefficients of the LP model.

Businesses rarely know with certainty what costs will be incurred, or the exact amount of resources that will be consumed or available in a given situation or time period. Thus, management might be skeptical of optimal solutions obtained using models that assume that all relevant factors are known with certainty. Sensitivity analysis can help overcome this skepticism and provide a better picture of how the solution to a problem will change if different factors in the model change. Sensitivity analysis also can help answer several practical managerial questions that might arise about the solution to an LP problem.

4.1 The Purpose of Sensitivity Analysis

As noted in Chapter 2, any problem that can be stated in the following form is an LP problem:

$$
\begin{array}{ll}
\text{MAX (or MIN):} & c_1X_1 + c_2X_2 + \cdots + c_nX_n \\
\text{Subject to:} & a_{11}X_1 + a_{12}X_2 + \cdots + a_{1n}X_n \leq b_1 \\
& \qquad\qquad\qquad \vdots \\
& a_{k1}X_1 + a_{k2}X_2 + \cdots + a_{kn}X_n \geq b_k \\
& \qquad\qquad\qquad \vdots \\
& a_{m1}X_1 + a_{m2}X_2 + \cdots + a_{mn}X_n = b_m
\end{array}
$$

All the coefficients in this model (the c_j, a_{ij}, and b_i) represent numeric constants. So, when we formulate and solve an LP problem, we implicitly assume that we can specify the exact values for these coefficients. However, in the real world, these coefficients might change from day to day or minute to minute. For example, the price a company charges for its products can change on a daily, weekly, or monthly basis. Similarly, if a skilled machinist calls in sick, a manufacturer might have less capacity to produce items on a given machine than was originally planned.

Realizing that such uncertainties exist, a manager should consider how sensitive an LP model's solution is to changes or estimation errors that might occur in: (1) the objective function coefficients (the c_j), (2) the constraint coefficients (the a_{ij}), and (3) the RHS values for the constraints (the b_i). A manager also might ask a number of "What if?" questions about these values. For example, what if the cost of a product increases by 7%? What if a reduction in setup time allows for additional capacity on a given machine? What if a worker's suggestion results in a product requiring only two hours of labor rather than three? Sensitivity analysis addresses these issues by assessing the sensitivity of the solution to uncertainty or estimation errors in the model coefficients, and also the solution's sensitivity to changes in model coefficients that might occur because of human intervention.

4.2 Approaches to Sensitivity Analysis

You can perform sensitivity analysis on an LP model in several ways. If you want to determine the effect of some change in the model, the most direct approach is simply to change the model and re-solve it. This approach is suitable if the model does not take an excessive amount of time to change or solve. In addition, if you are interested in studying the consequences of *simultaneously* changing several coefficients in the model, this might be the only practical approach to sensitivity analysis.

Solver also provides some sensitivity information after solving an LP problem. As mentioned in Chapter 3, one of the benefits of using the simplex method to solve LP problems is its speed—it is considerably faster than the other optimization techniques offered by Solver. However, another advantage of using the simplex method is that it provides more sensitivity analysis information than the other techniques. In particular, the simplex method provides us with information about:

- The range of values the objective function coefficients can assume without changing the optimal solution
- The impact on the optimal objective function value of increases or decreases in the availability of various constrained resources
- The impact on the optimal objective function value of forcing changes in the values of certain decision variables away from their optimal values
- The impact that changes in constraint coefficients will have on the optimal solution to the problem

4.3 An Example Problem

We will again use the Blue Ridge Hot Tubs problem to illustrate the types of sensitivity analysis information available using Solver. The LP formulation of the problem is repeated here, where X_1 represents the number of Aqua-Spas and X_2 represents the number of Hydro-Luxes to be produced:

$$
\begin{array}{llll}
\text{MAX:} & 350X_1 + 300X_2 & & \} \text{ profit} \\
\text{Subject to:} & 1X_1 + 1X_2 \leq 200 & & \} \text{ pump constraint} \\
& 9X_1 + 6X_2 \leq 1{,}566 & & \} \text{ labor constraint} \\
& 12X_1 + 16X_2 \leq 2{,}880 & & \} \text{ tubing constraint} \\
& X_1, X_2 \geq 0 & & \} \text{ nonnegativity conditions}
\end{array}
$$

FIGURE 4.1

*Spreadsheet model
for the Blue Ridge
Hot Tubs product
mix problem*

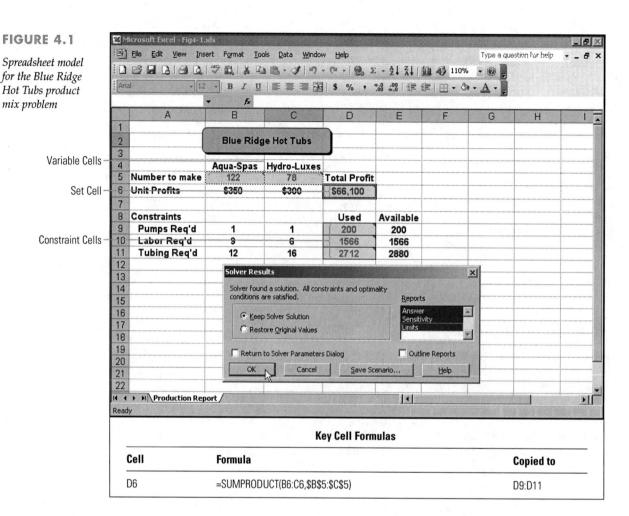

Key Cell Formulas		
Cell	**Formula**	**Copied to**
D6	=SUMPRODUCT(B6:C6,$B$5:$C$5)	D9:D11

This model is implemented in the spreadsheet shown in Figure 4.1 (and file Fig4-1.xls on your data disk). (See Chapter 3 for details on the procedure used to create and solve this spreadsheet model.)

After solving the LP model, Solver displays the Solver Results dialog box, shown in Figure 4.1. This dialog box provides three report options: Answer, Sensitivity, and Limits. You can select any of these reports after a model has been solved. To select all three reports, highlight the reports, and then click OK. To access each report, click the appropriate tab at the bottom of the screen.

4.4 The Answer Report

Figure 4.2 shows the Answer Report for the Blue Ridge Hot Tubs problem. This report summarizes the solution to the problem, and is fairly self-explanatory. The first section of the report summarizes the original and final (optimal) value of the set cell. The next section summarizes the original and final (optimal) values of the adjustable (or changing) cells representing the decision variables.

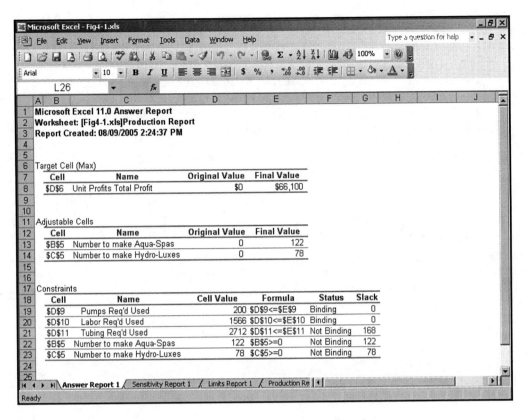

FIGURE 4.2

*Answer Report
for the hot tub
problem*

The final section of this report provides information about the constraints. In particular, the Cell Value column shows the final (optimal) value assumed by each constraint cell. Note that these values correspond to the final value assumed by the LHS formula of each constraint. The Formula column indicates the upper or lower bounds that apply to each constraint cell. The Status column indicates which constraints are binding and which are nonbinding. A constraint is binding if it is satisfied as a strict equality in the optimal solution; otherwise, it is nonbinding. Notice that the constraints for the number of pumps and amount of labor used are both binding, meaning that *all* the available pumps and labor hours will be used if this solution is implemented. Therefore, these constraints are preventing Blue Ridge Hot Tubs from achieving a higher level of profit.

Finally, the values in the Slack column indicate the difference between the LHS and RHS of each constraint. By definition, binding constraints have zero slack and nonbinding constraints have some positive level of slack. The values in the Slack column indicate that if this solution is implemented, all the available pumps and labor hours will be used, but 168 feet of tubing will be left over. The slack values for the nonnegativity conditions indicate the amounts by which the decision variables exceed their respective lower bounds of zero.

The Answer Report does not provide any information that could not be derived from the solution shown in the spreadsheet model. However, the format of this report gives a convenient summary of the solution that can be incorporated easily into a word-processing document as part of a written report to management.

Report Headings

When creating the reports described in this chapter, Solver will try to use various text entries from the original spreadsheet to generate meaningful headings and labels in the reports. Given the various ways in which a model can be implemented, Solver might not always produce meaningful headings. However, you can change any text entry to make the report more meaningful or descriptive.

4.5 The Sensitivity Report

Figure 4.3 shows the Sensitivity Report for the Blue Ridge Hot Tubs problem. This report summarizes information about the variable cells and constraints for our model. This information is useful in evaluating how sensitive the optimal solution is to changes in various coefficients in the model.

FIGURE 4.3

Sensitivity Report for the hot tub problem

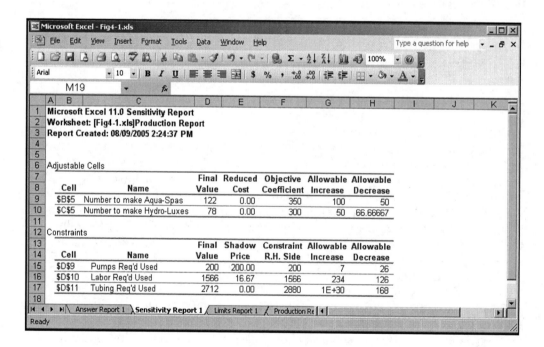

Microsoft Excel 11.0 Sensitivity Report
Worksheet: [Fig4-1.xls]Production Report
Report Created: 08/09/2005 2:24:37 PM

Adjustable Cells

Cell	Name	Final Value	Reduced Cost	Objective Coefficient	Allowable Increase	Allowable Decrease
$B$5	Number to make Aqua-Spas	122	0.00	350	100	50
$C$5	Number to make Hydro-Luxes	78	0.00	300	50	66.66667

Constraints

Cell	Name	Final Value	Shadow Price	Constraint R.H. Side	Allowable Increase	Allowable Decrease
$D$9	Pumps Req'd Used	200	200.00	200	7	26
$D$10	Labor Req'd Used	1566	16.67	1566	234	126
$D$11	Tubing Req'd Used	2712	0.00	2880	1E+30	168

4.5.1 CHANGES IN THE OBJECTIVE FUNCTION COEFFICIENTS

Chapter 2 introduced the level-curve approach to solving a graphical LP problem and showed how to use this approach to solve the Blue Ridge Hot Tubs problem. This graphical solution is repeated in Figure 4.4 (and file Fig4-4.xls on your data disk).

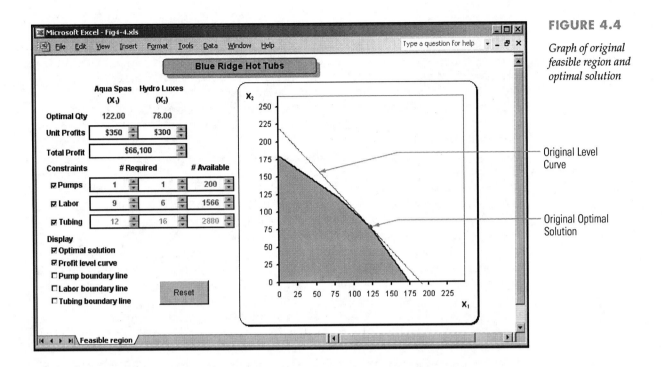

FIGURE 4.4

Graph of original feasible region and optimal solution

Original Level Curve

Original Optimal Solution

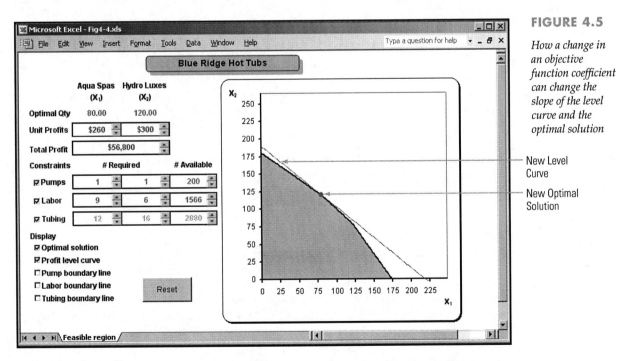

FIGURE 4.5

How a change in an objective function coefficient can change the slope of the level curve and the optimal solution

New Level Curve

New Optimal Solution

The slope of the original level curve in Figure 4.4 is determined by the coefficients in the objective function of the model (the values 350 and 300). In Figure 4.5, we can see that if the slope of the level curve were different, the extreme point represented by $X_1 = 80$, $X_2 = 120$ would be the optimal solution. Of course, the only way to change the level curve for the objective function is to change the coefficients in the objective function. So, if the objective function coefficients are at all uncertain, we might be interested in determining how much these values could change before the optimal solution would change.

For example, if the owner of Blue Ridge Hot Tubs does not have complete control over the costs of producing hot tubs (which is likely because he purchases the fiberglass hot tub shells from another company), the profit figures in the objective function of our LP model might not be the exact profits earned on hot tubs produced in the future. So before the manager decides to produce 122 Aqua-Spas and 78 Hydro-Luxes, he might want to determine how sensitive this solution is to the profit figures in the objective. That is, the manager might want to determine how much the profit figures could change before the optimal solution of $X_1 = 122$, $X_2 = 78$ would change. This information is provided in the Sensitivity Report shown in Figure 4.3.

The original objective function coefficients associated with the variable cells are listed in the Objective Coefficient column in Figure 4.3. The next two columns show the allowable increases and decreases in these values. For example, the objective function value associated with Aqua-Spas (or variable X_1) can increase by as much as $100 or decrease by as much as $50 without changing the optimal solution, assuming all other coefficients remain constant. (You can verify this by changing the profit coefficient for Aqua-Spas to any value in the range from $300 to $450 and re-solving the model.) Similarly, the objective function value associated with Hydro-Luxes (or variable X_2) can increase by $50 or decrease by approximately $66.67 without changing the optimal values of the decision variables, assuming all other coefficients remain constant. (Again, you can verify this by re-solving the model with different profit values for Hydro-Luxes.)

Software Note

When setting up a spreadsheet model for an LP problem for which you intend to generate a sensitivity report, it is a good idea to make sure that the cells corresponding to RHS values of constraints contain constants or formulas that do not involve the decision variables. Thus, any RHS formula related directly or indirectly to the decision variables should be moved algebraically to the left-hand side of the constraint before implementing your model. This will help to reduce problems in interpreting Solver's sensitivity report.

4.5.2 A NOTE ABOUT CONSTANCY

The phrase "assuming all other coefficients remain constant" in the previous paragraph reinforces that the allowable increases and decreases shown in the Sensitivity Report apply only if *all* the other coefficients in the LP model do not change. The objective coefficient for Aqua-Spas can assume any value from $300 to $450 without changing the optimal solution—*but this is guaranteed to be true only if all the other coefficients in the model remain constant (including the objective function coefficient for X_2).* Similarly, the objective function coefficient for X_2 can assume any value between $233.33 and $350 without changing the optimal solution—*but this is guaranteed to be true only if all the other coefficients in the model remain constant (including the objective function coefficient for X_1).* Later in this chapter, you will see how to determine whether the current solution remains optimal if changes are made in two or more objective coefficients at the same time.

4.5.3 ALTERNATE OPTIMAL SOLUTIONS

Sometimes, the allowable increase or allowable decrease for the objective function coefficient for one or more variables will equal zero. In the absence of degeneracy (to be described later), this indicates that alternate optimal solutions exist. Usually you can get Solver to produce an alternate optimal solution (when they exist) by: (1) adding a constraint to your model that holds the objective function at the current optimal value, and then (2) attempting to maximize or minimize the value of one of the decision variables that had an objective function coefficient with an allowable increase or decrease of zero. This approach sometimes involves some "trial and error" in step 2, but should cause Solver to produce an alternate optimal solution to your problem.

4.5.4 CHANGES IN THE RHS VALUES

As noted earlier, constraints that have zero slack in the optimal solution to an LP problem are called binding constraints. Binding constraints prevent us from further improving (that is, maximizing or minimizing) the objective function. For example, the Answer Report in Figure 4.2 indicates that the constraints for the number of pumps and hours of labor available are binding, whereas the constraint on the amount of tubing available is nonbinding. This is also evident in Figure 4.3 by comparing the Final Value column with the Constraint R.H. Side column. The values in the Final Value column represent the LHS values of each constraint at the optimal solution. A constraint is binding if its Final Value is equal to its Constraint R.H. Side value.

After solving an LP problem, you might want to determine how much better or worse the solution would be if we had more or less of a given resource. For example, Howie Jones might wonder how much more profit could be earned if additional pumps or labor hours were available. The Shadow Price column in Figure 4.3 provides the answers to such questions.

The shadow price for a constraint indicates the amount by which the objective function value changes given a unit *increase* in the RHS value of the constraint, assuming that all other coefficients remain constant. If a shadow price is positive, a unit increase in the RHS value of the associated constraint results in an increase in the optimal objective function value. If a shadow price is negative, a unit increase in the RHS value of the associated constraint results in a decrease in the optimal objective function value. To analyze the effects of decreases in the RHS values, you reverse the sign on the shadow price. That is, the negated shadow price for a constraint indicates the amount by which the optimal objective function value changes given a unit *decrease* in the RHS value of the constraint, assuming that all other coefficients remain constant. The shadow price values apply, provided that the increase or decrease in the RHS value falls within the allowable increase or allowable decrease limits in the Sensitivity Report for each constraint.

For example, Figure 4.3 indicates that the shadow price for the labor constraint is 16.67. Therefore, if the number of available labor hours increased by any amount in the range from 0 to 234 hours, the optimal objective function value changes (increases) by $16.67 for each additional labor hour. If the number of available labor hours decreased by any amount in the range from 0 to 126 hours, the optimal objective function value changes (decreases) by −$16.67 for each lost labor hour. A similar interpretation holds for the shadow price for the constraint on the number of pumps. (It is coincidental that the shadow price for the pump constraint (200) is the same as that constraint's RHS and Final Values.)

4.5.5 SHADOW PRICES FOR NONBINDING CONSTRAINTS

Now, let's consider the shadow price for the nonbinding tubing constraint. The tubing constraint has a shadow price of zero with an allowable increase of infinity and an allowable decrease of 168. Therefore, if the RHS value for the tubing constraint increases by *any* amount, the objective function value does not change (or changes by zero). This result is not surprising. Because the optimal solution to this problem leaves 168 feet of tubing unused, *additional* tubing will not produce a better solution. Furthermore, because the optimal solution includes 168 feet of unused tubing, we can reduce the RHS value of this constraint by 168 without affecting the optimal solution.

As this example illustrates, the shadow price of a nonbinding constraint is always zero. There is always some amount by which the RHS value of a nonbinding constraint can be changed without affecting the optimal solution.

4.5.6 A NOTE ABOUT SHADOW PRICES

One important point needs to be made concerning shadow prices. To illustrate this point, let's suppose that the RHS value of the labor constraint for our example problem increases by 162 hours (from 1,566 to 1,728) due to the addition of new workers. Because this increase is within the allowable increase listed for the labor constraint, you might expect that the optimal objective function value would increase by $16.67 \times 162 = \$2,700$. That is, the new optimal objective function value would be approximately $68,800 ($66,100 + $16.67 \times 162 = \$68,800$). Figure 4.6 shows the re-solved model after increasing the RHS value for the labor constraint by 162 labor hours to 1,728.

FIGURE 4.6

Solution to the revised hot tub problem with 162 additional labor hours

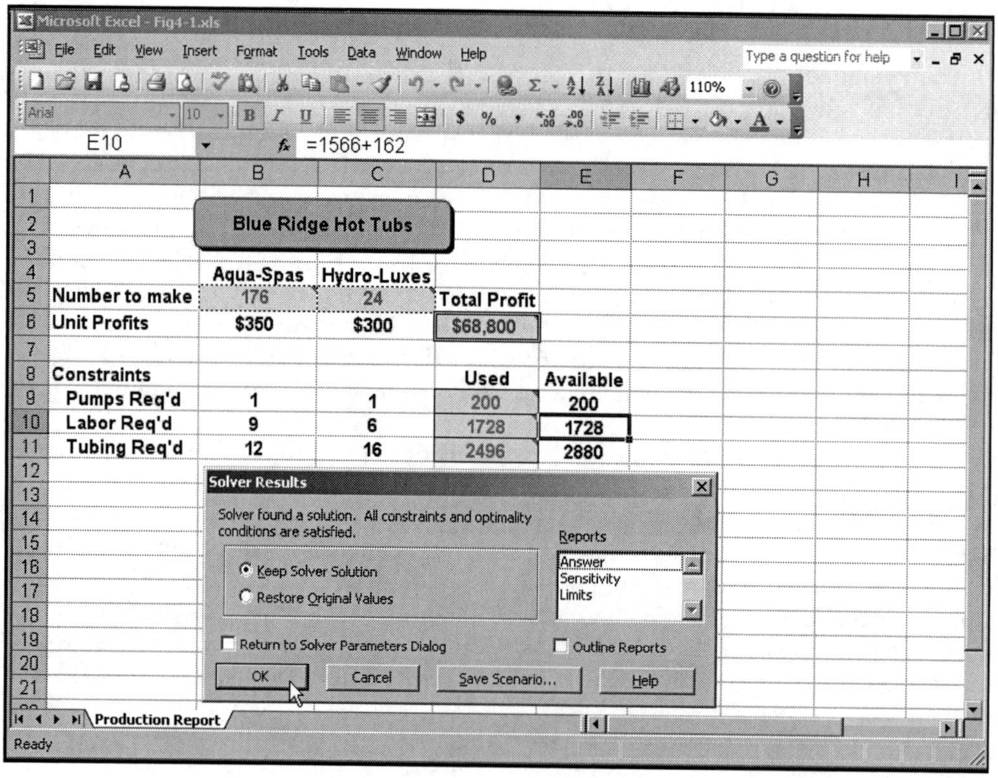

In Figure 4.6, the new optimal objective function value is $68,800, as expected. But this solution involves producing 176 Aqua-Spas and 24 Hydro-Luxes. That is, the optimal solution to the revised problem is *different* from the solution to the original problem shown in Figure 4.1. This is not surprising, because changing the RHS of a constraint also changes the feasible region for the problem. The effect of increasing the RHS of the labor constraint is shown graphically in Figure 4.7.

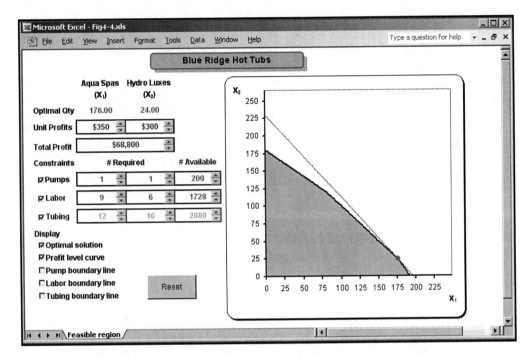

FIGURE 4.7

How a change in the RHS value of the labor constraint changes the feasible region and optimal solution

So, although shadow prices indicate how the objective function value changes if a given RHS value changes, they *do not* tell you which values the decision variables need to assume to achieve this new objective function value. Determining the new optimal values for the decision variables requires that you make the appropriate changes in the RHS value and re-solve the model.

Another Interpretation of Shadow Prices

Unfortunately, there is no one universally accepted way of reporting shadow prices for constraints. In some software packages, the signs of the shadow prices do not conform to the convention used by Solver. Regardless of which software package you use, there is another way to look at shadow prices that always should lead to a proper interpretation. The absolute value of the shadow price always indicates the amount by which the objective function will be *improved* if the corresponding constraint is *loosened*. A "less than or equal to" constraint is loosened by *increasing* its RHS value, whereas a "greater than or equal to" constraint is loosened by *decreasing* its RHS value. (The absolute value of the shadow price also can be interpreted as the amount by which the objective will be made *worse* if the corresponding constraint is *tightened*.)

4.5.7 SHADOW PRICES AND THE VALUE OF ADDITIONAL RESOURCES

In the previous example, an additional 162 hours of labor allowed us to increase profits by $2,700. A question then might arise as to how much we should be willing to pay to acquire these additional 162 hours of labor. The answer to this question is, "It depends. . . ."

If labor is a *variable* cost that was subtracted (along with other variable costs) from the selling price of the hot tubs to determine the marginal profits associated with each type of tub, we should be willing to pay up to $2,700 *above and beyond* what we ordinarily would pay to acquire 162 hours of labor. In this case, notice that both the original and revised profit figures of $66,100 and $68,800, respectively, represent the profit earned *after* the normal labor charge has been paid. Therefore, we could pay a premium of up to $2,700 to acquire the additional 162 hours of labor (or an extra $16.67 per additional labor hour) and still earn at least as much profit as we would have without the additional 162 hours of labor. Thus, if the normal labor rate is $12 per hour, we could pay up to $28.67 per hour to acquire each of the additional 162 hours of labor.

On the other hand, if labor is a sunk cost, which must be paid regardless of how many hot tubs are produced, it would not (or should not) have been subtracted from the selling price of the hot tubs in determining the marginal profit coefficients for each tub produced. In this case, we should be willing to pay a maximum of $16.67 per hour to acquire each of the additional 162 hours of labor.

4.5.8 OTHER USES OF SHADOW PRICES

Because shadow prices represent the marginal values of the resources in an LP problem, they can help us answer several other managerial questions that might arise. For example, suppose that Blue Ridge Hot Tubs is considering introducing a new model of hot tub called the Typhoon-Lagoon. Suppose that each unit of this new model requires 1 pump, 8 hours of labor, and 13 feet of tubing, and can be sold to generate a marginal profit of $320. Would production of this new model be profitable?

Because Blue Ridge Hot Tubs has limited resources, the production of any Typhoon-Lagoons would consume some of the resources currently devoted to the production of Aqua-Spas and Hydro-Luxes. So, producing Typhoon-Lagoons will reduce the number of pumps, labor hours, and tubing available for producing the other types of hot tubs. The shadow prices in Figure 4.3 indicate that each pump taken away from production of the current products will reduce profits by $200. Similarly, each labor hour taken away from the production of the current products will reduce profits by $16.67. The shadow price for the tubing constraint indicates that the supply of tubing can be reduced without adversely affecting profits.

Because each Typhoon-Lagoon requires 1 pump, 8 hours of labor, and 13 feet of tubing, the diversion of resources required to produce one unit of this new model would cause a reduction in profit of $200 \times 1 + $16.67 \times 8 + $0 \times 13 = $333.33. This reduction would be partially offset by the $320 increase in profit generated by each Typhoon-Lagoon. The net effect of producing each Typhoon-Lagoon would be a $13.33 reduction in profit ($320 − $333.33 = −$13.33). Therefore, the production of Typhoon-Lagoons would not be profitable (although the company might choose to produce a small number of Typhoon-Lagoons to enhance its product line for marketing purposes).

Another way to determine whether or not Typhoon-Lagoons should be produced is to add this alternative to our model and solve the resulting LP problem. The LP model for this revised problem is represented as follows, where X_1, X_2, and X_3 represent the number of Aqua-Spas, Hydro-Luxes, and Typhoon-Lagoons to be produced, respectively:

$$\text{MAX:} \quad 350X_1 + 300X_2 + 320X_3 \qquad \} \text{ profit}$$

$$\text{Subject to:} \quad 1X_1 + 1X_2 + 1X_3 \leq 200 \qquad \} \text{ pump constraint}$$

$$9X_1 + 6X_2 + 8X_3 \leq 1{,}566 \qquad \} \text{ labor constraint}$$

$$12X_1 + 16X_2 + 13X_3 \leq 2{,}880 \qquad \} \text{ tubing constraint}$$

$$X_1, X_2, X_3 \geq 0 \qquad \} \text{ nonnegativity conditions}$$

This model is implemented and solved in the spreadsheet, as shown in Figure 4.8. Notice that the optimal solution to this problem involves producing 122 Aqua-Spas ($X_1 = 122$), 78 Hydro-Luxes ($X_2 = 78$), and no Typhoon-Lagoons ($X_3 = 0$). So, as expected, the optimal solution does not involve producing Typhoon-Lagoons. Figure 4.9 shows the Sensitivity Report for our revised model.

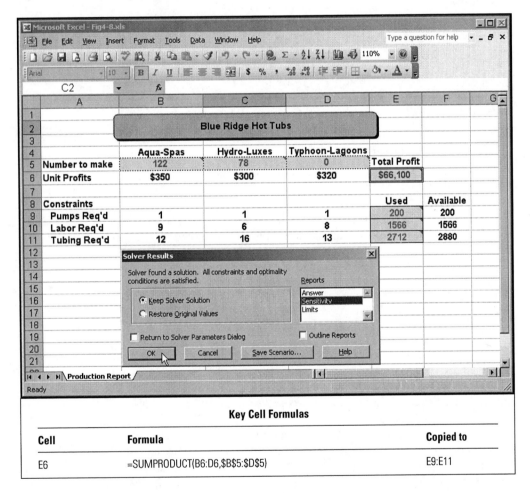

FIGURE 4.8

Spreadsheet model for the revised product mix problem with three hot tub models

4.5.9 THE MEANING OF THE REDUCED COSTS

The Sensitivity Report in Figure 4.9 for our revised model is identical to the sensitivity report for our original model *except* that it includes an additional row in the adjustable cells section. This row reports sensitivity information on the number of Typhoon-Lagoons

FIGURE 4.9

Sensitivity Report for the revised product mix problem with three hot tub models

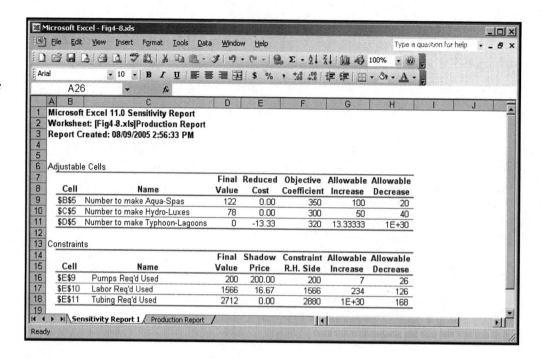

to produce. Notice that the Reduced Cost column indicates that the reduced cost value for Typhoon-Lagoons is −13.33. This is the same number that we calculated in the previous section when determining whether or not it would be profitable to produce Typhoon-Lagoons.

The reduced cost for each variable is equal to the per-unit amount that the product contributes to profits, minus the per-unit value of the resources it consumes (where the consumed resources are priced at their shadow prices). For example, the reduced cost of each variable in this problem is calculated as:

Reduced cost of Aqua-Spas $\quad= 350 - 200 \times 1 - 16.67 \times 9 - 0 \times 12 = 0$

Reduced cost of Hydro-Luxes $\quad= 300 - 200 \times 1 - 16.67 \times 6 - 0 \times 16 = 0$

Reduced cost of Typhoon-Lagoons $= 320 - 200 \times 1 - 16.67 \times 8 - 0 \times 13 = -13.33$

The allowable increase in the objective function coefficient for Typhoon-Lagoons equals 13.33. This means that the current solution will remain optimal provided that the marginal profit on Typhoon-Lagoons is less than or equal to $320 + $13.33 = $333.33 (because this would keep its reduced cost less than or equal to zero). However, if the marginal profit for Typhoon-Lagoons is more than $333.33, producing this product would be profitable and the optimal solution to the problem would change.

It is interesting to note that the shadow prices (marginal values) of the resources equate exactly with the marginal profits of the products that, at optimality, assume values between their simple lower and upper bounds. This will always be the case. In the optimal solution to an LP problem, the variables that assume values *between* their simple lower and upper bounds always have reduced cost values of zero. (In our example problem, all the variables have implicit simple upper bounds of positive infinity.) The variables with optimal values equal to their simple lower bounds have reduced cost values that are less than or equal to zero for maximization problems, or greater than or equal to zero for minimization problems. Variables with optimal values equal to their simple upper bounds have reduced cost values that are greater than or equal to zero for

FIGURE 4.10

Summary of optimal reduced cost values

Type of Problem	Optimal Value of Decision Variable	Optimal Value of Reduced Cost
Maximization	at simple lower bound	≤ 0
	between lower and upper bounds	$= 0$
	at simple upper bound	≥ 0
Minimization	at simple lower bound	≥ 0
	between lower and upper bounds	$= 0$
	at simple upper bound	≤ 0

maximization problems, or less than or equal to zero for minimization problems. Figure 4.10 summarizes these relationships.

Generally, at optimality, a variable assumes its largest possible value (or is set equal to its simple upper bound) if this variable helps improve the objective function value. In a maximization problem, the variable's reduced cost must be nonnegative to indicate that if the variable's value increased, the objective value would increase (improve). In a minimization problem, the variable's reduced cost must be nonpositive to indicate that if the variable's value increased, the objective value would decrease (improve).

Similar arguments can be made for the optimal reduced costs of variables at their lower bounds. At optimality, a variable assumes its smallest (lower bound) value if it cannot be used to improve the objective value. In a maximization problem, the variable's reduced cost must be nonpositive to indicate that if the variable's value increased, the objective value would decrease (worsen). In a minimization problem, the variable's reduced cost must be nonnegative to indicate that if the variable's value increased, the objective value would increase (worsen).

Key Points

Our discussion of Solver's sensitivity report highlights some key points concerning shadow prices and their relationship to reduced costs. These key points are summarized as:

- The shadow prices of resources equate the marginal value of the resources consumed with the marginal benefit of the goods being produced.
- Resources in excess supply have a shadow price (or marginal value) of zero.
- The reduced cost of a product is the difference between its marginal profit and the marginal value of the resources it consumes.
- Products whose marginal profits are less than the marginal value of the goods required for their production will not be produced in an optimal solution.

4.5.10 ANALYZING CHANGES IN CONSTRAINT COEFFICIENTS

Given what we know about reduced costs and shadow prices, we can now analyze how changes in some constraint coefficients affect the optimal solution to an LP problem. For example, it is unprofitable for Blue Ridge Hot Tubs to manufacture Typhoon-Lagoons assuming that each unit requires 8 hours of labor. However, what would happen if the product could be produced in only 7 hours? The reduced cost value for Typhoon-Lagoons is calculated as:

$$\$320 - \$200 \times 1 - \$16.67 \times 7 - \$0 \times 13 = \$3.31$$

Because this new reduced cost value is positive, producing Typhoon-Lagoons would be profitable in this scenario and the solution shown in Figure 4.8 no longer would be optimal. We could also reach this conclusion by changing the labor requirement for Typhoon-Lagoons in our spreadsheet model and re-solving the problem. In fact, we have to do this to determine the new optimal solution if each Typhoon-Lagoon requires only 7 hours of labor.

As another example, suppose that we wanted to know the maximum amount of labor that is required to assemble a Typhoon-Lagoon while keeping its production economically justifiable. The production of Typhoon-Lagoons would be profitable provided that the reduced cost for the product is greater than or equal to zero. If L_3 represents the amount of labor required to produce a Typhoon-Lagoon, we want to find the maximum value of L_3 that keeps the reduced cost for Typhoon-Lagoons greater than or equal to zero. That is, we want to find the maximum value of L_3 that satisfies the inequality:

$$\$320 - \$200 \times 1 - \$16.67 \times L_3 - \$0 \times 13 \geq 0$$

If we solve this inequality for L_3, we obtain:

$$L_3 \leq \frac{120}{16.67} = 7.20$$

Thus, the production of Typhoon-Lagoons would be economically justified provided that the labor required to produce them does not exceed 7.20 hours per unit. Similar types of questions can be answered using knowledge of the basic relationships between reduced costs, shadow prices, and optimality conditions.

4.5.11 SIMULTANEOUS CHANGES IN OBJECTIVE FUNCTION COEFFICIENTS

Earlier, we noted that the values in the Allowable Increase and Allowable Decrease columns in the Sensitivity Report for the objective function coefficients indicate the maximum amounts by which each objective coefficient can change without altering the optimal solution—*assuming that all other coefficients in the model remain constant.* A technique known as The 100% Rule determines whether the current solution remains optimal when more than one objective function coefficient changes. The following two situations could arise when applying this rule:

Case 1. All variables whose objective function coefficients change have non-zero reduced costs.

Case 2. At least one variable whose objective function coefficient changes has a reduced cost of zero.

In case 1, the current solution remains optimal provided that the objective function coefficient of each changed variable remains within the limits indicated in the Allowable Increase and Allowable Decrease columns of the Sensitivity Report.

Case 2 is a bit more tricky. In case 2, we must perform the following analysis where:

c_j = the original objective function coefficient for variable X_j

Δc_j = the planned change in c_j

I_j = the allowable increase in c_j given in the Sensitivity Report

D_j = the allowable decrease in c_j given in the Sensitivity Report

$$r_j = \begin{cases} \dfrac{\Delta c_j}{I_j}, & \text{if } \Delta c_j \geq 0 \\[2ex] \dfrac{-\Delta c_j}{D_j}, & \text{if } \Delta c_j < 0 \end{cases}$$

Notice that r_j measures the ratio of the planned change in c_j to the maximum allowable change for which the current solution remains optimal. If only one objective function coefficient changed, the current solution remains optimal provided that $r_j \leq 1$ (or, if r_j is expressed as a percentage, it must be less than or equal to 100%). Similarly, if more than one objective function coefficient changes, the current solution will remain optimal provided that $\Sigma r_j \leq 1$. (Note that if $\Sigma r_j > 1$, the current solution might remain optimal, but this is not guaranteed.)

4.5.12 A WARNING ABOUT DEGENERACY

The solution to an LP problem sometimes exhibits a mathematical anomaly known as *degeneracy*. The solution to an LP problem is degenerate if the RHS values of any of the constraints have an allowable increase or allowable decrease of zero. The presence of degeneracy affects our interpretation of the values on the sensitivity report in a number of important ways:

1. When the solution is degenerate, the methods mentioned earlier for detecting alternate optimal solutions cannot be relied upon.
2. When a solution is degenerate, the reduced costs for the variable cells may not be unique. Additionally, in this case, the objective function coefficients for variable cells must change by at least as much as (and possibly more than) their respective reduced costs before the optimal solution would change.
3. When the solution is degenerate, the allowable increases and decreases for the objective function coefficients still hold and, in fact, the coefficients might have to be changed substantially beyond the allowable increase and decrease limits before the optimal solution changes.
4. When the solution is degenerate, the given shadow prices and their ranges still might be interpreted in the usual way but they might not be unique. That is, a different set of shadow prices and ranges also might apply to the problem (even if the optimal solution is unique).

So before interpreting the results on a sensitivity report, you always should check first to see if the solution is degenerate because this has important ramifications for how the numbers on the report should be interpreted. A complete description of the degeneracy anomaly goes beyond the intended scope of this book. However, degeneracy is sometimes caused by having redundant constraints in an LP model. *Extreme caution* (and perhaps consultation with an expert in mathematical programming) is in order if important business decisions are being made based on the sensitivity report for a degenerate LP problem.

4.6 The Limits Report

The Limits Report for the original Blue Ridge Hot Tubs problem is shown in Figure 4.11. This report lists the optimal value of the set cell. It then summarizes the optimal values for each variable cell and indicates what values the set cell assumes if each variable cell is set to its upper or lower limits. The values in the Lower Limits column indicate the smallest value that each variable cell can assume while the values of all other variable cells remain constant and all the constraints are satisfied. The values in the Upper Limits column indicate the largest value that each variable cell can assume while the values of all other variable cells remain constant and all the constraints are satisfied.

FIGURE 4.11

Limits Report for the original Blue Ridge Hot Tubs problem

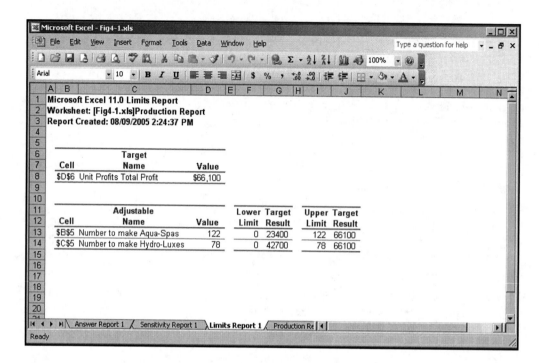

4.7 The Sensitivity Assistant Add-in (Optional)

This book comes with an Excel add-in called Sensitivity Assistant that provides two additional tools for performing sensitivity analysis on an *ad hoc* basis: Spider Tables and Solver Tables. A Spider Table summarizes the optimal value for one output cell as individual changes are made to various input cells. A Solver Table summarizes the optimal value of multiple output cells as changes are made to a single input cell. As illustrated in the following sections, these tools can be helpful in developing an understanding of how changes in various model parameters affect the optimal solution to a problem.

I n s t a l l i n g   t h e   S e n s i t i v i t y
A s s i s t a n t   A d d - I n

To use the Sensitivity Assistant add-in, it must first be installed on your computer. To do this:

1. Copy the file Sensitivity.xla from the CD-ROM accompanying this book to the folder on your hard drive containing the file Solver.xla. (On most cases, this is the folder: *d*:\Program Files\Microsoft Office\Office10\Library\Solver.)

(Continued)

---

2. In Excel, click Tools, Add-Ins, click the Browse button, locate the Sensitivity.xla file, and click OK.

This instructs your computer to open the Sensitivity Assistant add-in whenever you start Excel. It also causes the "Sensitivity Assistant . . ." option to be added to the Tools menu in Excel. You can deactivate the Sensitivity Assistant add-in at any time by using the Tools, Add-Ins command again.

4.7.1 CREATING SPIDER TABLES AND PLOTS

Recall that the optimal solution to the original Blue Ridge Hot Tubs problem involves producing 122 Aqua-Spas and 78 Hydro-Luxes for a total profit of $66,100. However, this solution assumes there will be exactly 200 pumps, 1,566 labor hours, and 2,880 feet of tubing available. In reality, pumps and tubing are sometimes defective, and workers sometimes call in sick. So, the owner of the company might wonder how sensitive the total profit is to changes in these resources. Although Solver's Sensitivity Report provides some information about this issue, a Spider Table and Plot is sometimes more helpful in communicating this information to management.

Again, a Spider Table summarizes the optimal value for one output cell as individual changes are made to various input cells. In this case, the output cell of interest is cell D6 representing total profit, and the input cells are E9, E10, and E11 representing the availability of pumps, labor, and tubing. Figure 4.12 (and file Fig4-12.xls on your data disk) shows how to set up a Spider Table for this problem.

The upper-left cell in a Spider Table should contain a formula referring to the output cell you want to track. Thus, in Figure 4.12, cell A14 contains a formula that returns the value of cell D6 representing total profit.

Formula for cell A14:   =D6

The remaining cells in the first row of a Spider Table should contain formulas referring to the input cells that you want to manipulate. Thus, cells B14, C14, and D14 contain formulas referring, respectively, to cells E9, E10, and E11, which represent the resource availability values that we want to manipulate.

Formula for cell B14:   =E9
Formula for cell C14:   =E10
Formula for cell D14:   =E11

The first cell in each remaining row of a Spider Table should contain a percentage value indicating an amount by which to adjust each of the input cells. Thus, in cells A15 through A25, we entered a series of percentages from 90% to 110%. The Spider Table tool will multiply the value of each of the input cells referenced in cells B14 through D14 by each of the percentages listed in cells A15 through A25, and will keep a record of the corresponding value of the output cell referenced in cell A14. Specifically, the Spider Table tool will first change the value in cell E9 (representing the number of pumps available) to 180 (or 90% of 200), re-solve the problem, and record the optimal profit in cell B15. It will then change the value in cell E9 to 184 (or 92% of 200), re-solve the problem, and record the optimal profit in cell B16. This process continues until all the input cells have been varied from 90% to 110% and the resulting optimal profit values recorded in the table.

FIGURE 4.12

Set up for creating a Spider Table and Plot

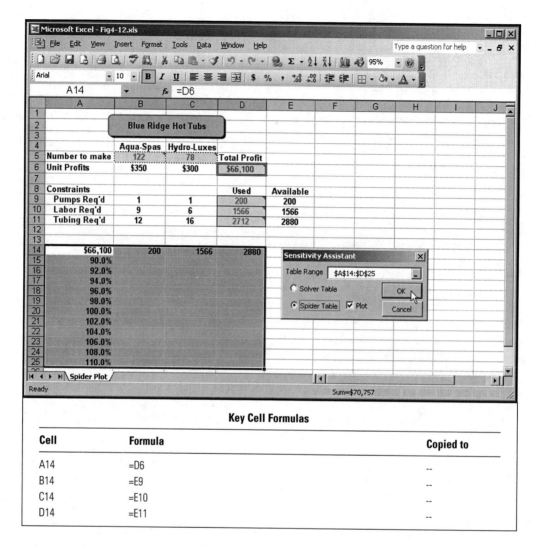

Key Cell Formulas

Cell	Formula	Copied to
A14	=D6	--
B14	=E9	--
C14	=E10	--
D14	=E11	--

To complete the Spider Table, we would proceed through the following steps. The resulting table and plot is shown in Figure 4.13.

1. Select the range A14:D25
2. Click Tools, Sensitivity Assistant
3. Select the Spider Table option
4. Click OK

The rationale for the name of this procedure should be readily apparent from the spider-like plot shown in Figure 4.13. The center point in the graph corresponds to the optimal solution to the original model with 100% of the pumps, labor, and tubing available. Each of the points in the graph show the effect on total profit of varying the original resource levels by the indicated percentage.

It is clear from Figure 4.13 that total profit is relatively insensitive to modest decreases or large increases in the availability of tubing. This is consistent with the sensitivity information regarding tubing shown earlier in Figure 4.9. The optimal solution to the original problem involved using all the pumps and all the labor hours, but only 2,712 feet of the 2,880 available feet of tubing. As a result, we could achieve the same level of profit even if the availability of tubing was reduced by 168 feet (or to about 94.2% of its original

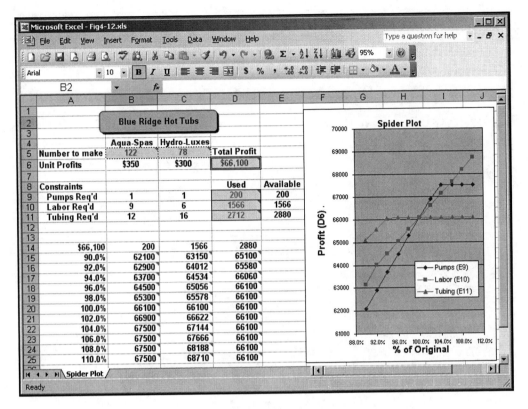

FIGURE 4.13

A Spider Table and
Plot showing the
relationship
between profit and
the availability of
pumps, labor, and
tubing

value). Similarly, because we are not using all of the available tubing, acquiring more tubing would only increase the surplus and not allow for any improvement in profit. Thus, our Spider Table and Plot suggest that the availability of tubing probably should not be a top concern in this problem. On the other hand, the Spider Plot suggests that changes in the availability of pumps and labor have a more pronounced effect on profit and the optimal solution to the problem.

Notes on Setting Up a Spider Table

1. The cell in the upper-left corner of the table range should contain a formula returning the value of the output cell you want to track.
2. The remaining cells in the first row of the table range should contain formulas referring to the input cells you want to manipulate.
3. The first cell in each remaining row of the table range should contain a percentage value indicating an amount by which to multiply each of the input cells.

4.7.2 CREATING A SOLVER TABLE

The Spider Plot in Figure 4.13 suggests that the total profit earned is most sensitive to changes in the available supply of pumps. We can create a Solver Table to study in greater detail the impact of changes in the available number of pumps. Recall that a Solver Table summarizes the optimal value of multiple output cells as changes are made

FIGURE 4.14

Set up for creating a Solver Table

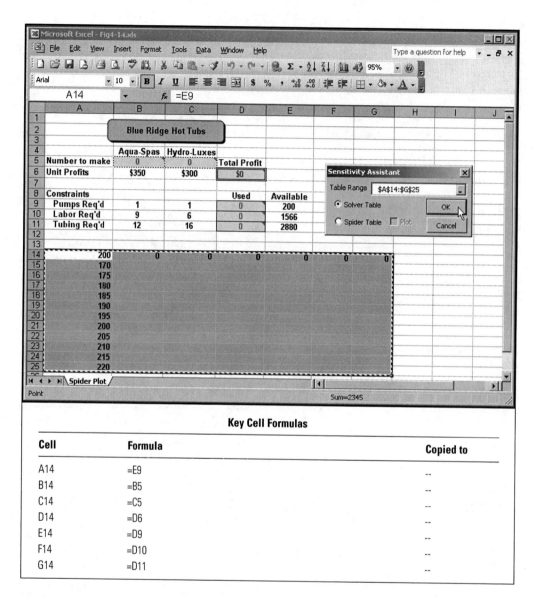

Cell	Formula	Copied to
A14	=E9	--
B14	=B5	--
C14	=C5	--
D14	=D6	--
E14	=D9	--
F14	=D10	--
G14	=D11	--

to a single input cell. In this case, the single input we want to change is cell E9, which represents the number of pumps available. We might want to track what happens to several output cells, including the optimal number of Aqua-Spas and Hydro-Luxes (cells B5 and B6), the total profit (cell D6), and the total amount of pumps, labor, and tubing used (cells D9, D10, and D11). Figure 4.14 (and file Fig4-14.xls on your data disk) shows how to set up the Solver Table for this problem.

The upper-left cell in a Solver Table should contain a formula referring to the input cell you want to manipulate. Thus, cell A14 contains a formula referring to cell E9, which represents the available number of pumps.

Formula for cell A14:   =E9

The remaining cells in the first row of a Solver Table should contain formulas returning the values of the various output cells you want to track. Thus, cells B14 through G14 each contain a formula referring to one of our output cells.

Formula for cell B14:	=B5
Formula for cell C14:	=C5
Formula for cell D14:	=D6
Formula for cell E14:	=D9
Formula for cell F14:	=D10
Formula for cell G14	=D11

The first cell in each of the remaining rows of the Solver Table should contain a value to be assumed by the input cell. In this case, we entered values from 170 to 220 (in multiples of five) in cells A15 to A25 as representative values for the input cell (E9) representing the available number of pumps. The Solver Table tool will substitute each of the values in cells A15 through A25 into the input cell (E9), re-solve the problem, and then record the resulting values for the output cells referenced in the first row of the table range.

To complete the Solver Table, we would proceed through the following steps. The resulting table and plot is shown in Figure 4.15.

1. Select the range A14:G25.
2. Click Tools, Sensitivity Assistant.
3. Select the Solver Table option.
4. Click OK.

Several interesting insights emerge from Figure 4.15. First, comparing columns A and E, as the number of available pumps increases from 170 up to 205, they are always all used. With about 175 pumps, we also begin to use all the available labor. However, when the number of available pumps increases to 210 or more, only 207 pumps can be used because we run out of both tubing and labor at that point. This suggests that the

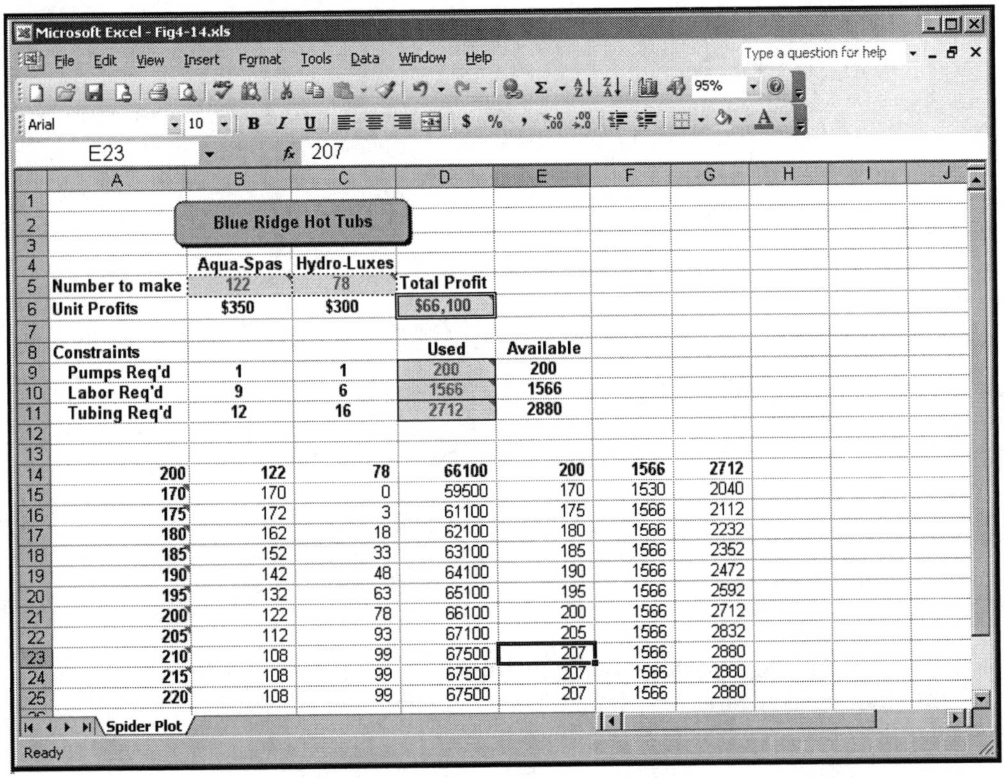

	A	B	C	D	E	F	G
2		Blue Ridge Hot Tubs					
4		Aqua-Spas	Hydro-Luxes				
5	Number to make	122	78	Total Profit			
6	Unit Profits	$350	$300	$66,100			
8	Constraints			Used	Available		
9	Pumps Req'd	1	1	200	200		
10	Labor Req'd	9	6	1566	1566		
11	Tubing Req'd	12	16	2712	2880		
14	200	122	78	66100	200	1566	2712
15	170	170	0	59500	170	1530	2040
16	175	172	3	61100	175	1566	2112
17	180	162	18	62100	180	1566	2232
18	185	152	33	63100	185	1566	2352
19	190	142	48	64100	190	1566	2472
20	195	132	63	65100	195	1566	2592
21	200	122	78	66100	200	1566	2712
22	205	112	93	67100	205	1566	2832
23	210	108	99	67500	207	1566	2880
24	215	108	99	67500	207	1566	2880
25	220	108	99	67500	207	1566	2880

FIGURE 4.15

Solver Table showing changes in the optimal solution, profit, and resource usage and the number of pumps changed

company should not be interested in getting more than 7 additional pumps unless it also can increase the amount of tubing and/or labor available.

Also note that the addition or subtraction of 5 pumps from the initial supply of 200 causes the optimal objective function value (column D) to change by $1,000. This suggests that if the company has 200 pumps, the marginal value of each pump is about $200 (i.e., $1000/5 = $200). Of course, this is equivalent to the *shadow price* of pumps shown earlier in Figure 4.9.

Finally, it is interesting to note that when the availability of pumps is between 175 and 205, each increase of 5 pumps causes the optimal number of Aqua-Spas to decrease by 10 and the optimal number of Hydro-Luxes to increase by 15. Thus, one advantage of the Solver Table over the Sensitivity Report is that it tells you not only how much the optimal value of the objective function changes as the number of pumps change, but it also can tell you how the optimal solution changes.

Notes on Setting Up a Solver Table

1. The cell in the upper-left corner of the table range should contain a formula referring to the input cell you want to manipulate.
2. The remaining cells in the first row of the table range should contain formulas returning the values of the output cells you want to track.
3. The first cell in each remaining row of the table range should contain a value to be assumed by the input cell.

4.7.3 COMMENTS

Additional Solver Tables and Spider Tables/Plots could be constructed to analyze every element of the model, including objective function and constraint coefficients. However, these techniques are considered 'computationally expensive' because they require the LP model to be solved repeatedly. For small problems such as Blue Ridge Hot Tubs, this is not really a problem. But as problem size and complexity increases, this approach to sensitivity analysis can become impractical.

4.8 The Simplex Method (Optional)

We have mentioned repeatedly that the simplex method is the preferred method for solving LP problems. This section provides an overview of the simplex method and shows how it relates to some of the items that appear on the Answer Report and the Sensitivity Report.

4.8.1 CREATING EQUALITY CONSTRAINTS USING SLACK VARIABLES

Because our original formulation of the LP model for the Blue Ridge Hot Tubs problem has only *two* decision variables (X_1 and X_2), you might be surprised to learn that Solver actually used *five* variables to solve this problem. As you saw in Chapter 2 when we plotted the boundary lines for the constraints in an LP problem, it is easier to work with "equal to" conditions rather than "less than or equal to," or "greater than or equal to" conditions. Similarly, the simplex method requires that *all* constraints in an LP model be expressed as equalities.

To solve an LP problem using the simplex method, Solver temporarily turns all inequality constraints into equality constraints by adding one new variable to each "less than or equal to" constraint and subtracting one new variable from each "greater than or equal to" constraint. The new variables used to create equality constraints are called slack variables.

For example, consider the less than or equal to constraint:

$$a_{k1}X_1 + a_{k2}X_2 + \cdots + a_{kn}X_n \leq b_k$$

Solver can turn this constraint into an equal to constraint by adding the nonnegative slack variable S_k to the LHS of the constraint:

$$a_{k1}X_1 + a_{k2}X_2 + \cdots + a_{kn}X_n + S_k = b_k$$

The variable S_k represents the amount by which $a_{k1}X_1 + a_{k2}X_2 + \cdots + a_{kn}X_n$ is less than b_k. Now consider the "greater than or equal to" constraint:

$$a_{k1}X_1 + a_{k2}X_2 + \cdots + a_{kn}X_n \geq b_k$$

Solver can turn this constraint into an "equal to" constraint by subtracting the non-negative slack variable S_k from the LHS of the constraint:

$$a_{k1}X_1 + a_{k2}X_2 + \cdots + a_{kn}X_n - S_k = b_k$$

In this case, the variable S_k represents the amount by which $a_{k1}X_1 + a_{k2}X_2 + \cdots + a_{kn}X_n$ exceeds b_k.

To solve the original Blue Ridge Hot Tubs problem using the simplex method, Solver actually solved the following modified problem involving *five* variables:

MAX:	$350X_1 + 300X_2$	} profit
Subject to:	$1X_1 + 1X_2 + S_1 = 200$	} pump constraint
	$9X_1 + 6X_2 + S_2 = 1{,}566$	} labor constraint
	$12X_1 + 16X_2 + S_3 = 2{,}880$	} tubing constraint
	$X_1, X_2, S_1, S_2, S_3 \geq 0$	} nonnegativity conditions

We will refer to X_1 and X_2 as the structural variables in the model to distinguish them from the slack variables.

Recall that we did not set up slack variables in the spreadsheet or include them in the formulas in the constraint cells. Solver automatically sets up the slack variables it needs to solve a particular problem. The only time Solver even mentions these variables is when it creates an Answer Report like the one shown in Figure 4.2. The values in the Slack column in the Answer Report correspond to the optimal values of the slack variables.

4.8.2 BASIC FEASIBLE SOLUTIONS

After all the inequality constraints in an LP problem have been converted into equalities (by adding or subtracting appropriate slack variables), the constraints in the LP model represent a system (or collection) of linear equations. If there are a total of n variables in a system of m equations, one strategy for finding a solution to the system of equations is to select any m variables and try to find values for them that solve the system, assuming that all other variables are set equal to their lower bounds (which usually are zero). This strategy requires more variables than constraints in the system of equations—or that $n \geq m$.

The m variables selected to solve the system of equations in an LP model are sometimes called basic variables, whereas the remaining variables are called **nonbasic variables**. If a solution to the system of equations can be obtained using a given set of basic variables (while the nonbasic variables are all set equal to zero), that solution is called a basic feasible solution. Every basic feasible solution corresponds to one of the extreme points of the feasible region for the LP problem, and we know that the optimal solution to the LP problem also occurs at an extreme point. So, the challenge in LP is to find the set of basic variables (and their optimal values) that produce the basic feasible solution corresponding to the optimal extreme point of the feasible region.

Because our modified problem involves three constraints and five variables, we could select three basic variables in ten different ways to form possible basic feasible solutions for the problem. Figure 4.16 summarizes the results for these ten options.

The first five solutions in Figure 4.16 are feasible and, therefore, represent basic feasible solutions to this problem. The remaining solutions are infeasible because they violate the nonnegativity conditions. The best feasible alternative shown in Figure 4.16 corresponds to the optimal solution to the problem. In particular, if X_1, X_2, and S_3 are selected as basic variables and S_1 and S_2 are nonbasic and assigned their lower bound values

FIGURE 4.16

Possible basic feasible solutions for the original Blue Ridge Hot Tubs problem

	Basic Variables	Nonbasic Variables	Solution	Objective Value
1	S_1, S_2, S_3	X_1, X_2	$X_1=0, X_2=0,$ $S_1=200, S_2=1566, S_3=2880$	0
2	X_1, S_1, S_3	X_2, S_2	$X_1=174, X_2=0,$ $S_1=26, S_2=0, S_3=792$	60,900
3	X_1, X_2, S_3	S_1, S_2	$X_1=122, X_2=78,$ $S_1=0, S_2=0, S_3=168$	66,100
4	X_1, X_2, S_2	S_1, S_3	$X_1=80, X_2=120,$ $S_1=0, S_2=126, S_3=0$	64,000
5	X_2, S_1, S_2	X_1, S_3	$X_1=0, X_2=180,$ $S_1=20, S_2=486, S_3=0$	54,000
6*	X_1, X_2, S_1	S_2, S_3	$X_1=108, X_2=99,$ $S_1=-7, S_2=0, S_3=0$	67,500
7*	X_1, S_1, S_2	X_2, S_3	$X_1=240, X_2=0,$ $S_1=-40, S_2=-594, S_3=0$	84,000
8*	X_1, S_2, S_3	X_2, S_1	$X_1=200, X_2=0,$ $S_1=0, S_2=-234, S_3=480$	70,000
9*	X_2, S_2, S_3	X_1, S_1	$X_1=0, X_2=200,$ $S_1=0, S_2=366, S_3=-320$	60,000
10*	X_2, S_1, S_3	X_1, S_2	$X_1=0, X_2=261,$ $S_1=-61, S_2=0, S_3=-1296$	78,300

Note: * denotes infeasible solutions

(zero), we try to find values for X_1, X_2, and S_3 that satisfy the following constraints:

$$1X_1 + 1X_2 \qquad\quad = \quad 200 \qquad \text{} \text{pump constraint}$$
$$9X_1 + 6X_2 \qquad\quad = 1{,}566 \qquad \text{} \text{labor constraint}$$
$$12X_1 + 16X_2 + S_3 = 2{,}880 \qquad \text{} \text{tubing constraint}$$

Notice that S_1 and S_2 in the modified "equal to" constraints are not included in the above constraint equations because we are assuming that the values of these nonbasic variables are equal to zero (their lower bounds). Using linear algebra, the simplex method determines that the values $X_1 = 122$, $X_2 = 78$, and $S_3 = 168$ satisfy the equations given above. So, a basic feasible solution to this problem is $X_1 = 122$, $X_2 = 78$, $S_1 = 0$, $S_2 = 0$, $S_3 = 168$. As indicated in Figure 4.16, this solution produces an objective function value of \$66,100. (Notice that the optimal values for the slack variables S_1, S_2, and S_3 also correspond to the values shown in the Answer Report in Figure 4.2 in the Slack column for constraint cells D9, D10, and D11.) Figure 4.17 shows the relationships between the basic feasible solutions listed in Figure 4.16 and the extreme points of the feasible region for this problem.

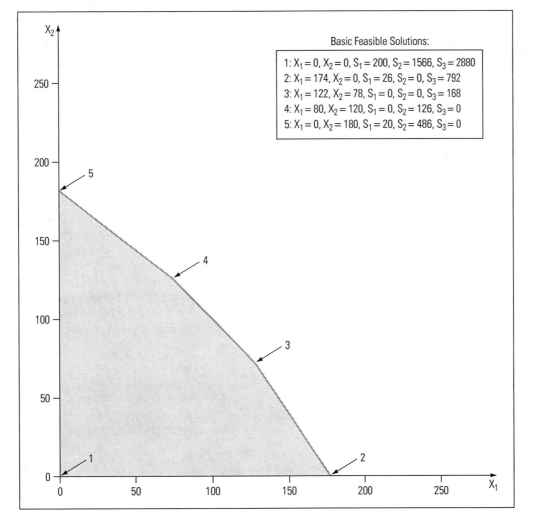

FIGURE 4.17

Illustration of the relationship between basic feasible solutions and extreme points

Basic Feasible Solutions:

1: $X_1 = 0$, $X_2 = 0$, $S_1 = 200$, $S_2 = 1566$, $S_3 = 2880$
2: $X_1 = 174$, $X_2 = 0$, $S_1 = 26$, $S_2 = 0$, $S_3 = 792$
3: $X_1 = 122$, $X_2 = 78$, $S_1 = 0$, $S_2 = 0$, $S_3 = 168$
4: $X_1 = 80$, $X_2 = 120$, $S_1 = 0$, $S_2 = 126$, $S_3 = 0$
5: $X_1 = 0$, $X_2 = 180$, $S_1 = 20$, $S_2 = 486$, $S_3 = 0$

4.8.3 FINDING THE BEST SOLUTION

The simplex method operates by first identifying any basic feasible solution (or extreme point) for an LP problem, and then moving to an adjacent extreme point, if such a move improves the value of the objective function. When no adjacent extreme point has a better objective function value, the current extreme point is optimal and the simplex method terminates.

The process of moving from one extreme point to an adjacent one is accomplished by switching one of the basic variables with one of the nonbasic variables to create a new basic feasible solution that corresponds to the adjacent extreme point. For example, in Figure 4.17, moving from the first basic feasible solution (point 1) to the second basic feasible solution (point 2) involves making X_1 a basic variable and S_2 a nonbasic variable. Similarly, we can move from point 2 to point 3 by switching basic variables with nonbasic variables. So, starting at point 1 in Figure 4.17, the simplex method could move to point 2, then to the optimal solution at point 3. Alternatively, the simplex method could move from point 1 through points 5 and 4 to reach the optimal solution at point 3. Thus, although there is no guarantee that the simplex method will take the shortest route to the optimal solution of an LP problem, it will find the optimal solution eventually.

To determine whether switching a basic and nonbasic variable will result in a better solution, the simplex method calculates the reduced cost for each nonbasic variable to determine if the objective function could be improved if any of these variables are substituted for one of the basic variables. (Note that unbounded solutions are detected easily in the simplex method by the existence of a nonbasic variable that could improve the objective value by an infinite amount if it were made basic.) This process continues until no further improvement in the objective function value is possible.

4.9 Summary

This chapter described the methods for assessing how sensitive an LP model is to various changes that might occur in the model or its optimal solution. The impact of changes in an LP model can be analyzed easily by re-solving the model. Solver also provides a significant amount of sensitivity information automatically. For LP problems, the maximum amount of sensitivity information is obtained by solving the problem using the simplex method. Before using the information on the Sensitivity Report, you always should check first for the presence of degeneracy because this can have a significant effect on how one should interpret the numbers on this report.

The simplex method considers only the extreme points of the feasible region, and is an efficient way of solving LP problems. In this method, slack variables are introduced first to convert all constraints to "equal to" constraints. The simplex method systematically moves to better and better corner point solutions until no adjacent extreme point provides an improved objective function value.

4.10 References

Bazaraa, M. and J. Jarvis. *Linear Programming and Network Flows*. New York: Wiley, 1990.

Eppen, G., F. Gould and C. Schmidt. *Introductory Management Science*, 4th ed., Englewood Cliffs, NJ: Prentice-Hall, 1993.

Shogan, A. *Management Science*. Englewood Cliffs, NJ: Prentice Hall, 1988.

Wagner, H. and D. Rubin. "Shadow Prices: Tips and Traps for Managers and Instructors," *Interfaces*, vol. 20, no. 4, 1990.

Winston, W. *Operations Research: Applications and Algorithms*. Belmont, CA: Duxbury Press, 1994.

THE WORLD OF MANAGEMENT SCIENCE

Fuel Management and Allocation Model Helps National Airlines Adapt to Cost and Supply Changes

Fuel is a major component in the cost structure of an airline. Price and availability of fuel can vary from one air terminal to the next, and it is sometimes advantageous for an aircraft to carry more than the necessary minimum for the next leg of its route. Fuel loaded for the purpose of taking advantage of price or availability at a specific location is said to be tankered. A disadvantage of tankering is that fuel consumption increases when an aircraft is carrying more weight.

The use of LP to determine when and where to fuel aircraft saved National Airlines several million dollars during the first two years of implementation. In particular, National Airlines saw its average fuel costs drop 11.75% during a period when the average fuel cost for all domestic trunk airlines increased by 2.87%.

The objective function in the Fuel Management and Allocation Model consists of fuel costs and increases in operating costs from tankering. The constraints in the model address availability, minimum reserves, and aircraft capacities.

A particularly useful feature of the Fuel Management and Allocation Model is a series of reports that assist management in modifying the fuel-loading plan when sudden changes occur in availability or price. Shadow prices, along with the associated range of applicability, provide information about supply changes. Information about changes in price per gallon comes from the allowable increase and decrease for objective function coefficients.

For example, the availability report might indicate that the optimal quantity to purchase at Los Angeles from Shell West is 2,718,013 gallons; but if its supply decreases and fuel must be purchased from the next most attractive vendor, total cost would increase at the rate of $0.0478 per gallon (the shadow price). This fuel would be replaced by a prior purchase of up to 159,293 gallons from Shell East at New Orleans, tankered to Los Angeles.

The price report shows, for example, that vendor substitutions should be made if the current price of Shell West at Los Angeles, $0.3074, increases to $0.32583 or decreases to $0.27036. The report also indicates what that substitution should be.

Source: Darnell, D. Wayne and Carolyn Loflin, "National Airlines Fuel Management and Allocation Model," *Interfaces*, vol. 7, no. 2, February 1977, pp 1–16.

Questions and Problems

1. Howie Jones used the following information to calculate the profit coefficients for Aqua-Spas and Hydro-Luxes: pumps cost $225 each, labor costs $12 per hour, tubing costs $2 per foot. In addition to pumps, labor, and tubing, the production of Aqua-Spas and Hydro-Luxes consumes, respectively, $243 and $246 per unit in other resources that are not in short supply. Using this information, Howie calculated the marginal profits on Aqua-Spas and Hydro-Luxes as:

	Aqua-Spas	Hydro-Luxes
Selling Price	$950	$875
Pump Cost	−$225	−$225
Labor Cost	−$108	−$72
Tubing Cost	−$24	−$32
Other Variable Costs	−$243	−$246
Marginal Profit	$350	$300

   Howie's accountant reviewed these calculations and thinks Howie made a mistake. For accounting purposes, factory overhead is assigned to products at a rate of $16 per labor hour. Howie's accountant argues that because Aqua-Spas require nine labor hours, the profit margin on this product should be $144 less. Similarly, because Hydro-Luxes require six labor hours, the profit margin on this product should be $96 less. Who is right and why?

2. A variable that assumes an optimal value between its lower and upper bounds has a reduced cost value of zero. Why must this be true? (*Hint:* What if such a variable's reduced cost value is not zero? What does this imply about the value of the objective function?)

3. Implement the following LP problem in a spreadsheet. Use Solver to solve the problem and create a Sensitivity Report. Use this information to answer the following questions:

$$\text{MAX:} \quad 4X_1 + 2X_2$$
$$\text{Subject to:} \quad 2X_1 + 4X_2 \leq 20$$
$$3X_1 + 5X_2 \leq 15$$
$$X_1, X_2 \geq 0$$

   a. What range of values can the objective function coefficient for variable X_1 assume without changing the optimal solution?

   b. Is the optimal solution to this problem unique, or are there alternate optimal solutions?

   c. How much does the objective function coefficient for variable X_2 have to increase before it enters the optimal solution at a strictly positive level?

   d. What is the optimal objective function value if X_2 equals 1?

   e. What is the optimal objective function value if the RHS value for the second constraint changes from 15 to 25?

   f. Is the current solution still optimal if the coefficient for X_2 in the second constraint changes from 5 to 1? Explain.

4. Implement the following LP model in a spreadsheet. Use Solver to solve the problem and create a Sensitivity Report. Use this information to answer the following questions:

$$\text{MAX:} \qquad 2X_1 + 4X_2$$
$$\text{Subject to:} \quad -X_1 + 2X_2 \leq \; 8$$
$$X_1 + 2X_2 \leq 12$$
$$X_1 + \; X_2 \geq \; 2$$
$$X_1, X_2 \geq \; 0$$

a. Which of the constraints are binding at the optimal solution?
b. Is the optimal solution to this problem unique, or is there an alternate optimal solution?
c. What is the optimal solution to this problem if the value of the objective function coefficient for variable X_1 is zero?
d. How much can the objective function coefficient for variable X_2 decrease before changing the optimal solution?
e. Given the objective in this problem, if management could increase the RHS value for any of the constraints for identical costs, which would you choose to increase and why?

5. Implement the following LP model in a spreadsheet. Use Solver to solve the problem and create a Sensitivity Report. Use this information to answer the following questions:

$$\text{MIN:} \qquad 5X_1 + 3X_2 + 4X_3$$
$$\text{Subject to:} \quad X_1 + \; X_2 + 2X_3 \geq 2$$
$$5X_1 + 3X_2 + 2X_3 \geq 1$$
$$X_1, X_2, X_3 \geq 0$$

a. What is the smallest value the objective function coefficient for X_3 can assume without changing the optimal solution?
b. What is the optimal objective function value if the objective function coefficient for X_3 changes to –1? (*Hint:* The answer to this question is not given in the Sensitivity Report. Consider what the new objective function is relative to the constraints.)
c. What is the optimal objective function value if the RHS value of the first constraint increases to 7?
d. What is the optimal objective function value if the RHS value of the first constraint decreases by 1?
e. Will the current solution remain optimal if the objective function coefficients for X_1 and X_3 both decrease by 1?

6. The CitruSun Corporation ships frozen orange juice concentrate from processing plants in Eustis and Clermont to distributors in Miami, Orlando, and Tallahassee. Each plant can produce 20 tons of concentrate each week. The company has just received orders of 10 tons from Miami for the coming week, 15 tons for Orlando, and 10 tons for Tallahassee. The cost per ton for supplying each of the distributors from each of the processing plants is shown in the following table.

	Miami	Orlando	Tallahassee
Eustis	$260	$220	$290
Clermont	$230	$240	$310

The company wants to determine the least costly plan for filling their orders for the coming week.
a. Formulate an LP model for this problem.
b. Implement the model in a spreadsheet and solve it.

   c. What is the optimal solution?

   d. Is the optimal solution degenerate?

   e. Is the optimal solution unique? If not, identify an alternate optimal solution for the problem.

   f. How would the solution change if the plant in Clermont is forced to shut for one day resulting in a loss of four tons of production capacity?

   g. What would the optimal objective function value be if the processing capacity in Eustis was reduced by five tons?

   h. Interpret the reduced cost for shipping from Eustis to Miami.

7. Use Solver to create Answer and Sensitivity Reports for question 15 at the end of Chapter 2 and answer the following questions:

   a. How much excess wiring and testing capacity exists in the optimal solution?

   b. What is the company's total profit if it has 10 additional hours of wiring capacity?

   c. By how much does the profit on alternators need to increase before their production is justified?

   d. Does the optimal solution change if the marginal profit on generators decreases by $50 and the marginal profit on alternators increases by $75?

   e. Suppose the marginal profit on generators decreases by $25. What is the maximum profit that can be earned on alternators without changing the optimal solution?

   f. Suppose the amount of wiring required on alternators is reduced to 1.5 hours. Does this change the optimal solution? Why or why not?

8. Use Solver to create Answer and Sensitivity Reports for question 18 at the end of Chapter 2 and answer the following questions:

   a. If the profit on Razors decreased to $35 would the optimal solution change?

   b. If the profit on Zoomers decreased to $35 would the optimal solution change?

   c. Interpret the shadow price for the supply of polymer.

   d. Why is the shadow price $0 for the constraint limiting the production of pocket bikes to no more than 700 units?

   e. Suppose the company could obtain 300 additional labor hours in production. What would the new optimal level of profit be?

9. Use Solver to create Answer and Sensitivity Reports for question 20 at the end of Chapter 2 and answer the following questions:

   a. How much can the price of watermelons drop before it is no longer optimal to plant any watermelons?

   b. How much does the price of cantaloupes have to increase before it is optimal to grow only cantaloupes?

   c. Suppose the price of watermelons drops by $60 per acre and the price of cantaloupes increases by $50 per acre. Is the current solution still optimal?

   d. Suppose the farmer can lease up to 20 acres of land from a neighboring farm to plant additional crops. How many acres should the farmer lease and what is the maximum amount he should pay to lease each acre?

10. Use Solver to create Answer and Sensitivity Reports for question 21 at the end of Chapter 2 and answer the following questions:

   a. If the profit on doors increased to $700 would the optimal solution change?

   b. If the profit on windows decreased to $200 would the optimal solution change?

   c. Explain the shadow price for the finishing process.

   d. If 20 additional hours of cutting capacity became available how much additional profit could the company earn?

    e. Suppose another company wanted to use 15 hours of Sanderson's sanding capacity and was willing to pay $400 per hour to acquire it? Should Sanderson agree to this? How (if at all) would your answer change if the company instead wanted 25 hours of sanding capacity?

11. Create a Sensitivity Report for Electro-Poly's make vs. buy problem in section 3.8 of Chapter 3 and answer the following questions.

    a. Is the solution degenerate?

    b. How much can the cost of making model 1 slip rings increase before it becomes more economical to buy some of them?

    c. Suppose the cost of buying model 2 slip rings decreased by $9 per unit. Would the optimal solution change?

    d. Assume workers in the wiring area normally make $12 per hour and get 50% more when they work overtime. Should Electro-Poly schedule these employees to work overtime to complete this job? If so, how much money would this save?

    e. Assume workers in the harnessing area normally make $12 per hour and get 50% more when they work overtime. Should Electro-Poly schedule these employees to work overtime to complete this job? If so, how much money would this save?

    f. Create a Spider plot that shows the effect of varying each of the wiring and harnessing requirements (in cells B17 thru D18) to 90% of their current levels in 1% increments. If Electro-Poly wanted to invest in training or new technology to reduce one of these values, which one offers the greatest potential for cost savings?

12. Use Solver to create a Sensitivity Report for question 12 at the end of Chapter 3 and answer the following questions:

    a. If the company could get 50 more units of routing capacity, should they do it? If so, how much should they be willing to pay for it?

    b. If the company could get 50 more units of sanding capacity, should they do it? If so, how much should they be willing to pay for it?

    c. Suppose the polishing time on country tables could be reduced from 2.5 to 2 units per table. How much should the company be willing to pay to achieve this improvement in efficiency?

    d. Contemporary tables sell for $450. By how much would the selling price have to decrease before we would no longer be willing to produce contemporary tables? Does this make sense? Explain.

13. Use Solver to create a Sensitivity Report for question 18 at the end of Chapter 3 and answer the following questions:

    a. Which of the constraints in the problem are binding?

    b. If the company was going to eliminate one of its products, which should it be?

    c. If the company could buy 1,000 additional memory chips at the usual cost, should they do it? If so, how much would profits increase?

    d. Suppose the manufacturing costs used in this analysis were estimated hastily and are known to be somewhat imprecise. For which products would you want more precise cost estimates before implementing this solution?

    e. Create a Spider Plot showing the sensitivity of the total profit to the selling price of each product (adjusting the original values by 90%, 92%, . . ., 110%). According to this graph, total profit is most sensitive to which product?

14. Use Solver to create a Sensitivity Report for question 20 at the end of Chapter 3 and answer the following questions:

    a. How much would electric trimmers have to cost for the company to consider purchasing these items rather than making them?

b. If the cost to make gas trimmers increased to $90 per unit, how would the optimal solution change?

c. How much should the company be willing to pay to acquire additional capacity in the assembly area? Explain.

d. How much should the company be willing to pay to acquire additional capacity in the production area? Explain.

e. Prepare a Spider Plot showing the sensitivity of the total cost to changes in costs to make and the costs to buy (adjusting the original values by of 90%, 92%, . . ., 110%). Which of these costs is the total cost most sensitive to?

f. Suppose the hours of production capacity available is uncertain and could vary from 9,500 to 10,500. How does the optimal solution change for every 100-hour change in production capacity within this range?

15. Use Solver to create a Sensitivity Report for question 22 at the end of Chapter 3 and answer the following questions.

a. Suppose the cost of the first two compounds increases by $1.00 per pound and the cost of the third compound increases by $0.50 per pound. Does the optimal solution change?

b. How does the solution change if the maximum amount of potassium allowed decreases from 45% to 40%?

c. How much does the cost of the mix increase if the specifications for CHEMIX change to require at least 31% sulfur? (*Hint:* Remember that the shadow price indicates the impact on the objective function if the RHS value of the associated constraint increases by 1.)

16. Use Solver to create a Sensitivity Report for question 23 at the end of Chapter 3 and answer the following questions.

a. What is the maximum level profit that can be achieved for this problem?

b. Are there alternate optimal solutions to this problem? If so, identify the solution that allows the most grade 5 oranges to be used in fruit baskets while still achieving the maximum profit identified in part a.

c. If Holiday could acquire 1,000 more pounds of grade 4 oranges at a cost of $2.65 per 100 pounds, should they do it? Why?

d. Create a Spider Table and Plot showing the change in the total profit obtained by changing the required grade of fruit baskets and juice from 90% to 110% in 1% increments. If the department of agriculture wants to increase the required rating of one of these products, which product should the company lobby for?

17. Use Solver to create a Sensitivity Report for question 24 at the end of Chapter 3 and answer the following questions:

a. Are there alternate optimal solutions to this problem? Explain.

b. What is the highest possible octane rating for regular gasoline, assuming the company wants to maximize its profits? What is the octane rating for supreme gasoline at this solution?

c. What is the highest possible octane rating for supreme gasoline, assuming the company wants to maximize its profits? What is the octane rating for regular gasoline at this solution?

d. Which of the two profit-maximizing solutions identified in parts b and c would you recommend that the company implement? Why?

e. If the company could buy another 150 barrels of input 2 at a cost of $17 per barrel, should they do it? Why?

18. Use Solver to create a Sensitivity Report for question 28 at the end of Chapter 3 and answer the following questions:

a. What total profit level is realized if 100 extra hours of labor are available?

b. Assume a marginal labor cost of $11 per hour in determining the unit profits of each of the three products. How much should management pay to acquire 100 additional labor hours?

c. Interpret the reduced cost value for tuners. Why are more tuners not being produced?

19. Use Solver to create a Sensitivity Report for question 29 at the end of Chapter 3 and answer the following questions:

a. Is the optimal solution unique? How can you tell?

b. Which location is receiving the fewest cars?

c. Suppose a particular car at location 1 must be sent to location 3 to meet a customer's request. How much does this increase costs for the company?

d. Suppose location 6 must have at least eight cars shipped to it. What impact does this have on the optimal objective function value?

20. Refer to the previous question. Suppose location 1 has 15 cars available rather than 16. Create a Sensitivity Report for this problem and answer the following questions:

a. Is the optimal solution unique? How can you tell?

b. According to the Sensitivity Report, by how much should the total cost increase if we force a car to be shipped from location 1 to location 3?

c. Add a constraint to the model to force one car to be shipped from location 1 to location 3. By how much did the total cost increase?

21. Use Solver to create a Sensitivity Report for question 30 at the end of chapter 3 and answer the following questions:

a. Is the solution unique?

b. If Sentry wants to increase their production capacity to meet more of the demand for their product, which plant should they use? Explain.

c. If the cost of shipping from Phoenix to Tacoma increased to $1.98 per unit, would the solution change? Explain.

d. Could the company make more money if they relaxed the restriction that each distributor must receive at least 80% of the predicted demand? Explain.

e. How much extra should the company charge the distributor in Tacoma if this distributor insisted on receiving 8,500 units?

22. Use Solver to create a Sensitivity Report for question 31 at the end of Chapter 3 and answer the following questions.

a. Is the solution degenerate?

b. Is the solution unique?

c. How much should the recycler be willing to pay to acquire more cardboard?

d. If the recycler could buy 50 more tons of newspaper at a cost of $18 per ton, should they do it? Why or why not?

e. What is the recycler's marginal cost of producing each of the three different types of pulp?

f. By how much would the cost of converting white office paper into newsprint have to drop before it would become economical to use white office paper for this purpose?

g. By how much would the yield of newsprint pulp per ton of cardboard have to increase before it would become economical to use cardboard for this purpose?

23. Use Solver to create a Sensitivity Report for question 35 at the end of Chapter 3 and answer the following questions.

a. Is the solution degenerate?

b. Is the solution unique?

c. How much can the profit per ton on commodity 1 decrease before the optimal solution would change?

d. Create a Spider Table and Plot showing the change in the total profit obtained by changing the profit per ton on each commodity from 95% to 105% in 1% increments. If the shipping company wanted to increase the price of transporting one of the commodities, which one would have the greatest influence on total profits?

24. Use Solver to create a Sensitivity Report for question 36 at the end of Chapter 3 and answer the following questions.
   a. Is the solution degenerate?
   b. Is the solution unique?
   c. Use a Solver Table to determine the maximum price the Pelletier Corporation should be willing to pay for a two-month lease.
   d. Suppose the company is not certain that it will need exactly 20,000 sq.ft. in month 3 and believes that the actual amount needed may be as low as 15,000 sq.ft. or as high as 25,000 sq. ft. Use a Solver Table to determine if this would have any effect on the leasing arrangements the company selects in months 1 and 2.

25. Refer to question 45 in Chapter 3 and create a Solver table to answer the following questions.
   a. Suppose the gas producer needs an extra 50,000 cf of storage capacity for the next 10 days and wants to buy this capacity from the gas trading firm. What is the least amount of money the gas trading company should demand to provide this capacity?
   b. How much should the gas trading company be willing to pay to increase their available storage capacity by 500,000 cf?

26. Consider the following LP problem:

$$\text{MAX:} \qquad 4X_1 + 2X_2$$
$$\text{Subject to:} \qquad 2X_1 + 4X_2 \leq 20$$
$$3X_1 + 5X_2 \leq 15$$
$$X_1, X_2 \geq 0$$

   a. Use slack variables to rewrite this problem so that all its constraints are "equal to" constraints.
   b. Identify the different sets of basic variables that might be used to obtain a solution to the problem.
   c. Of the possible sets of basic variables, which lead to feasible solutions and what are the values for all the variables at each of these solutions?
   d. Graph the feasible region for this problem and indicate which basic feasible solution corresponds to each of the extreme points of the feasible region.
   e. What is the value of the objective function at each of the basic feasible solutions?
   f. What is the optimal solution to the problem?
   g. Which constraints are binding at the optimal solution?

27. Consider the following LP problem:

$$\text{MAX:} \qquad 2X_1 + 4X_2$$
$$\text{Subject to:} \qquad -X_1 + 2X_2 \leq 8$$
$$X_1 + 2X_2 \leq 12$$
$$X_1 + X_2 \geq 2$$
$$X_1, X_2 \geq 0$$

   a. Use slack variables to rewrite this problem so that all its constraints are "equal to" constraints.
   b. Identify the different sets of basic variables that might be used to obtain a solution to the problem.

c. Of the possible sets of basic variables, which lead to feasible solutions and what are the values for all the variables at each of these solutions?

d. Graph the feasible region for this problem and indicate which basic feasible solution corresponds to each of the extreme points of the feasible region.

e. What is the value of the objective function at each of the basic feasible solutions?

f. What is the optimal solution to the problem?

g. Which constraints are binding at the optimal solution?

28. Consider the following LP problem:

$$\text{MIN:} \quad 5X_1 + 3X_2 + 4X_3$$
$$\text{Subject to:} \quad X_1 + X_2 + 2X_3 \geq 2$$
$$5X_1 + 3X_2 + 2X_3 \geq 1$$
$$X_1, X_2, X_3 \geq 0$$

a. Use slack variables to rewrite this problem so that all its constraints are "equal to" constraints.

b. Identify the different sets of basic variables that might be used to obtain a solution to the problem.

c. Of the possible sets of basic variables, which lead to feasible solutions and what are the values for all the variables at each of these solutions?

d. What is the value of the objective function at each of the basic feasible solutions?

e. What is the optimal solution to the problem?

f. Which constraints are binding at the optimal solution?

29. Consider the following constraint, where S is a slack variable:

$$2X_1 + 4X_2 + S = 16$$

a. What was the original constraint before the slack variable was included?

b. What value of S is associated with each of the following points:

i) $X_1 = 2, X_2 = 2$

ii) $X_1 = 8, X_2 = 0$

iii) $X_1 = 1, X_2 = 3$

iv) $X_1 = 4, X_2 = 1$

30. Consider the following constraint, where S is a slack variable:

$$3X_1 + 4X_2 - S = 12$$

a. What was the original constraint before the slack variable was included?

b. What value of S is associated with each of the following points:

i) $X_1 = 5, X_2 = 0$

ii) $X_1 = 2, X_2 = 2$

iii) $X_1 = 7, X_2 = 1$

iv) $X_1 = 4, X_2 = 0$

A Nut Case

The Molokai Nut Company (MNC) makes four different products from macadamia nuts grown in the Hawaiian Islands: chocolate-coated whole nuts (Whole), chocolate-coated nut clusters (Cluster), chocolate-coated nut crunch bars (Crunch), and plain roasted nuts (Roasted). The company is barely able to keep up with the increasing demand for these products. However, increasing raw material prices and foreign competition are forcing MNC to watch its margins to ensure it is operating in the most efficient manner possible. To meet marketing demands for the coming week, MNC needs to produce at least 1,000 pounds of the Whole product, between 400 and 500 pounds of the Cluster product, no more than 150 pounds of the Crunch product, and no more than 200 pounds of Roasted product.

Each pound of the Whole, Cluster, Crunch, and Roasted product contains, respectively, 60%, 40%, 20%, and 100% macadamia nuts with the remaining weight made up of chocolate coating. The company has 1100 pounds of nuts and 800 pounds of chocolate available for use in the next week. The various products are made using four different machines that hull the nuts, roast the nuts, coat the nuts in chocolate (if needed), and package the products. The following table summarizes the time required by each product on each machine. Each machine has 60 hours of time available in the coming week.

| | Minutes Required per Pound | | | |
Machine	Whole	Cluster	Crunch	Roasted
Hulling	1.00	1.00	1.00	1.00
Roasting	2.00	1.50	1.00	1.75
Coating	1.00	0.70	0.20	0.00
Packaging	2.50	1.60	1.25	1.00

The controller recently presented management with the following financial summary of MNC's average weekly operations over the past quarter. From this report, the controller is arguing that the company should cease producing its Cluster and Crunch products.

| | Product | | | | |
	Whole	Cluster	Crunch	Roasted	Total
Sales Revenue	$5,304	$1,800	$510	$925	$8,539
Variable Costs					
Direct materials	$1,331	$560	$144	$320	$2,355
Direct labor	$1,092	$400	$96	$130	$1,718
Manufacturing overhead	$333	$140	$36	$90	$599
Selling & Administrative	$540	$180	$62	$120	$902
Allocated Fixed Costs					
Manufacturing overhead	$688	$331	$99	$132	$1,250
Selling & Administrative	$578	$278	$83	$111	$1,050
Net Profit	$742	−$88	−$11	$22	$665
Units Sold	1040	500	150	200	1890
Net Profit Per Unit	$0.71	−$0.18	−$0.07	$0.11	$0.35

a. Do you agree with the controller's recommendation? Why or why not?
b. Formulate an LP model for this problem.
c. Create a spreadsheet model for this problem and solve it using Solver.
d. What is the optimal solution?
e. Create a sensitivity report for this solution and answer the following questions.
f. Is the solution degenerate?
g. Is the solution unique?

h. If MNC wanted to decrease the production on any product, which one would you recommend and why?

i. If MNC wanted to increase the production of any product, which one would you recommend and why?

j. Which resources are preventing MNS from making more money? If they could acquire more of this resource how much should they acquire & how much should they be willing to pay to acquire it?

k. How much should MNC be willing to pay to acquire more chocolate?

l. If the marketing department wanted to decrease the price of the Whole product by $0.25, would the optimal solution change?

m. Create a Spider plot showing the impact on net profit of changing each product's required time in the roasting process from between 70% to 130% of their original values in 5% increments. Interpret the information in the resulting chart.

n. Create a Spider plot showing the impact on net profit of changing the availability of nuts and chocolate from between 70% to 100% of their original values in 5% increments. Interpret the information in the resulting chart.

Parket Sisters

CASE 4.2

(Contributed by Jack Yurkiewicz, Lubin School of Business, Pace University, New York.)

Computers and word processors notwithstanding, the art of writing by hand recently entered a boom era. People are buying fountain pens again, and mechanical pencils are becoming more popular than ever. Joe Script, the president and CEO of Parket Sisters, a small but growing pen and pencil manufacturer, wants to establish a better foothold in the market. The writing market is divided into two main sectors. One, dominated by Mont Blanc, Cross, Parker Brothers, Waterman, Schaffer, and a few others, caters to people who want writing instruments. The product lines from these companies consist of pens and pencils of elaborate design, lifetime warranty, and high price. At the other end of the market are manufacturers like BIC, Pentel, and many companies from the far east, offering good quality items, low price, few trims, and limited diversity. These pens and pencils are meant to be used for a limited time and disposed of when the ink in a ballpoint pen runs out, or when the lead in a mechanical pencil won't retract or extend. In short, these items are not meant for repair.

Joe thinks that there must be a middle ground, and that is where he wants to position his company. Parket Sisters makes high-quality items, with limited trim and diversity, but also offers lifetime warranties. Furthermore, its pens and pencils are ergonomically efficient. Joe knows that some people want the status of the Mont Blanc Meisterstuck pen, for example, but he has never met a person who said that writing with such a pen is enjoyable. The pen is too large and clumsy for smooth writing. Parket Sisters' products, on the other hand, have a reputation for working well, are easy to hold and use, and cause limited "writer's fatigue."

Parket Sisters makes only three items—a ballpoint pen, a mechanical pencil, and a fountain pen. All are available in just one color, black, and are sold mostly in specialty stores and from better catalog companies. The per-unit profit of the items is $3.00 for the ballpoint pen, $3.00 for the mechanical pencil, and $5.00 for the fountain pen. These values take into account labor, the cost of materials, packing, quality control, and so on.

The company is trying to plan its production mix for each week. Joe believes that the company can sell any number of pens and pencils it produces, but production is currently limited by the available resources. Because of a recent strike and certain cash-flow problems, the suppliers of these resources are selling them to Parket Sisters in limited amounts. In particular, Joe can count on getting at most 1,000 ounces of plastic, 1,200 ounces of chrome, and 2,000 ounces of stainless steel each week from his suppliers, and these figures are not likely to change in the near future. Because of Joe's excellent reputation, the suppliers will sell Joe any amount (up to his limit) of the resources he needs when he requires them. That is, the suppliers do not require Joe to buy some fixed quantities of resources in advance of his production of pens and pencils; therefore, these resources can be considered variable costs rather than fixed costs for the pens and pencils.

Each ballpoint pen requires 1.2 ounces of plastic, 0.8 ounces of chrome, and 2 ounces of stainless steel. Each mechanical pencil requires 1.7 ounces of plastic, no chrome, and 3 ounces of stainless steel. Each fountain pen requires 1.2 ounces of plastic, 2.3 ounces of chrome, and 4.5 ounces of stainless steel. Joe believes LP could help him decide what his weekly product mix should consist of.

Getting his notes and notebooks, Joe grapples with the LP formulation. In addition to the constraints of the available resources, he recognizes that the model should include many other constraints (such as labor time availability and materials for packing). However, Joe wants to keep his model simple. He knows that eventually he'll have to take other constraints into account, but as a first-pass model, he'll restrict the constraints to just the three resources: plastic, chrome, and stainless steel.

With only these three constraints, Joe can formulate the problem easily as:

$$
\begin{aligned}
\text{MAX:} \qquad & 3.0X_1 + 3.0X_2 + 5.0X_3 \\
\text{Subject to:} \qquad & 1.2X_1 + 1.7X_2 + 1.2X_3 \leq 1{,}000 \\
& 0.8X_1 + 0X_2 + 2.3X_3 \leq 1{,}200 \\
& 2.0X_1 + 3.0X_2 + 4.5X_3 \leq 2{,}000 \\
& X_1, X_2, X_3 \geq 0
\end{aligned}
$$

where:

$$
\begin{aligned}
X_1 &= \text{the number of ballpoint pens} \\
X_2 &= \text{the number of mechanical pencils} \\
X_3 &= \text{the number of fountain pens}
\end{aligned}
$$

Joe's knowledge of Excel and the Solver feature is limited, so he asks you to enter and solve the problem for him, then answer the following questions. (Assume that each question is independent unless otherwise stated.)

a. What should the weekly product mix consist of, and what is the weekly net profit?
b. Is the optimal solution to question 1 degenerate? Explain your response.
c. Is the optimal solution from question 1 unique, or are there alternate answers to this question? Explain your response.
d. What is the marginal value of one more unit of chrome? Of plastic?
e. A local distributor has offered to sell Parket Sisters an additional 500 ounces of stainless steel for $0.60 per ounce more than it ordinarily pays. Should the company buy the steel at this price? Explain your response.
f. If Parket Sisters buys the additional 500 ounces of stainless steel noted in question 5, what is the new optimal product mix and what is the new optimal profit? Explain your response.
g. Suppose that the distributor offers to sell Parket Sisters some additional plastic at a price of only $1.00 over its usual cost of $5.00 per ounce. However, the distributor

will sell the plastic only in lot sizes of 500 ounces. Should Parket Sisters buy one such lot? Explain your response.

h. The distributor is willing to sell the plastic in lots of just 100 ounces instead of the usual 500-ounce lots, still at $1.00 over Parket Sisters' cost of $5.00 per ounce. How many lots (if any) should Parket Sisters buy? What is the optimal product mix if the company buys these lots, and what is the optimal profit?

i. Parket Sisters has an opportunity to sell some of its plastic for $6.50 per ounce to another company. The other company (which does not produce pens and pencils and, therefore, is not a competitor) wants to buy 300 ounces of plastic from Parket Sisters. Should Parket Sisters sell the plastic to the other company? What happens to Parket Sisters' product mix and overall profit if it does sell the plastic? Be as specific as possible.

j. The chrome supplier might have to fulfill an emergency order, and would be able to send only 1,000 ounces of chrome this week instead of the usual 1,200 ounces. If Parket Sisters receives only 1,000 ounces of chrome, what is the optimal product mix and optimal profit? Be as specific as possible.

k. The R&D department at Parket Sisters has been redesigning the mechanical pencil to make it more profitable. The new design requires 1.1 ounces of plastic, 2.0 ounces of chrome, and 2.0 ounces of stainless steel. If the company can sell one of these pencils at a net profit of $3.00, should it approve the new design? Explain your response.

l. If the per-unit profit on ballpoint pens decreases to $2.50, what is the optimal product mix and what is the company's total profit?

m. The marketing department suggested introducing a new felt tip pen that requires 1.8 ounces of plastic, 0.5 ounces of chrome, and 1.3 ounces of stainless steel. What profit must this product generate to make it worthwhile to produce?

n. What must the minimum per-unit profit of mechanical pencils be to make them worthwhile to produce?

o. Management believes that the company should produce at least 20 mechanical pencils per week to round out its product line. What effect would this have on overall profit? Give a numerical answer.

p. If the profit on a fountain pen is $6.75 instead of $5.00, what is the optimal product mix and optimal profit?

Kamm Industries

If your home or office is carpeted, there's a good chance that carpet came from Dalton, Georgia—also known as the "Carpet Capital of the World." Manufacturers in the Dalton area produce more than 70 percent of the total output of the $9 billion world-wide carpet industry. Competition in this industry is intense, which forces producers to strive for maximum efficiency and economies of scale. It also forces producers to continually evaluate investments in new technology.

Kamm Industries is one of the leading carpet producers in the Dalton area. Its owner, Geoff Kamm, has asked for your assistance in planning the production schedule for the next quarter (13 weeks). The company has orders for 15 different types of carpets that the company can produce on either of two types of looms: Dobbie looms and Pantera looms. Pantera looms produce standard tufted carpeting. Dobbie looms also can produce standard tufted carpeting, but they also allow the incorporation of designs (such as flowers or corporate logos) into the carpeting. The following table summarizes the orders for each type of carpet that must be produced in the coming quarter along with their production rates and costs on each type of loom, and the cost of subcontracting each order. Note that the first 4 orders involve special production requirements that can be achieved only on a Dobbie loom or via subcontracting. Assume that any portion of an order may be subcontracted.

| | Demand | Dobbie | | Pantera | | Subcontract |
Carpet	Yds	Yd/Hr	Cost/Yd	Yd/Hr	Cost/Yd	Cost/Yd
1	14,000	4.510	$2.66	na	na	$2.77
2	52,000	4.796	2.55	na	na	2.73
3	44,000	4.629	2.64	na	na	2.85
4	20,000	4.256	2.56	na	na	2.73
5	77,500	5.145	1.61	5.428	$1.60	1.76
6	109,500	3.806	1.62	3.935	1.61	1.76
7	120,000	4.168	1.64	4.316	1.61	1.76
8	60,000	5.251	1.48	5.356	1.47	1.59
9	7,500	5.223	1.50	5.277	1.50	1.71
10	69,500	5.216	1.44	5.419	1.42	1.63
11	68,500	3.744	1.64	3.835	1.64	1.80
12	83,000	4.157	1.57	4.291	1.56	1.78
13	10,000	4.422	1.49	4.558	1.48	1.63
14	381,000	5.281	1.31	5.353	1.30	1.44
15	64,000	4.222	1.51	4.288	1.50	1.69

Kamm currently owns and operates 15 Dobbie looms and 80 Pantera looms. To maximize efficiency and keep pace with demand, the company operates 24 hours a day, 7 days a week. Each machine is down for routine maintenance for approximately 2 hours per week. Create a spreadsheet model for this problem that can be used to determine the optimal production plan and answer the following questions.

a. What is the optimal production plan and associated cost?
b. Is the solution degenerate?
c. Is the solution unique?
d. What would happen to the total cost if one of the Dobbie machines broke and could not be used at all during the quarter?
e. What would happen to the total cost if an additional Dobbie machine was purchased and available for the quarter?
f. What would happen to the total cost if one of the Pantera machines broke and could not be used at all during the quarter?
g. What would happen to the total cost if an additional Pantera machine was purchased and available for the quarter?
h. Explain the shadow prices and the values in the "Allowable Increase" column of the Sensitivity Report for the products that are being outsourced.
i. How much money does it cost to produce carpet order 2? How much would the total cost decrease if that order were eliminated? Explain.
j. If the carpets in orders 5 through 15 all sell for the same amount, which type of carpet should Kamm encourage its sales force to sell more of? Why?
k. If the cost of buying the carpet in order 1 increased to $2.80 per yard, would the optimal solution change? Why?
l. If the cost of buying the carpet in order 15 decreased to $1.65 per yard, would the optimal solution change? Why?

Chapter 5

Network Modeling

5.0 Introduction

A number of practical decision problems in business fall into a category known as network flow problems. These problems share a common characteristic—they can be described or displayed in a graphical form known as a network. This chapter focuses on several types of network flow problems: transshipment problems, shortest path problems, maximal flow problems, transportation/assignment problems, and generalized network flow problems. Although specialized solution procedures exist for solving network flow problems, we will consider how to formulate and solve these problems as LP problems. We will also consider a different type of network problem known as the minimum spanning tree problem.

5.1 The Transshipment Problem

Let's begin our study of network flow problems by considering the transshipment problem. As you will see, most of the other types of network flow problems all can be viewed as simple variations of the transshipment problem. So, once you understand how to formulate and solve transshipment problems, the other types of problems will be easy to solve. The following example illustrates the transshipment problem.

> The Bavarian Motor Company (BMC) manufactures expensive luxury cars in Hamburg, Germany, and exports cars to sell in the United States. The exported cars are shipped from Hamburg to ports in Newark, New Jersey, and Jacksonville, Florida. From these ports, the cars are transported by rail or truck to distributors located in Boston, Massachusetts; Columbus, Ohio; Atlanta, Georgia; Richmond, Virginia; and Mobile, Alabama. Figure 5.1 shows the possible shipping routes available to the company along with the transportation cost for shipping each car along the indicated path.
>
> Currently, 200 cars are available at the port in Newark and 300 are available in Jacksonville. The numbers of cars needed by the distributors in Boston, Columbus, Atlanta, Richmond, and Mobile are 100, 60, 170, 80, and 70, respectively. BMC wants to determine the least costly way of transporting cars from the ports in Newark and Jacksonville to the cities where they are needed.

5.1.1 CHARACTERISTICS OF NETWORK FLOW PROBLEMS

Figure 5.1 illustrates a number of characteristics common to all network flow problems. All network flow problems can be represented as a collection of nodes connected by

FIGURE 5.1

Network representation of the BMC transshipment problem

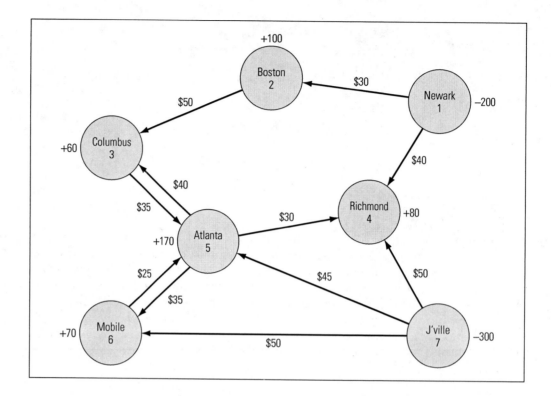

arcs. The circles in Figure 5.1 are called nodes in the terminology of network flow problems, and the lines connecting the nodes are called arcs. The arcs in a network indicate the valid paths, routes, or connections between the nodes in a network flow problem. When the lines connecting the nodes in a network are arrows that indicate a direction, the arcs in the network are called directed arcs. This chapter discusses directed arcs primarily but, for convenience, refers to them as arcs.

The notion of supply nodes (or sending nodes) and demand nodes (or receiving nodes) is another common element of network flow problems illustrated in Figure 5.1. The nodes representing the port cities of Newark and Jacksonville are both supply nodes because each has a supply of cars to send to other nodes in the network. Richmond represents a demand node because it demands to receive cars from the other nodes. All the other nodes in this network are transshipment nodes. Transshipment nodes can both send to and receive from other nodes in the network. For example, the node representing Atlanta in Figure 5.1 is a transshipment node because it can *receive* cars from Jacksonville, Mobile, and Columbus, and it also can send cars to Columbus, Mobile, and Richmond.

The net supply or demand for each node in the network is indicated by a positive or negative number next to each node. Positive numbers represent the *demand* at a given node, and negative numbers represent the *supply* available at a node. For example, the value +80 next to the node for Richmond indicates that the number of cars needs to increase by 80 — or that Richmond has a *demand* for 80 cars. The value −200 next to the node for Newark indicates that the number of cars can be reduced by 200 — or that Newark has a *supply* of 200 cars. A transshipment node can have either a net supply or demand, but not both. In this particular problem, all the transshipment nodes have demands. For example, the node representing Mobile in Figure 5.1 has a demand for 70 cars.

5.1.2 THE DECISION VARIABLES FOR NETWORK FLOW PROBLEMS

The goal in a network flow model is to determine how many items should be moved (or flow) across each of the arcs. In our example, BMC needs to determine the least costly method of transporting cars along the various arcs shown in Figure 5.1 to distribute cars where they are needed. Thus, each of the arcs in a network flow model represents a decision variable. Determining the optimal flow for each arc is the equivalent of determining the optimal value for the corresponding decision variable.

It is customary to use numbers to identify each node in a network flow problem. In Figure 5.1, the number 1 identifies the node for Newark, 2 identifies the node for Boston, and so on. You can assign numbers to the nodes in any manner, but it is best to use a series of consecutive integers. The node numbers provide a convenient way to identify the decision variables needed to formulate the LP model for the problem. For each arc in a network flow model, you need to define one decision variable as:

X_{ij} = the number of items shipped (or flowing) *from* node i *to* node j

The network in Figure 5.1 for our example problem contains 11 arcs. Therefore, the LP formulation of this model requires the following 11 decision variables:

X_{12} = the number of cars shipped *from* node 1 (Newark) *to* node 2 (Boston)

X_{14} = the number of cars shipped *from* node 1 (Newark) *to* node 4 (Richmond)

X_{23} = the number of cars shipped *from* node 2 (Boston) *to* node 3 (Columbus)

X_{35} = the number of cars shipped *from* node 3 (Columbus) *to* node 5 (Atlanta)

X_{53} = the number of cars shipped *from* node 5 (Atlanta) *to* node 3 (Columbus)

X_{54} = the number of cars shipped *from* node 5 (Atlanta) *to* node 4 (Richmond)

X_{56} = the number of cars shipped *from* node 5 (Atlanta) *to* node 6 (Mobile)

X_{65} = the number of cars shipped *from* node 6 (Mobile) *to* node 5 (Atlanta)

X_{74} = the number of cars shipped *from* node 7 (Jacksonville) *to* node 4 (Richmond)

X_{75} = the number of cars shipped *from* node 7 (Jacksonville) *to* node 5 (Atlanta)

X_{76} = the number of cars shipped *from* node 7 (Jacksonville) *to* node 6 (Mobile)

5.1.3 THE OBJECTIVE FUNCTION FOR NETWORK FLOW PROBLEMS

Each unit that flows from node i to node j in a network flow problem usually incurs some cost, c_{ij}. This cost might represent a monetary payment, a distance, or some other type of penalty. The objective in most network flow problems is to minimize the total cost, distance, or penalty that must be incurred to solve the problem. Such problems are known as *minimum cost network flow problems*.

In our example problem, different monetary costs must be paid for each car shipped across a given arc. For example, it costs \$30 to ship each car from node 1 (Newark) to node 2 (Boston). Because X_{12} represents the number of cars shipped from Newark to Boston, the total cost incurred by cars shipped along this path is determined by \$30X_{12}. Similar calculations can be done for the other arcs in the network. Because BMC is interested in minimizing the total shipping costs, the objective function for this problem is expressed as:

$$\text{MIN:} \quad +30X_{12} + 40X_{14} + 50X_{23} + 35X_{35} + 40X_{53} + 30X_{54}$$
$$+ 35X_{56} + 25X_{65} + 50X_{74} + 45X_{75} + 50X_{76}$$

5.1.4 THE CONSTRAINTS FOR NETWORK FLOW PROBLEMS

Just as the number of arcs in the network determines the number of variables in the LP formulation of a network flow problem, the number of nodes determines the number of constraints. In particular, there must be one constraint for each node. A simple set of rules, known as the *Balance-of-Flow Rules*, applies to constructing the constraints for minimum cost network flow problems. These rules are summarized as follows:

For Minimum Cost Network Flow Problems Where:	Apply This Balance-of-Flow Rule at Each Node:
Total Supply > Total Demand	Inflow − Outflow ≥ Supply or Demand
Total Supply < Total Demand	Inflow − Outflow ≤ Supply or Demand
Total Supply = Total Demand	Inflow − Outflow = Supply or Demand

Note that if the total supply in a network flow problem is less than the total demand, then it will be impossible to satisfy all the demand. The balance-of-flow rule listed for this case assumes that you want to determine the least costly way of distributing the available supply—knowing that it is impossible to satisfy all the demand.

So to apply the correct balance-of-flow rule, we first must compare the total supply in the network to the total demand. In our example problem, there is a total supply of 500 cars and a total demand for 480 cars. Because the total supply exceeds the total demand, we will use the first balance-of-flow rule to formulate our example problem. That is, at each node, we will create a constraint of the form:

$$\text{Inflow} - \text{Outflow} \geq \text{Supply or Demand}$$

For example, consider node 1 (Newark) in Figure 5.1. No arcs flow into this node but two arcs (represented by X_{12} and X_{14}) flow out of the node. According to the balance-of-flow rule, the constraint for this node is:

$$\text{Constraint for node 1:} \qquad -X_{12} - X_{14} \geq -200$$

Notice that the supply at this node is represented by −200 following the convention we established earlier. If we multiply both sides of this equation by −1, we see that it is equivalent to $+X_{12} + X_{14} \leq +200$. (Note that multiplying an inequality by −1 reverses the direction of the inequality.) This constraint indicates that the total number of cars flowing out of Newark must not exceed 200. So, if we include either form of this constraint in the model, we can ensure that no more than 200 cars will be shipped from Newark.

Now consider the constraint for node 2 (Boston) in Figure 5.1. Because Boston has a demand for 100 cars, the balance-of-flow rule requires that the total number of cars coming into Boston from Newark (via X_{12}) minus the total number of cars being shipped out of Boston to Columbus (via X_{23}) must leave at least 100 cars in Boston. This condition is imposed by the constraint:

$$\text{Constraint for node 2:} \qquad +X_{12} - X_{23} \geq +100$$

Note that this constraint makes it possible to leave more than the required number of cars in Boston (e.g., 200 cars could be shipped into Boston and only 50 shipped out, leaving 150 cars in Boston). However, because our objective is to minimize costs, we can be sure that an excess number of cars will never be shipped to any city, because that would result in unnecessary costs being incurred.

Using the balance-of-flow rule, the constraints for each of the remaining nodes in our example problem are represented as:

Constraint for node 3:	$+X_{23} + X_{53} - X_{35} \geq +60$
Constraint for node 4:	$+X_{14} + X_{54} + X_{74} \geq +80$
Constraint for node 5:	$+X_{35} + X_{65} + X_{75} - X_{53} - X_{54} - X_{56} \geq +170$
Constraint for node 6:	$+X_{56} + X_{76} - X_{65} \geq +70$
Constraint for node 7:	$-X_{74} - X_{75} - X_{76} \geq -300$

Again, each constraint indicates that the flow into a given node minus the flow out of that same node must be greater than or equal to the supply or demand at the node. So, if you draw a graph of a network flow problem like the one in Figure 5.1, it is easy to write out the constraints for the problem by following the balance-of-flow rule. Of course, we also need to specify the following nonnegativity condition for all the decision variables because negative flows should not occur on arcs:

$$X_{ij} \geq 0 \text{ for all } i \text{ and } j$$

5.1.5 IMPLEMENTING THE MODEL IN A SPREADSHEET

The formulation for the BMC transshipment problem is summarized as:

MIN: $+30X_{12} + 40X_{14} + 50X_{23} + 35X_{35} + 40X_{53}$
$+30X_{54} + 35X_{56} + 25X_{65} + 50X_{74} + 45X_{75}$ } total shipping cost
$+50X_{76}$

Subject to:

$-X_{12} - X_{14} \geq -200$	} flow constraint for node 1
$+X_{12} - X_{23} \geq +100$	} flow constraint for node 2
$+X_{23} + X_{53} - X_{35} \geq +60$	} flow constraint for node 3
$+X_{14} + X_{54} + X_{74} \geq +80$	} flow constraint for node 4
$+X_{35} + X_{65} + X_{75} - X_{53} - X_{54} - X_{56} \geq +170$	} flow constraint for node 5
$+X_{56} + X_{76} - X_{65} \geq +70$	} flow constraint for node 6
$-X_{74} - X_{75} - X_{76} \geq -300$	} flow constraint for node 7
$X_{ij} \geq 0 \text{ for all } i \text{ and } j$	} nonnegativity conditions

A convenient way to implement this type of problem is shown in Figure 5.2 (and in the file Fig5-2.xls on your data disk). In this spreadsheet, cells B6 through B16 are used to represent the decision variables for our model (or the number of cars that should flow between each of the cities listed). The unit cost of transporting cars between each city is listed in column G. The objective function for the model is then implemented in cell G18 as follows:

Formula for cell G18:   =SUMPRODUCT(B6:B16,G6:G16)

To implement the LHS formulas for the constraints in this model, we need to compute the total inflow minus the total outflow for each node. This is done in cells K6 through K12 as follows:

Formula for cell K6:   =SUMIF($E$6:$E$16,I6,$B$6:$B$16)−
(Copy to cells K7 through K12.)   SUMIF($C$6:$C$16,I6,$B$6:$B$16)

FIGURE 5.2

Spreadsheet implementation of the BMC transshipment problem

Constraint Cells

Variable Cells

Set Cell

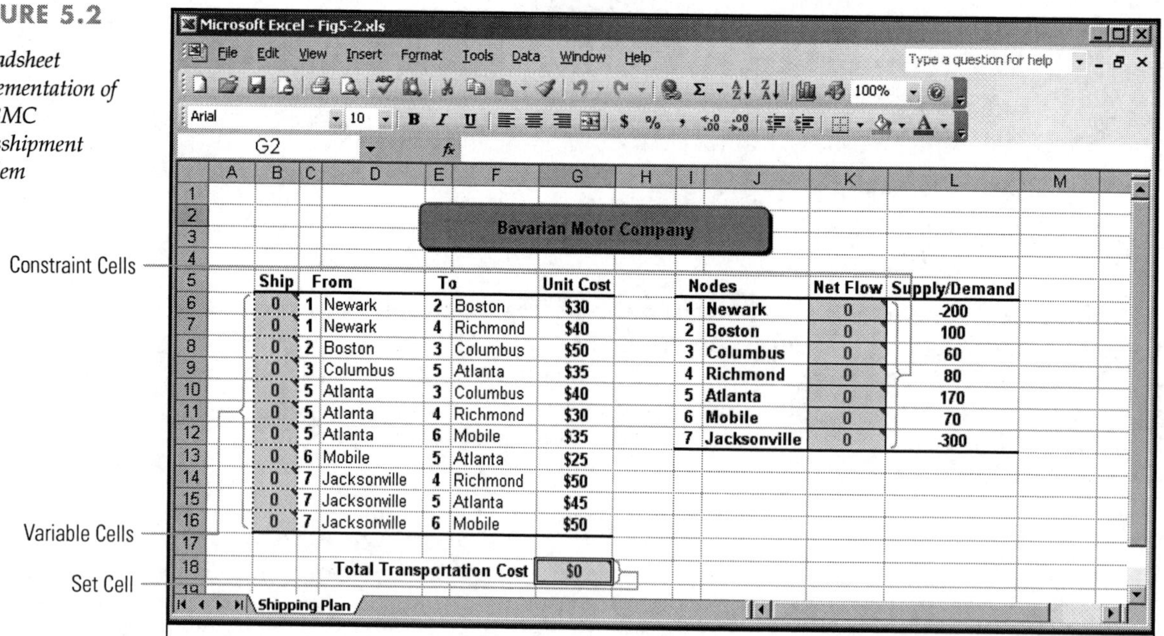

	Key Cell Formulas	
Cell	Formula	Copied to
D6	=VLOOKUP(C6,$I$6:$J$12,2)	D7:D16 and F6:F16
G18	=SUMPRODUCT(B6:B16,G6:G16)	--
K6	=SUMIF($E$6:$E$16,I6,$B$6:$B$16)- SUMIF($C$6:$C$16,I6,$B$6:$B$16)	K7:K12

The first SUMIF function in this formula compares the values in the range E6 through E16 to the value in I6 and, if a match occurs, sums the corresponding value in the range B6 through B16. Of course, this gives us the total number of cars flowing *into* Newark (which in this case will always be zero because none of the values in E6 through E16 match the value in I6). The next SUMIF function compares the values in the range C6 through C16 to the value in I6 and, if a match occurs, sums the corresponding values in the range B6 through B16. This gives us the total number of cars flowing *out of* Newark (which in this case will always equal the values in cells B6 and B7 because these are the only arcs flowing out of Newark). Copying this formula to cells K7 though K12 allows us to easily calculate the total inflow minus the total outflow for each of the nodes in our problem. The RHS values for these constraint cells are shown in cells L6 though L12.

Figure 5.3 shows the Solver parameters and options required to solve this model. The optimal solution to the problem is shown in Figure 5.4.

5.1.6 ANALYZING THE SOLUTION

Figure 5.4 shows the optimal solution for BMC's transshipment problem. The solution indicates that 120 cars should be shipped from Newark to Boston ($X_{12} = 120$), 80 cars from Newark to Richmond ($X_{14} = 80$), 20 cars from Boston to Columbus ($X_{23} = 20$), 40 cars from Atlanta to Columbus ($X_{53} = 40$), 210 cars from Jacksonville to Atlanta ($X_{75} = 210$), and 70 cars from Jacksonville to Mobile ($X_{76} = 70$). Cell G18 indicates that

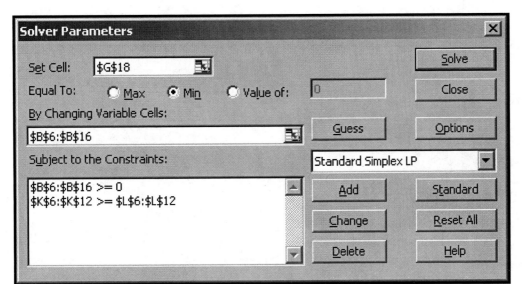

FIGURE 5.3

Solver parameters for the BMC transshipment problem

Ship	From	To	Unit Cost
120	1 Newark	2 Boston	$30
80	1 Newark	4 Richmond	$40
20	2 Boston	3 Columbus	$50
0	3 Columbus	5 Atlanta	$35
40	5 Atlanta	3 Columbus	$40
0	5 Atlanta	4 Richmond	$30
0	5 Atlanta	6 Mobile	$35
0	6 Mobile	5 Atlanta	$25
0	7 Jacksonville	4 Richmond	$50
210	7 Jacksonville	5 Atlanta	$45
70	7 Jacksonville	6 Mobile	$50
		Total Transportation Cost	$22,350

Nodes	Net Flow	Supply/Demand
1 Newark	-200	-200
2 Boston	100	100
3 Columbus	60	60
4 Richmond	80	80
5 Atlanta	170	170
6 Mobile	70	70
7 Jacksonville	-280	-300

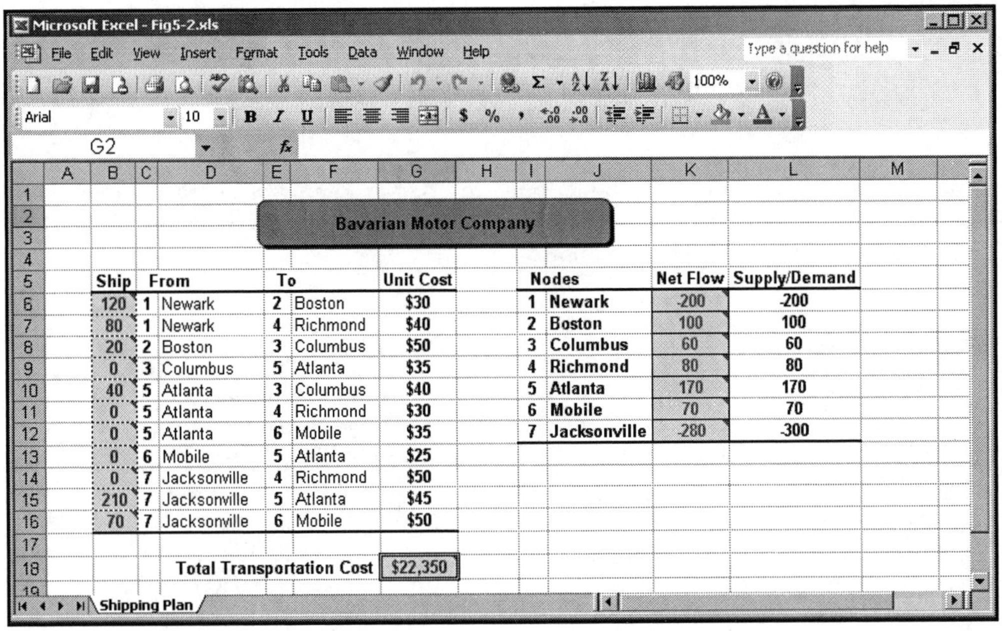

FIGURE 5.4

Optimal solution to the BMC transshipment problem

the total cost associated with this shipping plan is $22,350. The values of the constraint cells in K6 and K12 indicate, respectively, that all 200 cars available at Newark are being shipped and only 280 of the 300 cars available at Jacksonville are being shipped. A comparison of the remaining constraint cells in K7 through K11 with their RHS values in L7 through L11 reveals that the demand at each of these cities is being met by the net flow of cars through each city.

This solution is summarized graphically, as shown in Figure 5.5. The values in the boxes next to each arc indicate the optimal flows for the arcs. The optimal flow for all the other arcs in the problem, which are not shown in Figure 5.5, is 0. Notice that the amount flowing into each node minus the amount flowing out of each node is equal

FIGURE 5.5

Network representation of the optimal solution for the BMC transshipment problem

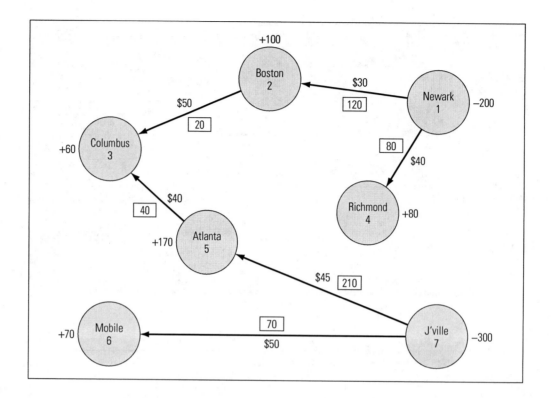

to the supply or demand at the node. For example, 210 cars are being shipped from Jacksonville to Atlanta. Atlanta will keep 170 of the cars (to satisfy the demand at this node) and send the extra 40 to Columbus.

5.2 The Shortest Path Problem

In many decision problems, we need to determine the shortest (or least costly) route or path through a network from a starting node to an ending node. For example, many cities are developing computerized models of their highways and streets to help emergency vehicles identify the quickest route to a given location. Each street intersection represents a potential node in a network, and the streets connecting the intersections represent arcs. Depending on the day of the week and the time of day, the time required to travel various streets can increase or decrease due to changes in traffic patterns. Road construction and maintenance also affect traffic flow patterns. So, the quickest route (or shortest path) for getting from one point in the city to another can change frequently. In emergency situations, lives or property can be lost or saved depending on how quickly emergency vehicles arrive where they are needed. The ability to quickly determine the shortest path to the location of an emergency situation is extremely useful in these situations. The following example illustrates another application of the shortest path problem.

The American Car Association (ACA) provides a variety of travel-related services to its members, including information on vacation destinations, discount hotel reservations, emergency road assistance, and travel route planning. This last service, travel route planning, is one of its most popular services. When members of the ACA are planning to take a driving trip, they call the organization's toll-free 800 number and indicate what cities they will be traveling from and to. The ACA then

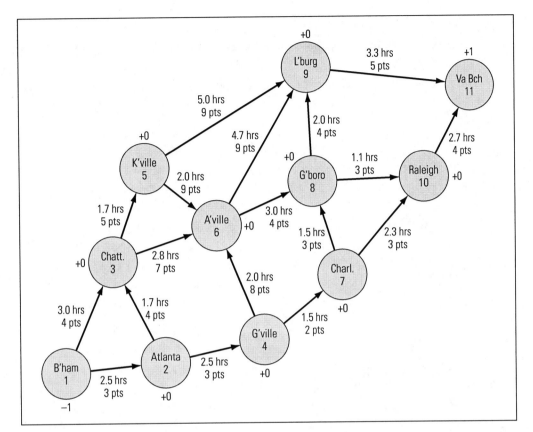

determines an optimal route for traveling between these cities. The ACA's computer databases of major highways and interstates are kept up-to-date with information on construction delays and detours and estimated travel times along various segments of roadways.

Members of the ACA often have different objectives in planning driving trips. Some are interested in identifying routes that minimize travel times. Others, with more leisure time on their hands, want to identify the most scenic route to their desired destination. The ACA wants to develop an automated system for identifying an optimal travel plan for its members.

To see how the ACA could benefit by solving shortest path problems, consider the simplified network shown in Figure 5.6 for a travel member who wants to drive from Birmingham, Alabama to Virginia Beach, Virginia. The nodes in this graph represent different cities and the arcs indicate the possible travel routes between the cities. For each arc, Figure 5.6 lists both the estimated driving time to travel the road represented by each arc and the number of points that route has received on the ACA's system for rating the scenic quality of the various routes.

Solving this problem as a network flow model requires the various nodes to have some supply or demand. In Figure 5.6, node 1 (Birmingham) has a supply of 1, node 11 (Virginia Beach) has a demand of 1, and all other nodes have a demand (or supply) of 0. If we view this model as a transshipment problem, we want to find either the quickest way or the most scenic way of shipping 1 unit of flow from node 1 to node 11. The route this unit of supply takes corresponds to either the shortest path or the most scenic path through the network, depending on which objective is being pursued.

5.2.1 AN LP MODEL FOR THE EXAMPLE PROBLEM

Using the balance-of-flow rule, the LP model to minimize the driving time in this problem is represented as:

MIN: $+2.5X_{12} + 3X_{13} + 1.7X_{23} + 2.5X_{24} + 1.7X_{35} + 2.8X_{36} + 2X_{46} + 1.5X_{47} + 2X_{56} + 5X_{59}$
$+ 3X_{68} + 4.7X_{69} + 1.5X_{78} + 2.3X_{7,10} + 2X_{89} + 1.1X_{8,10} + 3.3X_{9,11} + 2.7X_{10,11}$

Subject to:

$$-X_{12} - X_{13} \qquad\qquad = -1 \qquad \} \text{ flow constraint for node 1}$$
$$+X_{12} - X_{23} - X_{24} \qquad\qquad = 0 \qquad \} \text{ flow constraint for node 2}$$
$$+X_{13} + X_{23} - X_{35} - X_{36} \qquad = 0 \qquad \} \text{ flow constraint for node 3}$$
$$+X_{24} - X_{46} - X_{47} \qquad\qquad = 0 \qquad \} \text{ flow constraint for node 4}$$
$$+X_{35} - X_{56} - X_{59} \qquad\qquad = 0 \qquad \} \text{ flow constraint for node 5}$$
$$+X_{36} + X_{46} + X_{56} - X_{68} - X_{69} = 0 \qquad \} \text{ flow constraint for node 6}$$
$$+X_{47} - X_{78} - X_{7,10} \qquad\qquad = 0 \qquad \} \text{ flow constraint for node 7}$$
$$+X_{68} + X_{78} - X_{89} - X_{8,10} \qquad = 0 \qquad \} \text{ flow constraint for node 8}$$
$$+X_{59} + X_{69} + X_{89} - X_{9,11} \qquad = 0 \qquad \} \text{ flow constraint for node 9}$$
$$+X_{7,10} + X_{8,10} - X_{10,11} \qquad = 0 \qquad \} \text{ flow constraint for node 10}$$
$$+X_{9,11} + X_{10,11} \qquad\qquad = +1 \qquad \} \text{ flow constraint for node 11}$$
$$X_{ij} \geq 0 \text{ for all } i \text{ and } j \qquad\qquad \} \text{ nonnegativity conditions}$$

Because the total supply equals the total demand in this problem, the constraints should be stated as equalities. The first constraint in this model ensures that the 1 unit of supply available at node 1 is shipped to node 2 or node 3. The next nine constraints indicate that anything flowing to nodes 2 though node 10 must also flow out of these nodes because each has a demand of 0. For example, if the unit of supply leaves node 1 for node 2 (via X_{12}), the second constraint ensures that it will leave node 2 for node 3 or node 4 (via X_{23} or X_{24}). The last constraint indicates that the unit ultimately must flow to node 11. Thus, the solution to this problem indicates the quickest route for getting from node 1 (Birmingham) to node 11 (Virginia Beach).

5.2.2 THE SPREADSHEET MODEL AND SOLUTION

The optimal solution to this problem shown in Figure 5.7 (and in the file Fig5-7.xls on your data disk) was obtained using the Solver parameters and options shown in Figure 5.8. Notice that this model includes calculations of both the total expected driving time (cell G26) and total scenic rating points (cell H26) associated with any solution. Either of these cells can be chosen as the objective function according to the client's desires. However, the solution shown in Figure 5.7 minimizes the expected driving time.

The optimal solution shown in Figure 5.7 indicates that the quickest travel plan involves driving from node 1 (Birmingham) to node 2 (Atlanta), then to node 4 (Greenville), then to node 7 (Charlotte), then to node 10 (Raleigh), and finally to node 11 (Virginia Beach). The total expected driving time along this route is 11.5 hours. Also note that this route receives a rating of 15 points on the ACA's scenic rating scale.

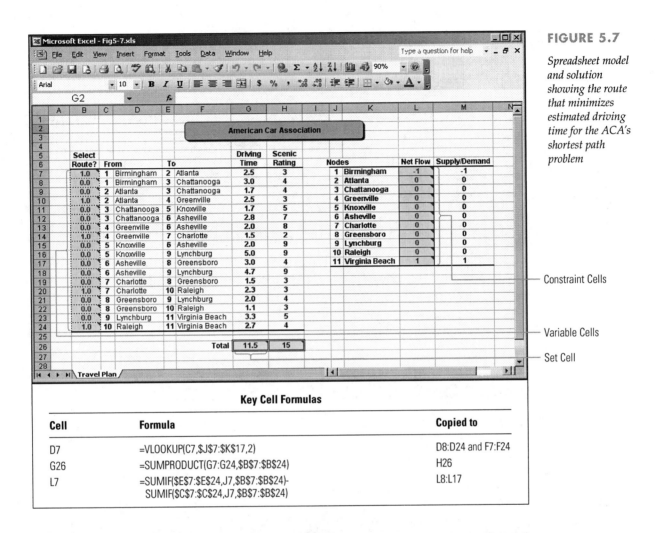

FIGURE 5.7

Spreadsheet model and solution showing the route that minimizes estimated driving time for the ACA's shortest path problem

— Constraint Cells

— Variable Cells

— Set Cell

Key Cell Formulas

Cell	Formula	Copied to
D7	=VLOOKUP(C7,$J$7:$K$17,2)	D8:D24 and F7:F24
G26	=SUMPRODUCT(G7:G24,$B$7:$B$24)	H26
L7	=SUMIF($E$7:$E$24,J7,$B$7:$B$24)- SUMIF($C$7:$C$24,J7,$B$7:$B$24)	L8:L17

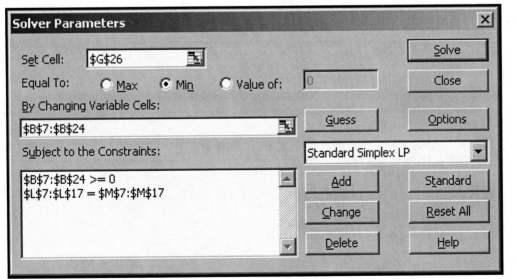

FIGURE 5.8

Solver parameters for the ACA's shortest path problem

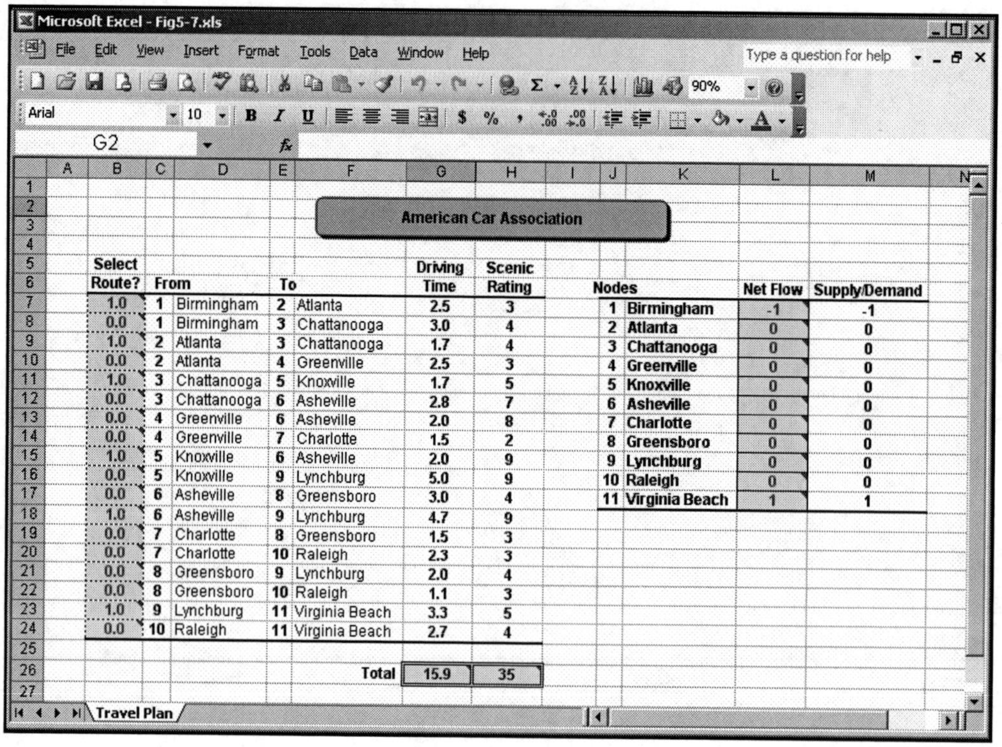

American Car Association

Select Route?	From		To		Driving Time	Scenic Rating
1.0	1	Birmingham	2	Atlanta	2.5	3
0.0	1	Birmingham	3	Chattanooga	3.0	4
1.0	2	Atlanta	3	Chattanooga	1.7	4
0.0	2	Atlanta	4	Greenville	2.5	3
1.0	3	Chattanooga	5	Knoxville	1.7	5
0.0	3	Chattanooga	6	Asheville	2.8	7
0.0	4	Greenville	6	Asheville	2.0	8
0.0	4	Greenville	7	Charlotte	1.5	2
1.0	5	Knoxville	6	Asheville	2.0	9
0.0	5	Knoxville	9	Lynchburg	5.0	9
0.0	6	Asheville	8	Greensboro	3.0	4
1.0	6	Asheville	9	Lynchburg	4.7	9
0.0	7	Charlotte	8	Greensboro	1.5	3
0.0	7	Charlotte	10	Raleigh	2.3	3
0.0	8	Greensboro	9	Lynchburg	2.0	4
0.0	8	Greensboro	10	Raleigh	1.1	3
1.0	9	Lynchburg	11	Virginia Beach	3.3	5
0.0	10	Raleigh	11	Virginia Beach	2.7	4
				Total	15.9	35

Nodes		Net Flow	Supply/Demand
1	Birmingham	-1	-1
2	Atlanta	0	0
3	Chattanooga	0	0
4	Greenville	0	0
5	Knoxville	0	0
6	Asheville	0	0
7	Charlotte	0	0
8	Greensboro	0	0
9	Lynchburg	0	0
10	Raleigh	0	0
11	Virginia Beach	1	1

FIGURE 5.9

Solution showing the most scenic route

Using this spreadsheet, we also can determine the most scenic route by instructing Solver to maximize the value in cell H26. Figure 5.9 shows the optimal solution obtained in this case. This travel plan involves driving from Birmingham to Atlanta, to Chattanooga, to Knoxville, to Asheville, to Lynchburg, and finally, to Virginia Beach. This itinerary receives a rating of 35 points on the ACA's scenic rating scale but takes almost 16 hours of driving time.

5.2.3 NETWORK FLOW MODELS AND INTEGER SOLUTIONS

Up to this point, each of the network flow models that we have solved generated integer solutions. If you use the simplex method to solve any minimum cost network flow model having integer constraint RHS values, then the optimal solution automatically assumes integer values. This property is helpful because the items flowing through most network flow models represent discrete units (such as cars or people).

Sometimes, it is tempting to place additional constraints (or side constraints) on a network model. For example, in the ACA problem, suppose that the customer wants to get to Virginia Beach in the most scenic way possible within 14 hours of driving time. We can easily add a constraint to the model to keep the total driving time G26 less than or equal to 14 hours. If we then re-solve the model to maximize the scenic rating in cell H26, we obtain the solution shown in Figure 5.10.

Unfortunately, this solution is useless because it produces fractional results. Thus, if we add *side constraints* to network flow problems that do not obey the balance-of-flow rule, we can no longer ensure that the solution to the LP formulation of the problems

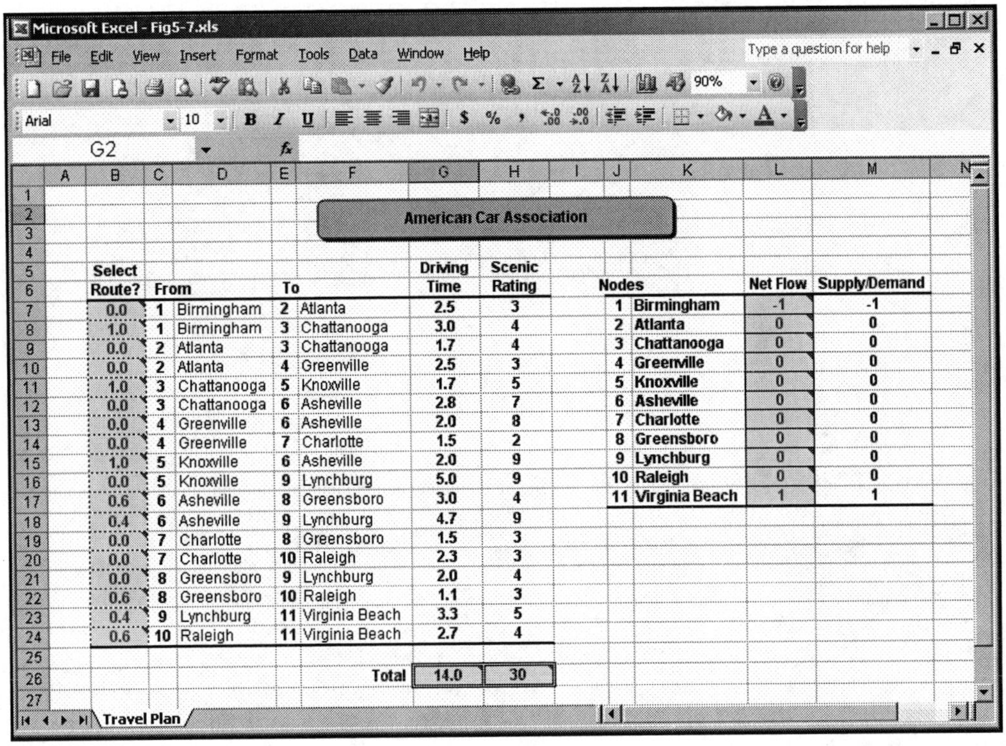

American Car Association

Select Route?	From		To		Driving Time	Scenic Rating
0.0	1	Birmingham	2	Atlanta	2.5	3
1.0	1	Birmingham	3	Chattanooga	3.0	4
0.0	2	Atlanta	3	Chattanooga	1.7	4
0.0	2	Atlanta	4	Greenville	2.5	3
1.0	3	Chattanooga	5	Knoxville	1.7	5
0.0	3	Chattanooga	6	Asheville	2.8	7
0.0	4	Greenville	6	Asheville	2.0	8
0.0	4	Greenville	7	Charlotte	1.5	2
1.0	5	Knoxville	6	Asheville	2.0	9
0.0	5	Knoxville	9	Lynchburg	5.0	9
0.6	6	Asheville	8	Greensboro	3.0	4
0.4	6	Asheville	9	Lynchburg	4.7	9
0.0	7	Charlotte	8	Greensboro	1.5	3
0.0	7	Charlotte	10	Raleigh	2.3	3
0.0	8	Greensboro	9	Lynchburg	2.0	4
0.6	8	Greensboro	10	Raleigh	1.1	3
0.4	9	Lynchburg	11	Virginia Beach	3.3	5
0.6	10	Raleigh	11	Virginia Beach	2.7	4
				Total	14.0	30

Nodes		Net Flow	Supply/Demand
1	Birmingham	-1	-1
2	Atlanta	0	0
3	Chattanooga	0	0
4	Greenville	0	0
5	Knoxville	0	0
6	Asheville	0	0
7	Charlotte	0	0
8	Greensboro	0	0
9	Lynchburg	0	0
10	Raleigh	0	0
11	Virginia Beach	1	1

FIGURE 5.10

Example of a non-integer solution to a network problem with side constraints

will be integral. If integer solutions are needed for such problems, the integer programming techniques discussed in Chapter 6 must be applied.

5.3 The Equipment Replacement Problem

The equipment replacement problem is a common type of business problem that can be modeled as a shortest path problem. This type of problem involves determining the least costly schedule for replacing equipment over a specified length of time. Consider the following example.

> Jose Maderos is the owner of Compu-Train, a small company that provides hands-on software education and training for businesses in and around Boulder, Colorado. Jose leases the computer equipment used in his business and he likes to keep the equipment up-to-date so that it will run the latest, state-of-the-art software in an efficient manner. Because of this, Jose wants to replace his equipment at least every two years.
>
> Jose is currently trying to decide between two different lease contracts his equipment supplier has proposed. Under both contracts Jose would be required to pay $62,000 initially to obtain the equipment he needs. However, the two contracts differ in terms of the amount Jose would have to pay in subsequent years to replace his equipment. Under the first contract, the price to acquire new equipment would increase by 6% per year, but he would be given a trade-in credit of 60% for any equipment that is one year old and 15% for any equipment that is two years old. Under the second contract, the price to acquire new equipment would increase by just 2% per year, but he would only be given a trade-in credit of 30% for any equipment that is one year old and 10% for any equipment that is two years old.

FIGURE 5.11

Network representation of Compu-Train's first contract alternative for their equipment replacement problem

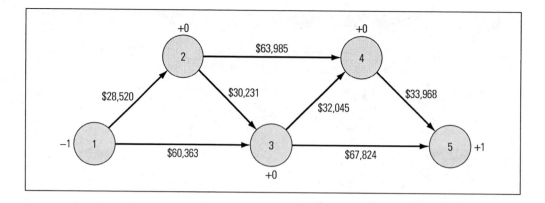

Jose realizes that no matter what he does, he will have to pay $62,000 to obtain the equipment initially. However, he wants to determine which contract would allow him to minimize the remaining leasing costs over the next five years and when he should replace his equipment under the selected contract.

Each of the two contracts Jose is considering can be modeled as a shortest path problem. Figure 5.11 shows how this would be accomplished for the first contract under consideration. Each node corresponds to a point in time during the next five years when Jose can replace his equipment. Each arc in this network represents a choice available to Jose. For example, the arc from node 1 to node 2 indicates that Jose can keep the equipment he initially acquires for one year and then replace it (at the beginning of year 2) for a net cost of $28,520 ($62,000 × 1.06 − 0.6 × $62,000 = $28,520). Alternatively, the arc from node 1 to node 3 indicates that Jose can keep his initial equipment for two years and replace it at the beginning of year 3 for a net cost of $60,363 ($62,000 × $1.06^2 − 0.15 × $62,000 = $60,363).

The arc from node 2 to node 3 indicates that if Jose replaces his initial equipment at the beginning of year 2, he can keep the new equipment for one year and replace it at the beginning of year 3 at a net cost of $30,231 ($62,000 × 1.06^2 − 0.60 × ($62,000 × 1.06) = $30,231). The remaining arcs and costs in the network can be interpreted in the same way. Jose's decision problem is to determine the least costly (or shortest) way of getting from node 1 to node 5 in this network.

5.3.1 THE SPREADSHEET MODEL AND SOLUTION

The LP formulation of Jose's decision problem can be generated from the graph in Figure 5.11 using the balance-of-flow rule in the same manner as the previous network flow problems. The spreadsheet model for this problem was implemented as shown in Figure 5.12 (and in the file Fig5-12.xls on your data disk) and solved using the settings shown in Figure 5.13. To assist Jose in comparing the two different alternatives he faces, notice that an area of the spreadsheet in Figure 5.12 has been reserved to represent assumptions about the annual increase in leasing costs (cell G5), and the trade-in values for one- and two-year old equipment (cells G6 and G7). The rest of the spreadsheet model uses these assumed values to compute the various costs. This enables us to change any of the assumptions and re-solve the model very easily.

The optimal solution to this problem shows that under the provisions of the first contract, Jose should replace his equipment at the beginning of each year at a total cost of $124,764. This amount is in addition to the $62,000 he has to pay up front at the beginning of year 1.

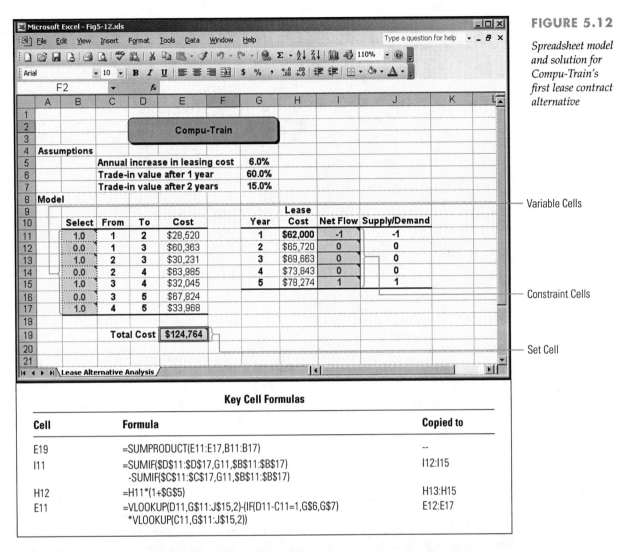

FIGURE 5.12

Spreadsheet model and solution for Compu-Train's first lease contract alternative

— Variable Cells

— Constraint Cells

— Set Cell

Key Cell Formulas

Cell	Formula	Copied to
E19	=SUMPRODUCT(E11:E17,B11:B17)	--
I11	=SUMIF($D$11:$D$17,G11,$B$11:$B$17) -SUMIF($C$11:$C$17,G11,$B$11:$B$17)	I12:I15
H12	=H11*(1+$G$5)	H13:H15
E11	=VLOOKUP(D11,G$11:J$15,2)-(IF(D11-C11=1,G$6,G$7) *VLOOKUP(C11,G$11:J$15,2))	E12:E17

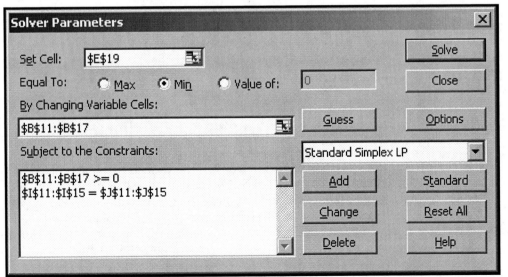

FIGURE 5.13

Solver parameters for Compu-Train's equipment replacement problem

FIGURE 5.14

Solution for Compu-Train's second lease contract alternative

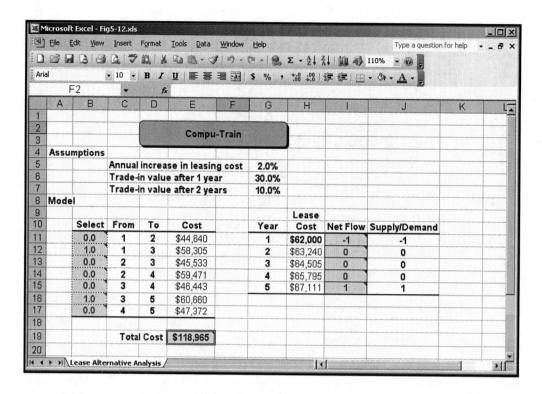

To determine the optimal replacement strategy and costs associated with the second contract, Jose could simply change the assumptions at the top of the spreadsheet and re-solve the model. The results of this are shown in Figure 5.14.

The optimal solution to this problem shows that under the provisions of the second contract, Jose should replace his equipment at the beginning of years 3 and 5 at a total cost of $118,965. Again, this amount is in addition to the $62,000 he has to pay up front at the beginning of year 1. Although the total costs under the second contract are lower than under the first, under the second contract Jose would be working with older equipment during years 2 and 4. Thus, although the solution to these two models makes the financial consequences of the two different alternatives clear, Jose still must decide for himself whether the benefits of the financial cost savings under the second contract outweigh the non-financial costs associated with using slightly out-of-date equipment during years 2 and 4. Of course, regardless of which contract Jose decides to go with, he will get to reconsider whether or not to upgrade his equipment at the beginning of each of the next 4 years.

Summary of Shortest Path Problems

You can model any shortest path problem as a transshipment problem by assigning a supply of 1 to the starting node, a demand of 1 to the ending node, and a demand of 0 to all other nodes in the network. Because the examples presented here involved only a small number of paths through each of the networks, it might have been easier to solve these problems simply by enumerating the paths and calculating the total distance of each one. However, in a problem with many nodes and arcs, an automated LP model is preferable to a manual solution approach.

5.4 Transportation/Assignment Problems

Chapter 3 presented an example of another type of network flow problem known as the transportation/assignment problem. The example involved the Tropicsun Company—a grower and distributor of fresh citrus products. The company wanted to determine the least expensive way to transport freshly picked fruit from three citrus groves to three processing plants. The network representation of the problem is repeated in Figure 5.15.

The network shown in Figure 5.15 differs from the earlier network flow problems in this chapter because it contains no transshipment nodes. Each node in Figure 5.15 is either a sending node or a receiving node. The lack of transshipment nodes is the key feature that distinguishes transportation/assignment problems from other types of network flow problems. As you saw in Chapter 3, this property allows you to set up and solve transportation/assignment problems conveniently in a matrix format in the spreadsheet. Although it is possible to solve transportation/assignment problems in the same way in which we solved transshipment problems, it is much easier to implement and solve these problems using the matrix approach described in Chapter 3.

Sometimes, transportation/assignment problems are *sparse* or not fully interconnected (meaning that not all the supply nodes have arcs connecting them to all the demand nodes). These "missing" arcs can be handled conveniently in the matrix approach to implementation by assigning arbitrarily large costs to the variable cells representing these arcs so that flow on these arcs becomes prohibitively expensive. However, as the number of missing arcs increases, the matrix approach to implementation becomes less and less computationally efficient compared to the procedure described in this chapter.

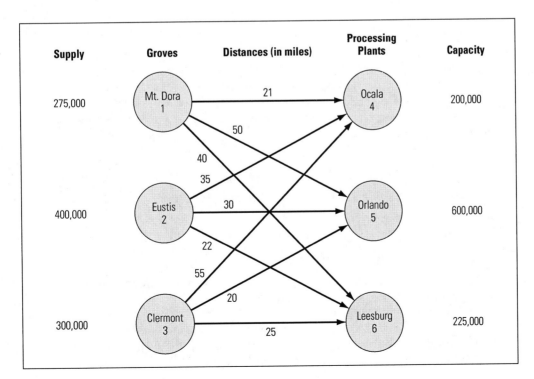

FIGURE 5.15

Network representation of Tropicsun's transportation/assignment problem

5.5 Generalized Network Flow Problems

In all of the network problems we have considered so far, the amount of flow that exited an arc was always the same as the amount that entered the arc. For example, if we put 40 cars on a train in Jacksonville and sent them to Atlanta, the same 40 cars came off the train in Atlanta. However, there are numerous examples of network flow problems in which a gain or loss occurs on flows across arcs. For instance, if oil or gas is shipped through a leaky pipeline, the amount of oil or gas arriving at the intended destination will be less than the amount originally placed in the pipeline. Similar loss-of-flow examples occur as a result of evaporation of liquids, spoilage of foods and other perishable items, or imperfections in raw materials entering production processes that result in a certain amount of scrap. Many financial cash flow problems can be modeled as network flow problems in which flow gains (or increases) occur in the form of interest or dividends as money flows through various investments. The following example illustrates the modeling changes required to accommodate these types of problems.

Nancy Grant is the owner of Coal Bank Hollow Recycling, a company that specializes in collecting and recycling paper products. Nancy's company uses two different recycling processes to convert newspaper, mixed paper, white office paper, and cardboard into paper pulp. The amount of paper pulp extracted from the recyclable materials and the cost of extracting the pulp differs depending on which recycling process is used. The following table summarizes the recycling processes:

Material	Recycling Process 1		Recycling Process 2	
	Cost per ton	Yield	Cost per Ton	Yield
Newspaper	$13	90%	$12	85%
Mixed Paper	$11	80%	$13	85%
White Office Paper	$9	95%	$10	90%
Cardboard	$13	75%	$14	85%

For instance, every ton of newspaper subjected to recycling process 1 costs $13 and yields 0.9 tons of paper pulp. The paper pulp produced by the two different recycling processes goes through other operations to be transformed into pulp for newsprint, packaging paper, or print stock quality paper. The yields associated with transforming the recycled pulp into pulp for the final products are summarized in the following table:

Pulp Source	Newsprint Pulp		Packaging Paper Pulp		Print Stock Pulp	
	Cost per Ton	Yield	Cost per Ton	Yield	Cost per Ton	Yield
Recycling Process 1	$5	95%	$6	90%	$8	90%
Recycling Process 2	$6	90%	$8	95%	$7	95%

For instance, a ton of pulp exiting recycling process 2 can be transformed into 0.95 tons of packaging paper at a cost of $8.

Nancy currently has 70 tons of newspaper, 50 tons of mixed paper, 30 tons of white office paper, and 40 tons of cardboard. She wants to determine the most efficient way of converting these materials into 60 tons of newsprint pulp, 40 tons of packaging paper pulp, and 50 tons of print stock pulp.

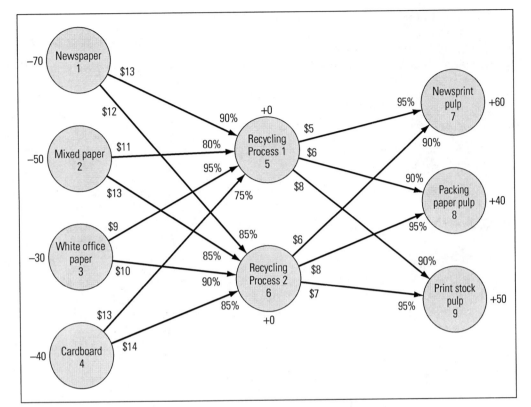

Figure 5.16 shows how Nancy's recycling problem can be viewed as a generalized network flow problem. The arcs in this graph indicate the possible flow of recycling material through the production process. On each arc, we have listed both the cost of flow along the arc and the reduction factor that applies to flow along the arc. For instance, the arc from node 1 to node 5 indicates that each ton of newspaper going to recycling process 1 costs $13 and yields 0.90 tons of paper pulp.

5.5.1 FORMULATING AN LP MODEL FOR THE RECYCLING PROBLEM

To formulate the LP model for this problem algebraically, we defined the decision variable X_{ij} to represent the tons of product flowing from node i to node j. The objective is then stated in the usual way as follows:

$$\text{MIN:} \quad 13X_{15} + 12X_{16} + 11X_{25} + 13X_{26} + 9X_{35} + 10X_{36} + 13X_{45} + 14X_{46} + 5X_{57} \\ + 6X_{58} + 8X_{59} + 6X_{67} + 8X_{68} + 7X_{69}$$

The constraints for this problem may be generated using the balance-of-flow rule for each node. The constraints for the first four nodes (representing the supply of newspaper, mixed paper, white office paper, and cardboard, respectively) are given by:

$$-X_{15} - X_{16} \geq -70 \quad \} \text{ flow constraint for node 1}$$
$$-X_{25} - X_{26} \geq -50 \quad \} \text{ flow constraint for node 2}$$
$$-X_{35} - X_{36} \geq -30 \quad \} \text{ flow constraint for node 3}$$
$$-X_{45} - X_{46} \geq -40 \quad \} \text{ flow constraint for node 4}$$

These constraints simply indicate that the amount of product flowing out of each of these nodes may not exceed the supply available at each node. (Recall that the constraint given for node 1 is equivalent to $+X_{15} + X_{16} \leq +70$.)

Applying the balance-of-flow rule at nodes 5 and 6 (representing the two recycling processes) we obtain:

$+0.9X_{15} + 0.8X_{25} + 0.95X_{35} + 0.75X_{45} - X_{57} - X_{58} - X_{59} \geq 0$ } flow constraint for node 5

$+0.85X_{16} + 0.85X_{26} + 0.9X_{36} + 0.85X_{46} - X_{67} - X_{68} - X_{69} \geq 0$ } flow constraint for node 6

To better understand the logic of these constraints, we will rewrite them in the following algebraically equivalent manner:

$+0.9X_{15} + 0.8X_{25} + 0.95X_{35} + 0.75X_{45} \geq +X_{57} + X_{58} + X_{59}$ } equivalent flow constraint for node 5

$+0.85X_{16} + 0.85X_{26} + 0.9X_{36} + 0.85X_{46} \geq +X_{67} + X_{68} + X_{69}$ } equivalent flow constraint for node 6

Notice that the constraint for node 5 requires that the amount being shipped from node 5 (given by $X_{57} + X_{58} + X_{59}$) cannot exceed the net amount that would be available at node 5 (given by $0.9X_{15} + 0.8X_{25} + 0.95X_{35} + 0.75X_{45}$). Thus, here the yield factors come into play in determining the amount of product that would be available from the recycling processes. A similar interpretation applies to the constraint for node 6.

Finally, applying the balance-of-flow rule to nodes 7, 8, and 9 we obtain the constraints:

$+0.95X_{57} + 0.90X_{67} \geq 60$ } flow constraint for node 7

$+0.9X_{58} + 0.95X_{68} \geq 40$ } flow constraint for node 8

$+0.9X_{59} + 0.95X_{69} \geq 50$ } flow constraint for node 9

The constraint for node 7 ensures that the final amount of product flowing to node 7 ($0.95X_{57} + 0.90X_{67}$) is sufficient to meet the demand for pulp at this node. Again, similar interpretations apply to the constraints for nodes 8 and 9.

5.5.2 IMPLEMENTING THE MODEL

The model for Coal Bank Hollow Recycling's generalized network flow problem is summarized as:

MIN: $13X_{15} + 12X_{16} + 11X_{25} + 13X_{26} + 9X_{35} + 10X_{36} + 13X_{45} + 14X_{46} + 5X_{57} + 6X_{58} + 8X_{59} + 6X_{67} + 8X_{68} + 7X_{69}$

Subject to:

$-X_{15} - X_{16} \geq -70$ } flow constraint for node 1

$-X_{25} - X_{26} \geq -50$ } flow constraint for node 2

$-X_{35} - X_{36} \geq -30$ } flow constraint for node 3

$-X_{45} - X_{46} \geq -40$ } flow constraint for node 4

$+0.9X_{15} + 0.8X_{25} + 0.95X_{35} + 0.75X_{45} - X_{57} - X_{58} - X_{59} \geq 0$ } flow constraint for node 5

$+0.85X_{16} + 0.85X_{26} + 0.9X_{36} + 0.85X_{46} - X_{67} - X_{68} - X_{69} \geq 0$ } flow constraint for node 6

$+0.95X_{57} + 0.90X_{67} \geq 60$ } flow constraint for node 7

$+0.9X_{58} + 0.95X_{68} \geq 40$ } flow constraint for node 8

$+0.9X_{59} + 0.95X_{69} \geq 50$ } flow constraint for node 9

$X_{ij} \geq 0$ for all i and j } nonnegativity conditions

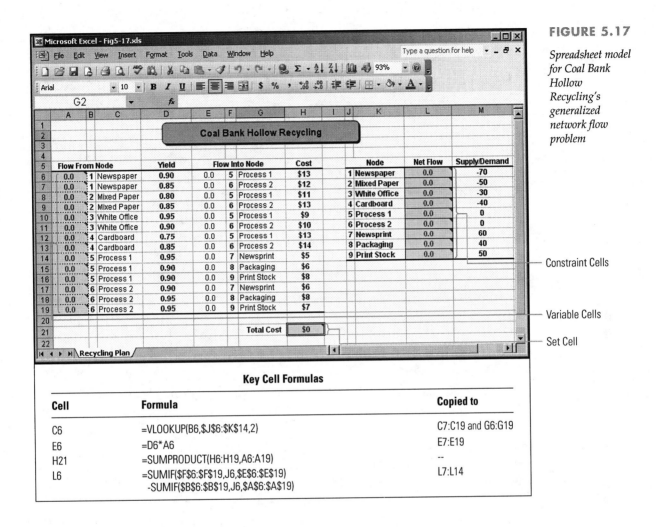

FIGURE 5.17

*Spreadsheet model
for Coal Bank
Hollow
Recycling's
generalized
network flow
problem*

In all the other network flow models we have seen up to this point, all the coefficients in all the constraints were implicitly always +1 or −1. This is not true in the above model. Thus, we must give special attention to the coefficients in the constraints as we implement this model in the spreadsheet. One approach to implementing this problem is shown in Figure 5.17 (and the file Fig5-17.xls on your data disk).

The spreadsheet in Figure 5.17 is very similar to those of the other network flow problems we have solved. Cells A6 through A19 represent the decision variables (arcs) for our model, and the corresponding unit cost associated with each variable is listed in the range from H6 through H19. The objective function is implemented in cell H21 as:

Formula for cell H21:   =SUMPRODUCT(H6:H19,A6:A19)

To implement the LHS formulas for our constraints, we no longer can simply sum the variables flowing into each node and subtract the variables flowing out of the nodes. Instead, we first need to multiply the variables flowing into a node by the appropriate yield factor. With the yield factors entered in column D, the yield-adjusted flow for each arc is computed in column E as follows:

Formula for cell E6:   =A6*D6

(Copy to cells E7 through E19.)

FIGURE 5.18

Solver parameters for the recycling problem

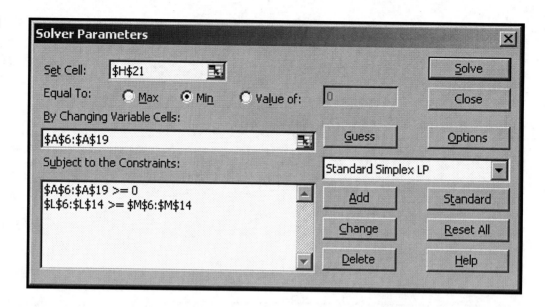

Now, to implement the LHS formulas for each node in cells L6 through L14, we will sum the yield-adjusted flows into each node and subtract the raw flow out of each node. This may be done as follows:

Formula for cell L6:   = SUMIF($F$6:$F$19,J6,$E$6:$E$19)–

(Copy to cells L7 through L14.)   SUMIF($B$6:$B$19,J6,$A$6:$A$19)

Notice that the first SUMIF function in this formula sums the appropriate yield-adjusted flows in column E while the second SUMIF sums the appropriate raw flow values from column A. Thus, although this formula is very similar to the ones used in earlier models, there is a critical difference here that must be carefully noted and understood. The RHS values for these constraint cells are listed in cells M6 through M14.

5.5.3 ANALYZING THE SOLUTION

The Solver parameters used to solve this problem are shown in Figure 5.18 and the optimal solution is shown in Figure 5.19.

In this solution, 43.4 tons of newspaper, 50 tons of mixed paper, and 30 tons of white office paper are assigned to recycling process 1 (i.e., $X_{15} = 43.4$, $X_{25} = 50$, $X_{35} = 30$). This recycling process then yields a total of 107.6 tons of pulp (i.e., $0.9 \times 43.3 + 0.8 \times 50 + 0.95 \times 30 = 107.6$) of which 63.2 tons are allocated to the production of newsprint pulp ($X_{57} = 63.2$) and 44.4 tons are allocated to the production of pulp for packaging paper ($X_{58} = 44.4$). This allows us to meet the demand for 60 tons of newsprint pulp ($0.95 \times 63.2 = 60$) and 40 tons of packaging paper ($0.90 \times 44.4 = 40$).

The remaining 26.6 tons of newspaper are combined with 35.4 tons of cardboard in recycling process 2 (i.e., $X_{16} = 26.6$, $X_{46} = 35.4$). This results in a yield of 52.6 tons of pulp (i.e., $0.85 \times 26.6 + 0.85 \times 35.4 = 52.6$), which is all devoted to the production of 50 tons of print stock quality pulp ($0.95 \times 52.6 = 50$).

It is important for Nancy to note that this production plan calls for the use of all her supply of newspaper, mixed paper, and white office paper, but leaves about 4.6 tons of cardboard left over. Thus, she should be able to lower her total costs further by acquiring more newspaper, mixed paper, or white office paper. It would be wise for her to see if she could trade her surplus cardboard to another recycler for the material that she lacks.

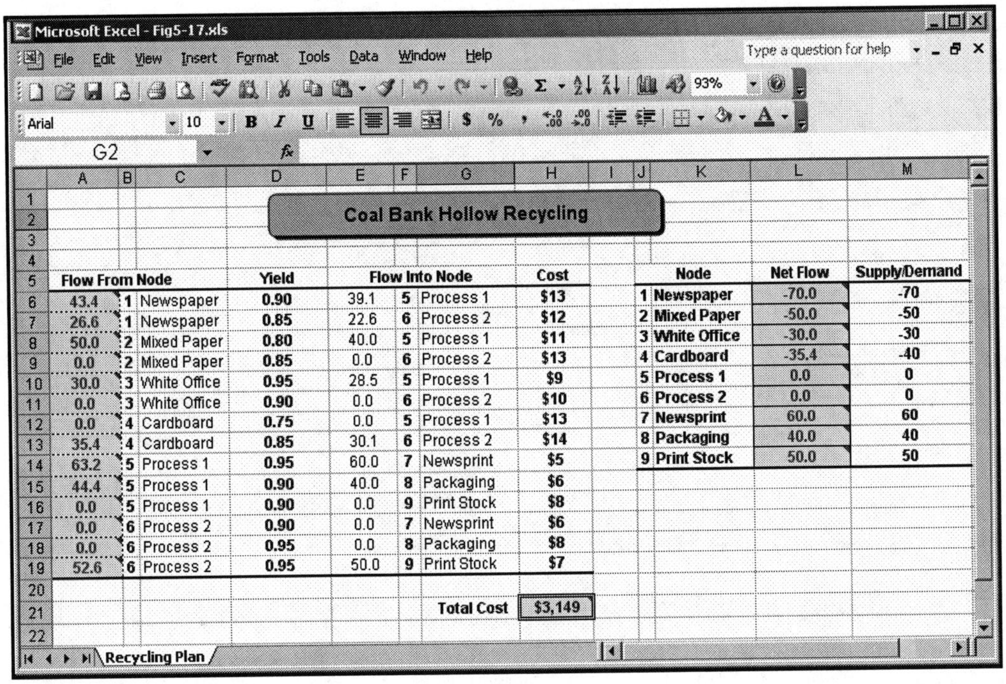

Flow From Node			Yield	Flow Into Node			Cost
43.4	1	Newspaper	0.90	39.1	5	Process 1	$13
26.6	1	Newspaper	0.85	22.6	6	Process 2	$12
50.0	2	Mixed Paper	0.80	40.0	5	Process 1	$11
0.0	2	Mixed Paper	0.85	0.0	6	Process 2	$13
30.0	3	White Office	0.95	28.5	5	Process 1	$9
0.0	3	White Office	0.90	0.0	6	Process 2	$10
0.0	4	Cardboard	0.75	0.0	5	Process 1	$13
35.4	4	Cardboard	0.85	30.1	6	Process 2	$14
63.2	5	Process 1	0.95	60.0	7	Newsprint	$5
44.4	5	Process 1	0.90	40.0	8	Packaging	$6
0.0	5	Process 1	0.90	0.0	9	Print Stock	$8
0.0	6	Process 2	0.90	0.0	7	Newsprint	$6
0.0	6	Process 2	0.95	0.0	8	Packaging	$8
52.6	6	Process 2	0.95	50.0	9	Print Stock	$7
						Total Cost	$3,149

Node		Net Flow	Supply/Demand
1	Newspaper	-70.0	-70
2	Mixed Paper	-50.0	-50
3	White Office	-30.0	-30
4	Cardboard	-35.4	-40
5	Process 1	0.0	0
6	Process 2	0.0	0
7	Newsprint	60.0	60
8	Packaging	40.0	40
9	Print Stock	50.0	50

FIGURE 5.19

Optimal solution to Coal Bank Hollow Recycling's generalized network flow problem

5.5.4 GENERALIZED NETWORK FLOW PROBLEMS AND FEASIBILITY

In generalized network flow problems, the gains and/or losses associated with flows across each arc *effectively* increase and/or decrease the supply available in the network. For example, consider what happens in Figure 5.16 if the supply of newspaper is reduced to 55 tons. Although it *appears* that the total supply in the network (175 tons) still exceeds the total demand (150 tons), if we try to solve the modified problem, Solver will tell us that the problem has no feasible solution. (You may verify this on your own.) So we are not able to satisfy all of the demand due to the loss of material that occurs in the production process.

The point being made here is that with generalized network flow problems, you cannot always tell before solving the problem if the total supply is adequate to meet the total demand. As a result, you cannot always know which balance-of-flow rule to apply. When the issue is unclear, it is safest[1] to first assume that all the demand can be met and (according to the balance-of-flow rule) use constraints of the form: Inflow − Outflow ≥ Supply or Demand. If the resulting problem is infeasible (and there are no errors in the model!), then we know all the demand cannot be satisfied and (according to the balance-of-flow rule) use constraints of the form: Inflow − Outflow ≤ Supply or Demand. In this later case, the solution will identify the least costly way of using the available supply to meet as much of the demand as possible.

Figures 5.20 and 5.21 show, respectively, the Solver parameters and optimal solution for this revised recycling problem with 55 tons of newspaper. Note that this solution uses all of the available supply of each of the recycling materials. Although the solution satisfies all the demand for newsprint pulp and packaging paper pulp, it falls almost 15 tons short of the total demand for print stock pulp.

[1] See question 3 at the end of this chapter for more on this issue.

FIGURE 5.20

Solver parameters for modified recycling problem

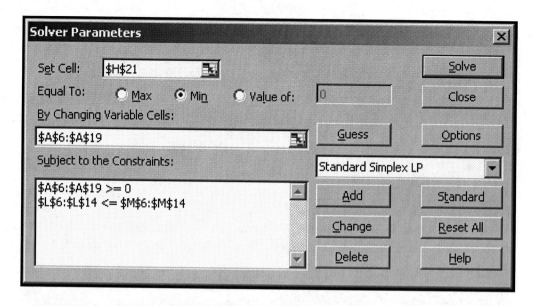

FIGURE 5.21

Optimal solution to modified recycling problem

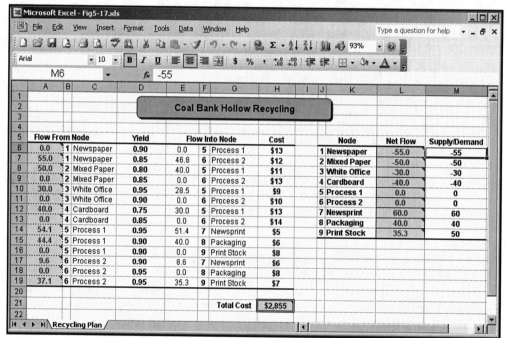

Important Modeling Point

For generalized network flow problems, the gains and/or losses associated with flows across each arc *effectively* increase and/or decrease the supply available in the network. As a result, it is sometimes difficult to tell in advance whether the total supply is adequate to meet the total demand in a generalized network flow problem. When in doubt, it is best to assume that the total supply is capable of satisfying the total demand and use Solver to prove (or refute) this assumption.

5.6 Maximal Flow Problems

The maximal flow problem (or max flow problem) is a type of network flow problem in which the goal is to determine the maximum amount of flow that can occur in the network. In a maximal flow problem, the amount of flow that can occur over each arc is limited by some capacity restriction. This type of network might be used to model the flow of oil in a pipeline (in which the amount of oil that can flow through a pipe in a unit of time is limited by the diameter of the pipe). Traffic engineers also use this type of network to determine the maximum number of cars that can travel through a collection of streets with different capacities imposed by the number of lanes in the streets and speed limits. The following example illustrates a max flow problem.

5.6.1 AN EXAMPLE OF A MAXIMAL FLOW PROBLEM

The Northwest Petroleum Company operates an oil field and refinery in Alaska. The crude obtained from the oil field is pumped through the network of pumping substations shown in Figure 5.22 to the company's refinery located 500 miles from the oil field. The amount of oil that can flow through each of the pipelines, represented by the arcs in the network, varies due to differing pipe diameters. The numbers next to the arcs in the network indicate the maximum amount of oil that can flow through the various pipelines (measured in thousands of barrels per hour). The company wants to determine the maximum number of barrels per hour that can flow from the oil field to the refinery.

The max flow problem appears to be very different from the network flow models described earlier because it does not include specific supplies or demands for the nodes. However, you can solve the max flow problem in the same way as a transshipment

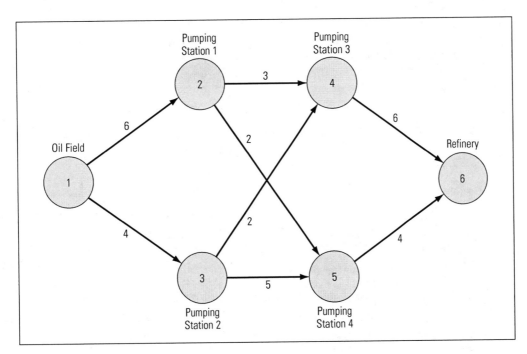

FIGURE 5.22

Network representation of Northwest Petroleum's oil refinery operation

FIGURE 5.23

Network structure of Northwest Petroleum's max flow problem

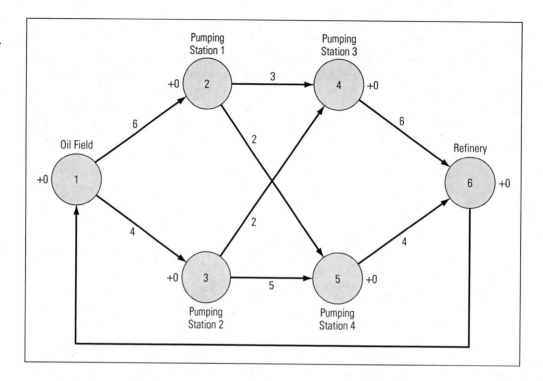

problem if you add a return arc from the ending node to the starting node, assign a demand of 0 to all the nodes in the network, and attempt to maximize the flow over the return arc. Figure 5.23 shows these modifications to the problem.

To understand the network in Figure 5.23, suppose that k units are shipped from node 6 to node 1 (where k represents some integer). Because node 6 has a supply of 0, it can send k units to node 1 only if these units can be returned through the network to node 6 (to balance the flow at node 6). The capacities on the arcs limit how many units can be returned to node 6. Therefore, the maximum flow through the network corresponds to the largest number of units that can be shipped from node 6 to node 1 and then returned through the network to node 6 (to balance the flow at this node). We can solve an LP model to determine the maximal flow by maximizing the flow from node 6 to node 1, given appropriate upper bounds on each arc and the usual balance-of-flow constraints. This model is represented as:

$$
\begin{aligned}
\text{MAX:} \quad & X_{61} \\
\text{Subject to:} \quad & +X_{61} - X_{12} - X_{13} = 0 \\
& +X_{12} - X_{24} - X_{25} = 0 \\
& +X_{13} - X_{34} - X_{35} = 0 \\
& +X_{24} + X_{34} - X_{46} = 0 \\
& +X_{25} + X_{35} - X_{56} = 0 \\
& +X_{46} + X_{56} - X_{61} = 0
\end{aligned}
$$

with the following bounds on the decision variables:

$$
\begin{array}{lll}
0 \le X_{12} \le 6 & 0 \le X_{25} \le 2 & 0 \le X_{46} \le 6 \\
0 \le X_{13} \le 4 & 0 \le X_{34} \le 2 & 0 \le X_{56} \le 4 \\
0 \le X_{24} \le 3 & 0 \le X_{35} \le 5 & 0 \le X_{61} \le \infty
\end{array}
$$

5.6.2 THE SPREADSHEET MODEL AND SOLUTION

This model is implemented in the spreadsheet shown in Figure 5.24 (and in the file Fig5-24.xls on your data disk). This spreadsheet model differs from the earlier network models in a few minor, but important, ways. First, column G in Figure 5.24 represents the upper bounds for each arc. Second, the objective function (or set cell) is represented by cell B16, which contains the formula:

$$\text{Formula in cell B16:} \quad =\text{B14}$$

Cell B14 represents the flow from node 6 to node 1 (or X_{61}). This cell corresponds to the variable that we want to maximize in the objective function of the LP model. The Solver parameters and options shown in Figure 5.25 are used to obtain the optimal solution shown in Figure 5.24.

Because the arcs leading to node 6 (X_{46} and X_{56}) have a total capacity for 10 units of flow, it might be surprising to learn that only 9 units can flow through the network. However, the optimal solution shown in Figure 5.24 indicates that the maximal flow through the network is just 9 units.

The optimal flows identified in Figure 5.24 for each arc are shown in the boxes next to the capacities for each arc in Figure 5.26. In Figure 5.26, the arc from node 5 to node 6 is at its full capacity of 4 units, whereas the arc from node 4 to node 6 is 1 unit below its full capacity of 6 units. Although the arc from node 4 to node 6 can carry 1 additional unit of flow, it is prevented from doing so because all the arcs flowing to node 4 (X_{24} and X_{34}) are at full capacity.

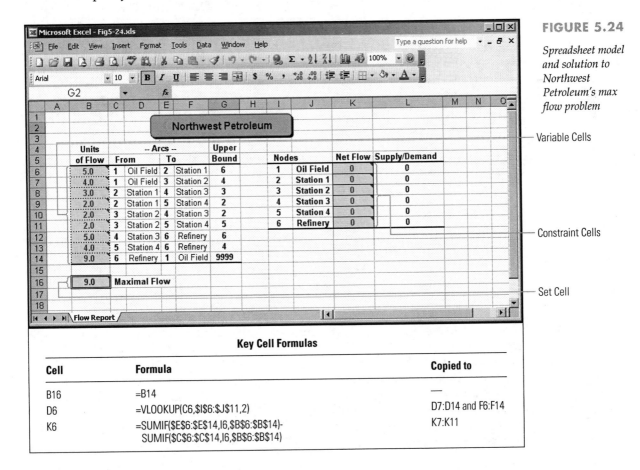

FIGURE 5.24

Spreadsheet model and solution to Northwest Petroleum's max flow problem

— Variable Cells

— Constraint Cells

— Set Cell

Key Cell Formulas

Cell	Formula	Copied to
B16	=B14	—
D6	=VLOOKUP(C6,$I$6:$J$11,2)	D7:D14 and F6:F14
K6	=SUMIF($E$6:$E$14,I6,$B$6:$B$14)- SUMIF($C$6:$C$14,I6,$B$6:$B$14)	K7:K11

FIGURE 5.25

Solver parameters for Northwest Petroleum's max flow problem

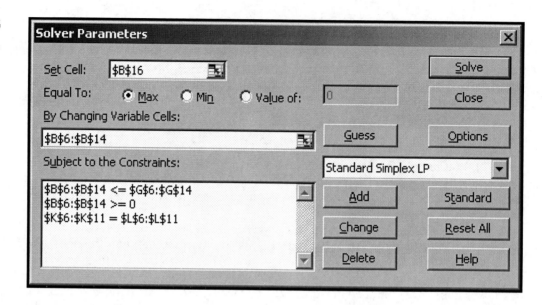

FIGURE 5.26

Network representation of the solution to Northwest Petroleum's max flow problem

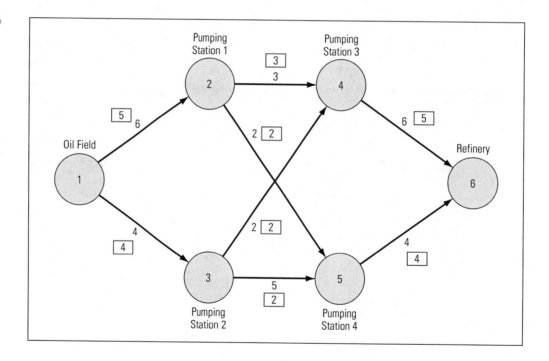

A graph like Figure 5.26, which summarizes the optimal flows in a max flow problem, is helpful in identifying where increases in flow capacity would be most effective. For example, from this graph, we can see that even though X_{24} and X_{34} are both at full capacity, increasing their capacity will not necessarily increase the flow through the network. Increasing the capacity of X_{24} would allow for an increased flow through the network because an additional unit could then flow from node 1 to node 2 to node 4 to node 6. However, increasing the capacity of X_{34} would not allow for an increase in the total flow because the arc from node 1 to node 3 is already at full capacity.

5.7 Special Modeling Considerations

A number of special conditions can arise in network flow problems that require a bit of creativity to model accurately. For example, it is easy to impose minimum or maximum flow restrictions on individual arcs in the networks by placing appropriate lower and upper bounds on the corresponding decision variables. However, in some network flow problems, minimum or maximum flow requirements may apply to the *total* flow emanating from a given node. For example, consider the network flow problem shown in Figure 5.27.

Now suppose that the total flow into node 3 must be at least 50 and the total flow into node 4 must be at least 60. We could enforce these conditions easily with the following constraints:

$$X_{13} + X_{23} \geq 50$$
$$X_{14} + X_{24} \geq 60$$

Unfortunately, these constraints do not conform to the balance-of-flow rule and would require us to impose *side constraints* on the model. An alternative approach to modeling this problem is shown in Figure 5.28.

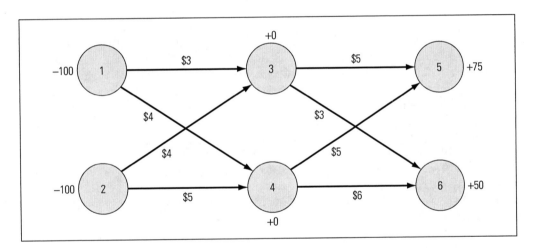

FIGURE 5.27

Example network flow problem

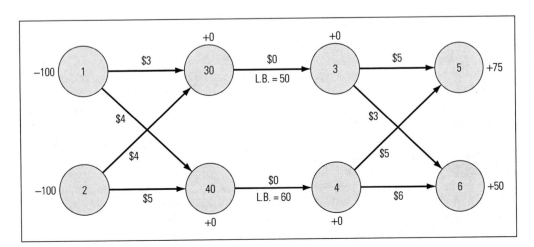

FIGURE 5.28

Revised network flow problem with lower bounds on the total flow into nodes 3 and 4

FIGURE 5.29

*Alternative
networks allowing
two different types
of flow between
two nodes*

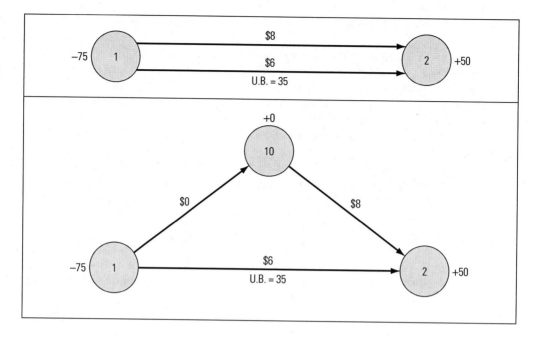

Two additional nodes and arcs were inserted in Figure 5.28. Note that the arc from node 30 to node 3 has a lower bound (L.B.) of 50. This will ensure that at least 50 units flow into node 3. Node 3 then must distribute this flow to nodes 5 and 6. Similarly, the arc connecting node 40 to node 4 ensures that at least 60 units will flow into node 4. The additional nodes and arcs added to Figure 5.28 are sometimes referred to as *dummy nodes* and *dummy arcs*.

As another example, consider the network in the upper portion of Figure 5.29 in which the flow between two nodes can occur at two different costs. One arc has a cost of $6 per unit of flow and an upper bound (U.B.) of 35. The other arc has a cost of $8 per unit of flow with no upper bound on the amount of flow allowed. Note that the minimum cost solution is to send 35 units of flow from node 1 to node 2 across the $6 arc and 15 units from node 1 to node 2 across the $8 arc.

To model this problem mathematically, we would like to have two arcs called X_{12} because both arcs go from node 1 to node 2. However, if both arcs are called X_{12}, there is no way to distinguish one from the other! A solution to this dilemma is shown in the lower portion of Figure 5.29 in which we inserted a dummy node and a dummy arc. Thus, there are now two distinct arcs flowing into node 2: X_{12} and $X_{10,2}$. Flow from node 1 to node 2 across the $8 arc now must first go through node 10.

As a final example, note that upper bounds (or capacity restrictions) on the arcs in a network flow might *effectively* limit the amount of supply that can be sent through the network to meet the demand. As a result, in a network flow problem with flow restrictions (upper bounds) on the arcs, it is sometimes difficult to tell in advance whether the total demand can be met—even if the total supply available exceeds the total demand. This again creates a potential problem in knowing which balance-of-flow rule to use. Consider the example in Figure 5.30.

The upper portion of Figure 5.30 shows a network with a total supply of 200 and total demand of 155. Because the total supply appears to exceed the total demand, we are inclined to apply the balance-of-flow rule that would generate constraints of the form: Inflow − Outflow ≥ Supply or Demand. This balance of flow rule requires the total

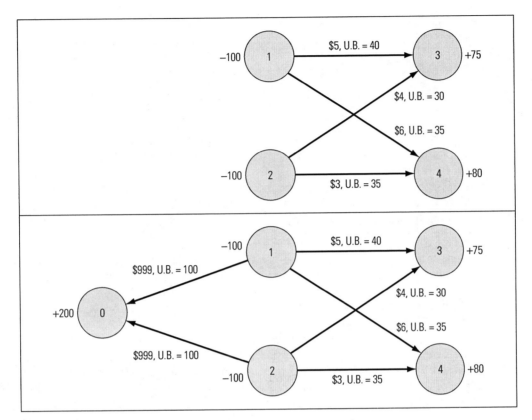

FIGURE 5.30

Example of using a dummy demand node

inflow to nodes 3 and 4 to be greater than or equal to their demands of 75 and 80, respectively. However, the upper bounds on the arcs leading into node 3 limit the total flow into this node to 70 units. Similarly, the total flow into node 4 is limited to 70. As a result, there is no feasible solution to the problem. In this case, we cannot resolve the infeasibility by reversing the constraints to be of the form: Inflow − Outflow ≤ Supply or Demand. Although this allows for less than the total amount demanded to be sent to nodes 3 and 4, it now *requires* all the supply to be sent out of nodes 1 and 2. Clearly, some of the 200 units of supply available from nodes 1 and 2 will have nowhere to go if the total flow into nodes 3 and 4 cannot exceed 140 units (as required by the upper bounds on the arcs).

A solution to this predicament is shown in the bottom half of Figure 5.30. Here, we added a dummy demand node (node 0) that is connected directly to nodes 1 and 2 with arcs that impose very large costs on flows to the dummy node. Note that the demand at this dummy node is equal to the total supply in the network. Now, the total demand exceeds the total supply so the balance-of-flow rule mandates we use constraints of the form: Inflow − Outflow ≤ Supply or Demand. Again, this allows for less than the total amount demanded to be sent to nodes 0, 3, and 4 but *requires* all the supply to be sent out of nodes 1 and 2. Due to the large costs associated with flows from nodes 1 and 2 to the dummy demand node, Solver will ensure that as much of the supply as possible is first sent to nodes 3 and 4. Any remaining supply at nodes 1 and 2 would then be sent to the dummy node. Of course, flows to the dummy node actually represent excess supply or inventory at nodes 1 and 2 that would not actually be shipped anywhere or incur any costs. But using a dummy node in this manner allows us to model and solve the problem accurately.

Dummy nodes and arcs can be helpful in modeling a variety of situations that occur naturally in network problems. The techniques illustrated here are three "tricks of the trade" in network modeling and might prove useful in some of the problems at the end of this chapter.

5.8 Minimal Spanning Tree Problems

Another type of network problem is known as the minimal spanning tree problem. This type of problem cannot be solved as an LP problem, but is solved easily using a simple manual algorithm.

For a network with n nodes, a **spanning tree** is a set of $n - 1$ arcs that connects all the nodes and contains no loops. A minimum spanning tree problem involves determining the set of arcs that connects all the nodes in a network while minimizing the total length (or cost) of the selected arcs. Consider the following example.

> Jon Fleming is responsible for setting up a local area network (LAN) in the design engineering department of Windstar Aerospace Company. A LAN consists of a number of individual computers connected to a centralized computer or file server. Each computer in the LAN can access information from the file server and communicate with the other computers in the LAN.
>
> Installing a LAN involves connecting all the computers together with communications cables. Not every computer has to be connected directly to the file server, but there must be some link between each computer in the network. Figure 5.31 summarizes all the possible connections that Jon could make. Each node in this figure represents one of the computers to be included in the LAN. Each line connecting the nodes represents a possible connection between pairs of computers. The dollar amount on each line represents the cost of making the connection.

The arcs in Figure 5.31 have no specific directional orientation, indicating that information can move in either direction across the arcs. Also note that the communication

FIGURE 5.31

Network representation of Windstar Aerospace's minimal spanning tree problem

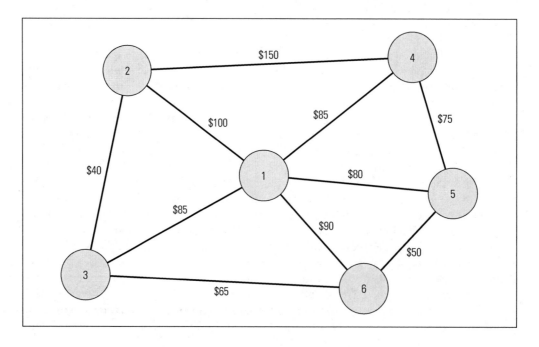

links represented by the arcs do not exist yet. Jon's challenge is to determine which links to establish. Because the network involves $n = 6$ nodes, a spanning tree for this problem consists of $n - 1 = 5$ arcs that results in a path existing between any pair of nodes. The objective is to find the minimal (least costly) spanning tree for this problem.

5.8.1 AN ALGORITHM FOR THE MINIMAL SPANNING TREE PROBLEM

You can apply a simple algorithm to solve minimal spanning tree problems. The steps to this algorithm are:

1. Select any node. Call this the current subnetwork.
2. Add to the current subnetwork the cheapest arc that connects any node within the current subnetwork to any node not in the current subnetwork. (Ties for the cheapest arc can be broken arbitrarily.) Call this the current subnetwork.
3. If all the nodes are in the subnetwork, stop; this is the optimal solution. Otherwise, return to step 2.

5.8.2 SOLVING THE EXAMPLE PROBLEM

You can program this algorithm easily or, for simple problems, execute it manually. The following steps illustrate how to execute the algorithm manually for the example problem shown in Figure 5.31.

Step 1. If we select node 1 in Figure 5.31, then node 1 is the current subnetwork.

Step 2. The cheapest arc connecting the current subnetwork to a node not in the current subnetwork is the $80 arc connecting nodes 1 and 5. This arc and node 5 are added to the current subnetwork.

Step 3. Four nodes (nodes 2, 3, 4, and 6) remain unconnected—therefore, return to step 2.

Step 2. The cheapest arc connecting the current subnetwork to a node not in the current subnetwork is the $50 arc connecting nodes 5 and 6. This arc and node 6 are added to the current subnetwork.

Step 3. Three nodes (nodes 2, 3, and 4) remain unconnected—therefore, return to step 2.

Step 2. The cheapest arc connecting the current subnetwork to a node not in the current subnetwork is the $65 arc connecting nodes 6 and 3. This arc and node 3 are added to the current subnetwork.

Step 3. Two nodes (nodes 2 and 4) remain unconnected—therefore, return to step 2.

Step 2. The cheapest arc connecting the current subnetwork to a node not in the current subnetwork is the $40 arc connecting nodes 3 and 2. This arc and node 2 are added to the current subnetwork.

Step 3. One node (node 4) remains unconnected—therefore, return to step 2.

Step 2. The cheapest arc connecting the current subnetwork to a node not in the current subnetwork is the $75 arc connecting nodes 5 and 4. This arc and node 4 are added to the current subnetwork.

Step 3. All the nodes are now connected. Stop; the current subnetwork is optimal.

Figure 5.32 shows the optimal (minimal) spanning tree generated by this algorithm. The algorithm described here produces the optimal (minimal) spanning tree regardless

FIGURE 5.32

Optimal solution to Windstar Aerospace's minimal spanning tree problem

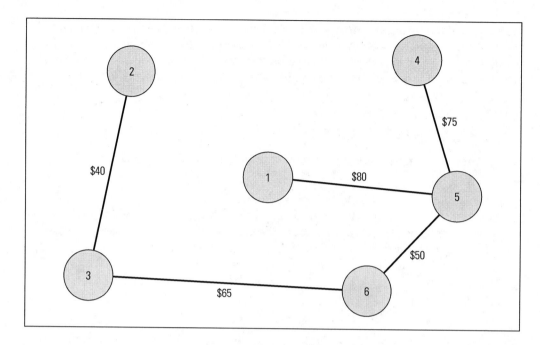

of which node is selected initially in step 1. You can verify this by solving the example problem again starting with a different node in step 1.

5.9 Summary

This chapter presented several business problems modeled as network flow problems, including transshipment problems, shortest path problems, maximal flow problems, transportation/assignment problems, and generalized network flow models. It also introduced the minimal spanning tree problem and presented a simple algorithm for solving this type of problem manually.

Although special algorithms exist for solving network flow problems, you can also formulate and solve them as LP problems. The constraints in an LP formulation of a network flow problem have a special structure that enables you to implement and solve these models easily in a spreadsheet. Although there might be more efficient ways of solving network flow problems, the methods discussed in this chapter are often the most practical. For extremely complex network flow problems, you might need to use a specialized algorithm. Unfortunately, you are unlikely to find this type of software at your local software store. However, various network optimization packages can be found in the technical/scientific directories on the Internet.

5.10 References

Glassey, R. and V. Gupta. "A Linear Programming Analysis of Paper Recycling," *Studies in Mathematical Programming*. New York: North–Holland, 1978.

Glover, F. and D. Klingman. "Network Applications in Industry and Government," *AIIE Transactions*, vol. 9, no. 4, 1977.

Glover, F., D. Klingman, and N. Phillips. *Network Models and Their Applications in Practice*. New York: Wiley, 1992.

Hansen, P. and R. Wendell. "A Note on Airline Commuting," *Interfaces*, vol. 11, no. 12, 1982.

Phillips, D. and A. Diaz. *Fundamentals of Network Analysis*. Englewood Cliffs, NJ: Prentice Hall, 1981.

Vemuganti, R., et al. "Network Models for Fleet Management," *Decision Sciences*, vol. 20, Winter 1989.

THE WORLD OF MANAGEMENT SCIENCE

Yellow Freight System Boosts Profits and Quality with Network Optimization

One of the largest motor carriers in the United States, Yellow Freight System, Inc. of Overland Park, Kansas, uses network modeling and optimization to assist management in load planning, routing empty trucks, routing trailers, dropping or adding direct service routes, and strategic planning of terminal size and location. The system, called SYSNET, operates on a network of Sun workstations optimizing over a million network flow variables. The company also uses a tactical planning room equipped with graphical display tools that allow planning meetings to be conducted interactively with the system.

The company competes in the less–than–truckload (LTL) segment of the trucking market. That is, they contract for shipments of any size, regardless of whether the shipment fills the trailer. To operate efficiently, Yellow Freight must consolidate and transfer shipments at 23 break–bulk terminals located throughout the United States. At these terminals, shipments might be reloaded into different trailers depending on the final destination. Each break–bulk terminal serves several end–of–line terminals, in a hub–and–spoke network. Normally, shipments are sent by truck to the break–bulk dedicated to the origination point. Local managers occasionally try to save costs by loading direct, which means bypassing a break–bulk and sending a truckload of consolidated shipments directly to the final destination. Before SYSNET, these decisions were made in the field without accurate information on how they would affect costs and reliability in the entire system.

Since its implementation in 1989, SYSNET has scored high with upper management. Often, the first response to a new proposal is, "Has it been run through SYSNET?" The benefits attributed to the new system include:

- an increase of 11.6% in freight loaded directly, saving $4.7 million annually
- better routing of trailers, saving $1 million annually
- savings of $1.42 million annually by increasing the average number of pounds loaded per trailer
- reduction in claims for damaged merchandise
- a 27% reduction in the number of late deliveries
- tactical planning projects with SYSNET in 1990 that identified $10 million in annual savings

Equally important has been the effect on the management philosophy and culture at Yellow Freight. Management now has greater control over network operations; tradition, intuition, and "gut feel" have been replaced with formal analytical tools; and Yellow Freight is better able to act as a partner with customers in total quality management and just–in–time inventory systems.

Source: Braklow, John W., William W. Graham, Stephen M. Hassler, Ken E. Peck and Warren B. Powell, "Interactive Optimization Improves Service and Performance for Yellow Freight System," *Interfaces*, 22:1, January–February 1992, pages 147–172.

Questions and Problems

1. This chapter followed the convention of using negative numbers to represent the supply at a node and positive numbers to represent the demand at a node. Another convention is just the opposite—using positive numbers to represent supply and negative numbers to represent demand. How would the balance-of-flow rule presented in this chapter need to be changed to accommodate this alternate convention?

2. To use the balance-of-flow rule presented in this chapter, constraints for supply nodes must have negative RHS values. Some LP software packages cannot solve problems in which the constraints have negative RHS values. How should the balance-of-flow rules be modified to produce LP models that can be solved with such software packages?

3. Consider the revised Coal Bank Hollow recycling problem discussed in section 5.5.4 of this chapter. We said that it is safest to assume the supply in a generalized network flow problem is capable of meeting the demand (until Solver proves otherwise).

   a. Solve the problem in Figure 5.17 (and file Fig5-17.xls on your data disk) assuming 80 tons of newspaper is available and that the supply is NOT adequate to meet the demand. How much of each of the raw recycling materials is used? How much demand for each product is met? What is the cost of this solution?

   b. Solve the problem again assuming that the supply is adequate to meet the demand. How much of each of the raw recycling materials is used? How much demand for each product is met? What is the cost of this solution?

   c. Which one is better? Why?

   d. Suppose there are 55 tons of newspaper available. Figure 5.21 shows the least cost solution for distributing the supply in this case. In that solution, the demand for newsprint pulp and packaging pulp is met but we are almost 15 tons short on print stock pulp. How much can this shortage be reduced (without creating shortages of the other products) and how much extra would it cost to do so?

4. Consider the generalized transportation problem shown in Figure 5.33. How can this problem be transformed into an equivalent transportation problem? Draw the network for the equivalent problem.

FIGURE 5.33

Graph of a generalized network flow problem

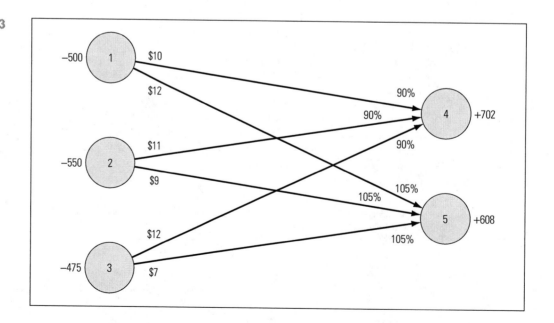

5. Draw the network representation of the following network flow problem.

MIN: $+7X_{12} + 6X_{14} + 3X_{23} + 4X_{24} + 5X_{32} + 9X_{43} + 8X_{52} + 5X_{54}$

Subject to: $-X_{12} - X_{14} = -5$

$+X_{12} + X_{52} + X_{32} - X_{23} - X_{24} = +4$

$-X_{32} + X_{23} + X_{43} = +8$

$+X_{14} + X_{24} + X_{54} - X_{43} = +0$

$-X_{52} - X_{54} = -7$

$X_{ij} \geq 0$ for all i and j

6. Draw the network representation of the following network flow problem. What kind of network flow problem is this?

MIN: $+2X_{13} + 6X_{14} + 5X_{15} + 4X_{23} + 3X_{24} + 7X_{25}$

Subject to: $-X_{13} - X_{14} - X_{15} = -8$

$-X_{23} - X_{24} - X_{25} = -7$

$+X_{13} + X_{23}$ $\quad = +5$

$+X_{14} + X_{24}$ $\quad = +5$

$+X_{15} + X_{25}$ $\quad = +5$

$X_{ij} \geq 0$ for all i and j

7. Refer to the equipment replacement problem discussed in section 5.3 of this chapter. In addition to the lease costs described for the problem, suppose that it costs Compu-Train $2,000 extra in labor costs whenever they replace their existing computers with new ones. What effect does this have on the formulation and solution of the problem? Which of the two leasing contracts is optimal in this case?

8. Suppose the X's in the following table indicate locations where fire sprinkler heads need to be installed in an existing building. The S indicates the location of the water source to supply these sprinklers. Assume that pipe can be run only vertically or horizontally (not diagonally) between the water source and the sprinkler heads.

	1	2	3	4	5	6	7
1		X					
2	X	X	X		X	X	X
3	X		X		X	X	X
4	X	X	X			X	X
5	X	X	X		X		X
6							
7	X						
8				S			X

a. Create a spanning tree showing how water can be brought to all the sprinkler heads using a minimal amount of pipe.

b. Suppose that it takes 10 feet of pipe to connect each cell in the table to each adjacent cell. How much pipe does your solution require?

9. SunNet is a residential Internet Service Provider (ISP) in the central Florida area. Presently, the company operates one centralized facility that all of its clients call into for Internet access. To improve service, the company is planning to open three satellite offices in the cities of Pine Hills, Eustis, and Sanford. The company has identified five different regions to be serviced by these three offices. The following table summarizes the number of customers in each region, the service capacity at each

office, and the average monthly per customer cost of providing service to each region from each office. Table entries of "n.a." indicate infeasible region-to-service-center combinations. SunNet would like to determine how many customers from each region to assign to each service center to minimize cost.

Region	Pine Hills	Eustis	Sanford	Customers
1	$6.50	$7.50	n.a.	30,000
2	$7.00	$8.00	n.a.	40,000
3	$8.25	$7.25	$6.75	25,000
4	n.a.	$7.75	$7.00	35,000
5	n.a.	$7.50	$6.75	33,000
Capacity	60,000	70,000	40,000	

a. Draw a network flow model to represent this problem.
b. Implement your model in Excel and solve it.
c. What is the optimal solution?

10. Acme Manufacturing makes a variety of household appliances at a single manufacturing facility. The expected demand for one of these appliances during the next four months is shown in the following table along with the expected production costs and the expected capacity for producing these items.

	Month			
	1	2	3	4
Demand	420	580	310	540
Production Cost	$49.00	$45.00	$46.00	$47.00
Production Capacity	500	520	450	550

Acme estimates that it costs $1.50 per month for each unit of this appliance carried in inventory at the end of each month. Currently, Acme has 120 units in inventory on hand for this product. To maintain a level workforce, the company wants to produce at least 400 units per month. They also want to maintain a safety stock of at least 50 units per month. Acme wants to determine how many of each appliance to manufacture during each of the next four months to meet the expected demand at the lowest possible total cost.

a. Draw a network flow model for this problem.
b. Create a spreadsheet model for this problem and solve it using Solver.
c. What is the optimal solution?
d. How much money could Acme save if they were willing to drop the restriction about producing at least 400 units per month?

11. Sunrise Swimwear manufactures ladies' swimwear in January through June of each year that is sold through retail outlets in March through August. The following table summarizes the monthly production capacity and retail demand (in 1000s), and inventory carrying costs (per 1000).

Month	Capacity	Demand	Carrying Cost	
			First Month	Other Months
January	16	—	$110	$55
February	18	—	$110	$55
March	20	14	$120	$55
April	28	20	$135	$55
May	29	26	$150	$55
June	36	33	$155	$55
July	—	28	—	—
August	—	10	—	—

a. Draw a network flow representation of this problem.
b. Implement a spreadsheet model for this problem.
c. What is the optimal solution?

12. Jacobs Manufacturing produces a popular custom accessory for pickup trucks at plants in Huntington, West Virginia and Bakersfield, California, and ships them to distributors in Dallas, Texas; Chicago, Illinois; Denver, Colorado; and Atlanta, Georgia. The plants in Huntington and Bakersfield have, respectively, the capacity to produce 3,000 and 4,000 units per month. For the month of October, costs of shipping a carton of 10 units from each plant to each distributor are summarized in the following table:

	Shipping Cost per Container			
	Dallas	Chicago	Denver	Atlanta
Huntington	$19	$15	$14	$12
Bakersfield	$16	$18	$11	$13

Jacobs has been notified that these shipping rates will each increase by $1.50 on November 1. Each distributor has ordered 1,500 units of Jacobs' product for October and 2,000 units for November. In any month, Jacobs can send each distributor up to 500 units more than they have ordered if Jacobs provides a $2 per unit discount on the excess (which the distributor must hold in inventory from one month to the next). In October, the per unit cost of production in Huntington and Bakersfield are $12 and $16, respectively. In November, Jacobs expects the cost of production at both plants to be $14 per unit. The company wants to develop production and distribution plan for the months of October and November that would allow them to meet the expected demand from each distributor at the minimum cost.

a. Draw a network flow model for this problem.
b. Implement your model in a spreadsheet and solve it.
c. What is the optimal solution?

13. A construction company wants to determine the optimal replacement policy for the earth mover it owns. The company has a policy of not keeping an earth mover for more than five years, and has estimated the annual operating costs and trade-in values for earth movers during each of the five years they might be kept as:

	Age in Years				
	0-1	1-2	2-3	3-4	4-5
Operating Cost	$8,000	$9,100	$10,700	$9,200	$11,000
Trade-in Value	$14,000	$9,000	$6,000	$3,500	$2,000

Assume that new earth movers currently cost $25,000 and are increasing in cost by 4.5% per year. The company wants to determine when it should plan on replacing its current, 2-year-old earth mover. Use a 5-year planning horizon.

a. Draw the network representation of this problem.
b. Write out the LP formulation of this problem.
c. Solve the problem using Solver. Interpret your solution.

14. The Ortega Food Company needs to ship 100 cases of hot tamales from its warehouse in San Diego to a distributor in New York City at minimum cost. The costs associated with shipping 100 cases between various cities are:

	To					
From	Los Angeles	Denver	St. Louis	Memphis	Chicago	New York
San Diego	5	13	—	45	—	105
Los Angeles	—	27	19	50	—	95
Denver	—	—	14	30	32	—
St. Louis	—	14	—	35	24	—
Memphis	—	—	35	—	18	25
Chicago	—	—	24	18	—	17

a. Draw the network representation of this problem.

b. Write out the LP formulation of this problem.

c. Solve the problem using Solver. Interpret your solution.

15. A cotton grower in south Georgia produces cotton on farms in Statesboro and Brooklet, ships it to cotton gins in Claxton and Millen, where it is processed, and then sends it to distribution centers in Savannah, Perry, and Valdosta, where it is sold to customers for $60 per ton. Any surplus cotton is sold to a government warehouse in Hinesville for $25 per ton. The cost of growing and harvesting a ton of cotton at the farms in Statesboro and Brooklet is $20 and $22, respectively. There are presently 700 and 500 tons of cotton available in Statesboro and Brooklet, respectively. The cost of transporting the cotton from the farms to the gins and the government warehouse is shown in the following table:

	Claxton	Millen	Hinesville
Statesboro	$4.00	$3.00	$4.50
Brooklet	$3.5	$3.00	$3.50

The gin in Claxton has the capacity to process 700 tons of cotton at a cost of $10 per ton. The gin in Millen can process 600 tons at a cost of $11 per ton. Each gin must use at least one half of its available capacity. The cost of shipping a ton of cotton from each gin to each distribution center is summarized in the following table:

	Savannah	Perry	Valdosta
Claxton	$10	$16	$15
Millen	$12	$18	$17

Assume that the demand for cotton in Savannah, Perry, and Valdosta is 400, 300, and 450 tons, respectively.

a. Draw a network flow model to represent this problem.

b. Implement your model in Excel and solve it.

c. What is the optimal solution?

16. The blood bank wants to determine the least expensive way to transport available blood donations from Pittsburg and Staunton to hospitals in Charleston, Roanoke, Richmond, Norfolk, and Suffolk. The supply and demand for donated blood is shown in Figure 5.34 along with the unit cost of shipping along each possible arc.

a. Create a spreadsheet model for this problem.

b. What is the optimal solution?

c. Suppose that no more than 1000 units of blood can be transported over any one arc. What is the optimal solution to this revised problem?

17. A furniture manufacturer has warehouses in cities represented by nodes 1, 2, and 3 in Figure 5.35. The values on the arcs indicate the per unit shipping costs required to transport living room suites between the various cities. The supply of living room

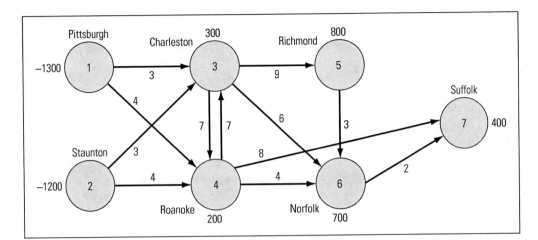

FIGURE 5.34

Network flow model for the blood bank problem

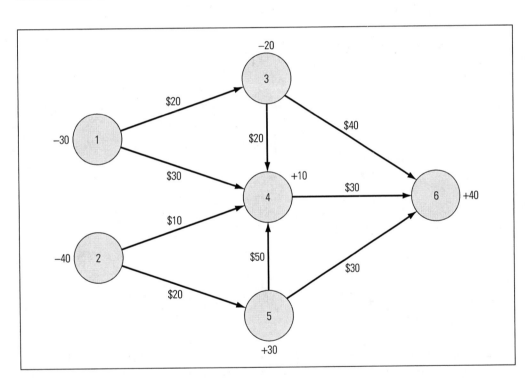

FIGURE 5.35

Network flow model for the furniture manufacturing problem

suites at each warehouse is indicated by the negative number next to nodes 1, 2, and 3. The demand for living room suites is indicated by the positive number next to the remaining nodes.

    a. Identify the supply, demand, and transshipment nodes in this problem.

    b. Use Solver to determine the least costly shipping plan for this problem.

18. The graph in Figure 5.36 represents various flows that can occur through a sewage treatment plant with the numbers on the arcs representing the maximum flow (in tons of sewage per hour) that can be accommodated. Formulate an LP model to determine the maximum tons of sewage per hour that can be processed by this plant.

19. A company has three warehouses that supply four stores with a given product. Each warehouse has 30 units of the product. Stores 1, 2, 3, and 4 require 20, 25, 30,

FIGURE 5.36

Network flow model for the sewage treatment plant

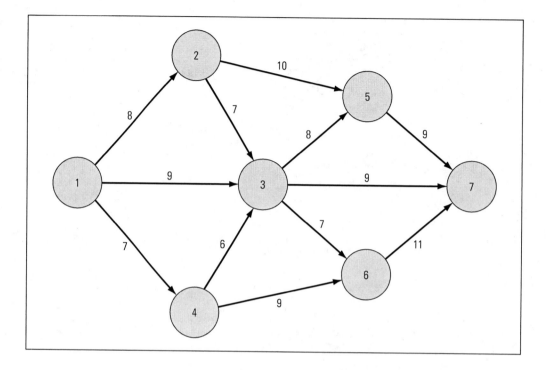

and 35 units of the product, respectively. The per unit shipping costs from each warehouse to each store are:

	Store			
Warehouse	**1**	**2**	**3**	**4**
1	5	4	6	5
2	3	6	4	4
3	4	3	3	2

a. Draw the network representation of this problem. What kind of problem is this?
b. Formulate an LP model to determine the least expensive shipping plan to fill the demands at the stores.
c. Solve the problem using Solver.
d. Suppose that shipments are not allowed between warehouse 1 and store 2 or between warehouse 2 and store 3. What is the easiest way to modify the spreadsheet so that you can solve this modified problem? What is the optimal solution to the modified problem?

20. A used-car broker needs to transport his inventory of cars from locations 1 and 2 in Figure 5.37 to used-car auctions being held at locations 4 and 5. The costs of transporting cars along each of the routes are indicated on the arcs. The trucks used to carry the cars can hold a maximum of 10 cars. Therefore, the maximum number of cars that can flow over any arc is 10.

a. Formulate an LP model to determine the least costly method of distributing the cars from locations 1 and 2 so that 20 cars will be available for sale at location 4, and 10 cars will be available for sale at location 5.
b. Use Solver to find the optimal solution to this problem.

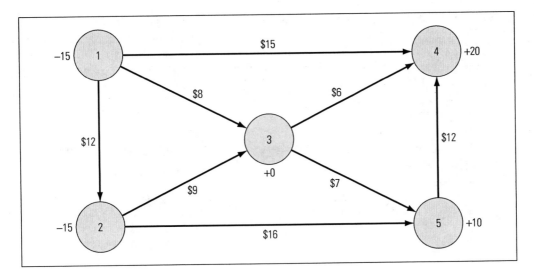

FIGURE 5.37

Network flow model for the used car problem

21. An information systems consultant who lives in Dallas must spend the majority of the month of March onsite with a client in San Diego. Her travel schedule for the month is as follows:

Leave Dallas	Leave San Diego
Monday, March 2	Friday, March 6
Monday, March 9	Thursday, March 12
Tuesday, March 17	Friday, March 20
Monday, March 23	Wednesday, March 25

The usual round-trip ticket price between Dallas and San Diego is $750. However, the airline offers a 25% discount if the dates on a round-trip ticket cover less than 7 nights and include a weekend. A 35% discount is offered for round-trip tickets covering 10 or more nights, and a 45% discount is available for round-trip tickets covering 20 or more nights. The consultant can purchase four round-trip tickets in any manner that allows her to leave Dallas and San Diego on the days indicated.

a. Draw a network flow model for this problem.
b. Implement the problem in a spreadsheet and solve it.
c. What is the optimal solution? How much does this save for four full-cost round-trip tickets?

22. The Conch Oil Company needs to transport 30 million barrels of crude oil from a port in Doha, Qatar in the Persian Gulf to three refineries throughout Europe. The refineries are in Rotterdam, Netherlands; Toulon, France; and Palermo, Italy, and require 6 million, 15 million, and 9 million barrels, respectively. The oil can be transported to the refineries in three different ways. First, oil may be shipped from Qatar to Rotterdam, Toulon, and Palermo on supertankers traveling around Africa at costs of $1.20, $1.40, and $1.35 per barrel, respectively. Conch is contractually obligated to send at least 25% of its oil via these supertankers. Alternatively, oil can be shipped from Doha to Suez, Egypt, at a cost of $0.35 per barrel, then through the Suez Canal to Port Said at a cost of $0.20 per barrel, then from Port

Said to Rotterdam, Toulon, and Palermo at per barrel costs of $0.27, $0.23, and $0.19, respectively. Finally, up to 15 million barrels of the oil shipped from Doha to Suez can then be sent via pipeline Damietta, Egypt, at $0.16 per barrel. From Damietta, it can shipped to Rotterdam, Toulon, and Palermo at costs of $0.25, $0.20, and $0.15, respectively.

a. Draw a network flow model for this problem.
b. Implement your model in a spreadsheet and solve it.
c. What is the optimal solution?

23. Omega Airlines has several nonstop flights between Atlanta and Los Angeles every day. The schedules of these flights are shown in the following table.

Flight	Departs Atlanta	Arrives in L.A.	Flight	Departs L.A.	Arrive in Atlanta
1	6 am	8 am	1	5 am	9 am
2	8 am	10 am	2	6 am	10 am
3	10 am	Noon	3	9 am	1 pm
4	Noon	2 pm	4	Noon	4 pm
5	4 pm	6 pm	5	2 pm	6 pm
6	6 pm	8 pm	6	5 pm	9 pm
7	7 pm	9 pm	7	7 pm	11 pm

Omega wants to determine the optimal way of assigning flight crews to these different flights. The company wants to ensure that the crews always return to the city from which they left each day. FAA regulations require at least one hour of rest for flight crews between flights. However, flight crews become irritated if they are forced to wait for extremely long periods of time between flights, so Omega wants to find an assignment of flight schedules that minimizes these waiting periods.

a. Draw a network flow model for this problem.
b. Implement the problem in a spreadsheet and solve it.
c. What is the optimal solution? What is the longest period of time that a flight crew has to wait between flights, according to your solution?
d. Are there alternate optimal solutions to this problem? If so, do any alternate optimal solutions result in a smaller maximum waiting period between flights?

24. A residential moving company needs to move a family from city 1 to city 12 in Figure 5.38 where the numbers on the arcs represents the driving distance in miles between cities.

a. Create a spreadsheet model for this problem.
b. What is the optimal solution?
c. Suppose that the moving company gets paid by the mile and, as a result, wants to determine the longest path from city 1 to city 12. What is the optimal solution?
d. Now suppose that travel is permissible in either direction between cities 6 and 9. Describe the optimal solution to this problem.

25. Joe Jones wants to establish a construction fund (or sinking fund) to pay for a new bowling alley he is having built. Construction of the bowling alley is expected to take six months and cost $300,000. Joe's contract with the construction company requires him to make payments of $50,000 at the end of the second and fourth months, and a final payment of $200,000 at the end of the sixth month when the

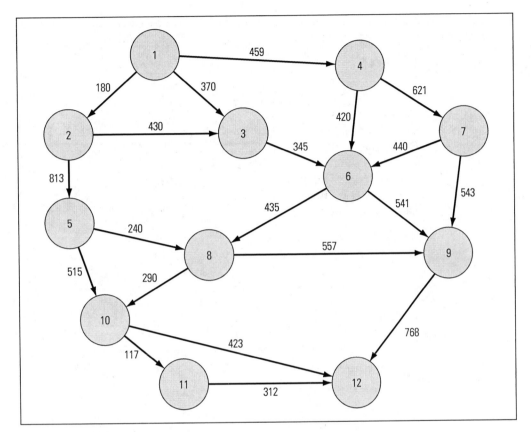

FIGURE 5.38

*Network flow
model for the
moving company
problem*

bowling alley is completed. Joe has identified four investments that he can use to establish the construction fund; these investments are summarized in the following table:

Investment	Available in Month	Months to Maturity	Yield at Maturity
A	1, 2, 3, 4, 5, 6	1	1.2%
B	1, 3, 5	2	3.5%
C	1, 4	3	5.8%
D	1	6	11.0%

The table indicates that investment A will be available at the beginning of each of the next six months, and funds invested in this manner mature in one month with a yield of 1.2%. Similarly, funds can be placed in investment C only at the beginning of months 1 and/or 4, and mature at the end of three months with a yield of 5.8%. Joe wants to minimize the amount of money he must invest in month 1 to meet the required payments for this project.

a. Draw a network flow model for this problem.

b. Create a spreadsheet model for this problem and solve it.

c. What is the optimal solution?

26. Telephone calls for the YakLine, a discount long distance carrier, are routed through a variety of switching devices that interconnect various network hubs in different

cities. The maximum number of calls that can be handled by each segment of their network is shown in the following table:

Network Segments	Calls (in 1,000s)
Washington, DC to Chicago	800
Washington, DC to Kansas City	650
Washington, DC to Dallas	700
Chicago to Dallas	725
Chicago to Denver	700
Kansas City to Denver	750
Kansas City to Dallas	625
Denver to San Francisco	900
Dallas to San Francisco	725

YakLine wants to determine the maximum number of calls that can go from their east coast operations hub in Washington, DC to their west coast operations hub in San Francisco.

a. Draw a network flow model for this problem.
b. Create a spreadsheet model for this problem and solve it.
c. What is the optimal solution?

27. Union Express has 60 tons of cargo that needs to be shipped from Boston to Dallas. The shipping capacity on each of the routes Union Express planes fly each night is shown in the following table:

Nightly Flight Segments	Capacity (in tons)
Boston to Baltimore	30
Boston to Pittsburgh	25
Boston to Cincinnati	35
Baltimore to Atlanta	10
Baltimore to Cincinnati	5
Pittsburgh to Atlanta	15
Pittsburgh to Chicago	20
Cincinnati to Chicago	15
Cincinnati to Memphis	5
Atlanta to Memphis	25
Atlanta to Dallas	10
Chicago to Memphis	20
Chicago to Dallas	15
Memphis to Dallas	30
Memphis to Chicago	15

Will Union Express be able to move all 60 tons from Boston to Dallas in one night?

a. Draw a network flow model for this problem.
b. Create a spreadsheet model for the problem and solve it.
c. What is the maximum flow for this network?

28. E-mail messages sent over the Internet are broken up into electronic packets that may take a variety of different paths to reach their destination where the original message is reassembled. Suppose that the nodes in the graph shown in Figure 5.39 represent a series of computer hubs on the Internet and the arcs represent connections between them. Suppose that the values on the arcs represent the number of packets per minute (in 1,000,000s) that can be transmitted over each arc.

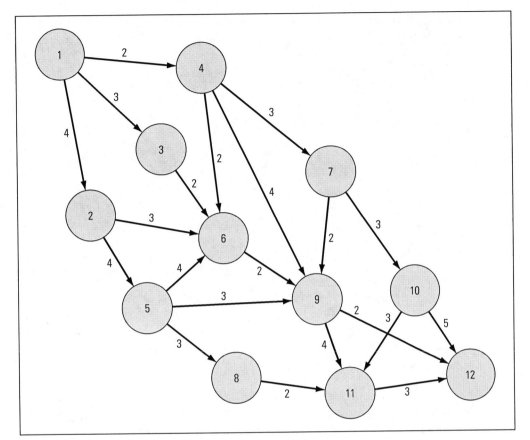

FIGURE 5.39

Network hubs and interconnections for the e-mail problem

a. Implement a network flow model to determine the maximum number of packets that can flow from node 1 to node 12 in one minute.

b. What is the maximum flow?

29. The Britts & Straggon company manufactures small engines at three different plants. From the plants, the engines are transported to two different warehouse facilities before being distributed to three wholesale distributors. The per unit manufacturing cost at each plant is shown in the following table in addition to the minimum required and maximum available daily production capacities.

Plant	Manufacturing Cost	Minimum Required Production	Maximum Production Capacity
1	$13	150	400
2	$15	150	300
3	$12	150	600

The unit cost of transporting engines from each plant to each warehouse is shown below.

Plant	Warehouse 1	Warehouse 2
1	$4	$5
2	$6	$4
3	$3	$5

FIGURE 5.40

Network flow model for the airport terminal problem

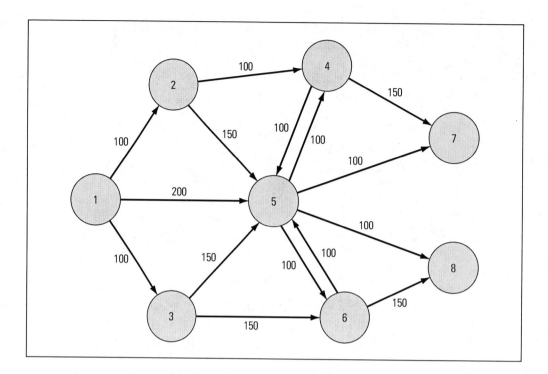

The unit cost of shipping engines from each warehouse to each distributor is shown in the following table along with the daily demand for each distributor.

Warehouse	Distributor 1	Distributor 2	Distributor 3
1	$6	$4	$3
2	$3	$5	$2
Demand	300	600	100

Each warehouse can process up to 500 engines per day.

a. Draw a network flow model to represent this problem.

b. Implement your model in Excel and solve it.

c. What is the optimal solution?

30. A new airport being built will have three terminals and two baggage pickup areas. An automated baggage delivery system has been designed to transport the baggage from each terminal to the two baggage pickup areas. This system is depicted graphically in Figure 5.40, where nodes 1, 2, and 3 represent the terminals, and nodes 7 and 8 represent the baggage pickup areas. The maximum number of bags per minute that can be handled by each part of the system is indicated by the value on each arc in the network.

a. Formulate an LP model to determine the maximum number of bags per minute that can be delivered by this system.

b. Use Solver to find the optimal solution to this problem.

31. Bull Dog Express runs a small airline that offers commuter flights between several cities in Georgia. The airline flies into and out of small airports only. These airports have limits on the number of flights Bull Dog Express can make each day. The airline can make five round-trip flights daily between Savannah and Macon, four round-trip flights daily between Macon and Albany, two round-trip flights daily between

Macon and Atlanta, two round-trip flights daily between Macon and Athens, two round-trip flights daily between Macon and Athens, two round-trip flights daily between Athens and Atlanta, and two round-trip flights daily from Albany to Atlanta. The airline wants to determine the maximum number of times connecting flights from Savannah to Atlanta can be offered in a single day.

a. Draw the network representation of this problem.

b. Formulate an LP model for this problem. What kind of problem is this?

c. Use Solver to determine the optimal solution to this problem.

32. The U.S. Department of Transportation (DOT) is planning to build a new interstate to run from Detroit, Michigan, to Charleston, South Carolina. Several different routes have been proposed. They are summarized in Figure 5.41, where node 1 represents Detroit and node 12 represents Charleston. The numbers on the arcs indicate the estimated construction costs of the various links (in millions of dollars). It is estimated that all of the routes will require approximately the same total driving time to make the trip from Detroit to Charleston. Thus, the DOT is interested in identifying the least costly alternative.

a. Formulate an LP model to determine the least costly construction plan.

b. Use Solver to determine the optimal solution to this problem.

33. A building contractor is designing the ductwork for the heating and air conditioning system in a new, single-story medical building. Figure 5.42 summarizes the possible connections between the primary air handling unit (node 1) and the various air outlets to be placed in the building (nodes 2 through 9). The arcs in the network represent possible ductwork connections, and the values on the arcs represent the feet of ductwork required.

FIGURE 5.41

Possible routes for the interstate construction problem

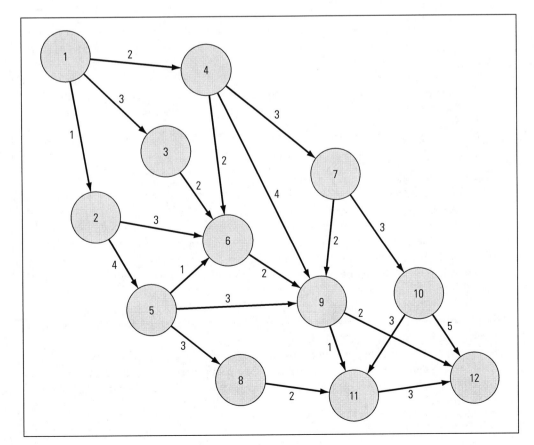

FIGURE 5.42

Network representation of the ductwork problem

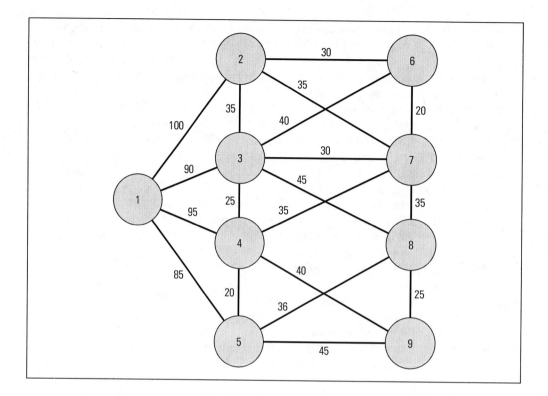

Starting at node 1, use the minimal spanning tree algorithm to determine how much ductwork should be installed to provide air access to each vent while requiring the least amount of ductwork.

34. The manager of catering services for the Roanoker Hotel has a problem. The banquet hall at the hotel is booked each evening during the coming week for groups who have reserved the following numbers of tables:

Day	Monday	Tuesday	Wednesday	Thursday	Friday
Tables Reserved	400	300	250	400	350

The hotel has 500 tablecloths that can be used for these banquets. However, the tablecloths used at each banquet will have to be cleaned before they can be used again. A local cleaning service will pick up the soiled tablecloths each evening after the banquet. It offers overnight cleaning for $2 per tablecloth, or 2-day service for $1 per tablecloth (*i.e.*, a tablecloth picked up Monday night can be ready Tuesday for $2 or ready for use Wednesday for $1). There are no tablecloth losses and all tablecloths must be cleaned. Due to the cleaner's capacity restrictions, the overnight service can be performed on up to only 250 tablecloths, and overnight service is not available on tablecloths picked up Friday night. All cloths used on Friday must be ready for use again by Monday. The hotel wants to determine the least costly plan for having its tablecloths cleaned.

a. Draw a network flow model for this problem. (*Hint:* Express the supplies and demands as minimum required and maximum allowable flows over selected arcs.)

b. Create a spreadsheet model for this problem and solve it. What is the optimal solution?

Hamilton & Jacobs

Hamilton & Jacobs (H&J) is a global investment company, providing start-up capital to promising new ventures around the world. Due to the nature of its business, H&J holds funds in a variety of countries and converts between currencies as needs arise in different parts of the world. Several months ago, the company moved $16 million into Japanese yen (JPY) when one U.S. dollar (USD) was worth 75 yen. Since that time, the value of the dollar has fallen sharply, where it now requires almost 110 yen to purchase one dollar.

Besides its holdings of yen, H&J also currently owns 6 million European EUROs and 30 million Swiss Francs (CHF). H&J's chief economic forecaster is predicting that all of the currencies it is presently holding will continue to gain strength against the dollar for the rest of the year. As a result, the company would like to convert all its surplus currency holdings back to U.S. dollars until the economic picture improves.

The bank H&J uses for currency conversions charges different transaction fees for converting between various currencies. The following table summarizes the transaction fees (expressed as a percentage of the amount converted) for US dollars (USD), Australian dollars (AUD), British pounds (GBP), European Euros (EURO), Indian Rupees (INR), Japanese yen (JPY), Singapore dollars (SGD), and Swiss Francs (CHF).

Transaction Fee Table

FROM/TO	USD	AUD	GBP	EUR	INR	JPY	SGD	CHF
USD	—	0.10%	0.50%	0.40%	0.40%	0.40%	0.25%	0.50%
AUD	0.10%	—	0.70%	0.50%	0.30%	0.30%	0.75%	0.75%
GBP	0.50%	0.70%	—	0.70%	0.70%	0.40%	0.45%	0.50%
EUR	0.40%	0.50%	0.70%	—	0.05%	0.10%	0.10%	0.10%
INR	0.40%	0.30%	0.70%	0.05%	—	0.20%	0.10%	0.10%
JPY	0.40%	0.30%	0.40%	0.10%	0.20%	—	0.05%	0.50%
SGD	0.25%	0.75%	0.45%	0.10%	0.10%	0.05%	—	0.50%
CHF	0.50%	0.75%	0.50%	0.10%	0.10%	0.50%	0.50%	—

Because it costs differing amounts to convert between various currencies, H&J determined that converting existing holdings directly into US dollars might not be the best strategy. Instead, it might be less expensive to convert existing holdings to an intermediate currency before converting the result back to US dollars. The following table summarizes the current exchange rates for converting from one currency to another.

Exchange Rate Table

From/To	USD	AUD	GBP	EUR	INR	JPY	SGD	CHF
USD	1	1.29249	0.55337	0.80425	43.5000	109.920	1.64790	1.24870
AUD	0.77370	1	0.42815	0.62225	33.6560	85.0451	1.27498	0.96612
GBP	1.80710	2.33566	1	1.45335	78.6088	198.636	2.97792	2.25652
EUR	1.24340	1.60708	0.68806	1	54.0879	136.675	2.04900	1.55263
INR	0.02299	0.02971	0.01272	0.01849	1	2.5269	0.03788	0.02871
JPY	0.00910	0.01176	0.00503	0.00732	0.39574	1	0.01499	0.01136
SGD	0.60683	0.78433	0.33581	0.48804	26.3972	66.7031	1	0.75775
CHF	0.80083	1.03507	0.44316	0.64407	34.8362	88.0275	1.31969	1

The exchange rate table indicates, for instance, that one Japanese yen can be converted into 0.00910 US dollars. So 100,000 yen would produce $910 US. However, the bank's 0.40% fee for this transaction would reduce the net amount received to

$910 \times (1 - 0.004) = \$906.36$. So H&J wants your assistance in determining the best way to convert all its non-US currency holdings back into US dollars.

a. Draw a network flow diagram for this problem.
b. Create a spreadsheet model for this problem and solve it.
c. What is the optimal solution?
d. If H&J converted each non-US currency it owns directly into US dollars, how many US dollars would it have?
e. Suppose that H&J wants to perform the same conversion but also leave $5 million in Australian dollars. What is the optimal solution in this case?

CASE 5.2   Old Dominion Energy

The United States is the biggest consumer of natural gas, and the second largest natural gas producer in the world. According to the U.S. Energy Information Administration (EIA), in 2001 the U.S. consumed 22.7 trillion cubic feet of natural gas. Stemming from phased deregulation, the transportation and delivery of natural gas from wellheads has grown since the '80s and there are now more than 278,000 miles of gas pipeline nationwide (see: http://www.platts.com/features/usgasguide/pipelines.shtml). With more electric power companies turning to natural gas as a cleaner-burning fuel, natural gas is expected to grow even more quickly over the next 20 years.

To ensure an adequate supply of natural gas, gas storage facilities have been built in numerous places along the pipeline. Energy companies can buy gas when prices are low and store it in these facilities for use or sale at a later date. Because energy consumption is influenced greatly by the weather (which is not entirely predictable), imbalances often arise in the supply and demand for gas in different parts of the country. Gas traders constantly monitor these market conditions and look for opportunities to sell gas from storage facilities when the price offered at a certain location is high enough. This decision is complicated because it costs different amounts of money to transport gas through different segments of the nationwide pipeline, and the capacity available in different parts of the pipeline is changing constantly. Thus, when traders see an opportunity to sell at a favorable price, they must quickly see how much capacity is available in the network and create deals with individual pipeline operators for the necessary capacity to move gas from storage to the buyer.

Bruce McDaniel is a gas trader for Old Dominion Energy (ODE), Inc. The network in Figure 5.43 represents a portion of the gas pipeline where ODE does business. The values next to each arc in this network are of the form (x,y) where x is the cost per thousand cubic feet (cf) of transporting gas along the arc, and y is the available transmission capacity of the arc in thousands of cubic feet. Note that the arcs in this network are bidirectional (i.e., gas can flow in either direction at the prices and capacities listed).

Bruce currently has 100,000 cf of gas in storage at Katy. Industrial customers in Joliet are offering $4.35 per thousand cf for up to 35,000 cf of gas. Buyers in Leidy are offering $4.63 per thousand cf for up to 60,000 cf of gas. Create a spreadsheet model to help Bruce answer the following questions.

a. Given the available capacity in the network, how much gas can be shipped from Katy to Leidy? From Katy to Joliet?
b. How much gas should Bruce offer to sell to Joliet and Leidy if he wants to maximize profits?
c. Is Bruce able to meet all the demand from both customers? If not, why not?
d. If Bruce wanted to try to pay more to obtain additional capacity on some of the pipelines, which ones should he investigate and why?

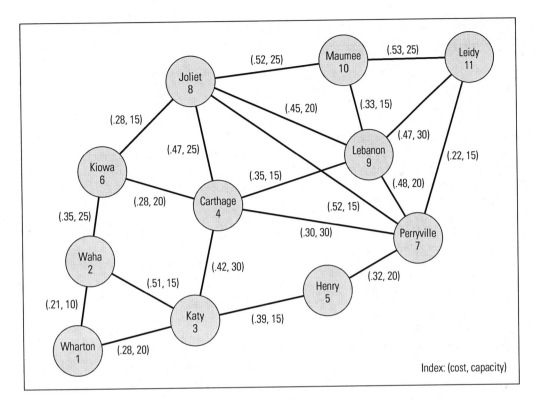

FIGURE 5.43

*Gas pipeline
network for
Old Dominion
Energy*

US Express

US Express is an overnight package delivery company based in Atlanta, Georgia. Jet fuel is one of the largest operating costs incurred by the company and they want your assistance in managing this cost. The price of jet fuel varies considerably at different airports around the country. As a result, it seems that it might be wise to "fill up" on jet fuel at airports where it is least expensive. However, the amount of fuel an airliner burns depends, in part, on the weight of the plane—and excess fuel makes an airplane heavier and, therefore, less fuel-efficient. Similarly, more fuel is burned on flights from the east coast to the west coast (going against the jet stream) than from the west coast to the east coast (going with the jet stream).

The following table summarizes the flight schedule (or rotation) flown nightly by one of the company's planes. For each flight segment, the table summarizes the minimum required and maximum allowable amount of fuel on board at takeoff and the cost of fuel at each point of departure. The final column provides a linear function relating fuel consumption to the amount of fuel on board at takeoff.

Segment	Depart	Arrive	Minimum Fuel Level at Takeoff (in 1000s)	Maximum Fuel Level at Takeoff (in 1000s)	Cost per Gallon	Fuel used in Flight with G Gallons (in 1000s) on Board at Takeoff
1	Atlanta	San Francisco	21	31	$0.92	$3.20 + 0.45 \times G$
2	San Francisco	Los Angeles	7	20	$0.85	$2.25 + 0.65 \times G$
3	Los Angeles	Chicago	18	31	$0.87	$1.80 + 0.35 \times G$
4	Chicago	Atlanta	16	31	$1.02	$2.20 + 0.60 \times G$

For instance, if the plane leaves Atlanta for San Francisco with 25,000 gallons on board, it should arrive in San Francisco with approximately $25 - (3.2 + 0.45 \times 25) = 10.55$ thousand gallons of fuel.

The company has many other planes that fly different schedules each night, so the potential cost savings from efficient fuel purchasing is quite significant. But before turning you loose on all of their flight schedules, the company wants you to create a spreadsheet model to determine the most economical fuel purchasing plan for the previous schedule. (*Hint:* Keep in mind that the most fuel you would purchase at any departure point is the maximum allowable fuel level for takeoff at that point. Also, assume that whatever fuel is on board when the plane returns to Atlanta at the end of the rotation will still be on board when the plane leaves Atlanta the next evening.)

a. Draw the network diagram for this problem.
b. Implement the model for this problem in your spreadsheet and solve it.
c. How much fuel should US Express purchase at each departure point and what is the cost of this purchasing plan?

CASE 5.4   The Major Electric Corporation

Henry Lee is the Vice President of Purchasing for the consumer electronics division of the Major Electric Corporation (MEC). The company recently introduced a new type of video camcorder that has taken the market by storm. Although Henry is pleased with the strong demand for this product in the marketplace, it has been a challenge to keep up with MEC's distributors' orders of this camcorder. His current challenge is how to meet requests from MEC's major distributors in Pittsburgh, Denver, Baltimore, and Houston who have placed orders of 10,000, 20,000, 30,000, and 25,000 units, respectively, for delivery in two months (there is a one-month manufacturing and one-month shipping lead time for this product).

MEC has contracts with companies in Hong Kong, Korea, and Singapore who manufacture camcorders for the company under the MEC label. These contracts require MEC to order a specified minimum number of units each month at a guaranteed per unit cost. The contracts also specify the maximum number of units that may be ordered at this price. The following table summarizes these contracts:

	Monthly Purchasing Contract Provisions		
Supplier	**Unit Cost**	**Minimum Required**	**Maximum Allowed**
Hong Kong	$375	20,000	30,000
Korea	$390	25,000	40,000
Singapore	$365	15,000	30,000

MEC also has a standing contract with a shipping company to transport product from each of these suppliers to ports in San Francisco and San Diego. The cost of shipping from each supplier to each port is given in the following table along with the minimum required and maximum allowable number of shipping cartons each month:

	Monthly Shipping Contract Provisions					
	San Francisco Requirements			San Diego Shipping Requirements		
Supplier	**Cost per Container**	**Minimum Containers**	**Maximum Containers**	**Cost per Container**	**Minimum Containers**	**Maximum Containers**
Hong Kong	$2,000	5	20	$2,300	5	20
Korea	$1,800	10	30	$2,100	10	30
Singapore	$2,400	5	25	$2,200	5	15

Under the terms of this contract, MEC guarantees it will send at least 20 but no more than 65 shipping containers to San Francisco each month, and at least 30 but no more than 70 shipping containers to San Diego each month.

Each shipping container can hold 1,000 video cameras and ultimately will be trucked from the seaports on to the distributors. Again, MEC has a standing contract with a trucking company to provide trucking services each month. The cost of trucking a shipping container from each port to each distributor is summarized in the following table.

Unit Shipping Cost per Container

	Pittsburgh	Denver	Baltimore	Houston
San Francisco	$1,100	$850	$1,200	$1,000
San Diego	$1,200	$1,000	$1,100	$900

As with the other contracts, to obtain the prices given above, MEC is required to use a certain minimum amount of trucking capacity on each route each month and may not exceed certain maximum shipping amounts without incurring cost penalties. These minimum and maximum shipping restrictions are summarized in the following table.

Minimum Required and Maximum Allowable Number of Shipping Containers per Month

	Pittsburgh		Denver		Baltimore		Houston	
	Min	Max	Min	Max	Min	Max	Min	Max
San Francisco	3	7	6	12	10	18	5	15
San Diego	4	6	5	14	5	20	10	20

Henry is left with the task of sorting through all this information to determine the least purchasing and distribution plan to fill the distributor's requests. But because he and his wife have tickets to the symphony for this evening, he has asked you to take a look at this problem and give him your recommendations at 9:00 tomorrow morning.

a. Create a network flow model for this problem. (*Hint:* Consider inserting intermediate nodes in your network to assist in meeting the minimum monthly purchase restrictions for each supplier and the minimum monthly shipping requirements for each port.)

b. Implement a spreadsheet model for this problem and solve it.

c. What is the optimal solution?

Chapter 6

Integer Linear Programming

6.0 Introduction

When some or all of the decision variables in an LP problem are restricted to assuming only integer values, the resulting problem is referred to as an integer linear programming (ILP) problem. Many practical business problems need integer solutions. For example, when scheduling workers, a company needs to determine the optimal number of employees to assign to each shift. If we formulate this problem as an LP problem, its optimal solution could involve allocating fractional numbers of workers (for example, 7.33 workers) to different shifts; but this is not an integer feasible solution. Similarly, if an airline is trying to decide how many 767s, 757s, and A-300s to purchase for its fleet, it must obtain an integer solution because the airline cannot buy fractions of planes.

This chapter discusses how to solve optimization problems in which certain decision variables must assume only integer values. This chapter also shows how the use of integer variables allows us to build more accurate models for a number of business problems.

6.1 Integrality Conditions

To illustrate some of the issues involved in an ILP problem, let's consider again the decision problem faced by Howie Jones, the owner of Blue Ridge Hot Tubs, described in Chapters 2, 3, and 4. This company sells two models of hot tubs, the Aqua-Spa and the Hydro-Lux, which it produces by purchasing prefabricated fiberglass hot tub shells and installing a common water pump and an appropriate amount of tubing. Each Aqua-Spa produced requires 1 pump, 9 hours of labor, and 12 feet of tubing, and contributes \$350 to profits. Each Hydro-Lux produced requires 1 pump, 6 hours of labor, and 16 feet of tubing, and contributes \$300 to profits. Assuming that the company has 200 pumps, 1,566 labor hours, and 2,880 feet of tubing available, we created the following LP formulation for this problem where X_1 and X_2 represent the number of Aqua-Spas and Hydro-Luxes to produce:

$$
\begin{array}{lll}
\text{MAX:} & 350X_1 + 300X_2 & \}\text{ profit} \\
\text{Subject to:} & 1X_1 + 1X_2 \le 200 & \}\text{ pump constraint} \\
& 9X_1 + 6X_2 \le 1{,}566 & \}\text{ labor constraint} \\
& 12X_1 + 16X_2 \le 2{,}880 & \}\text{ tubing constraint} \\
& X_1, X_2 \ge 0 & \}\text{ nonnegativity conditions}
\end{array}
$$

Blue Ridge Hot Tubs is undoubtedly interested in obtaining the best possible *integer solution* to this problem because hot tubs can be sold only as discrete units. Thus, we can be sure that the company wants to find the *optimal integer solution* to this problem. So, in addition to the constraints stated previously, we add the following integrality condition to the formulation of the problem:

$$X_1 \text{ and } X_2 \text{ must be integers}$$

An integrality condition indicates that some (or all) of the variables in the formulation must assume only integer values. We refer to such variables as the integer variables in a problem. In contrast, variables that are not required to assume strictly integer values are referred to as continuous variables. Although it is easy to state integrality conditions for a problem, such conditions often make a problem more difficult (and sometimes impossible) to solve.

6.2 Relaxation

One approach to finding the optimal integer solution to a problem is to relax, or ignore, the integrality conditions and solve the problem as if it were a standard LP problem where all the variables are assumed to be continuous. This model is sometimes referred to as the LP relaxation of the original ILP problem. Consider the following ILP problem:

$$
\begin{aligned}
\text{MAX:} \qquad & 2X_1 + 3X_2 \\
\text{Subject to:} \qquad & X_1 + 3X_2 \leq 8.25 \\
& 2.5X_1 + X_2 \leq 8.75 \\
& X_1, X_2 \geq 0 \\
& X_1, X_2 \text{ must be integers}
\end{aligned}
$$

The LP relaxation for this problem is represented by:

$$
\begin{aligned}
\text{MAX:} \qquad & 2X_1 + 3X_2 \\
\text{Subject to:} \qquad & X_1 + 3X_2 \leq 8.25 \\
& 2.5X_1 + X_2 \leq 8.75 \\
& X_1, X_2 \geq 0
\end{aligned}
$$

The only difference between the ILP and its LP relaxation is that all integrality conditions imposed by the ILP are dropped in the relaxation. However, as illustrated in Figure 6.1, this change has a significant impact on the feasible regions for the two problems.

As shown in Figure 6.1, the feasible region for the ILP consists of only 11 discrete points. On the other hand, the feasible region for its LP relaxation consists of an infinite number of points represented by the shaded area. This figure illustrates an important point about the relationship between the feasible region of an ILP and its LP relaxation. The feasible region of the LP relaxation of an ILP problem *always* encompasses *all* the feasible integer solutions to the original ILP problem. Although the relaxed feasible region might include additional noninteger solutions, it will *not* include any integer solutions that are not feasible solutions to the original ILP.

6.3 Solving the Relaxed Problem

The LP relaxation of an ILP problem is often easy to solve using the simplex method. As explained in Chapter 2, an optimal solution to an LP problem occurs at one of the corner points of its feasible region (assuming that the problem has a bounded optimal solution). Thus, if we are extremely lucky, the optimal solution to the LP relaxation of an

FIGURE 6.1

Integer feasible region vs. LP feasible region

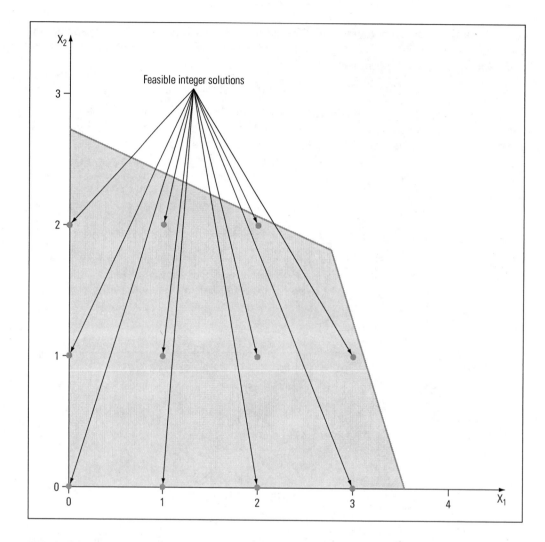

ILP problem might occur at an integer corner point of the relaxed feasible region. In this case, we find the optimal integer solution to the ILP problem simply by solving its LP relaxation. This is exactly what happened in Chapters 2 and 3 when we originally solved the relaxed LP model for the hot tub problem. Figure 6.2 (and the file Fig6-2.xls on your data disk) shows the solution to this problem.

The optimal solution to the relaxed LP formulation of the hot tub problem assigns integer values to the decision variables ($X_1 = 122$ and $X_2 = 78$). So in this case, the relaxed LP problem happens to have an integer-valued optimal solution. However, as you might expect, this will not always be the case.

Suppose, for example, that Blue Ridge Hot Tubs has only 1,520 hours of labor and 2,650 feet of tubing available during its next production cycle. The company might be interested in solving the following ILP problem:

$$
\begin{array}{lll}
\text{MAX:} & 350X_1 + 300X_2 & \text{\} profit} \\
\text{Subject to:} & 1X_1 + 1X_2 \leq 200 & \text{\} pump constraint} \\
& 9X_1 + 6X_2 \leq 1{,}520 & \text{\} labor constraint} \\
& 12X_1 + 16X_2 \leq 2{,}650 & \text{\} tubing constraint} \\
& X_1, X_2 \geq 0 & \text{\} nonnegativity conditions} \\
& X_1, X_2 \text{ must be integers} & \text{\} integrality conditions}
\end{array}
$$

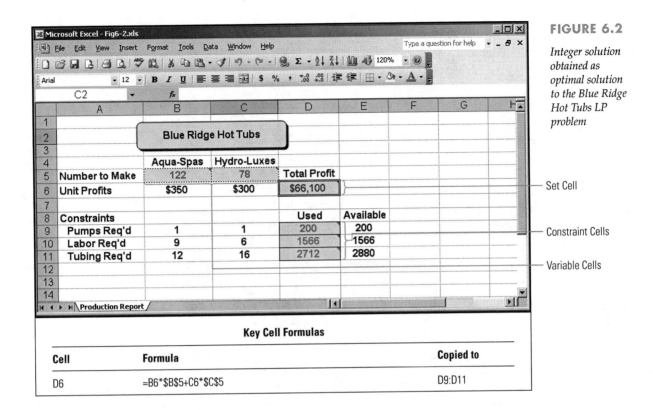

FIGURE 6.2

Integer solution obtained as optimal solution to the Blue Ridge Hot Tubs LP problem

Key Cell Formulas

Cell	Formula	Copied to
D6	=B6*$B$5+C6*$C$5	D9:D11

If we relax the integrality conditions and solve the resulting LP problem, we obtain the solution shown in Figure 6.3. This solution indicates that producing 116.9444 Aqua-Spas and 77.9167 Hydro-Luxes will generate a maximum profit of $64,306. But this solution violates the integrality conditions stated in the original problem. As a general rule, the optimal solution to the LP relaxation of an ILP problem is not guaranteed to produce an integer solution. In such cases, other techniques must be applied to find the optimal integer solution for the problem being solved. (There are some exceptions to this rule. In particular, the network flow problems discussed in Chapter 5 often can be viewed as ILP problems. For reasons that go beyond the scope of this text, the LP relaxation of network flow problems always will have integer solutions if the supplies and/or demands at each node are integers and the problem is solved using the simplex method.)

6.4 Bounds

Before discussing how to solve ILP problems, an important point must be made about the relationship between the optimal solution to an ILP problem and the optimal solution to its LP relaxation: *The objective function value for the optimal solution to the ILP problem can never be better than the objective function value for the optimal solution to its LP relaxation.*

For example, the solution shown in Figure 6.3 indicates that if the company could produce (and sell) fractional numbers of hot tubs, it could make a maximum profit of $64,306 by producing 116.9444 Aqua-Spas and 77.9167 Hydro-Luxes. No other feasible solution (integer or otherwise) could result in a better value of the objective function. If a better feasible solution existed, the optimization procedure would have identified this better solution as optimal because our aim was to maximize the value of the objective function.

FIGURE 6.3

*Noninteger
solution obtained
as optimal
solution to the
revised Blue Ridge
Hot Tubs LP
problem*

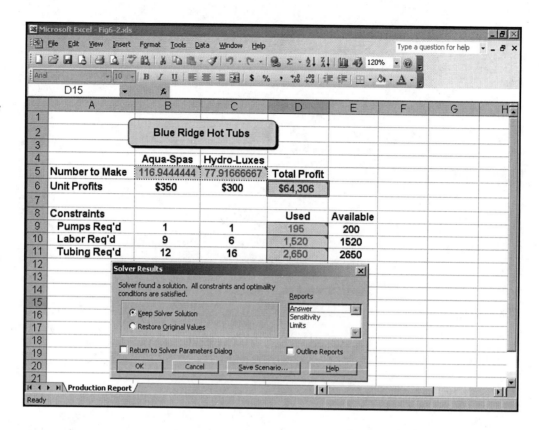

Although solving the LP relaxation of the revised hot tub problem might not provide the optimal integer solution to our original ILP problem, it does indicate that the objective function value of the optimal integer solution cannot possibly be greater than $64,306. This information can be important in helping us evaluate the quality of integer solutions we might discover during our search for the optimal solution.

> ### Key Concept
>
> For *maximization* problems, the objective function value at the optimal solution to the LP relaxation represents an *upper bound* on the optimal objective function value of the original ILP problem. For *minimization* problems, the objective function value at the optimal solution to the LP relaxation represents a *lower bound* on the optimal objective function value of the original ILP problem.

6.5 Rounding

As mentioned earlier, the solution to the LP relaxation of an ILP problem might satisfy the ILP problem's integrality conditions and, therefore, represent the optimal integer solution to the problem. But what should we do if this is not the case (as usually happens)? One technique that frequently is applied involves rounding the relaxed LP solution.

When the solution to the LP relaxation of an ILP problem does not result in an integer solution, it is tempting to think that simply rounding this solution will generate the optimal integer solution. Unfortunately, this is not the case. For example, if the values for the decision variables shown in Figure 6.3 are manually rounded up to their closest integer values, as shown in Figure 6.4, the resulting solution is infeasible. The company cannot manufacture 117 Aqua-Spas and 78 Hydro-Luxes because this would involve using more labor and tubing than are available.

Because rounding up does not always work, perhaps we should round down, or truncate, the values for the decision variables identified in the LP relaxation. As shown in Figure 6.5, this results in a feasible solution where 116 Aqua-Spas and 77 Hydro-Luxes are manufactured for a total profit of $63,700. However, this approach presents two possible problems. First, rounding down also could result in an infeasible solution, as shown in Figure 6.6.

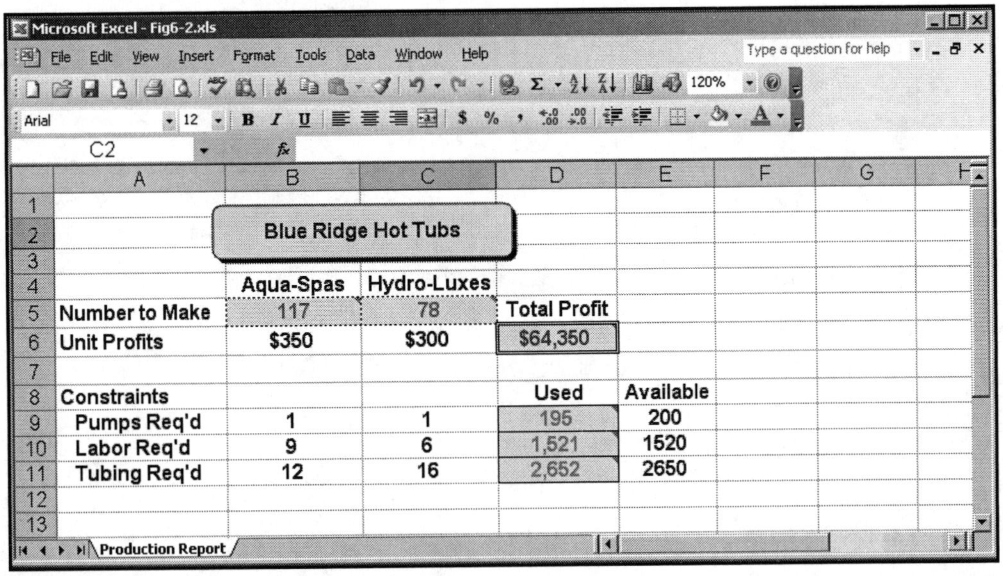

FIGURE 6.4

Infeasible integer solution obtained by rounding up

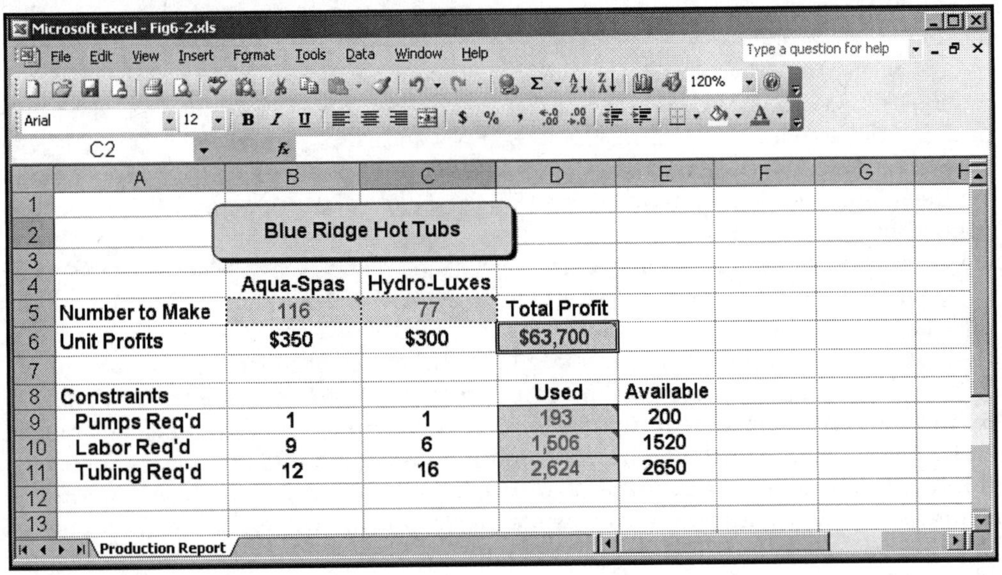

FIGURE 6.5

Feasible integer solution obtained by rounding down

FIGURE 6.6

How rounding down can result in an infeasible integer solution

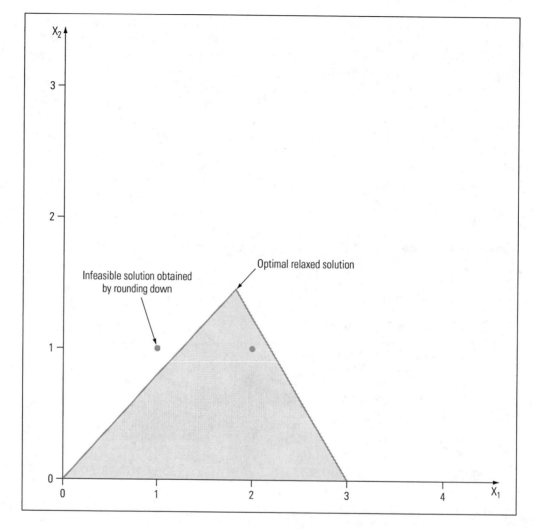

Another problem with rounding down is that even if it results in a feasible integer solution to the problem, there is no guarantee that it is the *optimal* integer solution. For example, the integer solution obtained by rounding down shown in Figure 6.5 produced a total profit of $63,700. However, as shown in Figure 6.7, a better integer solution exists for this problem. If the company produces 118 Aqua-Spas and 76 Hydro-Luxes, it can achieve a total profit of $64,100 (which is the optimal integer solution to this problem). Simply rounding the solution to the LP relaxation of an ILP problem is not guaranteed to provide the optimal integer solution. Although the integer solution obtained in this problem by rounding is very close to the optimal integer solution, rounding does not always work this well.

As we have seen, the solution to the LP relaxation of an ILP is not guaranteed to produce an integer solution, and rounding the solution to the LP relaxation is not guaranteed to produce the optimal integer solution. Therefore, we need another way to find the optimal integer solution to an ILP problem. Various procedures have been developed for this purpose. The most effective and widely used of these procedures is the branch-and-bound (B&B) algorithm. The B&B algorithm theoretically allows us to solve any ILP problem by solving a series of LP problems called candidate problems. For those who are interested, a discussion of how the B&B algorithm works is given at the end of this chapter.

6.6 Stopping Rules

Finding the optimal solution for simple ILP problems sometimes can require the evaluation of hundreds of candidate problems. More complex problems can require the evaluation of thousands of candidate problems, which can be a very time-consuming task even for the fastest computers. For this reason, many ILP packages allow you to specify a suboptimality tolerance of X% (where X is some numeric value), which tells the B&B algorithm to stop when it finds an integer solution that is no more than X% worse than the optimal integer solution. This is another area where obtaining upper or lower bounds on the optimal integer solution can be helpful.

As noted earlier, if we relax all the integrality conditions in an ILP with a maximization objective and solve the resulting LP problem, the objective function value at the optimal solution to the relaxed problem provides an upper bound on the optimal integer solution. For example, when we relaxed the integrality conditions for the revised Blue Ridge Hot Tubs problem and solved it as an LP, we obtained the solution shown in Figure 6.3, which has an objective function value of $64,306. Thus, we know that the optimal integer solution to this problem cannot have an objective function value greater than $64,306. Now, suppose that the owner of Blue Ridge Hot Tubs is willing to settle for any integer solution to their problem that is no more than 5% below the optimal integer solution. It is easy to determine that 95% of $64,306 is $61,090 (0.95 × $64,306 = $61,090). Therefore, any integer solution with an objective function value of at least $61,090 can be no worse than 5% below the optimal integer solution.

Specifying suboptimality tolerances can be helpful if you are willing to settle for a good but suboptimal solution to a difficult ILP problem. However, most B&B packages employ some sort of default suboptimality tolerance and, therefore, might produce a suboptimal solution to the ILP problem without indicating that a better solution might exist. (We will look at an example where this occurs shortly.) It is important to be aware of suboptimality tolerances because they can determine whether or not the true optimal solution to an ILP problem is found.

6.7 Solving ILP Problems Using Solver

Now that you have some understanding of the effort required to solve ILP problems, you can appreciate how using Solver simplifies this process. This section shows how to use Solver with the revised Blue Ridge Hot Tubs problem.

Figure 6.8 shows the Solver parameters required to solve the revised Blue Ridge Hot Tubs problem as a standard LP problem. However, none of these parameters indicate that the cells representing the decision variables (cells B5 and C5) must assume integer values. To communicate this to Solver, we need to add constraints to the problem by clicking the Add button.

Clicking this button displays the Add Constraint dialog box shown in Figure 6.9. In this dialog box, cells B5 through C5 are specified as the cell references for the additional constraints. Because we want these cells to assume only integer values, we need to select the int option from the drop-down menu, as shown in Figure 6.9.

After clicking the OK button, we return to the Solver Parameters dialog box shown in Figure 6.10. This dialog box now indicates that cells B5 and C5 are constrained to assume only integer values. We can now click the Solve button to determine the optimal solution to the problem, shown in Figure 6.11.

The Solver Results dialog box in Figure 6.11 indicates that Solver found a solution "within tolerance" that satisfies all constraints. Thus, we might suspect that the optimal integer solution to this problem involves producing 117 Aqua-Spas and 77 Hydro-Luxes for a total profit of $64,050. However, if you refer back to Figure 6.7, you will recall that

FIGURE 6.8

Solver parameters for the relaxed Blue Ridge Hot Tubs problem

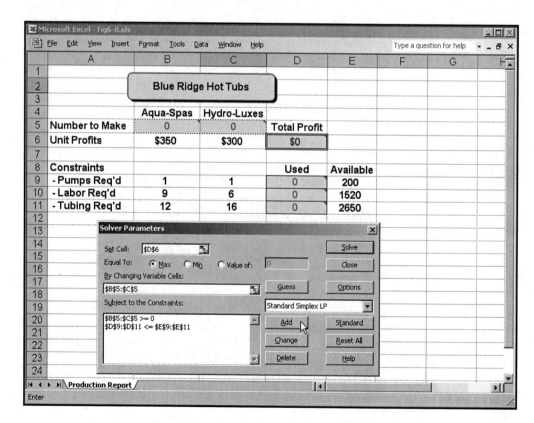

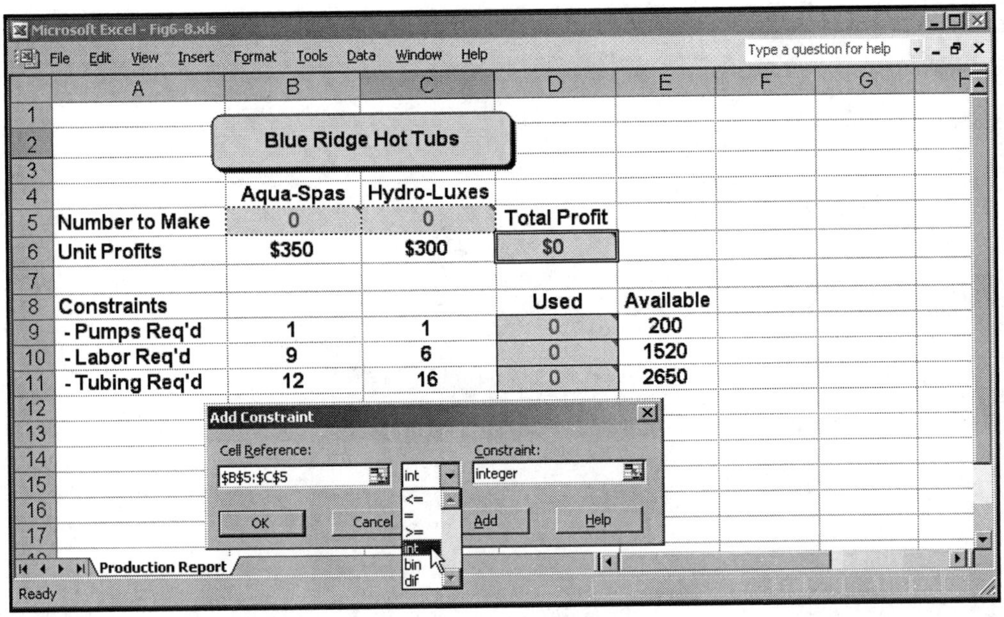

FIGURE 6.9

Selecting integer constraints

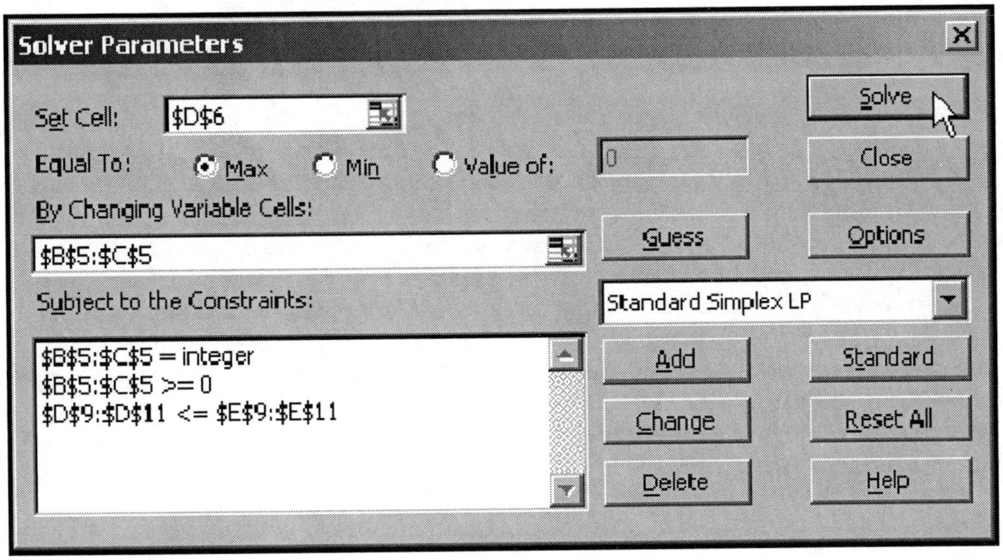

FIGURE 6.10

Solver parameters for the revised Blue Ridge Hot Tubs problem with integer constraints

an even better integer solution to this problem can be obtained by producing 118 Aqua-Spas and 76 Hydro-Luxes for a total profit of $64,100. So why did Solver select an integer solution with a total profit of $64,050 when a better integer solution exists? The answer lies in Solver's suboptimality tolerance factor.

By default, Solver uses a suboptimality tolerance factor of 5%. So, when Solver found the integer solution with the objective function value of $64,050 shown in Figure 6.11, it determined that this solution was within 5% of the optimal integer solution and, therefore, it abandoned its search. (Note the message in Figure 6.11, "Solver found an integer solution within tolerance.") To ensure that Solver finds the best possible

FIGURE 6.11

Solution to the revised Blue Ridge Hot Tubs problem with integer constraints

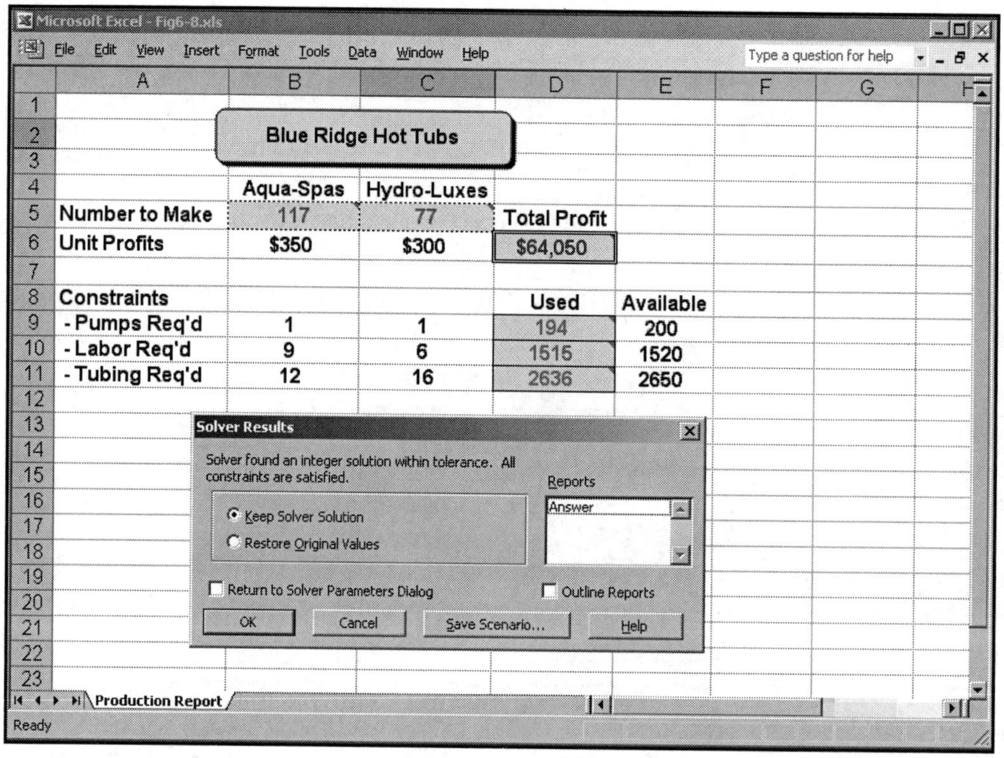

solution to an ILP problem, we must change its suboptimality tolerance factor by clicking the Options button in the Solver Parameters dialog box and then click the Integer Options button in the Solver Options dialog box. Figure 6.12 shows the resulting Integer Options dialog box.

As shown in Figure 6.12, you can set a number of options to control Solver's operations. The Tolerance option represents Solver's suboptimality tolerance value. To make sure that Solver finds the best possible solution to an ILP problem, we must change this setting from its default value of 0.05 to 0. If we do this and re-solve the current problem, we obtain the solution shown in Figure 6.13. This solution is the best possible integer solution to the problem.

FIGURE 6.12

Changing the suboptimality tolerance factor

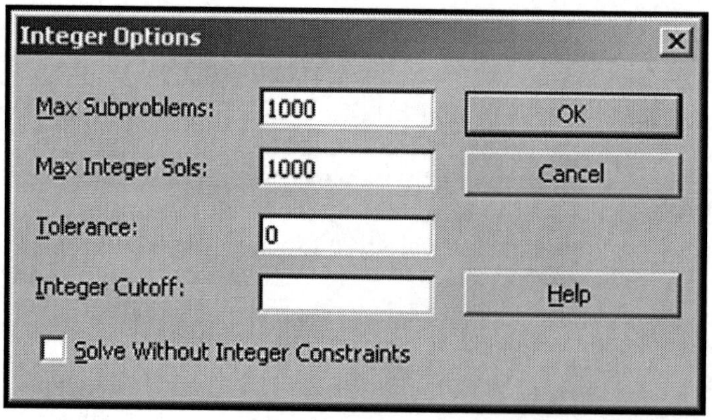

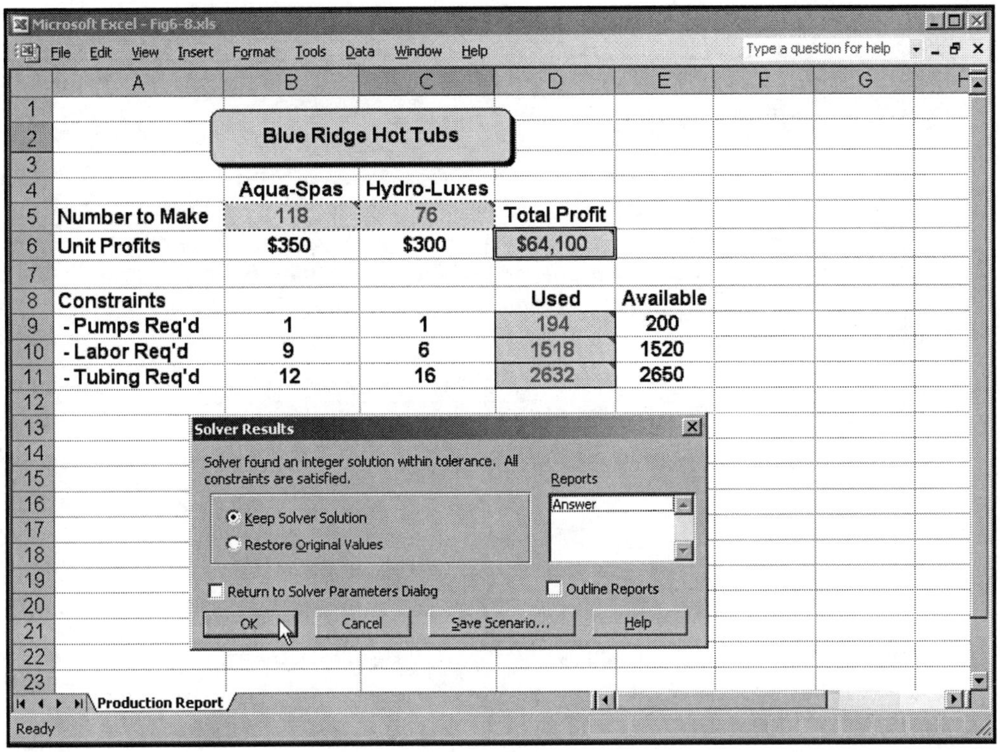

FIGURE 6.13

Optimal integer solution to the revised Blue Ridge Hot Tubs problem

6.8 Other ILP Problems

Many decision problems encountered in business can be modeled as ILPs. As we have seen from the Blue Ridge Hot Tubs example, some problems that are initially formulated as LP problems might turn into ILP formulations if they require integer solutions. However, the importance of ILP extends beyond simply allowing us to obtain integer solutions to LP problems.

The ability to constrain certain variables to assume only integer values enables us to model a number of important conditions more accurately. For example, up to this point, we have not considered the impact of quantity discounts, setup or lump-sum costs, or batch size restrictions on a given decision problem. Without ILP techniques, we could not model these decision issues. We now consider several examples that illustrate the expanded modeling capabilities available through the use of integer variables.

6.9 An Employee Scheduling Problem

Anyone responsible for creating work schedules for several employees can appreciate the difficulties in this task. It can be very difficult to develop a feasible schedule, much less an optimal schedule. Trying to ensure that a sufficient number of workers is available when needed is a complicated task when you must consider multiple shifts, rest breaks, and lunch or dinner breaks. However, some sophisticated LP models have been devised to solve these problems. Although a discussion of these models is beyond the scope of this text, we will consider a simple example of an employee scheduling problem to give you an idea of how LP models are applied in this area.

Air-Express is an express shipping service that guarantees overnight delivery of packages anywhere in the continental United States. The company has various operations centers, called hubs, at airports in major cities across the country. Packages are received at hubs from other locations and then shipped to intermediate hubs or to their final destinations.

The manager of the Air-Express hub in Baltimore, Maryland, is concerned about labor costs at the hub and is interested in determining the most effective way to schedule workers. The hub operates seven days a week, and the number of packages it handles each day varies from one day to the next. Using historical data on the average number of packages received each day, the manager estimates the number of workers needed to handle the packages as:

Day of Week	Workers Required
Sunday	18
Monday	27
Tuesday	22
Wednesday	26
Thursday	25
Friday	21
Saturday	19

The package handlers working for Air-Express are unionized and are guaranteed a five-day work week with two consecutive days off. The base wage for the handlers is $655 per week. Because most workers prefer to have Saturday or Sunday off, the union has negotiated bonuses of $25 per day for its members who work on these days. The possible shifts and salaries for package handlers are:

Shift	Days Off	Wage
1	Sunday and Monday	$680
2	Monday and Tuesday	$705
3	Tuesday and Wednesday	$705
4	Wednesday and Thursday	$705
5	Thursday and Friday	$705
6	Friday and Saturday	$680
7	Saturday and Sunday	$655

The manager wants to keep the total wage expense for the hub as low as possible. With this in mind, how many package handlers should be assigned to each shift if the manager wants to have a sufficient number of workers available each day?

6.9.1 DEFINING THE DECISION VARIABLES

In this problem, the manager must decide how many workers to assign to each shift. Because there are seven possible shifts, we need the following seven decision variables:

$$X_1 = \text{the number of workers assigned to shift 1}$$
$$X_2 = \text{the number of workers assigned to shift 2}$$
$$X_3 = \text{the number of workers assigned to shift 3}$$
$$X_4 = \text{the number of workers assigned to shift 4}$$
$$X_5 = \text{the number of workers assigned to shift 5}$$
$$X_6 = \text{the number of workers assigned to shift 6}$$
$$X_7 = \text{the number of workers assigned to shift 7}$$

6.9.2 DEFINING THE OBJECTIVE FUNCTION

The objective in this problem is to minimize the total wages paid. Each worker on shift 1 and 6 is paid \$680 per week, and each worker on shift 7 is paid \$655. All other workers are paid \$705 per week. Thus, the objective of minimizing the total wage expense is expressed as:

$$\text{MIN:}\quad 680X_1 + 705X_2 + 705X_3 + 705X_4 + 705X_5 + 680X_6 + 655X_7 \ \} \text{ total wage expense}$$

6.9.3 DEFINING THE CONSTRAINTS

The constraints for this problem must ensure that at least 18 workers are scheduled for Sunday, at least 27 are scheduled for Monday, and so on. We need one constraint for each day of the week.

To make sure that at least 18 workers are available on Sunday, we must determine which decision variables represent shifts that are scheduled to work on Sunday. Because shifts 1 and 7 are the only shifts that have Sunday scheduled as a day off, the remaining shifts, 2 through 6, all are scheduled to work on Sunday. The following constraint ensures that at least 18 workers are available on Sunday:

$$0X_1 + 1X_2 + 1X_3 + 1X_4 + 1X_5 + 1X_6 + 0X_7 \geq 18 \qquad \} \text{ workers required on Sunday}$$

Because workers on shifts 1 and 2 have Monday off, the constraint for Monday should ensure that the sum of the variables representing the number of workers on the remaining shifts, 3 through 7, is at least 27. This constraint is expressed as:

$$0X_1 + 0X_2 + 1X_3 + 1X_4 + 1X_5 + 1X_6 + 1X_7 \geq 27 \qquad \} \text{ workers required on Monday}$$

Constraints for the remaining days of the week are generated easily by applying the same logic used in generating the previous two constraints. The resulting constraints are stated as:

$$1X_1 + 0X_2 + 0X_3 + 1X_4 + 1X_5 + 1X_6 + 1X_7 \geq 22 \qquad \} \text{ workers required on Tuesday}$$
$$1X_1 + 1X_2 + 0X_3 + 0X_4 + 1X_5 + 1X_6 + 1X_7 \geq 26 \qquad \} \text{ workers required on Wednesday}$$
$$1X_1 + 1X_2 + 1X_3 + 0X_4 + 0X_5 + 1X_6 + 1X_7 \geq 25 \qquad \} \text{ workers required on Thursday}$$
$$1X_1 + 1X_2 + 1X_3 + 1X_4 + 0X_5 + 0X_6 + 1X_7 \geq 21 \qquad \} \text{ workers required on Friday}$$
$$1X_1 + 1X_2 + 1X_3 + 1X_4 + 1X_5 + 0X_6 + 0X_7 \geq 19 \qquad \} \text{ workers required on Saturday}$$

Finally, all our decision variables must assume nonnegative integer values. These conditions are stated as:

$$X_1, X_2, X_3, X_4, X_5, X_6, X_7 \geq 0$$

All X_i must be integers

6.9.4 A NOTE ABOUT THE CONSTRAINTS

At this point, you might wonder why the constraints for each day are "greater than or equal to" rather than "equal to" constraints. For example, if Air-Express needs only 19 people on Saturday, why do we have a constraint that allows *more* than 19 people to be scheduled? The answer to this question relates to feasibility. Suppose we restate the problem so that all the constraints are "equal to" constraints. There are two possible outcomes for this problem: (1) it might have a feasible optimal solution, or (2) it might not have a feasible solution.

In the first case, if the formulation using "equal to" constraints has a feasible optimal solution, this same solution also must be a feasible solution to our formulation using "greater than or equal to" constraints. Because both formulations have the same objective function, the solution to our original formulation could not be worse (in terms of the optimal objective function value) than a formulation using "equal to" constraints.

In the second case, if the formulation using "equal to" constraints has no feasible solution, there is no schedule where the *exact* number of employees required can be scheduled each day. To find a feasible solution in this case, we would need to make the constraints less restrictive by allowing for more than the required number of employees to be scheduled (that is, using "greater than or equal to" constraints).

Therefore, using "greater than or equal to" constraints does not preclude a solution where the exact number of workers needed is scheduled for each shift, if such a schedule is feasible and optimal. If such a schedule is not feasible or not optimal, the formulation using "greater than or equal to constraints" also guarantees that a feasible optimal solution to the problem will be obtained.

6.9.5 IMPLEMENTING THE MODEL

The LP model for the Air-Express scheduling problem is summarized as:

MIN: $680X_1 + 705X_2 + 705X_3 + 705X_4 + 705X_5 + 680X_6 + 655X_7$ } total wage expense

Subject to:

$0X_1 + 1X_2 + 1X_3 + 1X_4 + 1X_5 + 1X_6 + 0X_7 \geq 18$ } workers required on Sunday

$0X_1 + 0X_2 + 1X_3 + 1X_4 + 1X_5 + 1X_6 + 1X_7 \geq 27$ } workers required on Monday

$1X_1 + 0X_2 + 0X_3 + 1X_4 + 1X_5 + 1X_6 + 1X_7 \geq 22$ } workers required on Tuesday

$1X_1 + 1X_2 + 0X_3 + 0X_4 + 1X_5 + 1X_6 + 1X_7 \geq 26$ } workers required on Wednesday

$1X_1 + 1X_2 + 1X_3 + 0X_4 + 0X_5 + 1X_6 + 1X_7 \geq 25$ } workers required on Thursday

$1X_1 + 1X_2 + 1X_3 + 1X_4 + 0X_5 + 0X_6 + 1X_7 \geq 21$ } workers required on Friday

$1X_1 + 1X_2 + 1X_3 + 1X_4 + 1X_5 + 0X_6 + 0X_7 \geq 19$ } workers required on Saturday

$X_1, X_2, X_3, X_4, X_5, X_6, X_7 \geq 0$

All X_i must be integers

A convenient way of implementing this model is shown in Figure 6.14 (and in the file Fig6-14.xls on your data disk). Each row in the table shown in this spreadsheet corresponds to one of the seven shifts in the problem. For each day of the week, entries have been made to indicate which shifts are scheduled to be on or off. For example, shift 1 is scheduled off Sunday and Monday, and works on the remaining days of the week. Notice that the values for each day of the week in Figure 6.14 correspond directly to the coefficients in the constraint in our LP model for the same day of the week. The required number of workers for each day is listed in cells B13 through H13 and corresponds to the RHS values of each constraint. The wages to be paid to each worker on the various shifts are listed in cells J5 through J11 and correspond to the objective function coefficients in our model.

Cells I5 through I11 indicate the number of workers assigned to each shift, and correspond to the decision variables X_1 through X_7 in our algebraic formulation of the LP model. The LHS formula for each constraint is implemented easily using the

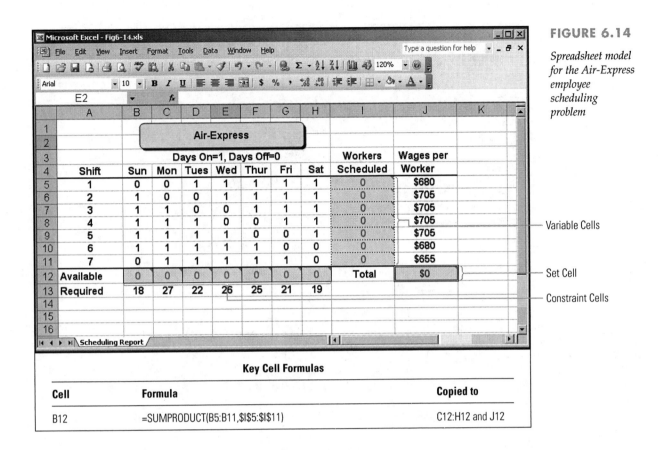

FIGURE 6.14

Spreadsheet model for the Air-Express employee scheduling problem

---

Key Cell Formulas

Cell	Formula	Copied to
B12	=SUMPRODUCT(B5:B11,$I$5:$I$11)	C12:H12 and J12

SUMPRODUCT( ) function. For example, the formula in cell B12 implements the LHS of the constraint for the number of workers needed on Sunday as:

Formula for cell B12:   =SUMPRODUCT(B5:B11,$I$5:$I$11)

(Copy to C12 through H12 and J12.)

This formula is then copied to cells C12 through H12 to implement the LHS formulas of the remaining constraints. With the coefficients for the objective function entered in cells J5 through J11, the previous formula also is copied to cell J12 to implement the objective function for this model.

6.9.6 SOLVING THE MODEL

Figure 6.15 shows the Solver parameters required to solve this problem. The optimal solution is shown in Figure 6.16.

6.9.7 ANALYZING THE SOLUTION

The optimal solution to this problem is shown in Figure 6.16. This solution ensures that the available number of employees is at least as great as the required number of employees for each day. The minimum total wage expense associated with this solution is $22,540.

FIGURE 6.15

Solver parameters for the Air-Express scheduling problem

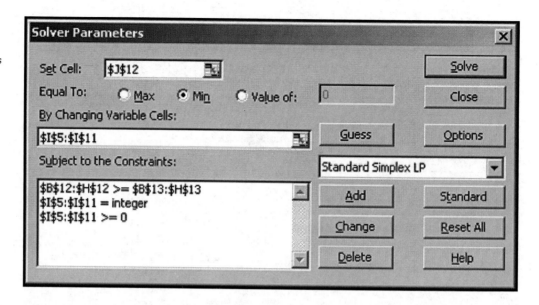

FIGURE 6.16

Optimal solution to the Air-Express employee scheduling problem

Shift	Sun	Mon	Tues	Wed	Thur	Fri	Sat	Workers Scheduled	Wages per Worker
Air-Express									
Days On=1, Days Off=0								Workers	Wages per
Shift	**Sun**	**Mon**	**Tues**	**Wed**	**Thur**	**Fri**	**Sat**	**Scheduled**	**Worker**
1	0	0	1	1	1	1	1	1	$680
2	1	0	0	1	1	1	1	5	$705
3	1	1	0	0	1	1	1	6	$705
4	1	1	1	0	0	1	1	1	$705
5	1	1	1	1	0	0	1	6	$705
6	1	1	1	1	1	0	0	0	$680
7	0	1	1	1	1	1	0	14	$655
Available	18	27	22	26	26	27	19	**Total**	$22,540
Required	18	27	22	26	25	21	19		

6.10 Binary Variables

As mentioned earlier, some LP problems naturally evolve into ILP problems when we realize that we need to obtain integer solutions. For example, in the Air-Express problem discussed in the previous section, we needed to determine the number of workers to assign to each of seven shifts. Because workers are discrete units, we needed to impose integrality conditions on the decision variables in this model representing the number of workers scheduled for each shift. To do so, we changed the continuous variables in the model into general integer variables, or variables that could assume any integer value (provided that the constraints of the problem are not violated). In many other situations, we might want to use binary integer variables (or binary variables), which can assume *only two* integer values: 0 and 1. Binary variables can be useful in several practical modeling situations, as illustrated in the following examples.

6.11 A Capital Budgeting Problem

In a capital budgeting problem, a decision maker is presented with several potential projects or investment alternatives and must determine which projects or investments to choose. The projects or investments typically require different amounts of various resources (for example, money, equipment, personnel) and generate different cash flows to the company. The cash flows for each project or investment are converted to a net present value (NPV). The problem is to determine which set of projects or investments to select to achieve the maximum possible NPV. Consider the following example:

> In his position as vice president of research and development (R&D) for CRT Technologies, Mark Schwartz is responsible for evaluating and choosing which R&D projects to support. The company received 18 R&D proposals from its scientists and engineers, and identified six projects as being consistent with the company's mission. However, the company does not have the funds available to undertake all six projects. Mark must determine which of the projects to select. The funding requirements for each project are summarized in the following table along with the NPV the company expects each project to generate.

| | | Capital (in $1,000s) Required in | | | | |
Project	Expected NPV (in $1,000s)	Year 1	Year 2	Year 3	Year 4	Year 5
1	$141	$ 75	$25	$20	$15	$10
2	$187	$ 90	$35	$ 0	$ 0	$30
3	$121	$ 60	$15	$15	$15	$15
4	$ 83	$ 30	$20	$10	$ 5	$ 5
5	$265	$100	$25	$20	$20	$20
6	$127	$ 50	$20	$10	$30	$40

> The company currently has $250,000 available to invest in new projects. It has budgeted $75,000 for continued support for these projects in year 2 and $50,000 per year for years 3, 4, and 5. Surplus funds in any year are reappropriated for other uses within the company and may not be carried over to future years.

6.11.1 DEFINING THE DECISION VARIABLES

Mark must decide which of the six projects to select. Thus, we need six variables to represent the alternatives under consideration. We will let $X_1, X_2, \ldots, X_6$ represent the six decision variables for this problem and assume they operate as:

$$X_i = \begin{cases} 1, \text{ if project } i \text{ is selected} \\ 0, \text{ otherwise} \end{cases} \quad i = 1, 2, \ldots, 6$$

Each decision variable in this problem is a binary variable that assumes the value 1 if the associated project is selected, or the value 0 if the associated project is not selected. In essence, each variable acts as an "on/off switch" to indicate whether or not a given project has been selected.

6.11.2 DEFINING THE OBJECTIVE FUNCTION

The objective in this problem is to maximize the total NPV of the selected projects. This is stated mathematically as:

$$\text{MAX:} \quad 141X_1 + 187X_2 + 121X_3 + 83X_4 + 265X_5 + 127X_6$$

Notice that this objective function simply sums the NPV figures for the selected projects.

6.11.3 DEFINING THE CONSTRAINTS

We need one capital constraint for each year to ensure that the selected projects do not require more capital than is available. This set of constraints is represented by:

$$
\begin{aligned}
75X_1 + 90X_2 + 60X_3 + 30X_4 + 100X_5 + 50X_6 &\le 250 \quad \}\ \text{year 1 capital constraint} \\
25X_1 + 35X_2 + 15X_3 + 20X_4 + 25X_5 + 20X_6 &\le 75 \quad \}\ \text{year 2 capital constraint} \\
20X_1 + 0X_2 + 15X_3 + 10X_4 + 20X_5 + 10X_6 &\le 50 \quad \}\ \text{year 3 capital constraint} \\
15X_1 + 0X_2 + 15X_3 + 5X_4 + 20X_5 + 30X_6 &\le 50 \quad \}\ \text{year 4 capital constraint} \\
10X_1 + 30X_2 + 15X_3 + 5X_4 + 20X_5 + 40X_6 &\le 50 \quad \}\ \text{year 5 capital constraint}
\end{aligned}
$$

6.11.4 SETTING UP THE BINARY VARIABLES

In our formulation of this problem, we assume that each decision variable is a binary variable. We must include this assumption in the formal statement of our model by adding the constraints:

$$\text{All } X_i \text{ must be binary}$$

Important Software Note

Starting with Excel 8.0 in Office 97, Solver provides a feature that allows you to indicate that certain variable cells represent binary variables. When you are adding constraints, the drop-down list box (see Figure 6.9) used to indicate the type of constraint ("<=", ">=", "=", "int") includes another option labeled "bin" for binary. If you are using Excel 8.0 (or Premium Solver for Education), you can simply select the "bin" option for variable cells that represent binary variables. However, if you are using an older version of Excel, you will need to add three sets of constraints (">=0", "<=1", and integer) to any variable cells that you want Solver to treat as binary variables.

6.11.5 IMPLEMENTING THE MODEL

The ILP model for the CRT Technologies project selection problem is summarized as:

$$
\begin{aligned}
\text{MAX:} \quad & 141X_1 + 187X_2 + 121X_3 + 83X_4 + 265X_5 + 127X_6 \\
\text{Subject to:} \quad & 75X_1 + 90X_2 + 60X_3 + 30X_4 + 100X_5 + 50X_6 \le 250 \\
& 25X_1 + 35X_2 + 15X_3 + 20X_4 + 25X_5 + 20X_6 \le 75 \\
& 20X_1 + 0X_2 + 15X_3 + 10X_4 + 20X_5 + 10X_6 \le 50 \\
& 15X_1 + 0X_2 + 15X_3 + 5X_4 + 20X_5 + 30X_6 \le 50 \\
& 10X_1 + 30X_2 + 15X_3 + 5X_4 + 20X_5 + 40X_6 \le 50 \\
& \text{All } X_i \text{ must be binary}
\end{aligned}
$$

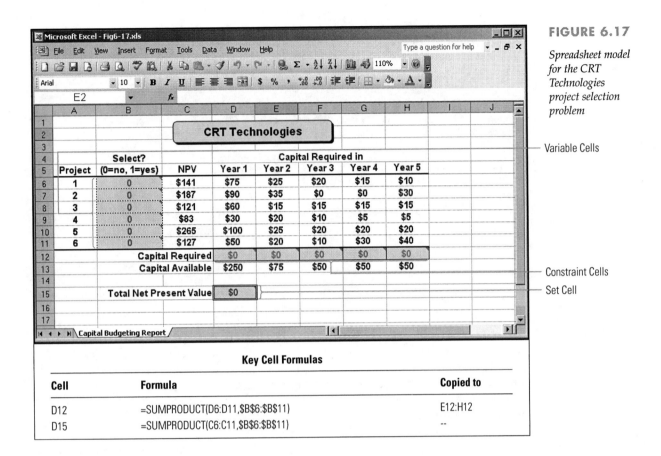

FIGURE 6.17

Spreadsheet model for the CRT Technologies project selection problem

— Variable Cells

— Constraint Cells
— Set Cell

Key Cell Formulas

Cell	Formula	Copied to
D12	=SUMPRODUCT(D6:D11,$B$6:$B$11)	E12:H12
D15	=SUMPRODUCT(C6:C11,$B$6:$B$11)	--

This model is implemented in the spreadsheet shown in Figure 6.17 (and in the file Fig6-17.xls on your data disk). In this spreadsheet, the data for each project are listed in separate rows.

Cells B6 through B11 contain values of 0 to indicate that they are reserved for representing the six variables in our algebraic model. The LHS formula for the capital constraint is entered in cell D12, then copied to cells E12 through H12, as:

Formula for cell D12:   =SUMPRODUCT(D6:D11,$B$6:$B$11)
(Copy to E12 through H12.)

The RHS values for the constraints are listed in cells D13 through H13. Finally, the objective function of the model is implemented in cell D15 as:

Formula for cell D15:   =SUMPRODUCT(C6:C11,$B$6:$B$11)

6.11.6 SOLVING THE MODEL

To solve this model, we must tell Solver where we have implemented our objective function, decision variables, and constraints. The Solver Parameters dialog box shown in Figure 6.18 indicates that the objective function is implemented in cell D15 and that the decision variables are represented by cells B6 through B11. Also, notice that only two sets of constraints are specified for this problem.

The first set of constraints ensures that cells B6 through B11 will operate as binary variables. Notice that we implemented these constraints by referring to the cells in the spreadsheet that represent our decision variables—we do not have to set up separate

FIGURE 6.18

Solver parameters for the CRT Technologies project selection problem

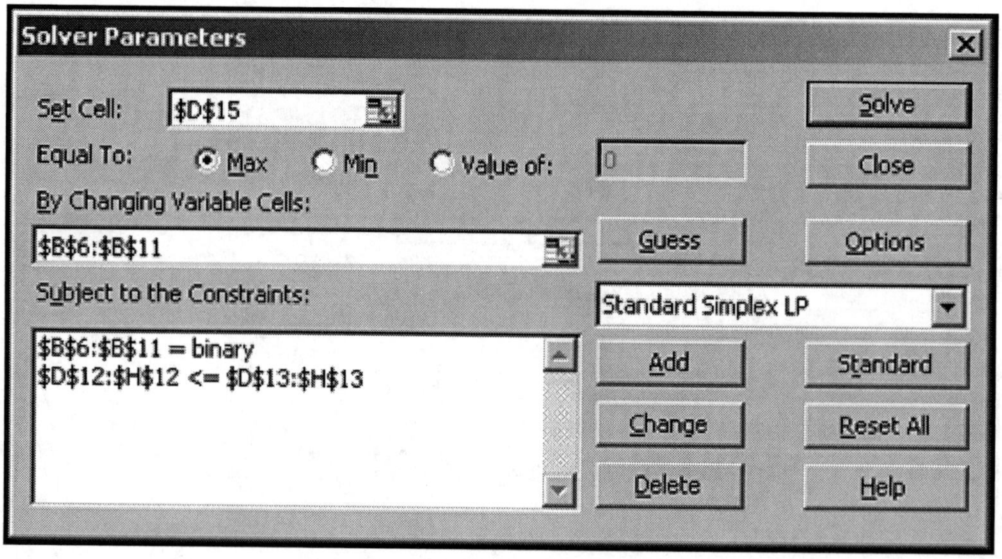

cells in the spreadsheet to implement these constraints. The last set of constraints shown in the dialog box indicates that the values in cells D12 through H12 must be less than or equal to the values in cells D13 through H13 when the problem is solved. These conditions correspond to the capital constraints in the problem.

Because this model contains six decision variables and each variable can assume only one of two values, at most $2^6 = 64$ possible integer solutions exist for this problem. Some of these integer solutions will not fall in the feasible region, so we might suspect that this problem will not be too difficult to solve optimally. If we set the suboptimality tolerance factor to 0 (in the Integer Options dialog box) and solve the problem, we obtain the solution shown in Figure 6.19.

FIGURE 6.19

Optimal integer solution to the CRT Technologies project selection problem

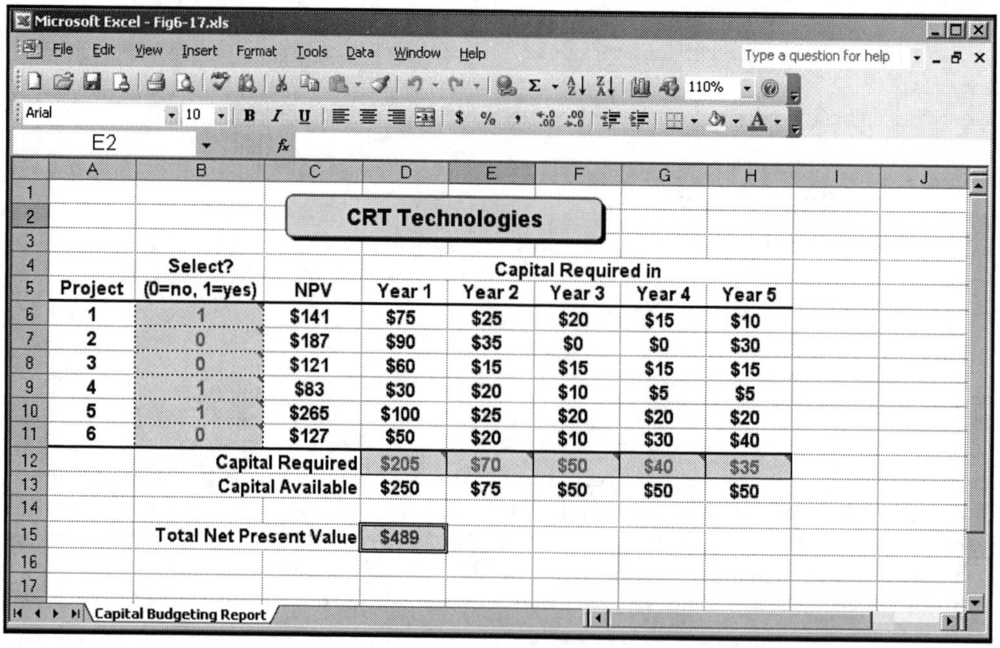

6.11.7 COMPARING THE OPTIMAL SOLUTION TO A HEURISTIC SOLUTION

The optimal solution shown in Figure 6.19 indicates that if CRT Technologies selects projects 1, 4, and 5, it can achieve a total NPV of $489,000. Although this solution does not use all of the capital available in each year, it is still the best possible integer solution to the problem.

Another approach to solving this problem is to create a ranked list of the projects in decreasing order by NPV and then select projects from this list, in order, until the capital is depleted. As shown in Figure 6.20, if we apply this heuristic to the current problem, we would select projects 5 and 2, but we could not select any more projects due to a lack of capital in year 5. This solution would generate a total NPV of $452,000. Again, we can see the potential benefit of optimization techniques over heuristic solution techniques.

6.12 Binary Variables and Logical Conditions

Binary variables can be used to model several logical conditions that might apply in a variety of problems. For example, in the CRT Technologies problem, several of the projects under consideration (for example, projects 1, 3, and 6) might represent alternative approaches for producing a certain part for a product. The company might want to limit the solution to include *no more than one* of these three alternatives. The following type of constraint accomplishes this restriction:

$$X_1 + X_3 + X_6 \leq 1$$

Because X_1, X_3, and X_6 represent binary variables, no more than one of them can assume the value 1 and still satisfy the previous constraint. If we want to ensure that the solution includes *exactly one* of these alternatives, we could include the following constraint in our model:

$$X_1 + X_3 + X_6 = 1$$

As an example of another type of logical condition, suppose that project 4 involves a cellular communications technology that will not be available to the company unless it undertakes project 5. In other words, the company cannot select project 4 unless it also selects project 5. This type of relationship can be imposed on the solution with the constraint:

$$X_4 - X_5 \leq 0$$

The four possible combinations of values for X_4 and X_5 and their relationships to the previous constraint are summarized as:

Value of			
X_4	X_5	Meaning	Feasible?
0	0	Do not select either project	Yes
1	1	Select both projects	Yes
0	1	Select 5, but not 4	Yes
1	0	Select 4, but not 5	No

As indicated in this table, the previous constraint prohibits any solution in which project 4 is selected and project 5 is not selected.

As these examples illustrate, you can model certain logical conditions using binary variables. Several problems at the end of this chapter allow you to use binary variables (and your own creativity) to formulate models for decision problems that involve these types of logical conditions.

6.13 The Fixed-Charge Problem

In most of the LP problems discussed in earlier chapters, we formulated objective functions to maximize profits or minimize costs. In each of these cases, we associated a per-unit cost or per-unit profit with each decision variable to create the objective function. However, in some situations, the decision to produce a product results in a lump-sum cost, or fixed charge, in addition to a per-unit cost or profit. These types of problems are known as fixed-charge or fixed-cost problems. The following are some examples of fixed costs:

- the cost to lease, rent, or purchase a piece of equipment or a vehicle that will be required if a particular action is taken
- the setup cost required to prepare a machine or production line to produce a different type of product
- the cost to construct a new production line or facility that will be required if a particular decision is made
- the cost of hiring additional personnel that will be required if a particular decision is made

In each of these examples, the fixed costs are *new* costs that will be incurred if a particular action or decision is made. In this respect, fixed costs are different from sunk costs, which are costs that will be incurred regardless of what decision is made. Sunk costs are irrelevant for decision-making purposes because, by definition, decisions do not influence these costs. On the other hand, fixed costs are important factors in decision making because the decision determines whether or not these costs will be incurred. The following example illustrates the formulation and solution of a fixed-charge problem.

> Remington Manufacturing is planning its next production cycle. The company can produce three products, each of which must undergo machining, grinding, and assembly operations. The following table below summarizes the hours of machining, grinding, and assembly required by each unit of each product, and the total hours of capacity available for each operation.

	Hours Required By			
Operation	**Product 1**	**Product 2**	**Product 3**	**Total Hours Available**
Machining	2	3	6	600
Grinding	6	3	4	300
Assembly	5	6	2	400

> The cost accounting department has estimated that each unit of product 1 manufactured and sold will contribute $48 to profit, and each unit of products 2 and 3 contributes $55 and $50, respectively. However, manufacturing a unit of product 1 requires a setup operation on the production line that costs $1,000. Similar setups are required for products 2 and 3 at costs of $800 and $900, respectively. The marketing department believes that it can sell all the products produced. Therefore, the management of Remington wants to determine the most profitable mix of products to produce.

6.13.1 DEFINING THE DECISION VARIABLES

Although only three products are under consideration in this problem, we need six variables to formulate the problem accurately. We can define these variables as:

$$X_i = \text{the amount of product } i \text{ to be produced, } i = 1, 2, 3$$

$$Y_i = \begin{cases} 1, \text{ if } X_i > 0 \\ 0, \text{ if } X_i = 0 \end{cases}, i = 1, 2, 3$$

We need three variables, X_1, X_2, and X_3, to correspond to the amount of products 1, 2, and 3 produced. Each of the X_i variables has a corresponding binary variable, Y_i, that will equal 1 if X_i assumes any positive value, or will equal 0 if X_i is 0. For now, do not be concerned about how this relationship between the X_i and Y_i is enforced. We will explore that soon.

6.13.2 DEFINING THE OBJECTIVE FUNCTION

Given our definition of the decision variables, the objective function for our model is stated as:

$$\text{MAX:} \quad 48X_1 + 55X_2 + 50X_3 - 1000Y_1 - 800Y_2 - 900Y_3$$

The first three terms in this function calculate the marginal profit generated by the number of products 1, 2, and 3 sold. The last three terms in this function subtract the fixed costs for the products produced. For example, if X_1 assumes a positive value, we know from our definition of the Y_i variables that Y_1 should equal 1. And if $Y_1 = 1$, the value of the objective function will be reduced by $1,000 to reflect payment of the setup cost. On the other hand, if $X_1 = 0$, we know that $Y_1 = 0$. Therefore, if no units of X_1 are produced, the setup cost for product 1 will not be incurred in the objective. Similar relationships exist between X_2 and Y_2 and between X_3 and Y_3.

6.13.3 DEFINING THE CONSTRAINTS

Several sets of constraints apply to this problem. Capacity constraints are needed to ensure that the number of machining, grinding, and assembly hours used does not exceed the number of hours available for each of these resources. These constraints are stated as:

$$2X_1 + 3X_2 + 6X_3 \leq 600 \quad \} \text{ machining constraint}$$
$$6X_1 + 3X_2 + 4X_3 \leq 300 \quad \} \text{ grinding constraint}$$
$$5X_1 + 6X_2 + 2X_3 \leq 400 \quad \} \text{ assembly constraint}$$

We also need to include nonnegativity conditions on the X_i variables as:

$$X_i \geq 0, i = 1, 2, 3$$

The following constraint on the Y_i variables is needed to ensure that they operate as binary variables:

$$\text{All } Y_i \text{ must be binary}$$

As mentioned earlier, we must ensure that the required relationship between the X_i and Y_i variables is enforced. In particular, the value of the Y_i variables can be determined from the X_i variables. Therefore, we need constraints to establish this *link* between the value of the Y_i variables and the X_i variables. These linking constraints are represented by:

$$X_1 \leq M_1 Y_1$$
$$X_2 \leq M_2 Y_2$$
$$X_3 \leq M_3 Y_3$$

In each of these constraints, the M_i is a numeric constant that represents an upper bound on the optimal value of the X_i. Let's assume that all the M_i are arbitrarily large numbers; for example, $M_i = 10{,}000$. Then each constraint sets up a link between the value of the X_i and the Y_i. For example, if any X_i variables in the previous constraints assume a value greater than 0, the corresponding Y_i variable must assume the value 1 or the constraint will be violated. On the other hand, if any of the X_i variables are equal to 0, the corresponding Y_i variables could equal 0 or 1 and still satisfy the constraint. However, if we consider the objective function to this problem, we know that when given a choice, Solver will always set the Y_i equal to 0 (rather than 1) because this results in a better objective function value. Therefore, we can conclude that if any X_i variables are equal to 0, Solver will set the corresponding Y_i variable equal to 0 because this is feasible, and it results in a better objective function value.

6.13.4 DETERMINING VALUES FOR "BIG M"

The M_i values used in the linking constraints sometimes are referred to as "Big M" values because they can be assigned arbitrarily large values. However, for reasons that go beyond the scope of this text, these types of problems are much easier to solve if the M_i values are kept as small as possible. As indicated earlier, the M_i values impose upper bounds on the values of the X_i. So, if a problem indicates that a company could manufacture and sell no more than 60 units of X_1, for example, we could let $M_1 = 60$.

However, even if upper bounds for the X_i are not indicated explicitly, it is sometimes easy to derive implicit upper bounds for these variables.

Let's consider the variable X_1 in the Remington problem. What is the maximum number of units of X_1 that can be produced in this problem? Referring back to our capacity constraints, if the company produced 0 units of X_2 and X_3, it would run out of machining capacity after producing $600/2 = 300$ units of X_1. Similarly, it would run out of grinding capacity after producing $300/6 = 50$ units of X_1, and it would run out of assembly capacity after producing $400/5 = 80$ units of X_1. Therefore, the maximum number of units of X_1 that the company can produce is 50. Using similar logic, we can determine that the maximum units of X_2 the company can produce is $MIN(600/3, 300/3, 400/6) = 66.67$, and the maximum units of X_3 is $MIN(600/6, 300/4, 400/2) = 75$. Thus, for this problem, reasonable upper bounds for X_1, X_2, and X_3 are represented by $M_1 = 50$, $M_2 = 67$, and $M_3 = 75$, respectively. (Note that the method illustrated here for obtaining reasonable values for the M_i does not apply if any of the coefficients in the machining, grinding, or assembly constraints are negative. Why is this?) When possible, you should determine reasonable values for the M_i in this type of problem. However, if this is not possible, you can assign arbitrarily large values to the M_i.

6.13.5 IMPLEMENTING THE MODEL

Using the values for the M_i calculated earlier, our ILP formulation of Remington's production planning model is summarized as:

MAX:	$48X_1 + 55X_2 + 50X_3 - 1000Y_1 - 800Y_2 - 900Y_3$		
Subject to:	$2X_1 + 3X_2 + 6X_3 \leq 600$	} machining constraint	
	$6X_1 + 3X_2 + 4X_3 \leq 300$	} grinding constraint	
	$5X_1 + 6X_2 + 2X_3 \leq 400$	} assembly constraint	
	$X_1 - 50Y_1 \leq 0$	} linking constraint	
	$X_2 - 67Y_2 \leq 0$	} linking constraint	
	$X_3 - 75Y_3 \leq 0$	} linking constraint	
	All Y_i must be binary	} binary constraints	
	$X_i \geq 0, i = 1, 2, 3$	} nonnegativity conditions	

This model expresses the linking constraints in a slightly different (but algebraically equivalent) manner, to follow our convention of having all the variables on the LHS of the inequality and a constant on the RHS. This model is implemented in the spreadsheet shown in Figure 6.21 (and in the file Fig6-21.xls on your data disk).

In the spreadsheet in Figure 6.21, cells B5, C5, and D5 represent the variables X_1, X_2, and X_3, and cells B15, C15, and D15 represent Y_1, Y_2, and Y_3. The coefficients for the objective function are in cells B7 through D8. The objective function is implemented in cell F8 with the formula:

Formula for cell F8: =SUMPRODUCT(B7:D7,B5:D5)−
SUMPRODUCT(B8:D8,B15:D15)

Cells B11 through D13 contain the coefficients for the machining, grinding, and assembly constraints. The LHS formulas for these constraints are implemented in cells E11 through E13, and cells F11 through F13 contain the RHS values for these constraints. Finally, the LHS formulas for the linking constraints are entered in cells B16 through D16 as:

Formula for cell B16:   =B5 − MIN($F$11/B11,$F$12/B12,$F$13/B13)*B15

(Copy to cells C16 through D16.)

FIGURE 6.21

Spreadsheet model for Remington's fixed-charge problem

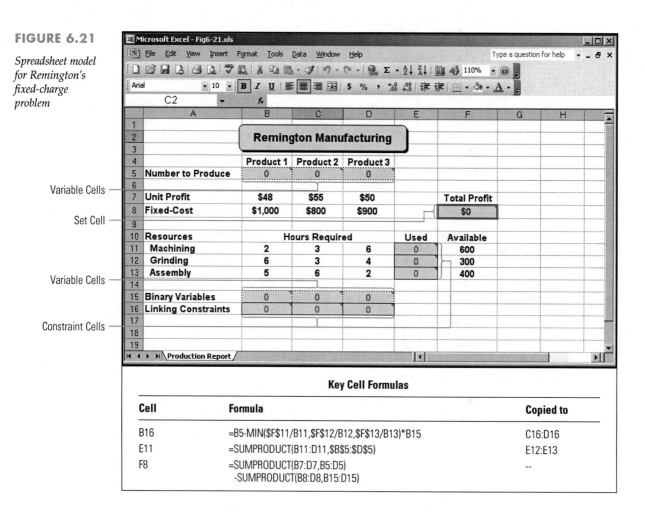

Variable Cells

Set Cell

Variable Cells

Constraint Cells

Key Cell Formulas

Cell	Formula	Copied to
B16	=B5-MIN($F$11/B11,$F$12/B12,$F$13/B13)*B15	C16:D16
E11	=SUMPRODUCT(B11:D11,$B$5:$D$5)	E12:E13
F8	=SUMPRODUCT(B7:D7,B5:D5) -SUMPRODUCT(B8:D8,B15:D15)	--

Instead of entering the values for M_i in these constraints, we implemented formulas that would calculate correct M_i values automatically if the user of this spreadsheet changed any of the coefficients or RHS values in the capacity constraints.

> ## Potential Pitfall
>
> Note that we are treating cells B15, C15, and D15, which represent the binary variables Y_1, Y_2, and Y_3, just like any other cells representing decision variables. We simply entered values of 0 into these cells to indicate that they represent decision variables. Ultimately, Solver will determine what values should be placed in these cells so that all the constraints are satisfied and the objective function is maximized. Some people try to make Solver's job "easier" by placing IF( ) functions in these cells to determine whether the values should be 0 or 1 depending on the values of cells B5, C5, and D5, which correspond to the variables X_1, X_2, and X_3. Although this approach seems to make sense, it can produce unwanted results. Using IF( ) functions in this way introduces *nonlinearities* in the spreadsheet model that can prevent Solver from finding the optimal solution to the problem. In Chapter 8, Nonlinear Programming, we will see that nonlinear programming problems can be very difficult to solve optimally. Thus, it is best to create a model so that it can be solved using linear optimization methods.

6.13.6 SOLVING THE MODEL

The Solver Parameters dialog box shown in Figure 6.22 indicates the settings required to solve this problem. Notice that the ranges B5 through D5 and B15 through D15, which correspond to the X_i and Y_i variables, are both listed as ranges of cells that can be changed. Also, notice that the necessary binary constraint is imposed on cells B15 through D15.

Because so few integer variables exist in this problem, we should be able to obtain an optimal integer solution easily. If we set the suboptimality tolerance to 0 in the Integer Options dialog box and instruct Solver to assume a linear model, we obtain the optimal solution to this problem, as shown in Figure 6.23.

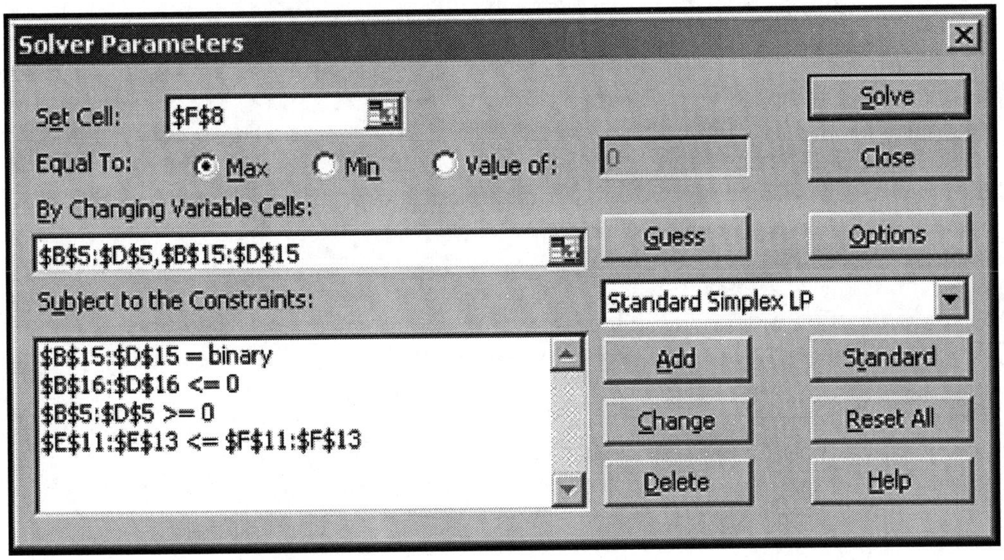

FIGURE 6.22

Solver parameters for Remington's fixed-charge problem

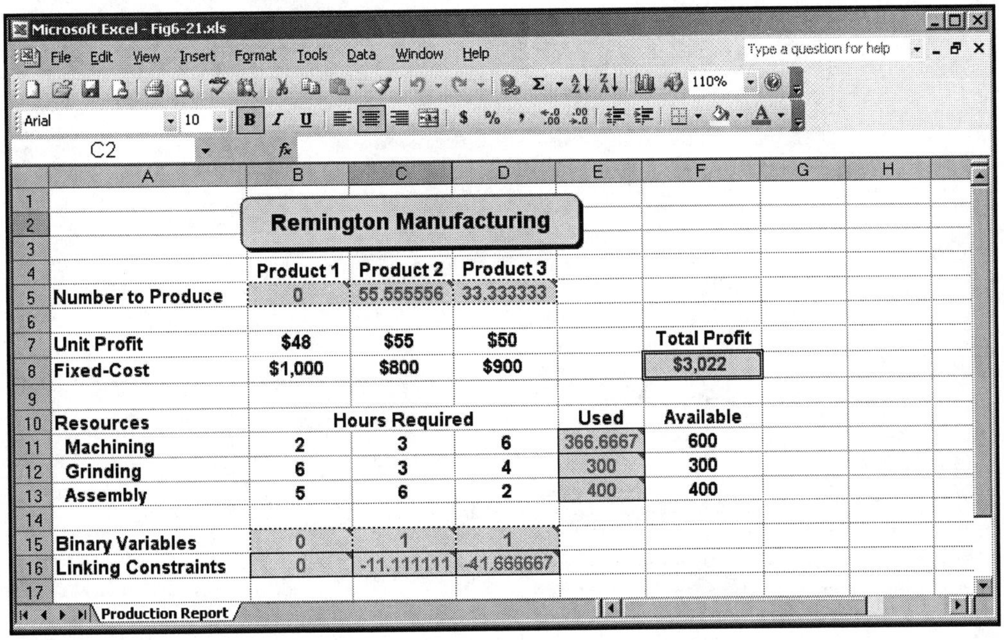

FIGURE 6.23

Optimal mixed-integer solution to Remington's fixed-charge problem

6.13.7 ANALYZING THE SOLUTION

The solution shown in Figure 6.23 indicates that the company should produce 0 units of product 1, 55.55 units of product 2, and 33.33 units of product 3 ($X_1 = 0$, $X_2 = 55.55$, and $X_3 = 33.33$). Solver assigned values of 0, 1, and 1 to cells B15, C15, and D15 ($Y_1 = 0$, $Y_2 = 1$, and $Y_3 = 1$). Thus, Solver maintained the proper relationship between the X_i and Y_i because the linking constraints were specified for this problem.

The values in B16, C16, and D16 indicate the amounts by which the values for X_1, X_2, and X_3 (in cells B5, C5, and D5) fall below the upper bounds imposed by their respective linking constraints. Thus, the optimal value of X_2 is approximately 11.11 units below its upper bound of 66.67 and the optimal value of X_3 is approximately 41.67 units below its upper bound of 75. Because the optimal value of Y_1 is zero, the linking constraint for X_1 and Y_1 imposes an upper bound of zero on X_1. Thus, the value in cell B16 indicates that the optimal value of X_1 is zero units below its upper bound of zero.

Because our formulation of this model did not specify that the X_i must be integers, we should not be surprised by the fractional values obtained for these variables in this solution. If we round the values of X_2 and X_3 down to 55 and 33, we obtain an integer feasible solution with an objective function value of $2,975. If we want to find the optimal all-integer solution, we can add the appropriate integrality condition for the X_i to the constraint set and then re-solve the problem. This optimal all-integer solution is shown in Figure 6.24.

Note that more computational effort is required to obtain the all-integer solution shown in Figure 6.24 versus the effort required to obtain the mixed-integer solution shown in Figure 6.23. This additional work resulted in only a $5 improvement in the objective function over the all-integer solution we obtained from rounding down the solution in Figure 6.23. This highlights two important points. First, problems involving binary integer variables are often easier to solve than problems involving general integer variables. Second, good near-optimal solutions often can be obtained by rounding, so this approach is not necessarily ineffective—and could be the only practical solution available for large ILPs that are difficult to solve.

FIGURE 6.24

Optimal all-integer solution to Remington's fixed-charge problem

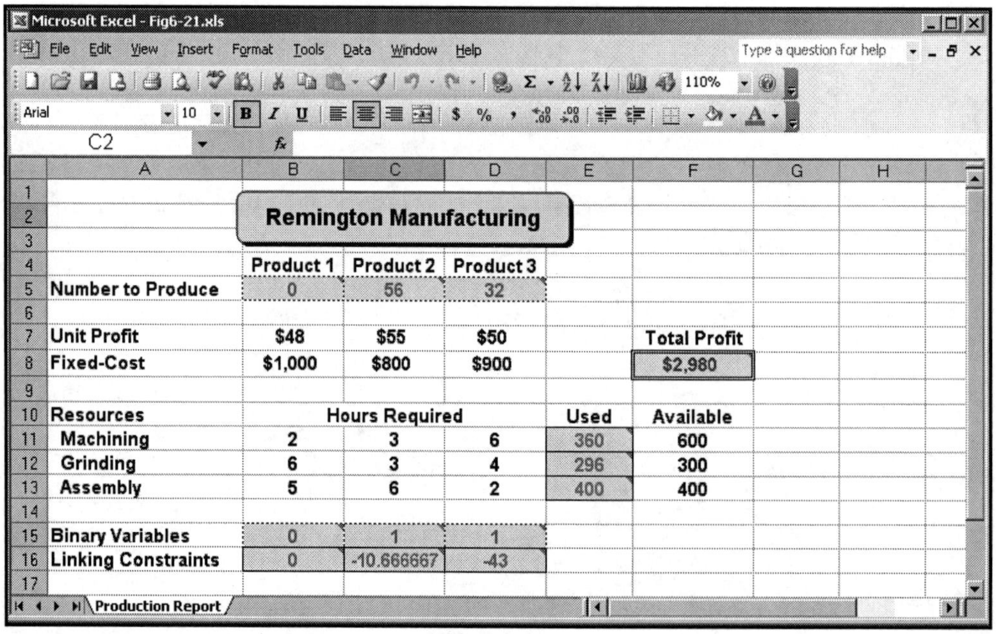

6.14 Minimum Order/Purchase Size

Many investment, production, and distribution problems have minimum purchase amounts or minimum production lot size requirements that must be met. For example, a particular investment opportunity might require a minimum investment of $25,000. Or, a supplier of a given part used in a production process might require a minimum order of 10 units. Similarly, many manufacturing companies have a policy of not producing any units of a given item unless a certain minimum lot size will be produced.

To see how these types of minimum order/purchase requirements can be modeled, suppose that in the previous problem, Remington Manufacturing did not want to produce any units of product 3 (X_3) unless it produced at least 40 units of this product. This type of restriction is modeled as:

$$X_3 \leq M_3 Y_3$$
$$X_3 \geq 40 Y_3$$

The first constraint is the same type of linking constraint described earlier, in which M_3 represents an upper bound on X_3 (or an arbitrarily large number) and Y_3 represents a binary variable. If X_3 assumes any positive value, Y_3 must equal 1 (if $X_3 > 0$, then $Y_3 = 1$). However, according to the second constraint, if Y_3 equals 1, then X_3 must be greater than or equal to 40 (if $Y_3 = 1$, then $X_3 \geq 40$). On the other hand, if X_3 equals 0, Y_3 also must equal 0 to satisfy both constraints. Together, these two constraints ensure that if X_3 assumes any positive value, that value must be at least 40. This example illustrates how binary variables can be used to model a practical condition that is likely to occur in a variety of decision problems.

6.15 Quantity Discounts

In all the LP problems considered to this point, we have assumed that the profit or cost coefficients in the objective function were constant. For example, consider our revised Blue Ridge Hot Tubs problem, which is represented by:

MAX:	$350X_1 + 300X_2$	} profit
Subject to:	$1X_1 + 1X_2 \leq 200$	} pump constraint
	$9X_1 + 6X_2 \leq 1,520$	} labor constraint
	$12X_1 + 16X_2 \leq 2,650$	} tubing constraint
	$X_1, X_2 \geq 0$	} nonnegativity conditions
	X_1, X_2 must be integers	} integrality conditions

This model assumes that *every* additional Aqua-Spa (X_1) manufactured and sold results in a $350 increase in profit. It also assumes that every additional Hydro-Lux (X_2) manufactured and sold results in a $300 increase in profit. However, as the production of these products increases, quantity discounts might be obtained on component parts that would cause the profit margin on these items to increase.

For example, suppose that if the company produces more than 75 Aqua-Spas, it will be able to obtain quantity discounts and other economies of scale that would increase the profit margin to $375 per unit for each unit produced in excess of 75. Similarly, suppose that if the company produces more than 50 Hydro-Luxes, it will be able to increase its profit margin to $325 for each unit produced in excess of 50. That is, each of the first 75 units of X_1 and the first 50 units of X_2 would produce profits of $350 and $300 per unit, respectively, and each additional unit of X_1 and X_2 would produce profits of $375 and $325 per unit, respectively. How do we model this type of problem?

6.15.1 FORMULATING THE MODEL

To accommodate the different profit rates that can be generated by producing Aqua-Spas and Hydro-Luxes, we need to define new variables for the problem, where

X_{11} = the number of Aqua-Spas produced at \$350 profit per unit

X_{12} = the number of Aqua-Spas produced at \$375 profit per unit

X_{21} = the number of Hydro-Luxes produced at \$300 profit per unit

X_{22} = the number of Hydro-Luxes produced at \$325 profit per unit

Using these variables, we can begin to reformulate our problem as:

MAX: $350X_{11} + 375X_{12} + 300X_{21} + 325X_{22}$

Subject to:
$$1X_{11} + 1X_{12} + 1X_{21} + 1X_{22} \leq 200 \quad \} \text{ pump constraint}$$
$$9X_{11} + 9X_{12} + 6X_{21} + 6X_{22} \leq 1{,}520 \quad \} \text{ labor constraint}$$
$$12X_{11} + 12X_{12} + 16X_{21} + 16X_{22} \leq 2{,}650 \quad \} \text{ tubing constraint}$$
$$\text{All } X_{ij} \geq 0 \quad \} \text{ simple lower bounds}$$
$$\text{All } X_{ij} \text{ must be integers} \quad \} \text{ integrality conditions}$$

This formulation is not complete. Notice that the variable X_{12} would always be preferred over X_{11} because X_{12} requires exactly the same resources as X_{11} and generates a larger per-unit profit. The same relationship holds between X_{22} and X_{21}. Thus, the optimal solution to the problem is $X_{11} = 0$, $X_{12} = 118$, $X_{21} = 0$, and $X_{22} = 76$. However, this solution is not allowable because we cannot produce any units of X_{12} until we have produced 75 units of X_{11}; and we cannot produce any units of X_{22} until we have produced 50 units of X_{21}. Therefore, we must identify some additional constraints to ensure that these conditions are met.

6.15.2 THE MISSING CONSTRAINTS

To ensure that the model does not allow any units of X_{12} to be produced unless we have produced 75 units of X_{11}, consider the constraints:

$$X_{12} \leq M_{12}Y_1$$
$$X_{11} \geq 75Y_1$$

In the first constraint, M_{12} represents some arbitrarily large numeric constant and Y_1 represents a binary variable. The first constraint requires that $Y_1 = 1$ if any units of X_{12} are produced (if $X_{12} > 0$, then $Y_1 = 1$). However, if $Y_1 = 1$, then the second constraint would require X_{11} to be at least 75. According to the second constraint, the only way that fewer than 75 units of X_{11} can be produced is if $Y_1 = 0$, which, by the first constraint, implies $X_{12} = 0$. These two constraints do not allow any units of X_{12} to be produced unless at least 75 units of X_{11} have been produced. The following constraints ensure that the model does not allow any units of X_{22} to be produced unless we have produced 50 units of X_{21}:

$$X_{22} \leq M_{22}Y_2$$
$$X_{21} \geq 50Y_2$$

If we include these new constraints in our previous formulation (along with the constraints necessary to make Y_1 and Y_2 operate as binary variables), we would have an accurate formulation of the decision problem. The optimal solution to this problem is $X_{11} = 75$, $X_{12} = 43$, $X_{21} = 50$, $X_{22} = 26$.

6.16 A Contract Award Problem

Other conditions often arise in decision problems that can be modeled effectively using binary variables. The following example, which involves awarding contracts, illustrates some of these conditions.

B&G Construction is a commercial building company located in Tampa, Florida. The company has recently signed contracts to construct four buildings in different locations throughout southern Florida. Each building project requires large amounts of cement to be delivered to the building sites. At B&G's request, three cement companies have submitted bids for supplying the cement for these jobs. The following table summarizes the prices the three companies charge per delivered ton of cement and the maximum amount of cement that each company can provide.

| | Cost per Delivered Ton of Cement | | | | |
	Project 1	Project 2	Project 3	Project 4	Max. Supply
Company 1	$120	$115	$130	$125	525
Company 2	$100	$150	$110	$105	450
Company 3	$140	$ 95	$145	$165	550
Total Tons Needed	450	275	300	350	

For example, Company 1 can supply a maximum of 525 tons of cement, and each ton delivered to projects 1, 2, 3, and 4 will cost $120, $115, $130, and $125, respectively. The costs vary primarily because of the different distances between the cement plants and the construction sites. The numbers in the last row of the table indicate the total amount of cement (in tons) required for each project.

In addition to the maximum supplies listed, each cement company placed special conditions on its bid. Specifically, Company 1 indicated that it will not supply orders of less than 150 tons for any of the construction projects. Company 2 indicated that it can supply more than 200 tons to no more than one of the projects. Company 3 indicated that it will only accept orders that total 200 tons, 400 tons, or 550 tons.

B&G can contract with more than one supplier to meet the cement requirements for a given project. The problem is to determine what amounts to purchase from each supplier to meet the demands for each project at the least total cost.

This problem seems like a transportation problem in which we want to determine how much cement should be shipped from each cement company to each construction project to meet the demands of the projects at a minimum cost. However, the special conditions imposed by each supplier require side constraints, which usually are not found in a standard transportation problem. First, we'll discuss the formulation of the objective function and the transportation constraints. Then, we'll consider how to implement the side constraints required by the special conditions in the problem.

6.16.1 FORMULATING THE MODEL: THE OBJECTIVE FUNCTION AND TRANSPORTATION CONSTRAINTS

To begin formulating this problem, we need to define our decision variables as:

X_{ij} = tons of cement purchased from company i for construction project j

The objective function to minimize total cost is represented by:

$$\text{MIN:} \quad 120X_{11} + 115X_{12} + 130X_{13} + 125X_{14}$$
$$+100X_{21} + 150X_{22} + 110X_{23} + 105X_{24}$$
$$+140X_{31} + \ 95X_{32} + 145X_{33} + 165X_{34}$$

To ensure that the maximum supply of cement from each company is not exceeded, we need the following constraints:

$$X_{11} + X_{12} + X_{13} + X_{14} \leq 525 \quad \} \text{ supply from company 1}$$
$$X_{21} + X_{22} + X_{23} + X_{24} \leq 450 \quad \} \text{ supply from company 2}$$
$$X_{31} + X_{32} + X_{33} + X_{34} \leq 550 \quad \} \text{ supply from company 3}$$

To ensure that the requirement for cement at each construction project is met, we need the following constraints:

$$X_{11} + X_{21} + X_{31} = 450 \quad \} \text{ demand for cement at project 1}$$
$$X_{12} + X_{22} + X_{32} = 275 \quad \} \text{ demand for cement at project 2}$$
$$X_{13} + X_{23} + X_{33} = 300 \quad \} \text{ demand for cement at project 3}$$
$$X_{14} + X_{24} + X_{34} = 350 \quad \} \text{ demand for cement at project 4}$$

6.16.2 IMPLEMENTING THE TRANSPORTATION CONSTRAINTS

The objective function and the constraints of this problem are implemented in the spreadsheet model shown in Figure 6.25 (and in the file Fig6-25.xls on your data disk).

In this spreadsheet, the costs per delivered ton of cement are shown in cells B6 through E8. Cells B12 through E14 represent the decision variables in the model. The objective function is entered in cell G17 as:

Formula for cell G17:   =SUMPRODUCT(B6:E8,B12:E14)

FIGURE 6.25

Spreadsheet model for the transportation portion of B&G's contract award problem

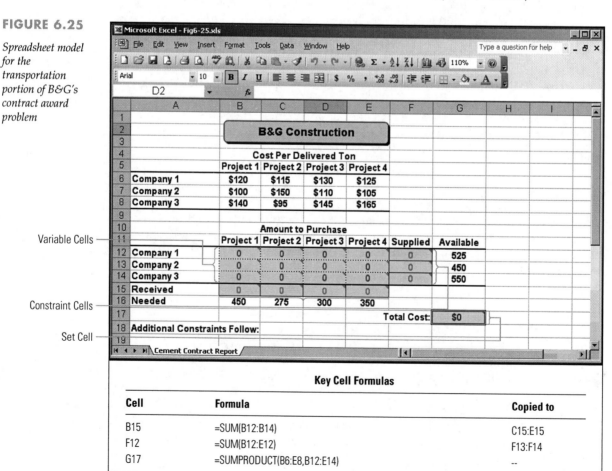

The LHS formulas of the supply constraints are entered in cells F12 through F14 as:

Formula for cell F12:   =SUM(B12:E12)

(Copy to F13 through F14.)

Cells G12 through G14 contain the RHS values for these constraints. The LHS formulas for the demand constraints are entered in cells B15 through E15 as:

Formula for cell B15:   =SUM(B12:B14)

(Copy to C15 through E15.)

Cells B16 through E16 contain the RHS values for these constraints.

6.16.3 FORMULATING THE MODEL: THE SIDE CONSTRAINTS

Company 1 indicated that it will not accept orders for less than 150 tons for any of the construction projects. This minimum-size order restriction is modeled by the following eight constraints, where the Y_{ij} represent binary variables:

$$X_{11} \leq 525Y_{11} \qquad \text{(implement as } X_{11} - 525Y_{11} \leq 0)$$
$$X_{12} \leq 525Y_{12} \qquad \text{(implement as } X_{12} - 525Y_{12} \leq 0)$$
$$X_{13} \leq 525Y_{13} \qquad \text{(implement as } X_{13} - 525Y_{13} \leq 0)$$
$$X_{14} \leq 525Y_{14} \qquad \text{(implement as } X_{14} - 525Y_{14} \leq 0)$$
$$X_{11} \geq 150Y_{11} \qquad \text{(implement as } X_{11} - 150Y_{11} \geq 0)$$
$$X_{12} \geq 150Y_{12} \qquad \text{(implement as } X_{12} - 150Y_{12} \geq 0)$$
$$X_{13} \geq 150Y_{13} \qquad \text{(implement as } X_{13} - 150Y_{13} \geq 0)$$
$$X_{14} \geq 150Y_{14} \qquad \text{(implement as } X_{14} - 150Y_{14} \geq 0)$$

Each constraint has an algebraically equivalent constraint, which ultimately will be used in implementing the constraint in the spreadsheet. The first four constraints represent linking constraints that ensure that if X_{11}, X_{12}, X_{13}, or X_{14} is greater than 0, then its associated binary variable (Y_{11}, Y_{12}, Y_{13}, or Y_{14}) must equal 1. (These constraints also indicate that 525 is the maximum value that can be assumed by X_{11}, X_{12}, X_{13}, and X_{14}.) The next four constraints ensure that if X_{11}, X_{12}, X_{13}, or X_{14} is greater than 0, it must be at least 150. We include these constraints in the formulation of this model to ensure that any order given to Company 1 is for at least 150 tons of cement.

Company 2 indicated that it can supply more than 200 tons to no more than one of the projects. This type of restriction is represented by the following set of constraints where, again, the Y_{ij} represent binary variables:

$$X_{21} \leq 200 + 250Y_{21} \qquad \text{(implement as } X_{21} - 200 - 250Y_{21} \leq 0)$$
$$X_{22} \leq 200 + 250Y_{22} \qquad \text{(implement as } X_{22} - 200 - 250Y_{22} \leq 0)$$
$$X_{23} \leq 200 + 250Y_{23} \qquad \text{(implement as } X_{23} - 200 - 250Y_{23} \leq 0)$$
$$X_{24} \leq 200 + 250Y_{24} \qquad \text{(implement as } X_{24} - 200 - 250Y_{24} \leq 0)$$
$$Y_{21} + Y_{22} + Y_{23} + Y_{24} \leq 1 \qquad \text{(implement as is)}$$

The first constraint indicates that the amount supplied from Company 2 for Project 1 must be less than 200 if $Y_{21} = 0$, or less than 450 (the maximum supply from company 2) if $Y_{21} = 1$. The next three constraints have similar interpretations for the amount supplied from Company 2 to Projects 2, 3, and 4, respectively. The last constraint indicates that at most, one of Y_{21}, Y_{22}, Y_{23}, and Y_{24} can equal 1. Therefore, only one of the projects can receive more than 200 tons of cement from Company 2.

The final set of constraints for this problem addresses Company 3's stipulation that it will accept only orders totaling 200, 400, or 550 tons. This type of condition is modeled using binary Y_{ij} variables as:

$$X_{31} + X_{32} + X_{33} + X_{34} = 200Y_{31} + 400Y_{32} + 550Y_{33}$$

$$\text{(implement as } X_{31} + X_{32} + X_{33} + X_{34} - 200Y_{31} - 400Y_{32} - 550Y_{33} = 0)$$

$$Y_{31} + Y_{32} + Y_{33} \leq 1 \text{ (implement as is)}$$

These constraints allow for the total amount ordered from Company 3 to assume four distinct values. If $Y_{31} = Y_{32} = Y_{33} = 0$, then no cement will be ordered from Company 3. If $Y_{31} = 1$, then 200 tons must be ordered. If $Y_{32} = 1$ then 400 tons must be ordered. Finally, if $Y_{33} = 1$, then 550 tons must be ordered from Company 3. These two constraints enforce the special condition imposed by Company 3.

6.16.4 IMPLEMENTING THE SIDE CONSTRAINTS

Although the side constraints in this problem allow us to impose important restrictions on the feasible solutions that can be considered, these constraints serve more of a "mechanical" purpose—to make the model work—but are not of primary interest to management. Thus, it is often convenient to implement side constraints in an out-of-the-way area of the spreadsheet so that they do not detract from the primary purpose of the spreadsheet, in this case, to determine how much cement to order from each potential supplier. Figure 6.26 shows how the side constraints for the current problem can be implemented in a spreadsheet.

To implement the side constraints for Company 1, we enter the batch-size restriction of 150 in cell B20 and reserve cells B21 through E21 to represent the binary variables Y_{11}, Y_{12}, Y_{13}, and Y_{14}. The LHS formulas for the linking constraints for Company 1 are implemented in cells B22 through E22 as:

Formula for cell B22:   =B12–$G$12*B21

(Copy to C22 through E22.)

Cell F22 contains a reminder for us to tell Solver that these cells must be less than or equal to 0. The LHS formulas for the batch-size constraints for Company 1 are implemented in cells B23 through E23 as:

Formula for cell B23:   =B12–$B$20*B21

(Copy to C23 through E23.)

Cell F23 contains a reminder for us to tell Solver that these cells must be greater than or equal to 0.

To implement the side constraints for Company 2, we enter the maximum supply value of 200 in cell B25 and reserve cells B26 through E26 to represent the binary variables Y_{21}, Y_{22}, Y_{23}, and Y_{24}. The LHS formulas for the maximum supply constraints are implemented in cells B27 through E27 as:

Formula for cell B27:   =B13–$B$25–($G$13–$B$25)*B26

(Copy to C27 through E27.)

Cell F27 reminds us to tell Solver that these cells must be less than or equal to 0. As discussed earlier, to ensure that no more than one order from Company 2 exceeds 200 tons, the sum of the binary variables for Company 2 cannot exceed 1. The LHS formula for this constraint is entered in cell E28 as:

Formula for cell E28:   =SUM(B26:E26)

Cell F28 reminds us to tell Solver that this cell must be less than or equal to 1.

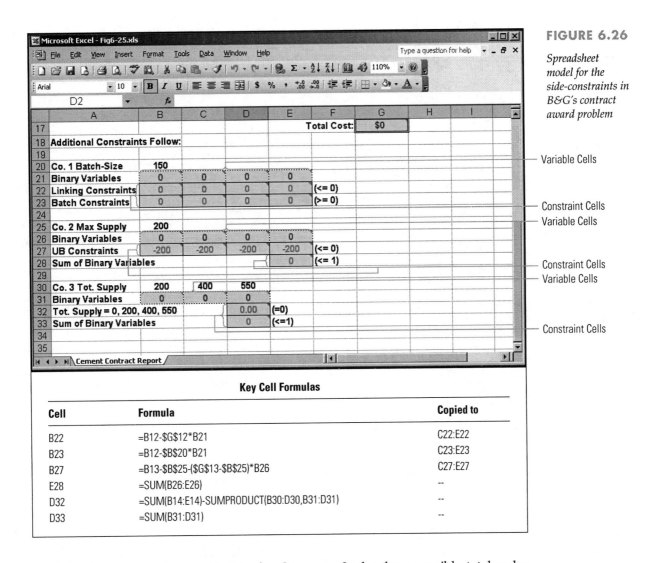

FIGURE 6.26

Spreadsheet model for the side-constraints in B&G's contract award problem

Key Cell Formulas

Cell	Formula	Copied to
B22	=B12-$G$12*B21	C22:E22
B23	=B12-$B$20*B21	C23:E23
B27	=B13-$B$25-($G$13-$B$25)*B26	C27:E27
E28	=SUM(B26:E26)	--
D32	=SUM(B14:E14)-SUMPRODUCT(B30:D30,B31:D31)	--
D33	=SUM(B31:D31)	--

To implement the side constraints for Company 3, the three possible total order amounts are entered in cells B30 through D30. Cells B31 through D31 are reserved to represent the binary variables Y_{31}, Y_{32}, and Y_{33}. The LHS formula for Company 3's total supply side constraint is entered in cell D32 as:

Formula for cell D32:   =SUM(B14:E14)–SUMPRODUCT(B30:D30,B31:D31)

Cell E32 reminds us to tell Solver that cell D32 must equal 0. Finally, to ensure that no more than one of the binary variables for company 3 is set equal to 1, we enter the sum of these variables in cell D33 as:

Formula for cell D33:   =SUM(B31:D31)

Cell E33 reminds us to tell Solver that this cell must be less than or equal to 1.

6.16.5 SOLVING THE MODEL

Because of the large number of variables and constraints in this problem, we summarized the Solver parameters required for this problem in Figure 6.27. Note that all of the cells representing binary variables must be identified as variable cells and must be constrained to assume only integer values between 0 and 1.

FIGURE 6.27

Solver parameters and options for B&G's contract award problem

Solver Parameters:

Set Target Cell: G17

Equal to: Min

By Changing Cells: B12:E14,B21:E21,B26:E26,B31:D31

Subject to the Constraints:

B12:E14 $\geq$ 0

B21:E21 = binary

B26:E26 = binary

B31:D31 = binary

F12:F14 $\geq$ G12:G14

B15:E15 = B16:E16

B22:E22 $\leq$ 0

B23:E23 $\geq$ 0

B27:E27 $\leq$ 0

E28 $\leq$ 1

D32 = 0

D33 $\leq$ 1

Solver Options:

Standard Simplex LP	Integer Tolerance = 0
Use Automatic Scaling	Iterations = 100

6.16.6 ANALYZING THE SOLUTION

An optimal solution to this problem is shown in Figure 6.28 (there are alternate optimal solutions to this problem). In this solution, the amounts of cement required by each construction project are met exactly. Also, each condition imposed by the side constraints for each company is met. Specifically, the orders awarded to Company 1 are for at least 150 tons; only one of the orders awarded to Company 2 exceeds 200 tons; and the sum of the orders awarded to Company 3 is exactly equal to 400 tons.

6.17 The Branch-and-Bound Algorithm (Optional)

As mentioned earlier, a special procedure, known as the branch-and-bound (B&B) algorithm, is required to solve ILPs. Although we can easily indicate the presence of integer variables in a model, it usually requires quite a bit of effort on Solver's part to actually solve an ILP problem using the B&B algorithm. To better appreciate and understand what is involved in the B&B algorithm, let's consider how it works.

The B&B algorithm starts by relaxing all the integrality conditions in an ILP and solving the resulting LP problem. As noted earlier, if we are lucky, the optimal solution to the relaxed LP problem might happen to satisfy the original integrality conditions. If

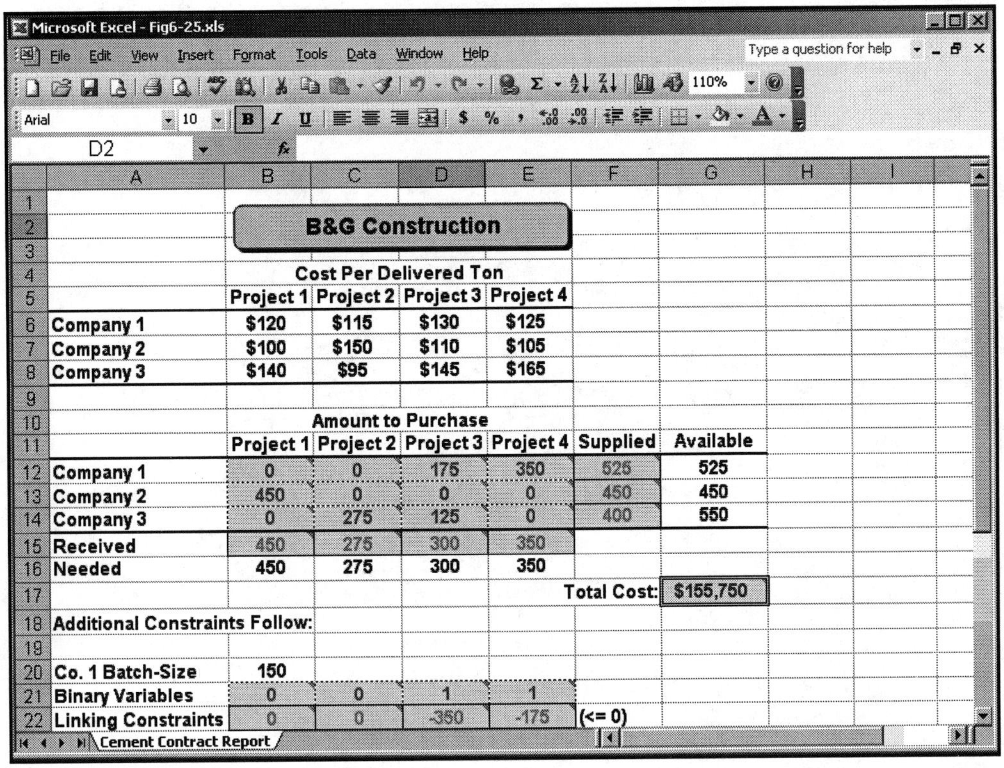

FIGURE 6.28

*Optimal solution
to B&G's contract
award problem*

this occurs, then we are done—the optimal solution to the LP relaxation is also the optimal solution to the ILP. However, it is more likely that the optimal solution to the LP will violate one or more of the original integrality conditions. For example, consider the problem for which the integer and relaxed feasible regions were shown in Figure 6.1 and are repeated in Figure 6.29:

$$\text{MAX:} \qquad 2X_1 + 3X_2$$
$$\text{Subject to:} \qquad X_1 + 3X_2 \leq 8.25$$
$$2.5X_1 + X_2 \leq 8.75$$
$$X_1, X_2 \geq 0$$
$$X_1, X_2 \text{ must be integers}$$

If we relax the integrality conditions in this problem and solve the resulting LP problem, we obtain the solution $X_1 = 2.769$, $X_2 = 1.826$ shown in Figure 6.29. This solution clearly violates the integrality conditions stated in the original problem. Part of the difficulty here is that none of the corner points of the relaxed feasible region are integer feasible (other than the origin). We know that the optimal solution to an LP problem will occur at a corner point of its feasible region but, in this case, none of those corner points (except the origin) correspond to integer solutions. Thus, we need to modify the problem so that the integer feasible solutions to the problem occur at corner points of the relaxed feasible region. This is accomplished by branching.

6.17.1 BRANCHING

Any integer variable in an ILP that assumes a fractional value in the optimal solution to the relaxed problem can be designated as a branching variable. For example, the

FIGURE 6.29

Solution to LP relaxation at noninteger corner point

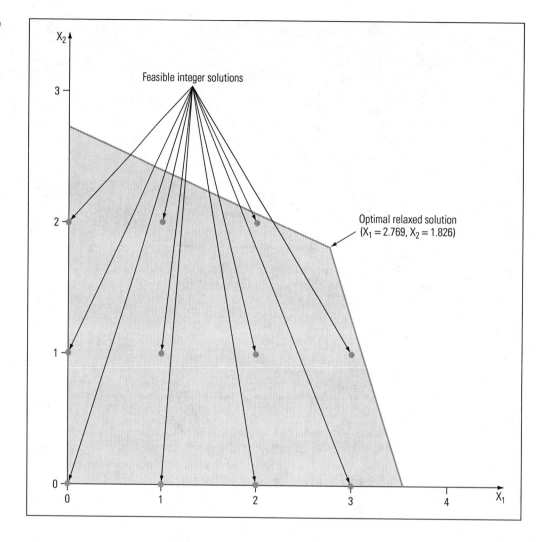

variables X_1 and X_2 in the previous problem should assume only integer values, but were assigned the values $X_1 = 2.769$ and $X_2 = 1.826$ in the optimal-solution to the LP relaxation of the problem. Either of these variables could be selected as branching variables.

Let's arbitrarily choose X_1 as our branching variable. Because the current value of X_1 is not integer feasible, we want to eliminate this solution from further consideration. Many other solutions in this same vicinity of the relaxed feasible region also can be eliminated. That is, X_1 must assume a value less than or equal to 2 ($X_1 \leq 2$) or greater than or equal to 3 ($X_1 \geq 3$) in the optimal integer solution to the ILP. Therefore, all other possible solutions where X_1 assumes values between 2 and 3 (such as the current solution where $X_1 = 2.769$) can be eliminated from consideration. By branching on X_1, our original ILP problem can be subdivided into the following two candidate problems:

Problem I:	MAX:	$2X_1 + 3X_2$
	Subject to:	$X_1 + 3X_2 \leq 8.25$
		$2.5X_1 + X_2 \leq 8.75$
		$X_1 \leq 2$
		$X_1, X_2 \geq 0$
		X_1, X_2 must be integers

Problem II: MAX: $2X_1 + 3X_2$

Subject to: $X_1 + 3X_2 \leq 8.25$

$2.5X_1 + X_2 \leq 8.75$

$X_1 \geq 3$

$X_1, X_2 \geq 0$

X_1, X_2 must be integers

The integer and relaxed feasible regions for each candidate problem are shown in Figure 6.30. Notice that a portion of the relaxed feasible region shown in Figure 6.29 has been eliminated in Figure 6.30, but none of the feasible integer solutions shown in Figure 6.29 have been eliminated. This is a general property of the branching operation in the B&B algorithm. Also notice that several feasible integer solutions now occur on the boundary lines of the feasible regions shown in Figure 6.30. More important, one of these feasible integer solutions occurs at an extreme point of the relaxed feasible region for problem I (at the point $X_1 = 2$, $X_2 = 0$). If we relax the integrality conditions in problem I and solve the resulting LP, we could obtain an integer solution because one of the corner points of the relaxed feasible region corresponds to such a point. (However, this integer feasible extreme point still might not be the optimal solution to the relaxed LP problem.)

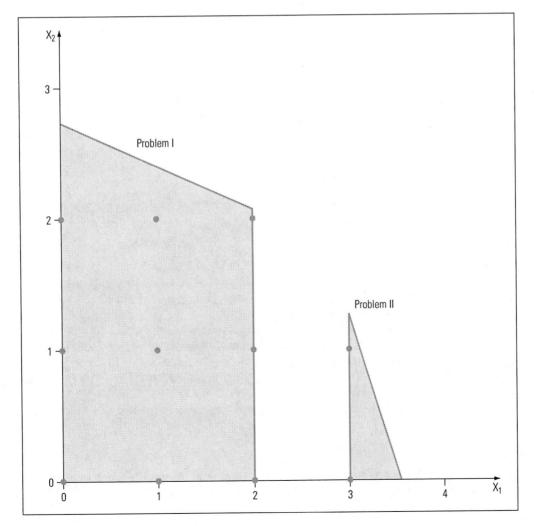

FIGURE 6.30

Feasible solutions to the candidate problems after the first branch

6.17.2 BOUNDING

The next step in the B&B algorithm is to select one of the existing candidate problems for further analysis. Let's arbitrarily select problem I. If we relax the integrality conditions in problem I and solve the resulting LP, we obtain the solution $X_1 = 2$, $X_2 = 2.083$ and an objective function value of 10.25. This value represents an upper bound on the best possible integer solution that can be obtained from problem I. That is, because the relaxed solution to problem I is not integer feasible, we have not yet found the best possible integer solution for this problem. However, we do know that the objective function value of the best possible integer solution that can be obtained from problem I can be no greater than 10.25. As we shall see, this information can be useful in reducing the amount of work required to locate the optimal integer solution to an ILP problem.

6.17.3 BRANCHING AGAIN

Because the relaxed solution to problem I is not entirely integer feasible, the B&B algorithm proceeds by selecting X_2 as a branching variable and creating two additional candidate problems from problem I. These problems are represented as:

Problem III:	MAX:	$2X_1 + 3X_2$
	Subject to:	$X_1 + 3X_2 \leq 8.25$
		$2.5X_1 + X_2 \leq 8.75$
		$X_1 \leq 2$
		$X_2 \leq 2$
		$X_1, X_2 \geq 0$
		X_1, X_2 must be integers
Problem IV:	MAX:	$2X_1 + 3X_2$
	Subject to:	$X_1 + 3X_2 \leq 8.25$
		$2.5X_1 + X_2 \leq 8.75$
		$X_1 \leq 2$
		$X_2 \geq 3$
		$X_1, X_2 \geq 0$
		X_1, X_2 must be integers

Problem III is created by adding the constraint $X_2 \leq 2$ to problem I. Problem IV is created by adding the constraint $X_2 \geq 3$ to problem I. Thus, our previous solution to problem I (where $X_2 = 2.083$) will be eliminated from consideration as a possible solution to the LP relaxations of problems III and IV.

Problem IV is infeasible because there are no feasible solutions where $X_2 \geq 3$. The integer and relaxed feasible regions for problems II and III are summarized in Figure 6.31.

All of the corner points to the relaxed feasible region of problem III correspond to integer feasible solutions. Thus, if we relax the integrality conditions in problem III and solve the resulting LP problem, we must obtain an integer feasible solution. The solution to problem III is represented by $X_1 = 2$, $X_2 = 2$ and has an objective function value of 10.

6.17.4 BOUNDING AGAIN

Although we have obtained an integer feasible solution to our problem, we won't know if it is the *optimal* integer solution until we evaluate the remaining candidate problem

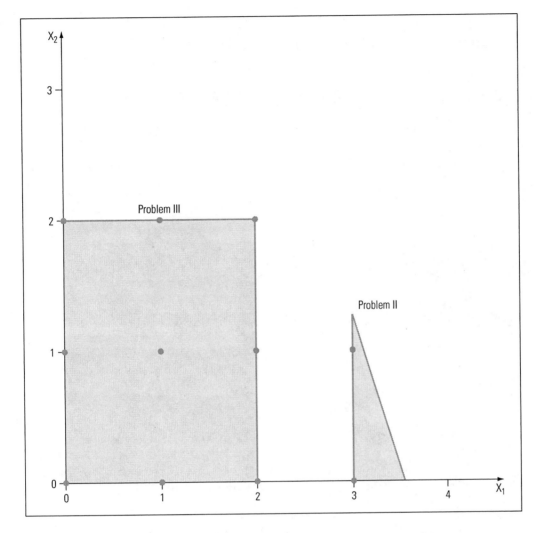

FIGURE 6.31

*Feasible solutions
to the candidate
problems after the
second branch*

(that is, problem II). If we relax the integrality conditions in problem II and solve the resulting LP problem, we obtain the solution $X_1 = 3$, $X_2 = 1.25$ with an objective function value of 9.75.

Because the solution to problem II is not integer feasible, we might be inclined to branch on X_2 in a further attempt to determine the best possible integer solution for problem II. However, this is not necessary. Earlier we noted that for *maximization* ILP problems, the objective function value at the optimal solution to the LP relaxation of the problem represents an *upper bound* on the optimal objective function value of the original ILP problem. This means that even though we do not yet know the optimal integer solution to problem II, we do know that its objective function value cannot be greater than 9.75. And because 9.75 is worse than the objective function value for the integer solution obtained from problem III, we cannot find a better integer solution by continuing to branch problem II. Therefore, problem II can be eliminated from further consideration. Because we have no more candidate problems to consider, we can conclude that the optimal integer solution to our problem is $X_1 = 2$, $X_2 = 2$ with an optimal objective function value of 10.

FIGURE 6.32

Branch-and-bound tree for the example problem

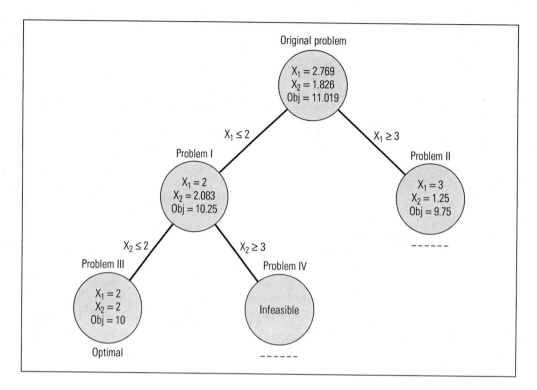

6.17.5 SUMMARY OF B&B EXAMPLE

The steps involved in the solution to our example problem can be represented graphically in the form of a *branch-and-bound tree*, as shown in Figure 6.32. Although Figure 6.29 indicates that 11 integer solutions exist for this problem, we do not have to locate all of them to prove that the integer solution we found is the optimal solution. The bounding operation of the B&B algorithm eliminated the need to explicitly enumerate all the integer feasible solutions and select the best of those as the optimal solution.

If the relaxed solution to problem II was greater than 10 (say 12.5), then the B&B algorithm would have continued branching from this problem in an attempt to find a better integer solution (an integer solution with an objective function value greater than 10). Similarly, if problem IV had a feasible noninteger solution, we would have needed to perform further branching from that problem if its relaxed objective value was better than that of the best known integer feasible solution. Thus, the first integer solution obtained using B&B will not always be the optimal integer solution. A more detailed description of the operations of the B&B algorithm is given in Figure 6.33.

6.18 Summary

This chapter discussed the issues involved in formulating and solving ILP problems. In some cases, acceptable integer solutions to ILP problems can be obtained by rounding the solution to the LP relaxation of the problem. However, this procedure can lead to suboptimal solutions, which still might be viable if you can show that the solution obtained by rounding is within an acceptable distance from the optimal integer solution. This approach might be the only practical way to obtain integer solutions for some ILP problems.

FIGURE 6.33

Detailed description of the B&B algorithm for solving ILP problems

THE BRANCH-AND-BOUND ALGORITHM

1. Relax all the integrality conditions in ILP and solve the resulting LP problem. If the optimal solution to the relaxed LP problem happens to satisfy the original integrality conditions, stop—this is the optimal integer solution. Otherwise, proceed to step 2.

2. If the problem being solved is a maximization problem let $Z_{best} = -$infinity. If it is a minimization problem, let $Z_{best} = +$infinity. (In general Z_{best} represents the objective function value of the best known integer solution as the algorithm proceeds.)

3. Let X_j represent one of the variables that violated the integrality conditions in the solution to the problem that was solved most recently and let b_j represent its noninteger value. Let $INT(b_j)$ represent the largest integer that is less than b_j. Create two new candidate problems: one by appending the constraint $X_j \leq INT(b_j)$ to the most recently solved LP problem, and the other by appending the constraint $X_j \geq INT(b_j) + 1$ to the most recently solved LP problem. Place both of these new LP problems in a list of candidate problems to be solved.

4. If the list of candidate problems is empty, proceed to step 9. Otherwise, remove a candidate problem from the list, relax any integrality conditions in the problem, and solve it.

5. If there is not a solution to the current candidate problem (that is, it is infeasible), proceed to step 4. Otherwise, let Z_{cp} denote the optimal objective function value for the current candidate problem.

6. If Z_{cp} is not better than Z_{best} (for a maximization problem $Z_{cp} \leq Z_{best}$ or for a minimization problem $Z_{cp} \geq Z_{best}$), proceed to step 4.

7. If the solution to the current candidate problem *does not* satisfy the original integrality conditions, proceed to step 3.

8. If the solution to the current candidate problem *does* satisfy the original integrality conditions, a better integer solution has been found. Thus, let $Z_{best} = Z_{cp}$ and save the solution obtained for this candidate problem. Then go back to step 4.

9. Stop. The optimal solution has been found and has an objective function value given by the current value of Z_{best}.

The B&B algorithm is a powerful technique for solving ILP problems. A great deal of skill and creativity is involved in formulating ILPs so that they can be solved efficiently using the B&B technique. Binary variables can be useful in overcoming a number of the simplifying assumptions often made in the formulation of LP models. Here again, quite a bit of creativity might be required on the part of the model builder to identify the constraints to implement various logical conditions in a given problem.

6.19 References

Bean, J., et al. "Selecting Tenants in a Shopping Mall. *Interfaces*, vol. 18, no. 2, 1988.

Blake, J. and J. Donald. "Mount Sinai Hospital Uses Integer Programming to Allocate Operating Room Time." *Interfaces*, vol. 32, no. 2, 2002.

Calloway, R., M. Cummins, and J. Freeland. "Solving Spreadsheet-Based Integer Programming Models: An Example From the Telecommunications Industry." *Decision Sciences*, vol. 21, 1990.

Nauss, R. and R. Markland. "Theory and Application of an Optimizing Procedure for the Lock Box Location Analysis." *Management Science*, vol. 27, no. 8, 1981.

Nemhauser, G. and L. Wolsey. *Integer and Combinatorial Optimization.* New York: Wiley, 1988.

Peiser, R. and S. Andrus. "Phasing of Income-Producing Real Estate." *Interfaces*, vol. 13, no. 1, 1983.

Schindler, S. and T. Semmel, "Station Staffing at Pan American World Airways." *Interfaces*, vol. 23, no. 3, 1993.

Stowe, J. "An Integer Programming Solution for the Optimal Credit Investigation/Credit Granting Sequence." *Financial Management*, vol. 14, Summer 1985.

Tavakoli, A. and C. Lightner. "Implementing a Mathematical Model for Locating EMS Vehicles in Fayetteville, NC." *Computers & Operations Research*, vol. 31, 2004.

THE WORLD OF MANAGEMENT SCIENCE

Who Eats the Float?—Maryland National Improves Check Clearing Operations and Cuts Costs

Maryland National Bank (MNB) of Baltimore typically processes about 500,000 checks worth over $250,000,000 each day. Those checks not drawn on MNB or a local bank must be cleared via the Federal Reserve System, a private clearing bank, or a "direct send" by courier service to the bank on which they were drawn.

Because funds are not available until the check clears, banks try to maximize the availability of current funds by reducing the float—the time interval required for a check to clear. Banks publish an availability schedule listing the number of days before funds from a deposited check are available to the customer. If clearing time is longer than the schedule, the bank must "eat the float." If the check is cleared through the Federal Reserve and clearing takes longer than the Federal Reserve availability schedule, then the Federal Reserve "eats the float." If clearing time is actually less than the local bank's availability schedule, the customer "eats the float." The cost of float is related to the daily cost of capital.

MNB uses a system based on binary integer LP to decide the timing and method to be used for each bundle of checks of a certain type (called a cash letter). Total clearing costs (the objective function) include float costs, clearing charges from the Federal Reserve or private clearing banks, and transportation costs for direct sends. Constraints ensure that exactly one method is chosen for each check type and that a method can be used only at a time that method is available. Use of this system saves the bank $100,000 annually.

Source: Markland, Robert E., and Robert M. Nauss, "Improving Transit Check Clearing Operations at Maryland National Bank," *Interfaces*, vol. 13, no. 1, February 1983, pp. 1–9.

Questions and Problems

1. As shown in Figure 6.1, the feasible region for an ILP consists of a relatively small, *finite* number of points, whereas the feasible region of its LP relaxation consists of an *infinite* number of points. Why, then, are ILPs so much harder to solve than LPs?

2. Identify reasonable values for M_{12} and M_{22} in the example on quantity discounts presented in section 6.15.2 of this chapter.

3. The following questions refer to the CRT Technologies project selection example presented in this chapter. Formulate a constraint to implement the conditions described in each of the following statements.

   a. Out of projects 1, 2, 4, and 6, CRT's management wants to select exactly two projects.

   b. Project 2 can be selected only if project 3 is selected and vice versa.

   c. Project 5 cannot be undertaken unless both projects 3 and 4 are also undertaken.

   d. If projects 2 and 4 are undertaken, then project 5 must also be undertaken.

4. In the CRT Technologies project selection example in this chapter, the problem indicates that surplus funds in any year are reappropriated and cannot be carried over to the next year. Suppose that this is no longer the case and surplus funds may be carried over to future years.

   a. Modify the spreadsheet model given for this problem to reflect this change in assumptions.

   b. What is the optimal solution to the revised problem?

5. The following questions refers to the Blue Ridge Hot Tubs example discussed in this chapter.

   a. Suppose Howie Jones has to purchase a single piece of equipment for $1,000 to produce any Aqua-Spas or Hydro-Luxes. How will this affect the formulation of the model of his decision problem?

   b. Suppose Howie must buy one piece of equipment that costs $900 to produce any Aqua-Spas and a different piece of equipment that costs $800 to produce any Hydro-Luxes. How will this affect the formulation of the model for his problem?

6. Garden City Beach is a popular summer vacation destination for thousands of people. Each summer, the city hires temporary lifeguards to ensure the safety of the vacationing public. Garden City's lifeguards are assigned to work five consecutive days each week and then have two days off. However, the city's insurance company requires that the city have at least the following number of lifeguards on duty each day of the week:

Minimum Number of Lifeguards Required Each Day

	Sunday	Monday	Tuesday	Wednesday	Thursday	Friday	Saturday
Lifeguards	18	17	16	16	16	14	19

The city manager would like to determine the minimum number of lifeguards that will have to be hired.

   a. Formulate an ILP for this problem.

   b. Implement your model in a spreadsheet and solve it.

   c. What is the optimal solution?

   d. Several lifeguards have expressed a preference to be off on Saturdays and Sundays. What is the maximum number of lifeguards that can be off on the weekend without increasing the total number of lifeguards required?

7. Snookers Restaurant is open from 8:00 am to 10:00 pm daily. Besides the hours that they are open for business, workers are needed an hour before opening and an hour after closing for setup and cleanup activities. The restaurant operates with both full-time and part-time workers on the following shifts:

Shift	Daily Pay Rate
7:00 am–11:00 am	$32
7:00 am–3:00 pm	$80
11:00 am–3:00 pm	$32
11:00 am–7:00 pm	$80
3:00 pm–7:00 pm	$32
3:00 pm–11:00 pm	$80
7:00 pm–11:00 pm	$32

The following numbers of workers are needed during each of the indicated time blocks.

Hours	Workers Needed
7:00 am–11:00 am	11
11:00 am–1:00 pm	24
1:00 pm–3:00 pm	16
3:00 pm–5:00 pm	10
5:00 pm–7:00 pm	22
7:00 pm–9:00 pm	17
9:00 pm–11:00 pm	6

At least one full-time worker must be available during the hour before opening and after closing. Additionally, at least 30% of the employees should be full-time (8-hour) workers during the restaurant's busy periods from 11:00 am–1:00 pm and 5:00 pm–7:00 pm.

a. Formulate an ILP for this problem with the objective of minimizing total daily labor costs.

b. Implement your model in a spreadsheet and solve it.

c. What is the optimal solution?

8. A power company is considering how to increase its generating capacity to meet expected demand in its growing service area. Currently, the company has 750 megawatts (MW) of generating capacity but projects that it will need the following minimum generating capacities in each of the next five years:

	Year				
	1	**2**	**3**	**4**	**5**
Minimum Capacity in Megawatts (MW)	780	860	950	1060	1180

The company can increase its generating capacity by purchasing four different types of generators: 10 MW, 25 MW, 50 MW, and/or 100 MW. The cost of acquiring and installing each of the four types of generators in each of the next five years is summarized in the following table:

	Cost of Generator (in $1,000s) in Year				
Generator Size	**1**	**2**	**3**	**4**	**5**
10 MW	$300	$250	$200	$170	$145
25 MW	$460	$375	$350	$280	$235
50 MW	$670	$558	$465	$380	$320
100 MW	$950	$790	$670	$550	$460

a. Formulate a mathematical programming model to determine the least costly way of expanding the company's generating assets to the minimum required levels.

b. Implement your model in a spreadsheet and solve it.

c. What is the optimal solution?

9. Health Care Systems of Florida (HCSF) is planning to build a number of new emergency-care clinics in central Florida. HCSF management has divided a map of the area into seven regions. They want to locate the emergency centers so that all seven regions will be conveniently served by at least one facility. Five possible sites

are available for constructing the new facilities. The regions that can be served conveniently by each site are indicated by X in the following table:

	Possible Building Sites				
Region	Sanford	Altamonte	Apopka	Casselberry	Maitland
1	X		X		
2	X	X		X	X
3		X		X	
4			X		X
5	X	X			
6			X		X
7				X	X
Cost ($1,000s)	$450	$650	$550	$500	$525

a. Formulate an ILP problem to determine which sites should be selected so as to provide convenient service to all locations in the least costly manner.
b. Implement your model in a spreadsheet and solve it.
c. What is the optimal solution?

10. Kentwood Electronics manufactures three components for stereo systems: CD players, tape decks, and stereo tuners. The wholesale price and manufacturing cost of each item are:

Component	Wholesale Price	Manufacturing Cost
CD Player	$150	$75
Tape Deck	$ 85	$35
Stereo Tuner	$ 70	$30

Each CD player produced requires three hours of assembly; each tape deck requires two hours of assembly; and each tuner requires one hour of assembly. However, the company manufactures these products only in batches of 150—partial batches are not allowed. The marketing department believes that it can sell no more than 150,000 CD players, 100,000 tape decks, and 90,000 stereo tuners. It expects a demand for at least 50,000 units of each item and wants to be able to meet this demand. If Kentwood has 400,000 hours of assembly time available, how many batches of CD players, tape decks, and stereo tuners should it produce to maximize profits while meeting the minimum demand figures supplied by marketing?

a. Formulate an ILP model for this problem. (*Hint:* Let your decision variables represent the number of batches of each item to produce.)
b. Create a spreadsheet model for this problem and solve it.
c. What is the optimal solution?

11. Radford Castings can produce brake shoes on six different machines. The following table summarizes the manufacturing costs associated with producing the brake shoes on each machine along with the available capacity on each machine. If the company has received an order for 1,800 brake shoes, how should it schedule these machines?

Machine	Fixed Cost	Variable Cost	Capacity
1	$1000	$21	500
2	$ 950	$23	600
3	$ 875	$25	750
4	$ 850	$24	400
5	$ 800	$20	600
6	$ 700	$26	800

a. Formulate an ILP model for this problem.
b. Create a spreadsheet model for this problem and solve it.
c. What is the optimal solution?

12. The teenage daughter of a recently deceased movie star inherited a number of items from her famous father's estate. Rather than convert these assets to cash immediately, her financial advisor has recommended that she let some of these assets appreciate in value before disposing of them. An appraiser has given the following estimates of the assets' worth (in $1,000s) for each of the next five years.

	Year 1	Year 2	Year 3	Year 4	Year 5
Car	$ 35	$ 37	$ 39	$ 42	$ 45
Piano	$ 16	$ 17	$ 18	$ 19	$ 20
Necklace	$125	$130	$136	$139	$144
Desk	$ 25	$ 27	$ 29	$ 30	$ 33
Golf Clubs	$ 40	$ 43	$ 46	$ 50	$ 52
Humidor	$ 5	$ 7	$ 8	$ 10	$ 11

Knowing this teenager's propensity to spend money, her financial advisor would like to develop a plan to dispose of these assets that will maximize the amount of money received and ensure that at least $30,000 of new funds become available each year to pay her college tuition.
a. Formulate an ILP model for this problem.
b. Create a spreadsheet model for this problem and solve it.
c. What is the optimal solution?

13. A developer of video game software has seven proposals for new games. Unfortunately, the company cannot develop all the proposals because its budget for new projects is limited to $950,000 and it has only 20 programmers to assign to new projects. The financial requirements, returns, and the number of programmers required by each project are summarized below. Projects 2 and 6 require specialized programming knowledge that only one of the programmers has. Both of these projects cannot be selected because the programmer with the necessary skills can be assigned to only one of the projects. (Note: All dollar amounts represent thousands.)

Project	Programmers Required	Capital Required	Estimated NPV
1	7	$250	$650
2	6	$175	$550
3	9	$300	$600
4	5	$150	$450
5	6	$145	$375
6	4	$160	$525
7	8	$325	$750

a. Formulate an ILP model for this problem.
b. Create a spreadsheet model for this problem and solve it.
c. What is the optimal solution?

14. Tropicsun is a leading grower and distributor of fresh citrus products with three large citrus groves scattered around central Florida in the cities of Mt. Dora, Eustis, and Clermont. Tropicsun currently has 275,000 bushels of citrus at the grove in Mt. Dora, 400,000 bushels at the grove in Eustis, and 300,000 at the grove in Clermont. Tropicsun has citrus processing plants in Ocala, Orlando, and Leesburg with processing capacities to handle 200,000, 600,000, and 225,000 bushels, respectively.

Tropicsun contracts with a local trucking company to transport its fruit from the groves to the processing plants. The trucking company charges a flat rate of $8 per mile regardless of how many bushels of fruit are transported. The following table summarizes the distances (in miles) between each grove and processing plant:

Distances (in Miles) Between Groves and Plants

| Grove | Processing Plant | | |
	Ocala	Orlando	Leesburg
Mt. Dora	21	50	40
Eustis	35	30	22
Clermont	55	20	25

Tropicsun wants to determine how many bushels to ship from each grove to each processing plant to minimize the total transportation cost.
a. Formulate an ILP model for this problem.
b. Create a spreadsheet model for this problem and solve it.
c. What is the optimal solution?

15. A real estate developer is planning to build an apartment building specifically for graduate students on a parcel of land adjacent to a major university. Four types of apartments can be included in the building: efficiencies, and one-, two-, or three-bedroom units. Each efficiency requires 500 square feet; each one-bedroom apartment requires 700 square feet; each two-bedroom apartment requires 800 square feet; and each three-bedroom unit requires 1,000 square feet. The developer believes that the building should include no more than 15 one-bedroom units, 22 two-bedroom units, and 10 three-bedroom units. Local zoning ordinances do not allow the developer to build more than 40 units in this particular building location. They restrict the building to a maximum of 40,000 square feet. The developer already has agreed to lease 5 one-bedroom units and 8 two-bedroom units to a local rental agency that is a "silent partner" in this endeavor. Market studies indicate that efficiencies can be rented for $350 per month, one-bedrooms for $450 per month, two-bedrooms for $550 per month, and three-bedrooms for $750 per month. How many rental units of each type should the developer include in the building plans to maximize the potential rental income from the building?
a. Formulate an LP model for this problem.
b. Create a spreadsheet model for this problem and solve it using Solver.
c. What is the optimal solution?
d. Which constraint in this model limits the builder's potential rental income from increasing any further?

16. Bellows Lumber Yard, Inc. stocks standard length 25-foot boards, which it cuts to custom lengths to fill individual customer orders. An order has just come in for 5,000 7-foot boards, 1,200 9-foot boards, and 300 11-foot boards. The lumber yard manager has identified six ways to cut the 25-foot boards to fill this order. The six cutting patterns are summarized in the following table.

Number of Boards Produced

Cutting Pattern	7 ft	9 ft	11 ft
1	3	0	0
2	2	1	0
3	2	0	1
4	1	2	0
5	0	1	1
6	0	0	2

One possibility (cutting pattern 1) is to cut a 25-foot board into three 7-foot boards, and not to cut any 9- or 11-foot boards. Note that cutting pattern 1 uses a total of 21 feet of board and leaves a 4-foot piece of scrap. Another possibility (cutting pattern 4) is to cut a 25-foot board into one 7-foot board and two 9-foot boards (using all 25 feet of the board). The remaining cutting patterns have similar interpretations. The lumber yard manager wants to fill this order using the fewest number of 25-foot boards as possible. To do this, the manager needs to determine how many 25-foot boards to run through each cutting pattern.

 a. Formulate an LP model for this problem.

 b. Create a spreadsheet model for this problem and solve it using Solver.

 c. What is the optimal solution?

 d. Suppose the manager wants to minimize waste. Would the solution change?

17. Howie's Carpet World has just received an order for carpets for a new office building. The order is for 4,000 yards of carpet 4 feet wide, 20,000 yards of carpet 9 feet wide, and 9,000 yards of carpet 12 feet wide. Howie can order two kinds of carpet rolls, which he will then have to cut to fill this order. One type of roll is 14 feet wide, 100 yards long, and costs $1,000 per roll; the other is 18 feet wide, 100 yards long, and costs $1,400 per roll. Howie needs to determine how many of the two types of carpet rolls to order and how they should be cut. He wants to do this in the least costly way possible.

 a. Formulate an LP model for this problem.

 b. Create a spreadsheet model for this problem and solve it using Solver.

 c. What is the optimal solution?

 d. Suppose Howie wants to minimize waste. Would the solution change?

18. A manufacturer is considering alternatives for building new plants, to be located closer to three of its primary customers with whom it intends to develop long-term, sole-supplier relationships. The net cost of manufacturing and transporting each unit of the product to its customers will vary depending on where the plant is built and the production capacity of the plant. These costs are summarized in the table below:

	Net Cost per Unit to Supply Customer		
Plant	X	Y	Z
1	35	30	45
2	45	40	50
3	70	65	50
4	20	45	25
5	65	45	45

The annual demand for products from customers X, Y, and Z is expected to be 40,000, 25,000, and 35,000 units, respectively. The annual production capacity and construction costs for each plant are:

Plant	Production Capacity	Construction Cost (in $1000s)
1	40,000	$1,325
2	30,000	$1,100
3	50,000	$1,500
4	20,000	$1,200
5	40,000	$1,400

The company wants to determine which plant to build to satisfy customer demand at a minimum total cost.

a. Formulate an ILP model for this problem.
b. Create a spreadsheet model for this problem and solve it.
c. What is the optimal solution?

19. Refer to the previous question. Suppose plants 1 and 2 represent different building alternatives for the same site (that is, only one of these plants can be built). Similarly, suppose plants 4 and 5 represent different building alternatives for another site.

a. What additional constraints are required to model these new conditions?
b. Revise the spreadsheet to reflect these additional constraints and solve the resulting problem.
c. What is the optimal solution?

20. A company manufactures three products: A, B, and C. The company currently has an order for three units of product A, 7 units of product B, and 4 units of product C. There is no inventory for any of these products. All three products require special processing that can be done on one of two machines. The cost of producing each product on each machine is summarized below:

Cost of Producing a Unit of Product

Machine	A	B	C
1	$13	$ 9	$10
2	$11	$12	$ 8

The time required to produce each product on each machine is summarized below:

Time (Hours) Needed to Produced a Unit of Product

Machine	A	B	C
1	0.4	1.1	0.9
2	0.5	1.2	1.3

Assume that machine 1 can be used for eight hours and machine 2 can be used for six hours. Each machine must undergo a special setup operation to prepare it to produce each product. After completing this setup for a product, any number of that product type can be produced. The setup costs for producing each product on each machine are summarized below.

Setup Costs for Producing

Machine	A	B	C
1	$55	$93	$60
2	$65	$58	$75

a. Formulate an ILP model to determine how many units of each product to produce on each machine to meet demand at a minimum cost.
b. Implement your model in a spreadsheet and solve it.
c. What is the optimal solution?

21. Clampett Oil purchases crude oil products from suppliers in Texas (TX), Oklahoma (OK), Pennsylvania (PA), and Alabama (AL), from which it refines four end-products: gasoline, kerosene, heating oil, and asphalt. Because of differences in the quality and chemical characteristics of the oil from the different suppliers, the amount of each end product that can be refined from a barrel of crude oil varies depending on the source of the crude. Additionally, the amount of crude available from each source varies, as does the cost of a barrel of crude from each supplier. These values

are summarized below. For example, the first line of this table indicates that a barrel of crude oil from Texas can be refined into 2 barrels of gasoline, 2.8 barrels of kerosene, 1.7 barrels of heating oil, or 2.4 barrels of asphalt. Each supplier requires a minimum purchase of at least 500 barrels.

Raw Material Characteristics

Crude Oils	Barrels Available	Possible Production Per Barrel				Cost Per Barrel	Trucking Cost
		Gas	Kero.	Heat	Asphalt		
TX	1,500	2.00	2.80	1.70	2.40	$22	$1,500
OK	2,000	1.80	2.30	1.75	1.90	$21	$1,700
PA	1,500	2.30	2.20	1.60	2.60	$22	$1,500
AL	1,800	2.10	2.60	1.90	2.40	$23	$1,400

The company owns a tanker truck that picks up whatever crude oil it purchases. This truck can hold 2,000 barrels of crude. The cost of sending the truck to pick up oil from the various locations is shown in the column labeled "Trucking Cost." The company's plans for its next production cycle specify 750 barrels of gasoline, 800 barrels of kerosene, 1,000 barrels of heating oil, and 300 barrels of asphalt to be produced.

a. Formulate an ILP model that can be solved to determine the purchasing plan that will allow the company to implement its production plan at the least cost.

b. Implement this model in a spreadsheet and solve it.

c. What is the optimal solution?

22. The Clampett Oil Company has a tanker truck that it uses to deliver fuel to customers. The tanker has five different storage compartments with capacities to hold 2,500, 2,000, 1,500, 1,800 and 2,300 gallons, respectively. The company has an order to deliver 2,700 gallons of diesel fuel; 3,500 gallons of regular unleaded gasoline; and 4,200 gallons of premium unleaded gasoline. If each storage compartment can hold only one type of fuel, how should Clampett Oil load the tanker? If it is impossible to load the truck with the full order, the company wants to minimize the total number of gallons by which the order is short. (*Hint:* Consider using slack variables to represent shortage amounts.)

a. Formulate an ILP model for this problem.

b. Implement this model in a spreadsheet and solve it.

c. What is the optimal solution?

23. Dan Boyd is a financial planner trying to determine how to invest $100,000 for one of his clients. The cash flows for the five investments under consideration are summarized in the following table:

Summary of Cash In-Flows and Out-Flows (at Beginning of Year)

	A	B	C	D	E
Year 1	−1.00	0.00	−1.00	0.00	−1.00
Year 2	+0.45	−1.00	0.00	0.00	0.00
Year 3	+1.05	0.00	0.00	−1.00	1.25
Year 4	0.00	+1.30	+1.65	+1.30	0.00

For example, if Dan invests $1 in investment A at the beginning of year 1, he will receive $0.45 at the beginning of year 2 and another $1.05 at the beginning of year 3.

Alternatively, he can invest $1 in investment B at the beginning of year 2 and receive $1.30 at the beginning of year 4. Entries of "0.00" in the above table indicate times when no cash inflows or outflows can occur. The minimum required investment for each of the possible investments is $50,000. Also, at the beginning of each year, Dan may also place any or all of the available money in a money market account that is expected to yield 5% per year. How should Dan plan his investments if he wants to maximize the amount of money available to his client at the end of year 4?

a. Formulate an ILP model for this problem.
b. Create a spreadsheet model for this problem and solve it using Solver.
c. What is the optimal solution?

24. The Mega-Bucks Corporation is planning its production schedule for the next four weeks and is forecasting the following demand for compound X—a key raw material used in its production process:

Forecasted Demand of Compound X

Week	1	2	3	4
Demand	400 lbs.	150 lbs.	200 lbs.	350 lbs.

The company currently has no compound X on hand. The supplier of this product delivers only in batch sizes that are multiples of 100 pounds (0, 100, 200, 300, and so on). The price of this material is $125 per 100 pounds. Deliveries can be arranged weekly, but there is a delivery charge of $50. Mega-Bucks estimates that it costs $15 for each 100 pounds of compound X held in inventory from one week to the next. Assuming that Mega-Bucks does not want more than 50 pounds of compound X in inventory at the end of week 4, how much should it order each week so that the demand for this product will be met in the least costly manner?

a. Formulate an ILP model for this problem.
b. Create a spreadsheet model for this problem and solve it using Solver.
c. What is the optimal solution?

25. An automobile manufacturer is considering mechanical design changes in one of its top-selling cars to reduce the weight of the car by at least 400 pounds to improve its fuel efficiency. Design engineers have identified ten changes that could be made in the car to make it lighter (for example, using composite body pieces rather than metal). The weight saved by each design change and the estimated costs of implementing each change are summarized below:

Design Change

	1	2	3	4	5	6	7	8	9	10
Weight Saved (lbs)	50	75	25	150	60	95	200	40	80	30
Cost (in $1,000s)	$150	$350	$50	$450	$90	$35	$650	$75	$110	$30

Changes 4 and 7 represent alternate ways of modifying the engine block and, therefore, only one of these options could be selected. The company wants to determine which changes to make to reduce the total weight of the car by at least 400 pounds in the least costly manner.

a. Formulate an ILP model for this problem.
b. Create a spreadsheet model for this problem and solve it.
c. What is the optimal solution?

26. Darten Restaurants owns and operates several different restaurant chains including Red Snapper and the Olive Grove. The company is considering opening a number of new units in Ohio. There are ten different sites available for the company to build

new restaurants, and the company can build either type of restaurant at a given site. The following table summarizes the estimated net present value (NPV) of the cash flows (in millions) resulting from locating each type of restaurant at each of the sites and also indicates which sites are within 15 miles of each other.

Site	Red Snapper NPV	Olive Grove NPV	Other Sites within 15 Miles
1	$11.8	$16.2	2, 3, 4
2	13.3	13.8	1, 3, 5
3	19.0	14.6	1, 2, 4, 5
4	17.8	12.4	1, 3
5	10.0	13.7	2, 3, 9
6	16.1	19.0	7
7	13.3	10.8	6, 8
8	18.8	15.2	7
9	17.2	15.9	5, 10
10	14.4	16.8	9

a. Suppose the company does not want to build two units from the same chain within 15 miles of each other (for example, it does not want to build two Red Snappers within 15 miles of each other, nor is it willing to build two Olive Groves within 15 miles of each other). Create a spreadsheet model to determine which (if any) restaurant it should build at each site to maximize total NPV.

b. What is the optimal solution?

c. Now suppose also that the company does not want to build a Red Snapper unless it also builds an Olive Grove at another site within 15 miles. Modify your spreadsheet model to determine which (if any) restaurant it should build at each site to maximize total NPV.

d. What is the optimal solution?

27. Paul Bergey is in charge of loading cargo ships for International Cargo Company (ICC) at the port in Newport News, Virginia. Paul is preparing a loading plan for an ICC freighter destined for Ghana. An agricultural commodities dealer would like to transport the following products aboard this ship.

Commodity	Amount Available (tons)	Volume per Ton (cubic feet)	Profit per Ton ($)
1	4,800	40	70
2	2,500	25	50
3	1,200	60	60
4	1,700	55	80

Paul can elect to load any and/or all of the available commodities. However, the ship has three cargo holds with the following capacity restrictions:

Cargo Hold	Weight Capacity (tons)	Volume Capacity (cubic feet)
Forward	3,000	145,000
Center	6,000	180,000
Rear	4,000	155,000

Only one type of commodity can be placed into any cargo hold. However, because of balance considerations, the weight in the forward cargo hold must be within 10%

of the weight in the rear cargo hold and the center cargo hold must be between 40% to 60% of the total weight on board.

   a. Formulate an ILP model for this problem.

   b. Create a spreadsheet model for this problem and solve it using Solver.

   c. What is the optimal solution?

28. KPS Communications is planning to bring wireless internet access to the town of Ames, Iowa. Using a geographic information system, KPS has divided Ames into the following 5 by 5 grid. The values in each block of the grid indicate the expected annual revenue (in $1,000s) KPS will receive if wireless internet service is provided to the geographic area represented by each block.

Expected Annual Revenue by Area (in $1,000s)

$34	$43	$62	$42	$34
$64	$43	$71	$48	$65
$57	$57	$51	$61	$30
$32	$38	$70	$56	$40
$68	$73	$30	$56	$44

KPS can build wireless towers in any block in the grid at a cost of $150,000 per tower. Each tower can provide wireless service to the block it is in and to all adjacent blocks. (Blocks are considered to be adjacent if they share a side. Blocks touching only at cornerpoints are not considered adjacent.) KPS would like to determine how many towers to build and where to build them to maximize profits in the first year of operations. (*Note:* If a block can receive wireless service from two different towers, the revenue for that block should be counted only once.)

   a. Create a spreadsheet model for this problem and solve it.

   b. What is the optimal solution and how much money will KPS make in the first year?

   c. Suppose KPS is required to provide wireless service to all of the blocks. What is the optimal solution and how much money will KPS make in the first year?

29. The emergency services coordinator for Clarke County is interested in locating the county's two ambulances to maximize the number of residents that can be reached within four minutes in emergency situations. The county is divided into five regions, and the average times required to travel from one region to the next are summarized below:

	To Region				
From Region	**1**	**2**	**3**	**4**	**5**
1	0	4	6	3	2
2	4	0	2	3	6
3	6	2	0	5	3
4	3	3	5	0	7
5	2	6	3	7	0

The population in regions 1, 2, 3, 4, and 5 are estimated as 45,000, 65,000, 28,000, 52,000, and 43,000, respectively. In which two regions should the ambulances be placed?

   a. Formulate an ILP model for this problem.

   b. Implement your model in a spreadsheet and solve it.

   c. What is the optimal solution?

30. Ken Stark is an operations analyst for an insurance company in Muncie, Indiana. Over the next 6 weeks the company needs to send 2,028,415 pieces of marketing literature to customers in the 16 states shown below.

State	Mailing Pieces
AZ	82,380
CA	212,954
CT	63,796
GA	136,562
IL	296,479
MA	99,070
ME	38,848
MN	86,207
MT	33,309
NC	170,997
NJ	104,974
NV	29,608
OH	260,858
OR	63,605
TX	214,076
VA	134,692
TOTAL	**2,028,415**

To coordinate with other marketing efforts, all the mailings for a given state must go out in the same week (i.e., if Ken decides to schedule mailings for Georgia in week 2, then all of the 136,562 pieces of mail for Georgia must be sent that week). Ken would like to balance the work load in each week as much as possible and, in particular, would like to minimize the maximum amount of mail to be processed in any given week during the 6-week period.

a. Create a spreadsheet model to determine which states should be processed each week to achieve Ken's objective.

b. What is the optimal solution?

31. The CoolAire Company manufactures air conditioners that are sold to five different retail customers across the United States. The company is evaluating its manufacturing and logistics strategy to ensure that it is operating in the most efficient manner possible. The company can produce air conditioners at six plants across the country and stock these units in any of four different warehouses. The cost of manufacturing and shipping a unit between each plant and warehouse is summarized in the following table along with the monthly capacity and fixed cost of operating each plant.

	Warehouse 1	Warehouse 2	Warehouse 3	Warehouse 4	Fixed Cost	Capacity
Plant 1	$700	$1,000	$900	$1,200	$55,000	300
Plant 2	$800	$ 500	$600	$ 700	$40,000	200
Plant 3	$850	$ 600	$700	$ 500	$45,000	300
Plant 4	$600	$ 800	$500	$ 600	$50,000	250
Plant 5	$500	$ 600	$450	$ 700	$42,000	350
Plant 6	$700	$ 600	$750	$ 500	$40,000	400

Similarly, the per-unit cost of shipping units from each warehouse to each customer is given below, along with the monthly fixed cost of operating each warehouse.

	Customer 1	Customer 2	Customer 3	Customer 4	Customer 5	Fixed Cost
Warehouse 1	$40	$80	$60	$90	$50	$40,000
Warehouse 2	$60	$50	$75	$40	$35	$50,000
Warehouse 3	$55	$40	$65	$60	$80	$35,000
Warehouse 4	$80	$30	$80	$50	$60	$60,000

The monthly demand from each customer is summarized below.

	Customer 1	Customer 2	Customer 3	Customer 4	Customer 5
Demand	200	300	200	150	250

CoolAire would like to determine which plants and warehouses it should operate to meet demand in the most cost-effective manner.

a. Create a spreadsheet model for this problem and solve it.

b. Which plants and warehouses should CoolAire operate?

c. What is the optimal shipping plan?

32. A blood bank wants to determine the least expensive way to transport available blood donations from Pittsburg and Staunton to hospitals in Charleston, Roanoke, Richmond, Norfolk, and Suffolk. Figure 6.34 shows the possible shipping paths between cities along with the per unit cost of shipping along each possible arc. Additionally, the courier service used by the blood bank charges a flat rate of $125 any time it makes a trip across any of these arcs, regardless of how many units of blood are transported. The van used by the courier service can carry a maximum of 200 units of blood. Assume that Pittsburg has 600 units of blood type O positive (O+) and 800 units of blood type AB available. Assume that Staunton has 500 units of O+ and 600 units of AB available. The following table summarizes the number of units of each blood type needed at the various hospitals:

	Units Needed	
Hospital	O+	AB
Charleston	100	200
Roanoke	100	100
Richmond	500	300
Norfolk	200	500
Suffolk	150	250

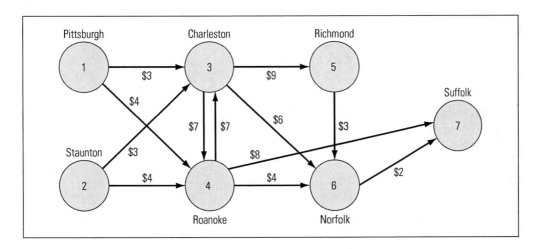

FIGURE 6.34

Possible shipping routes for the blood bank problem

a. Create a spreadsheet model for this problem.

b. What is the optimal solution?

c. Suppose that the courier service switches to a new type of van that can carry no more than 1000 units of blood between any two cities. What is the optimal solution to this revised problem?

33. CaroliNet is an Internet service provider for residential consumers in North Carolina. The company is planning to expand and offer Internet service in South Carolina. The company wants to establish a set of hubs throughout the state to ensure that all residents of the state can access at least one of their hubs via a local phone call. Local phone service is available between all adjacent counties throughout the state. Figure 6.35 (and the file FIG6-35.xls on your data disk) show an Excel spreadsheet with a matrix indicating county adjacencies throughout the state. That is, values of 1 in the matrix indicate counties that are adjacent to one another while values of 0 indicate counties that are not adjacent to one another. (Note that a county is also considered to be adjacent to itself.)

a. Assume CaroliNet wants to minimize the number of hubs it must install. In what counties should the hubs be installed?

b. Suppose CaroliNet is willing to install hubs in exactly ten different counties. In what counties should the hubs be installed if the company wants to maximize its service coverage?

34. Solve the following problem manually using the B&B algorithm. You can use the computer to solve the individual problems generated. Create a branch-and-bound tree to display the steps you complete.

FIGURE 6.35

County adjacency matrix for the CaroliNet ISP location problem

	Abbeville	Aiken	Allendale	Anderson	Bamberg	Barnwell	Beaufort	Berkeley	Calhoun	Charleston	Cherokee	Chester	Ch
Abbeville	1	0	0	1	0	0	0	0	0	0	0	0	
Aiken	0	1	0	0	0	1	0	0	0	0	0	0	
Allendale	0	0	1	0	1	1	0	0	0	0	0	0	
Anderson	1	0	0	1	0	0	0	0	0	0	0	0	
Bamberg	0	0	1	0	1	1	0	0	0	0	0	0	
Barnwell	0	1	1	0	1	1	0	0	0	0	0	0	
Beaufort	0	0	0	0	0	0	1	0	0	0	0	0	
Berkeley	0	0	0	0	0	0	0	1	0	1	0	0	
Calhoun	0	0	0	0	0	0	0	0	1	0	0	0	
Charleston	0	0	0	0	0	0	0	1	0	1	0	0	
Cherokee	0	0	0	0	0	0	0	0	0	0	1	0	
Chester	0	0	0	0	0	0	0	0	0	0	0	1	
Chesterfield	0	0	0	0	0	0	0	0	0	0	0	0	
Claredon	0	0	0	0	0	0	0	1	1	0	0	0	
Colleton	0	0	1	0	1	0	1	0	0	1	0	0	
Darlington	0	0	0	0	0	0	0	0	0	0	0	0	
Dillon	0	0	0	0	0	0	0	0	0	0	0	0	
Dorchester	0	0	0	0	1	0	0	1	0	1	0	0	
Edgefield	0	1	0	0	0	0	0	0	0	0	0	0	
Fairfield	0	0	0	0	0	0	0	0	0	0	0	1	
Florence	0	0	0	0	0	0	0	0	0	0	0	0	
Georgetown	0	0	0	0	0	0	0	1	0	0	0	0	
Greenville	1	0	0	1	0	0	0	0	0	0	0	0	
Greenwood	1	0	0	0	0	0	0	0	0	0	0	0	
Hampton	0	0	1	0	1	0	1	0	0	0	0	0	
Horry	0	0	0	0	0	0	0	0	0	0	0	0	
Jasper	0	0	0	0	0	0	1	0	0	0	0	0	
Kershaw	0	0	0	0	0	0	0	0	0	0	0	0	
Lancaster	0	0	0	0	0	0	0	0	0	0	0	1	
Laurens	1	0	0	1	0	0	0	0	0	0	0	0	

$$\text{MAX:} \qquad 6X_1 + 8X_2$$

$$\text{Subject to:} \qquad 6X_1 + 3X_2 \leq 18$$

$$2X_1 + 3X_2 \leq 9$$

$$X_1, X_2 \leq 0$$

$$X_1, X_2 \text{ must be integers}$$

34. During the execution of the B&B algorithm, many candidate problems are likely to be generated and awaiting further analysis. In the B&B example in this chapter, we chose the next candidate problem to analyze in a rather arbitrary way. What other, more structured ways might we use to select the next candidate problem? What are the pros and cons of these techniques?

Optimizing a Timber Harvest

CASE 6.1

The state of Virginia is one of the largest producers of wood furniture in the United States, with the furniture industry accounting for 50% of value added to wood materials. Over the past 40 years the inventory volume of wood in Virginia's forests has increased by 81 percent. Today, 15.4 million acres, which is well over half of the state, are covered in forest. Private owners hold 77% of this land. When making decisions about which trees to harvest, forestry professionals consider many factors and must follow numerous laws and regulations.

Figure 6.36 depicts a tract of forested land that has been sectioned off into 12 harvestable areas, indicated by dashed lines. Area 2 provides the only access to the forest via a paved road, so any timber cut ultimately must be transported out of the forest through area 2. Currently, there are no roads through this forest. So to harvest the timber, forest roads must be built. The allowable routes for these roads are also shown in Figure 6.36. They are determined largely by the geography of the land and by the location of streams and wildlife habitat.

Not all areas of the forest have to be harvested. However, to harvest any area, a forest road must be built to that area. The cost of building each section of forest road (in

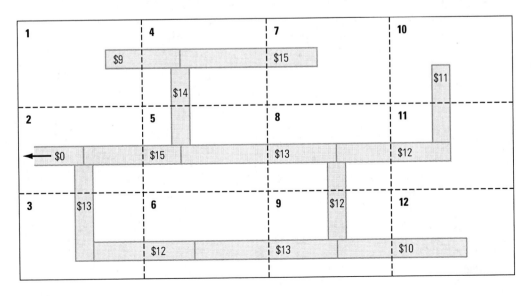

FIGURE 6.36

Forest diagram for the timber harvesting problem

$1000s) is indicated in the figure. Finally, the net value of the harvestable timber in each area is estimated as follows:

Area	Harvested Value (in $1000s)											
	1	2	3	4	5	6	7	8	9	10	11	12
Value	$15	$7	$10	$12	$8	$17	$14	$18	$13	$12	$10	$11

Which areas should be harvested and what roads should be built to make the most profitable use of this forest?

a. Create a spreadsheet model for this problem.
b. What is the optimal solution?
c. Suppose the cost of building the road connecting areas 4 and 5 dropped to $12,000. What impact does this have on the optimal solution?

CASE 6.2   Power Dispatching at Old Dominion

The demand for electricity varies greatly during the day. Because large amounts of electricity cannot be stored economically, electric power companies cannot manufacture electricity and hold it in inventory until it is needed. Instead, power companies must balance the production of power with the demand for power in real time. One of the greatest uncertainties in forecasting the demand for electricity is the weather. Most power companies employ meteorologists who constantly monitor weather patterns and update computer models that predict the demand for power over a rolling, seven-day planning horizon. This forecasted seven-day window of demand is referred to as the company's load profile. Typically it is updated every hour.

Every power company has a baseload demand that is relatively constant. To satisfy this baseload demand, a power company uses its most economical, low-cost power generating assets and keeps them running continuously. To meet additional demands for power above the baseload, a power company must dispatch (or turn on) other generators. These other generators are sometimes called "peakers," as they help the power company meet the highest demands or peak loads. It costs differing amounts of money to bring different types of peakers online. And because different peakers use different types of fuel (e.g., coal, gas, biomass), their operating costs per megawatt (MW) generated also differ. Thus, dispatchers for a power company continually have to decide which generator to bring online or turn off to meet their load profile with the least cost.

The Old Dominion Power (ODP) Company provides electrical power throughout Virginia and the Carolinas. Suppose ODP's peak-load profile (that is the estimated load above baseload) in MWs is currently estimated as follows:

	Day						
	1	2	3	4	5	6	7
Load (in MWs)	4,300	3,700	3,900	4,000	4,700	4,800	3,600

ODP currently has three peaking generators offline that are available to help meet this load. The generators have the following operating characteristics:

Generator Location	Startup Cost	Cost per Day	Maximum MW Capacity per Day
New River	$ 800	$200 + $5 per MW	2,100
Galax	$1,000	$300 + $4 per MW	1,900
James River	$ 700	$250 + $7 per MW	3,000

To get an offline generator up and running, a startup cost must be paid. Once a generator is running, it can continue to run indefinitely without having to pay this startup cost again. However, if the generator is turned off at any point, the setup cost must be paid again to get it back up and running. Each day that a generator runs, there is both a fixed and variable cost that must be paid. For example, any day that the New River generator is online, it incurs a fixed cost of $200 plus $5 per MW generated. So even if this generator is not producing any MWs, it still costs $200 per day to keep it running (so as to avoid a restart). When they are running, each generator can supply up to the maximum daily MWs listed in the final column of the table.

a. Formulate a mathematical programming model for ODP's power dispatching problem.
b. Implement your model in a spreadsheet and solve it.
c. What is the optimal solution?
d. Suppose ODP can buy power sometimes from a competitor. How much should ODP be willing to pay to acquire 300 MW of power on day 1? Explain your answer.
e. What concerns, if any, would you have about implementing this plan?

The MasterDebt Lockbox Problem   CASE 6.3

MasterDebt is a national credit card company with thousands of card holders located across the United States. Every day throughout the month, MasterDebt sends out statements to different customers summarizing their charges for the previous month. Customers then have 30 days to remit a payment for their bills. MasterDebt includes a pre-addressed envelope with each statement for customers to use in making their payments.

One of the critical problems facing MasterDebt involves determining what address to put on the pre-addressed envelopes sent to various parts of the country. The amount of time that elapses between when a customer writes his check and when MasterDebt receives the cash for the check is referred to as *float*. Checks can spend several days floating in the mail and in processing before being cashed. This float time represents lost revenue to MasterDebt because if they could receive and cash these checks immediately, they could earn additional interest on these funds.

To reduce the interest being lost from floating checks, MasterDebt would like to implement a lockbox system to speed the processing of checks. Under such a system, MasterDebt might have all their customers on the West Coast send their payments to a bank in Sacramento which, for a fee, processes the checks and deposits the proceeds in a MasterDebt account. Similarly, MasterDebt might arrange for a similar service with a bank on the East Coast for their customers there. Such lockbox systems are a common method that companies use to improve their cash flows.

MasterDebt has identified six different cities as possible lockbox sites. The annual fixed cost of operating a lockbox in each of the possible locations is given below.

Annual Lockbox Operating Costs (in $1,000s)

Sacramento	Denver	Chicago	Dallas	New York	Atlanta
$25	$30	$35	$35	$30	$35

An analysis was done to determine the average number of days that a check floats when sent from seven different regions of the country to each of these six cities. The results of this analysis are summarized below. This table indicates, for instance, that a check sent from the central region of the country to New York spends an average of three days in the mail and in processing before MasterDebt actually receives the cash for the check.

Average Days of Float Between Regions and Possible Lockbox Locations

	Sacramento	Denver	Chicago	Dallas	New York	Atlanta
Central	4	2	2	2	3	3
Mid-Atlantic	6	4	3	4	2	2
Midwest	3	2	3	2	5	4
Northeast	6	4	2	5	2	3
Northwest	2	3	5	4	6	7
Southeast	7	4	3	2	4	2
Southwest	2	3	6	2	7	6

Further analysis was done to determine the average amount of payments being sent from each region of the country. These results are given below.

Average Daily Payments (in $1,000s) by Region

	Payments
Central	$45
Mid-Atlantic	$65
Midwest	$50
Northeast	$90
Northwest	$70
Southeast	$80
Southwest	$60

Thus, if payments from the Central Region are sent to New York, on any given day there is an average of $135,000 in undeposited checks from the Central Region. Because MasterDebt can earn 15% on cash deposits, it would be losing $20,250 per year in potential interest on these checks alone.

a. Which of the six potential lockbox locations should MasterDebt use and to which lockbox location should each region be assigned?
b. How would your solution change if a maximum of four regions could be assigned to any lockbox location?

CASE 6.4   Removing Snow in Montreal

Based on: Campbell, J. and Langevin, A. "The Snow Disposal Assignment Problem." *Journal of the Operational Research Society*, 1995, pp. 919–929.

Snow removal and disposal are important and expensive activities in Montreal and many northern cities. Even though snow can be cleared from streets and sidewalks by plowing and shoveling, in prolonged sub-freezing temperatures, the resulting banks of accumulated snow can impede pedestrian and vehicular traffic and must be removed.

To allow timely removal and disposal of snow, a city is divided into several sectors and snow removal operations are carried out concurrently in each sector. In Montreal, accumulated snow is loaded onto trucks and hauled away to disposal sites (e.g., rivers, quarries, sewer chutes, surface holding areas). For contractual reasons, each sector may be assigned to only a *single* disposal site. (However, each disposal site may receive snow from multiple sectors.) The different types of disposal sites can accommodate different amounts of snow either because of the physical size of the disposal facility or environmental restrictions on the amount of snow (often contaminated by salt and de-icing chemicals) that can be dumped into rivers. The annual capacities for five different snow disposal sites are given below (in 1,000s of cubic meters).

	Disposal Site				
	1	**2**	**3**	**4**	**5**
Capacity	350	250	500	400	200

The cost of removing and disposing of snow depends mainly on the distance it must be trucked. For planning purposes, the city of Montreal uses the straight-line distance between the center of each sector to each of the various disposal sites as an approximation of the cost involved in transporting snow between these locations. The following table summarizes these distances (in kilometers) for ten sectors in the city.

	Disposal Site				
Sector	**1**	**2**	**3**	**4**	**5**
1	3.4	1.4	4.9	7.4	9.3
2	2.4	2.1	8.3	9.1	8.8
3	1.4	2.9	3.7	9.4	8.6
4	2.6	3.6	4.5	8.2	8.9
5	1.5	3.1	2.1	7.9	8.8
6	4.2	4.9	6.5	7.7	6.1
7	4.8	6.2	9.9	6.2	5.7
8	5.4	6.0	5.2	7.6	4.9
9	3.1	4.1	6.6	7.5	7.2
10	3.2	6.5	7.1	6.0	8.3

Using historical snowfall data, the city can estimate the annual volume of snow requiring removal in each sector as four times the length of streets in the sectors in meters (i.e., it is assumed that each linear meter of street generates four cubic meters of snow to remove over an entire year). The following table estimates the snow removal requirements (in 1,000s of cubic meters) for each sector in the coming year.

				Estimated Annual Snow Removal Requirements					
1	**2**	**3**	**4**	**5**	**6**	**7**	**8**	**9**	**10**
153	152	154	138	127	129	111	110	130	135

Questions

1. Create a spreadsheet that Montreal could use to determine the most efficient snow removal plan for the coming year. Assume it costs $0.10 to transport one cubic meter of snow one kilometer.
2. What is the optimal solution?
3. How much will it cost Montreal to implement your snow disposal plan?
4. Ignoring the capacity restrictions at the disposal sites, how many different assignments of sectors to disposal sites are possible?
5. Suppose Montreal can increase the capacity of a single disposal site by 100,000 cubic meters. Which disposal site's capacity (if any) should be increased and how much should the city be willing to pay to obtain this extra disposal capacity?

Chapter 9

Regression Analysis

9.0 Introduction

Regression analysis is a modeling technique for analyzing the relationship between a *continuous* (real-valued) dependent variable Y and one or more independent variables $X_1, X_2, \ldots, X_k$. The goal in regression analysis is to identify a function that describes, as closely as possible, the relationship between these variables so that we can predict what value the dependent variable will assume given specific values for the independent variables. This chapter shows how to estimate these functions and how to use them to make predictions in a business environment.

9.1 An Example

As a simple example of how regression analysis might be used, consider the relationship between sales for a company and the amount of money it spends on advertising. Few would question that the level of sales for a company will depend on or be influenced by advertising. Thus, we could view sales as the dependent variable Y and advertising as the independent variable X_1. Although some relationship exists between sales and advertising, we might not know the exact functional form of this relationship. Indeed, there probably is not an exact functional relationship between these variables.

We expect that sales for a company depend to some degree on the amount of money the company spends on advertising. But many other factors also might affect a company's sales, such as general economic conditions, the level of competition in the marketplace, product quality, and so on. Nevertheless, we might be interested in studying the relationship between the dependent variable sales (Y) and the independent variable advertising (X_1) and predicting the average level of sales expected for a given level of advertising. Regression analysis provides the tool for making such predictions.

To identify a function that describes the relationship between advertising and sales for a company, we first need to collect sample data to analyze. Suppose that we obtain the data shown in Figure 9.1 (and in the file Fig9-1.xls on your data disk) for a company on the level of sales observed for various levels of advertising expenditures in 10 different test markets around the country. We will assume that the different test markets are similar in terms of size and other demographic and economic characteristics. The main difference in each market is the level of advertising expenditure.

The data from Figure 9.1 are displayed graphically in Figure 9.2. This graph suggests a strong linear relationship between advertising expenditures and sales. Note that as advertising expenditures increase, sales increase proportionately. However, the relationship between advertising and sales is not perfect. For example, advertising expenditures

FIGURE 9.1

Sample data for advertising expenditures and observed sales

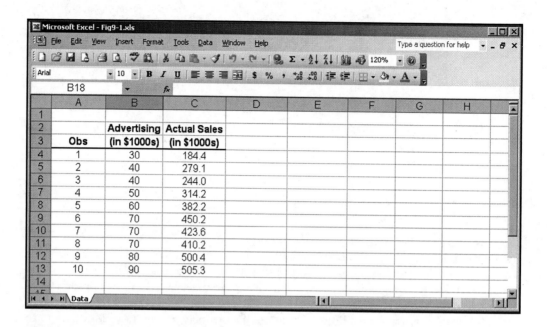

FIGURE 9.2

Scatter diagram for sales and advertising data

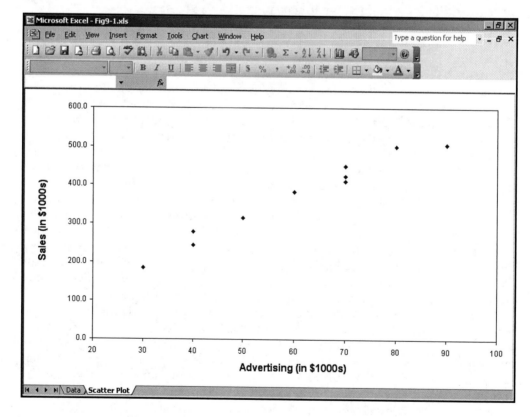

of $70,000 were used in three different test markets and resulted in three different levels of sales. Thus, the level of sales that occurs for a given level of advertising is subject to random fluctuation.

The random fluctuation, or scattering, of the points in Figure 9.2 suggests that some of the variation in sales is not accounted for by advertising expenditures. Because of the scattering of points, this type of graph is called a scatter diagram or scatter plot. So although there is not a perfect *functional* relationship between sales and advertising (where each level of advertising yields one unique level of sales), there does seem to be a *statistical* relationship between these variables (where each level of sales is associated with a range or distribution of possible sales values).

Creating a Scatter Plot

To create a scatter plot like the one shown in Figure 9.2:

1. Select cells B4 through C13 shown in Figure 9.1.
2. Click the Insert menu.
3. Click Chart.
4. Click XY (Scatter).

Excel's Chart Wizard then prompts you to make several selections concerning the type of chart you want and how it should be labeled and formatted. After Excel creates a basic chart, you can customize it in many ways. Double-click a chart element to display a dialog box with options for modifying the appearance of the element.

9.2 Regression Models

We will formalize the somewhat imprecise nature of a statistical relationship by adding an *error term* to what is otherwise a functional relationship. That is, in regression analysis, we consider models of the form:

$$Y = f(X_1, X_2, \ldots, X_k) + \varepsilon \qquad \textbf{9.1}$$

where ε represents a random disturbance, or error, term. Equation 9.1 is a regression model. The number of independent variables in a regression model differs from one application to another. Similarly, the form of $f(\cdot)$ varies from simple linear functions to more complex polynomial and nonlinear forms. In any case, the model in equation 9.1 conveys the two essential elements of a statistical relationship:

1. A tendency for the dependent variable Y to vary with the independent variable(s) in a systematic way, as expressed by $f(X_1, X_2, \ldots, X_k)$ in equation 9.1.
2. An element of *unsystematic* or random variation in the dependent variable, as expressed by ε in equation 9.1.

The regression model in equation 9.1 indicates that for any values assumed by the independent variables $X_1, \ldots, X_k$ there is a probability distribution that describes the possible values that can be assumed by the dependent variable Y. This is portrayed graphically in Figure 9.3 for the case of a single independent variable. The curve drawn in Figure 9.3 represents the regression line (or regression function). It denotes the *systematic* variation between the dependent and independent variables (represented by $f(X_1, X_2, \ldots, X_k)$ in equation 9.1). The probability distributions in Figure 9.3 denote the *unsystematic* variation in the dependent variable Y at different levels of the independent variable. This represents random variation in the dependent variable (represented by ε in equation 9.1) that cannot be accounted for by the independent variable.

FIGURE 9.3

*Diagram of the
distribution of Y
values at various
levels of X*

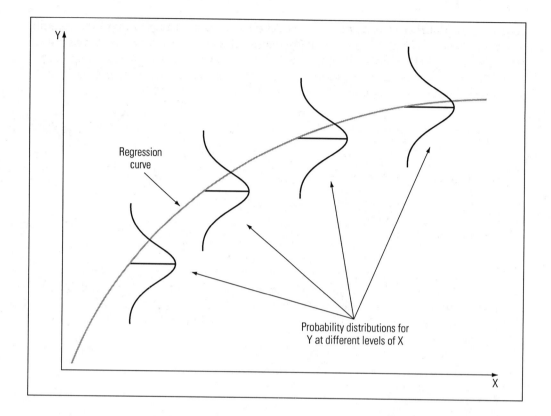

Notice that the regression function in Figure 9.3 passes through the mean, or average, value for each probability distribution. Therefore, the regression function indicates what value, on average, the dependent variable is expected to assume at various levels of the independent variable. If we want to predict what value the dependent variable Y would assume at some level of the independent variable, the best estimate we could make is given by the regression function. That is, our best estimate of the value that Y will assume at a given level of the independent variable X_1 is the mean (or average) of the distribution of values for Y at that level of X_1.

The actual value assumed by the dependent variable is likely to be somewhat different from our estimate because there is some random, unsystematic variation in the dependent variable that cannot be accounted for by our regression function. If we could repeatedly sample and observe actual values of Y at a given level of X_1, sometimes the actual value of Y would be higher than our estimated (mean) value and sometimes it would be lower. So, the difference between the actual value of Y and our predicted value of Y would, on average, tend toward 0. For this reason, we can assume that the error term ε in equation 9.1 has an average, or expected, value of 0 if the probability distributions for the dependent variable Y at the various levels of the independent variable are normally distributed (bell-shaped) as shown in Figure 9.3.

9.3 Simple Linear Regression Analysis

As mentioned earlier, the function $f(\cdot)$ in equation 9.1 can assume many forms. However, the scatter plot in Figure 9.2 suggests that a strong linear relationship exists between the independent variable in our example (advertising expenditures) and the dependent variable (sales). That is, we could draw a straight line through the data in Figure 9.2 that would fit the data fairly well. So, the formula of a straight line might account for the systematic variation between advertising and sales. Therefore, the following simple linear regression model might be an appropriate choice for describing the relationship between advertising and sales:

$$Y_i = \beta_0 + \beta_1 X_{1_i} + \varepsilon_i \qquad\qquad 9.2$$

In equation 9.2, Y_i denotes the *actual* sales value for the ith observation, X_{1_i} denotes the advertising expenditures associated with Y_i, and ε_i is an error term indicating that when X_{1_i} dollars are spent on advertising, sales might not always equal $\beta_0 + \beta_1 X_{1_i}$. The parameter β_0 represents a constant value (sometimes referred to as the Y-intercept because it represents the point where the line goes through the Y-axis) and β_1 represents the slope of the line (that is, the amount by which the line rises or falls per unit increase in X_1). Assuming that a straight line accounts for the systematic variation between Y and X_1, the error terms ε_i represent the amounts by which the actual levels of sales are scattered around the regression line. Again, if the errors are scattered randomly around the regression line, they should average out to 0 or have an expected value of 0.

The model in equation 9.2 is a simple model because it contains only one independent variable. It is linear because none of the parameters (β_0 and β_1) appear as an exponent in the model or are multiplied or divided by one another.

Conceptually, it is important to understand that we are assuming that a large population of Y values occurs at each level of X_1. The parameters β_0 and β_1 represent, respectively, the intercept and slope of the *true* regression line relating these populations. For this reason, β_0 and β_1 are sometimes referred to as population parameters. Usually we never know the exact numeric values for the population parameters in a given regression problem (we know that these values exist, but we don't know what they are). To determine the numeric values of the population parameters, we would have to look at the entire population of Y at each level of X_1—usually an impossible task. However, by taking a sample of Y values at selected levels of X_1 we can estimate the values of the population parameters. We will identify the estimated values of β_0 and β_1 as b_0 and b_1, respectively. The remaining problem is to determine the best values of b_0 and b_1 from our sample data.

9.4 Defining "Best Fit"

An infinite number of values could be assigned to b_0 and b_1. So, searching for the exact values for b_0 and b_1 to produce the line that best fits our sample data might seem like searching for a needle in a haystack—and it is certainly not something we want to do manually. To have the computer estimate the values for b_0 and b_1 that produce the line that best fits our data, we must give it some guidance and define what we mean by the best fit.

We will use the symbol $\hat{Y}_i$ to denote our estimated, or fitted, value of Y_i, which is defined as:

$$\hat{Y}_i = b_0 + b_1 X_{1_i} \qquad\qquad 9.3$$

We want to the find values for b_0 and b_1 that make all the *estimated* sales values ($\hat{Y}_i$) as close as possible to the *actual* sales values (Y_i). For example, the data in Figure 9.1 indicate that we spent \$30,000 on advertising ($X_{1_i} = 30$) and observed sales of \$184,400 ($Y_1 = 184.4$). So in equation 9.3, if we let $X_{1_i} = 30$, we want $\hat{Y}_i$ to assume a value that is as close as possible to 184.4. Similarly, in the three instances in Figure 9.1 where \$70,000 was spent on advertising ($X_{1_6} = X_{1_7} = X_{1_8} = 70$), we observed sales of \$450,200, \$423,600, and \$410,200 ($Y_6 = 450.2$, $Y_7 = 423.6$, $Y_8 = 410.2$). So in equation 9.3, if we let $X_{1_i} = 70$, we want Y_i to assume a value that is as close as possible to 450.2, 423.6, and 410.2.

If we could find values for b_0 and b_1 so that all the estimated sales values were exactly the same as all the actual sales values ($\hat{Y}_i = Y_i$ for all observations i), we would have the equation of the straight line that passes through each data point—in other words, the line would fit our data perfectly. This is impossible for the data in Figure 9.2 because a straight line could not be drawn to pass through each data point in the graph. In most regression problems, it is impossible to find a function that fits the data perfectly because most data sets contain some amount of unsystematic variation.

Although we are unlikely to find values for b_0 and b_1 that will allow us to fit our data perfectly, we will try to find values that make the differences between the estimated values for the dependent variable and the actual values for the dependent variable ($Y_i - \hat{Y}_i$) as small as possible. We refer to the difference $Y_i - \hat{Y}_i$ as the estimation error for observation i because it measures how far away the estimated value $\hat{Y}_i$ is from the actual value Y_i. The estimation errors in a regression problem are also referred to as *residuals*.

Although different criteria can be used to determine the best values for b_0 and b_1, the most widely used method determines the values that minimize the sum of squared estimation errors—or *error sum of squares* (ESS) for short. That is, we will attempt to find values for b_0 and b_1 that minimize:

$$\text{ESS} = \sum_{i=1}^{n} (Y_i - \hat{Y}_i)^2 = \sum_{i=1}^{n} [Y_i - (b_0 + b_1 X_{1_i})]^2 \qquad \textbf{9.4}$$

Several observations should be made concerning ESS. Because each estimation error is squared, the value of ESS will always be nonnegative and, therefore, the smallest value ESS can assume is 0. The only way for ESS to equal 0 is for all the individual estimation errors to be 0 ($Y_i - \hat{Y}_i = 0$ for all observations), in which case the estimated regression line would fit our data perfectly. Thus, minimizing ESS seems to be a good objective to use in searching for the best values of b_0 and b_1. Because regression analysis finds the values of the parameter estimates that minimize the sum of squared estimation errors, it is sometimes referred to as the method of least squares.

9.5 Solving the Problem Using Solver

We can calculate the optimal parameter estimates for a linear regression model in several ways. As in earlier chapters, we can use Solver to find the values for b_0 and b_1 that minimize the ESS quantity in equation 9.4.

Finding the optimal values for b_0 and b_1 in equation 9.4 is an unconstrained nonlinear optimization problem. Consider the spreadsheet in Figure 9.4.

In Figure 9.4, cells C15 and C16 represent the values for b_0 and b_1, respectively. These cells are labeled Intercept and Slope because b_0 represents the intercept in equation 9.3 and b_1 represents the slope. Values of 70 and 5 were entered for these cells as rough guesses of their optimal values.

To use Solver to calculate the optimal values of b_0 and b_1, we need to implement a formula in the spreadsheet that corresponds to the ESS calculation in equation 9.4. This formula represents the objective function to be minimized. To calculate the ESS, we first need to calculate the sales values estimated by the regression function in equation 9.3 for

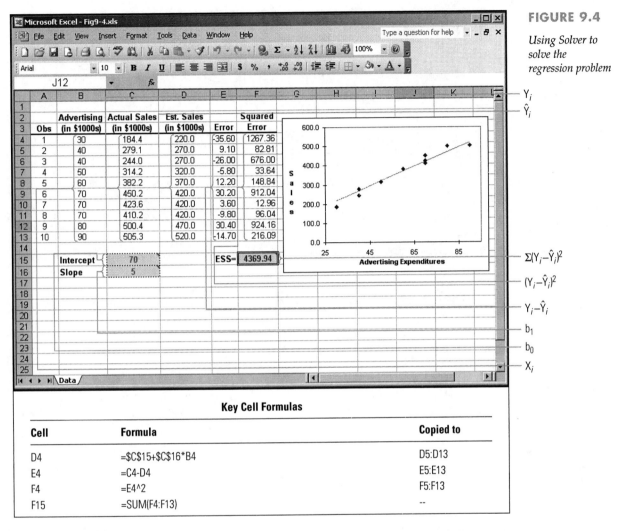

FIGURE 9.4

Using Solver to solve the regression problem

each observation in our sample. These estimated sales values ($\hat{Y}_i$) were created in column D as:

Formula for cell D4:   =\$C\$15+\$C\$16*B4

(Copy to D5 through D13.)

The estimation errors ($Y_i - \hat{Y}_i$) were calculated in column E as:

Formula for cell E4:   =C4–D4

(Copy to E5 through E13.)

The squared estimation errors (($Y_i - \hat{Y}_i)^2$) were calculated in column F as:

Formula for cell F4:   =E4^2

(Copy to F5 through F13.)

Finally, the sum of the squared estimation errors (ESS) was calculated in cell F15 as:

Formula for cell F15:   =SUM(F4:F13)

Note that the formula in cell F15 corresponds exactly to equation 9.4.

FIGURE 9.5

Solver parameters for the regression problem

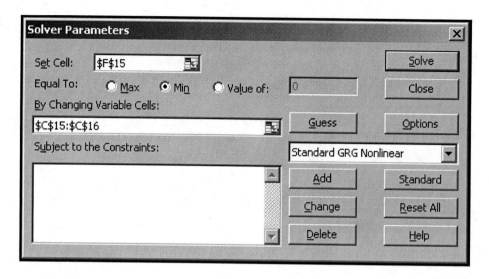

The graph in Figure 9.4 plots the line connecting the estimated sales values against the actual sales values. The intercept and slope of this line are determined by the values in C15 and C16. Although this line seems to fit our data fairly well, we do not know if this is the line that minimizes the ESS value. However, we can use the Solver parameters shown in Figure 9.5 to determine the values for C15 and C16 that minimize the ESS value in F15.

Figure 9.6 shows the optimal solution to this problem. In this spreadsheet, the intercept and slope of the line that best fits our data are $b_0 = 36.34235$ and $b_1 = 5.550293$, respectively. The ESS value of 3,336.244 associated with these optimal parameter estimates is better (or smaller) than the ESS value for the parameter estimates shown in Figure 9.4. No other values for b_0 and b_1 would result in an ESS value smaller than the one shown in Figure 9.6. Thus, the equation of the straight line that best fits our data according to the least squares criterion is represented by:

$$\hat{Y}_i = 36.34235 + 5.550291 X_{1_i} \qquad \qquad 9.5$$

FIGURE 9.6

Optimal solution to the regression problem

Obs	Advertising (in $1000s)	Actual Sales (in $1000s)	Est. Sales (in $1000s)	Error	Squared Error
1	30	184.4	202.9	-18.45	340.44
2	40	279.1	258.4	20.75	430.40
3	40	244.0	258.4	-14.35	206.04
4	50	314.2	313.9	0.34	0.12
5	60	382.2	369.4	12.84	164.87
6	70	450.2	424.9	25.34	641.98
7	70	423.6	424.9	-1.26	1.59
8	70	410.2	424.9	-14.66	215.00
9	80	500.4	480.4	20.03	401.37
10	90	505.3	535.9	-30.57	934.44
	Intercept	36.34235534		ESS=	3336.244
	Slope	5.550291294			

9.6 Solving the Problem Using the Regression Tool

In addition to Solver, Excel provides another tool for solving regression problems that is easier to use and provides more information about a regression problem. We will demonstrate the use of this regression tool by referring back to the original data for the current problem, shown in Figure 9.1. Before you can use the regression tool in Excel, you need to make sure that the Analysis ToolPak add-in is available. You can do this by completing the following steps:

1. Click the Tools menu.
2. Click Add-Ins.
3. Click Analysis ToolPak. (If Analysis ToolPak is not listed among your available add-ins, you will need to install it from your Microsoft Office CD.)

After ensuring that the Analysis ToolPak is available, you can access the regression tool by completing the following steps:

1. Click the Tools menu.
2. Click Data Analysis.
3. Click Regression.

After you choose the Regression command, the Regression dialog box appears, as shown in Figure 9.7. This dialog box presents many options and selections. At this point, we will focus on only three options: the Y-Range, the X-Range, and the Output-Range. The Y-Range corresponds to the range in the spreadsheet containing the sample

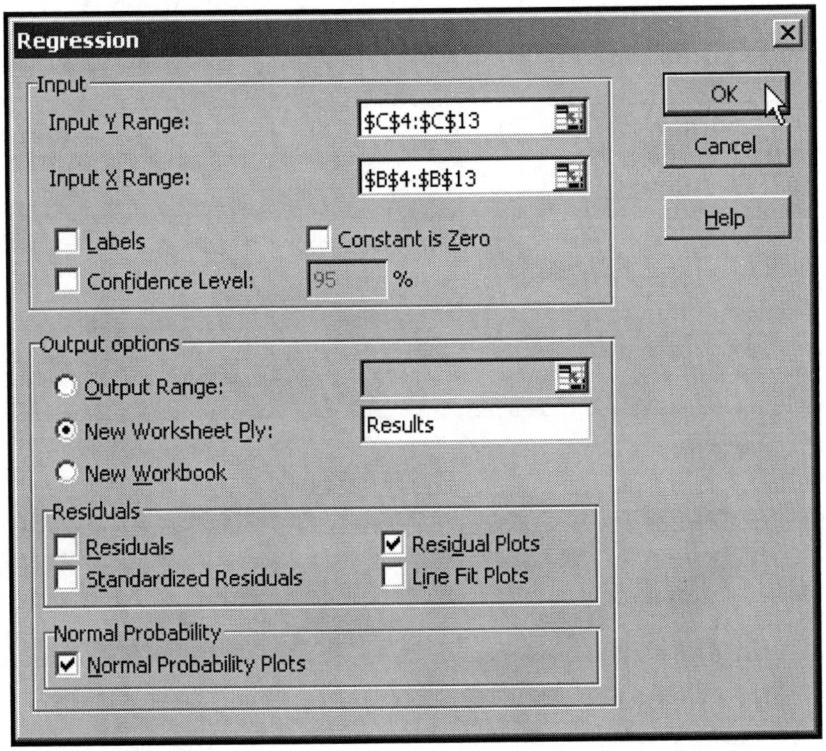

FIGURE 9.7

Regression dialog box

observations for the *dependent* variable (C4 through C13 for the example in Figure 9.1). The X-Range corresponds to the range in the spreadsheet containing the sample observations for the *independent* variable (B4 through B13 for the current example). We also need to specify the output range where we want the regression results to be reported. In Figure 9.7, we selected the New Worksheet Ply option to indicate that we want the regression results placed on a new sheet named "Results." With the dialog box selections complete, we can click the OK button and Excel will calculate the least squares values for b_0 and b_1 (along with other summary statistics).

Figure 9.8 shows the Results sheet for our example. For now, we will focus on only a few values in Figure 9.8. Note that the value labeled "Intercept" in cell B17 represents the optimal value for b_0 ($b_0 = 36.342$). The value representing the coefficient for "X Variable 1" in cell B18 represents the optimal value for b_1 ($b_1 = 5.550$). Thus, the estimated regression function is represented by:

$$\hat{Y}_i = b_0 + b_1 X_{1_i} = 36.342 + 5.550 X_{1_i} \qquad \textbf{9.6}$$

Equation 9.6 is essentially the same result we obtained earlier using Solver (see equation 9.5). Thus, we can calculate the parameter estimates for a regression function using either Solver or the regression tool shown in Figure 9.7. The advantage of the regression tool is that it does not require us to set up any special formulas or cells in the spreadsheet, and it produces additional statistical results about the problem under study.

FIGURE 9.8

Results for the regression calculations

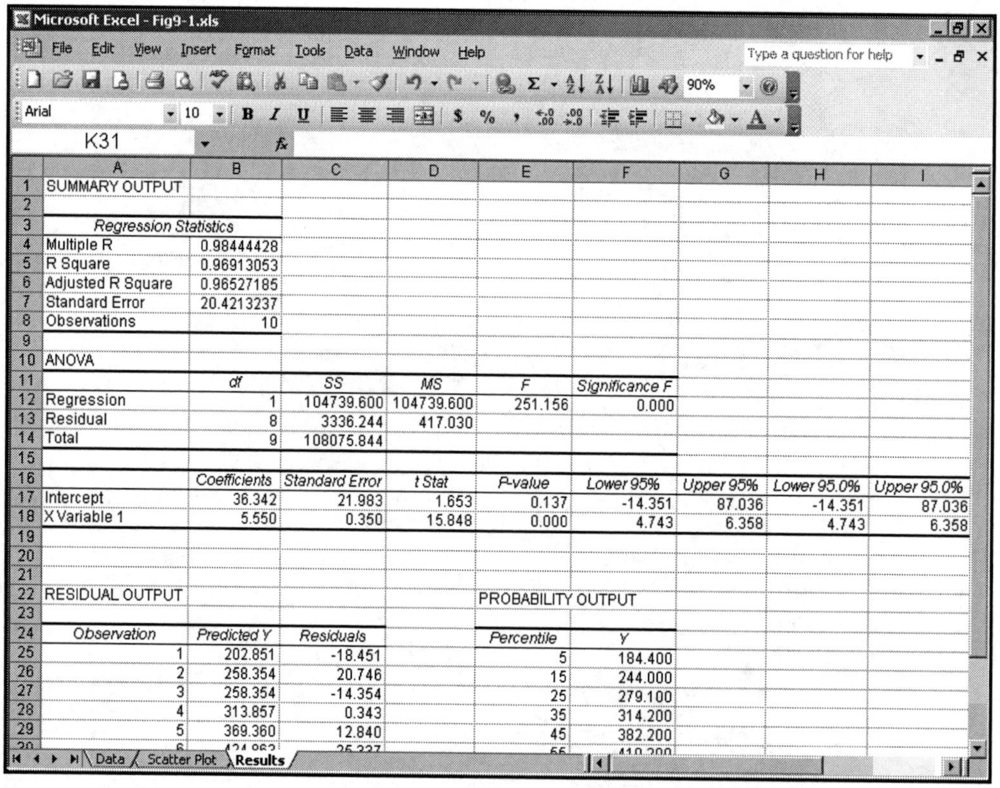

9.7 Evaluating the Fit

Our goal in the example problem is to identify the equation of a straight line that fits our data well. Having calculated the estimated regression line (using either Solver or the regression tool), we might be interested in determining how well the line fits our data. Using equation 9.6, we can compute the estimated or expected level of sales ($\hat{Y}_i$) for each observation in our sample. The $\hat{Y}_i$ values could be calculated in column D of Figure 9.9 as follows:

Formula for cell D4:   =36.342+5.550*B4

(Copy to D5 through D13.)

However, we can also use the TREND( ) function in Excel to compute the $\hat{Y}_i$ values in column D as follows:

Alternate Formula for cell D4:   =TREND($C$4:$C$13,$B$4:$B$13,B4)

(Copy to D5 through D13.)

This TREND( ) function computes the least squares linear regression line using a Y-range of C4 through C13 and an X-range of B4 through B13. It then uses this regression function to estimate the value of Y using the value of X given in cell B4. Thus, using the TREND( ) function, we don't have to worry about typing the wrong values for the estimated intercept or slope. Notice that the resulting estimated sales values shown in column D in Figure 9.9 match the predicted Y values shown toward the bottom on column B in Figure 9.8.

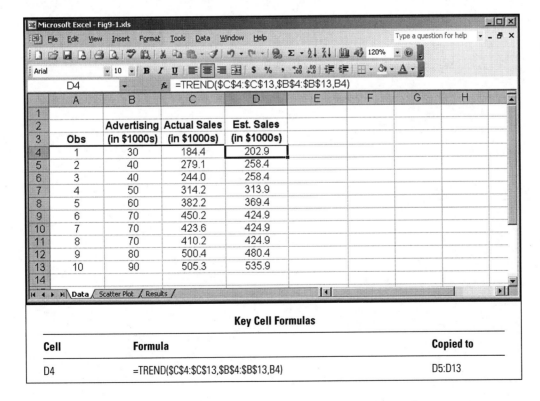

FIGURE 9.9

Estimated sales values at each level of advertising

Obs	Advertising (in $1000s)	Actual Sales (in $1000s)	Est. Sales (in $1000s)
1	30	184.4	202.9
2	40	279.1	258.4
3	40	244.0	258.4
4	50	314.2	313.9
5	60	382.2	369.4
6	70	450.2	424.9
7	70	423.6	424.9
8	70	410.2	424.9
9	80	500.4	480.4
10	90	505.3	535.9

Key Cell Formulas

Cell	Formula	Copied to
D4	=TREND($C$4:$C$13,$B$4:$B$13,B4)	D5:D13

A Note on the TREND( ) Function

The TREND( ) function can be used to calculate the estimated values for linear regression models. The format of the TREND( ) function is as follows:

TREND(Y-range, X-range, X-value for prediction)

where Y-range is the range in the spreadsheet containing the dependent Y variable, X-range is the range in the spreadsheet containing the independent X variable(s), and X-value for prediction is a cell (or cells) containing the values for the independent X variable(s) for which we want an estimated value of Y. The TREND( ) function has an advantage over the regression tool in that it is dynamically updated whenever any inputs to the function change. However, it does not provide the statistical information provided by the regression tool. It is best to use these two different approaches to doing regression in conjunction with one another.

Figure 9.10 shows a graph of the estimated regression function along with the actual sales data. This function represents the expected amount of sales that would occur for each value of the independent variable (that is, each value in column D of Figure 9.9 falls on this line). To insert this estimated trend line on the existing scatter plot:

1. Right-click on any of the data points in the scatter plot to select the series of data.
2. Select Add Trendline.
3. On the Type card, click Linear.
4. On the Options card, select the "Display equation on chart" and "Display R-squared value on chart."
5. Click OK.

FIGURE 9.10

Graph of the regression line through the actual sales data

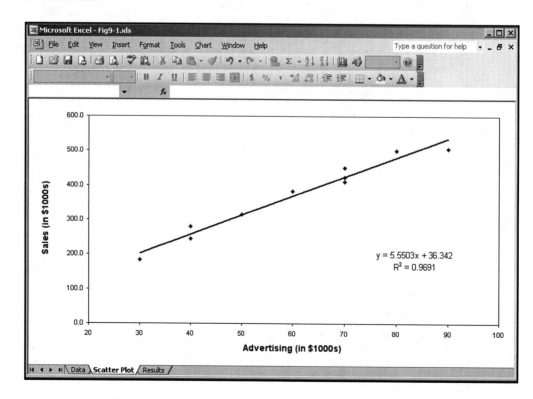

From this graph, we see that the regression function seems to fit the data reasonably well in this example. In particular, it seems that the actual sales values fluctuate around this line in a fairly unsystematic, or random, pattern. Thus, it appears that we have achieved our goal of identifying a function that accounts for most, if not all, of the systematic variation between the dependent and independent variables.

9.8 The R^2 Statistic

In Figure 9.8, the value labeled "R Square" in cell B5 (or "R^2" in Figure 9.10) provides a goodness-of-fit measure. This value represents the R^2 statistic (also referred to as the coefficient of determination). This statistic ranges in value from 0 to 1 ($0 \leq R^2 \leq 1$) and indicates the proportion of the total variation in the dependent variable Y around its mean (average) that is accounted for by the independent variable(s) in the estimated regression function.

The total variation in the dependent variable Y around its mean is described by a measure known as the *total sum of squares* (TSS), which is defined as:

$$TSS = \sum_{i=1}^{n} (Y_i - \bar{Y})^2 \tag{9.7}$$

The TSS equals the sum of the squared differences between each observation Y_i in the sample and the average value of Y, denoted in equation 9.7 by $\bar{Y}$. The difference between each observed value of Y_i and the average value $\bar{Y}$ can be decomposed into two parts as:

$$Y_i - \bar{Y}_i = (Y_i - \hat{Y}_i) + (\hat{Y}_i - \bar{Y}) \tag{9.8}$$

Figure 9.11 illustrates this decomposition for a hypothetical data point. The value $Y_i - \hat{Y}_i$ in equation 9.8 represents the estimation error, or the amount of the total deviation between Y_i and $\bar{Y}$ that is not accounted for by the regression function. The value $\hat{Y}_i - \bar{Y}$ in equation 9.8 represents the amount of the total deviation in Y_i from $\bar{Y}$ that is accounted for by the regression function.

The decomposition of the individual deviation in equation 9.8 also applies to the TSS in equation 9.7. That is, the *total sum of squares* (TSS) can be decomposed into the following two parts:

$$\sum_{i=1}^{n} (Y_i - \bar{Y})^2 = \sum_{i=1}^{n} (Y_i - \hat{Y}_i)^2 + \sum_{i=1}^{n} (\hat{Y}_i - \bar{Y})^2 \tag{9.9}$$
$$\text{TSS} \quad = \quad \text{ESS} \quad + \quad \text{RSS}$$

ESS is the quantity that is minimized in least squares regression. ESS represents the amount of variation in Y around its mean that the regression function cannot account for, or the amount of variation in the dependent variable that is unexplained by the regression function. Therefore, the *regression sum of squares* (RSS) represents the amount of variation in Y around its mean that the regression function can account for, or the amount of variation in the dependent variable that is explained by the regression function. In Figure 9.8, cells C12, C13, and C14 contain the values for RSS, ESS, and TSS, respectively.

Now consider the following definitions of the R^2 statistic:

$$R^2 = \frac{RSS}{TSS} = 1 - \frac{ESS}{TSS} \tag{9.10}$$

From the previous definition of TSS in equation 9.9, we can see that if ESS = 0 (which can occur only if the regression function fits the data perfectly), then TSS = RSS and, therefore, R^2 = 1. On the other hand, if RSS = 0 (which means that the regression function was unable to explain any of the variation in the behavior of the dependent variable Y),

FIGURE 9.11

Decomposition of the total deviation into error and regression components

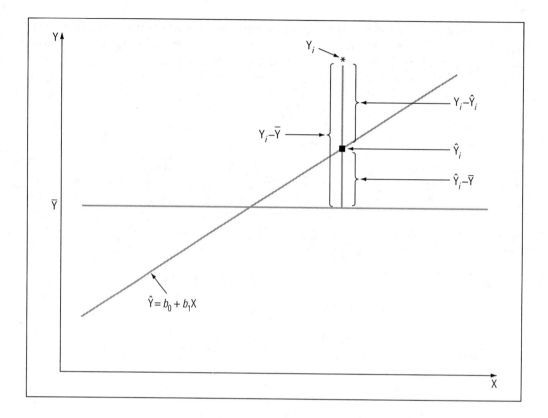

then TSS = ESS and $R^2 = 0$. So, the closer the R^2 statistic is to the value 1, the better the estimated regression function fits the data.

From cell B5 in Figure 9.8, we observe that the value of the R^2 statistic is approximately 0.969. This indicates that approximately 96.9% of the total variation in our dependent variable around its mean has been accounted for by the independent variable in our estimated regression function. Because this value is fairly close to the maximum possible R^2 value (1), this statistic indicates that the regression function we have estimated fits our data well. This is confirmed by the graph in Figure 9.10.

The multiple R statistic shown in cell B4 of the regression output in Figure 9.8 represents the strength of the linear relationship between actual and estimated values for the dependent variable. As with the R^2 statistic, the multiple R statistic varies between 0 and 1 with values near 1 indicating a good fit. When a regression model includes only one independent variable, the multiple R statistic is equivalent to the square root of the R^2 statistic. We'll focus on the R^2 statistic because its interpretation is more apparent than that of the multiple R statistic.

9.9 Making Predictions

Using the estimated regression in equation 9.6, we can make predictions about the level of sales expected for different levels of advertising expenditures. For example, suppose that the company wants to estimate the level of sales that would occur if $65,000 were spent on advertising in a given market. Assuming that the market in question is similar to those used in estimating the regression function, the expected sales level is estimated as:

$$\text{Estimated Sales} = b_0 + b_1 \times 65 = 36.342 + 5.550 \times 65 = 397.092$$
(in $1000s)

So, if the company spends $65,000 on advertising (in a market similar to those used to estimate the regression function), we would expect to observe sales of approximately $397,092. The *actual* level of sales is likely to differ somewhat from this value due to other random factors influencing sales.

9.9.1 THE STANDARD ERROR

A measure of the accuracy of the prediction obtained from a regression model is given by the standard deviation of the estimation errors—also known as the standard error, S_e. If we let n denote the number of observations in the data set, and k denote the number of independent variables in the regression model, the formula for the standard error is represented by:

$$S_e = \sqrt{\frac{\sum_{i=1}^{n} (Y_i - \hat{Y}_i)^2}{n - k - 1}}$$

9.11

The standard error measures the amount of scatter, or variation, in the actual data around the fitted regression function. Cell B7 in Figure 9.8 indicates that the standard error for our example problem is $S_e = 20.421$.

The standard error is useful in evaluating the level of uncertainty in predictions we make with a regression model. As a *very* rough rule of thumb, there is approximately a 68% chance of the actual level of sales falling within ± 1 standard error of the predicted value $\hat{Y}_i$. Alternatively, the chance of the actual level of sales falling within ± 2 standard errors of the predicted value $\hat{Y}_i$ is approximately 95%. In our example, if the company spends $65,000 on advertising, we could be roughly 95% confident that the actual level of sales observed would fall somewhere in the range from $356,250 to $437,934 ($\hat{Y}_i \pm 2S_e$).

9.9.2 PREDICTION INTERVALS FOR NEW VALUES OF Y

To calculate a more accurate confidence interval for a prediction, or prediction interval, of a new value of Y when $X_1 = X_{1_h}$, we first calculate the estimated value $\hat{Y}_h$ as:

$$\hat{Y}_h = b_0 + b_1 X_{1_h}$$

9.12

A $(1 - \alpha)\%$ prediction interval for a new value of Y when $X_1 = X_{1_h}$ is represented by:

$$\hat{Y}_h \pm t_{(1-\alpha/2;n-2)} S_p$$

9.13

where $t_{(1-\alpha/2;n-2)}$ represents the $1 - \alpha/2$ percentile of a t-distribution with $n - 2$ degrees of freedom, and S_p represents the standard prediction error defined by:

$$S_p = S_e \sqrt{1 + \frac{1}{n} + \frac{(X_{1_h} - \bar{X})^2}{\sum_{i=1}^{n} (X_{1_i} - \bar{X})^2}}$$

9.14

The rule of thumb presented earlier is a generalization of equation 9.13. Notice that S_p is always larger than S_e because the term under the square root symbol is always greater than 1. Also notice that the magnitude of the difference between S_p and S_e increases as the difference between X_{1_h} and $\bar{X}$ increases. Thus, the prediction intervals generated by the rule of thumb tend to underestimate the true amount of uncertainty involved in making predictions. This is illustrated in Figure 9.12.

As shown in Figure 9.12, for this example problem, there is not a lot of difference between the prediction intervals created using the rule of thumb and the more accurate prediction interval given in equation 9.13. In a situation requiring a precise prediction

FIGURE 9.12

Comparison of prediction intervals obtained using the rule of thumb and the more accurate statistical calculation

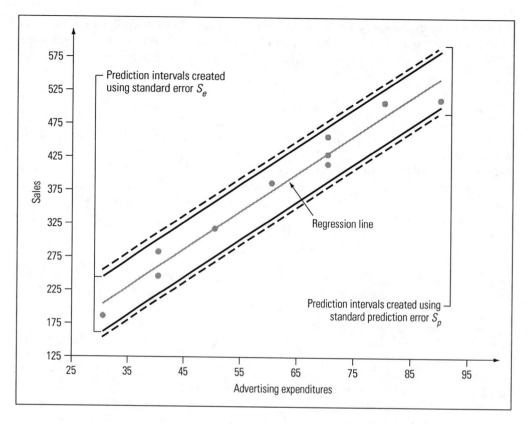

interval, the various quantities needed to construct the prediction interval in equation 9.13 can be computed easily in Excel. Figure 9.13 provides an example of a 95% prediction interval for a new value of sales when $65,000 is spent on advertising.

To create this prediction interval, we first use the TREND( ) function to calculate the estimated sales level ($\hat{Y}_h$) when advertising equals $65,000 ($X_{1_h} = 65$). The value 65 is entered in cell B17 to represent X_{1_h} and the estimated sales level ($\hat{Y}_h$) is calculated in cell D17 as:

Formula for cell D17:   =TREND($C$4:$C$13,$B$4:$B$13,B17)

The expected level of sales when $65,000 is spent on advertising is approximately $397,100. The standard error (S_e) shown in cell B19 is extracted from the Results sheet shown in Figure 9.8 as:

Formula for cell B19:   =Results!B7

The standard prediction error (S_p) is calculated in cell B20 as:

Formula for cell B20:   =B19*SQRT(1+1/10+
(B17–AVERAGE(B4:B13)) ^2/(10*VARP(B4:B13)))

The value 10 appearing in the preceding formula corresponds to the sample size n in equation 9.14. The appropriate t-value for a 95% confidence (or prediction) interval is calculated in cell B21 as:

Formula for cell B21:   =TINV(1–0.95,8)

The first argument in the preceding formula corresponds to 1 minus the desired confidence level (or $\alpha = 0.05$). The second argument corresponds to $n - 2$ ($10 - 2 = 8$). Cells E17 and F17 calculate the lower and upper limits of the prediction interval as:

Microsoft Excel - Fig9-1.xls

D17 =TREND($C$4:$C$13,$B$4:$B$13,B17)

	A	B	C	D	E	F	G	H
1								
2		Advertising	Actual Sales	Est. Sales				
3	Obs	(in $1000s)	(in $1000s)	(in $1000s)				
4	1	30	184.4	202.9				
5	2	40	279.1	258.4				
6	3	40	244.0	258.4				
7	4	50	314.2	313.9				
8	5	60	382.2	369.4				
9	6	70	450.2	424.9				
10	7	70	423.6	424.9				
11	8	70	410.2	424.9				
12	9	80	500.4	480.4				
13	10	90	505.3	535.9				
14								
15					95% Prediction Interval			
16					Lower Limit	Upper Limit		
17	Prediction	65	?	397.1	347.557	446.666		
18								
19	Se	20.4213						
20	Sp	21.48953						
21	t	2.30600						
22								

Data / Scatter Plot / Results

Key Cell Formulas

Cell	Formula	Copied to
D17	=TREND($C$4:$C$13,$B$4:$B$13,B17)	--
B19	=Results!B7	--
B20	=B19*SQRT(1+1/10+(B17-AVERAGE(B4:B13))^2/(10*VARP(B4:B13)))	--
B21	=TINV(1-0.95,8)	--
E17	=D17-B21*B20	--
F17	=D17+B21*B20	--

FIGURE 9.13

Example of calculating a prediction interval

Formula for cell E17: =D17–B21*B20

Formula for cell F17: =D17+B21*B20

The results indicate that when $65,000 is spent on advertising, we expect to observe sales of approximately $397,100, but realize that the actual sales level is likely to deviate somewhat from this value. However, we can be 95% confident that the actual sales value observed will fall somewhere in the range from $347,556 to $446,666. (Notice that this prediction interval is somewhat wider than the range from $356,250 to $437,934 generated earlier using the rule of thumb.)

9.9.3 CONFIDENCE INTERVALS FOR MEAN VALUES OF Y

At times, you might want to construct a confidence interval for the average, or mean, value of Y when $X_1 = X_{1_h}$. This involves a slightly different procedure from constructing a prediction interval for a new individual value of Y when $X_1 = X_{1_h}$. A $(1 - \alpha)$% confidence interval for the average value of Y when $X_1 = X_{1_h}$ is represented by:

$$\hat{Y}_h \pm t_{(1-\alpha/2;n-2)}S_a \qquad\qquad \textbf{9.15}$$

where $\hat{Y}_h$ is defined by equation 9.12, $t_{(1-\alpha/2;n-2)}$ represents the $1 - \alpha/2$ percentile of a t-distribution with $n - 2$ degrees of freedom, and S_a is represented by:

$$S_a = S_e \sqrt{\frac{1}{n} + \frac{(X_{1_h} - \bar{X})^2}{\sum\limits_{i=1}^{n}(X_{1_i} - \bar{X})^2}} \qquad\qquad \textbf{9.16}$$

Comparing the definition of S_a in equation 9.16 with that of S_p in equation 9.14 reveals that S_a will always be smaller than S_p. Therefore, the confidence interval for the average value of Y when $X_1 = X_{1_h}$ will be tighter (or cover a smaller range) than the prediction interval for a new value of Y when $X_1 = X_{1_h}$. This type of confidence interval can be implemented in a similar way to that described earlier for prediction intervals.

9.9.4 A NOTE ABOUT EXTRAPOLATION

Predictions made using an estimated regression function might have little or no validity for values of the independent variable that are substantially different from those represented in the sample. For example, the advertising expenditures represented in the sample in Figure 9.1 range from $30,000 to $90,000. Thus, we cannot assume that our model will give accurate estimates of sales levels at advertising expenditures significantly above or below this range of values, because the relationship between sales and advertising might be quite different outside this range.

9.10 Statistical Tests for Population Parameters

Recall that the parameter β_1 in equation 9.2 represents the slope of the *true* regression line (or the amount by which the dependent variable Y is expected to change given a unit change in X_1). If no linear relationship exists between the dependent and independent variables, the true value of β_1 for the model in equation 9.2 should be 0. As mentioned earlier, we cannot calculate or observe the true value of β_1 but instead must estimate its value using the sample statistic b_1. However, because the value of b_1 is based on a sample rather than on the entire population of possible values, its value probably is not exactly equal to the true (but unknown) value of β_1. Thus, we might want to determine how different the true value of β_1 is from its estimated value b_1. The regression results in Figure 9.8 provide a variety of information addressing this issue.

Cell B18 in Figure 9.8 indicates that the estimated value of β_1 is $b_1 = 5.550$. Cells F18 and G18 give the lower and upper limits of a 95% confidence interval for the true value of β_1. That is, we can be 95% confident that $4.74 \leq \beta_1 \leq 6.35$. This indicates that for every $1,000 increase in advertising, we would expect to see an increase in sales of approximately $4,740 to $6,350. Notice that this confidence interval does not include the value 0. Thus, we can be at least 95% confident that a linear relationship exists between advertising and sales ($\beta_1 \neq 0$). (If we want an interval other than a 95% confidence interval, we can use the Confidence Level option in the Regression dialog box, shown in Figure 9.7, to specify a different interval.)

The t-statistic and p-value listed in cells D18 and E18 in Figure 9.8 provide another way of testing whether $\beta_1 = 0$. According to statistical theory, if $\beta_1 = 0$, then the ratio of

b_1 to its standard error should follow a t-distribution with $n-2$ degrees of freedom. Thus, the t-statistic for testing if $\beta_1 = 0$ in cell D18 is:

$$t\text{-statistic in cell D18} = \frac{b_1}{\text{standard error or } b_1} = \frac{5.550}{0.35022} = 15.848$$

The p-value in cell E18 indicates the probability of obtaining an outcome that is more extreme than the observed test statistic value if $\beta_1 = 0$. In this case, the p-value is 0, indicating that there is virtually no chance that we will obtain an outcome as large as the observed value for b_1 if the true value of β_1 is 0. Therefore, we conclude that the true value of β_1 is not equal to 0. This is the same conclusion implied earlier by the confidence interval for β_1.

The t-statistic, p-value, and confidence interval for the intercept β_0 are listed in Figure 9.8 in row 17, and would be interpreted in the same way as demonstrated for β_1. Notice that the confidence interval for β_0 straddles the value 0 and, therefore, we cannot be certain that the intercept is significantly different from 0. The p-value for β_0 indicates that we have a 13.689% chance of obtaining an outcome more extreme than the observed value of b_0 if the true value of β_0 is 0. Both of these results indicate a fair chance that $\beta_0 = 0$.

9.10.1 ANALYSIS OF VARIANCE

The *analysis of variance* (ANOVA) results, shown in Figure 9.8, provide another way of testing whether or not $\beta_1 = 0$. The values in the MS column in the ANOVA table represent values known as the *mean squared regression* (MSR) and *mean squared error* (MSE), respectively. These values are computed by dividing the RSS and ESS values in C12 and C13 by the corresponding degrees of freedom values in cells B12 and B13.

If $\beta_1 = 0$, then the ratio of MSR to MSE follows an F-distribution. The statistic labeled "F" in cell E12 is:

$$F\text{-statistic in cell E12} = \frac{MSR}{MSE} = \frac{104739.6}{417.03} = 251.156$$

The value in F12 labeled "Significance F" is similar to the p-values described earlier, and indicates the probability of obtaining a value in excess of the observed value for the F-statistic if $\beta_1 = 0$. In this case, the significance of F is 0, indicating that there is virtually no chance that we would have obtained the observed value for b_1 if the true value of β_1 is 0. Therefore, we conclude that the true value of β_1 is not equal to 0. This is the same conclusion implied earlier by our previous analysis.

The F-statistic might seem a bit redundant, given that we can use the t-statistic to test whether or not $\beta_1 = 0$. However, the F-statistic serves a different purpose, which becomes apparent in multiple regression models with more than one independent variable. The F-statistic tests whether or not *all* of the β_i for *all* of the independent variables in a regression model are all simultaneously equal to 0. A simple linear regression model contains only one independent variable. In this case, the tests involving the F-statistic and the t-statistic are equivalent.

9.10.2 ASSUMPTIONS FOR THE STATISTICAL TESTS

The methods for constructing confidence intervals are based on important assumptions concerning the simple linear regression model presented in equation 9.2. Throughout this discussion, we assumed that the error terms ε_i are independent, normally distributed random variables with expected (or mean) values of 0 and constant variances. Thus, the statistical procedures for constructing intervals and performing t-tests apply only when these assumptions are true for a given set of data. As long as these assumptions are not seriously violated, the procedures described offer good approximations of the desired confidence intervals and *t*-tests. Various diagnostic checks can be performed on the residuals $(Y_i - \hat{Y}_i)$ to see whether or not our assumptions concerning the properties of the error terms are valid. These diagnostics are discussed in depth in most statistics books, but are not repeated in this text. Excel also provides basic diagnostics that can help determine whether assumptions about the error terms are violated.

The Regression dialog box (shown in Figure 9.7) provides two options for producing graphs that highlight serious violations of the error term assumptions. These options are Residual Plots and Normal Probability Plots. Figure 9.14 shows the graphs produced by these two options for our example problem.

The first graph in Figure 9.14 results from the Residual Plots option. This graph plots the residuals (or estimation errors) versus each independent variable in the regression model. Our example problem involves one independent variable—therefore, we have one residual plot. If the assumptions underlying the regression model are met, the residuals should fall within a horizontal band centered on zero and should display no systematic tendency to be positive or negative. The residual plot in Figure 9.14 indicates that the residuals for our example problem fall randomly within a range from -30 to $+30$. Thus, no serious problems are indicated by this graph.

The second graph in Figure 9.14 results from the Normal Probability Plot option. If the error terms in equation 9.2 are normally distributed random variables, the dependent variable in equation 9.2 is a normally distributed random variable prior to sampling. Thus, one way to evaluate whether we can assume that the error terms are normally distributed is to determine if we can assume that the dependent variable is normally distributed. The normal probability plot provides an easy way to evaluate whether the sample values on the dependent variable are consistent with the normality

FIGURE 9.14

Residual plot and normal probability plot for the example problem

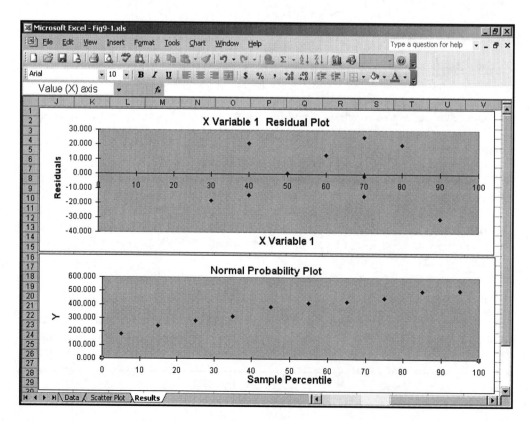

assumption. A plot that is approximately linear (such as the one in Figure 9.14) supports the assumption of normality.

If the residual plot shows a systematic tendency for the residuals to be positive or negative, this indicates that the function chosen to model the systematic variation between the dependent and independent variables is inadequate and that another functional form would be more appropriate. An example of this type of residual plot is given in the first graph in Figure 9.15.

If the residual plot indicates that the magnitude of the residuals is increasing (or decreasing) as the value of the independent variable increases, we would question the validity of the assumption of constant error variances. An example of this type of residual plot is given in the second graph in Figure 9.15. (Note that checking for increasing or decreasing magnitude in the residuals requires multiple observations on Y at the same value of X and at various levels of X.) In some cases, a simple transformation of the

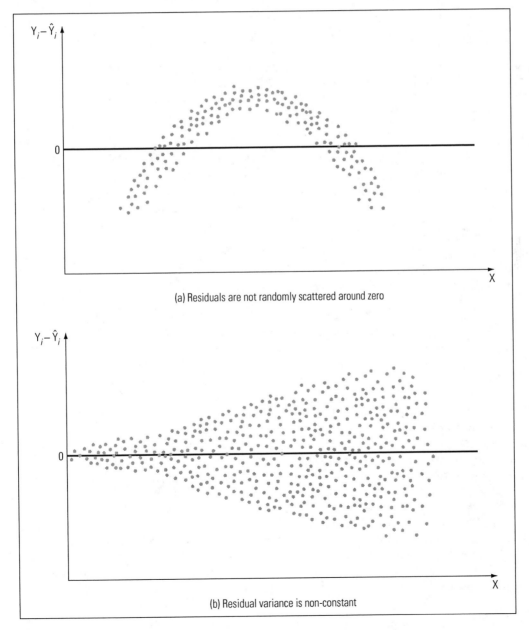

(a) Residuals are not randomly scattered around zero

(b) Residual variance is non-constant

FIGURE 9.15

Residual plots indicating that the fitted regression model is not adequate dependent variable can correct the problem of nonconstant error variances. Such transformations are discussed in more advanced texts on regression analysis.

9.10.3 A NOTE ABOUT STATISTICAL TESTS

Regardless of the form of the distribution of the error terms, least squares regression can always be used to fit regression curves to data to predict the value that the dependent variable will assume for a given level of the independent variables. Many decision makers never bother to look at residual plots or to construct confidence intervals for parameters in the regression models for the predictions they make. However, the accuracy of predictions made using regression models depends on how well the regression function fits the data. At the very least, we always should check to see how well a regression function fits a given data set. We can do so using residual plots, graphs of the actual data versus the estimated values, and the R^2 statistic.

9.11 Introduction to Multiple Regression

We have seen that regression analysis involves identifying a function that relates the *systematic* changes in a continuous dependent variable to the values of one or more independent variables. That is, our goal in regression analysis is to identify an appropriate representation of the function $f(\cdot)$ in:

$$Y = f(X_1, X_2, \ldots, X_k) + \varepsilon \qquad \textbf{9.17}$$

The previous sections in this chapter introduced some of the basic concepts of regression analysis by considering a special case of equation 9.17 that involves a *single* independent variable. Although such a model might be appropriate in some situations, a business person is far more likely to encounter situations involving more than one (or multiple) independent variables. We'll now consider how *multiple* regression analysis can be applied to these situations.

For the most part, multiple regression analysis is a direct extension of simple linear regression analysis. Although volumes have been written on this topic, we'll focus our attention on the multiple linear regression function represented by:

$$\hat{Y}_i = b_0 + b_1X_{1_i} + b_2X_{2_i} + \cdots + b_kX_{k_i} \qquad \textbf{9.18}$$

The regression function in equation 9.18 is similar to the simple linear regression function except that it allows for more than one (or "k") independent variables. Here again, $\hat{Y}_i$ represents the estimated value for the ith observation in our sample whose actual value is Y_i. The symbols $X_{1_i}, X_{2_i}, \ldots, X_{k_i}$ represent the observed values of the independent variables associated with observation i. Assuming that each of these variables vary in a linear fashion with the dependent variable Y, the function in equation 9.18 might be applied appropriately to a variety of problems.

We can easily visualize the equation of a straight line in our earlier discussion of regression analysis. In multiple regression analysis, the concepts are similar but the results are more difficult to visualize. Figure 9.16 shows an example of the type of regression surface we might fit using equation 9.18 if the regression function involves only two independent variables. With two independent variables, we fit a *plane* to our data. With three or more independent variables, we fit a *hyperplane* to our data. It is difficult to visualize or draw graphs in more than three dimensions, so we cannot actually see what a hyperplane looks like. However, just as a plane is a generalization of a straight line into three dimensions, a hyperplane is a generalization of a plane into more than three dimensions.

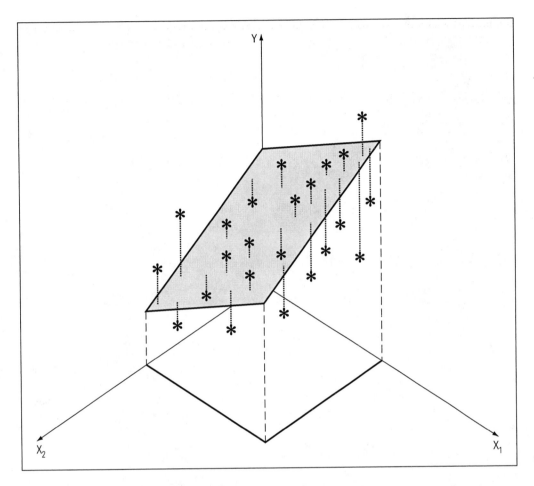

Regardless of the number of independent variables, the goal in multiple regression analysis is the same as the goal in a problem with a single independent variable. That is, we want to find the values for $b_0, b_1, \ldots, b_k$ in equation 9.18 that minimize the sum of squared estimation errors represented by:

$$\text{ESS} = \sum_{i=1}^{n} (Y_i - \hat{Y}_i)^2$$

We can use the method of least squares to determine the values for $b_0, b_1, \ldots, b_k$ that minimize ESS. This should allow us to identify the regression function that best fits our data.

9.12 A Multiple Regression Example

The following example illustrates how to perform multiple linear regression.

A real estate appraiser is interested in developing a regression model to help predict the fair market value of houses in a particular town. She visited the county courthouse and collected the data shown in Figure 9.17 (and in the file Fig9-17.xls on your data disk). The appraiser wants to determine if the selling price of the houses can be accounted for by the total square footage of living area, the size of the garage (as measured by the number of cars that can fit in the garage), and the number of bedrooms in each house. (Note that a garage size of 0 indicates that the house has no garage.)

FIGURE 9.17

Data for the real estate appraisal problem

	A	B	C	D	E
1		Sq. Feet	Size of		Price
2	Obs	(in 1000s)	Garage	Bedrooms	(in $1000s)
3	1	1.000	0	2	$65
4	2	1.100	0	2	$73
5	3	1.150	1	2	$85
6	4	1.400	0	3	$87
7	5	1.700	1	3	$98
8	6	1.900	0	3	$95
9	7	2.100	2	4	$125
10	8	1.800	1	4	$105
11	9	1.900	1	4	$125
12	10	2.100	2	4	$137
13	11	2.300	2	4	$150

In this example, the dependent variable Y represents the selling price of a house, and the independent variables X_1, X_2, and X_3 represent the total square footage, the size of the garage, and the number of bedrooms, respectively. To determine if the multiple linear regression function in equation 9.18 is appropriate for these data, we should first construct scatter plots between the dependent variable (selling price) and each independent variable, as shown in Figure 9.18. These graphs seem to indicate a

FIGURE 9.18

Scatter plots of the real estate appraisal problem

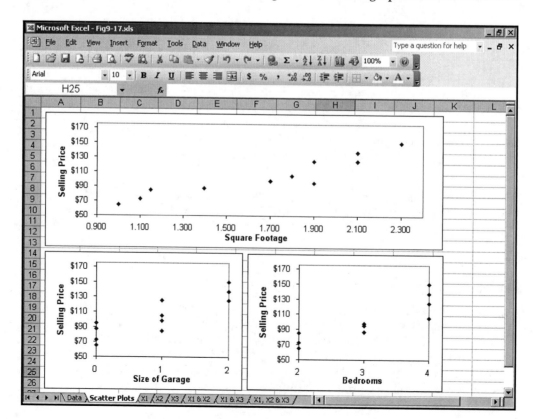

linear relationship between each independent variable and the dependent variable. Thus, we have reason to believe that a multiple linear regression function would be appropriate for these data.

9.13 Selecting the Model

In our discussion of modeling and problem-solving in Chapter 1, we noted that the best model is often the simplest model that accurately reflects the relevant characteristics of the problem being studied. This is particularly true in multiple regression models. The fact that a particular problem might involve numerous independent variables does not necessarily mean that all of the variables should be included in the regression function. If the data used to build a regression model represents a sample from a larger population of data, it is possible to over-analyze or *overfit* the data in the sample. That is, if we look too closely at a sample of data, we are likely to discover characteristics of the sample that are not representative (or which do not generalize) to the population from which the sample was drawn. This can lead to erroneous conclusions about the population being sampled. To avoid the problem of overfitting when building a multiple regression model, we should attempt to identify the *simplest* regression function that adequately accounts for the behavior of the dependent variable we are studying.

9.13.1 MODELS WITH ONE INDEPENDENT VARIABLE

With this idea of simplicity in mind, the real estate appraiser in our example problem might begin her analysis by trying to estimate the selling prices of the houses in the sample using a simple regression function with only one independent variable. The appraiser might first try to fit each of the following three simple linear regression functions to the data:

$$\hat{Y}_i = b_0 + b_1 X_{1_i} \qquad\qquad \textbf{9.19}$$
$$\hat{Y}_i = b_0 + b_2 X_{2_i} \qquad\qquad \textbf{9.20}$$
$$\hat{Y}_i = b_0 + b_3 X_{3_i} \qquad\qquad \textbf{9.21}$$

In equations 9.19 through 9.21, $\hat{Y}_i$ represents the estimated or fitted selling price for the ith observation in the sample, and X_{1_i}, X_{2_i}, and X_{3_i} represent the total square footage, size of garage, and number of bedrooms for this same observation i, respectively.

To obtain the optimal values for the b_i in each regression function, the appraiser must perform three separate regressions. She would do so in the same way as described earlier in our example involving the prediction of sales from advertising expenditures. Figure 9.19 summarizes the results of these three regression functions.

The values of the R^2 statistic in Figure 9.19 indicate the proportion of the total variation in the dependent variable around its mean accounted for by each of the three simple linear regression functions. (We will comment on the adjusted-R^2 and S_e values

Independent Variable in the Model	R^2	Adjusted-R^2	S_e	Parameter Estimates
X_1	0.870	0.855	10.299	$b_0 = 9.503$, $b_1 = 56.394$
X_2	0.759	0.731	14.030	$b_0 = 78.290$, $b_2 = 28.382$
X_3	0.793	0.770	12.982	$b_0 = 16.250$, $b_3 = 27.607$

FIGURE 9.19

Regression results for the three simple linear regression models

shortly.) The model that uses X_1 (square footage) as the independent variable accounts for 87% of the variation in Y (selling price). The model using X_2 (garage size) accounts for roughly 76% of the variation in Y, and the model that uses X_3 (number of bedrooms) as the independent variable accounts for about 79% of the variation in the selling price.

If the appraiser wants to use only one of the available independent variables in a simple linear regression model to predict the selling price of a house, it seems that X_1 would be the best choice because, according to the R^2 statistics, it accounts for more of the variation in selling price than either of the other two variables. In particular, X_1 accounts for about 87% of the variation in the dependent variable. This leaves approximately 13% of the variation in Y unaccounted for. Thus, the best linear regression function with one independent variable is represented by:

$$\hat{Y}_i = b_0 + b_1 X_{1_i} = 9.503 + 56.394\, X_{1_i} \qquad\qquad \textbf{9.22}$$

9.13.2 MODELS WITH TWO INDEPENDENT VARIABLES

Next, the appraiser might want to determine if one of the other two variables could be combined with X_1 in a *multiple* regression model to account for a significant portion of the remaining 13% variation in Y that was not accounted for by X_1. To do this, the appraiser could fit each of the following multiple regression functions to the data:

$$\hat{Y}_i = b_0 + b_1 X_{1_i} + b_2 X_{2_i} \qquad\qquad \textbf{9.23}$$
$$\hat{Y}_i = b_0 + b_1 X_{1_i} + b_3 X_{3_i} \qquad\qquad \textbf{9.24}$$

To determine the optimal values for the b_i in the regression model in equation 9.23, we would use the settings shown in the Regression dialog box in Figure 9.20. The Input X-Range in this dialog box is the range in Figure 9.17 that corresponds to the values for

FIGURE 9.20

Regression dialog box settings for the multiple regression model using square footage and garage size as independent variables

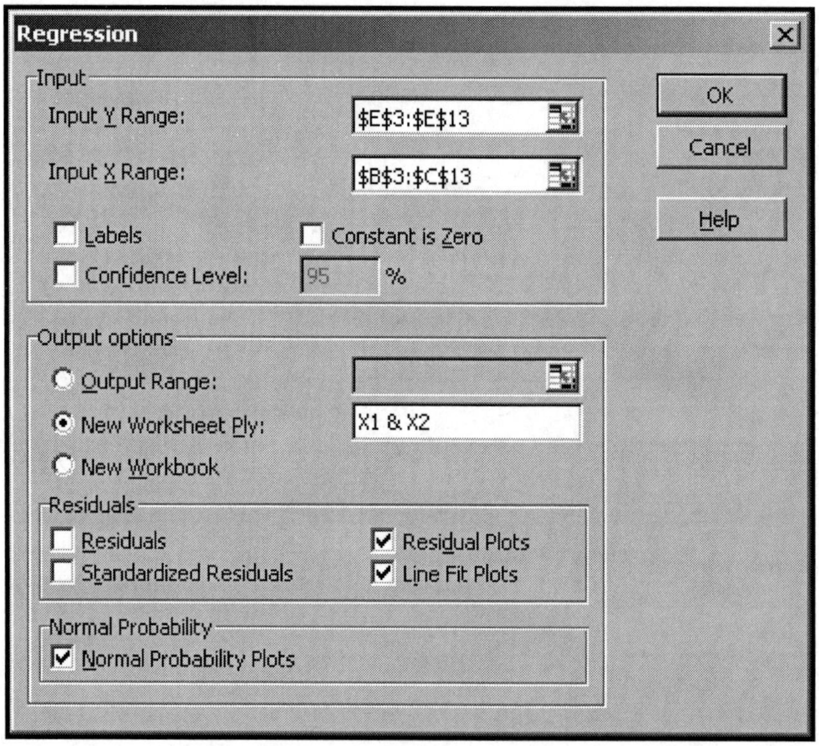

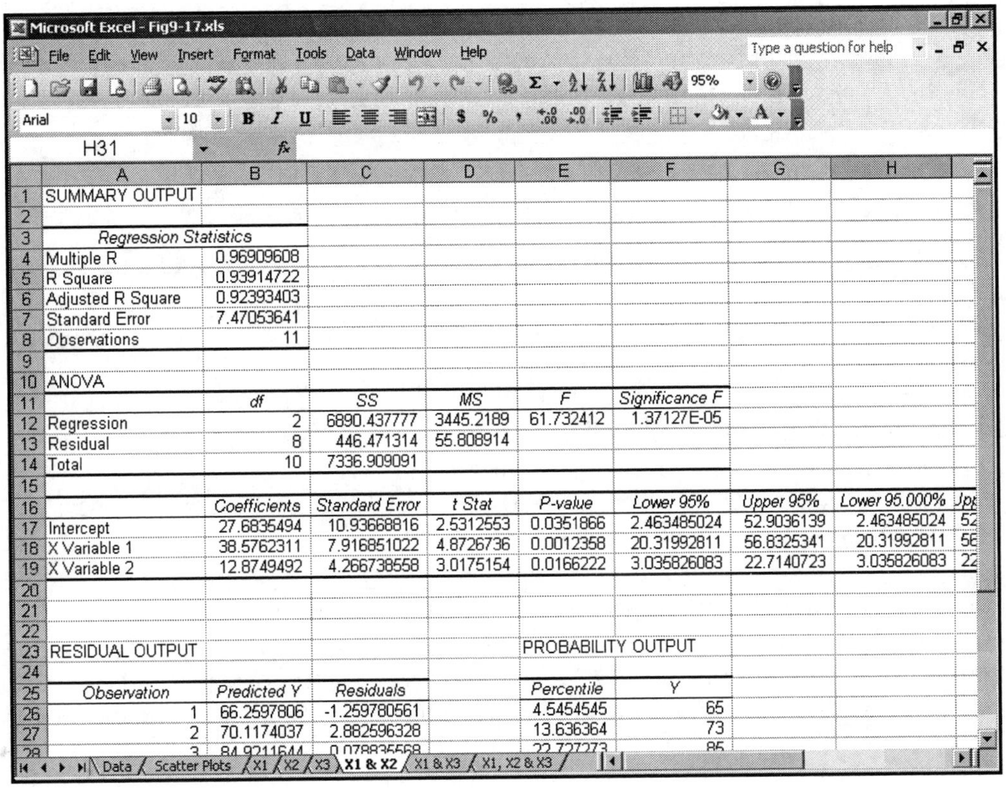

SUMMARY OUTPUT

Regression Statistics	
Multiple R	0.96909608
R Square	0.93914722
Adjusted R Square	0.92393403
Standard Error	7.47053641
Observations	11

ANOVA

	df	SS	MS	F	Significance F
Regression	2	6890.437777	3445.2189	61.732412	1.37127E-05
Residual	8	446.471314	55.808914		
Total	10	7336.909091			

	Coefficients	Standard Error	t Stat	P-value	Lower 95%	Upper 95%	Lower 95.000%	Upp
Intercept	27.6835494	10.93668816	2.5312553	0.0351866	2.463485024	52.9036139	2.463485024	52
X Variable 1	38.5762311	7.916851022	4.8726736	0.0012358	20.31992811	56.8325341	20.31992811	56
X Variable 2	12.8749492	4.266738558	3.0175154	0.0166222	3.035826083	22.7140723	3.035826083	22

RESIDUAL OUTPUT

Observation	Predicted Y	Residuals
1	66.2597806	-1.259780561
2	70.1174037	2.882596328

PROBABILITY OUTPUT

Percentile	Y
4.5454545	65
13.636364	73

FIGURE 9.21

Results of the multiple regression model using square footage and garage size as independent variables

X_1 (total square footage) and X_2 (garage size). After we click the OK button, Excel performs the appropriate calculations and displays the regression results shown in Figure 9.21.

Figure 9.21 lists *three* numbers in the Coefficients column. These numbers correspond to the parameter estimates b_0, b_1, and b_2. Note that the value listed for X Variable 1 is the coefficient for the first variable in the X Range (which, in some cases, might be X_2 or X_3, depending on how the data are arranged in the spreadsheet). The value for X Variable 2 corresponds to the second variable in the X-Range (which might be X_3 or X_1, depending on the arrangement of the data).

From the regression results in Figure 9.21, we know that when using X_1 (square footage) and X_2 (garage size) as independent variables, the estimated regression function is:

$$\hat{Y}_i = b_0 + b_1X_{1_i} + b_2X_{2_i} = 27.684 + 38.576X_{1_i} + 12.875X_{2_i} \tag{9.25}$$

Notice that adding the second independent variable caused the values of b_0 and b_1 to change from their earlier values shown in equation 9.22. Thus, the values assumed by the parameters in a regression model might vary depending on the number (and combination) of variables in the model.

We could obtain the values for the parameters in the second multiple regression model (in equation 9.24) in the same way. Note, however, that before issuing the Regression command again, we would need to rearrange the data in the spreadsheet so that the values for X_1 (total square footage) and X_3 (number of bedrooms) are located next to each other in one contiguous block. The regression tool in Excel (and in most other spreadsheet software packages) requires that the X-Range be represented by one contiguous block of cells.

FIGURE 9.22

Comparison of regression results for models with two independent variables versus the best model with one independent variable

Independent Variables in the Model	R^2	Adjusted-R^2	S_e	Parameter Estimates
X_1	0.870	0.855	10.299	$b_0 = 9.503$, $b_1 = 56.394$
X_1 and X_2	0.939	0.924	7.471	$b_0 = 27.684$, $b_1 = 38.576$, $b_2 = 12.875$
X_1 and X_3	0.877	0.847	10.609	$b_0 = 8.311$, $b_1 = 44.313$, $b_3 = 6.743$

Important Software Note

When using the regression tool, the values for the independent variables *must* be listed in *adjacent* columns in the spreadsheet and cannot be separated by any intervening columns. That is, the Input X-Range option in the Regression dialog box must always specify a contiguous block of numbers.

Figure 9.22 compares the regression results for the model in equation 9.24 and the results for the model in equation 9.23 versus the earlier results of the best simple linear regression model in equation 9.22, where X_1 was the only independent variable in the model.

These results indicate that when using X_1 (square footage) and X_3 (number of bedrooms) as independent variables, the estimated regression function is:

$$\hat{Y}_i = b_0 + b_1 X_{1_i} + b_3 X_{3_i} = 8.311 + 44.313 X_{1_i} + 6.743 X_{3_i} \qquad \textbf{9.26}$$

The appraiser was hoping that the inclusion of a second independent variable in the models in equation 9.23 and equation 9.24 might help to explain a significant portion of the remaining 13% of the variation in the dependent that was not accounted for by the simple linear regression function in equation 9.22. How can we tell if this happened?

9.13.3 INFLATING R^2

Figure 9.22 indicates that adding either X_2 or X_3 to the simple linear regression model caused the R^2 statistic to increase. This should not be surprising. As it turns out, the value of R^2 can never decrease as a result of adding an independent variable to a regression function. The reason for this is easy to see. From equation 9.10, recall that $R^2 = 1 - \text{ESS}/\text{TSS}$. Thus, the only way R^2 could decrease as the result of adding an independent variable (X_n) to the model would be if ESS *increased*. However, because the method of least squares attempts to minimize ESS, a new independent variable cannot cause ESS to increase because this variable simply could be ignored by setting $b_n = 0$. In other words, if adding the new independent variable does not help to reduce ESS, least squares regression simply would ignore the new variable.

When you add *any* independent variable to a regression function, the value of the R^2 statistic never can decrease, and usually will increase at least a little. Therefore, we can make the R^2 statistic arbitrarily large simply by including enough independent variables in the regression function—regardless of whether or not the new independent variables are related at all to the dependent variable. For example, the real estate appraiser probably could increase the value R^2 to some degree by including another independent variable in the model that represents the height of the mailbox at each house—which probably has little to do with the selling price of a house. This results in a model that overfits our data and might not generalize well to other data not included in the sample being analyzed.

9.13.4 THE ADJUSTED-R^2 STATISTIC

The value of the R^2 statistic can be inflated artificially by including independent variables in a regression function that have little or no logical connection with the dependent variable. Thus, another goodness-of-fit measure, known as the adjusted-R^2 statistic (denoted by R_a^2), has been suggested which accounts for the number of independent variables included in a regression model. The adjusted-R^2 statistic is defined as:

$$R_a^2 = 1 - \left(\frac{\text{ESS}}{\text{TSS}}\right)\left(\frac{n-1}{n-k-1}\right) \qquad \text{9.27}$$

where n represents the number of observations in the sample, and k represents the number of independent variables in the model. As variables are added to a regression model, the ratio of ESS to TSS in equation 9.27 will decrease (because ESS decreases and TSS remains constant), but the ratio of $n-1$ to $n-k-1$ will increase (because $n-1$ remains constant and $n-k-1$ decreases). Thus, if we add a variable to the model that does not reduce ESS enough to compensate for the increase in k, the adjusted-R^2 value will decrease.

The adjusted-R^2 value can be used as a rule of thumb to help us decide if an additional independent variable enhances the predictive ability of a model or if it simply inflates the R^2 statistic artificially. However, using the adjusted-R^2 statistic in this way is not foolproof and requires a good bit of judgment on the part of the person performing the analysis.

9.13.5 THE BEST MODEL WITH TWO INDEPENDENT VARIABLES

As shown in Figure 9.22, when X_2 (garage size) is introduced to the model, the adjusted-R^2 *increases* from 0.855 to 0.924. We can conclude from this increase that the addition of X_2 to the regression model helps to account for a significant portion of the remaining variation in Y that was not accounted for by X_1. On the other hand, when X_3 is introduced as an independent variable in the regression model, the adjusted-R^2 statistic in Figure 9.22 *decreases* (from 0.855 to 0.847). This indicates that adding this variable to the model does not help account for a significant portion of the remaining variation in Y if X_1 is already in the model. The best model with two independent variables is given in equation 9.25, which uses X_1 (total square footage) and X_2 (garage size) as predictors of selling price. According to the R^2 statistic in Figure 9.22, this model accounts for about 94% of the total variation in Y around its mean. This model leaves roughly 6% of the variation in Y unaccounted for.

9.13.6 MULTICOLLINEARITY

We should not be too surprised that no significant improvement was observed when X_3 (number of bedrooms) was added to the model containing X_1 (total square footage), because both of these variables represent similar factors. That is, the number of bedrooms in a house is closely related (or correlated) to the total square footage in the house. Thus, if we already have used total square footage to help explain variations in the selling prices of houses (as in the first regression function), adding information about the number of bedrooms is somewhat redundant. Our analysis confirms this.

The term **multicollinearity** is used to describe the situation when the independent variables in a regression model are correlated among themselves. Multicollinearity tends to increase the uncertainty associated with the parameters estimates (b_i) in a regression model and should be avoided whenever possible. Specialized procedures for detecting and correcting multicollinearity can be found in advanced texts on regression analysis.

9.13.7 THE MODEL WITH THREE INDEPENDENT VARIABLES

As a final test, the appraiser might want to see if X_3 (number of bedrooms) helps to explain a significant portion of the remaining 6% variation in Y that was not accounted for by the model using X_1 and X_2 as independent variables. This involves fitting the following multiple regression function to the data:

$$\hat{Y}_i = b_0 + b_1X_{1_i} + b_2X_{2_i} + b_3X_{3_i} \qquad \textbf{9.28}$$

Figure 9.23 shows the regression results for this model. The results of this model are also summarized for comparison purposes in Figure 9.24, along with the earlier results for the best model with one independent variable and the best model with two independent variables.

Figure 9.24 indicates that when X_3 is added to the model that contains X_1 and X_2, the R^2 statistic increases slightly (from 0.939 to 0.943). However, the adjusted-R^2 drops from

FIGURE 9.23

Results of regression model using all three independent variables

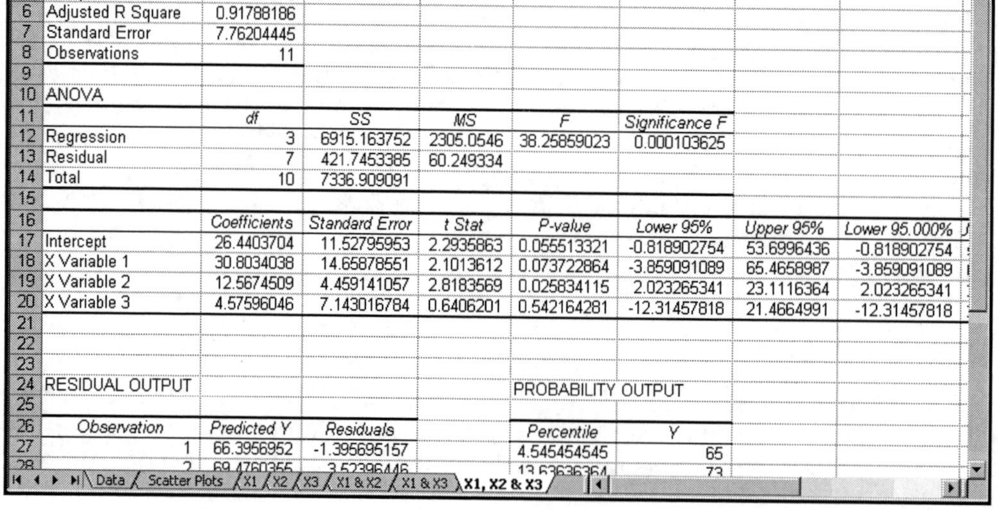

	A	B	C	D	E	F	G	H
1	SUMMARY OUTPUT							
2								
3	*Regression Statistics*							
4	Multiple R	0.9708333						
5	R Square	0.9425173						
6	Adjusted R Square	0.91788186						
7	Standard Error	7.76204445						
8	Observations	11						
9								
10	ANOVA							
11		*df*	*SS*	*MS*	*F*	*Significance F*		
12	Regression	3	6915.163752	2305.0546	38.25859023	0.000103625		
13	Residual	7	421.7453385	60.249334				
14	Total	10	7336.909091					
15								
16		*Coefficients*	*Standard Error*	*t Stat*	*P-value*	*Lower 95%*	*Upper 95%*	*Lower 95.000%*
17	Intercept	26.4403704	11.52795953	2.2935863	0.055513321	-0.818902754	53.6996436	-0.818902754
18	X Variable 1	30.8034038	14.65878551	2.1013612	0.073722864	-3.859091089	65.4658987	-3.859091089
19	X Variable 2	12.5674509	4.459141057	2.8183569	0.025834115	2.023265341	23.1116364	2.023265341
20	X Variable 3	4.57596046	7.143016784	0.6406201	0.542164281	-12.31457818	21.4664991	-12.31457818
21								
22								
23								
24	RESIDUAL OUTPUT				PROBABILITY OUTPUT			
25								
26	*Observation*	*Predicted Y*	*Residuals*		*Percentile*	*Y*		
27	1	66.3956952	-1.395695157		4.545454545	65		
28	2	69.4760355	3.52396446		13.63636364	73		

FIGURE 9.24

Comparison of regression results for the model with three independent variables versus the best models with one and two independent variables

Independent Variables in the Model	R^2	Adjusted-R^2	S_e	Parameter Estimates
X_1	0.870	0.855	10.299	$b_0 = 9.503$, $b_1 = 56.394$
X_1 and X_2	0.939	0.924	7.471	$b_0 = 27.684$, $b_1 = 38.576$, $b_2 = 12.875$
X_1, X_2, and X_3	0.943	0.918	7.762	$b_0 = 26.440$, $b_1 = 30.803$, $b_2 = 12.567$, $b_3 = 4.576$

0.924 to 0.918. Thus, it does not appear that adding information about X_3 (number of bedrooms) helps to explain selling prices in any significant way when X_1 (total square footage) and X_2 (size of garage) are already in the model.

It is also interesting to note that the best model with two independent variables also has the smallest standard error S_e. This means that the confidence intervals around any predictions made with this model will be narrower (or more precise) than those of the other models. It can be shown that the model with the highest adjusted-R^2 always has the smallest standard error. For this reason, the adjusted-R^2 statistic is sometimes the sole criterion used to select which multiple regression model to use in a given problem. However, other procedures for selecting regression models exist and are discussed in advanced texts on regression analysis.

9.14 Making Predictions

On the basis of this analysis, the appraiser most likely would choose to use the estimated regression model in equation 9.25, which includes X_1 (total square footage) and X_2 (garage size) as independent variables. For a house with X_{1_i} total square feet and space for X_{2_i} cars in its garage, the estimated selling price $\hat{Y}_i$ is:

$$\hat{Y}_i = 27.684 + 38.576X_{1_i} + 12.875X_{2_i}$$

For example, the expected selling price (or average market value) of a house with 2,100 square feet and a two-car garage is estimated as:

$$\hat{Y}_i = 27.684 + 38.576 \times 2.1 + 12.875 \times 2 = 134.444$$

or approximately \$134,444. Note that in making this prediction, we expressed the square footage of the house in the same units in which X_1 (total square footage variable) was expressed in the sample used to estimate the model. This should be done for all independent variables when making predictions.

The standard error of the estimation errors for this model is 7.471. Therefore, we should not be surprised to see prices for houses with 2,100 square feet and two-car garages varying within roughly ±2 standard errors (or ±\$14,942) of our estimate. That is, we expect prices on this type of house to be as low as \$119,502 or as high as \$149,386 depending on other factors not included in our analysis (such as age or condition of the roof, presence of a swimming pool, and so on).

As demonstrated earlier in the case of simple linear regression models, more accurate techniques exist for constructing prediction intervals using multiple regression models. In the case of a multiple regression model, the techniques used to construct prediction intervals require a basic knowledge of matrix algebra, which is not assumed in this text. The interested reader should consult advanced texts on multiple regression analysis for a description of how to construct more accurate prediction intervals using multiple regression models. Keep in mind that the simple rule of thumb described earlier gives an underestimated (narrower) approximation of the more accurate prediction interval.

9.15 Binary Independent Variables

As just mentioned, the appraiser might want to include other independent variables in her analysis. Some of these, such as age of the roof, could be measured numerically and be included as an independent variable. But how would we create variables to represent the presence of a swimming pool or the condition of the roof?

The presence of a swimming pool can be included in the analysis with a binary independent variable coded as:

$$X_{p_i} = \begin{cases} 1, \text{ if house } i \text{ has a pool} \\ 0, \text{ otherwise} \end{cases}$$

The condition of the roof could also be modeled with binary variables. Here, however, we might need more than one binary variable to model all the possible conditions. If some qualitative variable can assume p possible values, we need $p - 1$ binary variables to model the possible outcomes. For example, suppose that the condition of the roof could be rated as good, average, or poor. There are three possible values for the variable representing the condition of the roof; therefore, we need two binary variables to model these outcomes. These binary variables are coded as:

$$X_{r_i} = \begin{cases} 1, \text{ if the roof of house } i \text{ is in good condition} \\ 0, \text{ otherwise} \end{cases}$$

$$X_{r+1_i} = \begin{cases} 1, \text{ if the roof of house } i \text{ is in average condition} \\ 0, \text{ otherwise} \end{cases}$$

It might appear that we left out a coding for a roof in poor condition. However, note that this condition is implied when $X_{r_i} = 0$ and $X_{r+1_i} = 0$. That is, if the roof is *not* in good condition (as implied by $X_{r_i} = 0$) *and* the roof is *not* in average condition (as implied by $X_{r+1_i} = 0$), then the roof must be in poor condition. Thus, we need only two binary variables to represent three possible roof conditions. For reasons that go beyond the scope of this text, the computer could not perform the least squares calculations if we included a third binary variable to indicate houses with roofs in poor condition. Also, it would be inappropriate to model the condition of the roof with a single variable coded as 1 for good, 2 for average, and 3 for poor because this implies that the average condition is twice as bad as the good condition, and that the poor condition is three times as bad as the good condition and 1.5 times as bad as the average condition.

As this example illustrates, we can use binary variables as independent variables in regression analysis to model a variety of conditions that are likely to occur. In each case, the binary variables would be placed in the X-Range of the spreadsheet and appropriate b_i values would be calculated by the regression tool.

9.16 Statistical Tests for the Population Parameters

Statistical tests for the population parameters in a multiple regression model are performed in much the same way as for the simple regression model. As described earlier, the F-statistic tests whether or not *all* of the β_i for *all* of the independent variables are *all* simultaneously equal to 0 ($\beta_1 = \beta_2 = \cdots = \beta_k = 0$). The value in the regression results labeled Significance of F indicates the probability of this condition being true for the data under consideration.

In the case of a multiple regression model, the t-statistics for each independent variable require a slightly different interpretation due to the possible presence of multicollinearity. Each t-statistic can be used to test whether or not the associated population parameter $\beta_i = 0$ *given all the other independent variables in the model*. For example, consider the t-statistics and p-values associated with the variable X_1 shown in Figures 9.21 and 9.23. The p-value for X_1 in cell E18 of Figure 9.21 indicates only a 0.123% chance that $\beta_1 = 0$ when X_2 is the only other independent variable in the model. The p-value for X_1 in cell E18 of Figure 9.23 indicates a 7.37% chance that $\beta_1 = 0$ when X_2 *and* X_3 are also in the model. This illustrates one of the potential problems caused by multicollinearity. Because X_1 and X_3 are highly correlated, it is less certain that X_1 plays a significant (nonzero) role in accounting for the behavior of the dependent variable Y when X_3 is also in the model.

In Figure 9.23, the p-value associated with X_3 indicates a 54.2% chance that $\beta_3 = 0$ given the other variables in the model. Thus, if we had started our analysis by including all three independent variables in the model, the p-value for X_3 in Figure 9.23 suggests that it might be wise to drop X_3 from the model because there is a fairly good chance that it contributes 0 ($\beta_3 = 0$) to explaining the behavior of the dependent variable, given the other variables in the model. In this case, if we drop X_3 from the model, we end up with the same model selected using the adjusted-R^2 criterion.

The statistical tests considered here are valid only when the underlying errors around the regression function are normally distributed random variables with constant means and variances. The graphical diagnostics described earlier apply equally to the case of multiple regression. However, the various statistics presented give reasonably accurate results if the assumptions about the distribution of the error terms are not violated too seriously. Furthermore, the R^2 and adjusted-R^2 statistics are purely descriptive in nature and do not depend in any way on the assumptions about the distribution of the error terms.

9.17 Polynomial Regression

When introducing the multiple linear regression function in equation 9.18, we noted that this type of model might be appropriate when the independent variables vary in a linear fashion with the dependent variable. Business problems exist where there is *not* a linear relationship between the dependent and independent variables. For example, suppose that the real estate appraiser in our earlier example had collected the data in Figure 9.25 (and in the file Fig9-25.xls on your data disk) showing the total square footage and selling price for a number of houses. Figure 9.26 shows a scatter plot of these data.

Figure 9.26 indicates a very strong relationship between total square footage and the selling price of the houses in this sample. However, this relationship is *not* linear. Rather, more of a *curvilinear* relationship exists between these variables. Does this mean that linear regression analysis cannot be used with these data? Not at all.

The data in Figure 9.25 (plotted in Figure 9.26) indicate a *quadratic* relationship between square footage and selling price. So, to account adequately for the variation in the selling price of houses, we need to use the following type of regression function:

$$\hat{Y}_i = b_0 + b_1 X_{1_i} + b_2 X_{1_i}^2 \qquad\qquad \textbf{9.29}$$

where $\hat{Y}_i$ represents the estimated selling price of the ith house in our sample, and X_{1_i} represents the total square footage in the house. Notice that the second independent variable in equation 9.29 is the first independent variable squared (X_1^2).

FIGURE 9.25

Data for nonlinear regression example

Obs	Sq. Feet (in 1000s)	Price (in $1000s)
1	1.000	$69
2	1.100	$73
3	1.200	$76
4	1.400	$78
5	1.600	$86
6	1.800	$97
7	1.900	$103
8	1.900	$108
9	2.100	$129
10	2.100	$137
11	2.200	$160

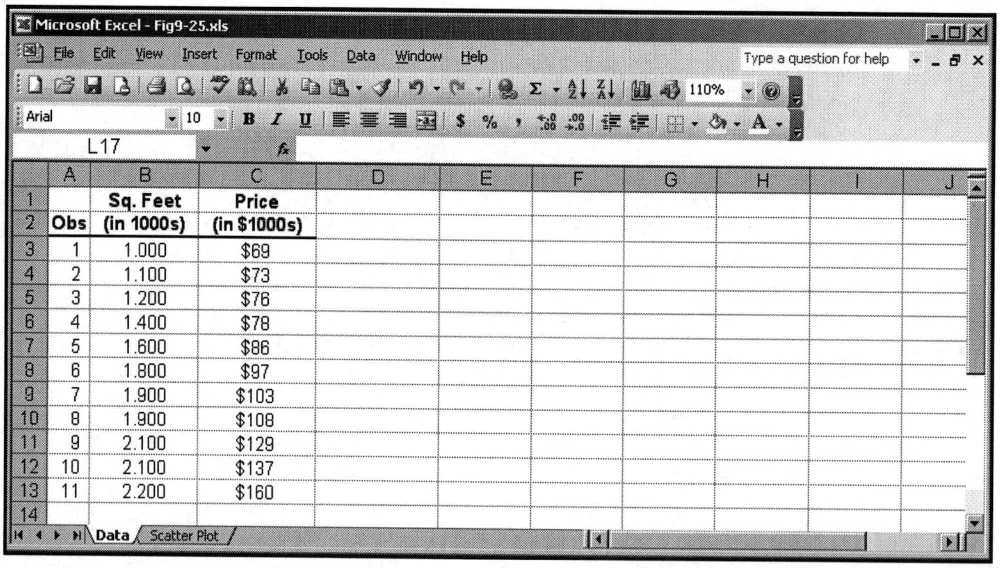

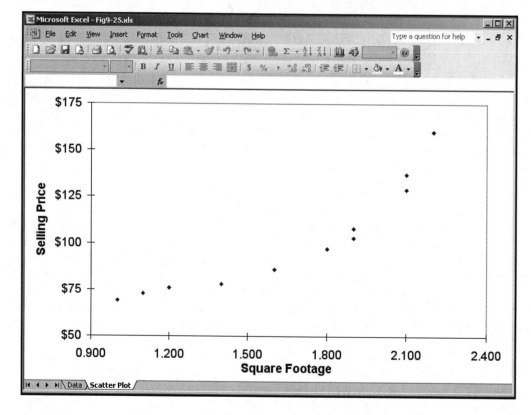

FIGURE 9.26

Scatter plot of data showing relationship between total square footage and selling price

9.17.1 EXPRESSING NONLINEAR RELATIONSHIPS USING LINEAR MODELS

Equation 9.29 is not a linear function because it contains the nonlinear variable X_1^2. It *is* linear with respect to the parameters that the computer must estimate—namely, b_0, b_1, and b_2. That is, none of the parameters in the regression function appear as an exponent or are multiplied together. Thus, we can use least squares regression to estimate the optimal values for b_0, b_1, and b_2. Note that if we define a new independent variable as $X_{2_i} = X_{1_i}^2$, then the regression function in equation 9.29 is equivalent to:

$$\hat{Y}_i = b_0 + b_1 X_{1_i} + b_2 X_{2_i} \qquad \textbf{9.30}$$

Equation 9.30 is equivalent to the multiple linear regression function in equation 9.29. As long as a regression function is linear with respect to its parameters, we can use Excel's regression analysis tool to find the least squares estimates for the parameters.

To fit the regression function in equation 9.30 to our data, we must create a second independent variable to represent the values of X_{2_i}, as shown in Figure 9.27.

Because the X-Range for the Regression command must be represented as one contiguous block, we inserted a new column between the square footage and selling price columns and placed the values of X_{2_i} in this column. Note that $X_{2_i} = X_{1_i}^2$ in column C in Figure 9.27:

Formula for cell C3:   =B3^2

(Copy to C4 through C13.)

The regression results are generated with a Y-Range of D3:D13 and an X-Range of B3:C13. Figure 9.28 shows the regression results.

In Figure 9.28, the estimated regression function is represented by:

$$\hat{Y}_i = b_0 + b_1 X_{1_i} + b_2 X_{2_i} = 194.9714 - 203.3812 X_{1_i} + 83.4063 X_{2_i} \qquad \textbf{9.31}$$

According to the R^2 statistic, this function accounts for 97.0% of the total variation in selling prices, so we expect that this function fits our data well. We can verify this by plotting the prices that would be estimated by the regression function in equation 9.31 for each observation in our sample against the actual selling prices.

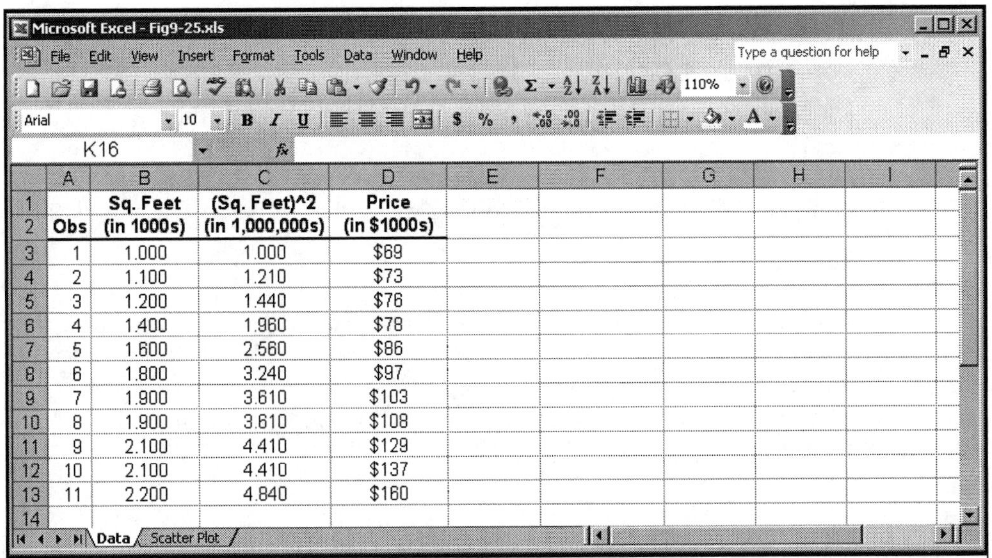

FIGURE 9.27

Modification of data to include squared independent variable

	Sq. Feet (in 1000s)	(Sq. Feet)^2 (in 1,000,000s)	Price (in $1000s)
Obs			
1	1.000	1.000	$69
2	1.100	1.210	$73
3	1.200	1.440	$76
4	1.400	1.960	$78
5	1.600	2.560	$86
6	1.800	3.240	$97
7	1.900	3.610	$103
8	1.900	3.610	$108
9	2.100	4.410	$129
10	2.100	4.410	$137
11	2.200	4.840	$160

Key Cell Formulas

Cell	Formula	Copied to
C3	=B3^2	C4:C13

FIGURE 9.28

Regression results for nonlinear example problem

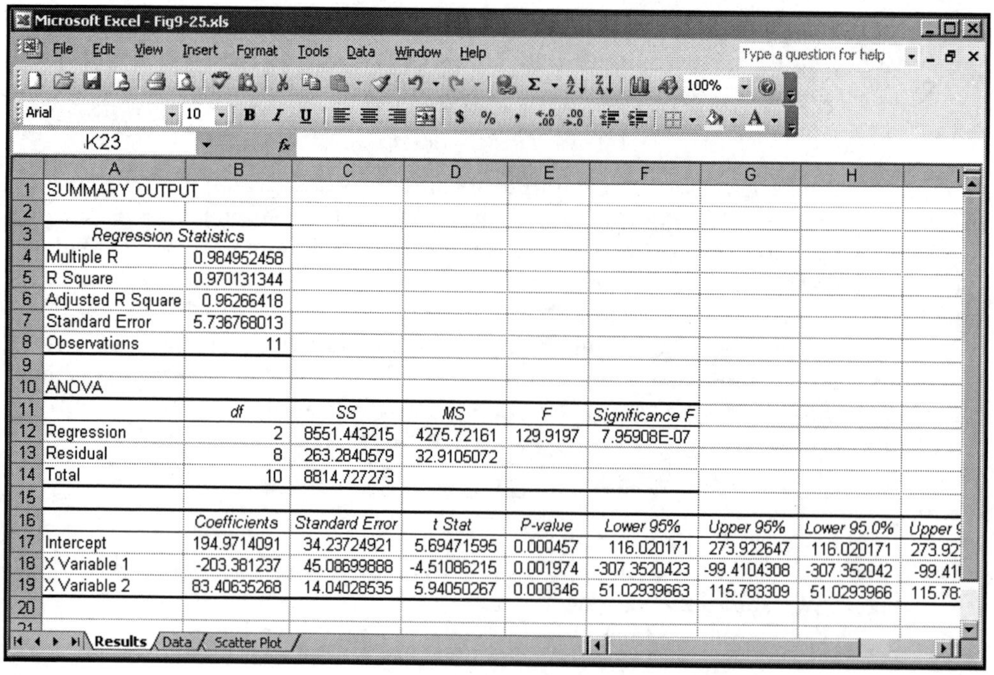

Microsoft Excel - Fig9-25.xls

	A	B	C	D	E	F	G	H	I
1	SUMMARY OUTPUT								
2									
3	*Regression Statistics*								
4	Multiple R	0.984952458							
5	R Square	0.970131344							
6	Adjusted R Square	0.96266418							
7	Standard Error	5.736768013							
8	Observations	11							
9									
10	ANOVA								
11		*df*	*SS*	*MS*	*F*	*Significance F*			
12	Regression	2	8551.443215	4275.72161	129.9197	7.95908E-07			
13	Residual	8	263.2840579	32.9105072					
14	Total	10	8814.727273						
15									
16		*Coefficients*	*Standard Error*	*t Stat*	*P-value*	*Lower 95%*	*Upper 95%*	*Lower 95.0%*	*Upper 9*
17	Intercept	194.9714091	34.23724921	5.69471595	0.000457	116.020171	273.922647	116.020171	273.92
18	X Variable 1	-203.381237	45.08699888	-4.51086215	0.001974	-307.3520423	-99.4104308	-307.352042	-99.41
19	X Variable 2	83.40635268	14.04028535	5.94050267	0.000346	51.02939663	115.783309	51.0293966	115.78
20									

Results / Data / Scatter Plot

To calculate the estimated selling prices, we applied the formula in equation 9.31 to each observation in the sample, as shown in Figure 9.29 where the following formula was entered in cell E3, then copied to cells E4 through E20:

Formula for cell E3: =TREND($D$3:$D$13,$B$3:$C$13,B3:C3)
(Copy to E4 through E13.)

Figure 9.30 shows a curve representing the estimated prices calculated in column E of Figure 9.29. This curve was added to our previous scatter plot as follows:

1. Right-click on any of the data points in the scatter plot to select the series of data.
2. Click Add Trendline.
3. On the Type card, click Polynomial and use an Order value of 2.
4. On the Options card, select Display Equation on Chart and Display R-squared Value on Chart.
5. Click OK.

This graph indicates that our regression model accounts for the nonlinear, quadratic relationship between the square footage and selling price of a house in a reasonably accurate manner.

Figure 9.31 shows the result obtained by fitting a third-order polynomial model to our data of the form:

$$\hat{Y}_i = b_0 + b_1X_{1_i} + b_2X_{1_i}^2 + b_3X_{1_i}^3 \qquad \textbf{9.32}$$

This model appears to provide an even better fit than the model shown in Figure 9.30. As you might imagine, we could continue to add higher order terms to the model and further increase the value of the R^2 statistic. Here again, the adjusted-R^2 statistic could help us select a model that provides a good fit to our data without overfitting the data.

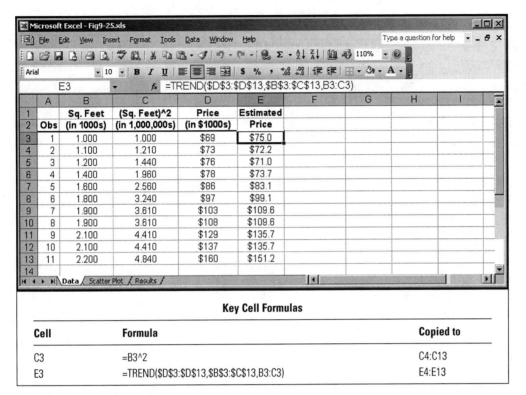

FIGURE 9.29

Estimated selling prices using a second order polynomial model

Key Cell Formulas

Cell	Formula	Copied to
C3	=B3^2	C4:C13
E3	=TREND($D$3:$D$13,$B$3:$C$13,B3:C3)	E4:E13

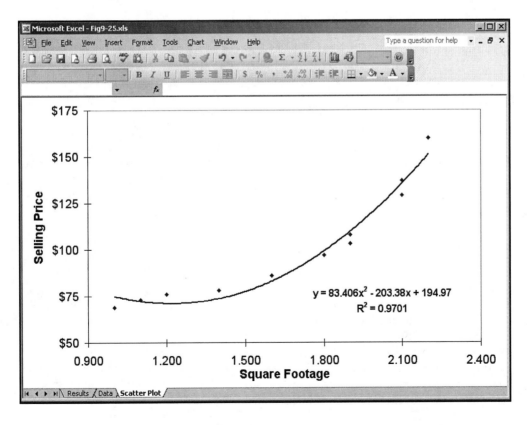

FIGURE 9.30

Plot of estimated regression function versus actual data

FIGURE 9.31

Plot of estimated regression function using a third order polynomial model

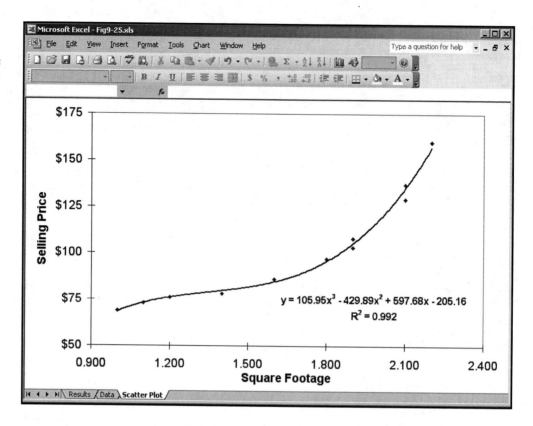

9.17.2 SUMMARY OF NONLINEAR REGRESSION

This brief example of a polynomial regression problem highlights the fact that regression analysis can be used not only in fitting straight lines or hyperplanes to linear data, but also in fitting other types of curved surfaces to nonlinear data. An in-depth discussion of nonlinear regression is beyond the intended scope of this book, but a wealth of information is available on this topic in numerous texts devoted solely to regression analysis.

This example should help you appreciate the importance of preparing scatter plots of each independent variable against the dependent variable in a regression problem to see if the relationship between the variables is linear or nonlinear. Relatively simple nonlinear relationships, such as the one described in the previous example, often can be accounted for by including squared or cubed terms in the model. In more complicated cases, sophisticated transformations of the dependent or independent variables might be required.

9.18 Summary

Regression analysis is a statistical technique that can be used to identify and analyze the relationship between one or more independent variables and a continuous dependent variable. This chapter presented an overview of some key issues involved in performing regression analysis and demonstrated some of the tools and methods available in Excel to assist managers in performing regression analysis.

The goal in regression analysis is to identify a function of the independent variables that adequately accounts for the behavior of the dependent variable. The method of least squares provides a way to determine the best values for the parameters in a regression model for a given sample of data. After identifying such a function, it can be used to predict what value the dependent variable will assume given specific values for the independent variables. Various statistical techniques are available for evaluating how well a given regression function fits a data set and for determining which independent variables are most helpful in explaining the behavior of the dependent variable. Although regression functions can assume a variety of forms, this chapter focused on linear regression models where a linear combination of the independent variables is used to model the dependent variable. Simple transformations of the independent variables can allow this type of model to fit both linear and nonlinear data sets.

9.19 References

Montgomery D. and E. Peck. *Introduction to Linear Regression Analysis.* New York: Wiley, 1991.
Neter, J., W. Wasserman, and M. Kutner. *Applied Linear Statistical Models.* Homewood, IL: Irwin, 1996.
Younger, M. *A First Course in Linear Regression.* Boston: Duxbury Press, 1985.

THE WORLD OF MANAGEMENT SCIENCE

Better Predictions Create Cost Savings for Ohio National Bank

The Ohio National Bank in Columbus must process checks for clearing in a timely manner, to minimize float. This had been difficult because of wide and seemingly unpredictable variations in the volume of checks received.

As checks pass through the processing center, they are encoded with the dollar amount in magnetic ink at the bottom of the check. This operation requires a staff of clerks, whose work schedules must be planned so that staffing is adequate during peak times. Because the bank could not accurately predict these peaks, deadlines often were missed and the clerks often were required to work overtime.

The variations in check volume seemed to be caused by changes in business activity brought about by the calendar—that is, volume was influenced by certain months, days of the week, days of the month, and proximity to certain holidays. A linear regression model was developed to predict staffing needs using a set of binary (dummy) independent variables representing these calendar effects. The regression study was very successful. The resulting model had a coefficient of determination (R^2) of 0.94 and a mean absolute percentage error of 6%. The bank then used these predictions as input to an LP shift-scheduling model that minimized the number of clerks needed to cover the predicted check volumes.

The planning process required data on check volumes and productivity estimates from the line supervisors in the encoding department. Initial reluctance of the supervisors to supply this information presented an obstacle to implementing the system. Eventually, this was overcome by taking time to explain the reasons for the data collection to the supervisors.

The new system provides estimated savings of $700,000 in float costs and $300,000 in labor costs. The close-out time of 10 pm is now met 98% of the time; previously, it was rarely met. Management has performed sensitivity analysis with the model to study the effects of productivity improvements associated with employing experienced full-time encoding clerks instead of part-time clerks.

Source: Krajewski, L. J. and L. P. Ritzman, "Shift Scheduling in Banking Operations: A Case Application." *Interfaces*, vol. 10, no. 2, April 1980, pp. 1–6.

Questions and Problems

1. Members of the Roanoke Health and Fitness Club pay an annual membership fee of $250 plus $3 each time they use the facility. Let X denote the number of times a person visits the club during the year. Let Y denote the total annual cost for membership in the club.
   a. What is the mathematical relationship between X and Y?
   b. Is this a functional or statistical relationship? Explain your answer.

2. In comparing two different regression models that were developed using the same data, we might say that the model with the higher R^2 value will provide the most accurate predictions. Is this true? Why or why not?

3. Show how R_a^2 and S_e are related algebraically (identify the function $f(\cdot)$ such that $R_a^2 = f(S_e)$).

4. Least squares regression finds the estimated values for the parameters in a regression model to minimize ESS $= \sum_{i=1}^{n} (Y_i - \hat{Y}_i)^2$. Why is it necessary to square the estimation errors? What problem might be encountered if we attempt to minimize just the sum of the estimation errors?

5. Suppose that you are interested in creating a prediction interval for Y at a particular value of X_1 (denoted by X_{1_h}) using a simple linear regression model, and that data has not yet been collected. For a given sample size n, how you would attempt to collect the sample data to make the most accurate prediction? (*Hint:* Consider equation 9.14.)

6. An accounting firm that specializes in auditing mining companies collected the data found in the file Dat9-6.xls on your data disk describing the long-term assets and long-term debt of its 12 clients.
   a. Prepare a scatter plot of the data. Does there appear to be a linear relationship between these variables?
   b. Develop a simple linear regression model that can be used to predict long-term debt from long-term assets. What is the estimated regression equation?
   c. Interpret the value of R^2.
   d. Suppose that the accounting firm has a client with total assets of $50,000,000. Construct an approximate 95% confidence interval for the amount of long-term debt that the firm expects this client to have.

7. The IRS wants to develop a method for detecting whether or not individuals have overstated their deductions for charitable contributions on their tax returns. To assist in this effort, the IRS supplied data found in the file Dat9-7.xls on your data disk listing the adjusted gross income (AGI) and charitable contributions for 11 taxpayers whose returns were audited and found to be correct.
   a. Prepare a scatter plot of the data. Does there appear to be a linear relationship between these variables?
   b. Develop a simple linear regression model that can be used to predict the level of charitable contributions from a return's AGI. What is the estimated regression equation?
   c. Interpret the value of R^2.
   d. How might the IRS use the regression results to identify returns with unusually high charitable contributions?

8. Roger Gallagher owns a used car lot that deals solely in used Corvettes. He wants to develop a regression model to help predict the price he can expect to receive for the cars he owns. He collected the data found in the file Dat9-8.xls on your data disk describing the mileage, model year, presence of a T-top, and selling price of a number of cars he has sold in recent months. Let Y represent the selling price, X_1 the mileage, X_2 the model year, and X_3 the presence (or absence) of a T-top.

a. If Roger wants to use a simple linear regression function to estimate the selling price of a car, which X variable do you recommend that he use?

b. Determine the parameter estimates for the regression function represented by:

$$\hat{Y}_i = b_0 + b_1 X_{1_i} + b_2 X_{2_i}$$

What is the estimated regression function? Does X_2 help to explain the selling price of the cars if X_1 is also in the model? What might be the reason for this?

c. Set up a binary variable (X_{3_i}) to indicate whether or not each car in the sample has a T-top. Determine the parameter estimates for the regression function represented by:

$$\hat{Y}_i = b_0 + b_1 X_{1_i} + b_3 X_{3_i}$$

Does X_3 help to explain the selling price of the cars if X_1 is also in the model? Explain.

d. According to the previous model, on average, how much does a T-top add to the value of a car?

e. Determine the parameter estimates for the regression function represented by:

$$\hat{Y}_i = b_0 + b_1 X_{1_i} + b_2 X_{2_i} + b_3 X_{3_i}$$

What is the estimated regression function?

f. Of all the regression functions considered here, which do you recommend that Roger use?

9. Refer to question 8. Prepare scatter plots of the values of X_1 and X_2 against Y.

a. Do these relationships seem to be linear or nonlinear?

b. Determine the parameter estimates for the regression function represented by:

$$\hat{Y}_i = b_0 + b_1 X_{1_i} + b_2 X_{2_i} + b_3 X_{3_i} + b_4 X_{4_i}$$

where $X_{4_i} = X_{2_i}^2$. What is the estimated regression function?

c. Consider the p-values for each β_i in this model. Do these values indicate that any of the independent variables should be dropped from the model?

10. Golden Years Easy Retirement Homes owns several adult care facilities throughout the southeast United States. A budget analyst for Golden Years has collected the data found in the file Dat9-10.xls on your data disk describing for each facility: the number of beds (X_1), the annual number of medical in-patient days (X_2), the total annual patient days (X_3), and whether or not the facility is in a rural location (X_4). The analyst would like to build a multiple regression model to estimate the annual nursing salaries (Y) that should be expected for each facility.

a. Prepare three scatter plots showing the relationship between the nursing salaries and each of the independent variables. What sort of relationship does each plot suggest?

b. If the budget analyst wanted to build a regression model using only one independent variable to predict the nursing salaries, what variable should be used?

c. If the budget analyst wanted to build a regression model using only two independent variables to predict the nursing salaries, what variables should be used?

d. If the budget analyst wanted to build a regression model using three independent variables to predict the nursing salaries, what variables should be used?

e. What set of independent variables results in the highest value for the adjusted R^2 statistic?

f. Suppose the personnel director chooses to use the regression function with all independent variables X_1, X_2 and X_3. What is the estimated regression function?

g. In your spreadsheet, calculate an estimated annual nursing salary for each facility using the regression function identified in part f. Based on this analysis which facilities, if any, should the budget analyst be concerned about? Explain your answer.

11. The O-rings in the booster rockets on the space shuttle are designed to expand when heated to seal different chambers of the rocket so that solid rocket fuel is not ignited prematurely. According to engineering specifications, the O-rings expand by some amount, say at least 5%, to ensure a safe launch. Hypothetical data on the amount of O-ring expansion and the atmospheric temperature in Fahrenheit at the time of several different launches are given in the file Dat9-11.xls on your data disk.

    a. Prepare a scatter plot of the data. Does there appear to be a linear relationship between these variables?
    b. Obtain a simple linear regression model to estimate the amount of O-ring expansion as a function of atmospheric temperature. What is the estimated regression function?
    c. Interpret the R^2 statistic for the model you obtained.
    d. Suppose that NASA officials are considering launching a space shuttle when the temperature is 29 degrees. What amount of O-ring expansion should they expect at this temperature, according to your model?
    e. On the basis of your analysis of these data, would you recommend that the shuttle be launched if the temperature is 29 degrees? Why or why not?

12. An analyst for Phidelity Investments wants to develop a regression model to predict the annual rate of return for a stock based on the price-earnings (PE) ratio of the stock and a measure of the stock's risk. The data found in the file Dat9-12.xls were collected for a random sample of stocks.

    a. Prepare scatter plots for each independent variable versus the dependent variable. What type of model do these scatter plots suggest might be appropriate for the data?
    b. Let Y = Return, X_1 = PE Ratio, and X_2 = Risk. Obtain the regression results for the following regression model:

    $$\hat{Y}_i = b_0 + b_1 X_{1_i} + b_2 X_{2_i}$$

    Interpret the value of R^2 for this model.
    c. Obtain the regression results for the following regression model:

    $$\hat{Y}_i = b_0 + b_1 X_{1_i} + b_2 X_{2_i} + b_3 X_{3_i} + b_4 X_{4_i}$$

    where $X_{3_i} = X_{1_i}^2$ and $X_{4_i} = X_{2_i}^2$. Interpret the value of R^2 for this model.
    d. Which of the previous two models would you recommend that the analyst use?

13. Oriented Strand Board (OSB) is manufactured by gluing woodchips together to form panels. Several panels are then bonded together to form a board. One of the factors influencing the strength of the final board is the amount of glue used in the production process. An OSB manufacturer conducted a test to determine the breaking point of a board based on the amount of glue used in the production process. In each test, a board was manufactured using a given amount of glue. Weight was then applied to determine the point at which the board would fail (or break). This test was performed 27 times using various amounts of glue. The data obtained from this testing may be found in the file Dat9-13.xls on your data disk.

    a. Prepare a scatter plot of this data.
    b. What type of regression function would you use to fit this data?

   c. Estimate the parameters of the regression function. What is the estimated regression function?

   d. Interpret the value of the R^2 statistic.

   e. Suppose the company wants to manufacture boards that will withstand up to 110 lbs. of pressure per square inch. How much glue should they use?

14. When interest rates decline, Patriot Bank has found that they get inundated with requests to refinance home mortgages. To better plan its staffing needs in the mortgage processing area of its operations, Patriot wants to develop a regression model to help predict the total number of mortgage applications (Y) each month as a function of the prime interest rate (X_1). The bank collected the data shown in the file Dat9-14.xls on your data disk representing the average prime interest rate and total number of mortgage applications in 20 different months.

   a. Prepare a scatter plot of these data.

   b. Fit the following regression model to the data:

$$\hat{Y}_i = b_0 + b_1 X_{1_i}$$

   Plot the number of monthly mortgage applications that are estimated by this model along with the actual values in the sample. How well does this model fit the data?

   c. Using the previous model, develop a 95% prediction interval for the number of mortgage applications Patriot could expect to receive in a month in which the interest rate is 6%. Interpret this interval.

   d. Fit the following regression model to the data:

$$\hat{Y}_i = b_0 + b_1 X_{1_i} + b_2 X_{2_i}$$

   where $X_{2_i} = X_{1_i}^2$. Plot the number of monthly mortgage applications that are estimated by this model along with the actual values in the sample. How well does this model fit the data?

   e. Using the previous model, develop a 95% prediction interval for the number of mortgage applications that Patriot could expect to receive in a month in which the interest rate is 6%. Interpret this interval.

   f. Which model would you suggest that Patriot Bank use, and why?

15. Creative Confectioners is planning to introduce a new brownie. A small-scale "taste test" was conducted to assess consumers' preferences (Y) with regard to moisture content (X_1) and sweetness (X_2). Data from the taste test may be found in the file Dat9-15.xls on your data disk.

   a. Prepare a scatter plot of moisture content versus preference. What type of relationship does your plot suggest?

   b. Prepare a scatter plot of sweetness versus preference. What type of relationship does your plot suggest?

   c. Estimate the parameters for the following regression function:

$$\hat{Y}_i = b_0 + b_1 X_{1_i} + b_2 X_{1_i}^2 + b_3 X_{2_i} + b_4 X_{2_i}^2$$

   What is the estimated regression function?

   d. Using the estimated regression function in part c, what is the expected preference rating of a brownie recipe with a moisture content of 7 and a sweetness rating of 9.5?

16. AutoReports is a consumer magazine that reports on the cost of maintaining various types of automobiles. The magazine collected the data found in the file Dat9-16.xls on your data disk describing the annual maintenance cost of a certain type of luxury imported automobile along with the age of the car (in years).

a. Prepare a scatter plot of these data.
b. Let Y = Maintenance Cost and X = Age. Fit the following regression model to the data:

$$\hat{Y}_i = b_0 + b_1 X_{1_i}$$

Plot the maintenance costs that are estimated by this model along with the actual costs in the sample. How well does this model fit the data?

c. Fit the following regression model to the data:

$$\hat{Y}_i = b_0 + b_1 X_{1_i} + b_2 X_{2_i}$$

where $X_{2_i} = X_{1_i}^2$. Plot the maintenance costs that are estimated by this model along with the actual costs in the sample. How well does this model fit the data?

d. Fit the following regression model to this data:

$$\hat{Y}_i = b_0 + b_1 X_{1_i} + b_2 X_{2_i} + b_3 X_{3_i}$$

where $X_{2_i} = X_{1_i}^2$ and $X_{3_i} = X_{1_i}^3$. Plot the maintenance costs that are estimated by this model along with the actual costs in the sample. How well does this model fit the data?

17. Duque Power Company wants to develop a regression model to help predict its daily peak power demand. This prediction is useful in determining how much generating capacity needs to be available (or purchased from competitors) on a daily basis. The daily peak power demand is influenced primarily by the weather and the day of the week. The file Dat9-17.xls on your data disk contains data summarizing Duque's daily peak demand and maximum daily temperature during the month of July last year.

a. Build a simple linear regression model to predict peak power demand using maximum daily temperature. What is the estimated regression equation?
b. Prepare a line chart plotting the actual peak demand data against the values predicted by this regression equation. How well does the model fit the data?
c. Interpret the R^2 statistic for this model.
d. Build a multiple linear regression model to predict peak power demand using maximum daily temperature and the day of the week as independent variables. (Note: This model will have seven independent variables.) What is the estimated regression equation?
e. Prepare a line chart plotting the actual peak demand data against the values predicted by this regression equation. How well does the model fit the data?
f. Interpret the R^2 statistic for this model.
g. Using the model you developed in part d above, what is the estimated peak power demand Duque should expect on a Wednesday in July when the daily high temperature is forecast to be 94?
h. Compute a 95% prediction interval for the estimate in the previous question. Explain the managerial implications of this interval for Duque.

18. An appraiser collected the data found in file Dat9-18.xls describing the auction selling price, diameter (in inches), and item type of several pieces of early 20th century metal tableware manufactured by a famous artisan. The item type variable is coded as follows: B=bowl, C=casserole pan, D=dish, T=tray, and P=plate. The appraiser wants to build a multiple regression model for this data to predict average selling prices of similar items.

a. Construct a multiple regression model for this problem. (*Hint:* Create binary independent variables to represent the item type data). What is the estimated regression function?

b. Interpret the value of the R^2 statistic for this model.

c. Construct an approximate 95% prediction interval for the expected selling price of an 18-inch diameter casserole pan. Interpret this interval.

d. What other variables not included in the model might help explain the remaining variation in auction selling prices for these items?

19. The personnel director for a small manufacturing company has collected the data found in the file Dat9-19.xls on your data disk describing the salary (Y) earned by each machinist in the factory along with the average performance rating (X_1) over the past 3 years, the years of service (X_2), and the number of different machines each employee is certified to operate (X_3).

The personnel director wants to build a regression model to estimate the average salary an employee should expect to receive based on his or her performance, years of service, and certifications.

a. Prepare three scatter plots showing the relationship between the salaries and each of the independent variables. What sort of relationship does each plot suggest?

b. If the personnel director wanted to build a regression model using only one independent variable to predict the salaries, what variable should be used?

c. If the personnel director wanted to build a regression model using only two independent variables to predict the salaries, what two variables should be used?

d. Compare the adjusted-R^2 statistics obtained in parts b and c with that of a regression model using all three independent variables. Which model would you recommend that the personnel director use?

e. Suppose the personnel director chooses to use the regression function with all three independent variables. What is the estimated regression function?

f. Suppose the company considers an employee's salary to be "fair" if it is within 1.5 standard errors of the value estimated by the regression function in part e. What salary range would be appropriate for an employee with 12 years of service, who has received average reviews of 4.5, and is certified to operate 4 pieces of machinery?

20. Caveat Emptor, Inc. is a home inspection service that provides prospective home buyers with a thorough assessment of the major systems in a house prior to the execution of the purchase contract. Prospective home buyers often ask the company for an estimate of the average monthly heating cost of the home during the winter. To answer this question, the company wants to build a regression model to help predict the average monthly heating cost (Y) as a function of the average outside temperature in winter (X_1), the amount of attic insulation in the house (X_2), the age of the furnace in the house (X_3), and the size of the house measured in square feet (X_4). Data on these variables for a number of homes was collected and may be found in the file Dat9-20.xls on your data disk.

a. Prepare scatter plots showing the relationship between the average heating cost and each of the potential independent variables. What sort of relationship does each plot suggest?

b. If the company wanted to build a regression model using only one independent variable to predict the average heating cost of these houses, what variable should be used?

c. If the company wanted to build a regression model using only two independent variables to predict the average heating cost of these houses, what variables should be used?

d. If the company wanted to build a regression model using only three independent variables to predict the average heating cost of these houses, what variables should be used?

    e. Suppose the company chooses to use the regression function with all four independent variables. What is the estimated regression function?

    f. Suppose the company decides to use the model with the highest adjusted R^2 statistic. Develop a 95% prediction interval for the average monthly heating cost of a house with 4 inches of attic insulation, a 5-year-old furnace, 2500 square feet, and in a location with an average outside winter temperature of 40. Interpret this interval.

21. Throughout our discussion of regression analysis, we used the Regression command to obtain the parameter estimates that minimize the sum of squared estimation errors. Suppose that we want to obtain parameter estimates that minimize the sum of the absolute value of the estimation errors, or:

$$\text{MIN: } \sum_{i=1}^{n} |Y_i - \hat{Y}_i|$$

    a. Use Solver to obtain the parameter estimates for a simple linear regression function that minimizes the sum of the absolute value of the estimation errors for the data in question 9.

    b. What advantages, if any, do you see in using this alternate objective to solve a regression problem?

    c. What disadvantages, if any, do you see in using this alternate objective to solve a regression problem?

22. Throughout our discussion of regression analysis, we used the Regression command to obtain the parameter estimates that minimize the sum of squared estimation errors. Suppose that we want to obtain parameter estimates that minimize the absolute value of the maximum estimation error, or:

$$\text{MIN: MAX } (|Y_1 - \hat{Y}_1|, |Y_2 - \hat{Y}_2|, \ldots, |Y_n - \hat{Y}_n|)$$

    a. Use Solver to obtain the parameter estimates for a simple linear regression function that minimizes the absolute value of the maximum estimation error for the data in question 9.

    b. What advantages, if any, do you see in using this alternate objective to solve a regression problem?

    c. What disadvantages, if any, do you see in using this alternate objective to solve a regression problem?

CASE 9.1   Diamonds Are Forever

(Inspired from actual events related by former Virginia Tech MBA student Brian Ellyson.)

With Christmas coming, Ryan Bellison was searching for the perfect gift for his wife. Ryan leaned back in his chair at the office and tried to think, after several years of marriage, of the one thing his wife had wanted during the years they pinched pennies to get through graduate school. Then he remembered the way her eyes had lit up last week when they walked by the jewelry store windows at the mall and she saw the diamond earrings. He knew he wanted to see that same look on her face Christmas morning. And so his hunt began for the perfect set of diamond earrings.

    Ryan's first order of business was to educate himself about the things to look for when buying diamonds. After perusing the Web, he learned about the "4Cs" of diamonds: cut, color, clarity, and carat (see: http://www.adiamondisforever.com). He knew his wife wanted round-cut earrings mounted in white gold settings, so he immediately narrowed his focus to evaluating color, clarity, and carat for that style earring.

After a bit of searching, Ryan located a number of earring sets that he would consider purchasing. But he knew the pricing of diamonds varied considerably and he wanted to make sure he didn't get ripped off. To assist in his decision making, Ryan decided to use regression analysis to develop a model to predict the retail price of different sets of round-cut earrings based on their color, clarity, and carat scores. He assembled the data in the file Diamonds.xls on your data disk for this purpose. Use this data to answer the following questions for Ryan.

a. Prepare scatter plots showing the relationship between the earring prices (Y) and each of the potential independent variables. What sort of relationship does each plot suggest?

b. Let X_1, X_2, and X_3 represent diamond color, clarity, and carats, respectively. If Ryan wanted to build a linear regression model to estimate earring prices using these variables, which variables would you recommend that he use? Why?

c. Suppose Ryan decides to use clarity (X_2) and carats (X_3) as independent variables in a regression model to predict earring prices. What is the estimated regression equation? What is the value of the R^2 and adjusted-R^2 statistics?

d. Use the regression equation identified in the previous question to create estimated prices for each of the earring sets in Ryan's sample. Which sets of earrings appear to be overpriced and which appear to be bargains? Based on this analysis, which set of earrings would you suggest that Ryan purchase?

e. Ryan now remembers that it is sometimes helps to perform a square root transformation on the dependent variable in a regression problem. Modify your spreadsheet to include a new dependent variable that is the square root on the earring prices (use Excel's SQRT( ) function). If Ryan wanted to build a linear regression model to estimate the square root of earring prices using the same independent variables as before, which variables would you recommend that he use? Why?

f. Suppose Ryan decides to use clarity (X_2) and carats (X_3) as independent variables in a regression model to predict the square root of the earring prices. What is the estimated regression equation? What is the value of the R^2 and adjusted-R^2 statistics?

g. Use the regression equation identified in the previous question to create estimated prices for each of the earring sets in Ryan's sample. (Remember, your model estimates the square root of the earring prices. So you must square the model's estimates to convert them to actually price estimates.) Which sets of earring appears to be overpriced and which appear to be bargains? Based on this analysis, which set of earrings would you suggest that Ryan purchase?

h. Ryan now also remembers that it sometimes helps to include interaction terms in a regression model—where you create a new independent variable as the product of two of the original variables. Modify your spreadsheet to include three new independent variables, X_4, X_5, and X_6, representing interaction terms where: $X_4 = X_1 \times X_2$, $X_5 = X_1 \times X_3$, and $X_6 = X_2 \times X_3$. There are now six potential independent variables. If Ryan wanted to build a linear regression model to estimate the square root of earring prices using the same independent variables as before, which variables would you recommend that he use? Why?

i. Suppose Ryan decides to use clarity (X_1), carats (X_3) and the interaction terms X_4 and X_5 as independent variables in a regression model to predict the square root of the earring prices. What is the estimated regression equation? What is the value of the R^2 and adjusted-R^2 statistics?

j. Use the regression equation identified in the previous question to create estimated prices for each of the earring sets in Ryan's sample. (Remember, your model estimates the square root of the earring prices. So you must square the model's estimates to convert them to actual price estimates.) Which sets of earrings appear to be overpriced and which appear to be bargains? Based on this analysis, which set of earrings would you suggest that Ryan purchase?

CASE 9.2 Fiasco in Florida

The 2000 U.S. Presidential election was one of the most controversial in history, with the final outcome ultimately being decided in a court of law rather than in the voting booth. At issue were the election results in Palm Beach, Florida. Palm Beach County used a so-called "butterfly" ballot where the candidates' names were arranged to the left and right of a center row of holes. Voters were to specify their preference by "punching" the appropriate hole next to the desired candidate. According to several news accounts, many voters in Palm Beach, Florida, claimed that they were confused by the ballot structure and might have voted inadvertently for Pat Buchanan when in fact they intended to vote for Al Gore. This allegedly contributed to Gore not obtaining enough votes to overtake George Bush's slim margin of victory in Florida—and ultimately cost Gore the election.

The file Votes.xls on your data disk contains the original vote totals by Florida county for Gore, Bush, and Buchanan as of November 8, 2000. (These data reflect the results prior to the hand recount that was done due to other problems with the election in Florida (*e.g.*, the "hanging chad" problem.)) Use the data in this file to answer the following questions.

a. What was George Bush's margin of victory in Florida?
b. Prepare a scatter plot showing the relationship between the number of votes received by Gore (X-axis) and Buchanan (Y-axis) in each county. Do there appear to be any outliers? If so, for what counties?
c. Estimate the parameters for a simple linear regression model for predicting the number of votes for Buchanan in each county (excluding Palm Beach County) as a function of the number of votes for Gore. What is the estimated regression equation?
d. Interpret the value for R^2 obtained using the equation from question 3.
e. Using the regression results from question 3, develop a 99% prediction interval for the number of votes you expect Buchanan to receive in Palm Beach County. What are the upper and lower limits of that interval? How does this compare with the actual number of votes reported for Buchanan in Palm Beach County?
f. Prepare a scatter plot showing the relationship between the number of votes received by Bush (X-axis) and Buchanan (Y-axis) in each county. Do there appear to be any outliers? If so, for what counties?
g. Estimate the parameters for a simple linear regression model for predicting the number of votes for Buchanan in each county (excluding Palm Beach County) as a function of the number of votes for Bush. What is the estimated regression equation?
h. Interpret the value for R^2 obtained using the equation from question 7.
i. Using the regression results from question 7, develop a 99% prediction interval for the number of votes you expect Buchanan to receive in Palm Beach County. What are the upper and lower limits of that interval? How does this compare with the actual number of votes reported for Buchanan in Palm Beach County?
j. What do these results suggest? What assumptions are being made by using regression analysis in this way?

The Georgia Public Service Commission

(Inspired by discussions with Mr. Nolan E. Ragsdale of Banks County, Georgia.)

Nolan Banks is an auditor for the Public Service Commission for the state of Georgia. The Public Service Commission is a government agency responsible for ensuring that utility companies throughout the state manage their operations efficiently so that they can provide quality services to the public at fair prices.

Georgia is the largest state east of the Mississippi River, and various communities and regions throughout the state have different companies that provide water, power, and phone service. These companies have a monopoly in the areas they serve and, therefore, could take unfair advantage of the public. One of Nolan's jobs is to visit the companies and audit their financial records to detect whether or not any abuse is occurring.

A major problem Nolan faces in his job is determining whether the expenses reported by the utility companies are reasonable. For example, when he reviews a financial report for a local phone company, he might see line maintenance costs of $1,345,948, and he needs to determine if this amount is reasonable. This determination is complicated because companies differ in size—so he cannot compare the costs of one company directly to those of another. Similarly, he cannot come up with a simple ratio to determine costs (such as 2% for the ratio of line maintenance costs to total revenue) because a single ratio might not be appropriate for companies of different sizes.

To help solve this problem, Nolan wants you to build a regression model to estimate what level of line maintenance expense would be expected for companies of different sizes. One measure of size for a phone company is the number of customers it has. Nolan collected the data in the file PhoneService.xls on your data disk representing the number of customers and line maintenance expenses of 12 companies that he audited in the past year and determined were being run in a reasonably efficient manner.

a. Enter the data in a spreadsheet.
b. Create a scatter diagram of these data.
c. Use regression to estimate the parameters for the following linear equation for the data.

$$\hat{Y} = b_0 + b_1 X_1$$

What is the estimated regression equation?
d. Interpret the value for R^2 obtained using the equation from question 3.
e. According to the equation in question 3, what level of line maintenance expense would be expected for a phone company with 75,000 customers? Show how you arrive at this value.
f. Suppose that a phone company with 75,000 customers reports a line maintenance expense of $1,500,000. Based on the results of the linear model, should Nolan view this amount as reasonable or excessive?
g. In your spreadsheet, calculate the estimated line maintenance expense that would be predicted by the regression function for each company in the sample. Plot the predicted values you calculate on your graph (connected with a line) along with the original data. Does it appear that a linear regression model is appropriate?
h. Use regression to estimate the parameters for the following quadratic equation for the data:

$$\hat{Y} = b_0 + b_1 X_1 + b_2 X_1^2$$

To do this, you must insert a new column in your spreadsheet next to the original X values. In this new column, calculate the values X_1^2. What is the new estimated regression equation for this model?

i.   Interpret the value for R^2 obtained using the equation in question 8.

j.   What is the value for the adjusted-R^2 statistic? What does this statistic tell you?

k.   What level of line maintenance expense would be expected for a phone company with 75,000 customers according to this new estimated regression function? Show how you arrive at this value.

l.   In your spreadsheet, calculate the estimated line maintenance expense that would be predicted by the quadratic regression function for each company in the sample. Plot these values on your graph (connected with a line) along with the original data and the original regression line.

m.   Suppose that a phone company with 75,000 customers reports a line maintenance expense of $1,500,000. Based on the results of the quadratic model, should Nolan view this amount as reasonable or excessive?

n.   Which of the two regression functions would you suggest that Nolan use for prediction purposes?

Chapter 11

Time Series Forecasting

11.0 Introduction

A time series is a set of observations on a quantitative variable collected over time. For example, every night the evening news reports the closing value of the Dow Jones Industrial Average. These closing values represent a series of values for a quantitative variable over time—or a time series. Most businesses keep track of a number of time series variables. Examples might include daily, weekly, monthly, or quarterly figures on sales, costs, profits, inventory, back orders, customer counts, and so on.

Businesses often are interested in forecasting future values of a time series variable. For example, if we could predict future closing values of the Dow Jones Industrial Average accurately, we could become very wealthy investing in the stock market by "buying low and selling high." In constructing business plans, most companies make some attempt to forecast the expected levels of sales, costs, profits, inventory, back orders, customer counts, and so on. These types of forecasts often are required inputs to the other types of modeling techniques discussed throughout this text.

In Chapter 9, we investigated how to build and use regression models to predict the behavior of a dependent variable using one or more independent variables that are believed to be related to the dependent variable in a *causal* fashion. That is, when building a regression model, we often select independent variables that are believed to cause the observed behavior of the dependent variable. Although sometimes we can use this same approach to build a causal regression model for a time series variable, we cannot always do so.

For example, if we do not know which causal independent variables are influencing a particular time series variable, we cannot build a regression model. And even if we do have some idea which causal variables are affecting a time series, there might not be any data available for those variables. If data on the causal variables are available, the best regression function estimated from these data might not fit the data well. Finally, even if the estimated regression function fits the data well, we might have to forecast the values of the causal independent variables to estimate future values of the dependent (time series) variable. Forecasting the causal independent variables might be more difficult than forecasting the original time series variable.

On The Importance of Forecasting...

"You do not plan to ship goods across the ocean, or to assemble merchandise for sale, or to borrow money without first trying to determine what the future may hold in store. Ensuring that the materials you order are delivered on time, seeing to it that the items you plan to sell are produced on schedule, and getting your sales facilities in place all must be planned before that moment when the customers show up and lay their money on the counter. The successful business executive is a forecaster first: purchasing, producing, marketing, pricing, and organizing all follow." —Peter Bernstein. Against the Gods: The Remarkable Story of Risk. New York: John. Wiley & Sons, 1996, pp. 21–22.

11.1 Time Series Methods

In many business planning situations, it is difficult, undesirable, or even impossible to forecast time series data using a causal regression model. However, if we can discover some sort of systematic variation in the past behavior of the time series variable, we can attempt to construct a model of this behavior to help us forecast its future behavior. For example, we might find a long-term upward (or downward) trend in the time series that might be expected to continue in the future. Or, we might discover some predictable seasonal fluctuations in the data that could help us make estimates about the future. As you may have surmised, time series forecasting is based largely on the maxim that history tends to repeat itself.

Techniques that analyze the past behavior of a time series variable to predict the future are sometimes referred to as *extrapolation* models. The general form of an extrapolation model is:

$$\hat{Y}_{t+1} = f(Y_t, Y_{t-1}, Y_{t-2}, \ldots)$$ **11.1**

where $\hat{Y}_{t+1}$ represents the *predicted* value for the time series variable in time period $t + 1$, Y_t represents the *actual* value of the time series variable in time period t, Y_{t-1} represents the *actual* value of the time series variable in time period $t - 1$, and so on. The goal of an extrapolation model is to identify a function $f(\cdot)$ for equation 11.1 that produces accurate forecasts of future values of the time series variable.

This chapter presents a variety of methods for analyzing time series data. We'll first discuss several techniques that are appropriate for *stationary* time series, where there is no significant upward or downward trend in the data over time. Then, we'll discuss techniques for handling *nonstationary* time series, where there is some upward or downward trend in the data over time. We'll also discuss techniques for modeling *seasonal* patterns in both stationary and nonstationary time series data.

11.2 Measuring Accuracy

Many methods are available for modeling time series data. In most cases, it is impossible to know in advance which method will be the most effective for a given set of data. Thus, a common approach to time series analysis involves trying several modeling techniques on a given data set and evaluating how well they explain the past behavior of the time series variable. We can evaluate these techniques by constructing line graphs that show the actual data versus the values predicted by the various modeling techniques. More formal quantitative measures of the accuracy (or "goodness of fit") of time series modeling techniques also exist. Four common accuracy measures are the mean absolute deviation (MAD), the mean absolute percent error (MAPE), the mean square error (MSE), and the root mean square error (RMSE). These quantities are defined as follows:

$$MAD = \frac{1}{n} \sum_i \left| Y_i - \hat{Y}_i \right|$$

$$MAPE = \frac{100}{n} \sum_i \left| \frac{Y_i - \hat{Y}_i}{Y_i} \right|$$

$$MSE = \frac{1}{n} \sum_i (Y_i - \hat{Y}_i)^2$$

$$RMSE = \sqrt{MSE}$$

In each of these formulas, Y_i represents the *actual* value for the ith observation in the time series and $\hat{Y}_i$ is the *forecasted* or predicted value for this observation. These quantities measure the differences between the actual values in the time series and the predicted, or fitted, values generated by the forecasting technique. The MSE and RMSE measures are closely related to the sum of square estimation errors criterion introduced in our discussion of regression analysis. Although all of these measures are commonly used in time series modeling, we will focus on the MSE measure because it is somewhat easier to calculate.

11.3 Stationary Models

The following example will be used to demonstrate several of the most common time series techniques for stationary data.

> Electra-City is a retail store that sells audio and video equipment for the home and car. Each month, the manager of the store must order merchandise from a distant warehouse. Currently, the manager is trying to estimate how many VCRs the store is likely to sell in the next month. To assist in this process, he has collected the data shown in Figure 11.1 (and in the file Fig11-1.xls on your data disk) on the number of VCRs sold in each of the previous 24 months. He wants to use these data in making his prediction.

After collecting the data for a time series variable, the next step in building a time series model is to inspect the data plotted over time. Figure 11.1 includes a plot of the VCR data. Notice that this plot does not suggest a strong upward or downward trend in the data. This plot suggests that the number of VCRs sold each month was somewhere between 30 and 40 units over the past two years with no continuing pattern or regularity from month to month. Thus, we expect that one of the extrapolation techniques discussed in the following sections would be an appropriate method for modeling these data.

FIGURE 11.1

Historical VCR sales data for the Electra-City forecasting problem

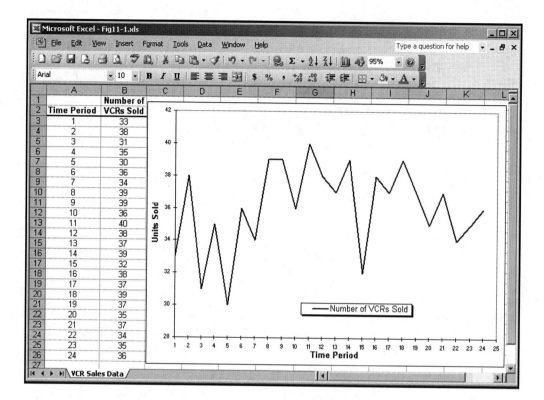

Creating a Line Graph

To create a scatter plot like the one shown in Figure 11.1:

1. Select cells A1 through B26.
2. Click the Insert menu.
3. Click Chart.
4. Click XY (Scatter).

Excel's Chart Wizard then prompts you to make several selections concerning how the chart should be labeled and formatted. After Excel creates a basic chart, you can customize it in many ways. Double-clicking a chart element displays a dialog box with options for modifying the appearance of the element.

11.4 Moving Averages

The moving average technique is probably the easiest extrapolation method for stationary data to use and understand. With this technique, the predicted value of the time series in period $t + 1$ (denoted by $\hat{Y}_{t+1}$) is simply the average of the k previous observations in the series; that is:

$$\hat{Y}_{t+1} = \frac{Y_t + Y_{t-1} + Y_{t-k+1}}{k}$$

11.2

The value k in equation 11.2 determines how many previous observations will be included in the moving average. No general method exists for determining what value of

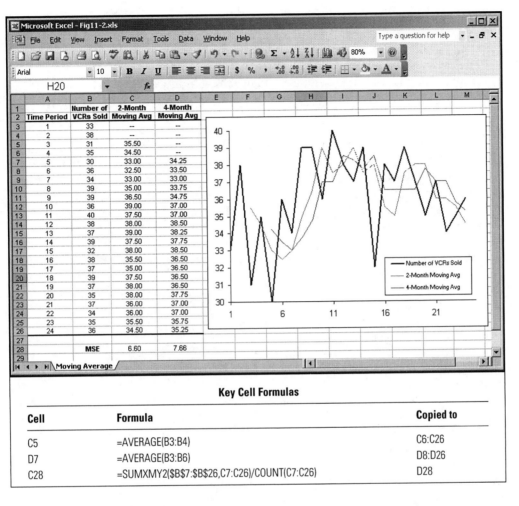

FIGURE 11.2

Moving average forecasts for the VCR sales data

Key Cell Formulas

Cell	Formula	Copied to
C5	=AVERAGE(B3:B4)	C6:C26
D7	=AVERAGE(B3:B6)	D8:D26
C28	=SUMXMY2($B$7:$B$26,C7:C26)/COUNT(C7:C26)	D28

k will be best for a particular time series. Therefore, we must try several values of k to see which gives the best results. This is illustrated in Figure 11.2 (and in the file Fig11-2.xls on your data disk) where the monthly number of VCRs sold for Electra-City is fit using moving average models with k values of 2 and 4.

We generated the moving average forecasts in Figure 11.2 using the AVERAGE( ) function. For example, the two-month moving average forecasts are generated by implementing the following formula in cell C5 and copying it to cells C6 through C26:

Formula for cell C5:   =AVERAGE(B3:B4)

(Copy to C6 through C26.)

The four-month moving average forecasts are generated by implementing the following formula in cell D7 and copying it to cells D8 through D26:

Formula for cell D7:   =AVERAGE(B3:B6)

(Copy to D8 through D26.)

The actual VCR sales data are plotted in Figure 11.2 along with the predicted values from the two moving average models. This graph shows that the predicted values tend to be less volatile, or smoother, than the actual data. This should not be surprising because the moving average technique tends to average out the peaks and valleys occurring in the original data. Thus, the moving average technique sometimes is referred to as a *smoothing* method. The larger the value of k (or the more past data points are averaged together), the smoother the moving average prediction will be.

We can evaluate the relative accuracy of the two moving average forecasting functions by comparing the MSE values for these two techniques shown in cells C28 and D28 in Figure 11.2. The following formula calculates these MSE values:

Formula for cell C28:   =SUMXMY2($B$7:$B$26,C7:C26)/COUNT(C7:C26)
(Copy to D28.)

Note that the SUMXMY2( ) function calculates the sum of squared differences between corresponding values in two different ranges. The COUNT( ) function returns the number of values in a range. Also note that the forecasts using the two-month moving average begin in time period 3 (cell C5) and the four-month moving average forecasts begin in time period 5 (cell D7). We are calculating the MSE values starting in time period 5 for both forecasting techniques so that we can make a fair comparison between them.

The MSE value describes the overall fit of the forecasting technique to the historical data. By comparing the MSE values for the two moving averages, we might conclude that the two-month moving average (with an MSE of 6.60) provides more accurate forecasts than the four-month moving average (with an MSE of 7.66). Note, however, that the MSE includes and weighs relatively old data with the same importance as the most recent data. Thus, selecting a forecast based on the total MSE of the forecasting functions might not be wise because a forecasting function might have achieved a lower total MSE by fitting older data points very well while being relatively inaccurate on more recent data.

Because we want to forecast *future* observations, we might be interested in how well the forecasting function performed on the most recent data. We can determine this by calculating other MSE values using only the most recent data. For example, if we calculate MSE values using only the last twelve time periods (periods 13 through 24), the four-month moving average produces an MSE of 6.01 and the two-month moving average produces an MSE of 6.02. These results are shown in the table below the graph in Figure 11.3. So an argument could be made that the four-month moving average model should be used to predict the future because it produced the most accurate predictions of the actual values observed during the past twelve time periods. Note, however, that there is no guarantee that the forecasting technique that has been most accurate recently will continue to be most accurate in the future.

11.4.1 FORECASTING WITH THE MOVING AVERAGE MODEL

Assuming (for simplicity) that the manager of Electra-City is satisfied with the accuracy of the two-month moving average model, the prediction of the number of VCRs to be sold in the next month (time period 25) is calculated as:

$$\hat{Y}_{25} = \frac{Y_{24} + Y_{23}}{2} = \frac{36 + 35}{2} = 35.5$$

To forecast *more* than one period into the future using the moving average technique, we must substitute forecasted values for unobserved actual values. For example, suppose that at the end of time period 24, we want to forecast the number of VCRs to be sold in time periods 25 *and* 26. Using a two-period moving average, the forecast for time period 26 is represented by:

$$\hat{Y}_{26} = \frac{Y_{25} + Y_{24}}{2}$$

However, at time period 24, we do not know the actual value for Y_{25}. We have to substitute $\hat{Y}_{25}$ for Y_{25} in the previous equation to generate the forecast for time period 26. Therefore, at time period 24, our estimate of the number of VCRs to be sold in time period 26 is:

$$\hat{Y}_{26} = \frac{\hat{Y}_{25} + Y_{24}}{2} = \frac{35.5 + 36}{2} = 35.75$$

Similarly, at time period 24, forecasts for periods 27 and 28 would be calculated as follows:

$$\hat{Y}_{27} = \frac{\hat{Y}_{26} + \hat{Y}_{25}}{2} = \frac{35.75 + 35.2}{2} = 35.63$$

$$\hat{Y}_{28} = \frac{\hat{Y}_{27} + \hat{Y}_{26}}{2} = \frac{35.63 + 35.75}{2} = 35.69$$

Figure 11.3 shows forecasts made at time period 24 for periods 25, 26, 27, and 28 for both the two-month and four-month moving average techniques.

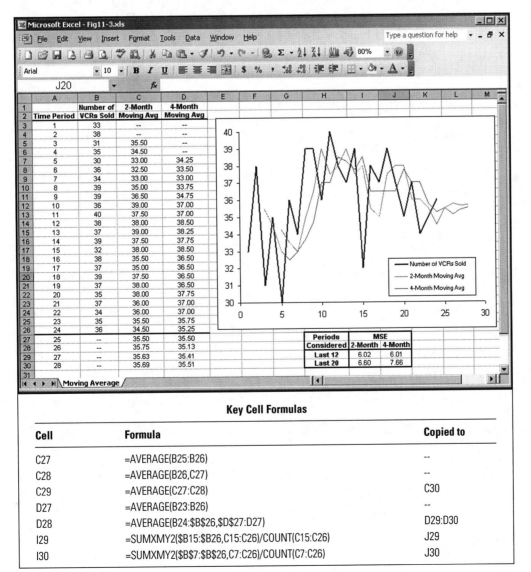

FIGURE 11.3

Forecasts of the VCR sales data

Key Cell Formulas

Cell	Formula	Copied to
C27	=AVERAGE(B25:B26)	--
C28	=AVERAGE(B26,C27)	--
C29	=AVERAGE(C27:C28)	C30
D27	=AVERAGE(B23:B26)	--
D28	=AVERAGE(B24:$B$26,$D$27:D27)	D29:D30
I29	=SUMXMY2($B$15:$B$26,C15:C26)/COUNT(C15:C26)	J29
I30	=SUMXMY2($B$7:$B$26,C7:C26)/COUNT(C7:C26)	J30

11.5 Weighted Moving Averages

One drawback of the moving average technique is that all the past data used in calculating the average are weighted equally. We can often obtain a more accurate forecast by assigning different weights to the data. The weighted moving average technique is a simple variation on the moving average technique that allows for weights to be assigned to the data being averaged. In the weighted moving average technique, the forecasting function is represented by:

$$\hat{Y}_{t+1} = w_1 Y_t + w_2 Y_{t-1} + \cdots + w_k Y_{t-k+1} \qquad \textbf{11.3}$$

where $0 \leq w_i \leq 1$ and $\Sigma_{i=1}^{k} w_i = 1$. Note that the simple moving average forecast in equation 11.2 is a special case of equation 11.3 where $w_1 = w_2 = \cdots = w_k = \frac{1}{k}$.

Although the weighted moving average offers greater flexibility than the moving average, it is also a bit more complicated. In addition to determining a value for k, we also must determine values for the weights w_i in equation 11.3. However, for a given value of k, we can use Solver to determine the values for w_i that minimize the MSE. The spreadsheet implementation of a two-month weighted moving average model for the Electra-City example is shown in Figure 11.4 (and in the file Fig11-4.xls on your data disk).

FIGURE 11.4

Spreadsheet implementation of the weighted moving average model

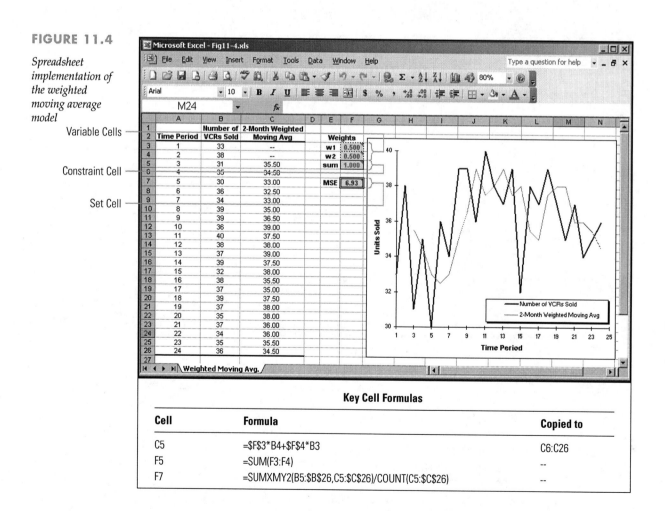

Key Cell Formulas		
Cell	**Formula**	**Copied to**
C5	=$F$3*B4+$F$4*B3	C6:C26
F5	=SUM(F3:F4)	--
F7	=SUMXMY2(B5:$B$26,C5:$C$26)/COUNT(C5:$C$26)	--

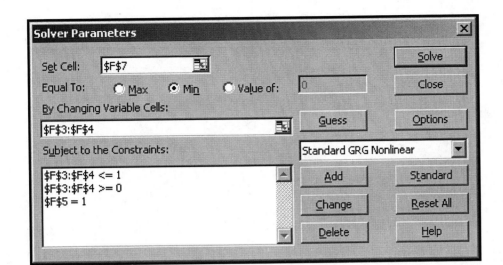

FIGURE 11.5

Solver parameters for the weighted moving average model

Cells F3 and F4 represent the weights w_1 and w_2, respectively. Cell F5 contains the sum of cells F3 and F4. The weighted average forecasting function is implemented in cell C5 with the following formula, which is copied to cells C6 through C26:

Formula for cell C5:   =$F$3*B4+$F$4*B3

(Copy to C6 through C26.)

Notice that with $w_1 = w_2 = 0.5$ the weighted average predictions are identical to those of the simple moving average method shown in Figure 11.2. The formula for the MSE is implemented in cell F7 as follows:

Formula for cell F7:   =SUMXMY2(B5:$B$26,C5:$C$26)/COUNT(C5:$C$26)

We can use the Solver parameters shown in Figure 11.5 to identify the values for the weights in cells F3 and F4 that minimize the MSE. Notice that this is a nonlinear optimization problem because the MSE represents a nonlinear objective function. Figure 11.6 shows the solution to this problem.

Notice that the optimal weights of $w_1 = 0.291$ and $w_2 = 0.709$ reduce the value of the MSE only slightly, from 6.93 to 6.29.

11.5.1 FORECASTING WITH THE WEIGHTED MOVING AVERAGE MODEL

Using the weighted moving average technique, the predicted number of VCRs to be sold at Electra-City in the next month (time period 25) is calculated as:

$$\hat{Y}_{25} = w_1 Y_{24} + w_2 Y_{23} = 0.291 \times 36 + 0.709 \times 35 = 35.29$$

We also can use the weighted moving average technique to forecast more than one time period into the future. However, as with the moving average technique, we must substitute forecasted values for unobserved actual values where needed. For example, suppose that at the end of time period 24, we want to forecast the number of VCRs to be sold in time periods 25 *and* 26. The weighted moving average forecast for time period 26 is represented by:

$$\hat{Y}_{26} = w_1 Y_{25} + w_2 Y_{24}$$

FIGURE 11.6

Optimal solution and forecasts with the weighted moving average model

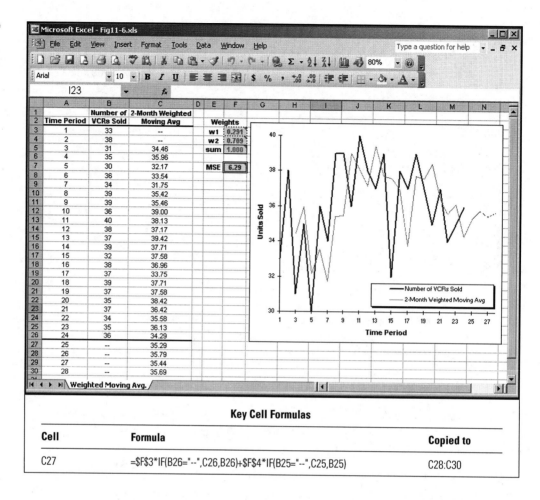

	Key Cell Formulas	
Cell	**Formula**	**Copied to**
C27	=$F$3*IF(B26="--",C26,B26)+$F$4*IF(B25="--",C25,B25)	C28:C30

However, at time period 24, we do not know the actual value for Y_{25}. As a result, we have to substitute $\hat{Y}_{25}$ for Y_{25} in the previous equation to generate the following forecast for time period 26:

$$\hat{Y}_{26} = w_1\hat{Y}_{25} + w_2Y_{24} = 0.291 \times 35.29 + 0.709 \times 36 = 35.79$$

Similarly, at time period 24, forecasts for time periods 27 and 28 would be computed as:

$$\hat{Y}_{27} = w_1\hat{Y}_{26} + w_2\hat{Y}_{25} = 0.291 \times 35.79 + 0.709 \times 35.29 = 35.44$$
$$\hat{Y}_{28} = w_1\hat{Y}_{27} + w_2\hat{Y}_{26} = 0.291 \times 35.44 + 0.709 \times 35.79 = 35.69$$

Figure 11.6 shows forecasts made at time period 24 for periods 25, 26, 27, and 28 for the two-month weighted average technique.

11.6 Exponential Smoothing

Exponential smoothing is another averaging technique for stationary data that allows weights to be assigned to past data. Exponential smoothing models assume the following form:

$$\hat{Y}_{t+1} = \hat{Y}_t + \alpha(Y_t - \hat{Y}_t) \qquad\qquad \textbf{11.4}$$

Equation 11.4 indicates that the predicted value for time period $t + 1$ ($\hat{Y}_{t+1}$) is equal to the predicted value for the previous period ($\hat{Y}_t$) plus an adjustment for the error made in predicting the previous period's value ($\alpha(Y_t - \hat{Y}_t)$). The parameter α in equation 11.4 can assume any value between 0 and 1 ($0 \leq \alpha \leq 1$).

It can be shown that the exponential smoothing formula in equation 11.4 is equivalent to:

$$\hat{Y}_{t+1} = \alpha Y_t + \alpha(1 - \alpha)Y_{t-1} + \alpha(1 - \alpha)^2 Y_{t-2} + \cdots + \alpha(1 - \alpha)^n Y_{t-n} + \cdots$$

As shown in the previous equation, the forecast $\hat{Y}_{t+1}$ in exponential smoothing is a weighted combination of all previous values in the time series where the most recent observation Y_t receives the heaviest weight (α), the next most recent observation Y_{t-1} receives the next heaviest weight ($\alpha(1 - \alpha)$), and so on.

In an exponential smoothing model, small values of α tend to produce sluggish forecasts that do not react quickly to changes in the data. A value of α near 1 produces a forecast that reacts more quickly to changes in the data. Figure 11.7 (and file Fig11-7.xls on your data disk) illustrates these relationships, showing the results of two exponential smoothing models for the VCR sales data with α-values of 0.1 and 0.9.

We can use Solver to determine the optimal value for α when building an exponential smoothing forecasting model for a particular data set. The spreadsheet implementation of the exponential smoothing forecasting model for the Electra-City example is shown in Figure 11.8 (and in the file Fig11-8.xls on your data disk).

In Figure 11.8, cell F3 represents α. In an exponential smoothing forecasting model, it is customary to assume that $\hat{Y}_1 = Y_1$. Thus, in Figure 11.8, cell C3 contains the following formula:

Formula for cell C3:   =B3

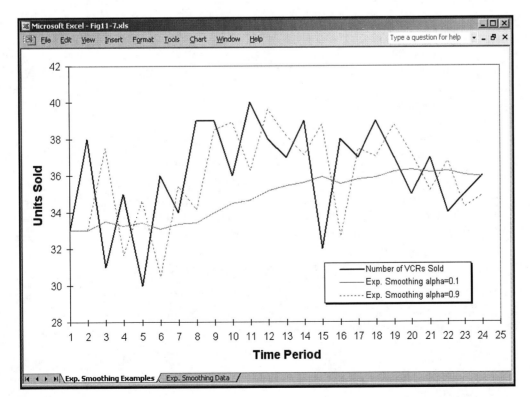

FIGURE 11.7

Two exponential smoothing models of the VCR sales data

FIGURE 11.8

Spreadsheet implementation of the exponential smoothing model

Variable Cell

Set Cell

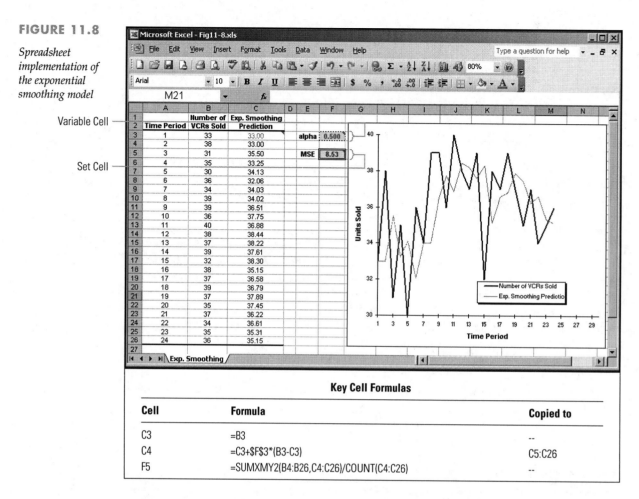

Key Cell Formulas

Cell	Formula	Copied to
C3	=B3	--
C4	=C3+$F$3*(B3-C3)	C5:C26
F5	=SUMXMY2(B4:B26,C4:C26)/COUNT(C4:C26)	--

The forecasting function in equation 11.4 begins for time period $t = 2$ with the following formula, which is implemented in cell C4 and copied to cells C5 through C26:

Formula for cell C4:   =C3+$F$3*(B3−C3)

(Copy to C5 through C26.)

The formula in cell F5 calculates the MSE value as:

Formula for cell F5:   =SUMXMY2(B4:B26,C4:C26)/COUNT(C4:C26)

We can use the Solver parameters and options shown in Figure 11.9 to identify the value for α that minimizes the MSE. Again, this is a nonlinear optimization problem because the MSE represents a nonlinear objective function. Figure 11.10 shows the solution to this problem. Notice that the optimal value for α is given in cell F3 as 0.268.

11.6.1 FORECASTING WITH THE EXPONENTIAL SMOOTHING MODEL

Using the exponential smoothing model, the predicted number of VCRs to be sold at Electra-City in the next month (time period 25) is calculated as:

$$\hat{Y}_{25} = \hat{Y}_{24} + \alpha(Y_{24} - \hat{Y}_{24}) = 35.74 + 0.268*(36 - 35.74) = 35.81$$

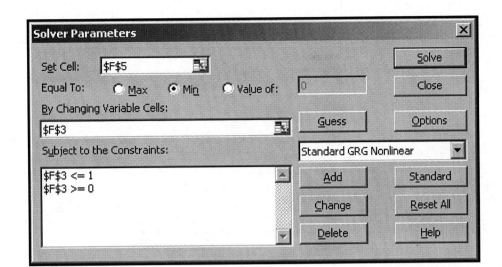

FIGURE 11.9

Solver parameters for the exponential smoothing model

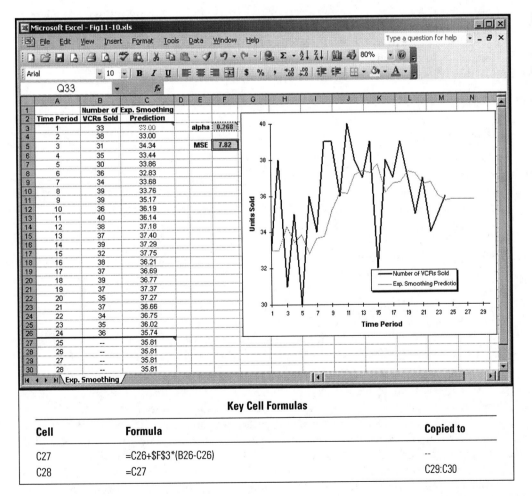

FIGURE 11.10

Optimal solution and forecasts for the exponential smoothing model

Key Cell Formulas

Cell	Formula	Copied to
C27	=C26+$F$3*(B26-C26)	--
C28	=C27	C29:C30

An interesting property of the exponential smoothing technique becomes apparent when we try to use it to forecast more than one time period into the future. For example, suppose that at time period 24, we want to forecast the number of VCRs to be sold in time periods 25 *and* 26. The forecast for time period 26 is represented by:

$$\hat{Y}_{26} = \hat{Y}_{25} + \alpha(Y_{25} - \hat{Y}_{25})$$

Because Y_{25} is unknown at time period 24, we must substitute $\hat{Y}_{25}$ for Y_{25} in the previous equation. However, in that case we obtain $\hat{Y}_{26} = \hat{Y}_{25}$. In fact, the forecast for all future time periods would equal $\hat{Y}_{25}$. So when using exponential smoothing, the forecast for *all* future time periods equal the same value. This is consistent with the underlying idea of a stationary time series. If a time series is stationary (or has no trend), it is reasonable to assume that the forecast of the next time period and all future time periods should equal the same value. Thus, the exponential smoothing forecasting model for all future time periods in the Electra-City example is represented by $\hat{Y}_t = 35.81$ (for $t = 25, 26, 27, \ldots$).

A Word of Caution About Forecasting...

Although we can use the moving average or exponential smoothing technique to forecast a value for any future time period, as the forecast horizon lengthens, our confidence in the accuracy of the forecast diminishes because there is no guarantee that the historical patterns on which the model is based will continue indefinitely into the future.

11.7 Seasonality

Many time series variables exhibit *seasonality*, or a regular, repeating pattern in the data. For example, in time series data for monthly fuel oil sales, we would expect to see regular jumps in the data during the winter months each year. Similarly, monthly or quarterly sales data for suntan lotion likely would show consistent peaks during the summer and valleys during the winter.

Two different types of seasonal effects are common in time series data: additive effects and multiplicative effects. Additive seasonal effects tend to be on the same order of magnitude each time a given season is encountered. Multiplicative seasonal effects tend to have an increasing effect each time a given season is encountered. Figure 11.11 (and the file Fig11-11.xls on your data disk) illustrates the difference between these two types of seasonal effects for stationary data.

We will use the following example to illustrate two techniques for modeling additive and multiplicative seasonality in stationary time series data.

Savannah Climate Control (SCC) sells and services residential heat pumps. Sales of heat pumps tend to be higher than average in the winter and summer quarters when temperatures are more extreme. Similarly, sales tend to be lower than average in the spring and fall quarters when temperatures are less extreme and homeowners can put off replacing inoperable heat pump units. The owner of SCC, Bill Cooter, has collected quarterly unit sales data for the past several years as shown in Figure 11.12 (and in file Fig11-12.xls on your data disk). He wants to analyze this data to create a model to estimate the number of units he will sell in each quarter of the year 2006.

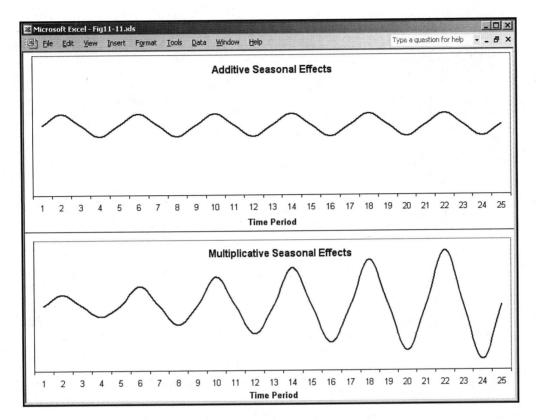

**FIGURE
11.11**

*Examples of
additive and
multiplicative
seasonal effects in
stationary data*

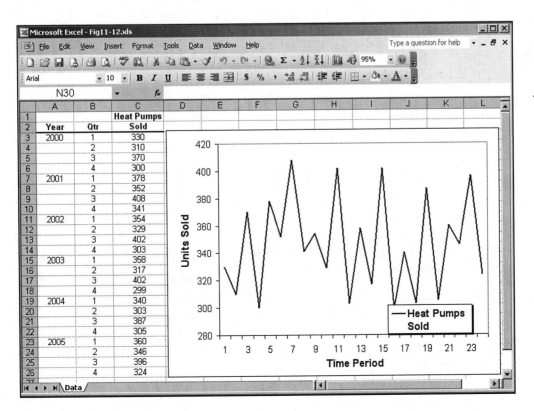

**FIGURE
11.12**

*Historical heat
pump sales data
for Savannah
Climate Control*

11.8 Stationary Data with Additive Seasonal Effects

The units sales data shown in Figure 11.12 indicate that unit sales tend to be high in quarters one and three (corresponding to the winter and summer months) and low in quarters two and four (corresponding to the spring and fall months). Thus, this data exhibits quarterly seasonal effects that likely can be modeled to make more accurate forecasts.

The following model is useful for modeling stationary time series data with additive seasonal effects:

$$\hat{Y}_{t+n} = E_t + S_{t+n-p} \qquad\qquad \textbf{11.5}$$

where

$$E_t = \alpha(Y_t - S_{t-p}) + (1 - \alpha)\, E_{t-1} \qquad\qquad \textbf{11.6}$$

$$S_t = \beta(Y_t - E_t) + (1 - \beta)S_{t-p} \qquad\qquad \textbf{11.7}$$

$$0 \le \alpha \le 1 \text{ and } 0 \le \beta \le 1$$

In this model, E_t represents the expected level of the time series in period t, and S_t represents the seasonal factor for period t. The constant p represents the number of seasonal periods in the data. Thus, for quarterly data $p = 4$ and for monthly data $p = 12$.

In equation 11.5, the forecast for time period $t + n$ is simply the expected level of the time series at period t adjusted upward or downward by the seasonal factor S_{t+n-p}. Equation 11.6 estimates the expected level for period t as a weighted average of the deseasonalized data for period t $(Y_t - S_{t-p})$ and the previous period's level (E_{t-1}). Equation 11.7 estimates the seasonal factor for period t as the weighted average of the estimated seasonal effect in period t $(Y_t - E_t)$ and the previous seasonal factor for that same season (S_{t-p}).

To use equations 11.5 through 11.7, we must initialize the estimated levels and seasonal factors for the first p time periods. There are numerous ways to do this. However, for convenience we will do this as follows:

$$E_t = \sum_{i=1}^{p} \frac{Y_i}{p}, \quad t = 1, 2, \ldots, p$$

$$S_t = Y_t - E_t, \quad t = 1, 2, \ldots, p$$

That is, we will use the average value of the first p time periods as the initial expected levels for each of these time periods. We then use the difference between the actual values and expected levels as the initial seasonal factors for the first p time periods. The spreadsheet implementation for this technique is shown in Figure 11.13 (and in file Fig11-13.xls on your data disk).

The initial expected level values for the first four time periods were entered into cells E3 through E6 as follows:

Formula for cell E3:   =AVERAGE($D$3:$D$6)

(Copy to cells E4 through E6.)

Next, the initial seasonal factors for the first four periods were entered into cells F3 through F6 as follows:

Formula for cell F3:   =D3-E3

(Copy to cells F4 through F6.)

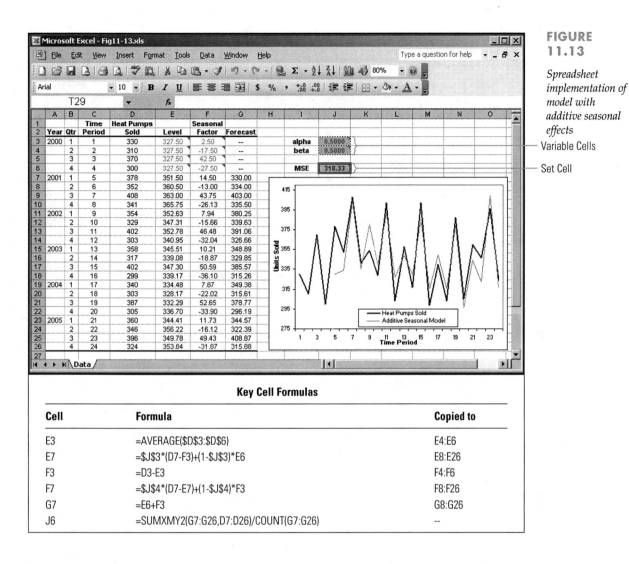

FIGURE 11.13

Spreadsheet implementation of model with additive seasonal effects

— Variable Cells

— Set Cell

Key Cell Formulas

Cell	Formula	Copied to
E3	=AVERAGE($D$3:$D$6)	E4:E6
E7	=$J$3*(D7-F3)+(1-$J$3)*E6	E8:E26
F3	=D3-E3	F4:F6
F7	=$J$4*(D7-E7)+(1-$J$4)*F3	F8:F26
G7	=E6+F3	G8:G26
J6	=SUMXMY2(G7:G26,D7:D26)/COUNT(G7:G26)	--

Cells J3 and J4 represent the values of α and β, respectively. The remaining expected levels and seasonal factors defined by equations 11.6 and 11.7 were then entered in columns E and F, respectively, as follows:

Formula for cell E7:   =$J$3*(D7-F3)+(1-$J$3)*E6

(Copy to cells E8 through E26.)

Formula for cell F7:   =$J$4*(D7-E7)+(1-$J$4)*F3

(Copy to cells F8 through F26.)

Now, according to equation 11.5, at any time period t, the prediction for time period $t + 1$ is given by:

$$\hat{Y}_{t+1} = E_t + S_{t+1-p}$$

Thus, at time period 4, we are able to calculate the prediction for time period 5 as follows:

Formula for cell G7:   =E6+F3

(Copy to cells G8 through G26.)

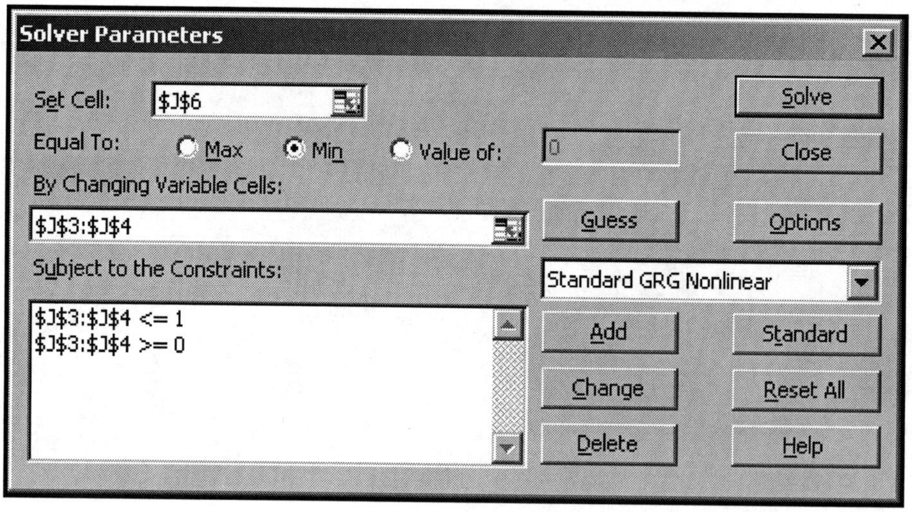

FIGURE 11.14

Solver parameters for the heat pump sales problem with seasonal additive effects

This formula is then copied to cells G8 through G26 to complete the one period ahead predictions for the remaining observations.

We can use Solver parameters shown in Figure 11.14 to determine the values of α and β that minimize the MSE for this problem, computed in cell J6 as follows:

Formula for cell J6:   =SUMXMY2(G7:G26,D7:D26)/COUNT(G7:G26)

Figure 11.15 shows the optimal solution to this problem along with a graph showing the actual sales data plotted against the values predicted by our model. Note that the predicted values fit the actual data reasonably well.

11.8.1 FORECASTING WITH THE MODEL

We can use the results in Figure 11.15 to compute forecasts for any future time period. According to equation 11.5, at time period 24, the forecast for time period $24 + n$ is given by:

$$\hat{Y}_{24+n} = E_{24} + S_{24+n-4}$$

Our forecasts for each quarter in the year 2006 would be calculated as follows:

$$\hat{Y}_{25} = E_{24} + S_{21} = 354.55 + 8.45 = 363.00$$
$$\hat{Y}_{26} = E_{24} + S_{22} = 354.55 - 17.82 = 336.73$$
$$\hat{Y}_{27} = E_{24} + S_{23} = 354.55 + 46.58 = 401.13$$
$$\hat{Y}_{28} = E_{24} + S_{24} = 354.55 - 31.73 = 322.81$$

Thus, each forecast is simply the expected level of the time series in period 24 adjusted by the relevant seasonal factor. The calculations for these forecasts were implemented in Figure 11.15 as follows:

Formula for cell G27:   =$E$26+F23
(Copy to cells G28 through G30)

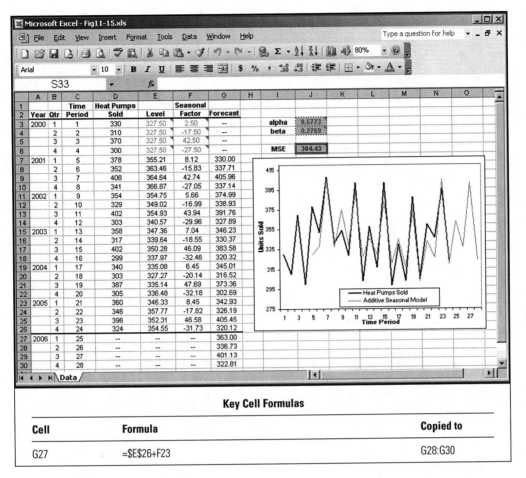

Key Cell Formulas

Cell	Formula	Copied to
G27	=$E$26+F23	G28:G30

A Note on Initializing Forecasting Models

It is important to note that the other methods can be used to initialize the base level (E_t) and seasonality (S_t) values used in the previous model and those presented later in this chapter. For instance, we could have used Solver to determine optimal (minimum MSE) values for the level and seasonality parameters along with the smoothing constants α and β. However, even if Solver is used to determine "optimal" initial values, there is no guarantee that the resulting forecasts will be any more accurate than if the initial values were determined using an alternative technique. When the data set being modeled is large, minor differences in the initial values are likely to have little impact on your forecasts. But as the size of the data set decreases, the impact of difference in the initial values becomes more pronounced.

11.9 Stationary Data with Multiplicative Seasonal Effects

A slight modification to the previous model makes it appropriate for modeling stationary time series data with multiplicative seasonal effects. In particular, the forecasting function becomes:

$$\hat{Y}_{t+n} = E_t \times S_{t+n-p} \qquad\qquad \textbf{11.8}$$

where

$$E_t = \alpha\,(Y_t/S_{t-p}) + (1 - \alpha)\,E_{t-1} \qquad\qquad \textbf{11.9}$$

$$S_t = \beta\,(Y_t/E_t) + (1 - \beta)S_{t-p} \qquad\qquad \textbf{11.10}$$

$$0 \le \alpha \le 1 \text{ and } 0 \le \beta \le 1$$

In this model, E_t again represents the expected level of the time series in period t, and S_t represents the seasonal factor for period t. The constant p represents the number of seasonal periods in the data.

In equation 11.8, the forecast for time period $t + n$ is simply the expected level of the time series at period t multiplied by the seasonal factor S_{t+n-p}. Equation 11.9 estimates the expected level for period t as a weighted average of the deseasonalized data for period t (Y_t / S_{t-p}) and the previous period's level (E_{t-1}). Equation 11.10 estimates the seasonal factor for period t as the weighted average of the estimated seasonal effect in period t (Y_t / E_t) and the previous seasonal factor for that same season (S_{t-p}).

To use equations 11.8 through 11.10, we must initialize the estimated levels and seasonal factors for the first p time periods. One simple way to do this is as follows:

$$E_t = \sum_{i=1}^{p} \frac{Y_i}{p}, \quad t = 1, 2, \ldots, p$$

$$S_t = Y_t/E_t, \quad t = 1, 2, \ldots, p$$

That is, we will use the average value of the first p time periods as the initial expected levels for each of these time periods. We then use the ratio of the actual values to the expected levels as the initial seasonal factors for the first p time periods.

The spreadsheet implementation for this technique is shown in Figure 11.16 (and in file Fig11-16.xls on your data disk).

The initial expected level values for the first four time periods were entered into cells E3 through E6 as follows:

> Formula for cell E3:   =AVERAGE($D$3:$D$6)
>
> (Copy to cells E4 through E6.)

Next, the initial seasonal factors for the first four periods were entered into cells F3 through F6 as follows:

> Formula for cell F3:   =D3/E3
>
> (Copy to cells F4 through F6.)

Cells J3 and J4 represent the values of α and β, respectively. The remaining expected levels and seasonal factors defined by equations 11.9 and 11.10 were then entered in columns E and F, respectively, as follows:

> Formula for cell E7:   =$J$3*(D7/F3)+(1-$J$3)*E6
>
> (Copy to cells E8 through E26.)

> Formula for cell F7:   =$J$4*(D7/E7)+(1-$J$4)*F3
>
> (Copy to cells F8 through F26.)

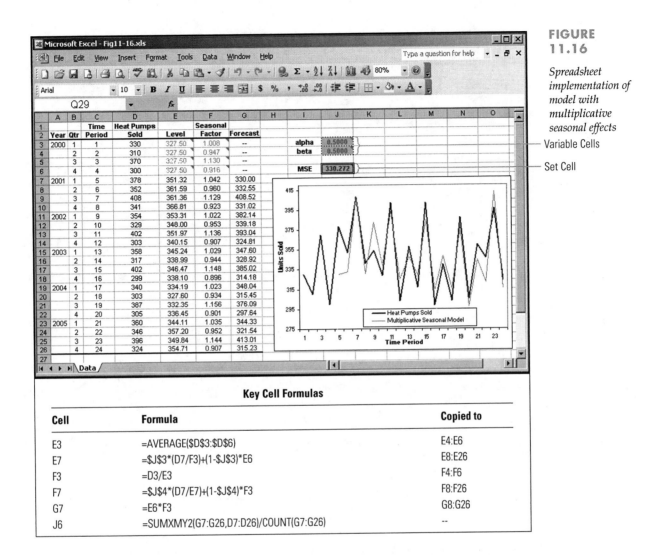

FIGURE
11.16

*Spreadsheet
implementation of
model with
multiplicative
seasonal effects*

— Variable Cells

— Set Cell

Key Cell Formulas

Cell	Formula	Copied to
E3	=AVERAGE($D$3:$D$6)	E4:E6
E7	=$J$3*(D7/F3)+(1-$J$3)*E6	E8:E26
F3	=D3/E3	F4:F6
F7	=$J$4*(D7/E7)+(1-$J$4)*F3	F8:F26
G7	=E6*F3	G8:G26
J6	=SUMXMY2(G7:G26,D7:D26)/COUNT(G7:G26)	--

Now, according to equation 11.8, at any time period t, the prediction for time period $t + 1$ is given by:

$$\hat{Y}_{t+1} = E_t \times S_{t+1-p}$$

Thus, at time period 4, we are able to calculate the prediction for time period 5 as follows:

Formula for cell G7:   =E6*F3

(Copy to cells G8 through G26.)

This formula is then copied to cells G8 through G26 to complete the one period ahead predictions for the remaining observations.

We can use the Solver parameters shown in Figure 11.17 to determine the values of α and β that minimize the MSE for this problem, computed in cell J6 as follows:

Formula for cell J6:   =SUMXMY2(G7:G26,D7:D26)/COUNT(G7:G26)

Figure 11.18 shows the optimal solution to this problem along with a graph showing the actual sales data plotted against the values predicted by our model. Note that the predicted values fit the actual data reasonably well.

FIGURE
11.17

Solver parameters
for the heat pump
sales problem with
multiplicative
seasonal effects

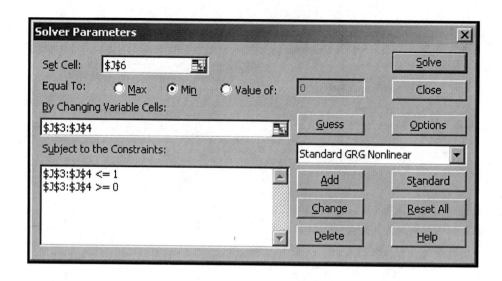

FIGURE
11.18

Optimal solution
to the heat pump
sales problem with
multiplicative
seasonal effects

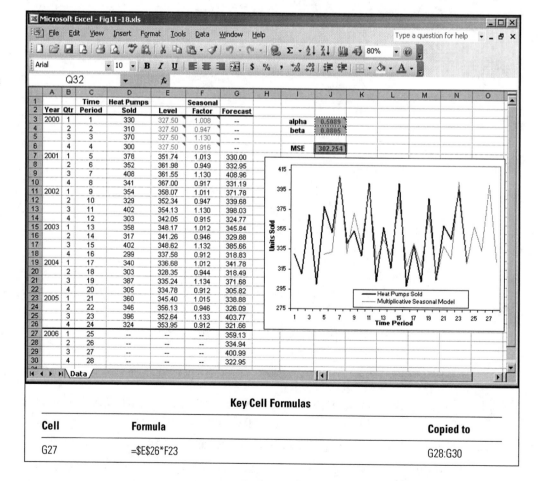

11.9.1 FORECASTING WITH THE MODEL

We can use the results in Figure 11.18 to compute forecasts for any future time period. According to equation 11.8, at time period 24, the forecast for time period $24 + n$ is given by:

$$\hat{Y}_{24+n} = E_{24} \times S_{24+n-4}$$

Our forecasts for each quarter in the year 2006 would then be calculated as follows:

$$\hat{Y}_{25} = E_{24} \times S_{21} = 353.95 \times 1.015 = 359.13$$
$$\hat{Y}_{26} = E_{24} \times S_{22} = 353.95 \times 0.946 = 334.94$$
$$\hat{Y}_{27} = E_{24} \times S_{23} = 353.95 \times 1.133 = 400.99$$
$$\hat{Y}_{28} = E_{24} \times S_{24} = 353.95 \times 0.912 = 322.95$$

Thus, each forecast is simply the expected level of the time series in period 24 multiplied by the relevant seasonal factor. The calculations for these forecasts were implemented in Figure 11.18 as follows:

Formula for cell G27:   =$E$26*F23

(Copy to cells G28 through G30)

11.10 Trend Models

The forecasting techniques presented so far are appropriate for stationary time series data in which there is no significant trend in the data over time. However, it is not unusual for time series data to exhibit some type of upward or downward trend over time. Trend is the long-term sweep or general direction of movement in a time series. It reflects the net influence of long-term factors that affect the time series in a fairly consistent and gradual way over time. In other words, the trend reflects changes in the data that occur with the passage of time.

Because the moving average, weighted moving average, and exponential smoothing techniques use some average of the previous values to forecast future values, they consistently *underestimate* the actual values if there is an upward trend in the data. For example, consider the time series data given by 2, 4, 6, 8, 10, 12, 14, 16, and 18. These data show a clear upward trend leading us to expect that the next value in the time series should be 20. However, the forecasting techniques discussed up to this point would forecast that the next value in the series is less than or equal to 18 because no weighted average of the given data could exceed 18. Similarly, if there is a downward trend in the data over time, all of the methods discussed so far would produce predictions that *overestimate* the actual values in the time series. In the following sections, we will consider several techniques that are appropriate for nonstationary time series involving an upward or downward trend in the data over time.

11.10.1 AN EXAMPLE

The following example will be used to illustrate a variety of techniques for modeling trends in time series data.

WaterCraft, Inc. is a manufacturer of personal watercraft (also known as jet skis). Throughout its first five years of operation, the company has enjoyed a fairly steady growth in sales of its products. The officers of the company are preparing sales and manufacturing plans for the coming year. A critical input to these plans involves a forecast of the level of sales that the company expects to achieve. Quarterly sales data for the company during the past five years are given in Figure 11.19 (and in the file Fig11-19.xls on your data disk).

**FIGURE
11.19**

*Historical sales
data for the
WaterCraft sales
forecasting
problem*

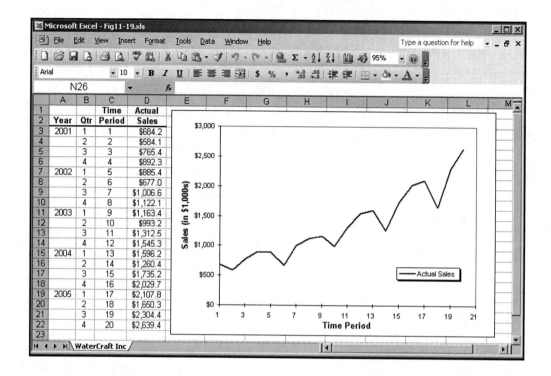

The plot of the data in Figure 11.19 suggests a fairly strong upward trend in the data over time. Thus, to forecast the value of this time series variable, we can use one of the forecasting techniques discussed in the following sections. These techniques account for a trend in the data.

11.11 Double Moving Average

As its name implies, the double moving average technique involves taking the average of averages. Let M_t be the moving average for the past k time periods (including t):

$$M_t = (Y_t + Y_{t-1} + \cdots + Y_{t-k+1})/k$$

The double moving average D_t for the last k time periods (including period t) is the average of the moving averages:

$$D_t = (M_t + M_{t-1} + \cdots + M_{t-k+1})/k$$

The double moving average forecasting function is then given by:

$$\hat{Y}_{t+n} = E_t + nT_t \qquad \qquad \textbf{11.11}$$

where:

$$E_t = 2M_t - D_t$$
$$T_t = 2(M_t - D_t)/(k-1)$$

The values of E_t and T_t are derived by minimizing the sum of squared errors using the last k periods of data. Note that E_t represents the estimated level of the time series at period t and T_t represents the estimated trend. Thus, at period t, the forecast n periods into the future would be $E_t + nT_t$ as indicated in equation 11.11.

Figure 11.20 (and file Fig11-20.xls on your data disk) shows how the double moving average technique with $k = 4$ can be applied to the sales data for WaterCraft, Inc.

FIGURE 11.20

Spreadsheet implementation of the double moving average technique

Key Cell Formulas

Cell	Formula	Copied to
E6	=AVERAGE(D3:D6)	E7:E22
F9	=AVERAGE(E6:E9)	F10:F22
G9	=2*E9-F9	G10:G22
H9	=2*(E9-F9)/(4-1)	H10:H22
I10	=G9+H9	I11:I22
I23	=$G$22+B23*$H$22	I24:I26

First, the four period moving averages (M_t) and double moving averages (D_t) are calculated in columns E and F, respectively, as follows:

Formula for cell E6:   =AVERAGE(D3:D6)

(Copy to cells E7 through E22.)

Formula for cell F9:   =AVERAGE(E6:E9)

(Copy to cells F10 through F22.)

The estimated level (E_t) and trend (T_t) values for each period are calculated in columns G and H, respectively, as follows:

Formula for cell G9:   =2*E9-F9

(Copy to cells G10 through G22.)

Formula for cell H9:   =2*(E9-F9)/(4-1)

(Copy to cells H10 through H22.)

FIGURE
11.21

*Plot of double
moving average
predictions versus
actual WaterCraft
sales data*

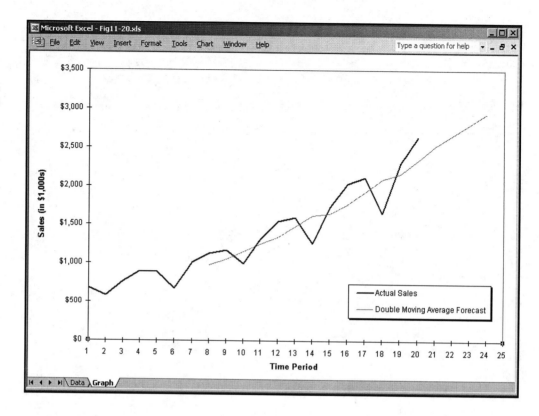

The predicted values for time periods 8 through 20 are then calculated in column I as follows:

Formula for cell I10:   =G9+H9

(Copy to cells I11 through I22.)

Figure 11.21 graphs the actual sales data against the values predicted by our model. Note that the predicted values seem to follow the upward trend in the actual data reasonably well.

11.11.1 FORECASTING WITH THE MODEL

We can use the results in Figure 11.20 to compute trend forecasts for any future time period. According to equation 11.11, at time period 20, the forecast for time period $20 + n$ is given by:

$$\hat{Y}_{20+n} = E_{20} + nT_{20}$$

The values of E_{20} and T_{20} are given in Figure 11.20 in cells G22 and H22, respectively ($E_{20} = 2385.33$ and $T_{20} = 139.9$). So at time period 20, trend forecasts for time periods 21, 22, 23, and 24 are computed as:

$$\hat{Y}_{21} = E_{20} + 1 \times T_{20} = 2385.33 + 1 \times 139.9 = 2525.23$$
$$\hat{Y}_{22} = E_{20} + 2 \times T_{20} = 2385.33 + 2 \times 139.9 = 2665.13$$
$$\hat{Y}_{23} = E_{20} + 3 \times T_{20} = 2385.33 + 3 \times 139.9 = 2805.03$$
$$\hat{Y}_{24} = E_{20} + 4 \times T_{20} = 2385.33 + 4 \times 139.9 = 2944.94$$

The calculations for these forecasts were implemented in Figure 11.20 as follows:

Formula for cell I23:   =$G$22+B23*$H$22

(Copy to cells I24 through I26.)

11.12 Double Exponential Smoothing (Holt's Method)

Double exponential smoothing (also known as Holt's method) is often an effective forecasting tool for time series data that exhibits a linear trend. After observing the value of the time series at period t (Y_t), Holt's method computes an estimate of the base, or expected, level of the time series (E_t), and the expected rate of increase or decrease (trend) per period (T_t). The forecasting function in Holt's method is represented by:

$$\hat{Y}_{t+n} = E_t + nT_t \qquad\qquad \textbf{11.12}$$

where

$$E_t = \alpha Y_t + (1 - \alpha)(E_{t-1} + T_{t-1}) \qquad\qquad \textbf{11.13}$$

$$T_t = \beta(E_t - E_{t-1}) + (1 - \beta)T_{t-1} \qquad\qquad \textbf{11.14}$$

We can use the forecasting function in equation 11.12 to obtain forecasts n time periods into the future where $n = 1, 2, 3$, and so on. The forecast for time period $t + n$ (or $\hat{Y}_{t+n}$) is the base level at time period t (given by E_t) plus the expected influence of the trend during the next n time periods (given by nT_t).

The smoothing parameters α and β in equations 11.13 and 11.14 can assume any value between 0 and 1 ($0 \leq \alpha \leq 1, 0 \leq \beta \leq 1$). If there is an upward trend in the data, E_t tends to be larger than E_{t-1}, making the quantity $E_t - E_{t-1}$ in equation 11.14 positive. This tends to increase the value of the trend adjustment factor T_t. Alternatively, if there is a downward trend in the data, E_t tends to be smaller than E_{t-1}, making the quantity $E_t - E_{t-1}$ in equation 11.14 negative. This tends to decrease the value of the trend adjustment factor T_t.

Although Holt's method might appear to be more complicated than the techniques discussed earlier, it is a simple three-step process:

1. Compute the base level E_t for time period t using equation 11.13.
2. Compute the expected trend value T_t for time period t using equation 11.14.
3. Compute the final forecast $\hat{Y}_{t+n}$ for time period $t + n$ using equation 11.12.

The spreadsheet implementation of Holt's method for the WaterCraft problem is shown in Figure 11.22 (and in the file Fig11-22.xls on your data disk).

Cells J3 and J4 represent the values of α and β, respectively. Column E implements the base levels for each time period as required in step 1 (that is, this column contains the E_t values). Equation 11.6 assumes that for any time period t the base level for the previous time period (E_{t-1}) is known. It is customary to assume that $E_1 = Y_1$, as reflected by the formula in cell E3:

Formula for cell E3:   =D3

The remaining E_t values are calculated using equation 11.13 in cells E4 through E22 as:

Formula for cell E4:   =$J$3*D4+(1−$J$3)*(E3+F3)

(Copy to E5 through E22.)

FIGURE
11.22

*Spreadsheet
implementation of
Holt's method*

Variable Cells ——

Set Cell ——

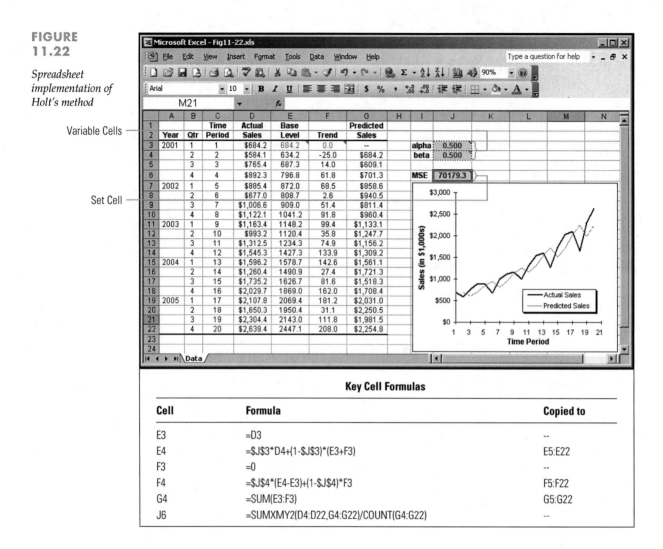

Key Cell Formulas		
Cell	**Formula**	**Copied to**
E3	=D3	--
E4	=$J$3*D4+(1-$J$3)*(E3+F3)	E5:E22
F3	=0	--
F4	=$J$4*(E4-E3)+(1-$J$4)*F3	F5:F22
G4	=SUM(E3:F3)	G5:G22
J6	=SUMXMY2(D4:D22,G4:G22)/COUNT(G4:G22)	--

Column F implements the expected trend values for each time period as required in step 2 (that is, this column contains the T_t values). Equation 11.14 assumes that for any time period t, the expected trend value at the previous time period (T_{t-1}) is known. So, we assume as an initial trend estimate that $T_t = 0$ (although any other initial trend estimate could be used), as reflected by the formula in cell F3:

Formula for cell F3:   =0

The remaining T_t values are calculated using equation 11.14 in cells F4 through F22 as:

Formula for cell F4:   =$J$4*(E4−E3)+(1−$J$4)*F3

(Copy to F5 through F22.)

According to equation 11.12, at any time period t, the forecast for time period $t + 1$ is represented by:

$$\hat{Y}_{t+1} = E_t + 1 \times T_t$$

At time period $t = 1$ shown in Figure 11.22, the forecast for time period $t = 2$ (shown in cell G4) is obtained by summing the values in cells E3 and F3, which correspond to

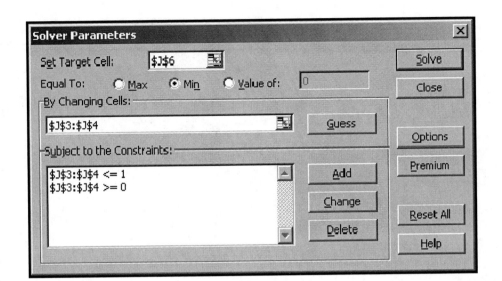

**FIGURE
11.23**

*Solver parameters
and options for
Holt's method*

E_1 and T_1, respectively. Thus, the forecast for time period $t = 2$ is implemented in cell G4 as:

Formula for cell G4:   =SUM(E3:F3)

(Copy to G5 through G22.)

This formula is copied to cells G5 through G22 to compute the predictions made using Holt's method for the remaining time periods.

We can use Solver to determine the values for α and β that minimize the MSE. The MSE for the predicted values is calculated in cell J6 as:

Formula for cell J6:   =SUMXMY2(D4:D22,G4:G22)/COUNT(G4:G22)

We can use the Solver parameters and options shown in Figure 11.23 to identify the values for α and β that minimize the nonlinear MSE objective. Figure 11.24 shows the solution to this problem. The graph in Figure 11.24 indicates that the predictions obtained using Holt's method follow the trend in the data quite well.

11.12.1 FORECASTING WITH HOLT'S METHOD

We can use the results in Figure 11.24 to compute forecasts for any future time period. According to equation 11.12, at time period 20, the forecast for time period $20 + n$ is represented by:

$$\hat{Y}_{20+n} = E_{20} + nT_{20}$$

The values of E_{20} and T_{20} are given in Figure 11.24 in cells E22 and F22, respectively ($E_{20} = 2336.8$ and $T_{20} = 152.1$). So at time period 20, forecasts for time periods 21, 22, 23, and 24 are computed as:

$$\hat{Y}_{21} = E_{20} + 1 \times T_{20} = 2336.8 + 1 \times 152.1 = 2{,}488.9$$
$$\hat{Y}_{22} = E_{20} + 2 \times T_{20} = 2336.8 + 2 \times 152.1 = 2{,}641.0$$
$$\hat{Y}_{23} = E_{20} + 3 \times T_{20} = 2336.8 + 3 \times 152.1 = 2{,}793.1$$
$$\hat{Y}_{24} = E_{20} + 4 \times T_{20} = 2336.8 + 4 \times 152.1 = 2{,}945.2$$

FIGURE 11.24

Optimal solution and forecasts using Holt's method

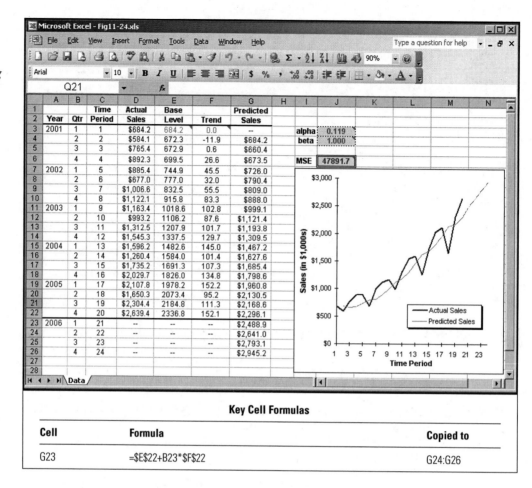

Key Cell Formulas

Cell	Formula	Copied to
G23	=$E$22+B23*$F$22	G24:G26

The calculations for these forecasts were implemented in Figure 11.24 as follows:

Formula for cell G23:   =$E$22+B23*$F$22

(Copy to cells G23 through G26.)

11.13 Holt-Winter's Method for Additive Seasonal Effects

In addition to having an upward or downward trend, nonstationary data also may exhibit seasonal effects. Here again, the seasonal effects might be additive or multiplicative in nature. Holt-Winter's method is another forecasting technique that we can apply to time series exhibiting trend and seasonality. We discuss the Holt-Winter's method for *additive* seasonal effects in this section.

To demonstrate Holt-Winter's method for additive seasonal effects, let p represent the number of seasons in the time series (for quarterly data, $p = 4$; for monthly data, $p = 12$). The forecasting function is then given by:

$$\hat{Y}_{t+n} = E_t + nT_t + S_{t+n-p} \qquad \textbf{11.15}$$

where

$$E_t = \alpha(Y_t - S_{t-p}) + (1 - \alpha)(E_{t-1} + T_{t-1}) \qquad \textbf{11.16}$$

$$T_t = \beta(E_t - E_{t-1}) + (1 - \beta)T_{t-1} \qquad \textbf{11.17}$$

$$S_t = \gamma(Y_t - E_t) + (1 - \gamma)S_{t-p} \qquad \textbf{11.18}$$

We can use the forecasting function in equation 11.15 to obtain forecasts n time periods into the future where $n = 1, 2, \ldots, p$. The forecast for time period $t + n$ ($\hat{Y}_{t+n}$) is obtained in equation 11.15 by adjusting the expected base level at time period $t + n$ (given by $E_t + nT_t$) by the most recent estimate of the seasonality associated with this time period (given by S_{t+n-p}). The smoothing parameters α, β, and γ (gamma) in equations 11.16, 11.17, and 11.18 can assume any value between 0 and 1 ($0 \le \alpha \le 1, 0 \le \beta \le 1, 0 \le \gamma \le 1$).

The expected base level of the time series in time period t (E_t) is updated in equation 11.16, which takes a weighted average of the following two values:

- $E_{t-1} + T_{t-1}$, which represents the expected base level of the time series at time period t before observing the actual value at time period t (given by Y_t).
- $Y_t - S_{t-p}$, which represents the deseasonalized estimate of the base level of the time series at time period t after observing Y_t.

The estimated per-period trend factor T_t is updated using equation 11.17, which is identical to the procedure in equation 11.14 used in Holt's method. The estimated seasonal adjustment factor for each time period is calculated using equation 11.18, which takes a weighted average of the following two quantities:

- S_{t-p}, which represents the most recent seasonal index for the season in which time period t occurs.
- $Y_t - E_t$, which represents an estimate of the seasonality associated with time period t after observing Y_t.

Holt-Winter's method is basically a four-step process:

1. Compute the base level E_t for time period t using equation 11.16.
2. Compute the estimated trend value T_t for time period t using equation 11.17.
3. Compute the estimated seasonal factor S_t for time period t using equation 11.18.
4. Compute the final forecast $\hat{Y}_{t+n}$ for time period $t + n$ using equation 11.15.

The spreadsheet implementation of Holt-Winter's method for the WaterCraft data is shown in Figure 11.25 (and in the file Fig11-25.xls on your data disk). Cells K3, K4, and K5 represent the values of α, β, and γ, respectively.

Equations 11.16 and 11.18 assume that at time period t an estimate of the seasonal factor from time period $t - p$ exists or that there is a value for S_{t-p}. Thus, our first task in implementing this method is to estimate values for $S_1, S_2, \ldots, S_p$ (or, in this case, S_1, S_2, S_3, and S_4). One easy way to make these initial estimates is to let:

$$S_t = Y_t - \sum_{i=1}^{p} \frac{Y_i}{p}, t = 1, 2, \ldots, p \qquad \textbf{11.19}$$

Equation 11.19 indicates that the initial seasonal estimate S_t for each of the first p time periods is the difference between the observed value in time period Y_t and the average value observed during the first p periods. In our example, the first four seasonal factors shown in column G in Figure 11.25 are calculated using equation 11.19 as:

Formula for cell G3:   =D3-AVERAGE($D$3:$D$6)

(Copy to G4 through G6.)

FIGURE 11.25

Spreadsheet implementation of Holt-Winter's method for additive seasonal effects

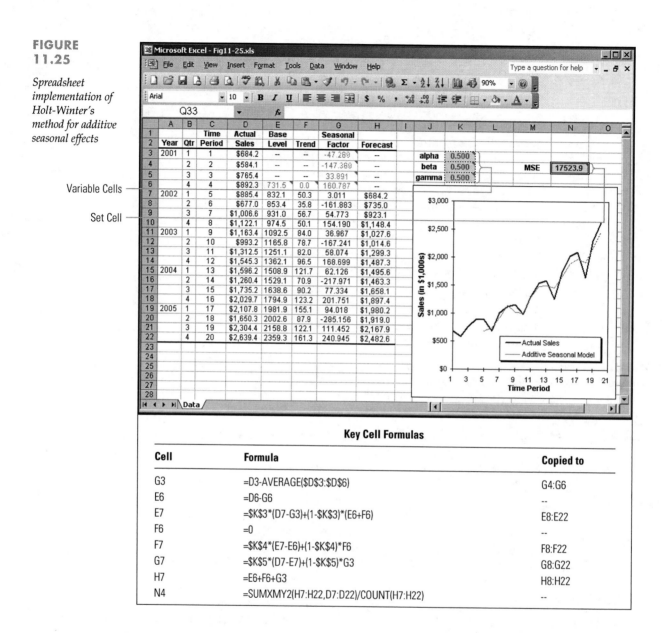

Key Cell Formulas

Cell	Formula	Copied to
G3	=D3-AVERAGE($D$3:$D$6)	G4:G6
E6	=D6-G6	--
E7	=$K$3*(D7-G3)+(1-$K$3)*(E6+F6)	E8:E22
F6	=0	--
F7	=$K$4*(E7-E6)+(1-$K$4)*F6	F8:F22
G7	=$K$5*(D7-E7)+(1-$K$5)*G3	G8:G22
H7	=E6+F6+G3	H8:H22
N4	=SUMXMY2(H7:H22,D7:D22)/COUNT(H7:H22)	--

The first E_t value that can be computed using equation 11.16 occurs at time period $p + 1$ (in our example, time period 5) because this is the first time period for which S_{t-p} is known. However, to compute E_5 using equation 11.16, we also need to know E_4 (which cannot be computed using equation 11.16 because S_0 is undefined) and T_4 (which cannot be computed using equation 11.17 because E_4 and E_3 are undefined). Thus, we assume $E_4 = Y_4 - S_4$ (so that $E_4 + S_4 = Y_4$) and $T_4 = 0$, as reflected by placing the following formulas in cells E6 and F6:

Formula for cell E6:   =D6-G6

Formula for cell F6:   =0

We generated the remaining E_t values using equation 11.16, which is implemented in Figure 11.25 as:

Formula for cell E7:   = $K$3*(D7-G3)+(1-$K$3)*(E6+F6)

(Copy to E8 through E22.)

We generated the remaining T_t values using equation 11.17, which is implemented in Figure 11.25 as:

Formula for cell F7:   =$K$4*(E7−E6)+(1−$K$4)*F6

(Copy to F8 through F22.)

We used equation 11.18 to generate the remaining S_t values in Figure 11.25 as:

Formula for cell G7:   =$K$5*(D7-E7)+(1−$K$5)*G3

(Copy to G8 through G22.)

Finally, at time period 4, we can use the forecasting function in equation 11.15 to predict one period ahead for time period 5. This is implemented in Figure 11.25 as:

Formula for cell H7:   =E6+F6+G3

(Copy to H8 through H22.)

Before making predictions using this method, we want to identify optimal values for α, β, and γ. We can use Solver to determine the values for α, β, and γ that minimize the MSE. The MSE for the predicted values is calculated in cell N4 as:

Formula for cell N4:   =SUMXMY2(H7:H22, D7:D22)/COUNT(H7:H22)

We can use the Solver parameters and options shown in Figure 11.26 to identify the values for α, β, and γ that minimize the nonlinear MSE objective. Figure 11.27 shows the solution to this problem.

Figure 11.27 displays a graph of the predictions obtained using Holt-Winter's method and the actual data. This graph indicates that the forecasting function fits the data reasonably well. However, it does appear that the seasonal effects in the data might be becoming more pronounced over time—suggesting that a model with multiplicative seasonal effects might be more appropriate in this case.

11.13.1 FORECASTING WITH HOLT-WINTER'S ADDITIVE METHOD

We can use the results in Figure 11.27 to compute forecasts for any future time period. According to equation 11.15, at time period 20 the forecast for time period $20 + n$ is represented by:

$$\hat{Y}_{20+n} = E_{20} + nT_{20} + S_{20+n-p}$$

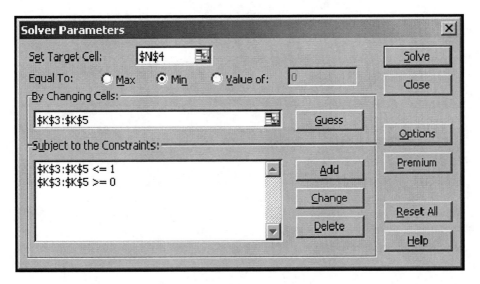

FIGURE 11.26

Solver parameters and options for Holt-Winter's method

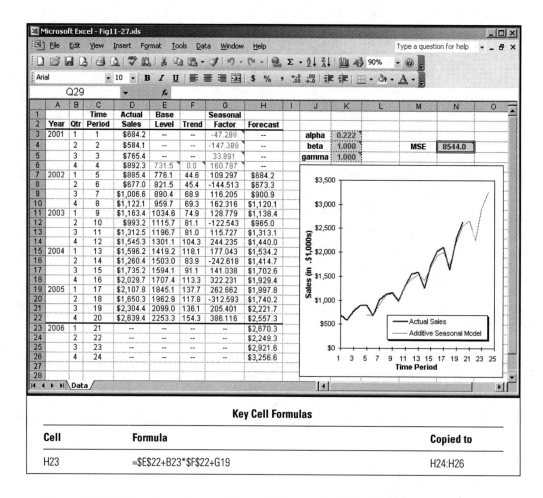

Cell	Formula	Copied to
H23	=$E$22+B23*$F$22+G19	H24:H26

Figure 11.27 shows the values of E_{20} and T_{20} in cells E22 and F22, respectively (E_{20} = 2253.3 and T_{20} = 154.3). At time period 20, forecasts for time periods 21, 22, 23, and 24 are computed as:

$$\hat{Y}_{21} = E_{20} + 1 \times T_{20} + S_{17} = 2{,}253.3 + 1 \times 154.3 + 262.662 = 2{,}670.3$$

$$\hat{Y}_{22} = E_{20} + 2 \times T_{20} + S_{18} = 2{,}253.3 + 2 \times 154.3 - 312.593 = 2{,}249.3$$

$$\hat{Y}_{23} = E_{20} + 3 \times T_{20} + S_{19} = 2{,}253.3 + 3 \times 154.3 + 205.401 = 2{,}921.6$$

$$\hat{Y}_{24} = E_{20} + 4 \times T_{20} + S_{20} = 2{,}253.3 + 4 \times 154.3 + 386.116 = 3{,}256.6$$

The calculations for these forecasts were implemented in Figure 11.27 as follows:

Formula for cell H23:=$E$22+B23*$F$22+G19

(Copy to cells H24 through H26.)

11.14 Holt-Winter's Method for Multiplicative Seasonal Effects

As noted previously, the graph in Figure 11.27 indicates that the seasonal effects in the data might be becoming more pronounced over time. As a result, it might be more appropriate to model this data with the Holt-Winter method for *multiplicative* seasonal effects. Fortunately, this technique is very similar to Holt-Winter's method for additive seasonal effects.

To demonstrate Holt-Winter's method for multiplicative seasonal effects, we again let p represent the number of seasons in the time series (for quarterly data, $p = 4$; for monthly data, $p = 12$). The forecasting function is then given by:

$$\hat{Y}_{t+n} = (E_t + nT_t)S_{t+n-p} \qquad \textbf{11.20}$$

where

$$E_t = \alpha \frac{Y_t}{S_{t-p}} + (1 - \alpha)(E_{t-1} + T_{t-1}) \qquad \textbf{11.21}$$

$$T_t = \beta(E_t - E_{t-1}) + (1 - \beta)T_{t-1} \qquad \textbf{11.22}$$

$$S_t = \gamma \frac{Y_t}{E_t} + (1 - \gamma)S_{t-p} \qquad \textbf{11.23}$$

Here, the forecast for time period $t + n$ ($\hat{Y}_{t+n}$) is obtained from equation 11.20 by *multiplying* the expected base level at time period $t + n$ (given by $E_t + nT_t$) by the most recent estimate of the seasonality associated with this time period (given by S_{t+n-p}). The smoothing parameters α, β, and γ (gamma) in equations 11.21, 11.22, and 11.23 again can assume any value between 0 and 1 ($0 \leq \alpha \leq 1, 0 \leq \beta \leq 1, 0 \leq \gamma \leq 1$).

The expected base level of the time series in time period t (E_t) is updated in equation 11.21, which takes a weighted average of the following two values:

- $E_{t-1} + T_{t-1}$, which represents the expected base level of the time series at time period t before observing the actual value at time period t (given by Y_t).
- $\frac{Y_t}{S_{t-p}}$, which represents the deseasonalized estimate of the base level of the time series at time period t after observing Y_t.

The estimated seasonal adjustment factor for each time period is calculated using equation 11.23, which takes a weighted average of the following two quantities:

- S_{t-p}, which represents the most recent seasonal index for the season in which time period t occurs.
- $\frac{Y_t}{E_t}$, which represents an estimate of the seasonality associated with time period t after observing Y_t.

The spreadsheet implementation of Holt-Winter's method for the WaterCraft data is shown in Figure 11.28 (and in the file Fig11-28.xls on your data disk). Cells K3, K4, and K5 represent the values of α, β, and γ, respectively.

Equations 11.21 and 11.23 assume that at time period t, an estimate of the seasonal index from time period $t-p$ exists or that there is a value for S_{t-p}. Thus, we need to estimate values for $S_1, S_2, \ldots, S_p$. An easy way to do this is to let:

$$S_t = \frac{Y_t}{\displaystyle\sum_{i=1}^{p} \frac{Y_i}{p}}, \quad t = 1, 2, \ldots, p \qquad \textbf{11.24}$$

Equation 11.24 indicates that the initial seasonal estimate S_t for each of the first p time periods is the ratio of the observed value in time period Y_t divided by the average value observed during the first p periods. In our example, the first four seasonal factors shown in column G in Figure 11.28 are calculated using equation 11.19 as:

Formula for cell G3:　　　=D3/AVERAGE($D$3:$D$6)

(Copy to G4 through G6.)

Variable Cells

Set Cell

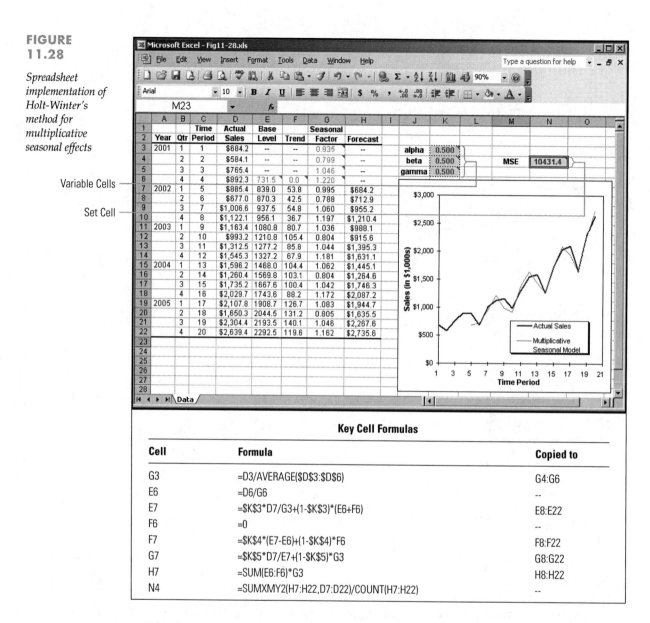

Key Cell Formulas

Cell	Formula	Copied to
G3	=D3/AVERAGE($D$3:$D$6)	G4:G6
E6	=D6/G6	--
E7	=$K$3*D7/G3+(1-$K$3)*(E6+F6)	E8:E22
F6	=0	--
F7	=$K$4*(E7-E6)+(1-$K$4)*F6	F8:F22
G7	=$K$5*D7/E7+(1-$K$5)*G3	G8:G22
H7	=SUM(E6:F6)*G3	H8:H22
N4	=SUMXMY2(H7:H22,D7:D22)/COUNT(H7:H22)	--

The first E_t value that can be computed using equation 11.21 occurs at time period $p + 1$ (in our example, time period 5) because this is the first time period for which S_{t-p} is known. However, to compute E_5 using equation 11.21, we also need to know E_4 (which cannot be computed using equation 11.16 because S_0 is undefined) and T_4 (which cannot be computed using equation 11.22 because E_4 and E_3 are undefined). Thus, we assume $E_4 = Y_4/S_4$ (so that $E_4 \times S_4 = Y_4$) and $T_4 = 0$, as reflected by placing the following formulas in cells E6 and F6:

Formula for cell E6:   =D6/G6

Formula for cell F6:   =0

We generated the remaining E_t values using equation 11.21, which is implemented in Figure 11.28 as:

Formula for cell E7:   =$K$3*D7/G3+(1−$K$3)*(E6+F6)

(Copy to E8 through E22.)

We generated the remaining T_t values using equation 11.22, which is implemented as:

Formula for cell F7:   =$K$4*(E7−E6)+(1−$K$4)*F6

(Copy to F8 through F22.)

We used equation 11.23 to generate the remaining S_t values as:

Formula for cell G7:   =$K$5*D7/E7+(1−$K$5)*G3

(Copy to G8 through G22.)

Finally, at time period 4, we can use the forecasting function in equation 11.20 to predict one period ahead for time period 5. This is implemented as:

Formula for cell H7:   =SUM(E6:F6)*G3

(Copy to H8 through H22.)

Before making predictions using this method, we want to identify optimal values for α, β, and γ. We can use Solver to determine the values for α, β, and γ that minimize the MSE. The MSE for the predicted values is calculated in cell N4 as:

Formula for cell N4:   =SUMXMY2(H7:H22,D7:D22)/COUNT(H7:H22)

We can use the Solver parameters and options shown in Figure 11.29 to identify the values for α, β, and γ that minimize the nonlinear MSE objective. Figure 11.30 shows the solution to this problem.

Figure 11.30 displays a graph of the predictions obtained using Holt-Winter's multiplicative method and the actual data. Comparing this graph to the one in Figure 11.27, it seems that the multiplicative model produces a forecasting function that might fit the data better.

11.14.1 FORECASTING WITH HOLT-WINTER'S MULTIPLICATIVE METHOD

We can use the results in Figure 11.30 to compute forecasts for any future time period. According to equation 11.15, at time period 20 the forecast for time period $20 + n$ is represented by:

$$\hat{Y}_{20+n} = (E_{20} + nT_{20})S_{20+n-p}$$

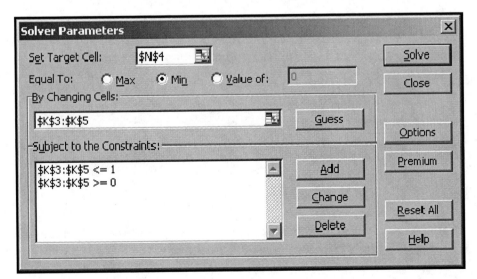

FIGURE 11.29

Solver parameters and options for Holt-Winter's multiplicative method

FIGURE 11.30

Optimal solution for Holt-Winter's method for multiplicative seasonal effects

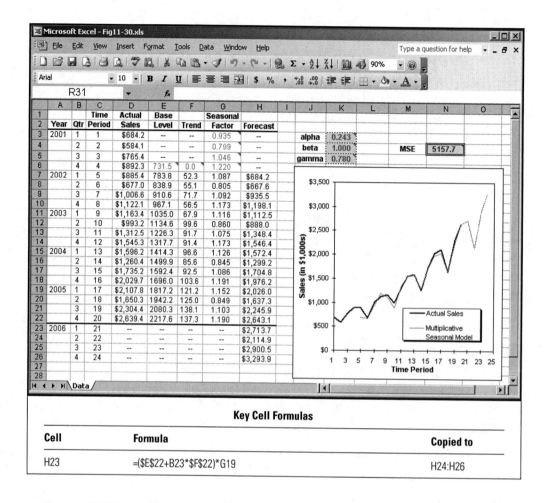

Key Cell Formulas

Cell	Formula	Copied to
H23	=($E$22+B23*$F$22)*G19	H24:H26

Figure 11.30 shows the values of E_{20} and T_{20} in cells E22 and F22, respectively (E_{20} = 2217.6 and T_{20} = 137.3). At time period 20, forecasts for time periods 21, 22, 23, and 24 are computed as:

$$\hat{Y}_{21} = (E_{20} + 1 \times T_{20})S_{17} = (2217.6 + 1 \times 137.3)1.152 = 2{,}713.7$$

$$\hat{Y}_{22} = (E_{20} + 2 \times T_{20})S_{18} = (2217.6 + 2 \times 137.3)0.849 = 2{,}114.9$$

$$\hat{Y}_{23} = (E_{20} + 3 \times T_{20})S_{19} = (2217.6 + 3 \times 137.3)1.103 = 2{,}900.5$$

$$\hat{Y}_{24} = (E_{20} + 4 \times T_{20})S_{20} = (2217.6 + 4 \times 137.3)1.190 = 3{,}293.9$$

The calculations for these forecasts were implemented in Figure 11.30 as follows:

Formula for cell H23:   =($E$22+B23*$F$22)*G19
(Copy to cells H24 through H26.)

11.15 Modeling Time Series Trends Using Regression

As mentioned in the introduction, we can build a regression model of a time series if data are available for one or more independent variables that account for the systematic movements in the time series. However, even if no independent variables have a *causal* relationship with the time series, some independent variables might have a *predictive* relationship with the time series. A predictor variable does not have a cause-and-effect relationship with the time series. Yet the behavior of a predictor variable might be correlated with that of the time series in a way that helps us forecast future values of the time series. In the following sections, we will consider how to use predictor variables as independent variables in regression models for time series data.

As mentioned earlier, trend is the long-term sweep or general direction of movement in a time series that reflects changes in the data over time. The mere passage of time does not cause the trend in the time series. But like the consistent passage of time, the trend of a time series reflects the steady upward or downward movement in the general direction of the series. Thus, time itself might represent a predictor variable that could be useful in accounting for the trend in a time series.

11.16 Linear Trend Model

To see how we might use time as an independent variable, consider the following linear regression model:

$$Y_t = \beta_0 + \beta_1 X_{1_t} + \varepsilon_t \tag{11.25}$$

where $X_{1_t} = t$. That is, the independent variable X_{1_t} represents the time period t ($X_{1_1} = 1$, $X_{1_2} = 2$, $X_{1_3} = 3$, and so on). The regression model in equation 11.25 assumes that the *systematic* variation in the time series (Y_t) can be described by the regression function $\beta_0 + \beta_1 X_{1_t}$ (which is a linear function of time). The error term ε_t in equation 11.25 represents the *unsystematic*, or random, variation in the time series not accounted for by our model. Because the values of Y_t are assumed to vary randomly around (above and below) the regression function $\beta_0 + \beta_1 X_{1_t}$, the average (or expected) value of ε_t is 0. Thus, if we use ordinary least squares to estimate the parameters in equation 11.25, our best estimate of Y_t for any time period t is:

$$\hat{Y}_t = b_0 + b_1 X_{1_t} \tag{11.26}$$

In equation 11.26, the estimated value of the time series at time period t ($\hat{Y}_t$) is a linear function of the independent variable, which is coded to represent time. Thus, equation 11.26 represents the equation of the line passing through the time series that minimizes the sum of squared differences between the actual values (Y_t) and the estimated values ($\hat{Y}_t$). We might interpret this line to represent the linear trend in the data.

An example of this technique is shown in Figure 11.31 (and in the file Fig11-31.xls on your data disk) for the quarterly sales data for WaterCraft. We can use the Time Period values in cells C3 through C22 as the values for the independent variable X_1 in our regression model. Thus, we can use the Regression command settings shown in Figure 11.32 to obtain the values for b_0 and b_1 required for the estimated regression function for these data.

Figure 11.33 shows the results of the Regression command, which indicate that the estimated regression function is:

$$\hat{Y}_t = 375.17 + 92.6255 X_{1_t} \tag{11.27}$$

Figure 11.31 shows the predicted sales level for each time period in column E (labeled "Linear Trend") where the following formula is entered in cell E3 and copied to cells E4 through E26:

Formula for cell E3:   =TREND($D$3:$D$22,$C$3:$C$22,C3)

(Copy to E4 through E26.)

FIGURE 11.31

Spreadsheet implementation of the linear trend model

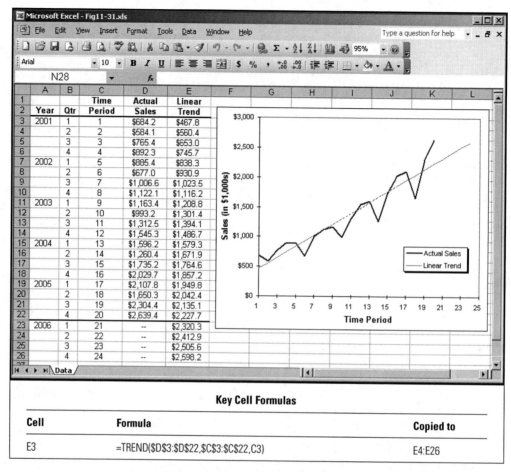

Key Cell Formulas

Cell	Formula	Copied to
E3	=TREND($D$3:$D$22,$C$3:$C$22,C3)	E4:E26

FIGURE 11.32

Regression command settings for the linear trend model

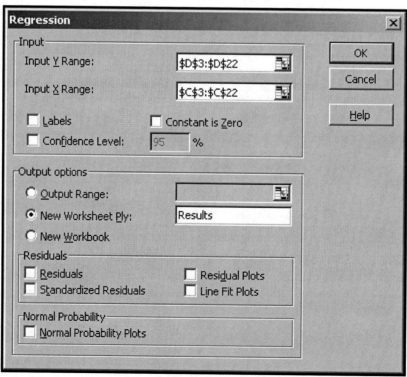

FIGURE
11.33

*Regression results
for the linear trend
model*

Microsoft Excel - Fig11-31.xls

	A	B	C	D	E	F	G	H	I
1	SUMMARY OUTPUT								
2									
3	*Regression Statistics*								
4	Multiple R	0.9341411							
5	R Square	0.8726197							
6	Adjusted R Square	0.865543							
7	Standard Error	215.10166							
8	Observations	20							
9									
10	ANOVA								
11		*df*	*SS*	*MS*	*F*	*Significance F*			
12	Regression	1	5705355.628	5705356	123.309	1.74046E-09			
13	Residual	18	832837.0251	46268.7					
14	Total	19	6538192.653						
15									
16		*Coefficients*	*Standard Error*	*t Stat*	*P-value*	*Lower 95%*	*Upper 95%*	*Lower 95.0%*	*Upper 95.0%*
17	Intercept	375.17	99.92148676	3.75465	0.00145	165.2427463	585.097253	165.242746	585.0972533
18	X Variable 1	92.625494	8.341284553	11.1045	1.7E-09	75.10110551	110.149883	75.1011055	110.1498826
19									

11.16.1 FORECASTING WITH THE LINEAR TREND MODEL

We can use equation 11.27 to generate forecasts of sales for any future time period t by setting $X_{1_t} = t$. For example, forecasts for time periods 21, 22, 23, and 24 are computed as:

$$\hat{Y}_{21} = 375.17 + 92.6255 \times 21 = 2{,}320.3$$
$$\hat{Y}_{22} = 375.17 + 92.6255 \times 22 = 2{,}412.9$$
$$\hat{Y}_{23} = 375.17 + 92.6255 \times 23 = 2{,}505.6$$
$$\hat{Y}_{24} = 375.17 + 92.6255 \times 24 = 2{,}598.2$$

Note that these forecasts were calculated using the TREND( ) function in cells E23 through E26 in Figure 11.31.

Again, as the forecast horizon lengthens, our confidence in the accuracy of the forecasts diminishes because there is no guarantee that the historical trends on which the model is based will continue indefinitely into the future.

> ### A Note on the TREND( ) Function
>
> The TREND( ) function can be used to calculate the estimated values for linear regression models. The format of the TREND( ) function is as follows:
>
> TREND(Y-range, X-range, X-value for prediction)
>
> where Y-range is the range in the spreadsheet containing the dependent Y variable, X-range is the range in the spreadsheet containing the independent X variable(s), and X-value for prediction is a cell (or cells) containing the values for the independent X variable(s) for which we want an estimated value of Y. The TREND( ) function has an advantage over the regression tool in that it is dynamically updated whenever any inputs to the function change. However, it does not provide the statistical information provided by the regression tool. It is best to use these two different approaches to doing regression in conjunction with one another.

11.17 Quadratic Trend Model

Although the graph of the estimated linear regression function shown in Figure 11.31 accounts for the upward trend in the data, the actual values do not appear to be scattered randomly around the trend line, as was assumed by our regression model in equation 11.25. An observation is more likely to be substantially below the line or only slightly above the line. This suggests that the linear trend model might not be appropriate for this data.

As an alternative, we might try fitting a curved trend line to the data using the following quadratic model:

$$Y_t = \beta_0 + \beta_1 X_{1_t} + \beta_2 X_{2_t} + \varepsilon_t \qquad \textbf{11.28}$$

where $X_{1_t} = t$ and $X_{2_t} = t^2$. The resulting *estimated* regression function for this model is:

$$\hat{Y}_t = b_0 + b_1 X_{1_t} + b_2 X_{2_t} \qquad \textbf{11.29}$$

To estimate the quadratic trend function, we must add a column to the spreadsheet to represent the additional independent variable $X_{2_t} = t^2$. This can be accomplished as shown in Figure 11.34 (and in the file Fig11-34.xls on your data disk) by inserting a new column D and placing the values t^2 in this column. Thus, the following formula is entered in cell D3 and copied to cells D4 through D26:

Formula for cell D3:   =C3^2

(Copy to D4 through D26.)

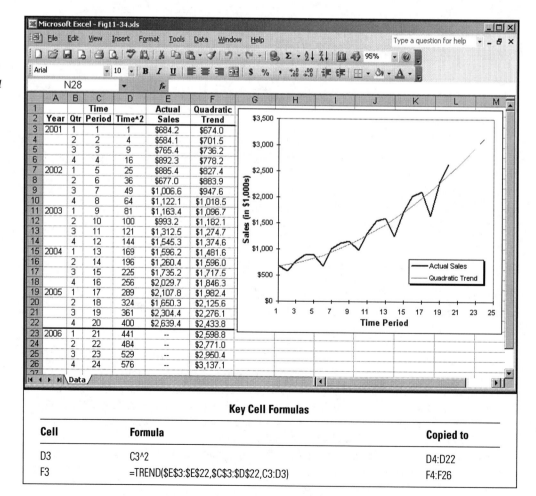

Key Cell Formulas

Cell	Formula	Copied to
D3	C3^2	D4:D22
F3	=TREND($E$3:$E$22,$C$3:$D$22,C3:D3)	F4:F26

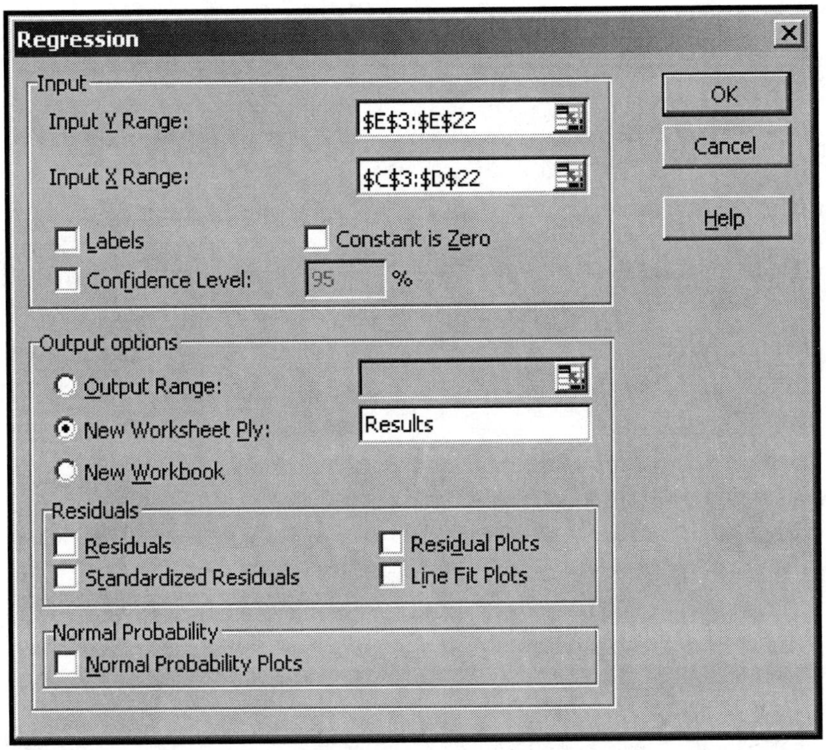

FIGURE 11.35

Regression command settings for the quadratic trend model

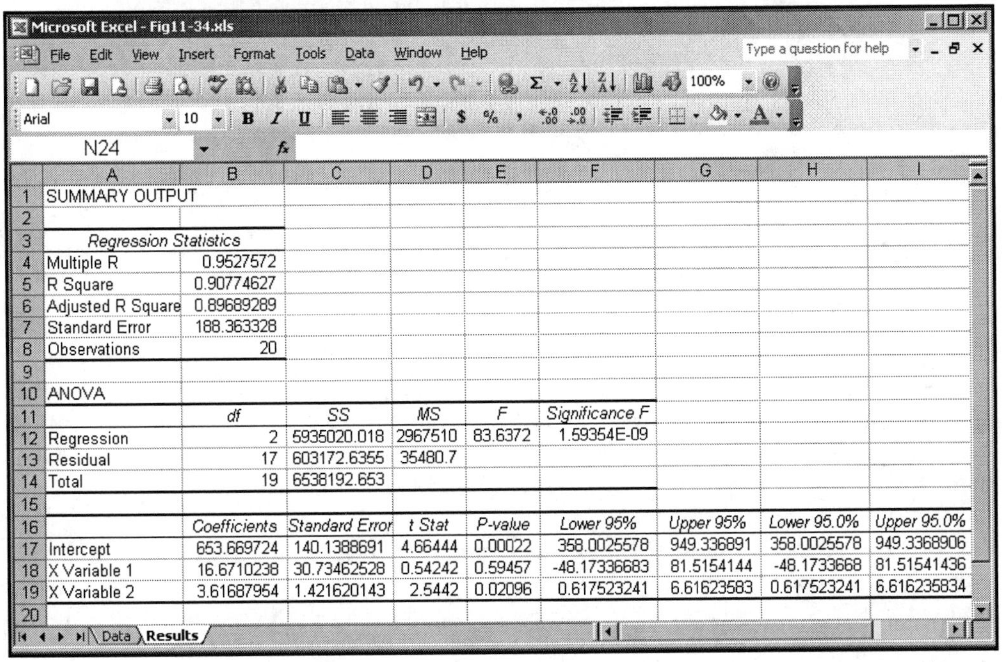

SUMMARY OUTPUT

Regression Statistics	
Multiple R	0.9527572
R Square	0.90774627
Adjusted R Square	0.89689289
Standard Error	188.363328
Observations	20

ANOVA

	df	SS	MS	F	Significance F
Regression	2	5935020.018	2967510	83.6372	1.59354E-09
Residual	17	603172.6355	35480.7		
Total	19	6538192.653			

	Coefficients	Standard Error	t Stat	P-value	Lower 95%	Upper 95%	Lower 95.0%	Upper 95.0%
Intercept	653.669724	140.1388691	4.66444	0.00022	358.0025578	949.336891	358.0025578	949.3368906
X Variable 1	16.6710238	30.73462528	0.54242	0.59457	-48.17336683	81.5154144	-48.1733668	81.51541436
X Variable 2	3.61687954	1.421620143	2.5442	0.02096	0.617523241	6.61623583	0.617523241	6.616235834

FIGURE 11.36

Regression results for the quadratic trend model

We can obtain the values of b_0, b_1, and b_2 required for the estimated regression function for this data using the Regression command settings shown in Figure 11.35.

Figure 11.36 shows the results of the Regression command, which indicate that the estimated regression function is:

$$\hat{Y}_t = 653.67 + 16.671\, X_{1_t} + 3.617\, X_{2_t} \qquad \textbf{11.30}$$

Figure 11.34 shows the estimated sales level for each time period in column F (labeled "Quadratic Trend") where the following formula is entered in cell F3 and copied to cells F4 through F26:

Formula for cell F3:   =TREND($E$3:$E$22,$C$3:$D$22,C3:D3)
(Copy to F4 through F26.)

Figure 11.34 also shows a graph of the sales levels predicted by the quadratic trend model versus the actual data. Notice that the quadratic trend curve fits the data better than the straight trend line shown in Figure 11.31. In particular, the deviations of the actual values above and below this curve are now more balanced.

11.17.1 FORECASTING WITH THE QUADRATIC TREND MODEL

We can use equation 11.30 to generate forecasts of sales for any future time period t by setting $X_{1_t} = t$ and $X_{2_t} = t^2$. For example, forecasts for time periods 21, 22, 23, and 24 are computed as:

$$\hat{Y}_{21} = 653.67 + 16.671 \times 21 + 3.617 \times (21)^2 = 2{,}598.8$$
$$\hat{Y}_{22} = 653.67 + 16.671 \times 22 + 3.617 \times (22)^2 = 2{,}771.0$$
$$\hat{Y}_{23} = 653.67 + 16.671 \times 23 + 3.617 \times (23)^2 = 2{,}950.4$$
$$\hat{Y}_{24} = 653.67 + 16.671 \times 24 + 3.617 \times (24)^2 = 3{,}137.1$$

Note that these forecasts were calculated using the TREND( ) function in cells F23 through F26 in Figure 11.34.

As with earlier models, as the forecast horizon lengthens, our confidence in the accuracy of the forecasts diminishes because there is no guarantee that the historical trends on which the model is based will continue indefinitely into the future.

11.18 Modeling Seasonality with Regression Models

The goal of any forecasting procedure is to develop a model that accounts for as much of the systematic variation in the past behavior of a time series as possible. The assumption is that a model that accurately explains what happened in the past will be useful in predicting what will happen in the future. Do the trend models shown in Figures 11.31 and 11.34 adequately account for all the systematic variation in the time series data?

All these graphs show a fairly regular pattern of fluctuation around the trend line. Notice that each point below the trend line is followed by three points at or above the trend line. This suggests that some additional *systematic* (or predictable) variation in the time series exists that is not accounted for by these models.

Figures 11.31 and 11.34 suggest that the data in the graphs include seasonal effects. In the second quarter of each year, sales drop well below the trend lines, whereas sales in the remaining quarters are at or above the trend line. Forecasts of future values for this time series would be more accurate if they reflected these systematic seasonal effects. The following sections discuss several techniques for modeling seasonal effects in time series data.

11.19 Adjusting Trend Predictions with Seasonal Indices

A simple and effective way of modeling multiplicative seasonal effects in a time series is to develop seasonal indices that reflect the average percentage by which observations in each season differ from their projected trend values. In the WaterCraft example, observations occurring in the second quarter fall below the values predicted using a trend model. Similarly, observations in the first, third, and fourth quarters are at or above the values predicted using a trend model. Thus, if we can determine seasonal indices representing the average amount by which the observations in a given quarter fall above or below the trend line, we could multiply our trend projections by these amounts and increase the accuracy of our forecasts.

We will demonstrate the calculation of multiplicative seasonal indices for the quadratic trend model developed earlier. However, we also could use this technique with any of the other trend or smoothing models discussed in this chapter. In Figure 11.37 (and in the file Fig11-37.xls on your data disk), columns A through F repeat the calculations for the quadratic trend model discussed earlier.

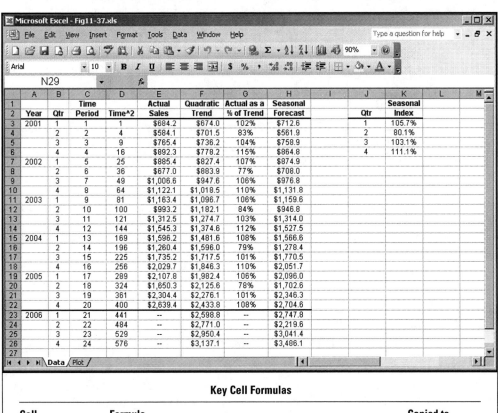

FIGURE 11.37

Spreadsheet implementation to calculate seasonal indices and seasonal forecasts for the quadratic trend model

Year	Qtr	Time Period	Time^2	Actual Sales	Quadratic Trend	Actual as a % of Trend	Seasonal Forecast		Qtr	Seasonal Index
2001	1	1	1	$684.2	$674.0	102%	$712.6		1	105.7%
	2	2	4	$584.1	$701.5	83%	$561.9		2	80.1%
	3	3	9	$765.4	$736.2	104%	$758.9		3	103.1%
	4	4	16	$892.3	$778.2	115%	$864.8		4	111.1%
2002	1	5	25	$885.4	$827.4	107%	$874.9			
	2	6	36	$677.0	$883.9	77%	$708.0			
	3	7	49	$1,006.6	$947.6	106%	$976.8			
	4	8	64	$1,122.1	$1,018.5	110%	$1,131.8			
2003	1	9	81	$1,163.4	$1,096.7	106%	$1,159.6			
	2	10	100	$993.2	$1,182.1	84%	$946.8			
	3	11	121	$1,312.5	$1,274.7	103%	$1,314.0			
	4	12	144	$1,545.3	$1,374.6	112%	$1,527.5			
2004	1	13	169	$1,596.2	$1,481.6	108%	$1,566.6			
	2	14	196	$1,260.4	$1,596.0	79%	$1,278.4			
	3	15	225	$1,735.2	$1,717.5	101%	$1,770.5			
	4	16	256	$2,029.7	$1,846.3	110%	$2,051.7			
2005	1	17	289	$2,107.8	$1,982.4	106%	$2,096.0			
	2	18	324	$1,650.3	$2,125.6	78%	$1,702.6			
	3	19	361	$2,304.4	$2,276.1	101%	$2,346.3			
	4	20	400	$2,639.4	$2,433.8	108%	$2,704.6			
2006	1	21	441	--	$2,598.8	--	$2,747.8			
	2	22	484	--	$2,771.0	--	$2,219.6			
	3	23	529	--	$2,950.4	--	$3,041.4			
	4	24	576	--	$3,137.1	--	$3,486.1			

Key Cell Formulas

Cell	Formula	Copied to
D3	=C3^2	D4:D26
F3	=TREND($E$3:$E$22,$C$3:$D$22,C3:D3)	F4:F26
G3	=E3/F3	G4:G22
K3	=SUMIF($B$3:$B$22,J3,$G$3:$G$22)/COUNTIF($B$3:$B$22,J3)	K4:K6
H3	=F3*VLOOKUP(B3,$J$3:$K$6,2)	H4:H26

11.19.1 COMPUTING SEASONAL INDICES

The goal in developing seasonal indices is to determine the average percentage by which observations in each season differ from the values projected for them using the trend model. To accomplish this, in column G of Figure 11.37, we calculated the ratio of each actual value in column E to its corresponding projected trend value shown in column F as:

Formula for cell G3:   =E3/F3

(Copy to G4 through G22.)

The value in cell G3 indicates that the actual value in time period 1 was 102% of (or approximately 2% larger than) its estimated trend value. The value in cell G4 indicates that the actual value in time period 2 was 83% of (or approximately 17% smaller than) its estimated trend value. The remaining values in column G have similar interpretations.

We obtain the seasonal index for each quarter by computing the average of the values in column G on a quarter-by-quarter basis. For example, the seasonal index for quarter 1 equals the average of the values in cells G3, G7, G11, G15, and G19. The seasonal index for quarter 2 equals the average of the values in cells G4, G8, G12, G16, and G20. Similar computations are required to calculate seasonal indices for quarters 3 and 4. We can use separate AVERAGE( ) functions for each quarter to compute these averages. However, for large data sets, such an approach would be tedious and prone to error. Thus, the averages shown in cells K3 through K6 are calculated as:

Formula for cell K3:   =SUMIF($B$3:$B$22,J3,$G$3:$G$22)/

(Copy to K4 through K6.)   COUNTIF($B$3:$B$22,J3)

The SUMIF( ) and COUNTIF( ) functions perform conditional sums and counts. The SUMIF( ) function in the previous formula sums the values in cells G3 through G22 for which the corresponding value in cells B3 through B22 equals the value in cell J3. This corresponds to the sum of the values in column G that occur in quarter 1. The COUNTIF( ) function in the previous equation counts the number of elements in cells B3 through B22 that equal the value in cell J3—or the number of quarter 1 observations.

The seasonal index for quarter 1 shown in cell K3 indicates that, on average, the actual sales value in the first quarter of any given year will be 105.7% of (or 5.7% larger than) the estimated trend value for the same time period. Similarly, the seasonal index for quarter 2 shown in cell K4 indicates that, on average, the actual sales value in the second quarter of any given year will be 80.1% of (or approximately 20% less than) the estimated trend value for the same time period. The seasonal indices for the third and fourth quarters have similar interpretations.

We can use the calculated seasonal indices to refine or adjust the trend estimates. This is accomplished in column H of Figure 11.37 as:

Formula for cell H3:   =F3*VLOOKUP(B3,$J$3:$K$6,2)

(Copy to H4 through H26.)

This formula takes the estimated trend value for each time period and multiplies it by the appropriate seasonal index for the quarter in which the time period occurs. The trend estimates for quarter 1 observations are multiplied by 105.7%, the trend estimates for quarter 2 observations are multiplied by 80.1%, and so on for quarters 3 and 4 observations.

Figure 11.38 shows a graph of the actual sales data versus the seasonal forecast calculated in column H of Figure 11.37. As this graph illustrates, the use of seasonal indices is very effective on this particular data set.

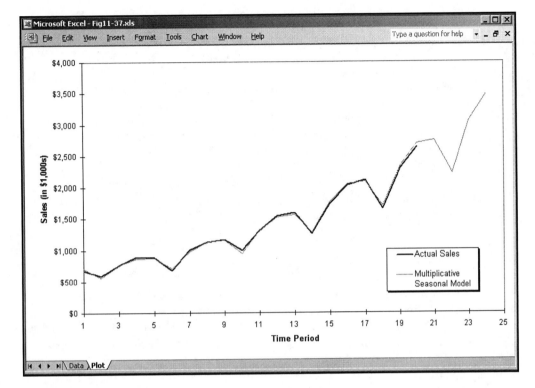

FIGURE 11.38

Plots of the predictions obtained using seasonal indices versus the actual WaterCraft sales data

11.19.2 FORECASTING WITH SEASONAL INDICES

We can use the seasonal indices to adjust trend projections of future time periods for the expected effects of seasonality. Earlier, we used the quadratic trend model to obtain the following forecasts of the expected level of sales in time periods 21, 22, 23, and 24:

$$\hat{Y}_{21} = 653.67 + 16.671 \times 21 + 3.617 \times (21)^2 = 2{,}598.8$$
$$\hat{Y}_{22} = 653.67 + 16.671 \times 22 + 3.617 \times (22)^2 = 2{,}771.0$$
$$\hat{Y}_{23} = 653.67 + 16.671 \times 23 + 3.617 \times (23)^2 = 2{,}950.4$$
$$\hat{Y}_{24} = 653.67 + 16.671 \times 24 + 3.617 \times (24)^2 = 3{,}137.1$$

To adjust these trend forecasts for the expected effects of seasonality, we multiply each of them by the appropriate seasonal index. Because time periods 21, 22, 23, and 24 occur in quarters 1, 2, 3, and 4, respectively, the seasonal forecasts are computed as:

Seasonal forecast for time period 21 = 2,598.9 × 105.7% = 2,747.8

Seasonal forecast for time period 22 = 2,771.1 × 80.1% = 2,219.6

Seasonal forecast for time period 23 = 2,950.5 × 103.1% = 3,041.4

Seasonal forecast for time period 24 = 3,137.2 × 111.1% = 3,486.1

These forecasts also are calculated in Figure 11.37. Note that although we demonstrated the calculation of multiplicative seasonal indices, additive seasonal indices could easily be obtained in a very similar manner.

> ### Summary of the Calculation and Use of Seasonal Indices
>
> 1. Create a trend model and calculate the estimated value ($\hat{Y}_t$) for each observation in the sample.
> 2. For each observation, calculate the ratio of the actual value to the predicted trend value: $Y_t / \hat{Y}_t$. (For additive seasonal effects, compute the difference: $Y_t - \hat{Y}_t$.)
> 3. For each season, compute the average of the values calculated in step 2. These are the seasonal indices.
> 4. Multiply any forecast produced by the trend model by the appropriate seasonal index calculated in step 3. (For additive seasonal effects, add the appropriate seasonal index to the forecast.)

11.19.3 REFINING THE SEASONAL INDICES

Although the approach for calculating seasonal indices illustrated in Figure 11.37 has considerable intuitive appeal, note that these seasonal adjustment factors are not necessarily optimal. Figure 11.39 shows a very similar approach to calculating seasonal indices that uses Solver to simultaneously determine the optimal values of the seasonal indices and the parameters of the quadratic trend model.

In Figure 11.39, cells J9, J10, and J11 are used to represent, respectively, the estimated values of b_0, b_1, and b_2 in the following quadratic trend model (where $X_{1_t} = t$ and $X_{2_t} = t^2$):

$$\hat{Y}_t = b_0 + b_1 X_{1_t} + b_2 X_{2_t}.$$

Note that the values shown in cells J9, J10, and J11 correspond to the least square estimates shown in Figure 11.36.

The quadratic trend estimates are then calculated in column F as follows:

Formula for cell F3:   =$J$9+$J$10*C3+$J$11*D3

(Copy to F4 through F22.)

Cells J3 through J6 represent the seasonal adjustment factors for each quarter. Note that the values shown in these cells correspond to the average seasonal adjustment values shown in Figure 11.37. Thus, the seasonal forecasts shown in column G of Figure 11.39 are computed as follows:

Formula for cell G3:   = F3*VLOOKUP(B3,$I$3:$J$6,2)

(Copy to G4 through G22.)

The forecasts shown in Figure 11.39 are exactly the same as those in Figure 11.37 and result in a MSE of 922.46 as shown in cell J13. However, we can use the Solver parameters shown in Figure 11.40 to determine values for the trend and seasonal parameters that minimize the MSE.

Figure 11.41 shows the optimal solution to this problem. Thus, using Solver to "fine-tune" the parameters for the model, we are able to reduce the MSE to approximately 400.

Note that the Solver model in Figure 11.40 used to solve this problem includes a constraint that requires the average of the seasonal indices in cell J7 to equal one (or 100%). To understand the reason for this, suppose that the seasonal indices average to something other than one, for example 105%. This suggests that the trend estimate is, on average, about 5% too low. Thus, if the seasonal indices do not average to 100%, there is some upward or downward bias in the trend component of the model. (Similarly, if the model included additive seasonal effects, they should be constrained to average to zero.)

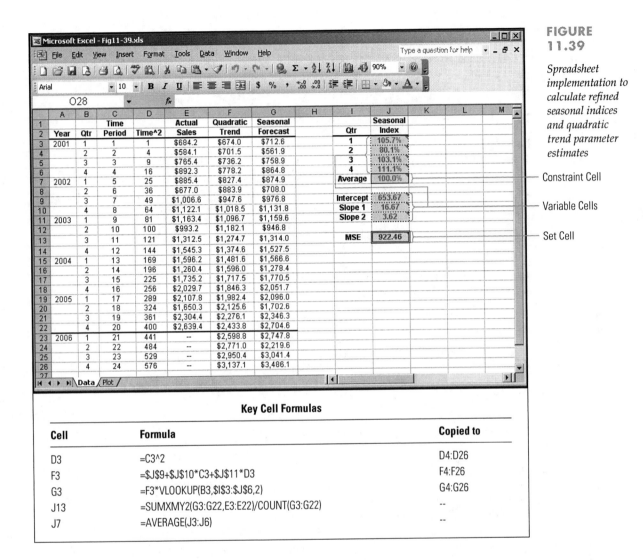

FIGURE
11.39

*Spreadsheet
implementation to
calculate refined
seasonal indices
and quadratic
trend parameter
estimates*

— Constraint Cell

— Variable Cells

— Set Cell

Key Cell Formulas

Cell	Formula	Copied to
D3	=C3^2	D4:D26
F3	=$J$9+$J$10*C3+$J$11*D3	F4:F26
G3	=F3*VLOOKUP(B3,$I$3:$J$6,2)	G4:G26
J13	=SUMXMY2(G3:G22,E3:E22)/COUNT(G3:G22)	--
J7	=AVERAGE(J3:J6)	--

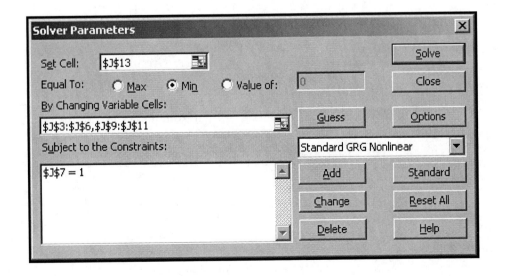

FIGURE
11.40

*Solver parameters
for calculating
refined seasonal
indices and
quadratic trend
parameter
estimates*

FIGURE 11.41

Optimal solution for calculating refined seasonal indices and quadratic trend parameter estimates

	A	B	C	D	E	F	G	H	I	J	K	L	M
1			Time		Actual	Quadratic	Seasonal			Seasonal			
2	Year	Qtr	Period	Time^2	Sales	Trend	Forecast		Qtr	Index			
3	2001	1	1	1	$684.2	$663.7	$708.7		1	106.8%			
4		2	2	4	$584.1	$697.5	$554.6		2	79.5%			
5		3	3	9	$765.4	$737.5	$757.7		3	102.7%			
6		4	4	16	$892.3	$783.9	$869.8		4	111.0%			
7	2002	1	5	25	$885.4	$836.5	$893.3		Average	100.0%			
8		2	6	36	$677.0	$895.5	$712.1						
9		3	7	49	$1,006.6	$960.7	$986.9		Intercept	636.24			
10		4	8	64	$1,122.1	$1,032.2	$1,145.4		Slope 1	24.32			
11	2003	1	9	81	$1,163.4	$1,110.0	$1,185.4		Slope 2	3.15			
12		2	10	100	$993.2	$1,194.2	$949.6						
13		3	11	121	$1,312.5	$1,284.6	$1,319.7		MSE	400.16			
14		4	12	144	$1,545.3	$1,381.3	$1,532.7						
15	2004	1	13	169	$1,596.2	$1,484.3	$1,585.0						
16		2	14	196	$1,260.4	$1,593.5	$1,267.2						
17		3	15	225	$1,735.2	$1,709.1	$1,755.8						
18		4	16	256	$2,029.7	$1,831.0	$2,031.7						
19	2005	1	17	289	$2,107.8	$1,959.2	$2,092.1						
20		2	18	324	$1,650.3	$2,093.6	$1,664.9						
21		3	19	361	$2,304.4	$2,234.4	$2,295.5						
22		4	20	400	$2,639.4	$2,381.4	$2,642.5						
23	2006	1	21	441	--	$2,534.8	$2,706.8						
24		2	22	484	--	$2,694.4	$2,142.6						
25		3	23	529	--	$2,860.4	$2,938.5						
26		4	24	576	--	$3,032.6	$3,365.0						

11.20 Seasonal Regression Models

As discussed in Chapter 9, an indicator variable is a binary variable that assumes a value of 0 or 1 to indicate whether or not a certain condition is true. To model additive seasonal effects in a time series, we might set up several indicator variables to indicate which season each observation represents. In general, if there are p seasons, we need $p - 1$ indicator variables in our model. For example, the WaterCraft sales data were collected on a quarterly basis. Because we have four seasons to model ($p = 4$), we need three indicator variables, which we define as:

$$X_{3_t} = \begin{cases} 1, \text{ if } Y_t \text{ is from quarter 1} \\ 0, \text{ otherwise} \end{cases}$$

$$X_{4_t} = \begin{cases} 1, \text{ if } Y_t \text{ is from quarter 2} \\ 0, \text{ otherwise} \end{cases}$$

$$X_{5_t} = \begin{cases} 1, \text{ if } Y_t \text{ is from quarter 3} \\ 0, \text{ otherwise} \end{cases}$$

Notice that the definitions of X_{3_t}, X_{4_t}, and X_{5_t} assign a unique coding for the variables to each quarter in our data. These codings are summarized as:

	Value of		
Quarter	X_{3_t}	X_{4_t}	X_{5_t}
1	1	0	0
2	0	1	0
3	0	0	1
4	0	0	0

Together, the values of X_{3_t}, X_{4_t}, and X_{5_t} indicate in which quarter observation Y_t occurs.

11.20.1 THE SEASONAL MODEL

We might expect that the following regression function would be appropriate for the time series data in our example:

$$Y_t = \beta_0 + \beta_1 X_{1_t} + \beta_2 X_{2_t} + \beta_3 X_{3_t} + \beta_4 X_{4_t} + \beta_5 X_{5_t} + \varepsilon_t \qquad \textbf{11.31}$$

where, $X_{1_t} = t$ and $X_{2_t} = t^2$. This regression model combines the variables that account for a quadratic trend in the data with additional indicator variables discussed earlier to account for any additive systematic seasonal differences.

To better understand the effect of the indicator variables, notice that for observations occurring in the fourth quarter, the model in equation 11.31 reduces to:

$$Y_t = \beta_0 + \beta_1 X_{1_t} + \beta_2 X_{2_t} + \varepsilon_t \qquad \textbf{11.32}$$

because in the fourth quarter $X_{3_t} = X_{4_t} = X_{5_t} = 0$. For observations occurring in the first quarter, we can express equation 11.31 as:

$$Y_t = (\beta_0 + \beta_3) + \beta_1 X_{1_t} + \beta_2 X_{2_t} + \varepsilon_t \qquad \textbf{11.33}$$

because, by definition, in the first quarter $X_{3_t} = 1$ and $X_{4_t} = X_{5_t} = 0$. Similarly, for observations in the second and third quarters, the model in equation 11.31 reduces to:

For the second quarter: $\quad Y_t = (\beta_0 + \beta_4) + \beta_1 X_{1_t} + \beta_2 X_{2_t} + \varepsilon_t \qquad \textbf{11.34}$

For the third quarter: $\quad Y_t = (\beta_0 + \beta_5) + \beta_1 X_{1_t} + \beta_2 X_{2_t} + \varepsilon_t \qquad \textbf{11.35}$

Equations 11.32 through 11.35 show that the values β_3, β_4, and β_5 in equation 11.31 indicate the average amounts by which the values of observations in the first, second, and third quarters are expected to differ from observations in the fourth quarter. That is, β_3, β_4, and β_5 indicate the expected effects of seasonality in the first, second, and third quarters, respectively, relative to the fourth quarter.

An example of the seasonal regression function in equation 11.31 is given in Figure 11.42 (and in the file Fig11-42.xls on your data disk).

The major difference between Figures 11.37 and 11.42 is the addition of the data in columns E, F, and G in Figure 11.42. These columns represent the indicator values for the independent variables X_{3_t}, X_{4_t}, and X_{5_t}, respectively. We created these values by entering the following formula in cell E3 and copying it to E4 through G22:

Formula for cell E3: $\quad$ =IF($B3=E$2,1,0)

(Copy to E4 through E26.)

In Figure 11.42, column I (labeled "Seasonal Model") shows the predicted sales level for each time period where the following formula is entered in cell I3 and copied to cells I4 through I22:

Formula for cell I3: $\quad$ =TREND($H$3:$H$22,$C$3:$G$22,C3:G3)

(Copy to I4 through I26.)

We can obtain the values of b_0, b_1, b_2, b_3, b_4, and b_5 required for the estimated regression function using the Regression command settings shown in Figure 11.43. Figure 11.44 shows the results of this command, which indicate that the estimated regression function is:

$$\hat{Y}_t = 824.472 + 17.319 X_{1_t} + 3.485 X_{2_t} - 86.805 X_{3_t} - 424.736 X_{4_t} - 123.453 X_{5_t} \qquad \textbf{11.36}$$

The coefficients for the indicator variables are given by $b_3 = -86.805$, $b_4 = -424.736$, and $b_5 = -123.453$. Because X_{3_t} is the indicator variable for quarter 1 observations, the value of b_3 indicates that, on average, the sales level in quarter 1 of any year is expected to be approximately \$86,805 lower than the level expected for quarter 4. The value of b_4 indicates that the typical sales value in quarter 2 of any given year is expected to be approximately \$424,736 less than the level expected in quarter 4. Finally, the value of b_5

FIGURE
11.42

*Spreadsheet
implementation of
the seasonal
regression model*

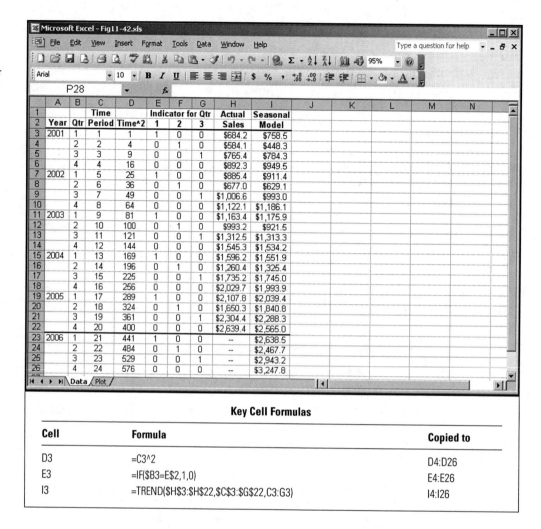

Key Cell Formulas

Cell	Formula	Copied to
D3	=C3^2	D4:D26
E3	=IF($B3=E$2,1,0)	E4:E26
I3	=TREND($H$3:$H$22,$C$3:$G$22,C3:G3)	I4:I26

indicates that the typical sales value in quarter 3 is expected to be approximately $123,453 less than the level expected in quarter 4.

In Figure 11.44, notice that $R^2 = 0.986$, suggesting that the estimated regression function fits the data very well. This is also evident from the graph in Figure 11.45, which shows the actual data versus the predictions of the seasonal forecasting model.

11.20.2 FORECASTING WITH THE SEASONAL REGRESSION MODEL

We can use the estimated regression function in equation 11.36 to forecast an expected level of sales for any future time period by assigning appropriate values to the independent variables. For example, forecasts of WaterCraft's sales in the next four quarters are represented by:

$$\hat{Y}_{21} = 824.472 + 17.319(21) + 3.485(21^2) - 86.805(1) - 424.736(0) - 123.453(0) = 2,638.5$$
$$\hat{Y}_{22} = 824.472 + 17.319(22) + 3.485(22^2) - 86.805(0) - 424.736(1) - 123.453(0) = 2,467.7$$
$$\hat{Y}_{23} = 824.472 + 17.319(23) + 3.485(23^2) - 86.805(0) - 424.736(0) - 123.453(1) = 2,943.2$$
$$\hat{Y}_{24} = 824.472 + 17.319(24) + 3.485(24^2) - 86.805(0) - 424.736(0) - 123.453(0) = 3,247.8$$

Note that these forecasts were calculated using the TREND( ) function in Figure 11.42.

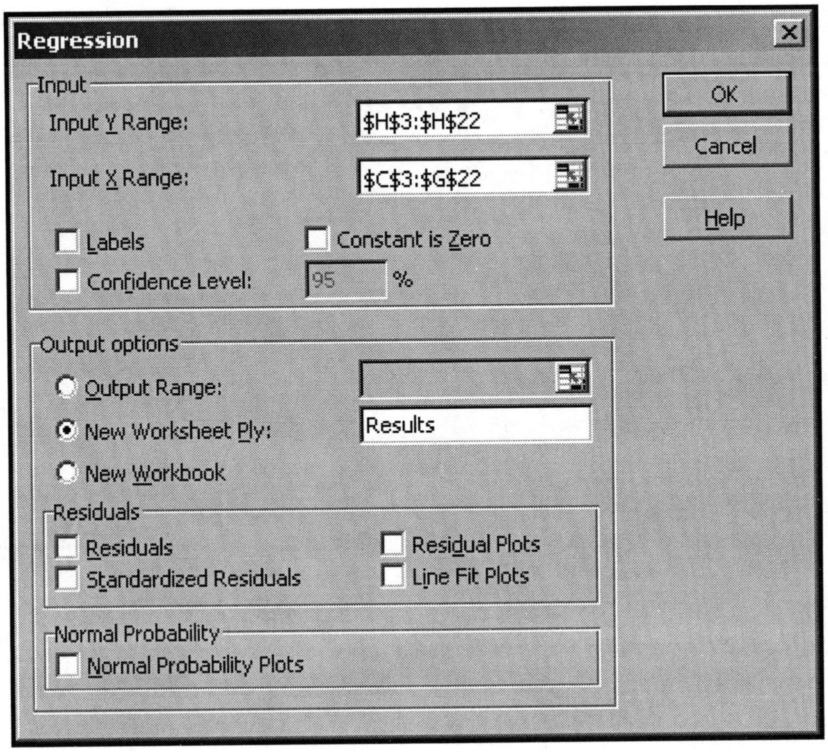

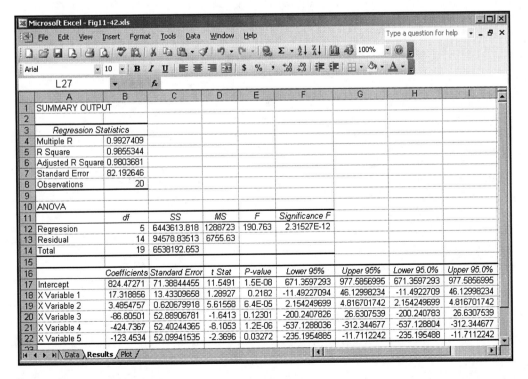

FIGURE 11.43

Regression command settings for the seasonal regression model

	A	B	C	D	E	F	G	H	I
1	SUMMARY OUTPUT								
2									
3	*Regression Statistics*								
4	Multiple R	0.9927409							
5	R Square	0.9855344							
6	Adjusted R Square	0.9803681							
7	Standard Error	82.192646							
8	Observations	20							
9									
10	ANOVA								
11		*df*	*SS*	*MS*	*F*	*Significance F*			
12	Regression	5	6443613.818	1288723	190.763	2.31527E-12			
13	Residual	14	94578.83513	6755.63					
14	Total	19	6538192.653						
15									
16		*Coefficients*	*Standard Error*	*t Stat*	*P-value*	*Lower 95%*	*Upper 95%*	*Lower 95.0%*	*Upper 95.0%*
17	Intercept	824.47271	71.38844455	11.5491	1.5E-08	671.3597293	977.5856995	671.3597293	977.5856995
18	X Variable 1	17.318856	13.43309658	1.28927	0.2182	-11.49227094	46.12998234	-11.4922709	46.12998234
19	X Variable 2	3.4854757	0.620679918	5.61558	6.4E-05	2.154249699	4.816701742	2.154249699	4.816701742
20	X Variable 3	-86.80501	52.88906781	-1.6413	0.12301	-200.2407826	26.6307539	-200.240783	26.6307539
21	X Variable 4	-424.7367	52.40244365	-8.1053	1.2E-06	-537.1288036	-312.344677	-537.128804	-312.344677
22	X Variable 5	-123.4534	52.09941535	-2.3696	0.03272	-235.1954885	-11.7112242	-235.195488	-11.7112242

FIGURE 11.44

Regression results for the seasonal regression model

**FIGURE
11.45**

*Plot of seasonal
regression model
predictions versus
actual WaterCraft
sales data*

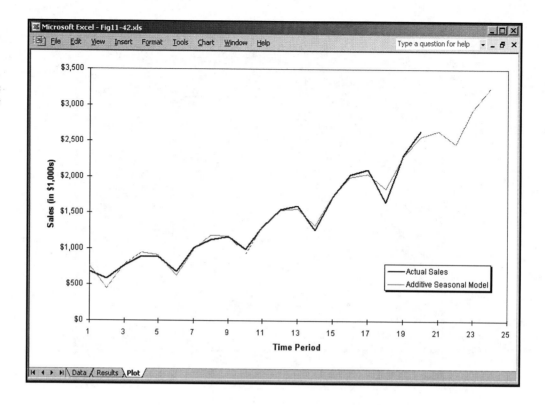

11.21 Crystal Ball Predictor

Given the complexity of some of the forecasting techniques described earlier, you probably have thought it would be nice if there was an Excel add-in to assist in carrying out some of these time series techniques. Fortunately, there is an Excel add-in called Crystal Ball Predictor (or CB Predictor) that automatically implements many of the techniques described in this chapter. CB Predictor is part of the Crystal Ball suite of Excel add-ins found on the CD-ROM accompanying this book.

About Crystal Ball...

Crystal Ball is a suite of Excel add-ins created and distributed by Decisioneering, Inc. in Denver, Colorado. Decisioneering graciously allows 140-day trial versions of its software to be distributed with this book. If you want to use this software beyond the scope of this course, please contact Decisioneering about acquiring a commercial version of their product (see http://www.decisioneering.com). Decisioneering also offers one- and two-year software licenses to students at a very modest cost.

11.21.1 USING CB PREDICTOR

When Crystal Ball is installed and loaded, it inserts several new menu options in Excel. CB Predictor can be launched from the new Run menu option shown in Figure 11.46

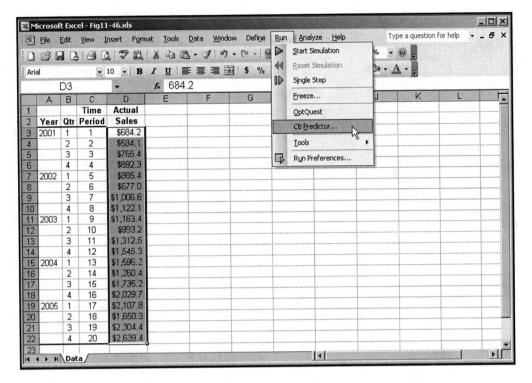

FIGURE 11.46

Crystal Ball menu option for CB Predictor

(and file Fig11-46.xls). (If you do not see this menu option, first make sure that Crystal Ball is installed on your machine, then click Tools, Add-Ins and then select the Crystal Ball option.)

CB Predictor provides a very easy-to-use interface that walks you through the process of finding an appropriate time series model for a given set of data. The first dialog card, shown in Figure 11.47, prompts you to enter the range in the spreadsheet containing the time series data you want to analyze.

The next dialog card in CB Predictor, shown in Figure 11.48, allows you to indicate the type of data you have (*e.g.*, hourly, daily, weekly, monthly, quarterly) and type of seasonality that might be present in the data. Note that if you select the "no seasonality" option, CB Predictor will not attempt to use any of the seasonal techniques to model the data.

The next dialog card in CB Predictor, shown in Figure 11.49, presents the "Method Gallery." This dialog card shows examples of the various time series techniques available in CB Predictor and allows you to select the ones you want to try. Descriptions of each method can be displayed by double-clicking on any of the example graphs on this card.

If you click the Preview button shown in Figure 11.49, CB Predictor fits all the selected techniques to your data and determines which technique is best. (By default, CB Predictor uses the RMSE statistic to determine which technique is best.) It then displays the graph in Figure 11.50 showing the actual data vs. fitted values for the best technique. You can also show the results easily for any of the other techniques simply by changing the selection in the "Method" drop-down list box.

Finally, the Results dialog card , shown in Figure 11.51, allows you to indicate the number of periods into the future that you want to forecast. Because any forecast is uncertain, CB Predictor also gives you the option to select confidence intervals for the

FIGURE 11.47

CB Predictor's Input Data dialog card

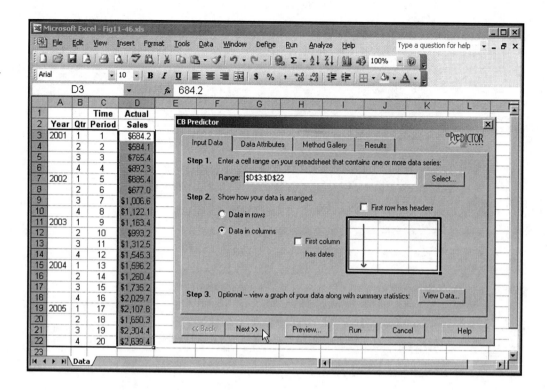

FIGURE 11.48

CB Predictor's Data Attributes dialog card

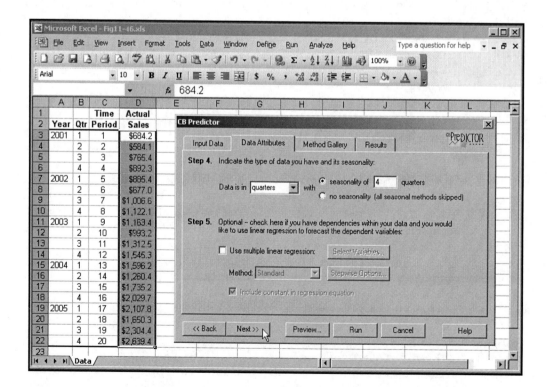

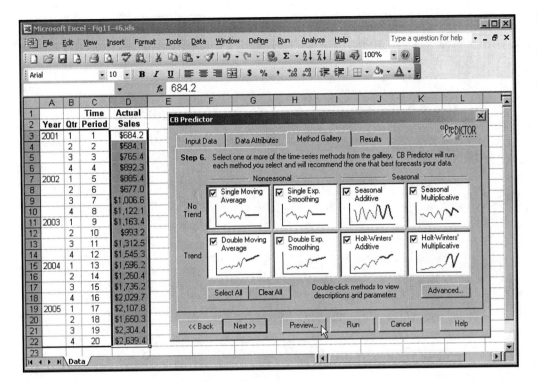

FIGURE 11.49

CB Predictor's Method Gallery dialog card

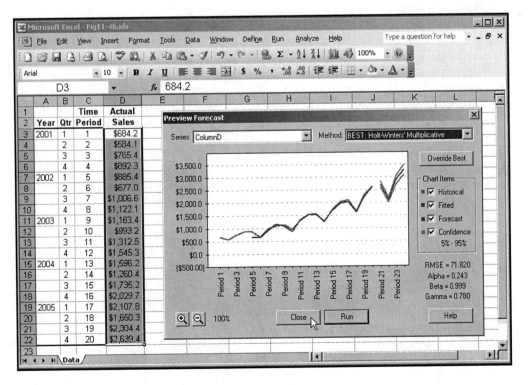

FIGURE 11.50

CB Predictor's Preview Forecast window

**FIGURE
11.51**

*CB Predictor's
Results dialog card*

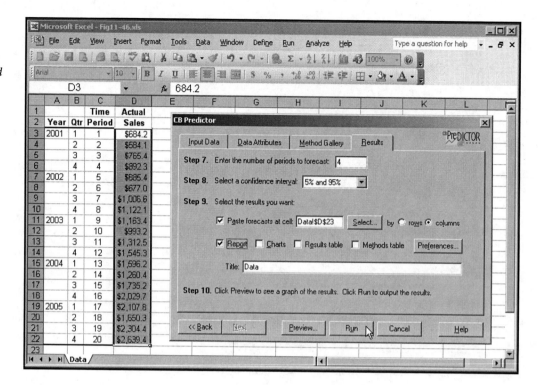

predictions to create lower and upper bounds on the forecasts' accuracy in the future. Various options also are given to indicate where the forecasts should be written in your worksheet. CB Predictor also will produce various reports and charts summarizing the results of the analysis. In Figure 11.51, we have selected the "Reports" and "Methods table" results options. Clicking the Run button in Figure 11.51 causes CB Predictor to carry out the indicated actions.

A portion of the Reports sheet created by CB Predictor is shown in Figure 11.52. Note that the report shows the forecasted values four time periods into the future along with the lower and upper limits of the confidence intervals for these predictions. The chart shown in Figure 11.52 displays the actual values of the time series data along with the fitted values and the forecasted values.

Figure 11.53 shows two of the Methods tables created by CB Predictor. These tables provide a summary of the relative performance of the different time series technique on the given data set. In this case, Holt-Winter's Multiplicative method had the best (lowest) value of the RMSE, MAD, and MAPE statistics. However, it is possible that the forecasting technique with the best value on one of these statistics might not have the best value on all the statistics.

The Durbin-Watson (DW) statistic in Figure 11.53 describes the amount of *autocorrelation* in a time series. Autocorrelation refers to the degree to which a previous data point in a time series is correlated to the next data point. The DW statistic ranges in value from 0 to 4. A DW value less than 1 indicates positive autocorrelation, whereas DW values greater than 3 indicate negative autocorrelation. DW values near 2 indicate no significant autocorrelation in the data.

Thiel's U statistic indicates how well each forecasting method does compared with a naïve forecast (such as using the last period's value as the forecast of the next period). Thiel's U will equal 1 if a forecasting technique is essentially no better than using a naïve

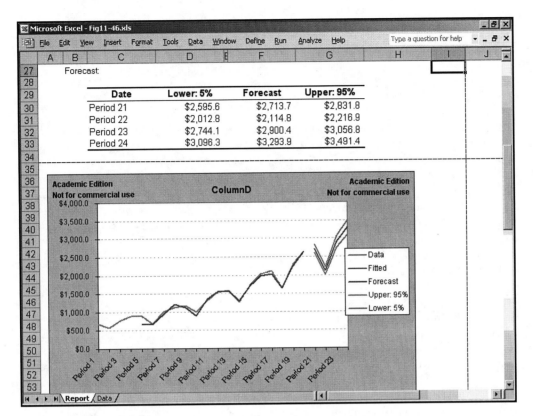

FIGURE 11.52

CB Predictor's Report sheet

Microsoft Excel - Fig11-46.xls

| | File | Edit | View | Insert | Format | Tools | Data | Window | Define | Run | Analyze | Help | Type a question for help |

| | A | B | C | D | E | F | G | H | I | J |

27   Forecast:

28

29

	Date	Lower: 5%	Forecast	Upper: 95%
30	Period 21	$2,595.6	$2,713.7	$2,831.8
31	Period 22	$2,012.8	$2,114.8	$2,216.9
32	Period 23	$2,744.1	$2,900.4	$3,056.8
33	Period 24	$3,096.3	$3,293.9	$3,491.4

ColumnD

Data
Fitted
Forecast
Upper: 95%
Lower: 5%

Report / Data

FIGURE 11.53

CB Predictor's Methods table

Microsoft Excel - Fig11-46.xls

| | File | Edit | View | Insert | Format | Tools | Data | Window | Define | Run | Analyze | Help | Type a question for help |

| | A | B | C | D | E | F | G | H | I | J |

56

57   Method Errors:

58

		Method	RMSE	MAD	MAPE
59					
60	Best:	Holt-Winters' Multiplicative	71.82	53.404	4.50%
61	2nd:	Holt-Winters' Additive	92.461	74.127	5.38%
62	3rd:	Seasonal Multiplicative	152.38	126.66	9.01%
63	4th:	Seasonal Additive	182.47	161.22	10.62%
64	5th:	Double Exponential Smoothing	223.6	197.71	15.07%
65	6th:	Double Moving Average	225.29	197.68	12.50%
66	7th:	Single Exponential Smoothing	287.17	249.24	18.16%
67	8th:	Single Moving Average	289.66	237.52	17.58%

68

69

70   Method Statistics:

71

		Method	Durbin-Watson	Theil's U
72				
73	Best:	Holt-Winters' Multiplicative	1.5	0.305
74	2nd:	Holt-Winters' Additive	1.689	0.343
75	3rd:	Seasonal Multiplicative	0.915	0.491
76	4th:	Seasonal Additive	1.021	0.561
77	5th:	Double Exponential Smoothing	1.824	0.729
78	6th:	Double Moving Average	2.061	0.62
79	7th:	Single Exponential Smoothing	1.77	0.956
80	8th:	Single Moving Average	2.08	1

81

82

Report / Data

forecast. Thiel's U values less than 1 indicate that a technique is better than using a naïve forecast. Values greater than 1 indicate that a technique is actually worse than using a naïve forecast.

11.22 Combining Forecasts

Given the number and variety of forecasting techniques available, it can be a challenge to settle on a *single* method to use in predicting future values of a time series variable. Indeed, the state-of-the-art research in time series forecasting suggests that we should *not* use a single forecasting method. Rather, we can obtain more accurate forecasts by combining the forecasts from several methods into a composite forecast.

For example, suppose that we used three methods to build forecasting models of the same time series variable. We denote the predicted value for time period t using each of these methods as F_{1_t}, F_{2_t}, and F_{3_t}, respectively. One simple approach to combining these forecasts into a composite forecast $\hat{Y}_t$ might involve taking a linear combination of the individual forecasts as:

$$\hat{Y}_t = b_0 + b_1 F_{1_t} + b_2 F_{2_t} + b_3 F_{3_t}$$

11.37

We could determine the values for the b_i using Solver or least squares regression to minimize the MSE between the combined forecast $\hat{Y}_t$ and the actual data. The combined forecast $\hat{Y}_t$ in equation 11.37 will be at least as accurate as any of the individual forecasting techniques. To see this, suppose that F_{1_t} is the most accurate of the individual forecasting techniques. If $b_1 = 1$ and $b_0 = b_2 = b_3 = 0$, then our combined forecast would be $\hat{Y}_t = F_{1_t}$. Thus, b_0, b_2, and b_3 would be assigned nonzero values only if this helps to reduce the MSE and produce more accurate predictions.

In Chapter 9, we noted that adding independent variables to a regression model can never decrease the value of the R^2 statistic. Therefore, it is important to ensure that each independent variable in a multiple regression model accounts for a significant portion of the variation in the dependent variable and does not simply inflate the value of R^2. Similarly, combining forecasts can never increase the value of the MSE. Thus, when combining forecasts, we must ensure that each forecasting technique plays a significant role in accounting for the behavior of the dependent time series variable. The adjusted-R^2 statistic (described in Chapter 9) also can be applied to the problem of selecting forecasting techniques to combine in time series analysis.

11.23 Summary

This chapter presented several methods for forecasting future values of a time series variable. The chapter discussed time series methods for stationary data (without a strong upward or downward trend), nonstationary data (with a strong upward or downward linear or nonlinear trend), and data with repeating seasonal patterns. In each case, the goal is to fit models to the past behavior of a time series and use the models to project future values.

Because time series vary in nature (for example, with and without trend, with and without seasonality), it helps to be aware of the different forecasting techniques and the types of problems for which they are intended. There are many other time series modeling techniques besides those discussed in this chapter. Descriptions of these other techniques can be found in texts devoted to time series analysis.

In modeling time series data, it is often useful to try several techniques and then compare them based on measures of forecast accuracy, including a graphical inspection of how well the model fits the historical data. Crystal Ball Predictor is an Excel add-in for time series forecasting that makes it very easy to apply several time series techniques to a data set and compare their accuracy. If no one procedure is clearly better than the others, it might be wise to combine the forecasts from the different procedures using a weighted average or some other method.

11.24 References

Clemen, R. T. "Combining Forecasts: A Review and Annotated Bibliography." *International Journal of Forecasting*, vol. 5, 1989.

Clements, D. and R. Reid. "Analytical MS/OR Tools Applied to a Plant Closure." *Interfaces*, vol. 24, no. 2, 1994.

Gardner, E. "Exponential Smoothing: The State of the Art." *Journal of Forecasting*, vol. 4, no. 1, 1985.

Georgoff, D. and R. Murdick. "Managers Guide to Forecasting." *Harvard Business Review*, vol. 64, no. 1, 1986.

Makridakis, S. and S. Wheelwright. *Forecasting: Methods and Applications.* New York: Wiley, 1986.

Pindyck, R. and D. Rubinfeld. *Econometric Models and Economic Forecasts.* New York: McGraw-Hill, 1989.

THE WORLD OF MANAGEMENT SCIENCE

Check Processing Revisited: The Chemical Bank Experience

Chemical Bank of New York employs more than 500 people to process checks averaging $2 billion per day. Scheduling shifts for these employees requires accurate predictions of check flows. This is done with a regression model that forecasts daily check volume using independent variables that represent calendar effects. The regression model used by Ohio National Bank (see "Better Predictions Create Cost Savings for Ohio National Bank" in Chapter 9) is based on this Chemical Bank model.

The binary independent variables in the regression model represent months, days of the month, weekdays, and holidays. Of 54 possible variables, 29 were used in the model to yield a coefficient of determination (R^2) of 0.83 and a standard deviation of 142.6.

The forecast errors, or residuals, were examined for patterns that would suggest the possibility of improving the model. Analysts noticed a tendency for overpredictions to follow one another and underpredictions to follow one another, implying that check volumes could be predicted not only by calendar effects but also by the recent history of prediction errors.

An exponential smoothing model was used to forecast the residuals. The regression model combined with the exponential smoothing model then became the complete model for predicting check volumes. Fine-tuning was accomplished by investigating different values of the smoothing constant (α) from 0.05 to 0.50. A smoothing constant of 0.2 produced the best results, reducing the standard deviation from 142.6 to 131.8. Examination of the residuals for the complete model showed nothing but random variations, indicating that the exponential smoothing procedure was working as well as could be expected.

Although the complete model provides better forecasts on the average, it occasionally overreacts and increases the error for some periods. Nevertheless, the complete model is considered to be preferable to regression alone.

Source: Kevin Boyd and Vincent A. Mabert. "A Two Stage Forecasting Approach at Chemical Bank of New York for Check Processing." *Journal of Bank Research*, vol. 8, no. 2, Summer 1977, pages 101–107.

Questions and Problems

1. What is the result of using regression analysis to estimate a linear trend model for a stationary time series?

2. A manufacturing company uses a certain type of steel rod in one of its products. The design specifications for this rod indicate that it must be between 0.353 to 0.357 inches in diameter. The machine that manufactures these rods is set up to produce them at 0.355 inches in diameter, but there is some variation in its output. Provided that the machine is producing rods within 0.353 to 0.357 inches in diameter, its output is considered acceptable or within control limits. Management uses a control chart to track the diameter of the rods being produced by the machine over time so that remedial measures can be taken if the machine begins to produce unacceptable rods. Figure 11.54 shows an example of this type of chart.

    Unacceptable rods represent waste. Thus, management wants to develop a procedure to predict when the machine will start producing rods that are outside the control limits, so it can take action to prevent the production of rods that must be scrapped. Of the time series models discussed in this chapter, which is the most appropriate tool for this problem? Explain your answer.

3. Each month, Joe's Auto Parts uses exponential smoothing (with $\alpha = 0.25$) to predict the number of cans of brake fluid that will be sold during the next month. In June, Joe forecast that he would sell 37 cans of brake fluid during July. Joe actually sold 43 cans in July.
    a. What is Joe's forecast for brake fluid sales in August and September?
    b. Suppose that Joe sells 32 cans of brake fluid in August. What is the revised forecast for September?

Questions 4 through 10 refer to the data in the file on your data disk named **SmallBusiness.xls** representing annual sales (in $1000s) for a small business.

4. Prepare a line graph of these data. Do the data appear to be stationary or nonstationary?

FIGURE 11.54

Graph for rod manufacturing problem

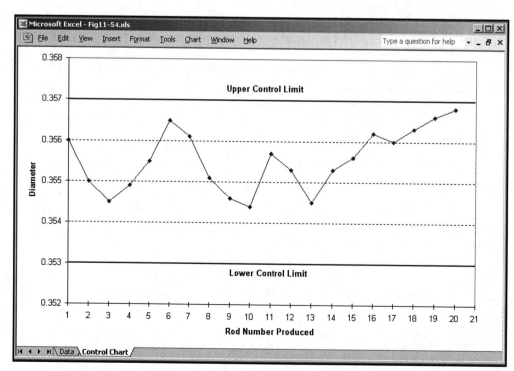

5. Compute the two-period and four-period moving average predictions for the data set.
   a. Prepare a line graph comparing the moving average predictions against the original data.
   b. Do the moving averages tend to overestimate or underestimate the actual data? Why?
   c. Compute forecasts for the next two years using the two-period and four-period moving average techniques.
6. Use Solver to determine the weights for a three-period weighted moving average that minimizes the MSE for the data set.
   a. What are the optimal values for the weights?
   b. Prepare a line graph comparing the weighted moving average predictions against the original data.
   c. What are the forecasts for the next two years using this technique?
7. Create a Double Moving Average model (with $k = 4$) for the data set.
   a. Prepare a line graph comparing the Double Moving Average predictions against the original data.
   b. What are the forecasts for the next two years using this technique?
8. Create an exponential smoothing model that minimizes the MSE for the data set. Use Solver to determine the optimal value of α.
   a. What is the optimal value of α?
   b. Prepare a line graph comparing the exponential smoothing predictions against the original data.
   c. What are the forecasts for the next two years using this technique?
9. Use Holt's method to create a model that minimizes the MSE for the data set. Use Solver to determine the optimal values of α and β.
   a. What are the optimal values of α and β?
   b. Prepare a line graph comparing the predictions from Holt's method versus the original data.
   c. What are the forecasts for the next two years using this technique?
10. Use regression analysis to fit a linear trend model to the data set.
    a. What is the estimated regression function?
    b. Interpret the R^2 value for your model.
    c. Prepare a line graph comparing the linear trend predictions against the original data.
    d. What are the forecasts for the next two years using this technique?
    e. Fit a quadratic trend model to these data. What is the estimated regression function?
    f. Compare the adjusted-R^2 value for this model to that of the linear trend model. What is implied by this comparison?
    g. Prepare a line graph comparing the quadratic trend predictions against the original data.
    h. What are the forecasts for the next two years using this technique?
    i. If you had to choose between the linear and quadratic trend models, which would you use? Why?

Questions 11 through 14 refer to the data in the file on your data disk named **FamilyHomePrices.xls** representing actual average sales prices of existing single family homes in the United States over a number of years.

11. Prepare a line graph of these data. Do the data appear to be stationary or nonstationary?
12. Create a Double Moving Average model (with $k = 2$) for the data set.
    a. Prepare a line graph comparing the Double Moving Average predictions against the original data.
    b. What are the forecasts for the next two years using this technique?

13. Use Holt's method to create a model that minimizes the MSE for the data set. Use Solver to determine the optimal values of α and β.
    a. What are the optimal values of α and β?
    b. Prepare a line graph comparing the predictions from Holt's method versus the original data.
    c. What are the forecasts for the next two years using this technique?

14. Use regression analysis to answer the following questions.
    a. Fit a linear trend model to the data set. What is the estimated regression function?
    b. Interpret the R^2 value for your model.
    c. Prepare a line graph comparing the linear trend predictions against the original data.
    d. What are the forecasts for the next two years using this technique?
    e. Fit a quadratic trend model to these data. What is the estimated regression function?
    f. Compare the adjusted-R^2 value for this model to that of the linear trend model. What is implied by this comparison?
    g. Prepare a line graph comparing the quadratic trend predictions against the original data.
    h. What are the forecasts for the next two years using this technique?
    i. If you had to choose between the linear and quadratic trend models, which would you use? Why?

Questions 15 through 22 refer to the data in the file on your data disk named **SUVSales.xls** representing quarterly data on the number of four-wheel drive sport-utility vehicles sold by a local car dealer during the past three years.

15. Use regression analysis to fit a linear trend model to the data set.
    a. What is the estimated regression function?
    b. Interpret the R^2 value for your model.
    c. Prepare a line graph comparing the linear trend predictions against the original data.
    d. What are the forecasts for each quarter in 2006 using this technique?
    e. Calculate seasonal indices for each quarter using the results of the linear trend model.
    f. Use these seasonal indices to compute seasonal forecasts for each quarter in 2006.

16. Use regression analysis to fit a quadratic trend model to the data set.
    a. What is the estimated regression function?
    b. Compare the adjusted-R^2 value for this model to that of the linear trend model. What is implied by this comparison?
    c. Prepare a line graph comparing the quadratic trend predictions against the original data.
    d. What are the forecasts for each quarter in 2006 using this technique?
    e. Calculate seasonal indices for each quarter using the results of the quadratic trend model.
    f. Use these seasonal indices to compute seasonal forecasts for each quarter in 2006.

17. Use the additive seasonal technique for stationary data to model the data. Use Solver to determine the optimal values of α and β.
    a. What are the optimal values of α and β?
    b. Prepare a line graph comparing the predictions from this method against the original data.
    c. What are the forecasts for each quarter in 2006 using this technique?

18. Use the multiplicative seasonal technique for stationary data to model the data. Use Solver to determine the optimal values of α and β.
    a. What are the optimal values of α and β?
    b. Prepare a line graph comparing the predictions from this method against the original data.
    c. What are the forecasts for each quarter in 2006 using this technique?
19. Use Holt's method to create a model that minimizes the MSE for the data set. Use Solver to determine the optimal values of α and β.
    a. What are the optimal values of α and β?
    b. Prepare a line graph comparing the predictions from Holt's method against the original data.
    c. What are the forecasts for each quarter in 2006 using this technique?
    d. Calculate multiplicative seasonal indices for each quarter using the results of Holt's method.
    e. Use these seasonal indices to compute seasonal forecasts for each quarter in 2006.
20. Use Holt-Winter's additive method to create a seasonal model that minimizes the MSE for the data set. Use Solver to determine the optimal values of α, β, and γ.
    a. What are the optimal values of α, β, and γ?
    b. Prepare a line graph comparing the predictions from this method against the original data.
    c. What are the forecasts for each quarter in 2006 using this technique?
21. Use Holt-Winter's multiplicative method to create a seasonal model that minimizes the MSE for the data set. Use Solver to determine the optimal values of α, β, and γ.
    a. What are the optimal values of α, β, and γ?
    b. Prepare a line graph comparing the predictions from this method against the original data.
    c. What are the forecasts for each quarter in 2006 using this technique?
22. Use regression analysis to fit an additive seasonal model with linear trend to the data set.
    a. What is the estimated regression function?
    b. Interpret the R^2 value for your model.
    c. Interpret the parameter estimates corresponding to the indicator variables in your model.
    d. Prepare a line graph comparing the linear trend predictions against the original data.
    e. What are the forecasts for each quarter in 2006 using this technique?

Questions 23 through 27 refer to the data in the file on your data disk named **CalfPrices.xls** representing the selling price of three-month-old calves at a livestock auction during the past 22 weeks.

23. Prepare a line graph of these data. Do the data appear to be stationary or nonstationary?
24. Compute the two-period and four-period moving average predictions for the data set.
    a. Prepare a line graph comparing the moving average predictions against the original data.
    b. Compute the MSE for each of the two moving averages. Which appears to provide the best fit for this data set?
    c. Compute forecasts for the next two weeks using the two-period and four-period moving average techniques.

25. Use Solver to determine the weights for a four-period weighted moving average on the data set that minimizes the MSE.
    a. What are the optimal values for the weights?
    b. Prepare a line graph comparing the weighted moving average predictions against the original data.
    c. What are the forecasts for weeks 23 and 24 using this technique?
26. Create an exponential smoothing model that minimizes the MSE for the data set. Use Solver to estimate the optimal value of α.
    a. What is the optimal value of α?
    b. Prepare a line graph comparing the exponential smoothing predictions against the original data.
    c. What are the forecasts for weeks 23 and 24 using this technique?
27. Use Holt's method to create a model that minimizes the MSE for the data set. Use Solver to estimate the optimal values of α and β.
    a. What are the optimal values of α and β?
    b. Are these values surprising? Why or why not?

Questions 28 through 32 refer to the data in the file on your data disk named **HealthClaims.xls** representing two years of monthly health insurance claims for a self-insured company.

28. Use regression analysis to fit a linear trend model to the data set.
    a. What is the estimated regression function?
    b. Interpret the R^2 value for your model.
    c. Prepare a line graph comparing the linear trend predictions against the original data.
    d. What are the forecasts for each of the first six months in 2006 using this technique?
    e. Calculate multiplicative seasonal indices for each month using the results of the linear trend model.
    f. Use these seasonal indices to compute seasonal forecasts for the first six months in 2006.
    g. Calculate additive seasonal indices for each month using the results of the linear trend model.
    h. Use these seasonal indices to compute seasonal forecasts for the first six months in 2006.
29. Use regression analysis to fit a quadratic trend model to the data set.
    a. What is the estimated regression function?
    b. Compare the adjusted-R^2 value for this model to that of the linear trend model. What is implied by this comparison?
    c. Prepare a line graph comparing the quadratic trend predictions against the original data.
    d. What are the forecasts for each of the first six months in 2006 using this technique?
    e. Calculate multiplicative seasonal indices for each month using the results of the quadratic trend model.
    f. Use these seasonal indices to compute seasonal forecasts for each of the first six months in 2006.
    g. Calculate additive seasonal indices for each month using the results of the quadratic trend model.
    h. Use these seasonal indices to compute seasonal forecasts for each of the first six months in 2006.
30. Use Holt's method to create a model that minimizes the MSE for the data set. Use Solver to determine the optimal values of α and β.

a. What are the optimal values of α and β?
b. Prepare a line graph comparing the predictions from Holt's method against the original data.
c. What are the forecasts for each of the first six months in 2006 using this technique?
d. Calculate multiplicative seasonal indices for each month using the results of Holt's method.
e. Use these seasonal indices to compute seasonal forecasts for each of the first six months in 2006.
f. Calculate additive seasonal indices for each month using the results of Holt's method.
g. Use these seasonal indices to compute seasonal forecasts for each of the first six months in 2006.

31. Use Holt-Winter's additive method to create a seasonal model that minimizes the MSE for the data set. Use Solver to determine the optimal values of α, β, and γ.
    a. What are the optimal values of α, β, and γ?
    b. Prepare a line graph comparing the predictions from this method against the original data.
    c. What are the forecasts for each of the first six months in 2006 using this technique?

32. Use Holt-Winter's multiplicative method to create a seasonal model that minimizes the MSE for the data set. Use Solver to determine the optimal values of α, β, and γ.
    a. What are the optimal values of α, β, and γ?
    b. Prepare a line graph comparing the predictions from this method against the original data.
    c. What are the forecasts for each of the first six months in 2006 using this technique?

Questions 33 through 36 refer to the data in the file on your data disk named **LaborForce.xls** containing monthly data on the number of workers in the U.S. civilian labor force (in 1000s) from January 1998 through October 2005.

33. Prepare a line graph of these data. Do the data appear to be stationary or nonstationary?

34. Create a Double Moving Average model (with $k = 4$) for the data set.
    a. Prepare a line graph comparing the Double Moving Average predictions against the original data.
    b. What are the forecasts for the next four months using this technique?

35. Use Holt's method to create a model that minimizes the MSE for the data set. Use Solver to estimate the optimal values of α and β.
    a. What are the optimal values of α and β?
    b. Prepare a line graph comparing the predictions from Holt's method against the original data.
    c. What are the forecasts for the next four months using this technique?

36. Use regression analysis to answer the following questions.
    a. Fit a linear trend model to the data set. What is the estimated regression function?
    b. Interpret the R^2 value for your model.
    c. Prepare a line graph comparing the linear trend predictions against the original data.
    d. What are the forecasts for the next two years using this technique?
    e. Fit a quadratic trend model to these data. What is the estimated regression function?
    f. Compare the adjusted-R^2 value for this model to that of the linear trend model. What is implied by this comparison?
    g. Prepare a line graph comparing the quadratic trend predictions against the original data.

h. What are the forecasts for the next two years using this technique?

i. If you had to choose between the linear and quadratic trend models, which would you use? Why?

Questions 37 through 43 refer to the data in the file on your data disk named **MortgageRates.xls** containing average monthly 30-year mortgage rates from January 1999 through October 2005.

37. Prepare a line graph of these data. Do the data appear to be stationary or nonstationary?

38. Compute the two-period and four-period moving average predictions for the data set.
    a. Prepare a line graph comparing the moving average predictions against the original data.
    b. Compute the MSE for each of the two moving averages. Which appears to provide the best fit for this data set?
    c. Compute forecasts for the next two months using the two-period and four-period moving average techniques.

39. Use Solver to determine the weights for a four-period weighted moving average on the data set that minimizes the MSE.
    a. What are the optimal values for the weights?
    b. Prepare a line graph comparing the weighted moving average predictions against the original data.
    c. What are the forecasts for the next two months using this technique?

40. Create an exponential smoothing model that minimizes the MSE for the data set. Use Solver to estimate the optimal value of α.
    a. What is the optimal value of α?
    b. Prepare a line graph comparing the exponential smoothing predictions against the original data.
    c. What are the forecasts for the next two months using this technique?

41. Create a Double Moving Average model (with $k = 4$) for the data set.
    a. Prepare a line graph comparing the Double Moving Average predictions against the original data.
    b. What are the forecasts for the next two months using this technique?

42. Use Holt's method to create a model that minimizes the MSE for the data set. Use Solver to estimate the optimal values of α and β.
    a. What are the optimal values of α and β?
    b. Prepare a line graph comparing the predictions from Holt's method against the original data.
    c. What are the forecasts for the next two months using this technique?

43. Use regression to estimate the parameters of a 6th order polynomial model for this data. That is, estimate the least squares estimates for the parameters in the following estimated regression equation:

$$\hat{Y}_t = b_0 + b_1 t + b_2 t^2 + b_3 t^3 + b_4 t^4 + b_5 t^5 + b_6 t^6$$

    a. What are the optimal values of $b_0, b_1, \ldots, b_6$?
    b. What are the forecasts for the next two months using this technique?
    c. Comment on the appropriateness of this technique.

Questions 44 through 48 refer to the data in the file on your data disk named **ChemicalDemand.xls** containing monthly data on the demand for a chemical product over a two year period.

44. Prepare a line graph of these data. Do the data appear to be stationary or nonstationary?

45. Use the additive seasonal technique for stationary data to model the data. Use Solver to determine the optimal values of α and β.
   a. What are the optimal values of α and β?
   b. Prepare a line graph comparing the predictions from this method against the original data.
   c. What are the forecasts for the next four months using this technique?

46. Use the multiplicative seasonal technique for stationary data to model the data. Use Solver to determine the optimal values of α and β.
   a. What are the optimal values of α and β?
   b. Prepare a line graph comparing the predictions from this method against the original data.
   c. What are the forecasts for the next four months using this technique?

47. Use Holt-Winter's additive method to create a seasonal model that minimizes the MSE for the data set. Use Solver to determine the optimal values of α, β, and γ.
   a. What are the optimal values of α, β, and γ?
   b. Prepare a line graph comparing the predictions from this method against the original data.
   c. What are the forecasts for the next four months using this technique?

48. Use Holt-Winter's multiplicative method to create a seasonal model that minimizes the MSE for the data set. Use Solver to determine the optimal values of α, β, and γ.
   a. What are the optimal values of α, β, and γ?
   b. Prepare a line graph comparing the predictions from this method against the original data.
   c. What are the forecasts for the next four months using this technique?

Questions 49 through 53 refer to the data in the file on your data disk named **ProductionHours.xls** containing monthly data on the average number of hours worked each week by production workers in the United States from January 1998 through October 2005.

49. Prepare a line graph of these data. Do the data appear to be stationary or non-stationary?

50. Use the additive seasonal technique for stationary data to model the data. Use Solver to determine the optimal values of α and β.
   a. What are the optimal values of α and β?
   b. Prepare a line graph comparing the predictions from this method against the original data.
   c. What are the forecasts for the next four months using this technique?

51. Use the multiplicative seasonal technique for stationary data to model the data. Use Solver to determine the optimal values of α and β.
   a. What are the optimal values of α and β?
   b. Prepare a line graph comparing the predictions from this method against the original data.
   c. What are the forecasts for the next four months using this technique?

52. Use Holt-Winter's additive method to create a seasonal model that minimizes the MSE for the data set. Use Solver to determine the optimal values of α, β, and γ.
   a. What are the optimal values of α, β, and γ?
   b. Prepare a line graph comparing the predictions from this method against the original data.
   c. What are the forecasts for the next four months using this technique?

53. Use Holt-Winter's multiplicative method to create a seasonal model that minimizes the MSE for the data set. Use Solver to determine the optimal values of α, β, and γ.
   a. What are the optimal values of α, β, and γ?

b. Prepare a line graph comparing the predictions from this method against the original data.

c. What are the forecasts for the next four months using this technique?

Questions 54 through 58 refer to the data in the file on your data disk named **QtrlySales.xls** containing quarterly sales data for a Norwegian export company from 1993 through 2005.

54. Prepare a line graph of these data. Do the data appear to be stationary or nonstationary?

55. Use the additive seasonal technique for stationary data to model the data. Use Solver to determine the optimal values of α and β.
    a. What are the optimal values of α and β?
    b. Prepare a line graph comparing the predictions from this method against the original data.
    c. What are the forecasts for the next four quarters using this technique?

56. Use the multiplicative seasonal technique for stationary data to model the data. Use Solver to determine the optimal values of α and β.
    a. What are the optimal values of α and β?
    b. Prepare a line graph comparing the predictions from this method against the original data.
    c. What are the forecasts for the next four quarters using this technique?

57. Use Holt-Winter's additive method to create a seasonal model that minimizes the MSE for the data set. Use Solver to determine the optimal values of α, β, and γ.
    a. What are the optimal values of α, β, and γ?
    b. Prepare a line graph comparing the predictions from this method against the original data.
    c. What are the forecasts for the next four quarters using this technique?

58. Use Holt-Winter's multiplicative method to create a seasonal model that minimizes the MSE for the data set. Use Solver to determine the optimal values of α, β, and γ.
    a. What are the optimal values of α, β, and γ?
    b. Prepare a line graph comparing the predictions from this method against the original data.
    c. What are the forecasts for the next four quarters using this technique?

CASE 11.1 PB Chemical Corporation

Mac Brown knew something had to change. As the new Vice President of Sales & Marketing for the PB Chemical Company, Mac understood that when you sell a commodity product, where there is minimal difference between the quality and price, customer service and proactive selling effort usually are the difference between success and failure. Unfortunately, PB's sales staff was using a fairly random method of soliciting sales, where they would work through an alphabetical list of customers, making phone calls to those who had not paced any orders that month. Often, the difference between whether PB or a competitor got an order simply boiled down to who called at the time the customer needed materials. If the BP salespersons called too soon, they didn't get an order. And if they waited too long for a customer to call, they often lost business to a competitor.

Mac decided it was time for PB to be a bit more proactive and sophisticated in its sales efforts. He first convinced his counterparts at PB's largest customers that they could create a more efficient supply chain if they shared their monthly usage data of various chemicals with PB. That way, PB could better anticipate its customers' needs for various products. This, in turn, would reduce PB's need to hold inventory as safety stock and would allow PB to operate more efficiently, and pass some of these cost savings on to its customers.

PB's five largest customers (that account for 85% of PB's sales) agreed to share their monthly product use data. Now it was up to Mac to decide what to do with the data. It has been quite a while since Mac actually did any demand forecasting on his own and he is far too busy with PB's strategic planning committee to be bothered by such details anyway. So Mac called one of the firm's top business analysts, Dee Hamrick, and dumped the problem in her lap. Specifically, Mac asked her to come up with a plan for forecasting demand for BP's products and using these forecasts for maximum advantage.

a. What issues should Dee consider in coming up with forecasts for BP's various products? How would you suggest she go about creating forecasts for each product?
b. Should Dee try to forecast aggregate monthly product demand for all customers, or individual monthly product demand for each customer? Which of these forecasts would be more accurate? Which of these forecasts would be more useful (and to whom)?
c. Given the available data, how might Dee and Mac judge or gauge the accuracy of each product forecast?
d. Suppose Dee's technical staff could come up with a way of accurately forecasting monthly demand for BP's products. How should PB use this information for strategic advantage?
e. What other information should Dee suggest that Mac try to get from BP's customers?

Forecasting COLAs

Tarrows, Pearson, Foster and Zuligar (TPF&Z) is one of the largest actuarial consulting firms in the United States. In addition to providing its clients with expert advice on executive compensation programs and employee benefits programs, TPF&Z also helps its clients determine the amounts of money they must contribute annually to defined benefit retirement programs.

Most companies offer two different types of retirement programs to their employees: defined contribution plans and defined benefit plans. Under a defined contribution plan, the company contributes a fixed percentage of an employee's earning to fund the employee's retirement. Individual employees covered by this type of plan determine how their money is to be invested (e.g., stocks, bonds, or fixed-income securities), and whatever the employees are able to accumulate over the years constitutes their retirement fund. In a defined benefit plan, the company provides covered employees with retirement benefits that usually are calculated as a percentage of the employee's final salary (or sometimes an average of the employee's highest five years of earnings). Thus, under a defined benefit plan, the company is obligated to make payments to retired employees, but the company must determine how much of its earnings to set aside each year to cover these future obligations. Actuarial firms like TPF&Z assist companies in making this determination.

Several of TPF&Z's clients offer employees defined benefit retirement plans that allow for cost of living adjustments (COLAs). Here, employees' retirement benefits still are based on some measure of their final earnings, but these benefits are increased over time as the cost of living rises. These COLAs often are tied to the national consumer price index (CPI), which tracks the cost of a fixed-market basket of items over time. Each month, the Federal government calculates and publishes the CPI. Monthly CPI data from January 1991 through October 2005 is given in the following table (and in the file **CPIData.xls** on your data disk).

To assist their clients in determining the amount of money to accrue during a year for their annual contribution to their defined benefit programs, TPF&Z must forecast the value of the CPI one year into the future. Pension assets represent the largest single source of investment funds in the world. As a result, small changes or differences in TPF&Z's CPI forecast translate into hundreds of millions of dollars in corporate earnings being diverted from the bottom line into pension reserves. Needless to say, the partners of TPF&Z want their CPI forecasts to be as accurate as possible.

Consumer Price Index Data 1991–2005

Month	1991	1992	1993	1994	1995	1996	1997	1998	1999	2000	2001	2002	2003	2004	2005
1	134.6	138.1	142.6	146.2	150.3	154.4	159.1	161.6	164.3	166.6	175.1	177.1	181.7	185.2	190.7
2	134.8	138.6	143.1	146.7	150.9	154.9	159.6	161.9	164.5	168.8	175.8	177.8	183.1	186.2	191.8
3	135.0	139.3	143.6	147.2	151.4	155.7	160.0	162.2	165.0	169.8	176.2	178.8	184.2	187.4	193.3
4	135.2	139.5	144.0	147.4	151.9	156.3	160.2	162.5	166.2	171.2	176.9	179.8	183.8	188.0	194.6
5	135.6	139.7	144.2	147.5	152.2	156.6	160.1	162.8	166.2	171.3	177.7	179.8	183.5	189.1	194.4
6	136.0	140.2	144.4	148.0	152.5	156.7	160.3	163.0	166.2	171.5	178.0	179.9	183.7	189.7	194.5
7	136.2	140.5	144.4	148.4	152.5	157.0	160.5	163.2	166.7	172.4	177.5	180.1	183.9	189.4	195.4
8	136.6	140.9	144.8	149.0	152.9	157.3	160.8	163.4	167.1	172.8	177.5	180.7	184.6	189.5	196.4
9	137.2	141.3	145.1	149.4	153.2	157.8	161.2	163.6	167.9	173.7	178.3	181.0	185.2	189.9	198.8
10	137.4	141.8	145.7	149.5	153.7	158.3	161.6	164.0	168.2	174.0	177.7	181.3	185.0	190.9	193.2
11	137.8	142.0	145.8	149.7	153.6	158.6	161.5	164.0	168.3	174.1	177.4	181.3	184.5	191.0	—
12	137.9	141.9	145.8	149.7	153.5	158.6	161.3	163.9	168.3	174.0	176.7	180.9	184.3	190.3	—

a. Prepare a plot of the CPI data. Based on this plot, which of the time series forecasting techniques covered in this chapter would *not* be appropriate for forecasting this time series?

b. Apply Holt's method to this data set and use Solver to find the values of α (alpha) and β (beta) that minimize the MSE between the actual and predicted CPI values. What is the MSE using this technique? What is the forecasted CPI value for November 2005 and November 2006 using this technique?

c. Apply linear regression to model the CPI as a function of time. What is the MSE using this technique? What is the forecasted CPI value for November 2005 and November 2006 using this technique?

d. Create a graph showing the actual CPI values plotted along with the predicted values obtained using Holt's method and the linear regression model. Which forecasting technique seems to fit the actual CPI data the best? Based on this graph, do you think it is appropriate to use linear regression on this data set? Explain your answer.

e. A partner of the firm has looked at your graph and asked you to repeat your analysis excluding the data prior to 1997. What MSE do you obtain using Holt's method? What MSE do you obtain using linear regression? What is the forecasted CPI value for November 2005 and November 2006 using each technique?

f. Graph your results again. Which forecasting technique seems to fit the actual CPI data the best? Based on this graph, do you think it is appropriate to use linear regression on this data set? Explain your answer.

g. The same partner is pleased with your new results but has one final request. She wants to consider if it is possible to combine the predictions obtained using Holt's method and linear regression to obtain a composite forecast that is more accurate than either technique used in isolation. The partner wants you to combine the predictions in the following manner:

$$\text{Combined Prediction} = \mathbf{w} \times H + (1 - \mathbf{w}) \times R$$

where H represents the predictions from Holt's method, R represents the predictions obtained using the linear regression model, and $\mathbf{w}$ is a weighting parameter between 0 and 1. Use Solver to determine the value of $\mathbf{w}$ that minimizes the MSE between the actual CPI values and the combined predictions. What is the optimal value of $\mathbf{w}$ and what is the associated MSE? What is the forecasted CPI value for November 2005 and November 2006 using this technique?

h.   What CPI forecast for November 2005 and November 2006 would you recommend that TPF&Z actually use?

i.   Use CB Predictor to determine the best forecasting function for this data based on minimum RMSE. What technique does CB Predictor suggest?

Strategic Planning at Fysco Foods

CASE 11.3

Fysco Foods, Inc. is one of the largest suppliers of institutional and commercial food products in the United States. Fortunately for Fysco, the demand for "food away from home" has been growing steadily over the past 22 years as shown in the following table (and the file **FyscoFoods.xls** on your data disk). Note that this table breaks the total expenditures on food away from home (shown in the final column) into six component parts (*e.g.*, eating & drinking places, hotels & motels, etc).

As part of its strategic planning process, each year Fsyco generates forecasts of the total market demand in each of the six food away from home expenditure categories. This helps the company allocate its marketing resources among the various customers represented in each category.

a.   Prepare line graphs of each of the six expenditure categories. Indicate whether each category appears to be stationary or nonstationary.

b.   Use Holt's method to create models for each expenditure category. Use Solver to estimate the values of α and β that minimize the MSE. What are the optimal values of α and β and the MSE for each model? What is the forecast for next year for each expenditure category?

c.   Estimate linear regression models for each expenditure category. What is the estimated regression equation and MSE for each model? What is the forecast for next year for each expenditure category?

d.   Fysco's Vice President of Marketing has a new idea for forecasting market demand. For each expenditure category, she wants you to estimate the growth rate represented by g in the following equation: $\hat{Y}_{t+1} = Y_t(1 + g)$. That is, the estimated value for time period $t + 1$ is equal to the actual value in the previous time period (t) multiplied by one plus the growth rate g. Use Solver to identify the optimal (minimum MSE) growth rate for each expenditure category. What is the growth rate for each category? What is the forecast for next year for each expenditure category?

e.   Which of the three forecasting techniques considered here would you recommend that Fysco use for each expenditure category?

Total Food Away from Home Expenditures (in millions)

Year	Eating & Drinking Places[1]	Hotels & Motels[1]	Retail Stores, Direct Selling[2]	Recreational Places[3]	Schools & Colleges[4]	All Other[5]	Total[6]
1	75,883	5,906	8,158	3,040	11,115	16,194	120,296
2	83,358	6,639	8,830	2,979	11,357	17,751	130,914
3	90,390	6,888	9,256	2,887	11,692	18,663	139,776
4	98,710	7,660	9,827	3,271	12,338	19,077	150,883
5	105,836	8,409	10,315	3,489	12,950	20,047	161,046
6	111,760	9,168	10,499	3,737	13,534	20,133	168,831
7	121,699	9,665	11,116	4,059	14,401	20,755	181,695
8	146,194	11,117	12,063	4,331	14,300	21,122	209,127
9	160,855	11,905	13,211	5,144	14,929	22,887	228,930
10	171,157	12,179	14,440	6,151	15,728	24,581	244,236
11	183,484	12,508	16,053	7,316	16,767	26,198	262,326
12	188,228	12,460	16,750	8,079	17,959	27,108	270,584
13	183,014	13,204	13,588	8,602	18,983	27,946	265,338
14	195,835	13,362	13,777	9,275	19,844	28,031	280,124
15	205,768	13,880	14,210	9,791	21,086	28,208	292,943
16	214,274	14,195	14,333	10,574	22,093	28,597	304,066
17	221,735	14,504	14,475	11,354	22,993	28,981	314,043
18	235,597	15,469	14,407	8,290	24,071	30,926	328,760
19	248,716	15,800	15,198	9,750	25,141	31,926	346,530
20	260,495	16,623	16,397	10,400	26,256	33,560	363,730
21	275,695	17,440	16,591	11,177	27,016	34,508	382,427
22	290,655	17,899	16,881	11,809	28,012	35,004	400,259

Notes:

[1] Includes tips.

[2] Includes vending machine operators but not vending machines operated by organization.

[3] Motion picture theaters, bowling alleys, pool parlors, sports arenas, camps, amusement parks, golf and country clubs.

[4] Includes school food subsidies.

[5] Military exchanges and clubs; railroad dining cars; airlines; food service in manufacturing plants, institutions, hospitals, boarding houses, fraternities and sororities, and civic and social organizations; and food supplied to military forces.

[6] Computed from unrounded data.

Chapter 12

Introduction to Simulation Using Crystal Ball

12.0 Introduction

Chapter 1 discussed how the calculations in a spreadsheet can be viewed as a mathematical model that defines a functional relationship between various input variables (or independent variables) and one or more bottom-line performance measures (or dependent variables). The following equation expresses this relationship:

$$Y = f(X_1, X_2, \ldots, X_k)$$

In many spreadsheets, the values of various input cells are determined by the person using the spreadsheet. These input cells correspond to the independent variables $X_1, X_2, \ldots, X_k$ in the previous equation. Various formulas (represented by $f(\cdot)$ above) are entered in other cells of the spreadsheet to transform the values of the input cells into some bottom-line output (denoted by Y above). Simulation is a technique that is helpful in analyzing models in which the value to be assumed by one or more independent variables is uncertain.

This chapter discusses how to perform simulation using a popular commercial spreadsheet add-in called Crystal Ball, created and distributed by Decisioneering, Inc. A limited-life (140-day) version of Crystal Ball and related products comes on the CD-ROM accompanying this book. Decisioneering offers students one- and two-year extensions of this software at very affordable prices. You can find additional information about Crystal Ball and these extension options at http://www.decisioneering.com.

12.1 Random Variables and Risk

To compute a value for the bottom-line performance measure of a spreadsheet model, each input cell must be assigned a specific value so that all the related calculations can be performed. However, some uncertainty often exists regarding the value that should be assumed by one or more independent variables (or input cells) in the spreadsheet. This is particularly true in spreadsheet models that represent future conditions. A random variable is any variable whose value cannot be predicted or set with certainty. Thus, many input variables in a spreadsheet model represent random variables whose actual values cannot be determined with certainty.

For example, projections of the cost of raw materials, future interest rates, future numbers of employees, and expected product demand are random variables because their true values are unknown and will be determined in the future. If we cannot say with certainty what value one or more input variables in a model will assume, we also cannot say with certainty what value the dependent variable will assume. This uncertainty associated with the value of the dependent variable introduces an element of risk to the decision-making problem. Specifically, if the dependent variable represents some bottom-line performance measure that managers use to make decisions, and its value is uncertain, any decisions made on the basis of this value are based on uncertain (or incomplete) information. When such a decision is made, some chance exists that the decision will not produce the intended results. This chance, or uncertainty, represents an element of risk in the decision-making problem.

The term "risk" also implies the *potential* for loss. The fact that a decision's outcome is uncertain does not mean that the decision is particularly risky. For example, whenever we put money into a soft-drink machine, there is a chance that the machine will take our money and not deliver the product. However, most of us would not consider this risk to be particularly great. From past experience, we know that the chance of not receiving the product is small. But even if the machine takes our money and does not deliver the product, most of us would not consider this to be a tremendous loss. Thus, the amount of risk involved in a given decision-making situation is a function of the uncertainty in the outcome of the decision and the magnitude of the potential loss. A proper assessment of the risk present in a decision-making situation should address both of these issues, as the examples in this chapter will demonstrate.

12.2 Why Analyze Risk?

Many spreadsheets built by business people contain *estimated* values for the uncertain input variables in their models. If a manager cannot say with certainty what value a particular cell in a spreadsheet will assume, this cell most likely represents a random variable. Ordinarily, the manager will attempt to make an informed guess about the values such cells will assume. The manager hopes that inserting the expected, or most likely, values for all the uncertain cells in a spreadsheet will provide the most likely value for the cell containing the bottom-line performance measure (Y). The problem with this type of analysis is that it tells the decision maker nothing about the variability of the performance measure.

For example, in analyzing a particular investment opportunity, we might determine that the expected return on a $1,000 investment is $10,000 within two years. But how much variability exists in the possible outcomes? If all the potential outcomes are scattered closely around $10,000 (say from $9,000 to $11,000), then the investment opportunity still might be attractive. If, on the other hand, the potential outcomes are scattered widely around $10,000 (say from $-$30,000 up to $+$50,000), then the investment opportunity might be unattractive. Although these two scenarios might have the same expected or average value, the risks involved are quite different. Thus, even if we can determine the expected outcome of a decision using a spreadsheet, it is just as important, if not more so, to consider the risk involved in the decision.

12.3 Methods of Risk Analysis

Several techniques are available to help managers analyze risk. Three of the most common are best-case/worst-case analysis, what-if analysis, and simulation. Of these methods, simulation is the most powerful and, therefore, is the technique that we will focus on in this chapter. Although the other techniques might not be completely effective in risk analysis, they probably are used more often than simulation by most managers in business today. This is largely because most managers are unaware of the spreadsheet's ability to perform simulation and of the benefits provided by this technique. So before discussing simulation, let's first look briefly at the other methods of risk analysis to understand their strengths and weaknesses.

12.3.1 BEST-CASE/WORST-CASE ANALYSIS

If we don't know what value a particular cell in a spreadsheet will assume, we could enter a number that we think is the most likely value for the uncertain cell. If we enter such numbers for all the uncertain cells in the spreadsheet, we can easily calculate the most likely value of the bottom-line performance measure. This is also called the base-case scenario. However, this scenario gives us no information about how far away the actual outcome might be from this expected, or most likely, value.

One simple solution to this problem is to calculate the value of the bottom-line performance measure using the best-case, or most optimistic, and worst-case, or most pessimistic, values for the uncertain input cells. These additional scenarios show the range of possible values that might be assumed by the bottom-line performance measure. As indicated in the earlier example about the $1,000 investment, knowing the range of possible outcomes helps us assess the risk involved in different alternatives. However, simply knowing the best-case and worst-case outcomes tells us nothing about the distribution of possible values within this range, nor does it tell us the probability of either scenario occurring.

Figure 12.1 displays several probability distributions that might be associated with the value of a bottom-line performance measure within a given range. Each of these distributions describes variables that have identical ranges and similar average values. But each distribution is very different in terms of the risk it represents to the decision maker. The appeal of best-case/worst-case analysis is that it is easy to do. Its weakness is that it tells us nothing about the shape of the distribution associated with the bottom-line

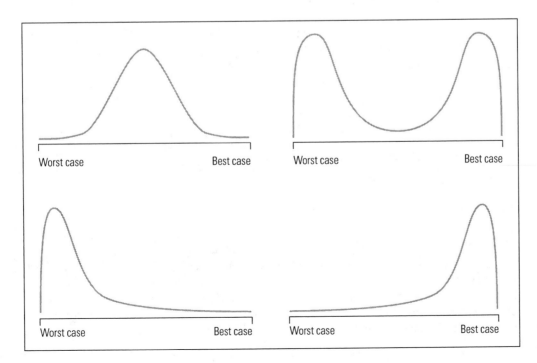

FIGURE 12.1

Possible distributions of performance measure values within a given range

performance measure. As we will see later, knowing the shape of the distribution of the bottom-line performance measure can be critically important in helping us answer several managerial questions.

12.3.2 WHAT-IF ANALYSIS

Before the introduction of electronic spreadsheets in the early 1980s, the use of best-case/worst-case analysis often was the only feasible way for a manager to analyze the risk associated with a decision. This process was extremely time-consuming, error prone, and tedious, using only paper, pencil, and calculator to recalculate the performance measure of a model using different values for the uncertain inputs. The arrival of personal computers and electronic spreadsheets made it much easier for a manager to play out a large number of scenarios in addition to the best and worst cases—which is the essence of what-if analysis.

In what-if analysis, a manager changes the values of the uncertain input variables to see what happens to the bottom-line performance measure. By making a series of such changes, a manager can gain some insight into how sensitive the performance measure is to changes to the input variables. Although many managers perform this type of manual what-if analysis, it has three major flaws.

First, if the values selected for the independent variables are based only on the manager's judgment, the resulting sample values of the performance measure are likely to be biased. That is, if several uncertain variables can each assume some range of values, it would be difficult to ensure that the manager tests a fair, or representative, sample of all possible combinations of these values. To select values for the uncertain variables that correctly reflect their random variations, the values must be randomly selected from a distribution, or pool, of values that reflects the appropriate range of possible values, and the appropriate relative frequencies of these variables.

Second, hundreds or thousands of what-if scenarios might be required to create a valid representation of the underlying variability in the bottom-line performance measure. No one would want to perform these scenarios manually, nor could anyone make sense of the resulting stream of numbers that would flash on the screen.

The third problem with what-if analysis is that the insight that the manager might gain from playing out various scenarios is of little value when recommending a decision to top management. What-if analysis simply does not supply the manager with the tangible evidence (facts and figures) needed to justify why a given decision was made or recommended. Additionally, what-if analysis does not address the problem identified in our earlier discussion of best-case/worst-case analysis—it does not allow us to estimate the distribution of the performance measure in a formal enough manner. Thus, what-if analysis is a step in the right direction, but it is not quite a large enough step to allow managers to analyze risk effectively in the decisions they face.

12.3.3 SIMULATION

Simulation is a technique that measures and describes various characteristics of the bottom-line performance measure of a model when one or more values for the independent variables are uncertain. If any independent variables in a model are random variables, the dependent variable (Y) also represents a random variable. The objective in simulation is to describe the distribution and characteristics of the possible values of the bottom-line performance measure Y, given the possible values and behavior of the independent variables $X_1, X_2, \ldots, X_k$.

The idea behind simulation is similar to the notion of playing out many what-if scenarios. The difference is that the process of assigning values to the cells in the spreadsheet that represent random variables is automated so that: (1) the values are assigned in a non-biased way, and (2) the spreadsheet user is relieved of the burden of determining these values. With simulation, we repeatedly and randomly generate sample values for each uncertain input variable ($X_1, X_2, \ldots, X_k$) in our model and then compute the resulting value of our bottom-line performance measure (Y). We can then use the sample values of Y to estimate the true distribution and other characteristics of the performance measure Y. For example, we can use the sample observations to construct a frequency distribution of the performance measure, to estimate the range of values over which the performance measure might vary, to estimate its mean and variance, and to estimate the probability that the actual value of the performance measure will be greater than (or less than) a particular value. All these measures provide greater insight into the risk associated with a given decision than a single value calculated based on the expected values for the uncertain independent variables.

On Uncertainty and Decision-Making...

"Uncertainty is the most difficult thing about decision-making. In the face of uncertainty, some people react with paralysis, or they do exhaustive research to avoid making a decision. The best decision-making happens when the mental environment is focused. In a physical environment, you focus on something physical. In tennis, that might be the spinning seams of the ball. In a mental environment, you focus on the facts at hand. That fine-tuned focus doesn't leave room for fears and doubts to enter. Doubts knock at the door of our consciousness, but you don't have to have them in for tea and crumpets."—Timothy Gallwey, author of *The Inner Game of Tennis* and *The Inner Game of Work*.

12.4 A Corporate Health Insurance Example

The following example demonstrates the mechanics of preparing a spreadsheet model for risk analysis using simulation. The example presents a fairly simple model to illustrate the process and give a sense of the amount of effort involved. However, the process for performing simulation is basically the same regardless of the size of the model.

Lisa Pon has just been hired as an analyst in the corporate planning department of Hungry Dawg Restaurants. Her first assignment is to determine how much money the company needs to accrue in the coming year to pay for its employees' health insurance claims. Hungry Dawg is a large, growing chain of restaurants that specializes in traditional southern foods. The company has become large enough that it no longer buys insurance from a private insurance company. The company is now self-insured, meaning that it pays health insurance claims with its own money (although it contracts with an outside company to handle the administrative details of processing claims and writing checks).

FIGURE 12.2

Original corporate health insurance model with expected values for uncertain variables

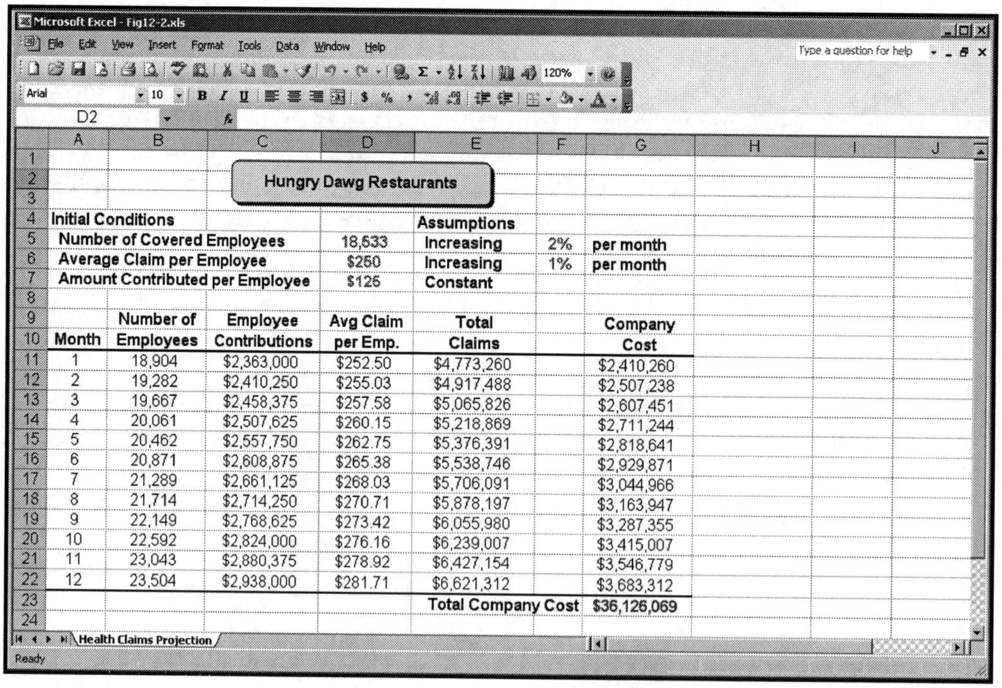

Hungry Dawg Restaurants

Initial Conditions		**Assumptions**	
Number of Covered Employees	18,533	Increasing	2% per month
Average Claim per Employee	$250	Increasing	1% per month
Amount Contributed per Employee	$125	Constant	

Month	Number of Employees	Employee Contributions	Avg Claim per Emp.	Total Claims	Company Cost
1	18,904	$2,363,000	$252.50	$4,773,260	$2,410,260
2	19,282	$2,410,250	$255.03	$4,917,488	$2,507,238
3	19,667	$2,458,375	$257.58	$5,065,826	$2,607,451
4	20,061	$2,507,625	$260.15	$5,218,869	$2,711,244
5	20,462	$2,557,750	$262.75	$5,376,391	$2,818,641
6	20,871	$2,608,875	$265.38	$5,538,746	$2,929,871
7	21,289	$2,661,125	$268.03	$5,706,091	$3,044,966
8	21,714	$2,714,250	$270.71	$5,878,197	$3,163,947
9	22,149	$2,768,625	$273.42	$6,055,980	$3,287,355
10	22,592	$2,824,000	$276.16	$6,239,007	$3,415,007
11	23,043	$2,880,375	$278.92	$6,427,154	$3,546,779
12	23,504	$2,938,000	$281.71	$6,621,312	$3,683,312
				Total Company Cost	$36,126,069

The money the company uses to pay claims comes from two sources: employee contributions (or premiums deducted from employees' paychecks), and company funds (the company must pay whatever costs are not covered by employee contributions). Each employee covered by the health plan contributes $125 per month. However, the number of employees covered by the plan changes from month to month as employees are hired and fired, quit, or simply add or drop health insurance coverage. A total of 18,533 employees were covered by the plan last month. The average monthly health claim per covered employee was $250 last month.

An example of how most analysts would model this problem is shown in Figure 12.2 (and in the file Fig12-2.xls on your data disk). The spreadsheet begins with a listing of the initial conditions and assumptions for the problem. For example, cell D5 indicates that 18,533 employees currently are covered by the health plan, and cell D6 indicates that the average monthly claim per covered employee is $250. The average monthly contribution per employee is $125, as shown in cell D7. The values in cells D5 and D6 are unlikely to stay the same for the entire year. Thus, we need to make some assumptions about the rate at which these values are likely to increase during the year. For example, we might assume that the number of covered employees will increase by about 2% per month, and that the average claim per employee will increase at a rate of 1% per month. These assumptions are reflected in cells F5 and F6. The average contribution per employee is assumed to be constant over the coming year.

Using the assumed rate of increase in the number of covered employees (cell F5), we can create formulas for cells B11 through B22 that cause the number of covered employees to increase by the assumed amount each month. (The details of these formulas are covered later.) The expected monthly employee contributions shown in column C are calculated as $125 times the number of employees in each month. We can use the assumed rate of increase in average monthly claims (cell F6) to create formulas for cells D11 through D22 that cause the average claim per employee to increase at the assumed rate.

The total claims for each month (shown in column E) are calculated as the average claim figures in column D times the number of employees for each month in column B. Because the company must pay for any claims that are not covered by the employee contributions, the company cost figures in column G are calculated as the total claims minus the employee contributions (column E minus column C). Finally, cell G23 sums the company cost figures listed in column G, and shows that the company can expect to contribute $36,126,069 of its revenues toward paying the health insurance claims of its employees in the coming year.

12.4.1 A CRITIQUE OF THE BASE CASE MODEL

Now, let's consider the model we just described. The example model assumes that the number of covered employees will increase by *exactly* 2% each month and that the average claim per covered employee will increase by *exactly* 1% each month. Although these values might be reasonable approximations of what might happen, they are unlikely to reflect exactly what will happen. In fact, the number of employees covered by the health plan each month is likely to vary randomly around the average increase per month—that is, the number might decrease in some months and increase by more than 2% in others. Similarly, the average claim per covered employee might be lower than expected in certain months and higher than expected in others.

Both of these figures are likely to exhibit some uncertainty or random behavior, even if they do move in the general upward direction assumed throughout the year. So, we cannot say with certainty that the total cost figure of $36,126,069 is exactly what the company will have to contribute toward health claims in the coming year. It is simply a prediction of what might happen. The actual outcome could be smaller or larger than this estimate. Using the original model, we have no idea how much larger or smaller the actual result could be—nor do we have any idea of how the actual values are distributed around this estimate. We do not know if there is a 10%, 50%, or 90% chance of the actual total costs exceeding this estimate. To determine the variability or risk inherent in the bottom-line performance measure of total company costs, we will apply the technique of simulation to our model.

12.5 Spreadsheet Simulation Using Crystal Ball

To perform simulation in a spreadsheet, we must first place a random number generator (RNG) in each cell that represents a random, or uncertain, independent variable. Each RNG provides a sample observation from an appropriate distribution that represents the range and frequency of possible values for the variable. After the RNGs are in place, a new value of the bottom-line performance measure is computed every time new sample values are generated for the uncertain input cells. We can sample the spreadsheet n times, where n is the desired number of replications or scenarios, and the value of the bottom-line performance measure will be stored after each replication. We then analyze these stored observations to gain insights into the behavior and characteristics of the performance measure.

The process of simulation involves a lot of work but, fortunately, the spreadsheet can do most of the work for us fairly easily. In particular, the spreadsheet add-in package Crystal Ball is designed specifically to make spreadsheet simulation a simple process. The Crystal Ball software provides the following capabilities, which are not otherwise available while working in Excel: additional tools that are helpful in generating the

FIGURE 12.3

The Crystal Ball toolbar in Excel

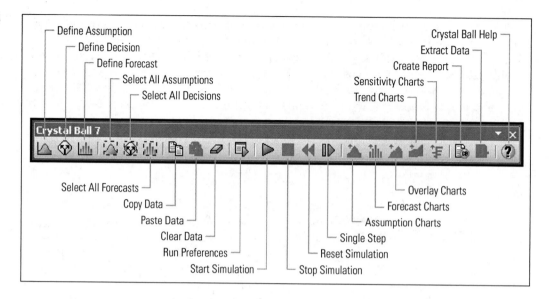

random numbers needed in simulation; additional commands that are helpful in setting up and running the simulation; and graphical and statistical summaries of the simulation data. As we shall see, these capabilities make simulation a relatively easy technique to apply in spreadsheets.

12.5.1 STARTING CRYSTAL BALL

If you are running Crystal Ball from a local area network (LAN) or in a computer lab, your instructor or LAN coordinator should give you directions on how to access this software. If you have installed Crystal Ball on your own computer, you can load Crystal Ball in Windows as follows:

1. Click Start.
2. Click Programs.
3. Click Crystal Ball 7.
4. Click Crystal Ball.

This loads Crystal Ball in a new instance of Excel and causes the De*fi*ne, *R*un, and *A*nalyze menus to appear on Excel's main menu bar. Crystal Ball also provides the custom toolbar shown in Figure 12.3. We will refer to the various buttons on this toolbar throughout this chapter. You can display this toolbar in Excel as follows:

1. Click View.
2. Click Toolbars.
3. Check the Crystal Ball 7 option.

12.6 Random Number Generators

As mentioned earlier, the first step in spreadsheet simulation is to place an RNG in each cell that contains an uncertain value. Each RNG will generate (or return) a number that represents a randomly selected value from a distribution, or pool, of values. The distributions that these samples are taken from should be representative of the underlying pool of values expected to occur in each uncertain cell. Crystal Ball refers to such cells as *assumption cells.* To create the RNGs required for simulating a spreadsheet model,

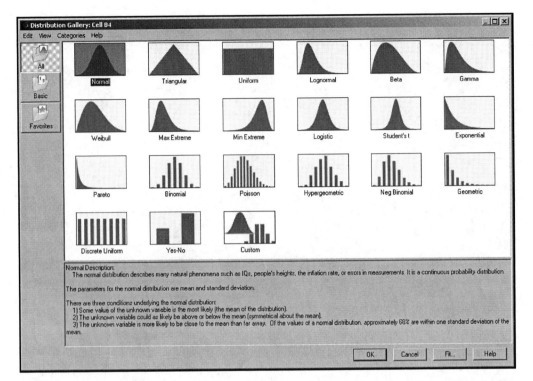

FIGURE 12.4

The Crystal Ball Distribution Gallery

Crystal Ball provides the Distribution Gallery tool shown in Figure 12.4. (The Distribution Gallery is launched by clicking the Define Assumption button on the Crystal Ball toolbar, or by clicking Define, Define Assumption on Excel's main menu bar.)

The distributions shown in Figure 12.4 allow us to generate a variety of random numbers easily. For example, if we think that the behavior of a particular uncertain cell (perhaps representing the average health insurance claim per employee in a given month) could be modeled as a normally distributed random variable with a mean of $250 and standard deviation of $3, we could double-click the Normal distribution button in Figure 12.4. This launches the dialog in Figure 12.5 that allows us to indicate the mean and standard deviation for the assumption (or uncertain) cell in question. (The entries for the mean and standard deviation also could be formulas that refer to other cells in the spreadsheet.) Whenever Crystal Ball creates a new replication of the spreadsheet, the value in this assumption cell would be a randomly selected value from a normal distribution with a mean of 250 and standard deviation of 3.

As a different example, suppose that an assumption cell in a spreadsheet (perhaps representing the number of gallons of white ceiling paint sold on a given day at a paint store) has a 30% chance of assuming the value 10, a 50% chance of assuming the value 15, and a 20% chance of assuming the value 20. We could model the behavior of this random variable using the Custom distribution from Crystal Ball's distribution gallery as shown in Figure 12.6. If we used Crystal Ball to replicate this spreadsheet many times, it would randomly choose the value 10 for this assumption cell approximately 30% of the time, the value 15 approximately 50% of the time, and the value 20 approximately 20% of the time.

Each of the RNGs in Figure 12.4 require different parameters that allow us to generate random numbers from probability distributions with a wide variety of shapes. Figures 12.7 and 12.8 illustrate some example distributions. Additional information about each distribution is available by clicking the Help button on any of the Crystal Ball dialogs or by selecting Help, Crystal Ball on Excel's main menu bar.

FIGURE 12.5

Example of creating a normally distributed assumption cell

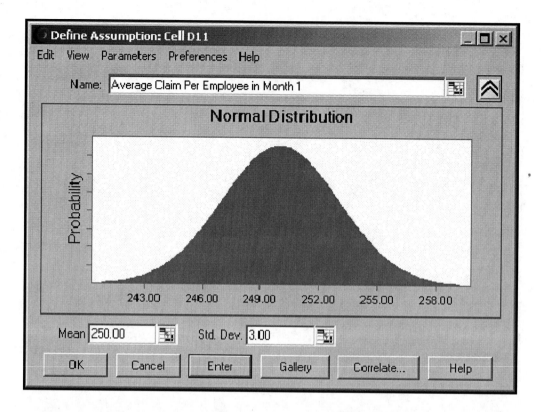

FIGURE 12.6

Example of creating a custom distribution for an assumption cell

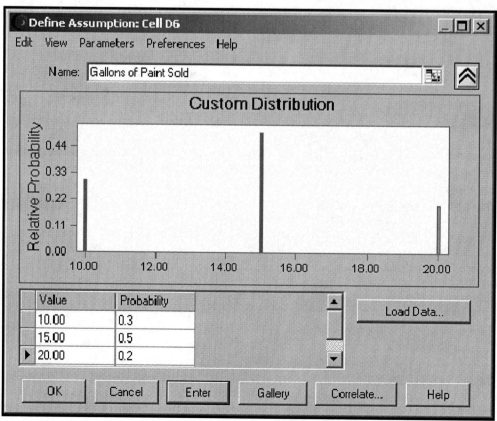

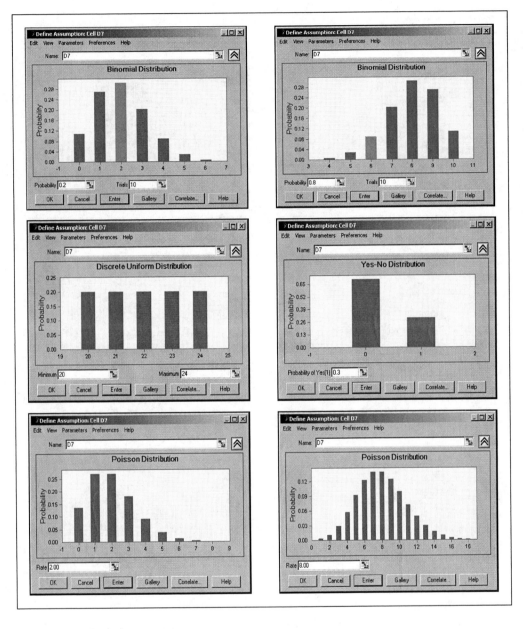

FIGURE 12.7

*Examples of
selected discrete
distributions*

12.6.1 DISCRETE VS. CONTINUOUS RANDOM VARIABLES

An important distinction exists between the graphs in Figures 12.7 and 12.8. In particular, the RNGs depicted in Figure 12.7 generate *discrete* outcomes, whereas those represented in Figure 12.8 generate *continuous* outcomes. That is, some of the RNGs displayed in Figure 12.4 can return only a distinct set of individual values, whereas the other RNGs can return any value from an infinite set of values. The distinction between discrete and continuous random variables is very important.

For example, the number of defective tires on a new car is a discrete random variable because it can assume only one of five distinct values: 0, 1, 2, 3, or 4. On the other hand, the amount of fuel in a new car is a continuous random variable because it can assume any value between 0 and the maximum capacity of the fuel tank. Thus, when selecting

FIGURE 12.8

Examples of selected continuous distributions

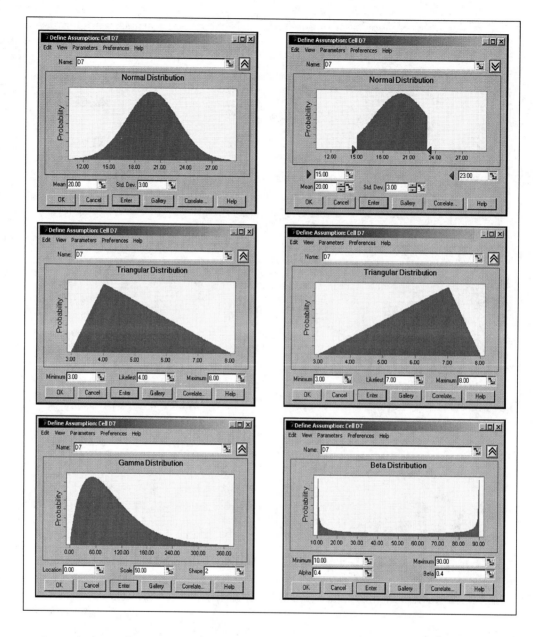

an RNG for an uncertain variable in a model, it is important to consider whether the variable can assume discrete or continuous values.

12.7 Preparing the Model for Simulation

To apply simulation to the model for Hungry Dawg Restaurants described earlier, first we must select appropriate RNGs for the uncertain variables in the model. If available, historical data on the uncertain variables could be analyzed to determine appropriate RNGs for these variables. (Crystal Ball's Batch Fit tool can be used for this purpose.) If past data are not available, or if we have some reason to expect the future behavior of a variable to be significantly different from the past, then we must use judgment in selecting appropriate RNGs to model the random behavior of the uncertain variables.

For our example problem, let's assume that by analyzing historical data, we determined that the change in the number of covered employees from one month to the next is expected to vary uniformly between a 3% decrease and a 7% increase. (Note that this should cause the *average* change in the number of employees to be a 2% increase, because 0.02 is the midpoint between −0.03 and +0.07.) Further, assume that we can model the average monthly claim per covered employee as a normally distributed random variable with the mean increasing by 1% per month and a standard deviation of approximately $3. (Note that this will cause the *average* increase in claims per covered employee from one month to the next to be approximately 1%.) These assumptions are reflected in cells F5 through H6 at the top of Figure 12.9 (and in the file Fig12-9.xls on your data disk).

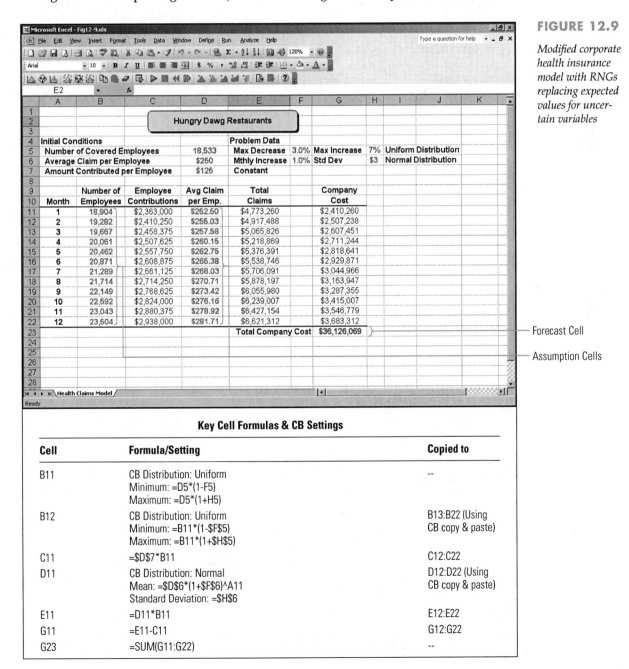

FIGURE 12.9

Modified corporate health insurance model with RNGs replacing expected values for uncertain variables

Key Cell Formulas & CB Settings

Cell	Formula/Setting	Copied to
B11	CB Distribution: Uniform Minimum: =D5*(1-F5) Maximum: =D5*(1+H5)	--
B12	CB Distribution: Uniform Minimum: =B11*(1-$F$5) Maximum: =B11*(1+$H$5)	B13:B22 (Using CB copy & paste)
C11	=$D$7*B11	C12:C22
D11	CB Distribution: Normal Mean: =$D$6*(1+$F$6)^A11 Standard Deviation: =$H$6	D12:D22 (Using CB copy & paste)
E11	=D11*B11	E12:E22
G11	=E11-C11	G12:G22
G23	=SUM(G11:G22)	--

12.7.1 DEFINING ASSUMPTIONS FOR THE NUMBER OF COVERED EMPLOYEES

To randomly generate the appropriate number of employees covered by the health plan each month, we will use the Uniform distribution shown in Figure 12.4. Because the change in the number of employees from one month to the next can vary between a 3% decrease and a 7% increase, the number of employees in any month should be between a minimum of 97% and a maximum of 107% of the number of employees in the previous month. Thus, the number of employees in month 1 (represented by cell B11) should vary uniformly between 97% and 107% of the number of employees given in cell D5. Using Crystal Ball, we place this assumption on cell B11 as follows:

1. Select cell B11.
2. Click Define, Assumption.
3. Select the Uniform distribution.
4. In the Name text box type: Employees in Month 1
5. For the Minimum parameter type the formula: =D5*(1-F5)
6. For the Minimum parameter type the formula: =D5*(1+H5)

The resulting Define Assumption dialog box is shown in Figure 12.10. Notice that we are instructing Crystal Ball to treat cell B11 as an assumption (or uncertain) cell whose value is a uniformly distributed random variable between a minimum of 97% (or 1-F5) of the value in D5 and a maximum of 107% (or 1+H5) of the value in cell D5. So when we run the simulation, Crystal Ball will randomly select values between 17,977 and 19,830 for cell B11.

FIGURE 12.10

Defining the assumptions cell for cell B11

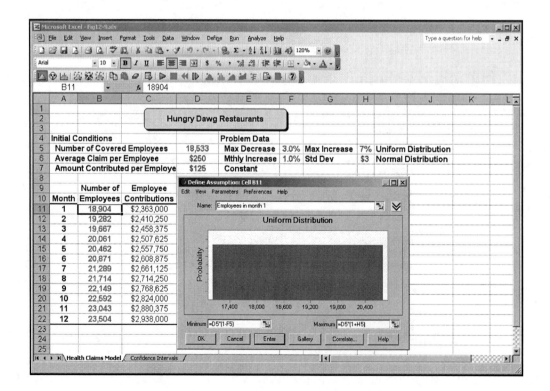

Do You Want to See the Formulas or the Numbers?

Using the Define Assumption dialog as shown in Figure 12.10, you can use the Parameters, Show Cell References command (or Ctrl+ ~) to instruct Crystal Ball to show either the formulas that define the minimum and maximum values or the values produced by the formulas.

When you click OK on the Define Assumption dialog shown in Figure 12.10, Crystal Ball automatically changes the background color of cell B11 to green to indicate that it is now an assumption cell. If you want assumption cells to be indicated by a different color you may indicate your preference using the Define, Cell Preferences command.

Next, we need to place similar assumptions on the number of employees in months 2 through 12 (cells B12 through B22). Again, the number of employees in each month should be between a minimum of 97% and a maximum of 107% of the number of employees in the previous month. We could define the assumptions for each cell individually, just as we did for month 1 (cell B11). However, it is also possible to copy and paste assumption definitions from one cell to other cells when the formulas that describe the distribution follow a common pattern. So if we are careful about how we create the formulas that define the minimum and maximum values for number of employees in month 2 (for cell B12), we can copy the assumptions about that cell to the remaining cells for months 3 through 12 (cells B13 through B22).

Figure 12.11 shows the Define Assumptions dialog box for cell B12. Notice that the formulas for the minimum and maximum number of employees are =B11*(1-$F$5) and

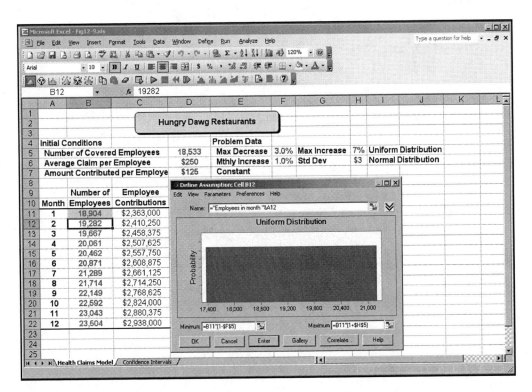

FIGURE 12.11

Defining the assumptions for cell B12

=B11*(1+$H$5), respectively. The dollar signs embedded in the references to cells F5 and H5 indicate that these are absolute cell references that should not change if the definition for this assumption cell is ever copied to another cell. The reference to B11 lacks the dollar signs and will change in the customary relative fashion if the definition for this assumption cell is copied elsewhere. Also notice that the name being defined for cell B12 is given by the formula: ="Employees in month "&A12. (Because the value in cell A12 is two (2), this formula evaluates to the text string "Employees in month 2".) When defining cells whose definitions will be copied, it is good practice to use formulas like this (when possible) for creating names so that these items are identified clearly in subsequent Crystal Ball reports and charts.

Once our assumptions about cell B12 are properly recorded, we can copy its assumption cell definition to cells B13 through B22. However, it is _**critical**_ that we use Crystal Ball's copy and paste commands to do this. Excel's copy and paste command **_will not work_** on assumption cell definitions. Thus, to copy the assumption cell definitions from cell B12 to cells B13 through B22:

1. Select cell B12.
2. Click Define, Copy Data (or click the Copy Data button on the Crystal Ball menu bar).
3 Select cells B13 through B22.
4. Click Define, Paste Data (or click the Paste Data button on the Crystal Ball menu bar).

Important Software Issue

To copy assumption cell definitions, you must use Crystal Ball's copy data and paste data commands. Excel's copy and paste commands do not work on assumption cell definitions.

12.7.2 DEFINING ASSUMPTIONS FOR THE AVERAGE MONTHLY CLAIM PER EMPLOYEE

To randomly generate the appropriate average claims per covered employee in each month, we will use the Normal distribution shown in Figure 12.4. This distribution requires that we supply the value of the mean and standard deviation of the distribution from which we want to sample. The assumed $3 standard deviation for the average monthly claim, shown in cell H6 in Figure 12.11, is constant from month to month. Thus, we need only to determine the proper mean value for each month.

In this case, the mean for any given month should be 1% larger than the mean in the previous month. For example, the mean for month 1 is:

$$\text{Mean in month 1} = (\text{original mean}) \times 1.01$$

and the mean for month 2 is:

$$\text{Mean in month 2} = (\text{mean in month 1}) \times 1.01$$

If we substitute the previous definition of the mean in month 1 into the previous equation, we obtain,

$$\text{Mean in month 2} = (\text{original mean}) \times (1.01)^2$$

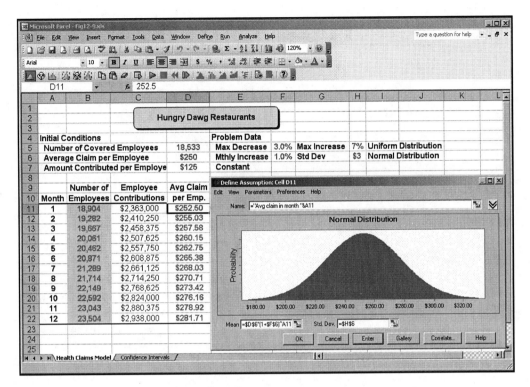

FIGURE
12.12

*Defining the
assumptions for
cell D11*

Similarly, the mean in month 3 is:

Mean in month 3 = (mean in month 2) × 1.01 = (original mean) × $(1.01)^3$

So in general, the mean for month n is:

Mean in month n = (original mean) × $(1.01)^n$

Thus, to generate the average claim per covered employee for month 1, we use the assumption cell definition for cell D11 shown in Figure 12.12.

Notice that the mean for cell D11 is defined by the formula: =$D$6*(1+$F$6)^A11. This formula implements the general definition of the mean in month n. Similarly, the standard deviation, which is assumed to be constant in all months, is defined by the formula: =$H$6. So after entering our assumptions for cell D11, we can copy this definition to cells D11 through D22 to complete the assumption cell specifications related to the average claim per employee each month. Again, it is ___critical___ that we use Crystal Ball's copy and paste commands to do this because Excel's copy and paste command *will not work* on assumption cell definitions.

12.7.3 DEFINING ASSUMPTIONS FOR THE AVERAGE MONTHLY CLAIM PER EMPLOYEE

After entering the appropriate RNGs via our assumption cell definitions, you can use Crystal Ball's Run, Single Step command (or click the Single Step button on the Crystal Ball menu bar) to automatically select new values for all the cells in the spreadsheet that represent uncertain (or random) values. Similarly, with each replication, a new value for the bottom-line performance measure (total company cost) appears in cell G23. Thus, by executing the Single Step command several times, we can observe representative values of the company's total cost for health claims. This also helps to verify that we implemented the RNGs correctly and that they are generating appropriate values for each uncertain cell.

Why Don't Your Numbers Change?

By default, Crystal Ball displays the mean (or average) value of the distribution for cells containing RNG functions. To make Crystal Ball display new values for your RNG cells whenever you click the Single Step button, click Cell, Cell Preferences, and deselect the check box labeled "Set to Distribution Mean."

12.8 Running the Simulation

The next step in performing the simulation involves recalculating the spreadsheet several hundred or several thousand times and recording the resulting values generated for the output cell, or bottom-line performance measure. Fortunately, Crystal Ball can do this for us if we indicate: 1) which cell(s) in the spreadsheet we want to track, and 2) how many times we want it to replicate the model.

12.8.1 SELECTING THE OUTPUT CELLS TO TRACK

We can use the Define Forecast button on the Crystal Ball toolbar (see Figure 12.3) to indicate the output cell (or cells) that we want Crystal Ball to track during the simulation. In the current example, cell G23 represents the output cell we want Crystal Ball to track. To indicate this:

1. Click cell G23.
2. Click the Define Forecast button on the Crystal Ball toolbar (or click Define, Define Forecast).
   (This causes the dialog box in Figure 12.13 to appear. If you see a button labeled More, click it.)
3. Make the indicated selections.
4. Click OK.

In some simulations, we might want to analyze several performance measures. In such a case, we can follow the preceding procedure repeatedly to select additional output cells to track.

Software Note...

When you define assumption, decision, or forecast cells, Crystal Ball automatically changes the background color of the cells to distinguish these cells from others on the spreadsheet. You can change the default colors Crystal Ball uses (or suppress this behavior entirely) by clicking Define, Cell Preferences.

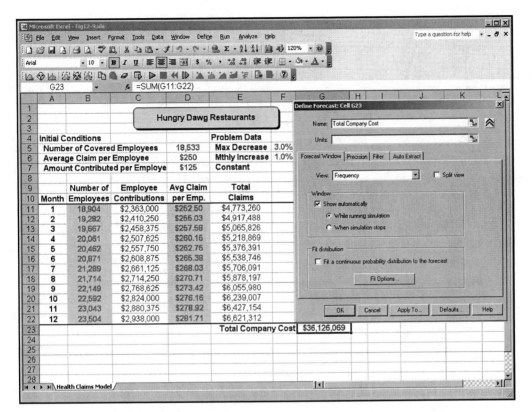

FIGURE
12.13

*Defining the
forecast cell*

12.8.2 SELECTING THE NUMBER OF ITERATIONS

Figure 12.14 shows the Trials card in the Run Preferences dialog box for Crystal Ball. The "Maximum Number of Trials" option in this dialog box allows us to specify the number of iterations (or replications) to include in our simulation. Thus, to indicate that we want to perform 5000 replications of our model:

1. Click the Run Preferences button on the Crystal Ball toolbar (or click Run, Run Preferences).
2. Type 5000 in the box labeled "Maximum Number of Trials."
3. Click OK.

12.8.3 DETERMINING THE SAMPLE SIZE

You might wonder why we selected 5000 replications. Why not 500, or 8000? Unfortunately, there is no easy answer to this question. Remember that the goal in simulation is to estimate various characteristics about the bottom-line performance measure(s) under consideration. For example, we might want to estimate the mean value of the performance measure and the shape of its probability distribution. However, a different value of the bottom-line performance measure occurs each time we manually recalculate the model in Figure 12.8. Thus, there is an infinite number of possibilities—or an infinite population—of total company cost values associated with this model.

We cannot analyze all of these infinite possibilities. But by taking a large enough sample from this infinite population, we can make reasonably accurate estimates about the characteristics of the underlying infinite population of values. The larger the sample we

FIGURE 12.14

Trials options in the Run Preferences dialog box

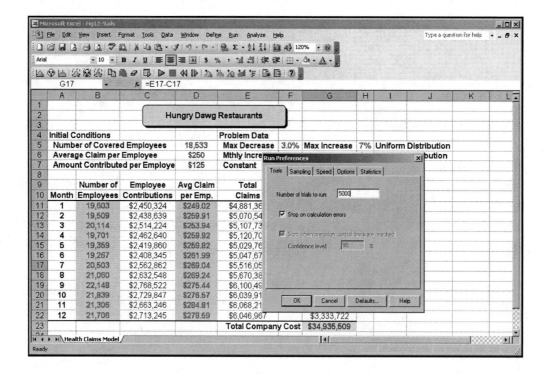

take (that is, the more replications we do), the more accurate our final results will be. But, performing many replications takes time, so we must make a trade-off in terms of estimation accuracy versus convenience. Thus, there is no simple answer to the question of how many replications to perform, but, as a bare minimum you should always perform at least 1000 replications, and more as time permits or accuracy demands.

12.8.4 RUNNING THE SIMULATION

Having identified the output cells to track and the number of replications to perform, we now need to instruct Crystal Ball to perform the simulation by clicking the Start button on the Crystal Ball toolbar in Figure 12.3 (or by clicking Run, Run). Crystal Ball then begins to perform the specified number of replications. Depending on the number of iterations selected, the size of the model, and the speed of your computer, it could take anywhere from several seconds to several minutes for these computations to be carried out.

For our example problem, Crystal Ball performs 5000 recalculations of the model, keeping track of the value in cell G23 for each replication. By default, Crystal Ball updates the computer screen after each replication, which can be very time-consuming. If you select the "When simulation stops" option shown in Figure 12.13, Crystal Ball will not update the screen after each replication and will perform the replications more quickly.

12.9 Data Analysis

As mentioned earlier, the objective of performing simulation is to estimate various characteristics of the performance measure resulting from uncertainty in some or all of the input variables. After performing the replications, Crystal Ball summarizes the output data, as shown in Figure 12.15. The summary statistics and frequency chart are shown simultaneously by clicking View, Split View.

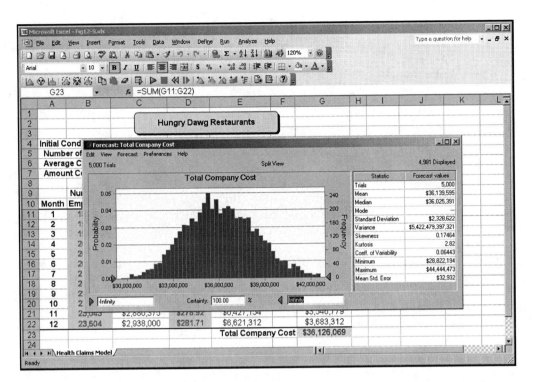

**FIGURE
12.15**

*Summary
statistics and
histogram for
simulation results*

12.9.1 THE BEST CASE AND THE WORST CASE

As shown in Figure 12.15, the average (or mean) value for cell G23 is approximately $36.1 million. (If you are working through this example on a computer, the graphs and statistics you generate might be somewhat different from the results shown here because you might be working with a different sample of 5000 observations.) However, decision makers usually want to know the best-case and worst-case scenarios to get an idea of the range of possible outcomes they might face. This information is available from the simulation results, as shown by the Minimum and Maximum values listed in Figure 12.15.

Although the average total cost value observed in the 5000 replications is $36.1 million, in one case the total cost is approximately $28.8 million (representing the best case) and in another case the total cost is approximately $44.4 million (representing the worst case). These figures should give the decision maker a good idea about the range of possible cost values that might occur. Note that these values might be difficult to determine manually in a complex model with many uncertain independent variables.

12.9.2 THE DISTRIBUTION OF THE OUTPUT CELL

The best- and worst-case scenarios are the most extreme outcomes, and might not be likely to occur. To determine the likelihood of these outcomes requires that we know something about the shape of the distribution of our bottom-line performance measure. A histogram of the simulation data for cell G23 also appears in Figure 12.15. This graph provides a visual summary of the approximate shape of the probability distribution associated with the output cell tracked by Crystal Ball during the simulation.

As shown in Figure 12.15, the shape of the distribution associated with the total cost variable is fairly bell-shaped, with a maximum value around $44 million and a minimum value around $29 million. Thus, we now have a clear idea of the shape of the distribution associated with our bottom-line performance measure—one of the goals in simulation.

If we tracked more than one output cell during the simulation, we could display histograms of the values occurring in these other cells by clicking Analyze, Forecast Charts.

12.9.3 VIEWING THE CUMULATIVE DISTRIBUTION OF THE OUTPUT CELLS

At times, we might want to view a graph of the cumulative probability distribution associated with one of the output cells tracked during a simulation. For example, suppose that the chief financial officer (CFO) for Hungry Dawg would prefer to accrue an excess amount of money to pay health claims rather than not accrue enough money. The CFO might want to know what amount the company should accrue so that there is only a 10% chance of coming up short of funds at the end of the year. So, how much money would you recommend be accrued?

Figure 12.16 shows a graph of the cumulative probability distribution of the values that occurred in cell G23 during the simulation. This graph could help us answer the preceding question. To change the graph shown in Figure 12.15 to the graph and statistics shown in Figure 12.16:

1. Click View.
2. De-select Frequency.
3. Select Cumulative Frequency.
4. De-select Statistics.
5. Select Percentiles.
6. Click and drag the right-hand arrowhead on the X-axis until the certainty level is 90%.

FIGURE 12.16

Cumulative frequency distribution and percentiles of possible total costs

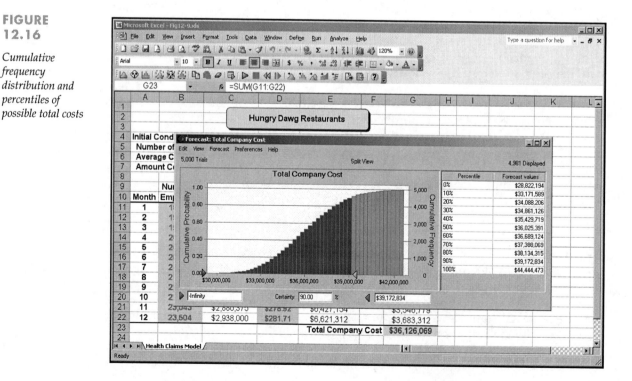

This graph displays the probability of the selected output cell taking on a value smaller than each value on the X-axis. For example, this graph indicates that approximately a 25% chance exists of the output cell (Total Company Cost) assuming a value smaller than approximately $34.5 million. Similarly, this graph indicates that roughly a 75% chance exists of total costs being less than approximately $38 million (or a 25% chance of total costs exceeding approximately $38 million). Thus, from this graph, we would estimate that roughly a 10% chance exists of the company's costs exceeding approximately $39.2 million.

12.9.4 OBTAINING OTHER CUMULATIVE PROBABILITIES

We also can answer the CFO's question from information in the Percentiles window shown in Figure 12.16. This window reveals several percentile values for the output cell G23. For example, the 10th percentile of the values generated for the output cell is approximately $33.2 million—or 10% of the 5000 values generated for cell G23 are less than or equal to this value. Similarly, the 90th percentile of the distribution of values is approximately $39.2 million. Thus, based on these results, if the company accrues $39.2 million, we would expect that only a 10% chance exists of the actual company costs exceeding this amount.

The ability to perform this type of analysis demonstrates the power and value of simulation and Crystal Ball. For example, how could we have answered the CFO's question about how much money to accrue using best-case/worst-case analysis or what-if analysis? The fact is, we could not have answered the question with any degree of accuracy without using simulation.

12.10 Incorporating Graphs and Statistics into a Spreadsheet

At times, you will want to save some of the graphs or statistics created by Crystal Ball. You can do so by selecting the Create Report option found on the Analyze menu. This option displays the dialog box shown in Figure 12.17. This dialog box provides options for saving different results to Excel. Crystal Ball automatically saves all the selected graphs and statistics in a worksheet in a new workbook.

Similarly, you might want to save the individual trial or replication data generated during the simulation to a separate file for further analysis. You can do so by selecting the Extract Data option from the Run menu. This option displays the dialog box shown in Figure 12.18. Here again, Crystal Ball automatically saves all the selected data items in a worksheet in a new workbook.

12.11 The Uncertainty of Sampling

To this point, we have used simulation to generate 5000 observations on our bottom-line performance measure and then calculated various statistics to describe the characteristics and behavior of the performance measure. For example, Figure 12.15 indicates that the mean company cost value in our sample is $36,139,595, and Figure 12.16 shows that a 90% chance exists of this performance measure assuming a value less than $39,172,834. But what if we repeat this process and generate another 5000 observations? Would the

FIGURE 12.17

Saving charts and statistics from the simulation

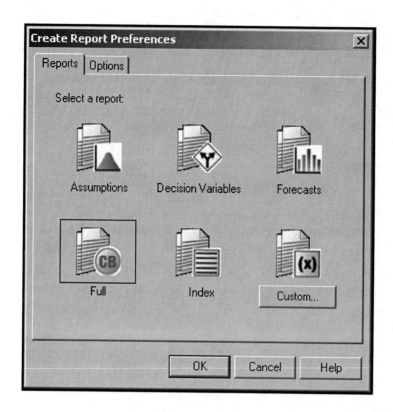

FIGURE 12.18

Saving data from the simulation

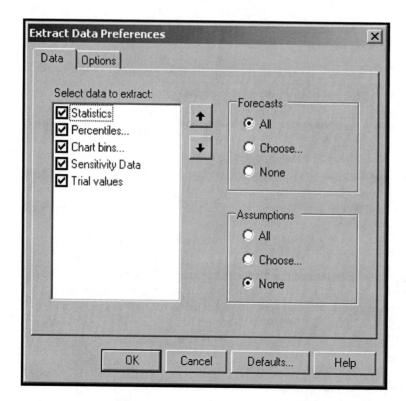

sample mean for the new 5000 observations also be exactly \$36,139,595? Or would exactly 90% of the observations in the new sample be less than \$39,172,834?

The answer to both these questions is "probably not." The sample of 5000 observations used in our analysis was taken from a population of values that theoretically is infinite in size. That is, if we had enough time and our computer had enough memory, we could generate an infinite number of values for our bottom-line performance measure. Theoretically, we then could analyze this infinite population of values to determine its true mean value, its true standard deviation, and the true probability of the performance measure being less than \$39,172,834. Unfortunately, we do not have the time or computer resources to determine these true characteristics (or parameters) of the population. The best we can do is take a sample from this population and, based on our sample, make estimates about the true characteristics of the underlying population. Our estimates will differ depending on the sample we choose and the size of the sample.

So, the mean of the sample we take probably is not equal to the true mean we would observe if we could analyze the entire population of values for our performance measure. The sample mean we calculate is just an estimate of the true population mean. In our example problem, we estimated that a 90% chance exists for our output variable to assume a value less than \$39,172,834. However, this most likely is not equal to the true probability we would calculate if we could analyze the entire population. Thus, there is some element of uncertainty surrounding the statistical estimates resulting from simulation because we are using a sample to make inferences about the population. Fortunately, there are ways of measuring and describing the amount of uncertainty present in some of the estimates we make about the population under study. Typically this is done by constructing confidence intervals for the population parameters being estimated.

12.11.1 CONSTRUCTING A CONFIDENCE INTERVAL FOR THE TRUE POPULATION MEAN

Constructing a confidence interval for the true population mean is a simple process. If $\bar{y}$ and s represent, respectively, the mean and standard deviation of a sample of size n from any population, then assuming n is sufficiently large ($n \geq 30$), the Central Limit Theorem tells us that the lower and upper limits of a 95% confidence interval for the true mean of the population are represented by:

$$95\% \text{ Lower Confidence Limit} = \bar{y} - 1.96 \times \frac{s}{\sqrt{n}}$$

$$95\% \text{ Upper Confidence Limit} = \bar{y} + 1.96 \times \frac{s}{\sqrt{n}}$$

Although we can be fairly certain that the sample mean we calculate from our sample data is not equal to the true population mean, we can be 95% confident that the true mean of the population falls somewhere between the lower and upper limits given previously. If we want a 90% or 99% confidence interval, we must change the value 1.96 in the previous equation to 1.645 or 2.575, respectively. The values 1.645, 1.96, and 2.575 represent the 95, 97.5, and 99.5 percentiles of the standard normal distribution. Any percentile of the standard normal distribution can be obtained easily using Excel's NORMSINV( ) function.

For our example, the lower and upper limits of a 95% confidence interval for the true mean of the population of total company cost values can be calculated easily, as shown

FIGURE 12.19

Confidence intervals for the population mean and population proportion

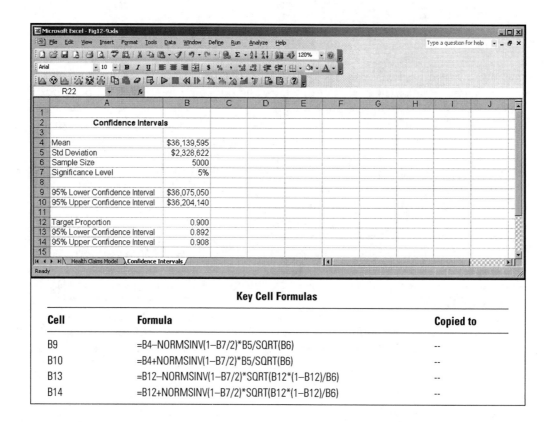

	Cell	Formula	Copied to
Key Cell Formulas			
	B9	=B4−NORMSINV(1−B7/2)*B5/SQRT(B6)	--
	B10	=B4+NORMSINV(1−B7/2)*B5/SQRT(B6)	--
	B13	=B12−NORMSINV(1−B7/2)*SQRT(B12*(1−B12)/B6)	--
	B14	=B12+NORMSINV(1−B7/2)*SQRT(B12*(1−B12)/B6)	--

in cells B9 and B10 in Figure 12.19. (The sample mean and standard deviation shown in Figure 12.19 were obtained from Figure 12.15.) The formulas for these cells are:

Formula for cell B9: $=$B4$-$NORMSINV$(1-$B7$/2)*$B5$/$SQRT(B6)

Formula for cell B10: $=$B4$+$NORMSINV$(1-$B7$/2)*$B5$/$SQRT(B6)

Thus, we can be 95% confident that the true mean of the population of total company cost values falls somewhere in the interval from \$36,075,050 to \$36,204,140.

12.11.2 CONSTRUCTING A CONFIDENCE INTERVAL FOR A POPULATION PROPORTION

In our example, we estimated that 90% of the population of total company cost values fall below \$39,172,834 based on our sample of 5000 observations. However, if we could evaluate the entire population of total cost values, we might find that only 80% of these values fall below \$39,172,834. Or, we might find that 99% of the entire population falls below this mark. It would be helpful to determine how accurate the 90% value is. So, at times, we might want to construct a confidence interval for the true proportion of a population that falls below (or above) some value, for example Y_p.

To see how this is done, let $\bar{p}$ denote the proportion of observations in a sample of size n that falls below some value Y_p. Assuming that n is sufficiently large ($n \geq 30$), the Central Limit Theorem tells us that the lower and upper limits of a 95% confidence interval for the true proportion of the population falling below Y_p are represented by:

$$95\% \text{ Lower Confidence Limit} = \bar{p} - 1.96 \times \sqrt{\frac{\bar{p}(1-\bar{p})}{n}}$$

$$95\% \text{ Upper Confidence Limit} = \bar{p} + 1.96 \times \sqrt{\frac{\bar{p}(1-\bar{p})}{n}}$$

Although we can be fairly certain that the proportion of observations falling below Y_p in our sample is not equal to the true proportion of the population falling below Y_p, we can be 95% confident that the true proportion of the population falling below Y_p is contained within the lower and upper limits given previously. Again, if we want a 90% or 99% confidence interval, we must change the value 1.96 in the previous equations to 1.645 or 2.575, respectively.

Using these formulas, we can calculate the lower and upper limits of a 95% confidence interval for the true proportion of the population falling below $39,172,834. From our simulation results, we know that 90% of the observations in our sample are less than $39,172,834. Thus, our estimated value of $\bar{p}$ is 0.90. This value was entered into cell B12 in Figure 12.19. The upper and lower limits of a 95% confidence interval for the true proportion of the population falling below $39,172,834 are calculated in cells B13 and B14 of Figure 12.19 using the following formulas:

Formula for cell B13:   =B12−NORMSINV(1−B7/2)*SQRT(B12*(1−B12)/B6)

Formula for cell B14:   =B12+NORMSINV(1−B7/2)*SQRT(B12*(1−B12)/B6)

We can be 95% confident that the true proportion of the population of total cost values falling below $39,172,834 is between 0.892 and 0.908. Because this interval is fairly tight around the value 0.90, we can be reasonably certain that the $39.2 million figure quoted to the CFO has approximately a 10% chance of being exceeded.

12.11.3 SAMPLE SIZES AND CONFIDENCE INTERVAL WIDTHS

The formulas for the confidence intervals in the previous section depend directly on the number of replications (n) in the simulation. As the number of replications (n) increases, the width of the confidence interval decreases (or becomes more precise). Thus, for a given level of confidence (for example, 95%), the only way to make the upper and lower limits of the interval closer together (or tighter) is to make n larger—that is, use a larger sample size. A larger sample should provide more information about the population and, therefore, allow us to be more accurate in estimating the true parameters of the population.

12.12 The Benefits of Simulation

What have we accomplished through simulation? Are we really better off than if we had just used the results of the original model proposed in Figure 12.2? The estimated value for the expected total cost to the company in Figure 12.2 is comparable to that obtained through simulation (although this might not always be the case). But remember that the goal of modeling is to give us greater insight into a problem to help us make more informed decisions.

The results of our simulation analysis do give us greater insight into the example problem. In particular, we now have some idea of the best- and worst-case total cost outcomes for the company. We have a better idea of the distribution and variability of the possible outcomes, and a more precise idea about where the mean of the distribution is located. We also now have a way of determining how likely it is for the actual outcome to fall above or below some value. Thus, in addition to our greater insight and understanding of the problem, we also have solid empirical evidence (the facts and figures) to support our recommendations.

Applying Simulation in Personal Financial Planning

A recent article in the *Wall Street Journal* highlighted the importance of simulation in evaluating the risk in personal financial investments. "Many people are taking a lot more risk than they realize. They are walking around with a false sense of security," said Christopher Cordaro, an investment adviser at Bugen Stuart Korn & Cordaro of Chatham, N.J. Using one online retirement calculator, after entering information about your finances and assumptions about investment gains, the screen shows a green or red light indicating whether you have saved enough to retire. What is doesn't tell you is whether there is a 95% chance or just a 60% chance that your plan will succeed. "How certain are you about the green light—is it just about to turn yellow and you're just sneaking by?" Mr. Cordaro asked.

Although any planning is better than nothing, traditional planning models spit out answers that create "the illusion that the number is a certainty, when it isn't," said Ross Levin, a Minneapolis investment adviser who uses simulation. Mutual-fund firm T. Rowe Price applied simulation to its recently launched Retirement Income Manager, a personalized consultation service that helps retirees understand how much income they can afford without outliving their assets or depleting funds they want to leave to heirs. A number of independent financial planning companies are now also using simulation software (see the Advisor Tools section of http://www.financeware.com).

In the face of widely divergent possibilities, the number crunching involved in simulation can bring some peace of mind. Steven Haas of Randolph, N.J., was not sure whether he had saved enough to accept an early retirement package from AT&T at age 53. After his financial advisor used simulation to determine he had a 95% probability that his money would last until he reached age 110, Mr. Haas took the package and retired. Mr. Haas reported that by using simulation, "I found that even under significantly negative scenarios we could live comfortably. It relieved a lot of anxiety."

Adapted from "Monte Carlo Financial Simulator May Be A Good Bet For Planning," *Wall Street Journal*, Section C1, April 27, 2000 by Karen Hube.

12.13 Additional Uses of Simulation

Earlier, we indicated that simulation is a technique that *describes* the behavior or characteristics of a bottom-line performance measure. The next several examples show how describing the behavior of a performance measure gives a manager a useful tool in determining the optimal value for one or more controllable parameters in a decision problem. These examples reinforce the mechanics of using simulation, and also demonstrate some additional capabilities of Crystal Ball.

12.14 A Reservation Management Example

Businesses that allow customers to make reservations for services (such as airlines, hotels, and car rental companies) know that some percentage of the reservations made will not be used for one reason or another, leaving these companies with a difficult decision problem. If they accept reservations for only the number of customers that actually can be served, then a portion of the company's assets will be underutilized when some customers with reservations fail to arrive. On the other hand, if they over-book (or accept more reservations than can be handled), then at times, more customers will arrive than can be served. This typically results in additional financial costs to the company and often generates ill-will among those customers who cannot be served. The following example illustrates how simulation might be used to help a company deter-mine the optimal number of reservations to accept.

> Marty Ford is an operations analyst for Piedmont Commuter Airlines (PCA). Re-cently, Marty was asked to make a recommendation on how many reservations PCA should book on Flight 343—a flight from a small regional airport in New England to a major hub at Boston's Logan airport. The plane used on Flight 343 is a small twin-engine turbo-prop with 19 passenger seats available. PCA sells nonrefundable tick-ets for Flight 343 for $150 per seat.
>
> Industry statistics show that for every ticket sold for a commuter flight, a 0.10 probability exists that the ticket holder will not be on the flight. Thus, if PCA sells 19 tickets for this flight, there is a fairly good chance that one or more seats on the plane will be empty. Of course, empty seats represent lost potential revenue to the company. On the other hand, if PCA overbooks this flight and more than 19 passen-gers show up, some of them will have to be bumped to a later flight.
>
> To compensate for the inconvenience of being bumped, PCA gives these pas-sengers vouchers for a free meal, a free flight at a later date, and sometimes also pays for them to stay overnight in a hotel near the airport. PCA pays an average of $325 (including the cost of lost goodwill) for each passenger that gets bumped. Marty wants to determine if PCA can increase profits by overbooking this flight and, if so, how many reservations should be accepted to produce the maximum average profit. To assist in the analysis, Marty analyzed market research data for this flight that reveals the following probability distribution of demand for this flight:

Seats Demanded	14	15	16	17	18	19	20	21	22	23	24	25
Probability	0.03	0.05	0.07	0.09	0.11	0.15	0.18	0.14	0.08	0.05	0.03	0.02

12.14.1 IMPLEMENTING THE MODEL

A spreadsheet model for this problem is shown in Figure 12.20 (and in the file Fig12-20.xls on your data disk). The spreadsheet begins by listing the relevant data from the problem, including the number of seats available on the plane, the price PCA charges for each seat, the probability of a no-show (a ticketed passenger not arriving in time for the flight), the cost of bumping passengers, and the number of reservations that will be accepted.

The distribution of demand for seats on the flight is summarized in columns E and F. With this data, cell C10 is defined as an assumption cell representing the random num-ber of seats demanded for a particular flight using Crystal Ball's Custom distribution with the settings shown in Figure 21.21.

**FIGURE
12.20**

*Spreadsheet model
for the overbooking
problem*

Decision Cell

Assumption Cells

Forecast Cell

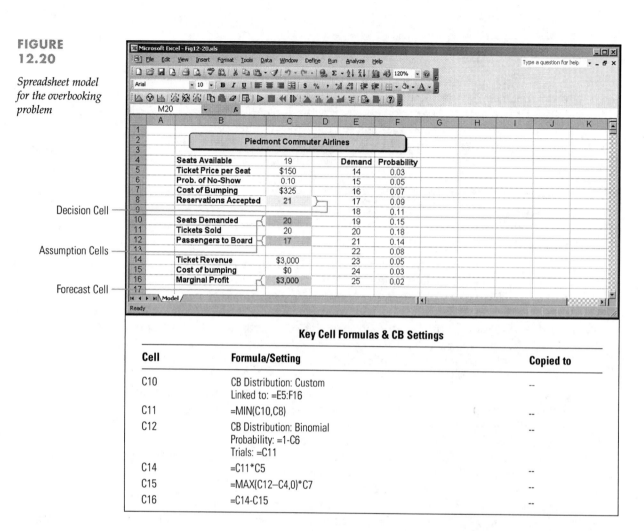

The number of tickets actually sold for a flight cannot exceed the number of reservations the company is willing to accept. Thus, the number of tickets sold is calculated in cell C11 as follows:

Formula for cell C11:   =MIN(C10,C8)

Because each ticketed passenger has a 0.10 probability of being a no-show, a 0.9 probability exists that each ticketed passenger will arrive in time to board the flight. So the number of passengers present to board the flight can be modeled as a Binomial random variable. The Binomial RNG returns the number of "successes" in a sample of size n where each trial has a probability p of "success." In this case, the sample size is the number of tickets sold (cell C11) and the probability of "success" is 0.9 – the probability that each ticketed passenger will arrive in time to board the flight (or 1-C6). Thus, Crystal Ball's Binomial distribution is used to define cell C12 as an assumption cell that models the number of ticketed passengers that actually arrive for a flight as shown in Figure 12.22.

Cell C14 represents the ticket revenue that PCA earns based on the number of tickets it sells for each flight. The formula for this cell is:

Formula for cell C14:   =C11*C5

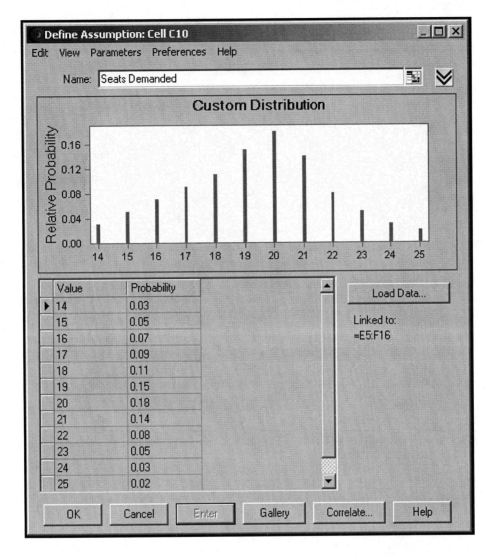

FIGURE 12.21

Defining the assumptions for cell C10

Cell C15 computes the costs PCA incurs when passengers must be bumped (i.e., when the number of passengers wanting to board exceeds the number of available seats).

Formula for cell C15:   =MAX(C12−C4,0)*C7

Finally, cell C16 computes the marginal profit PCA earns on each flight.

Formula for cell C16:   =C14−C15

12.14.2 USING THE DECISION TABLE TOOL

Marty wants to determine the number of reservations to accept that, on average, will result in the highest marginal profit. To do so, he needs to simulate what would happen to the marginal profit cell (C16) if 19, 20, 21, . . . , 25 reservations were accepted. Fortunately, Crystal Ball includes a tool called Decision Table that simplifies this type of

**FIGURE
12.22**

*Defining the
assumptions for
cell C12*

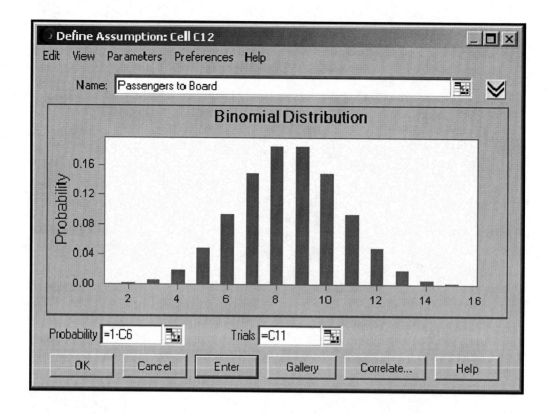

analysis. To use Decision Table, first indicate the marginal profit cell (C16) to be a forecast cell in the usual way:

1. Select C16.
2. Click the Define Forecast button on the Crystal Ball toolbar (or click Define, Define Forecast on the main menu).

Next, define cell C8 (number of reservations accepted) to be a decision variable that may assume integer values from 19 to 25. To do this:

1. Select cell C8.
2. Click Define, Define Decision.
3. Fill in the values shown in Figure 12.23.
4. Click OK.

When comparing different values for one or more decision variables (*i.e.*, different solutions), it is best if each possible solution is evaluated using exactly the same series of random numbers. In this way, any difference in the performance of two possible solutions can be attributed to the decision variables' values and not the result of a more favorable set of random numbers for one of the solutions. You can ensure that Crystal Ball uses the same set of random numbers for each simulation by selecting the "Use Same Sequence of Random Numbers" option and supplying an "Initial Seed Value" under the Sampling option on Crystal Ball's Run Preferences dialog box shown in Figure 12.24.

The Sampling Method options shown in Figure 12.21 also affect the accuracy of the results of a simulation run. Using the Monte Carlo option, Crystal Ball is free to select any value for a particular RNG during each replication of the model. For example,

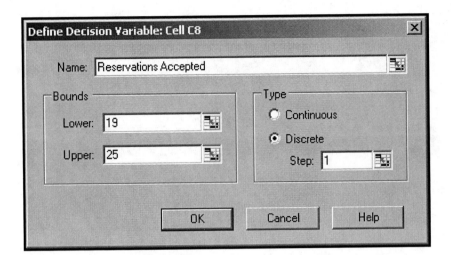

FIGURE
12.23

Defining reservations accepted as a decision variable

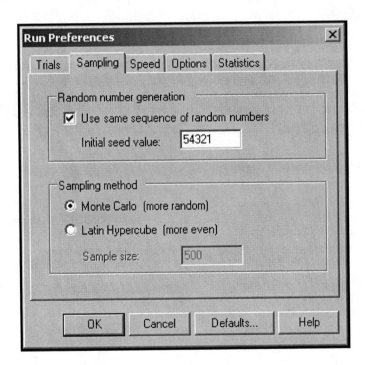

FIGURE
12.24

Crystal Ball's Run Preferences dialog

Crystal Ball might repeatedly generate several very extreme (and rare!) values from the upper tail of a normal distribution. The Latin Hypercube option guards against this by ensuring that a fair representation of values is generated from the entire distribution for each RNG. As you might imagine, the Latin Hypercube sampling option requires a bit more work during each replication of the model, but it tends to generate more accurate simulation results in a fewer number of trials.

After setting a random number seed as shown in Figure 12.24, we are ready to use the Decision Table tool. To invoke the Decision Table tool:

1. Click Run, Tools, Decision Table.
2. Click Decision Table.

FIGURE
12.25

*Specifying the
target cell for the
Decision Table tool*

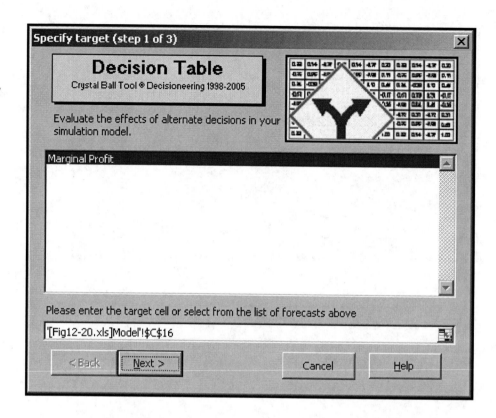

The dialog box shown in Figure 12.25 appears prompting us to select the forecast (or target) cell we want to track. Here, we select the "Marginal Profit" option and click the Next button.

In the next dialog box, shown in Figure 12.26, we select the decision variable we want to evaluate. In this case there is only one variable (Reservations Accepted). However, the Decision Table tool allows you to select up to two decision variables to analyze simultaneously.

The next dialog box, shown in Figure 12.27, allows us to specify the number of values to test for each decision variable and the number of iterations (trials) to use for each resulting simulation run. In our case, there are seven possible discrete values for Reservations Accepted (i.e., 19, 20, 21, . . . , 25) and we want to test them all. However, for continuous decision variables that can assume any value within some interval, it is impossible to test all the possible values, and we must tell the Decision Table tool the number of possible values to try.

When you click the Start button in Figure 12.27, the Decision Table tool runs a separate simulation for each of the seven possible values we indicated for the decision variable. When it is finished, the Decision Table tool creates a new workbook like the one shown in Figure 12.28 summarizing the average value of the forecast cell (Marginal Profit) for each of the seven simulations. These values indicate that the average marginal profit reaches a maximum value of $2,782 when PCA accepts 21 reservations. We can easily create a bar chart from this data to graphically represent the differences in the average profits under each scenario.

You can also select one or more of the average profit values on row 2 in Figure 12.28 and display a Trend Chart, Overlay Chart, or Forecast Chart for the selected values.

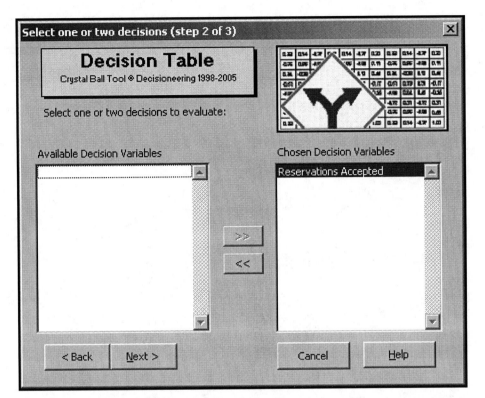

FIGURE 12.26

Choosing the decision variable with the Decision Table tool

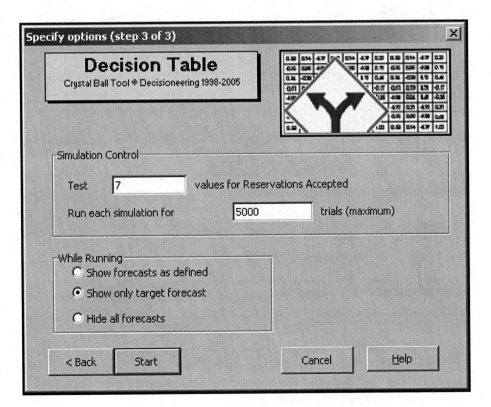

FIGURE 12.27

Setting options with the Decision Table tool

**FIGURE
12.28**

*Results of the
Decision Table tool*

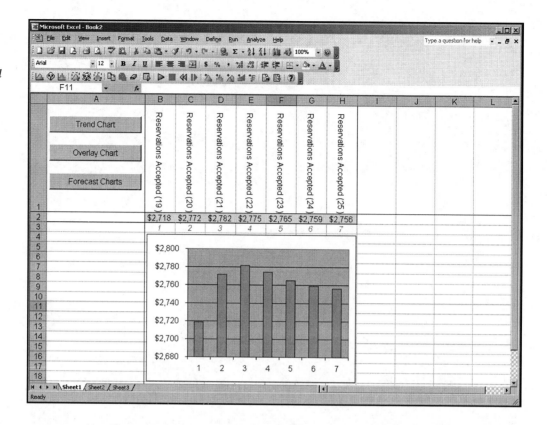

**FIGURE
12.29**

*Overlay chart
comparing
outcome
distributions
for 21 and 25
reservations
accepted*

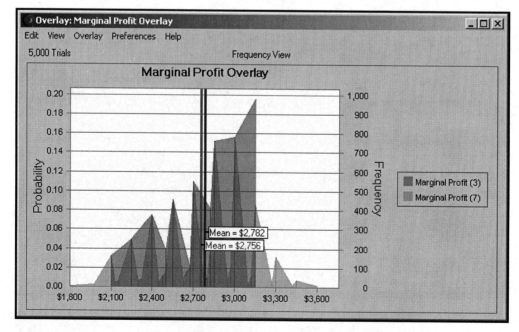

Figure 12.29 shows an Overlay Chart comparing the distributions of values generated in simulation 3 (where up to 21 reservations were accepted) and simulation 7 (where up to 25 reservations were accepted). This type of chart is often helpful in comparing the riskiness of different decision alternatives.

12.15 An Inventory Control Example

According to the *Wall Street Journal*, U.S. businesses recently had a combined inventory worth $884.77 billion. Because so much money is tied up in inventories, businesses face many important decisions regarding the management of these assets. Frequently asked questions regarding inventory include:

- What's the best level of inventory for a business to maintain?
- When should goods be reordered (or manufactured)?
- How much safety stock should be held in inventory?

The study of inventory control principles is split into two distinct areas—one assumes that demand is known (or deterministic), and the other assumes that demand is random (or stochastic). If demand is known, various formulas can be derived that provide answers to the previous questions (an example of one such formula is given in the discussion of the EOQ model in Chapter 8.) However, when demand for a product is uncertain or random, answers to the previous questions cannot be expressed in terms of a simple formula. In these situations, the technique of simulation proves to be a useful tool, as illustrated in the following example.

Laura Tanner is the owner of Millennium Computer Corporation (MCC), a retail computer store in Austin, Texas. Competition in retail computer sales is fierce—both in terms of price and service. Laura is concerned about the number of stockouts occurring on a popular type of computer monitor. Stockouts are very costly to the business because when customers cannot buy this item at MCC, they simply buy it from a competing store and MCC loses the sale (there are no back orders). Laura measures the effects of stockouts on her business in terms of service level, or the percentage of total demand that can be satisfied from inventory.

Laura has been following the policy of ordering 50 monitors whenever her daily ending inventory position (defined as ending inventory on hand plus outstanding orders) falls below her reorder point of 28 units. Laura places the order at the beginning of the next day. Orders are delivered at the beginning of the day and, therefore, can be used to satisfy demand on that day. For example, if the ending inventory position on day 2 is less than 28, Laura places the order at the beginning of day 3. If the actual time between order and delivery, or lead time, turns out to be four days, then the order arrives at the start of day 7.

The current level of on-hand inventory is 50 units and no orders are pending. MCC sells an average of six monitors per day. However, the actual number sold on any given day can vary. By reviewing her sales records for the past several months, Laura determined that the actual daily demand for this monitor is a random variable that can be described by the following probability distribution:

Units Demanded	0	1	2	3	4	5	6	7	8	9	10
Probability	0.01	0.02	0.04	0.06	0.09	0.14	0.18	0.22	0.16	0.06	0.02

The manufacturer of this computer monitor is located in California. Although it takes an average of four days for MCC to receive an order from this company, Laura has determined that the lead time of a shipment of monitors is also a random variable that can be described by the following probability distribution:

Lead Time (days)	3	4	5
Probability	0.2	0.6	0.2

One way to guard against stockouts and improve the service level is to increase the reorder point for the item so that more inventory is on hand to meet the demand occurring during the lead time. However, there are holding costs associated with keeping more inventory on hand. Laura wants to evaluate her current ordering policy for this item and determine if it might be possible to improve the service level without increasing the average amount of inventory on hand.

12.15.1 IMPLEMENTING THE MODEL

To solve this problem, we need to build a model to represent the inventory of computer monitors during an average month of 30 days. This model must account for the random daily demands that can occur and the random lead times encountered when orders are placed. To facilitate this, we first entered the data for these variables as shown in Figure 12.30 (and in the file Fig12-30.xls on your data disk). We will use this data in conjunction with Crystal Ball's Custom distribution to create assumption cells representing the random order lead times and daily demand values needed for this problem.

Figure 12.31 shows a model representing 30 days of inventory activity. Notice that cells M5 and M6 have been reserved to represent, respectively, the reorder point and order quantity for the model.

The inventory on hand at the beginning of each day is calculated in column B in Figure 12.31. The beginning inventory for each day is simply the ending inventory from the previous day. The formulas in column B are:

Formula for cell B6:	=50
Formula for cell B7:	=F6

(Copy to B8 through B35.)

Column C represents the number of units scheduled to be received each day. We will discuss the formulas in column C after we discuss columns H, I, and J, which relate to ordering and order lead times.

FIGURE
12.30

*RNG data for
MCC's inventory
problem*

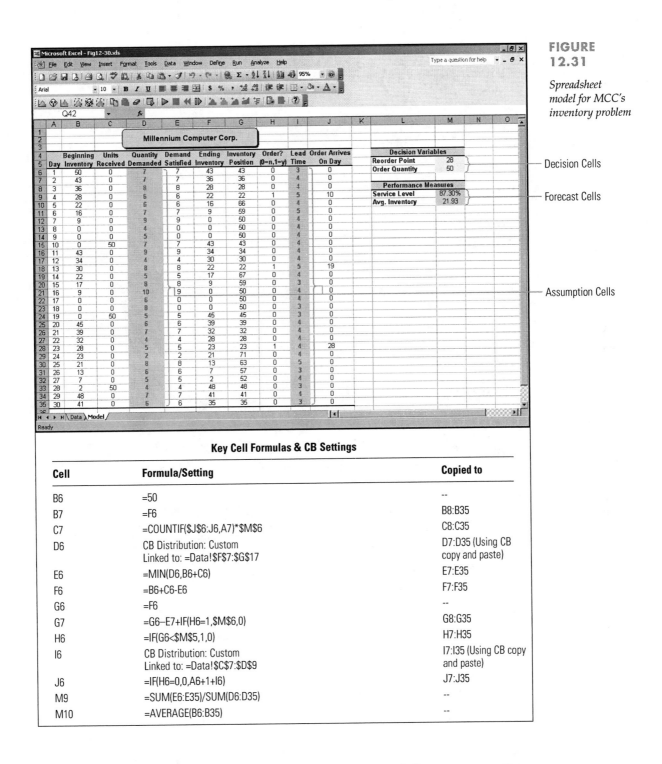

FIGURE 12.31

Spreadsheet model for MCC's inventory problem

— Decision Cells

— Forecast Cells

— Assumption Cells

Key Cell Formulas & CB Settings

Cell	Formula/Setting	Copied to
B6	=50	--
B7	=F6	B8:B35
C7	=COUNTIF($J$6:J6,A7)*$M$6	C8:C35
D6	CB Distribution: Custom Linked to: =Data!$F$7:$G$17	D7:D35 (Using CB copy and paste)
E6	=MIN(D6,B6+C6)	E7:E35
F6	=B6+C6-E6	F7:F35
G6	=F6	--
G7	=G6-E7+IF(H6=1,$M$6,0)	G8:G35
H6	=IF(G6<$M$5,1,0)	H7:H35
I6	CB Distribution: Custom Linked to: =Data!$C$7:$D$9	I7:I35 (Using CB copy and paste)
J6	=IF(H6=0,0,A6+1+I6)	J7:J35
M9	=SUM(E6:E35)/SUM(D6:D35)	--
M10	=AVERAGE(B6:B35)	--

In column D, we use Crystal Ball's Custom distribution to define our assumptions about the random behavior of daily demand for monitors. Figure 12.32 shows the Define Assumption dialog box for cell D6. This definition was also copied to cells D7 through D35 (using Crystal Ball's copy data and paste data commands).

Because it is possible for demand to exceed the available supply, column E indicates how much of the daily demand can be met. If the beginning inventory (in column B)

**FIGURE
12.32**

*Defining the
assumptions for
cell D6*

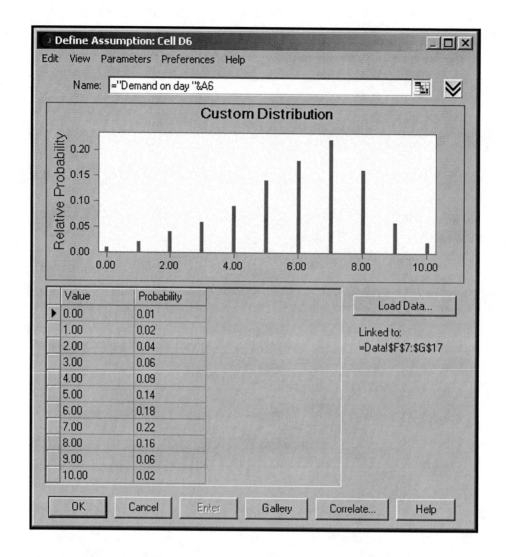

plus the ordered units received (in column C) is greater than or equal to the actual demand, then all the demand can be satisfied; otherwise, MCC can sell only as many units as are available. This condition is modeled as:

Formula for cell E6:   =MIN(D6,B6+C6)
(Copy to E7 through E35.)

The values in column F represent the on-hand inventory at the end of each day, and are calculated as:

Formula for cell F6:   =B6+C6−E6
(Copy to F7 through F35.)

To determine whether to place an order, we first must calculate the inventory position, which was defined earlier as the ending inventory plus any outstanding orders. This is implemented in column G as:

Formula for cell G6:   =F6

Formula for cell G7:   =G6−E7+IF(H6=1,$M$6,0)
(Copy to G8 through G35.)

Column H indicates if an order should be placed based on inventory position and the reorder point, as:

Formula for cell H6:   =IF(G6<$M$5,1,0)

(Copy to H7 through H35.)

In column I, we use Crystal Ball's Custom distribution to define our assumptions about the random behavior of order lead times. Figure 12.33 shows the Define Assumption dialog box for cell I6. This definition was also copied to cells I7 through I35 (using Crystal Ball's copy data and paste data commands). Note that column I generates an order lead time for each day, irrespective of if an order is actually placed on a given day. If no order is placed on a given day, the associated lead time value in Column I is ignored.

If an order is placed (as indicated by column H), column J indicates the day on which the order will be received based on its random lead time in column I. This is done as:

Formula for cell J6:   =IF(H6=0,0,A6+1+I6)

(Copy to J7 through J35.)

The values in column C are coordinated with those in column J. The nonzero values in column J indicate the days on which orders will be received. For example, cell J9 indicates that an order will be received on day 10. The actual receipt of this order is reflected by the value of 50 in cell C15, which represents the receipt of an order at the beginning of day 10. The formula in cell C15 that achieves this is:

Formula for cell C15:   =COUNTIF($J$6:J14,A15)*$M$6

This formula counts how many times the value in cell A15 (representing day 10) appears as a scheduled receipt day between days 1 through 9 in column J. This represents

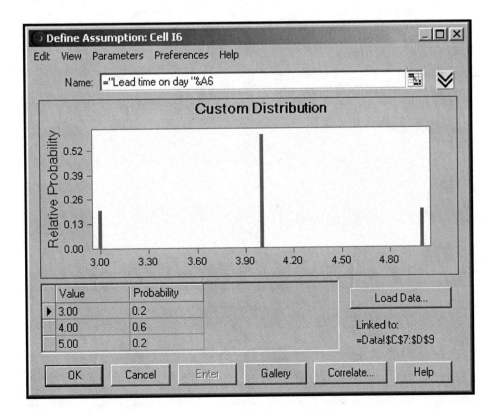

FIGURE
12.33

*Defining the
assumptions
for cell I6*

the number of orders scheduled to be received on day 10. We then multiply this by the order quantity (50), given in cell M6 to determine the total units to be received on day 10. Thus, the values in column C are generated as:

Formula for cell C6:   =0

Formula for cell C7:   =COUNTIF($J$6:J6,A7)*$M$6
(Copy to C8 through C35.)

The service level for the model is calculated in cell M9 using the values in columns D and E as:

Formula for cell M9:   =SUM(E6:E35)/SUM(D6:D35)

Again, the service level represents the proportion of total demand that can be satisfied from inventory. The value in cell M9 indicates that in the scenario shown, 87.30% of the total demand is satisfied.

The average inventory level is calculated in cell M10 by averaging the values in column B. This is accomplished as follows:

Formula for cell M10:   =AVERAGE(B6:B35)

12.15.2 REPLICATING THE MODEL

The model in Figure 12.31 indicates one possible scenario that could occur if Laura uses a reorder point of 28 units for the computer monitor. Figure 12.34 shows the results of using Crystal Ball to replicate this model 5000 times, tracking the values in cells M9 (service level) and M10 (average inventory) as forecast cells.

Figure 12.34 indicates that MCC's current reorder point (28 units) and order quantity (50 units) results in an average service level of approximately 96.2% (with a minimum

FIGURE 12.34

Results of 5000 replications of the MCC model

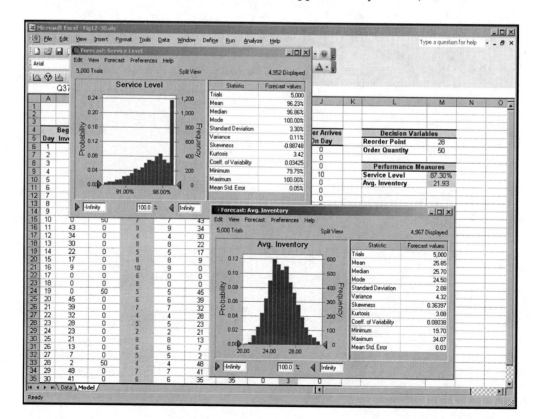

value of 79.8% and a maximum value of 100%) and an average inventory level of almost 26 monitors (with a minimum value of 19.7 and a maximum value of 34.07).

12.15.3 OPTIMIZING THE MODEL

Suppose Laura wants to determine a reorder point and order quantity that provides an average service level of 98% while keeping the average inventory level as low as possible. One way to do this is to run additional simulations at various reorder point and inventory level combinations trying to find the combination of settings that produce the desired behavior. However, as you might imagine, this could be very time-consuming.

Fortunately, Crystal Ball Professional includes a product called OptQuest that is designed to solve this type of problem. To use OptQuest, first we must use Crystal Ball to define cells M5 (reorder point) and M6 (order quantity) to be decision variable cells. We will assume that Laura wants to consider discrete reorder points in the range from 20 and 50 and discrete order quantity values in the range from 20 to 70. To do this:

1. Select cells M5 and M6.
2. Click the Define Decision button on the Crystal Ball toolbar (or click Define, Define Decision).
3. Enter lower and upper bounds for each cell and a discrete step size of 1.
4. Click OK.

Note that cells M9 (service level) and M10 (average inventory level) should already be selected as forecast cells from our earlier simulation run.

Again, when comparing different values for one or more decision variables, it is best if each possible solution is evaluated using exactly the same series of random numbers. We can ensure that Crystal Ball uses the same set of random numbers for each simulation by selecting the "Use same sequence of random numbers" option and supplying an "Initial seed value" under the Sampling option on Crystal Ball's Run Preferences dialog box (shown earlier in Figure 12.24).

After the decision variable cells, forecast cells, random number seed, and an Assumption cell are specified using Crystal Ball, you may start an OptQuest session for the model as follows:

1. Click Run, OptQuest.
2. In OptQuest, click File, New.

The resulting OptQuest screen is shown in Figure 12.35. This screen shows the decision variables for the current problem along with the bounds and restrictions we have placed on these variables. Click the OK button on this screen to accept these selections.

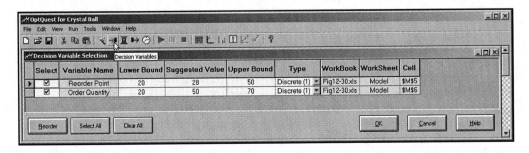

FIGURE 12.35

OptQuest's Decision Variable Selection screen

FIGURE 12.36

OptQuest's Forecast Selection screen

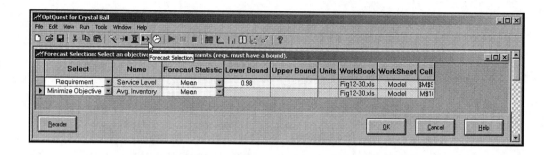

FIGURE 12.37

OptQuest's Options screen

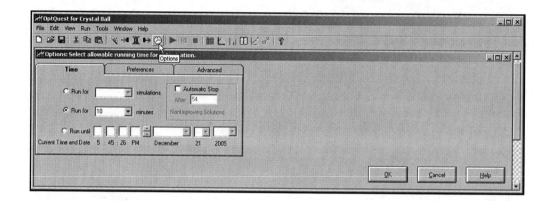

The next step is to tell OptQuest about the objectives we want it to pursue. This is done using the Forecast Selection window shown in Figure 12.36.

In the window shown in Figure 12.36, we indicated that we want OptQuest to minimize the value of the "Avg. Inventory" cell. We also placed a lower bound of 0.98 on the "Service Level" cell and indicated that this is a requirement that must be enforced. (Note that you can make changes to the various cells in the Forecast Selection window by clicking on the appropriate cell.) Click the OK button on this screen to accept these selections.

Next, we use the Options window shown in Figure 12.37 to indicate the amount of time we want OptQuest to search for solutions to the problem. Remember that a separate simulation must be run for each combination of the decision variables that OptQuest chooses. OptQuest uses several heuristics to search intelligently for the best combination of decision variables. However, this is still inherently a very computationally intensive and time-consuming process and complicated models may take hours (or days) of solution time. Note that we are giving OptQuest ten minutes to search for a solution to the MCC problem.

With all the appropriate options set, click the Start button (or click Run, Start). OptQuest then runs multiple simulations using different combinations of values for the decision variables. The Performance Graph and Status and Solutions windows shown in Figure 12.38 provide a summary of OptQuest's efforts on the problem. Ultimately, OptQuest found that a reorder point of 34 and order quantity of 20 resulted in an average service level of 98.4% while requiring an average inventory of approximately 18.3 units per month. Thus, MCC can simultaneously increase its service level and reduce its average inventory level by using the new ordering policy identified by OptQuest.

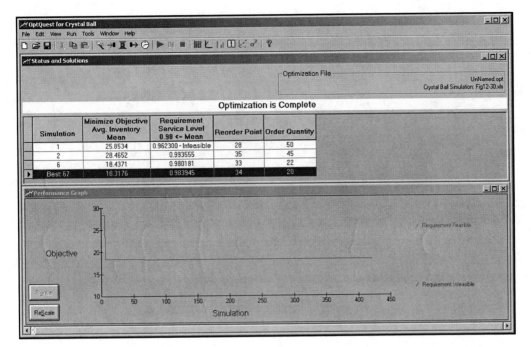

FIGURE 12.38

OptQuest results

A Tip on Using OptQuest...

When using OptQuest to solve a problem, it is often a good idea to reduce the number of trials that Crystal Ball performs during each simulation. This allows OptQuest to explore more possible combinations of decision variable values (solutions) in the allotted amount of time. Then after OptQuest identifies a solution for the problem, you can implement that solution in your model (click Edit, Copy to Excel in OptQuest) and rerun Crystal Ball with a higher number of trials to get a better idea of how well the suggested solution actually performs.

12.15.4 COMPARING THE ORIGINAL AND OPTIMAL ORDERING POLICIES

MCC's manager should be pleased with the new ordering policy OptQuest identified, but she may have other questions about how the reorder point and order quantity will affect the physical storage requirements for this inventory item. Figure 12.39 shows two separate charts illustrating the variability in daily ending inventory under the original and optimal ordering policies. Clearly, in addition to its other benefits, the new ordering policy also requires a more consistent and smaller amount of storage space for this inventory item.

The charts in Figure 12.39 were created using Crystal Ball's Analyze, Trend Charts command. To collect the data for these charts, each of the ending inventory cells shown in column F of Figure 12.31 were defined to be Crystal Ball forecast cells. Two separate simulations then were run: one with the original reorder point and order

FIGURE
12.39

*Comparison
of original and
optimal inventory
policies*

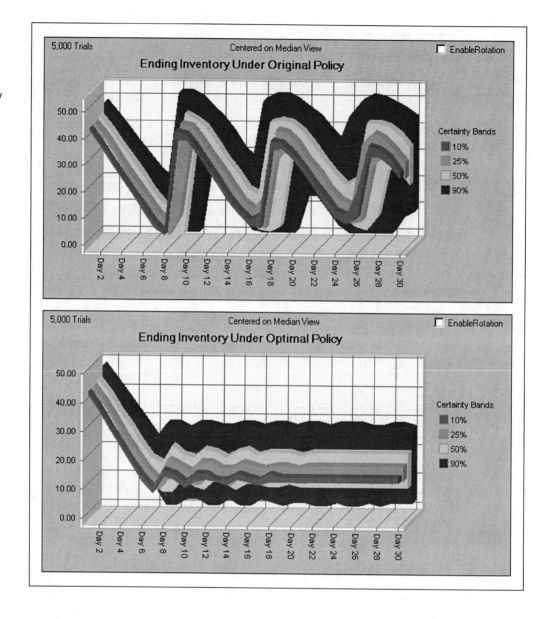

quantity values (in cells M5 and M6, respectively), and the other with the optimal reorder point and order quantity values identified by OptQuest. After each simulation, a trend chart was created from the forecast cells representing the daily ending inventory values.

12.16 A Project Selection Example

In Chapter 6, we saw how Solver can be used in project selection problems in which the payoff for each project is assumed to be known with certainty. In many cases, a great deal of uncertainty exists with respect to the ultimate payoff that will be received if a particular project is undertaken. In these situations, Crystal Ball and OptQuest offer an alternate means for deciding which project(s) to undertake. Consider the following example.

> TRC Technologies has $2 million to invest in new R&D projects. The following table summarizes the initial cost, probability of success, and revenue potential for each of the projects.

Project	Initial Cost ($1000s)	Probability of Success	Revenue Potential ($1000s)		
			Min.	Most Likely	Max.
1	$250.0	90%	$ 600	$ 750	$ 900
2	$650.0	70%	$1,250	$1,500	$1,600
3	$250.0	60%	$ 500	$ 600	$ 750
4	$500.0	40%	$1,600	$1,800	$1,900
5	$700.0	80%	$1,150	$1,200	$1,400
6	$ 30.0	60%	$ 150	$ 180	$ 250
7	$350.0	70%	$ 750	$ 900	$1,000
8	$ 70.0	90%	$ 220	$ 250	$ 320

> TRC's management wants to determine the set of projects that will maximize the firm's expected profit.

12.16.1 A SPREADSHEET MODEL

A spreadsheet model for this problem is shown in Figure 12.40 (and the file Fig12-40.xls on your data disk). Cells C6 through C13 in this spreadsheet indicate which projects will be selected. Using Crystal Ball, we can define these cells to be decision variables that must take on discrete values between zero and one—or operate as binary variables. The values shown in cells C6 though C13 were assigned arbitrarily. We will use OptQuest to determine the optimal values for these variables.

In cell D14, we compute the total initial investment required by the selected projects as follows:

Formula for cell D14:   =SUMPRODUCT(D6:D13,C6:C13)

In cell D16, we calculate the amount of unused or surplus investment funds. Using Crystal Ball, we will define this to be a forecast cell. Using OptQuest, we can place a lower bound requirement of zero on the value of this cell to ensure that the projects selected do not require more than $2 million in initial investment funds.

Formula for cell D16:   =D15−D14

The potential success or failure of each project may be modeled using Crystal Ball's Yes-No distribution. This distribution randomly returns a value of either 1 (representing "Yes" or success) or 0 (representing "No" or failure) according to a specified probability of success. The probability of success for each project is given in column E. Thus, we model the potential success of project 1 in cell F6 using the Crystal Ball Define Assumption settings shown in Figure 12.41. This definition also was copied to cells F7 through F13 (using Crystal Ball's copy data and paste data commands).

There is also uncertainty about the revenue that each project might generate. Because we have estimates of the minimum, most likely, and maximum possible revenue for

**FIGURE
12.40**

*Spreadsheet
model for TRC
Technologies'
project selection
problem*

Decision Cells

Assumption Cells

Forecast Cells

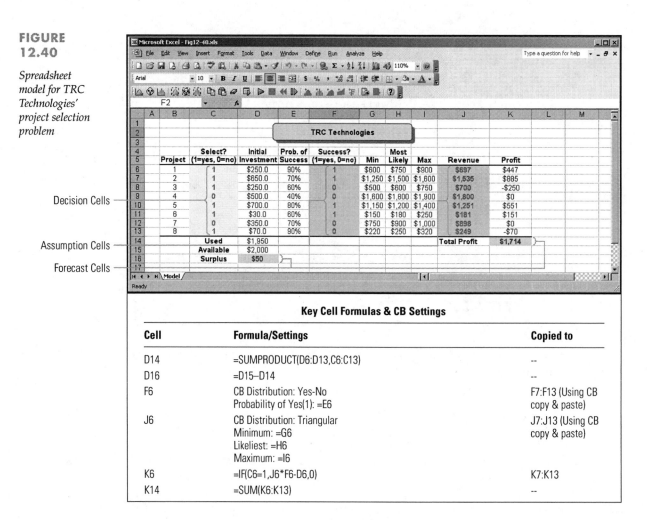

Key Cell Formulas & CB Settings

Cell	Formula/Settings	Copied to
D14	=SUMPRODUCT(D6:D13,C6:C13)	--
D16	=D15–D14	--
F6	CB Distribution: Yes-No Probability of Yes(1): =E6	F7:F13 (Using CB copy & paste)
J6	CB Distribution: Triangular Minimum: =G6 Likeliest: =H6 Maximum: =I6	J7:J13 (Using CB copy & paste)
K6	=IF(C6=1,J6*F6-D6,0)	K7:K13
K14	=SUM(K6:K13)	--

each project, we will model the revenues for selected, successful projects using a triangular distribution. We accomplish this for project 1 in cell J6 as shown in Figure 12.42. This definition also was copied to cells J7 through J13 (using Crystal Ball's copy data and paste data commands).

Note that each project's potential success or failure must be generated independently of whether or not the project is selected (even though only selected projects have the potential to be successful). Similarly, each project's potential revenue must be generated independently of whether or the not the project is successful (even though only successful projects generate revenue). Thus, in column K we must compute the profit for each project carefully based on whether the project is selected and, if selected, whether it is also successful. This is accomplished in column K as follows:

Formula for cell K6:   =IF(C6=1,J6*F6-D6,0)
(Copy to cells K7 through K13.)

Finally, cell K14 computes the total profit for each replication of the model. We will define this as a forecast cell using Crystal Ball and attempt to maximize its value using OptQuest.

Formula for cell K14:   =SUM(K6:K13)

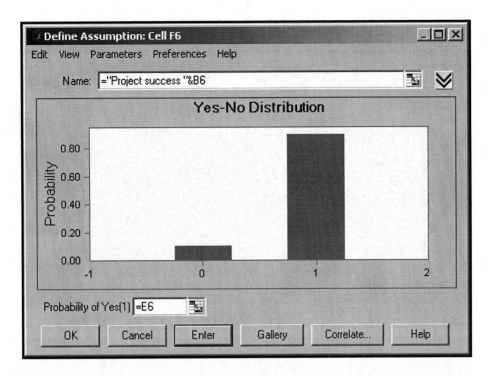

FIGURE
12.41

*Defining the
assumptions for
cell F6*

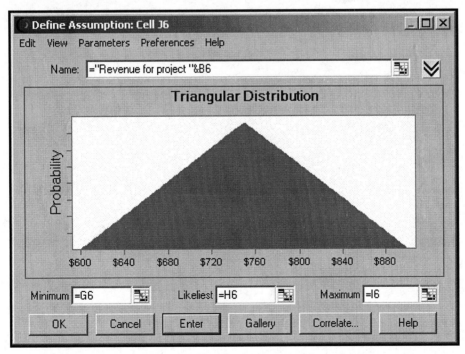

FIGURE
12.42

*Defining the
assumptions for
cell J6*

12.16.2 SOLVING THE PROBLEM WITH OptQUEST

The OptQuest settings used to solve this problem are shown in Figure 12.43 and the optimal solution is shown in Figure 12.44. This solution involves selecting projects 1, 2, 4, 6, 7, and 8, requiring an initial investment of $1.85 million and resulting in an expected profit of approximately $1.5 million.

FIGURE
12.43

*OptQuest settings
for the project
selection problem*

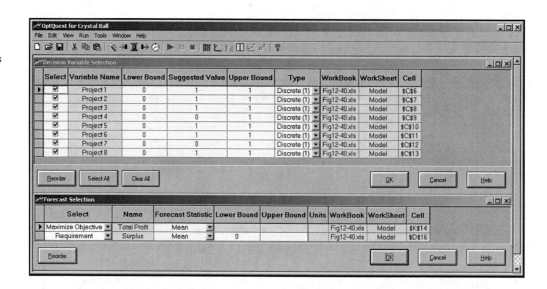

FIGURE
12.44

*Optimal solution
to the project
selection problem*

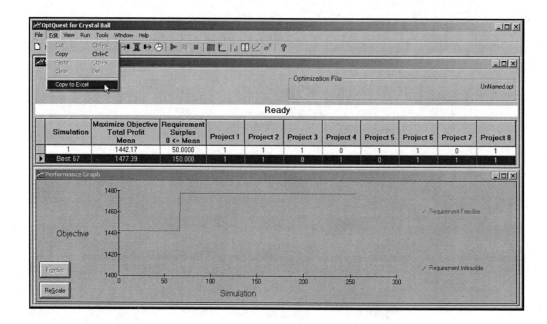

To investigate this solution in a bit more detail, we can copy it back into Crystal Ball (click Edit, Copy to Excel in OptQuest), and view the statistics and frequency distribution associated with the solution. These results are shown in Figures 12.45.

Although the expected (mean) profit associated with this solution is approximately $1.5 million, the range of the possible outcomes is fairly wide (approximately $5.5 million). The worst-case outcome observed with this solution resulted in approximately a $1.6 million loss, whereas the best-case outcome resulted in approximately a $3.86 million profit. Because each of the projects is a one-time occurrence that either can succeed or fail, the decision makers in this problem do not have the luxury of selecting this set of projects over and over and realizing the average profit level of $1.5 million over time. Also, we see that there is about a 10% chance of losing money if this solution

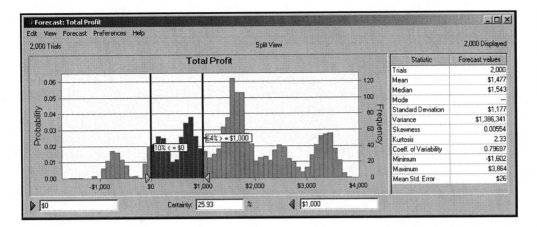

FIGURE 12.45

Results for the project selection problem

is implemented, but about a 64% chance of making at least $1 million. Thus, there is a significant risk associated with this solution that is not apparent if one simply looks at its expected profit level of $1.5 million.

12.16.3 CONSIDERING OTHER SOLUTIONS

The decision makers in this problem might be interested in considering other alternatives. Because each of the projects has the potential to fail and lose money, the only way to completely avoid the possibility of a loss is not to invest in any of the projects. Unfortunately, this also completely avoids the possibility of earning profit! In most situations, greater levels of risk are required to achieve higher levels of return.

After considering the earlier solution and their attitudes toward risk and return, suppose the decision makers at TRC decide that they are comfortable with a 10% chance of losing money. But while assuming this risk, they want to ensure that they maximize the chance of earning a profit of at least $1 million. The OptQuest Forecast Selections settings required to solve this revised problem are shown in Figure 12.46. Notice that now

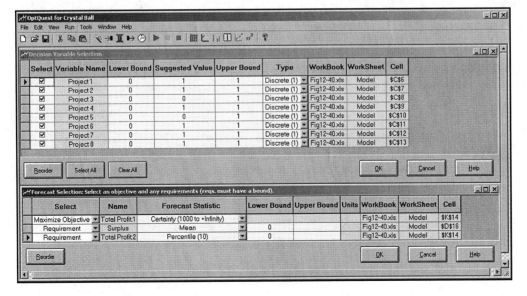

FIGURE 12.46

OptQuest settings for the revised project selection problem

we are attempting to maximize the number of times that the forecasted profit value (in cell K14 in Figure 12.40) falls above $1 million (as opposed to maximizing the average profit value). We have implemented a requirement that the 10th percentile of the distribution of forecasted profit values be greater than zero (or have a lower bound of 0). This should ensure that the resulting solution will have at most a 10% chance of losing money. To place more than one requirement on the same forecast cell (as was done for cell K14 in Figure 12.46), in OptQuest's Forecast Selection window,

1. Click anywhere on the row corresponding to the forecast cell you want to duplicate.
2. Click Edit, Duplicate.

> ## Placing Multiple Requirements on the Same Forecast Cell...
>
> To place more than one requirement on the same forecast cell (as done in Figure 12.46), in OptQuest's Forecast Selection window, click anywhere on the row corresponding to the forecast cell you want to duplicate. Then click Edit, Duplicate.

OptQuest's solution to this problem is shown in Figure 12.47. This solution indicates that TRC should accept projects 1, 2, 3, 5, 6, and 8, consuming $1.95 million in initial capital. To investigate this solution in more detail, we copy this solution back into our spreadsheet (in OptQuest click Edit, Copy to Excel) and generate the solution statistics and frequency distribution shown in Figure 12.48.

In Figure 12.48, notice that the expected (mean) profit for this solution is about $1.44 million, representing a decrease of approximately $35,000 from the earlier solution.

FIGURE 12.47

OptQuest solution for the revised project selection problem

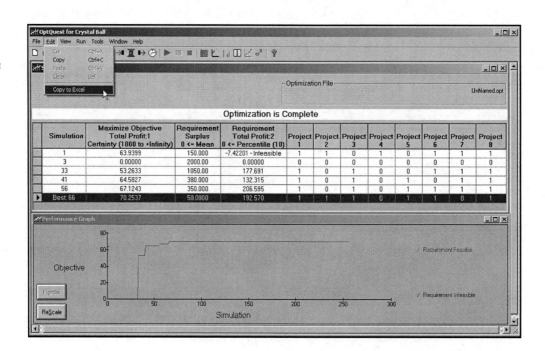

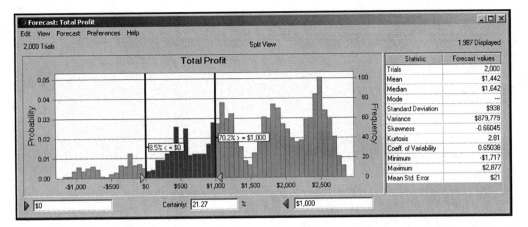

FIGURE 12.48

Statistics for the revised project selection problem

The range of possible outcomes also has decreased to about $4.6 million, with a worst-case outcome of a $1.7 million loss, and a best-case outcome of approximately a $2.9 million profit. This solution *reduces* the chances of realizing a loss to approximately 8.5% and *increases* the chances of making at least $1 million to approximately 70.2%. Thus, although the best possible outcome realized under this solution ($2.9 million) is not as large as that of the earlier solution ($3.86 million), it reduces the downside risk in the problem and makes it more likely for the company to earn at least $1 million—but it also requires a slightly larger initial investment. It is also interesting to note that the probability of *all* the selected projects being successful under this solution is 0.1633 (i.e., 0.1633 = .9 × .7 × .6 × .8 × .6 × .9), whereas the probability of all selected projects being successful under the first solution is only 0.0953 (i.e., 0.0953 = .9 × .7 × .4 × .6 × .7 × .9).

So, what is the best solution to this problem? It depends on the risk attitudes and preferences of the decision makers at TRC. However, the simulation techniques that we have described clearly provide valuable insights into the risks associated with various solutions.

12.17 A Portfolio Optimization Example

In Chapter 8, we saw how Solver can be used to analyze potential tradeoffs between risk and return for a given set of stocks using the idea of an *efficient frontier*. The efficient frontier represents the highest level of return a portfolio can achieve for any given level of risk. Whereas portfolio optimization and efficient frontier analysis is most commonly associated with financial instruments such as stocks and bonds, it also can be applied to physical assets. OptQuest contains an efficient frontier calculation process that makes identifying the efficient frontier a relatively simple process. This will be illustrated using the following example.

In recent years, a fundamental shift occurred in power plant asset ownership. Traditionally, a single regulated utility would own a given power plant. Today, more and more power plants are owned by merchant generators that provide power to a competitive wholesale marketplace. This makes is possible for an investor to buy, for example, 10% of ten different generating assets rather than 100% of a single power plant. As a result, non-traditional power plant owners have emerged in the form of investment groups, private equity funds, and energy hedge funds.

The McDaniel Group is a private investment company in Richmond, VA, that currently has a total of $1 billion that it wants to invest in power generation assets. Five different types of investments are possible: natural gas, oil, coal, nuclear, and wind-powered plants. The following table summarizes the megawatts (MW) of generation capacity that can be purchased per each $1 million investment in the various types of power plants.

	Generation Capacity per Million $ Invested				
Fuel Type	Gas	Coal	Oil	Nuclear	Wind
MWs	2.0	1.2	3.5	1.0	0.5

The return on each type of investment varies randomly and is determined primarily by fluctuations in fuel prices and the spot price (or current market value) of electricity. Assume that the McDaniel Group analyzed historical data to determine that the return per MW produced by each type of plant can be modeled as normally distributed random variables with the following means and standard deviations.

	Normal Distribution Return Parameters by Fuel Type				
	Gas	Coal	Oil	Nuclear	Wind
Mean	16%	12%	10%	9%	8%
Std Dev	12%	6%	4%	3%	1%

Additionally, while analyzing the historical data on operating costs, it was observed that many of the returns are correlated. For example, when the returns from plants fueled by natural gas are high (due to low gas prices), returns from plants fueled by coal and oil tend to be low. So there is a negative correlation between the returns from gas plants and the returns from coal and oil plants. The following table summarizes all the pairwise correlations between the returns from different types of power plants.

	Correlations Between Returns by Fuel Type				
	Gas	Coal	Oil	Nuclear	Wind
Gas	1	−0.49	−0.31	0.16	0.12
Coal		1	−0.41	0.11	0.07
Oil			1	0.13	0.09
Nuclear				1	0.04
Wind					1

The McDaniel Group would like to determine the efficient frontier for its investment options in power generation assets.

12.17.1 A SPREADSHEET MODEL

A spreadsheet model for this problem is shown in Figure 12.49 (and the file Fig12-49.xls on your data disk). Cells D5 through D9 in this spreadsheet indicate how much money (in millions) will be invested in each type of generation asset. Using Crystal Ball, we can define these cells to be decision variables that must take on values between zero and $1,000. The values shown in cells D5 though D19 were assigned arbitrarily. We will use OptQuest to determine the optimal values for these variables. In OptQuest, we also will create a constraint that requires these values to sum to $1,000 (or $1 billion).

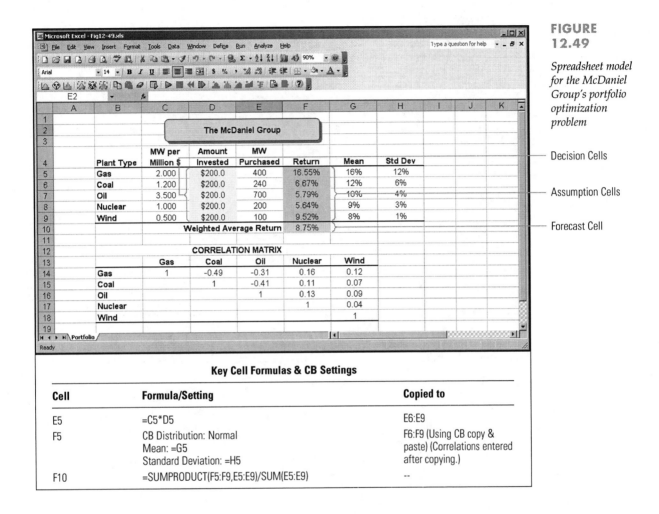

FIGURE 12.49

Spreadsheet model for the McDaniel Group's portfolio optimization problem

— Decision Cells

— Assumption Cells

— Forecast Cell

Key Cell Formulas & CB Settings

Cell	Formula/Setting	Copied to
E5	=C5*D5	E6:E9
F5	CB Distribution: Normal Mean: =G5 Standard Deviation: =H5	F6:F9 (Using CB copy & paste) (Correlations entered after copying.)
F10	=SUMPRODUCT(F5:F9,E5:E9)/SUM(E5:E9)	--

In column E we compute the number of MW of generation capacity purchased in each asset category as follows:

Formula for cell E5:   =C5*D5

(Copy to cells E6 through E9.)

The assumption cells representing the random return for each asset category are implemented in column F using Crystal Ball's Normal distribution with the means and standard deviations specified in columns G and H, respectively. We accomplish this for investments in gas-fueled plants in cell F5 as shown in Figure 12.50. This definition also was copied to cells F6 through F9 (using Crystal Ball's copy data and paste data commands).

The "Correlate . . ." button on Crystal Ball's Define Assumption dialog box (shown in Figure 12.50) allows us to define correlations among the random variables (or assumption cells) in our spreadsheet models. However, there is not an accurate way to copy correlations from one assumption cell to another assumption cell. So first we must define all our assumption cells and then go back and individually specify any correlations between them. The Define Correlation dialog box for cell F5 is shown in Figure 12.51. The "Choose . . ." button on this dialog box allows you to select any assumption cells on the spreadsheet and individually specify their correlations to the assumption cell being

FIGURE 12.50

Defining the assumptions for cell F5

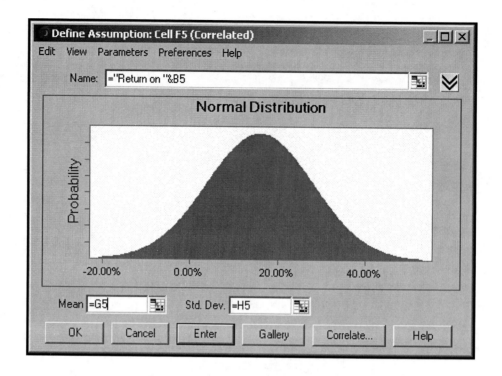

defined. In Figure 12.51 we indicated that the return on gas-fueled plants (represented by cell F5) is correlated with the returns on the other types of plants as indicated by the values in cells D14 through G14 on our spreadsheet model (shown in Figure 12.49). The graph in Figure 12.51 shows an example of the assumed negative correlation between the return of gas assets (assumption cell F5) and the return on coal assets (assumption cell F6). Again, using Crystal Ball's Define Correlation dialog, we have to enter the correlations repeatedly for each individual assumption cell.

Finally, in cell F10, we calculate the weighted average return on investments. Using Crystal Ball, we will define this to be a forecast cell:

Formula for cell F10:   =SUMPRODUCT(F5:F9,E5:E9)/SUM(E5:E9)

FIGURE 12.51

Defining correlations for cell F5

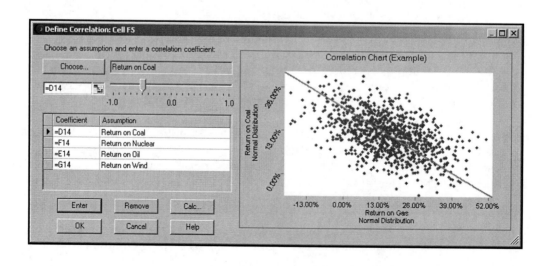

Another Way of Specifying Correlations...

Crystal Ball also offers a Correlation Matrix tool (launched by the command Run, Tools, Correlation Matrix) that allows you to upload an entire correlation matrix in a small number of steps. The Correlation Matrix tool is especially useful if you have many correlated assumption cells.

12.17.2 SOLVING THE PROBLEM WITH OptQUEST

The OptQuest settings used to solve this problem are shown in Figure 12.52. The Decision Variable Selection window indicates that we are asking OptQuest to determine the optimal amounts (in millions) to invest in gas, coal, oil, nuclear and wind generation assets, represented by cells D5 through D9, respectively, on our spreadsheet. The Constraints window indicates that the sum of the decision variables must equal 1000 (which is equivalent to $1 billion).

Recall that the McDaniel Group is interested in examining solutions on the efficient frontier of its possible investment options, these power generation assets. This requires determining the portfolios that provide the maximum expected (or average) return at a variety of different risk levels. In this case, we will define risk to be the standard deviation of a portfolio's weighted average return. Thus, in the Forecast Selection window, we indicate that our objective is to maximize the mean value of the weighted average return calculated in cell F10 in our spreadsheet. Finally, we also specify a variable requirement on the allowable upper bound of the standard deviation of the weighted

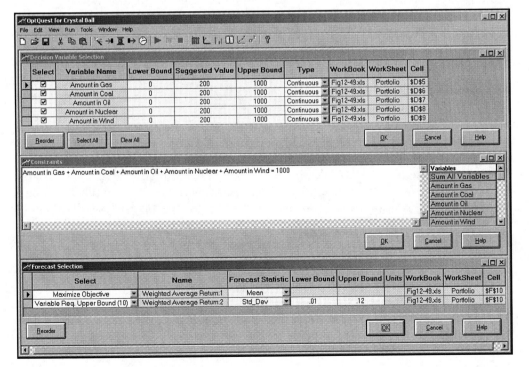

FIGURE 12.52

OptQuest settings for the portfolio optimization problem

FIGURE 12.53

Efficient frontier for the portfolio optimization problem

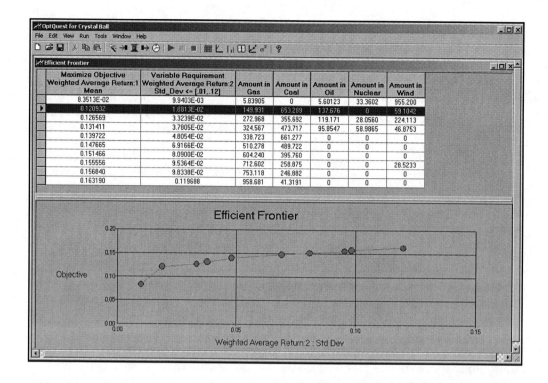

average return via the forecast selection labeled "Variable Req. Upper Bound (10)." When you select a variable required upper (or lower) bound on a forecast cell statistic, OptQuest will prompt you to indicate the number of possible upper (or lower) bounds you want to consider. In this case, we indicated we want to investigate 10 different upper bound values for the standard deviation of the forecast cell. The indicated lower and upper bounds of 1% and 12%, respectively, defined the range over which the standard deviation's upper bound will be allowed to vary. (Note that 1% and 12% were selected since they correspond, respectively, to the standard deviations on the returns for the least risky and most risky individual assets available in our portfolio). With these forecast selection settings, OptQuest will automatically identify portfolios that provide the maximum expected return for 10 different levels of risk as measured by portfolio return standard deviations between 1% and 12%.

Figure 12.53 displays OptQuest's Efficient Frontier window summarizing the ten portfolios it found and their relative trade-offs in terms of risk and return. The expected returns on these portfolios vary from 8.3% to 16.3% with standard deviations varying from approximately 1% to 12% with higher expected returns being associated with higher levels of risk. Determining the portfolio that is optimal for the McDaniel Group depends on the firm's preferences for risk versus return. But this analysis should help the firm identify a portfolio that provides the maximum return for the desired level of risk—or the minimum level of risk for the desired level of return.

12.18 Summary

This chapter introduced the concept of risk analysis and simulation. Many of the input cells in a spreadsheet represent random variables whose values cannot be determined with certainty. Any uncertainty in the input cells flows through the spreadsheet model to create a related uncertainty in the value of the output cell(s). Decisions made on the basis of these uncertain values involve some degree of risk.

Various methods of risk analysis are available, including best-case/worst-case analysis, what-if analysis, and simulation. Of these three methods, simulation is the only technique that provides hard evidence (facts and figures) that can be used objectively in making decisions. This chapter introduced the use of the Crystal Ball add-in to perform spreadsheet simulation. To simulate a model, RNGs are used to select representative values for each uncertain independent variable in the model. This process is repeated over and over to generate a sample of representative values for the dependent variable(s) in the model. The variability and distribution of the sample values for the dependent variable(s) can then be analyzed to gain insight into the possible outcomes that might occur. We also illustrated the use of OptQuest in determining the optimal value of controllable parameters or decision variables in simulation models.

12.19 References

Banks, J. and J. Carson. *Discrete-Event Simulation*. Englewood Cliffs, NJ: Prentice Hall, 1984. *Crystal Ball 2000 User Manual*. Decisioneering, Inc., Denver, CO, 2001.

Evans, J. and D. Olson. *Introduction to Simulation and Risk Analysis*. Upper Saddle River, NJ: Prentice Hall, 1998.

Hamzawi, S. "Management and Planning of Airport Gate Capacity: A Microcomputer-Based Gate Assignment Simulation Model." *Transportation Planning and Technology*, vol. 11, 1986.

Kaplan, A. and S. Frazza. "Empirical Inventory Simulation: A Case Study." *Decision Sciences*, vol. 14, January 1983.

Khoshnevis, B. *Discrete Systems Simulation*. New York: McGraw-Hill, 1994.

Law, A. and W. Kelton. *Simulation Modeling and Analysis*. New York: McGraw-Hill, 1990.

Marcus, A. "The Magellan Fund and Market Efficiency." *Journal of Portfolio Management*, Fall 1990. *OptQuest for Crystal Ball 2000 User Manual*. Decisioneering Inc., Denver, CO, 2001.

Russell, R. and R. Hickle. "Simulation of a CD Portfolio." *Interfaces*, vol. 16, no. 3, 1986.

Vollman, T., W. Berry and C. Whybark. *Manufacturing Planning and Control Systems*. Homewood, IL: Irwin, 1987.

Watson, H. *Computer Simulation in Business*. New York: Wiley, 1981.

THE WORLD OF MANAGEMENT SCIENCE

The U.S. Postal Service Moves to the Fast Lane

Mail flows into the U.S. Postal Service at the rate of 500 million pieces per day, and it comes in many forms. There are standard-sized letters with 9-digit ZIP codes (with or without imprinted bar codes), 5-digit ZIP codes, typed addresses that can be read by optical character readers, handwritten addresses that are barely decipherable, Christmas cards in red envelopes addressed in red ink, and so on. The enormous task of sorting all these pieces at the sending post office and at the destination has caused postal management to consider and adopt many new forms of technology. These include operator-assisted mechanized sorters, optical character readers (last-line and multiple-line), and bar code sorters. Implementation of new technology brings with it associated policy decisions, such as rate discounts for bar coding by the customer, finer sorting at the origin, and so on.

(Continued)

A simulation model called META (model for evaluating technology alternatives) assists management in evaluating new technologies, configurations, and operating plans. Using distributions based on experience or projections of the effects of new policies, META simulates a random stream of mail of different types; routes the mail through the system configuration being tested; and prints reports detailing total pieces handled, capacity utilization, work hours required, space requirements, and cost.

META has been used on several projects associated with the Postal Service corporate automation plan. These include facilities planning, benefits of alternative sorting plans, justification of efforts to enhance address readability, planning studies for reducing the time that carriers spend sorting vs. delivering, and identification of mail types that offer the greatest potential for cost savings.

According to the Associate Postmaster General, ". . . META became the vehicle to help steer our organization on an entirely new course at a speed we had never before experienced."

Source: Cebry, Michael E., Anura H. deSilva and Fred J. DiLisio. "Management Science in Automating Postal Operations: Facility and Equipment Planning in the United States Postal Service." *Interfaces*, vol. 22, no. 1, January–February 1992, pages 110–130.

Questions and Problems

1. Under what condition(s) is it appropriate to use simulation to analyze a model? That is, what characteristics should a model possess for simulation to be used?

2. The graph of the probability distribution of a normally distributed random variable with a mean of 20 and standard deviation of 3 is shown in Figure 12.8. The Excel function =NORMINV(Rand( ),20,3) also returns randomly generated observations from this distribution.
   a. Use Excel's NORMINV( ) function to generate 100 sample values from this distribution.
   b. Produce a histogram of the 100 sample values that you generated. Does your histogram look like the graph for this distribution in Figure 12.8?
   c. Repeat this experiment, with 1,000 sample values.
   d. Produce a histogram for the 1,000 sample values you generated. Does the histogram now more closely resemble the graph in Figure 12.8 for this distribution?
   e. Why does your second histogram look more "normal" than the first one?

3. Refer to the Hungry Dawg Restaurant example presented in this chapter. Health claim costs actually tend to be seasonal, with higher levels of claims occurring during the summer months (when kids are out of school and more likely to injure themselves) and during December (when people schedule elective procedures before the next year's deductible must be paid). The following table summarizes the seasonal adjustment factors that apply to RNGs for average claims in the Hungry Dawg problem. For instance, the average claim for month 6 should be multiplied by 115% and claims for month 1 should be multiplied by 80%.

Month	1	2	3	4	5	6	7	8	9	10	11	12
Seasonal Factor	0.80	0.85	0.87	0.92	0.93	1.15	1.20	1.18	1.03	0.95	0.98	1.14

Suppose that the company maintains an account from which it pays health insurance claims. Assume that there is $2.5 million in the account at the beginning of month 1. Each month, employee contributions are deposited into this account and claims are paid from the account.

a. Modify the spreadsheet shown in Figure 12.9 to include the cash flows in this account. If the company deposits $3 million into this account every month, what is the probability that the account will have insufficient funds to pay claims at some point during the year? Use 5000 replications. (*Hint*: You can use the COUNTIF( ) function to count the number of months in a year in which the ending balance in the account is below 0.)

b. If the company wants to deposit an equal amount of money in this account each month, what should this amount be if they want there to only be a 5% chance of having insufficient funds?

4. One of the examples in this chapter dealt with determining the optimal reorder point for a computer monitor sold by Millennium Computer Corp. Suppose that it costs MCC $0.30 per day in holding costs for each monitor in beginning inventory, and it costs $20 to place an order. Each monitor sold generates a profit of $45, and each lost sale results in an opportunity cost of $65 (including the lost profit of $45 and $20 in lost goodwill). Modify the spreadsheet shown in Figure 12.31 to determine the reorder point and order quantity that maximize the average monthly profit associated with this monitor.

5. A debate recently erupted about the optimal strategy for playing a game on the TV show called "Let's Make a Deal." In one of the games on this show, the contestant would be given the choice of prizes behind three closed doors. A valuable prize was behind one door and worthless prizes were behind the other two doors. After the contestant selected a door, the host would open one of the two remaining doors to reveal one of the worthless prizes. Then, before opening the selected door, the host would give the contestant the opportunity to switch the selection to the other door that had not been opened. The question is, should the contestant switch?

a. Suppose a contestant is allowed to play this game 500 times, always picks door number 1, and never switches when given the option. If the valuable prize is equally likely to be behind each door at the beginning of each play, how many times would the contestant win the valuable prize? Use simulation to answer this question.

b. Now suppose the contestant is allowed to play this game another 500 times. This time the player always selects door number 1 initially and switches when given the option. Using simulation, how many times would the contestant win the valuable prize?

c. If you were a contestant on this show, what would you do if given the option of switching doors?

6. Suppose that a product must go through an assembly line that consists of five sequential operations. The time it takes to complete each operation is normally distributed with a mean of 180 seconds and standard deviation of 5 seconds. Let X denote the cycle time for the line, so that after X seconds each operation is supposed to be finished and ready to pass the product to the next operation in the assembly line.

a. If the cycle time X = 180 seconds, what is the probability that all five operations will be completed?

b. What cycle time will ensure that all operations are finished 98% of the time?

7. Suppose that a product must go through an assembly line that consists of five sequential operations. The time it takes to complete each operation is normally

distributed with a mean of 180 seconds and standard deviation of 5 seconds. Define the flow time to be the total time it takes a product to go through the assembly line from start to finish.

a. What is the mean and standard deviation of the flow time? What is the probability that the total time will be less than 920 seconds?

b. Now assume that the time required to complete each operation has a 0.40 correlation with the operation time immediately preceding it. What is the mean and standard deviation of the flow time? What is the probability that the total time will be less than 920 seconds?

c. Now assume that the time required to complete each operation has a −0.40 correlation with the operation time immediately preceding it. What is the mean and standard deviation of the flow time? What is the probability that the total time will be less than 920 seconds?

d. Explain the effects of positive and negative correlations on the previous results.

8. WVTU is a television station that has 20 thirty-second advertising slots during its regularly scheduled programming each evening. The station is now selling advertising for the first few days in November. It could sell all the slots immediately for $4,500 each, but because November 7 will be Election Day, the station manager knows she might be able to sell slots at the last minute to political candidates in tight races for $8,000 each. The demand for these last minute slots is estimated as follows:

					Demand						
8	**9**	**10**	**11**	**12**	**13**	**14**	**15**	**16**	**17**	**18**	**19**
Probability 0.03	0.05	0.10	0.15	0.20	0.15	0.10	0.05	0.05	0.05	0.05	0.02

Slots not sold in advance and not sold to political candidates at the last minute can be sold to local advertisers for $2,000.

a. If the station manager sells all the advertising slots in advance, how much revenue will the station receive?

b. How many advertising slots should be sold in advance if the station manager wants to maximize expected revenue?

c. If the station manager sells in advance the number of slots identified in the previous question, what is the probability that the total revenue received will exceed the amount identified in part a where all slots are sold in advance?

9. The owner of a ski apparel store in Winter Park, CO, must decide in July how many ski jackets to order for the following ski season. Each ski jacket costs $54 each and can be sold during the ski season for $145. Any unsold jackets at the end of the season are sold for $45. The demand for jackets is expected to follow a Poisson distribution with a average rate of 80. The store owner can order jackets in lot sizes of 10 units.

a. How many jackets should the store owner order if she wants to maximize her expected profit?

b. What are the best-case and worst-case outcomes the owner might face for this product if she implements your suggestion?

c. How likely is it that the store owner will make at least $7,000 if she implements your suggestion?

d. How likely is it that the store owner will make between $6,000 to $7,000 if she implements your suggestion?

10. The owner of a golf shop in Myrtle Beach, SC, must decide how many sets of beginner golf clubs to order for the coming tourist season. Demand for golf clubs is random but follows a Poisson distribution with the average demand rates indicated in

the following table for each month. The expected selling price of the clubs also is shown for each month.

	May	June	July	August	September	October
Average Demand	60	90	70	50	30	40
Selling Price	$145	$140	$130	$110	$80	$60

In May, each set of clubs can be ordered at a cost of $75. This price is expected to drop 5% a month during the remainder of the season. Each month, the owner of the shop also gives away a free set of clubs to anyone who makes a hole-in-one from a short practice tee next to the shop. The number of people making a hole-in-one on this tee each month follows a Poisson distribution with a mean of 3. Any sets of clubs left over at the end of October are sold for $45 per set.

a. How many sets of clubs should the shop owner order if he wants to maximize the expected profit on this product?

b. What are the best-case and worst-case outcomes the owner might face on this product if he implements your suggestion?

c. How likely is it that the store owner will make at least $17,000 if he implements your suggestion?

d. How likely is it that the store owner will make between $12,000 to $14,000 if he implements your suggestion?

e. What percentage of the total demand for this product (excluding the free give-aways) will the owner be able to meet if he implements your suggestion?

11. Large Lots is planning a seven-day promotion on a discontinued model of 31" color television sets. At a price of $575 per set, the daily demand for this type of TV has been estimated as follows:

	Units Demanded per Day					
	0	**1**	**2**	**3**	**4**	**5**
Probability	0.15	0.20	0.30	0.20	0.10	0.05

Large Lots can order up to 50 of these TVs from a surplus dealer at a cost of $325. This dealer has offered to buy back any unsold sets at the end of the promotion for $250 each.

a. How many TVs should Large Lots order if it wants to maximize the expected profit on this promotion?

b. What is the expected level of profit?

c. Suppose the surplus dealer will buy back a maximum of only four sets at the end of the promotion. Would this change your answer? If so, how?

12. The monthly demand for the latest computer at Newland Computers follows a normal distribution with a mean of 350 and standard deviation of 75. Newland purchases these computers for $1,200 and sells them for $2,300. It costs the company $100 to place an order and $12 for every computer held in inventory at the end of each month. Currently, the company places an order for 1000 computers whenever the inventory at the end of a month falls below 100 units. Assume that the beginning inventory is 400 units, unmet demand in any month is lost to competitors, and orders placed at the end of one month arrive at the beginning of the next month.

a. Create a spreadsheet model to simulate the profit that the company will earn on this product over the next two years. Use 5000 replications. What is the average level of profit the company will earn?

b. Suppose that the company wants to determine the optimum reorder point and order quantity. Which combination of reorder point and order quantity will provide the highest average profit over the next two years?

13. The manager of Moore's Catalog Showroom is trying to predict how much revenue will be generated by each major department in the store during 2006. The manager has estimated the minimum and maximum growth rates possible for revenues in each department. The manager believes that any of the possible growth rates between the minimum and maximum values are equally likely to occur. These estimates are summarized in the following table:

		Growth Rates	
Department	2005 Revenues	Minimum	Maximum
Electronics	$6,342,213	2%	10%
Garden Supplies	$1,203,231	−4%	5%
Jewelry	$4,367,342	−2%	6%
Sporting Goods	$3,543,532	−1%	8%
Toys	$4,342,132	4%	15%

Create a spreadsheet to simulate the total revenues that could occur in the coming year. Run 5000 replications of the model and do the following:

a. Construct a 95% confidence interval for the average level of revenues that the manager could expect for 2006.

b. According to your model, what are the chances that total revenues in 2006 will be more than 5% larger than those in 2005?

14. The Harriet Hotel in downtown Boston has 100 rooms that rent for $150 per night. It costs the hotel $30 per room in variable costs (cleaning, bathroom items, etc.) each night a room is occupied. For each reservation accepted, there is a 5% chance that the guest will not arrive. If the hotel overbooks, it costs $200 to compensate guests whose reservations cannot be honored.

a. How many reservations should the hotel accept if it wants to maximize the average daily profit? Use 1000 replications for each reservation level that you consider.

15. Lynn Price recently completed her MBA and accepted a job with an electronics manufacturing company. Although she likes her job, she also is looking forward to retiring one day. To ensure that her retirement is comfortable, Lynn intends to invest $3,000 of her salary into a tax-sheltered retirement fund at the end of each year. Lynn is not certain what rate of return this investment will earn each year, but she expects that each year's rate of return could be modeled appropriately as a normally distributed random variable with a mean of 12.5% and standard deviation of 2%.

a. If Lynn is 30 years old, how much money should she expect to have in her retirement fund at age 60? (Use 5000 replications.)

b. Construct a 95% confidence interval for the average amount that Lynn will have at age 60.

c. What is the probability that Lynn will have more than $1 million in her retirement fund when she reaches age 60?

d. How much should Lynn invest each year if she wants there to be a 90% chance of having at least $1 million in her retirement fund at age 60?

e. Suppose that Lynn contributes $3,000 annually to her retirement fund for eight years and then terminates these annual contributions. How much of her salary would she have contributed to this retirement plan and how much money could she expect to have accumulated at age 60?

f. Now suppose that Lynn contributes nothing to her retirement fund for eight years and then begins contributing $3,000 annually until age 60. How much of her salary would she have contributed to this retirement plan and how much money could she expect to have accumulated at age 60?

g. What should Lynn (and you) learn from the answers to questions e and f?

16. Employees of Georgia-Atlantic are permitted to contribute a portion of their earnings (in increments of $500) to a flexible spending account from which they can pay medical expenses not covered by the company's health insurance program. Contributions to an employee's "flex" account are not subject to income taxes. However, the employee forfeits any amount contributed to the "flex" account that is not spent during the year. Suppose Greg Davis makes $60,000 per year from Georgia-Atlantic and pays a marginal tax rate of 33%. Greg and his wife estimate that in the coming year their normal medical expenses not covered by the health insurance program could be as small as $500, as large as $5,000, and most likely about $1,300. However, Greg also believes there is a 5% chance that an abnormal medical event could occur which might add $10,000 to the normal expenses paid from their flex account. If their uncovered medical claims exceed their contribution to their "flex" account, they will have to cover these expenses with the after-tax money Greg brings home.

a. Use simulation to determine the amount of money Greg should contribute to his flexible spending account in the coming year if he wants to maximize his disposable income (after taxes and all medical expenses are paid). Use 5000 replications for each level of "flex" account contribution you consider.

17. Acme Equipment Company is considering the development of a new machine that would be marketed to tire manufacturers. Research and development costs for the project are expected to be about $4 million but could vary between $3 and $6 million. The market life for the product is estimated to be 3 to 8 years with all intervening possibilities being equally likely. The company thinks it will sell 250 units per year, but acknowledges that this figure could be as low as 50 or as high as 350. The company will sell the machine for about $23,000. Finally, the cost of manufacturing the machine is expected to be $14,000 but could be as low as $12,000 or as high as $18,000. The company's cost of capital is 15%.

a. Use appropriate RNGs to create a spreadsheet to calculate the possible net present values (NPVs) that could result from taking on this project.

b. Replicate the model 5000 times. What is the expected NPV for this project?

c. What is the probability of this project generating a positive NPV for the company?

18. Representatives from the American Heart Association are planning to go door-to-door throughout a community, soliciting contributions. From past experience, they know that when someone answers the door, 80% of the time it is a female and 20% of the time it is a male. They also know that 70% of the females who answer the door make a donation, whereas only 40% of the males who answer the door make donations. The amount of money that females contribute follows a normal distribution with a mean of $20 and standard deviation of $3. The amount of money that males contribute follows a normal distribution with a mean of $10 and standard deviation of $2.

a. Create a spreadsheet model that simulates what might happen whenever a representative of the American Heart Association knocks on a door and someone answers.

b. Replicate your model 5000 times. What is the average contribution the Heart Association can expect to receive when someone answers the door?

c. Suppose that the Heart Association plans to visit 300 homes on a given Saturday. If no one is home at 25% of the residences, what is the total amount that the Heart Association can expect to receive in donations?

19. Techsburg, Inc. uses a stamping machine to manufacture aluminum bodies for light-weight miniature aircraft used for military reconnaissance. Currently, forms in the stamping machine are changed after every 60 hours of operation or whenever a form breaks, whichever happens first. The lifetime of each form follows a Weibull distribution with location, scale, and shape parameters of 50, 25, and 2, respectively. The machine is operated 5840 hours per year. It costs $800 to replace the stamping forms. If a form breaks before its scheduled replacement time (or in less than 60 hours of use), the shop loses 8 hours of production time. However, if a form lasts until its scheduled replacement after 60 hours of use, the shop only loses 2 hours of production time. The company estimates that each hour of lost production time costs $1200.

    a. On average, how much does Techsburg spend maintaining this stamping machine per year?
    b. Suppose Techsburg wanted to minimize its total maintenance cost for the stamping machine. How often should the company plan on changing the stamping forms and how much money would it save?
    c. Suppose the cost to replace the stamping forms is expected to increase. What impact should this have on the optimal planned replacement time of the forms? Explain.
    d. Suppose the cost of lost production time is increased. What effect should this have on the optimal planned replacement time of the forms? Explain.

20. After spending ten years as an assistant manager for a large restaurant chain, Ray Clark has decided to become his own boss. The owner of a local submarine sandwich store wants to sell the store to Ray for $65,000, to be paid in installments of $13,000 in each of the next five years. According to the current owner, the store brings in revenue of about $110,000 per year and incurs operating costs of about 63% of sales. Thus, once the store is paid for, Ray should make about $35,000–$40,000 per year before taxes. Until the store is paid for, he will make substantially less—but he will be his own boss. Realizing that some uncertainty is involved in this decision, Ray wants to simulate what level of net income he can expect to earn during the next five years as he operates and pays for the store. In particular, he wants to see what could happen if sales are allowed to vary uniformly between $90,000 and $120,000, and if operating costs are allowed to vary uniformly between 60% and 65% of sales. Assume that Ray's payments for the store are not deductible for tax purposes and that he is in the 28% tax bracket.

    a. Create a spreadsheet model to simulate the annual net income Ray would receive during each of the next five years if he decides to buy the store.
    b. Given the money he has in savings, Ray thinks he can get by for the next five years if he can make at least $12,000 from the store each year. Replicate the model 5000 times and track: 1) the minimum amount of money Ray makes over the five-year period represented by each replication, and 2) the total amount Ray makes during the five-year period represented by each replication.
    c. What is the probability that Ray will make at least $12,000 in each of the next five years?
    d. What is the probability that Ray will make at least $60,000 total over the next five years?

21. Road Racer Sports, Inc. is a mail-order business dedicated to the running enthusiast. The company sends out full-color catalogs several times a year to several hundred

thousand people on its mailing list. Production and mailing costs are fairly expensive for direct mail advertising, averaging about $3.25 per catalog. As a result, management does not want to continue sending catalogs to persons who do not buy enough to cover the costs of the catalogs they receive. Currently, the company removes customers from their mailing list if they receive six consecutive catalogs without placing an order. The following table summarizes the probability of a customer placing an order.

Last Order	Prob. of Order
1 catalog ago	0.40
2 catalogs ago	0.34
3 catalogs ago	0.25
4 catalogs ago	0.17
5 catalogs ago	0.09
6 catalogs ago	0.03

According to the first row in this table, if customers receive a catalog and place an order, there is a 40% chance they will place another order when they receive their next catalog. The second row indicates there is a 34% chance that customers will receive a catalog, place an order, and then not order again until they receive two more catalogs. The remaining rows in this table have similar interpretations.

a. How much profit must the company earn on an average order in order to cover the cost of printing and distributing the catalogs?

b. Approximately what percentage of the names on the mailing list will be purged before each catalog mailing?

22. Sammy Slick works for a company that allows him to contribute up to 10% of his earnings into a tax-deferred savings plan. The company matches a portion of the contributions its employees make based on the organization's financial performance. Although the minimum match is 25% of the employee's contributions and the maximum match is 100%, in most years the company match is about 50%. Sammy is currently 30 years old and makes $35,000. He wants to retire at age 60. He expects his salary to increase in any given year to be at least 2% per year, at most 6%, and most likely 3%. The funds contributed by Sammy and his employer are invested in mutual funds. Sammy expects the annual return on his investments to vary according to a normal distribution with a mean of 12.5% and standard deviation of 2%.

a. If Sammy contributes 10% of his income to this plan, how much money could he expect to have at age 60?

b. Suppose Sammy makes 10% contributions to this plan for eight years, from age 30 to 37, and then stops contributing. How much of his own money would he have invested and how much money could he expect to have at age 60?

c. Now suppose Sammy contributes nothing to the plan his first eight years and then contributes 10% for 23 years from age 38 to age 60. How much of his own money would he have invested and how much money could he expect to have at age 60?

d. What do you learn from Sammy's example?

23. Podcessories manufactures several accessories for a popular digital music player. The company is trying to decide whether to discontinue one of the items in this product line. Discontinuing the item would save the company $600,000 in fixed costs (consisting of leases on building and machinery) during the coming year. However, the company is anticipating that it might receive an order for 60,000 units from a large discount retailer that could be very profitable. Unfortunately, the company is

being forced to decide about renewing the leases required to continue this item before knowing if it will receive the large order from the discount retailer. The variable cost per unit for this item is $6. The regular selling price of the item is $12 per unit. However, the company has offered the discount retailer a price of $10.50 per unit due to the size of its potential order. Podcessories believes there is a 60% chance it will receive the order from the discount retailer. Additionally, it believes general demand for this product (apart from the discount retailer's order) will vary between 45,000 to 115,000 units with a most likely outcome of 75,000 units.

a. Create a spreadsheet model for this problem.

b. How much money might the company lose next year (worst case) if it continues this line?

c. How much money might the company make next year (best case) if it continues this line?

d. If the company loses money, on average how much could it expect to lose? (*Hint*: Use the filter option under the forecast window's preferences command.)

e. If the company makes money, on average how much could it expect to make? (*Hint*: Use the filter option under the forecast window's preferences command.)

f. What other actions might you suggest this company take to improve its chance of making a decision with a good outcome?

24. Bob Davidson owns a newsstand outside the Waterstone office building complex in Atlanta, near Hartsfield International Airport. He buys his papers wholesale at $0.50 per paper and sells them for $0.75. Bob wonders what is the optimal number of papers to order each day. Based on history, he has found that demand (even though it is discrete) can be modeled by a normal distribution with a mean of 50 and standard deviation of 5. When he has more papers than customers, he can recycle all the extra papers the next day and receive $0.05 per paper. On the other hand, if he has more customers than papers, he loses some goodwill in addition to the lost profit on the potential sale of $0.25. Bob estimates the incremental lost goodwill costs five days' worth of business (that is, dissatisfied customers will go to a competitor the next week, but come back to him the week after that).

a. Create a spreadsheet model to determine the optimal number of papers to order each day. Use 5000 replications and round the demand values generated by the normal RNG to the closest integer value.

b. Construct a 95% confidence interval for the expected payoff from the optimal decision.

25. Vinton Auto Insurance is trying to decide how much money to keep in liquid assets to cover insurance claims. In the past, the company held some of the premiums it received in interest-bearing checking accounts and put the rest into investments that are not quite as liquid, but tend to generate a higher investment return. The company wants to study cash flows to determine how much money it should keep in liquid assets to pay claims. After reviewing historical data, the company determined that the average repair bill per claim is normally distributed with a mean of $1,700 and standard deviation of $400. It also determined that the number of repair claims filed each week is a random variable that follows the probability distribution shown in the following table:

Number of Claims	1	2	3	4	5	6	7	8	9
Probability	0.1	0.1	0	0.2	0.3	0.1	0.1	0.1	0.1

In addition to repair claims, the company also receives claims for cars that have been "totaled" and cannot be repaired. A 20% chance of receiving this type of claim exists in any week. These claims for "totaled" cars typically cost anywhere from $2,000 to $35,000, with $13,000 being the most common cost.

a. Create a spreadsheet model of the total claims cost incurred by the company in any week.

b. Replicate the model 5000 times and create a histogram of the distribution of total cost values that were generated.

c. What is the average cost that the company should expect to pay each week?

d. Suppose that the company decides to keep $20,000 cash on hand to pay claims. What is the probability that this amount would not be adequate to cover claims in any week?

e. Create a 95% confidence interval for the true probability of claims exceeding $20,000 in a given week.

26. Executives at Meds-R-Us have decided to build a new production facility for the company's best-selling high-blood-pressure drug. The problem they now face is determining the size of the facility (in terms of production capacity). Last year, the company sold 1,085,000 units of this drug at a price of $13 per unit. They estimate the demand for the drug to be normally distributed with a mean increasing by approximately 59,000 units per year over the next 10 years with a standard deviation of 30,000 units. They expect the price of the drug to increase with inflation at a rate of 3% per year. Variable production costs currently are $9 per unit and are expected to increase in future years at the rate of inflation. Other operating costs are expected to be $1.50 per unit of capacity in the first year of operation, increasing at the rate of inflation in subsequent years. The plant construction cost is expected to be $18 million for 1 million units of annual production capacity. The company can increase the annual production capacity above this level at a cost of $12 per unit of additional capacity. Assume that the company must pay for the plant when it is completed and all other cash flows occur at the end of each year. The company uses a 10% discount rate on cash flows for financial decisions.

a. Create a spreadsheet model to compute the net present value (NPV) for this decision.

b. What is the expected NPV for a plant with a production capacity of 1.2 million units per year?

c. What is the expected NPV for a plant with a production capacity of 1.4 million units per year?

d. How large a plant should the company build if they want to be 90% certain of obtaining a positive NPV for this project?

27. The owner of a local car dealership has just received a call from a regional distributor stating that a $5,000 bonus will be awarded if the owner's dealership sells at least 10 new cars next Saturday. On an average Saturday, this dealership has 75 potential customers look at new cars, but there is no way to determine exactly how many customers will come this particular Saturday. The owner is fairly certain that the number would not be less than 40, but also thinks it would be unrealistic to expect more than 120 (which is the largest number of customers ever to show up in one day). The owner determined that, on average, about one out of ten customers who look at cars at the dealership actually purchases a car—or, a 0.10 probability (or 10% chance) exists that any given customer will buy a new car.

a. Create a spreadsheet model for this problem and generate 5000 random outcomes for the number of cars the dealership might sell next Saturday.

b. What is the probability that the dealership will earn the $5,000 bonus?

c. If you were this dealer, what is the maximum amount of money you would be willing to spend on sales incentives to try to earn this bonus?

28. Dr. Sarah Benson is an ophthalmologist who, in addition to prescribing glasses and contact lenses, performs optical laser surgery to correct nearsightedness. This surgery is fairly easy and inexpensive to perform. Thus, it represents a potential gold mine for her practice. To inform the public about this procedure, Dr. Benson advertises in the local paper and holds information sessions in her office one night a week at which she shows a videotape about the procedure and answers any questions that potential patients might have. The room where these meetings are held can seat ten people, and reservations are required. The number of people attending each session varies from week to week. Dr. Benson cancels the meeting if two or fewer people have made reservations. Using data from the previous year, Dr. Benson determined that the distribution of reservations is as follows:

Number of Reservations	0	1	2	3	4	5	6	7	8	9	10
Probability	0.02	0.05	0.08	0.16	0.26	0.18	0.11	0.07	0.05	0.01	0.01

Using data from the past year, Dr. Benson determined that each person who attends an information session has a 0.25 probability of electing to have the surgery. Of those who do not, most cite the cost of the procedure—$2,000—as their major concern.

a. On average, how much revenue does Dr. Benson's practice in laser surgery generate each week? (Use 5000 replications.)

b. On average, how much revenue would the laser surgery generate each week if Dr. Benson did not cancel sessions with two or fewer reservations?

c. Dr. Benson believes that 40% of the people attending the information sessions would have the surgery if she reduced the price to $1,500. Under this scenario, how much revenue could Dr. Benson expect to realize per week from laser surgery?

29. Calls to the 24-hour customer support line for Richman Financial Services occur randomly following a Poisson distribution with the following average rates during different hours of the day:

Time Period	Avg Calls Per Hour	Time Period	Avg Calls Per Hour
Midnight–1 A.M.	2	Noon–1 P.M.	35
1 A.M.–2 A.M.	2	1 P.M.–2 P.M.	20
2 A.M.–3 A.M.	2	2 P.M.–3 P.M.	20
3 A.M.–4 A.M.	4	3 P.M.–4 P.M.	20
4 A.M.–5 A.M.	4	4 P.M.–5 P.M.	18
5 A.M.–6 A.M.	8	5 P.M.–6 P.M.	18
6 A.M.–7 A.M.	12	6 P.M.–7 P.M.	15
7 A.M.–8 A.M.	18	7 P.M.–8 P.M.	10
8 A.M.–9 A.M.	25	8 P.M.–9 P.M.	6
9 A.M.–10 A.M.	30	9 P.M.–10 P.M.	5
10 A.M.–11 A.M.	25	10 P.M.–11 P.M.	4
11 A.M.–Noon	20	11 P.M.–Midnight	2

The Richman customer service representatives spend approximately seven minutes on each call and are assigned to work eight-hour shifts that begin at the top of each hour. Richman wants to ensure that, on average, they can provide a 98% service level.

a. Determine the customer service schedule that allows Richman to achieve its service level objective using the fewest number of employees.

b. According to your solution, how many customer service representatives should Richman employ and how should they be scheduled?

30. A European call option gives a person the right to buy a particular stock at a given price (the strike price) on a specific date in the future (the expiration date). This type of call option typically is sold at the net present value of the expected value of the option on its expiration date. Suppose you own a call option with a strike price of $54. If the stock is worth $59 on the expiration date, you would exercise your option and buy the stock, making a $5 profit. On the other hand, if the stock is worth $47 on the expiration date, you would not exercise your option and make $0 profit. Researchers have suggested the following model for simulating the movement of stock prices:

$$P_{k+1} = P_k \left(1 + (\mu t + z\sigma\sqrt{t}\right)$$

where:

P_k = price of the stock at time period k

$\mu = v + 0.5\sigma^2$

v = the stock's expected annual growth rate

σ = the standard deviation on the stock's annual growth rate

t = time period interval (expressed in years)

z = a random observation from a normal distribution with mean 0 and standard deviation of 1.

Suppose that a stock has an initial price (P_0) of $80, an expected annual growth rate (v) of 15%, and a standard deviation (σ) of 25%.
  a. Create a spreadsheet model to simulate this stock's price behavior for the next 13 weeks (note $t = 1/52$ because the time period is weekly).
  b. Suppose you are interested in purchasing a call option with a strike price of $75 and an expiration date at week 13. On average, how much profit would you earn with this option? (Use 5000 replications.)
  c. Assume that a risk-free discount rate is 6%. How much should you be willing to pay for this option today? (*Hint*: Use Excel's NPV function.)
  d. If you purchase the option, what is the probability that you will make a profit?
31. Refer to the previous question. Another type of option is the Asian option. Its payoff is not based on the price of the stock on the expiration date but, instead, on the average price of the stock over the lifetime of the option.
  Suppose a stock has an initial price (P_0) of $80, an expected annual growth rate (v) of 15%, and a standard deviation (σ) of 25%.
  a. Create a spreadsheet model to simulate this stock's price behavior for the next 13 weeks (note $t = 1/52$ because the time period is weekly).
  b. Suppose you are interested in purchasing a call option with a strike price of $75 and an expiration date at week 13. On average, how much profit would you earn with this option? (Use 5000 replications.)
  c. Assume a risk-free discount rate is 6%. How much should you be willing to pay for this option today? (*Hint*: Use Excel's NPV function.)
  d. If you purchase the option, what is the probability that you will make a profit?
32. Amanda Green is interested in investing in the following set of mutual funds whose returns are all normally distributed with the indicated means and standard deviations:

	Windsor	Columbus	Vanguard	Integrity	Nottingham
Mean	17.0%	14.0%	11.0%	8.0%	5.0%
Std Dev	9.0%	6.5%	5.0%	3.5%	2.0%

The correlations between the mutual funds are as follows:

	Windsor	Columbus	Vanguard	Integrity	Nottingham
Windsor	1	0.1	0.05	0.3	0.6
Columbus		1	0.2	0.15	0.1
Vanguard			1	0.1	0.2
Integrity				1	0.4
Nottingham					1

a. What is the expected return and standard deviation on a portfolio where Amanda invests her money equally in all five mutual funds?

b. Suppose Amanda is willing to assume the risk associated with a 5% standard deviation in returns on her portfolio. What portfolio will give her the greatest expected return for this level of risk?

c. Construct the efficient frontier for this portfolio. How would you explain this graph to Amanda?

33. Martin manufacturing company uses a piece of machinery that has three different bushings that periodically fail in service. The probability distribution of the life of each bushing is identical and is summarized by the following table.

	Bushing Life (operating hours)									
	1000	1100	1200	1300	1400	1500	1600	1700	1800	1900
Probability	0.08	0.13	0.25	0.15	0.12	0.09	0.07	0.05	0.04	0.02

When a bushing fails, the machine stops, a repair person is called, and a new bushing is installed. Each bushing costs $35. Downtime for the machine costs the company an estimated $15 per minute. The direct on-site cost for the repair person is $50 per hour. The amount of time required for the repair person to arrive after a bushing fails is approximately normally distributed with a mean of 10 minutes and standard deviation of 2 minutes. The amount of time required to change a bushing follows a triangular distribution with minimum, most likely, and maximum values of 15, 20, and 30 minutes, respectively.

a. On average, what is the total bushing-related cost that Martin incurs to operate this machine for 20,000 hours?

b. Martin is considering implementing another repair policy: if any of the bushings fail, all three are replaced. What is the total bushing-related cost that Martin incurs to operate this machine for 20,000 hours under this policy?

c. Should Martin implement the new policy?

34. Michael Abrams runs a specialty clothing store that sells collegiate sports apparel. One of his primary business opportunities involves selling custom screenprinted sweatshirts for college football bowl games. He is trying to determine how many sweatshirts to produce for the upcoming Tangerine Bowl game. During the month before the game, Michael plans to sell his sweatshirts for $25 apiece. At this price, he believes the demand for sweatshirts will be triangularly distributed with a minimum demand of 10,000, maximum demand of 30,000 and a most likely demand of 18,000. During the month after the game, Michael plans to sell any remaining sweatshirts for $12 apiece. At this price, he believes the demand for sweatshirts will be triangularly distributed with a minimum demand of 2,000, maximum demand of 7,000, and a most likely demand of 5,000. Two months after the game, Michael plans to sell any remaining sweatshirts to a surplus store that has agreed to buy up to 2,000

sweatshirts for a price of $3 per shirt. Michael can order custom screenprinted sweatshirts for $8 apiece in lot sizes of 3,000.

a. On average, how much profit would Michael earn if he orders 18,000 sweatshirts? Use 5000 replications.

b. How many sweatshirts should he order if he wants to maximize his expected profit? Again use 5000 replications in each simulation you perform.

35. The Major Motors Corporation is trying to decide whether to introduce a new midsize car. The directors of the company only want to produce the car if it has at least an 80% chance of generating a positive net present value over the next ten years. If the company decides to produce the car, it will have to pay an uncertain initial start-up cost that is estimated to follow a triangular distribution with a minimum value of $2 billion, maximum value of $2.4 billion, and a most likely value of $2.1 billion. In the first year, the company would produce 100,000 units. Demand during the first year is uncertain but expected to be normally distributed with a mean of 95,000 and standard deviation of 7,000. For any year in which the demand exceeds production, production will be increased by 5% in the following year. For any year in which the production exceeds demand, production will be decreased by 5% in the next year, and the excess cars will be sold to a rental car company at a 20% discount. After the first year, the demand in any year will be modeled as a normally distributed random variable with a mean equal to the actual demand in the previous year and standard deviation of 7,000. In the first year, the sales price of the car will be $13,000 and the total variable cost per car is expected to be $9,500. Both the selling price and variable cost is expected to increase each year at the rate of inflation, which is assumed to be uniformly distributed between 2% and 7%. The company uses a discount rate of 9% to discount future cash flows.

a. Create a spreadsheet model for this problem and replicate it 5000 times. What is the minimum, average, and maximum NPV Major Motors can expect if it decides to produce this car? (*Hint*: Consider using the NPV( ) function to discount the profits Major Motors would earn each year.)

b. What is the probability of Major Motors earning a positive NPV over the next ten years?

c. Should Major Motors produce this car?

36. Each year, the Schriber Corporation must determine how much to contribute to the company's pension plan. The company uses a ten-year planning horizon to determine the contribution which, if made annually in each of the next ten years, would allow for only a 10% chance of the fund running short of money. The company then makes that contribution in the current year and repeats this process in each subsequent year to determine the specific amount to contribute each year. (Last year, the company contributed $23 million to the plan.) The pension plan covers two types of employees: hourly and salaried. In the current year, there will be 6,000 former hourly employees and 3,000 former salaried employees receiving benefits from the plan. The change in the number of retired hourly employees from one year to the next is expected to vary according to a normal distribution with a mean of 4% and standard deviation of 1%. The change in the number of retired salaried employees from one year to the next is expected to vary between 1% and 4% according to a truncated normal distribution with a mean of 2% and standard deviation of 1%. Currently, hourly retirees receive an average benefit of $15,000 per year, whereas salaried retirees receive an average annual benefit of $40,000. Both of these averages are expected to increase annually with the rate of inflation, which is assumed to vary between 2% and 7% according to a triangular distribution with a most likely value of 3.5%. The current balance in the company's pension fund is $1.5 billion. Investments in this

fund earn an annual return that is assumed to be normally distributed with a mean of 12% and standard deviation of 2%. Create a spreadsheet model for this problem and use simulation to determine the pension fund contribution that the company should make in the current year. What is your recommendation?

CASE 12.1   Live Well, Die Broke

(Inspired by a presentation given by Dr. John Charnes, University of Kansas, at the 2005 Crystal Ball Users Group meeting.)

For investment advisors, a major consideration in planning for a client in retirement is the determination of a withdrawal amount that will provide the client with the funds necessary to maintain a desired standard of living throughout the client's remaining lifetime. If a client withdraws too much or if investment returns fall below expectations, there is a danger of either running out of funds or reducing the desired standard of living. A sustainable retirement withdrawal is the inflation-adjusted monetary amount a client can withdraw periodically from retirement funds for an assumed planning horizon. This amount cannot be determined with complete certainty because of the random nature of investment returns. Usually, the sustainable retirement withdrawal is determined by limiting the probability of running out of funds to some specified level, such as 5%. The sustainable retirement withdrawal amount typically is expressed as a percentage of the initial value of the assets in the retirement portfolio, but is actually the inflation-adjusted monetary amount that the client would like each year for living expenses.

Assume that an investment advisor, Roy Dodson, is assisting a widowed client in determining a sustainable retirement withdrawal. The client is a 59 year-old woman who will turn 60 in two months. She has $1,000,000 in a tax-deferred retirement account that will be the primary source of her retirement income. Roy has designed a portfolio for his client with returns that he expects to be normally distributed with a mean of 8% and a standard deviation of 2%. Withdrawals will be made at the beginning of each year on the client's birthday.

Roy assumes that the inflation rate will be 3%, based on long-term historic data. So if her withdrawal at the beginning of the first year is $40,000, her inflation-adjusted withdrawal at the beginning of the second year will be $41,200, and third year's withdrawal will be $42,436, etc.

For his initial analysis, Roy wants to assume that his client will live until age 90. In consultation with his client, he also wants to limit the chance that she will run out of money before her death to a maximum of 5%.

a. What is the maximum amount that Roy should advise his client to withdraw on her 60th birthday? If she lives until age 90, how much should the client expect to leave to her heirs?

b. Roy is now concerned about basing his analysis on the assumption that his client will live to age 90. After all, she is healthy and might live to be 110, or she could be in a car accident and die at age 62. To account for this uncertainty in the client's age at death, Roy would like to model the client's remaining life expectancy as a random variable between 0 and 50 years that follows a lognormal distribution with a mean of 20 and standard deviation of 10 (rounded to the nearest integer). Under this assumption, what is the maximum amount that Roy should advise his client to withdraw on her 60th birthday and how much should the client expect to leave to her heirs? *Hint:* Modify your spreadsheet to accommodate ages up to 110 and use a VLOOKUP( ) function to return the client's ending balance in her randomly determined year of death.)

c. Roy is pleased to now be modeling the uncertainty in his client's life expectancy. But he is now curious about limiting to 5% the chance that his client will run out of money before her death. In particular, he is wondering how sensitive the sustainable withdrawal amount is to changes in this 5% assumption. To answer this question, create an efficient frontier showing the maximum sustainable withdrawal amount as the chance of running out of money is varied from 1% to 10%. How should Roy explain the meaning of this chart to his client?

d. Suppose that Roy's client has three children and wants there to be a 95% chance that they will each inherit at least $250,000 when she dies. Under this assumption, what is the maximum amount that Roy should advise his client to withdraw on her 60th birthday and how much should the client expect to leave to her heirs?

Death and Taxes

Benjamin Franklin once said, "In this world nothing is certain but death and taxes." Although that might be true, there is often great uncertainty involved in when one will encounter death and how much one must pay in taxes before arriving there. Another Benjamin made a very significant contribution toward assessing the uncertainty associated with both death and taxes. Benjamin Gompertz (1779–1865) was a British mathematician who, by studying Mediterranean fruit flies, theorized that mortality rates increase at an exponential rate as age increases (*i.e.*, as an organism gets older, its chance of dying per unit of time increases exponentially). Gompertz's Law of Mortality has since become a cornerstone of actuarial and financial planning activities.

In a group of people of a given age (for example, 65), some proportion of those people will not live another year. Let q_x represent the proportion of people of age x who will die before reaching age $x + 1$. The value q_x is sometimes referred to as the *mortality rate* at age x. The following formula, based on Gompertz's Law, is sometimes used to model mortality rates.

$$q_x = 1 - \text{EXP}\left(\frac{(\text{LN}(1-q_{x-1}))^2}{\text{LN}(1-q_{x-2})}\right)$$

Mortality rates play an important role in numerous financial planning and retirement decisions. For instance, most individuals do not want to retire unless they are reasonably certain that they have enough assets to sustain themselves financially for the rest of their life. The uncertainties associated with this sort of decision create a perfect application for spreadsheet simulation.

The following questions give you the opportunity to explore several issues that actuaries and financial planners face on a daily basis. Assume the mortality rates for males at ages 63 and 64 are $q_{63} = 0.0235$ and $q_{64} = 0.0262$, respectively, and those of females at ages 63 and 64 are $q_{63} = 0.0208$ and $q_{64} = 0.0225$, respectively.

a. On average, to what age should a 65-year-old male expect to live?
b. What is the probability of a 65-year-old male living to at least age 80?
c. What is the probability of a 65-year-old male living to exactly age 80?
d. On average, to what age should a 70-year-old male expect to live?
e. What is the probability of a 70-year-old male living to at least age 80?
f. What is the probability of a 70-year-old male living to exactly age 80?
g. Suppose a 65-year-old male has $1,200,000 in retirement investments earning an 8% interest rate. Assume he intends to withdraw $100,000 in his first year of retirement and 3% more in subsequent years to adjust for inflation. Annual interest earnings are credited on the beginning balance minus one half the amount withdrawn. For

example, in the first year interest earnings would be $0.08 \times (\$1,200,000 - \$100,000/2) = \$92,000$. What is the probability that this individual would outlive his retirement assets (assuming he spends all that he withdraws each year)?

h. Refer to the previous question. Suppose the interest rate each year can be modeled as a normally distributed random variable with a mean of 8% and standard deviation of 1.5%. Further suppose that the rate of inflation each year can be described as a random variable following a triangular distribution with minimum, most likely, and maximum values of 2%, 3%, and 5%, respectively. Under these conditions, what is the probability that this individual would outlive his retirement assets (assuming that he spends all he withdraws each year)?

i. Suppose that the person described in the previous question has a 65-year-old wife who is joint owner of the retirement assets described earlier. What is the probability that the retirement assets would be depleted before both spouses die (assuming they spend all they withdraw each year)?

j. Refer to the previous question. How much money should this couple plan on withdrawing in the first year if they want there to be a maximum of a 5% chance of depleting their retirement assets before they both die?

CASE 12.3   The Sound's Alive Company

(Contributed by Dr. Jack Yurkiewicz, Lubin School of Business, Pace University.)

Marissa Jones is the president and CEO of Sound's Alive, a company that manufactures and sells a line of speakers, CD players, receivers, high-definition televisions, and other items geared for the home entertainment market. Respected throughout the industry for bringing many high-quality, innovative products to market, Marissa is considering adding a speaker system to her product line.

The speaker market has changed dramatically during the last several years. Originally, high-fidelity aficionados knew that to reproduce sound covering the fullest range of frequencies—from the lowest kettle drum to the highest violin—a speaker system had to be large and heavy. The speaker had various drivers: a woofer to reproduce the low notes, a tweeter for the high notes, and a mid-range driver for the broad spectrum of frequencies in between. Many speaker systems had a minimum of three drivers, but some had even more. The trouble was that such a system was too large for anything but the biggest rooms, and consumers were reluctant to spend thousands of dollars and give up valuable wall space to get the excellent sound these speakers could reproduce.

The trend has changed during the past several years. Consumers still want good sound, but they want it from smaller boxes. Therefore, the satellite system became popular. Consisting of two small boxes that house either one driver (to cover the mid-range and high frequencies) or two (a mid-range and tweeter), a satellite system can be mounted easily on walls or shelves. To reproduce the low notes, a separate subwoofer that is approximately the size of a cube 18 inches on a side also is needed. This subwoofer can be placed anywhere in the room. Taking up less space than a typical large speaker system and sounding almost as good, yet costing hundreds of dollars less, these satellite systems are hot items in the high-fidelity market.

Recently, the separate wings of home entertainment—high fidelity (receivers, speakers, CD players, CDs, cassettes, and so on), television (large screen monitors, video cassette recorders, laser players), and computers (games with sounds, virtual reality software, and so on)—have merged into the home theater concept. To simulate the movie environment, a home theater system requires the traditional stereo speaker system plus additional speakers placed in the rear of the room so that viewers are literally surrounded with sound. Although the rear speakers do not have to match the high quality of the front speakers and, therefore, can be less expensive, most consumers choose a system in which the front and rear speakers are of equal quality, reproducing the full range of frequencies with equal fidelity.

This is the speaker market that Marissa wants to enter. She is considering having Sound's Alive manufacture and sell a home theater system that consists of seven speakers. Three small speakers—each with one dome tweeter that could reproduce the frequency range of 200 Hertz to 20,000 Hertz (upper-low frequencies to the highest frequencies)—would be placed in front, and three similar speakers would be placed strategically around the sides and back of the room. To reproduce the lowest frequencies (from 35 Hertz to 200 Hertz), a single subwoofer also would be part of the system. This subwoofer is revolutionary because it is smaller than the ordinary subwoofer, only 10 inches per side, and it has a built-in amplifier to power it. Consumers and critics are thrilled with the music from early prototype systems, claiming that these speakers have the best balance of sound and size. Marissa is extremely encouraged by these early reviews, and although her company has never produced a product with its house label on it (having always sold systems from established high-fidelity companies), she believes that Sound's Alive should enter the home theater market with this product.

Phase One: Projecting Profits

Marissa decides to create a spreadsheet that will project profits over the next several years. After consulting with economists, market analysts, employees in her own company, and employees from other companies that sell house brand components, Marissa is confident that the gross revenues for these speakers in 2007 would be around $6 million. She also must figure that a small percentage of speakers will be damaged in transit, or some will be returned by dissatisfied customers shortly after the sales. These returns and allowances (R&As) usually are calculated as 2% of the gross revenues. Hence, the net revenues are simply the gross revenues minus the R&As. Marissa believes that the 2007 labor costs for these speakers will be $995,100. The cost of materials (including boxes to ship the speakers) should be $915,350 for 2007. Finally, her overhead costs (rent, lighting, heating in winter, air conditioning in summer, security, and so on) for 2007 should be $1,536,120. Thus, the cost of goods sold is the sum of labor, material, and overhead costs. Marissa figures the gross profit as the difference between the net revenues and the cost of goods sold. In addition, she must consider the selling, general, and administrative (SG&A) expenses. These expenses are more difficult to estimate, but the standard industry practice is to use 18% of the net revenues as the nominal percentage value for these expenses. Therefore, Marissa's profit *before taxes* is the gross profit minus the SG&A value. To calculate taxes, Marissa multiplies her profits before taxes times the tax rate, currently 30%. If her company is operating at a loss, however, no taxes would have to be paid. Finally, Marissa's net (or after tax) profit is simply the difference between the profit before taxes and the actual taxes paid.

To determine the numbers for 2008 through 2010, Marissa assumes that gross revenues, labor costs, material costs, and overhead costs will increase over the years. Although the rates of increase for these items are difficult to estimate, Marissa figures that gross revenues will increase by 9% per year, labor costs will increase by 4% per year, material costs will increase by 6% per year, and overhead costs will increase by 3% per year. She figures that the tax rate will not change from the 30% mark, and she assumes that the SG&A value will remain at 18%.

FIGURE 12.54

Spreadsheet template for the Sound's Alive case

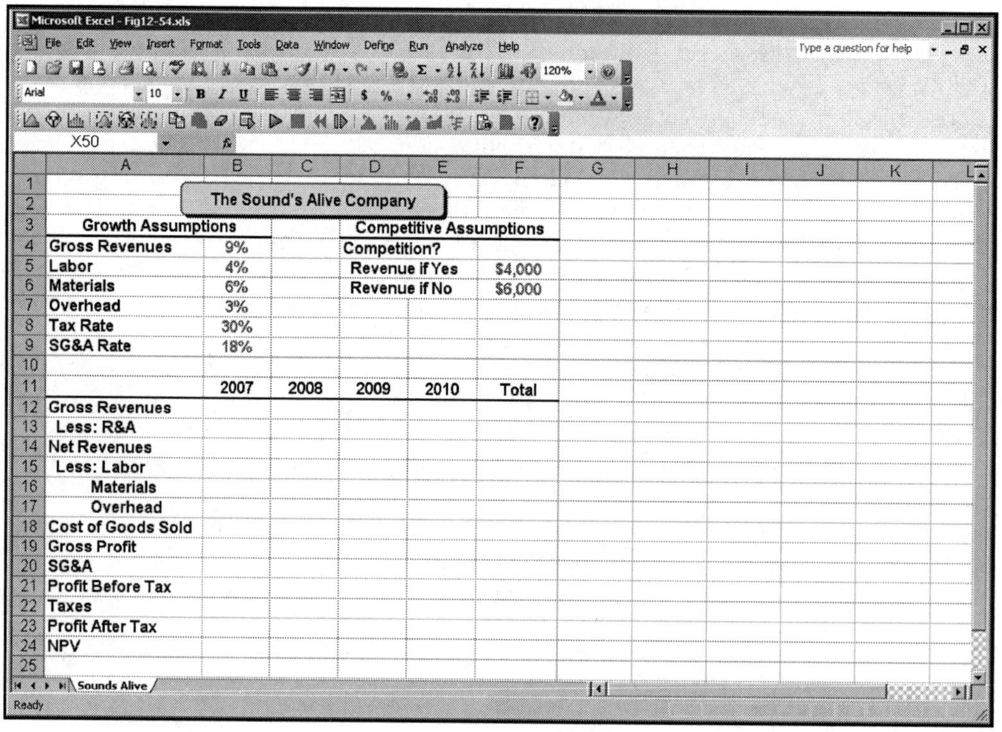

	A	B	C	D	E	F
1						
2		The Sound's Alive Company				
3	Growth Assumptions			Competitive Assumptions		
4	Gross Revenues	9%		Competition?		
5	Labor	4%		Revenue if Yes		$4,000
6	Materials	6%		Revenue if No		$6,000
7	Overhead	3%				
8	Tax Rate	30%				
9	SG&A Rate	18%				
10						
11		2007	2008	2009	2010	Total
12	Gross Revenues					
13	Less: R&A					
14	Net Revenues					
15	Less: Labor					
16	Materials					
17	Overhead					
18	Cost of Goods Sold					
19	Gross Profit					
20	SG&A					
21	Profit Before Tax					
22	Taxes					
23	Profit After Tax					
24	NPV					
25						

The basic layout of the spreadsheet that Marissa creates is shown in Figure 12-54 (and in the file Fig12-54.xls on your data disk). (Ignore the Competitive Assumptions section for now; we will consider it later.) Construct the spreadsheet, determine the values for the years 2007 through 2010, and then determine the totals for the four years.

Marissa not only wants to determine her net profits for 2007 through 2010, she also must justify her decisions to the company's Board of Trustees. Should she even consider entering this market, from a financial point of view? One way to answer this question is to find the net present value (NPV) of the net profits for 2007 through 2010. Use Excel's NPV capability to find the NPV, at the current interest rate of 5%, of the profit values for 2007 through 2010.

To avoid large values in the spreadsheet, enter all dollar calculations in thousands. For example, enter labor costs as 995.10 and overhead costs as 1536.12.

Phase Two: Bringing Competition into the Model

With her spreadsheet complete, Marissa is confident that entering the home theater speaker market would be lucrative for Sound's Alive. However, she has not considered one factor in her calculations—competition. The current market leader and company she is most concerned about is the Bose Corporation. Bose pioneered the concept of a satellite speaker system, and its AMT series is very successful. Marissa is concerned that Bose will enter the home market, cutting into her gross revenues. If Bose does enter the market, Marissa believes that Sound's Alive still would make money; however, she would have to revise her gross revenues estimate from $6 million to $4 million for 2007.

To account for the competition factor, Marissa revises her spreadsheet by adding a Competitive Assumptions section. Cell F4 will contain either a 0 (no competition) or a 1 (if Bose enters the market). Cells F5 and F6 provide the gross revenue estimates (in thousands of dollars) for the two possibilities. Modify your spreadsheet to take these options into account. Use the IF( ) function for the gross revenues for 2007 (cell B12). If Bose does enter the market, not only would Marissa's gross revenues be lower, but the labor, materials, and overhead costs also would be lower because Sound's Alive would be making and selling fewer speakers. Marissa thinks that if Bose enters the market, her 2007 labor costs would be $859,170; 2007 material costs would be $702,950; and 2007 overhead costs would be $1,288,750. She believes that her growth rate assumptions would stay the same whether or not Bose enters the market. Add these possible values to your spreadsheet using the IF( ) function in the appropriate cells.

Look at the net profits for 2007 through 2010. In particular, examine the NPV for the two scenarios: Bose does or does not enter the home theater speaker market.

Phase Three: Bringing Uncertainty into the Model

Jim Allison, the chief of operations at Sound's Alive and a quantitative methods specialist, plays a key role in providing Marissa with estimates for the various revenues and costs. He is uneasy about the basic estimates for the growth rates. For example, although market research indicates that a 9% gross revenue increase per year is reasonable, Jim knows that if this value is 7%, for example, the profit values and the NPV would be quite different. Even more troublesome is a potential tax increase, which would hit Sound's Alive hard. Jim believes that the tax rate could vary around the expected 30% figure. Finally, Jim is uncomfortable with the industry's standard estimate of 18% for the SG&A rate. Jim thinks that this value could be higher or even lower.

The Sound's Alive problem is too complicated for solving with what-if analysis because seven assumed values could change: the growth rates for gross revenues, labor, materials, overhead costs, tax rate, SG&A percent, and whether or not Bose enters the market. Jim believes that a Monte Carlo simulation would be a better approach. Jim thinks that the behavior of these variables can be modeled as follows:

Gross Revenues (%): normally distributed, mean = 9.9, std dev = 1.4

Labor Growth (%): normally distributed, mean = 3.45, std dev = 1.0

Materials (%)	Probability
4	0.10
5	0.15
6	0.15
7	0.25
8	0.25
9	0.10

Overhead (%)	Probability
2	0.20
3	0.35
4	0.25
5	0.20

Tax Rate (%)	Probability
30	0.15
32	0.30
34	0.30
36	0.25

SG&A (%)	Probability
15	0.05
16	0.10
17	0.20
18	0.25
19	0.20
20	0.20

Finally, Jim and Marissa agree that there is a 50/50 chance that Bose will enter the market.

a. Use simulation to analyze the Sound's Alive problem. Based on your results, what is the expected net profit for the years 2007 through 2010, and what is the expected NPV for this business venture?

b. The Board of Trustees told Marissa that the stockholders would feel comfortable with this business venture if its NPV is at least $5 million. What are the chances that Sound's Alive home theater venture will result in an NPV of $5 million or more?

CASE 12.4   The Foxridge Investment Group

(Inspired by a case written by MBA students Fred Hirsch and Ray Rogers for Professor Larry Weatherford at the University of Wyoming.)

The Foxridge Investment Group buys and sells rental income properties in Southwest Virginia. Bill Hunter, president of Foxridge, has asked for your assistance in analyzing a small apartment building the group is interested in purchasing.

The property in question is a small two-story structure with three rental units on each floor. The purchase price of the property is $170,000 representing $30,000 in land value and $140,000 in buildings and improvements. Foxridge will depreciate the buildings and improvements value on a straight-line basis over 27.5 years. The Foxridge Group will make a down payment of $40,000 to acquire the property and finance the remainder of the purchase price over 20 years with an 11% fixed-rate loan with payments due annually. Figure 12.55 (and the file Fig12-55.xls on your data disk) summarizes this and other pertinent information.

FIGURE 12.55

Assumptions for the Foxridge Investment Group

Foxridge Investment Group	
Acquisition Data	
Land Value	$30,000
Buildings/Improvements	$140,000
Purchase Price	$170,000
Financing Data	
Down Payment	$40,000
Amount Financed	$130,000
APR	11.0%
Term	20
Annual Payment	$16,325
Economic Assumptions	
Annual Gross Rental Income	$35,000
Rental Income Growth Rate	4.0%
V&C Allowance	3.0%
Operating Expenses	45.0%
Tax Rate	28.0%
Property Value Growth Rate	2.5%
Sales Commission	5.0%
Discount Rate	12.0%

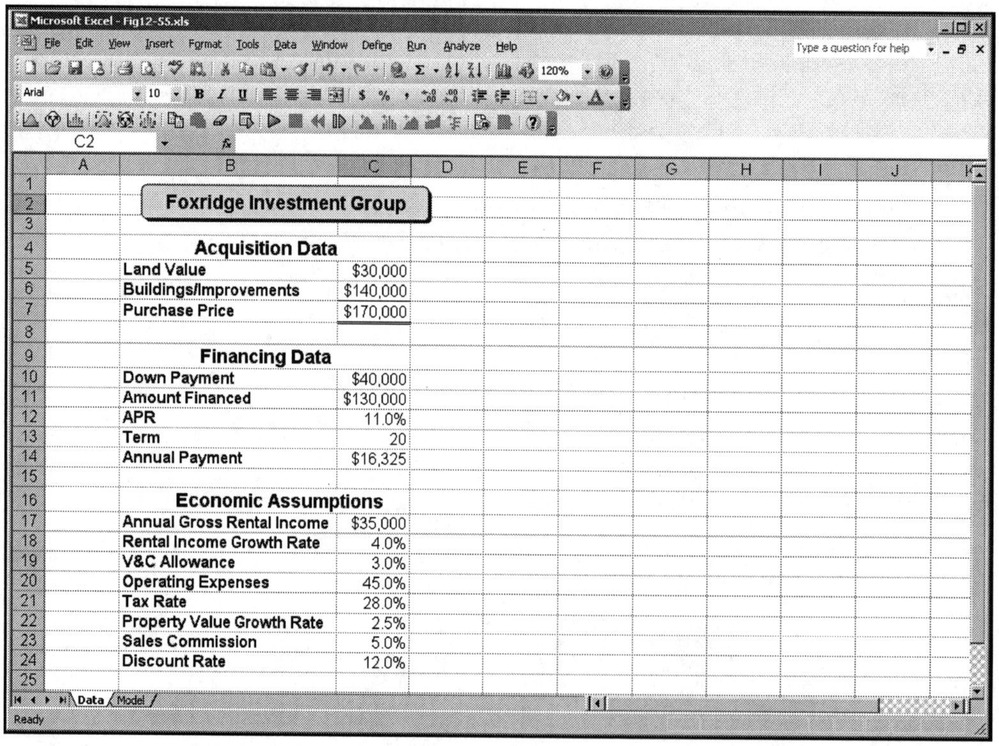

If all units are fully occupied, Mr. Hunter expects the property to generate rental income of $35,000 in the first year and expects to increase the rent at the rate of inflation (currently 4%). Because vacancies occur and some residents might not always be able to pay their rent, Mr. Hunter factors in a 3% vacancy & collection (V&C) allowance against rental income. Operating expenses are expected to be approximately 45% of rental income. The group's marginal tax rate is 28%.

If the group decides to purchase this property, their plan is to hold it for five years and then sell it to another investor. Presently, property values in this area are increasing at a rate of approximately 2.5% per year. The group will have to pay a sales commission of 5% of the gross selling price when they sell the property.

Figure 12.56 shows a spreadsheet model that Mr. Hunter developed to analyze this problem. This model first uses the data and assumptions given in Figure 12.55 to generate the expected net cash flows in each of the next five years. It then provides a final summary of the proceeds expected from selling the property at the end of five years. The total net present value (NPV) of the project is then calculated in cell I18 using the discount rate of 12% in cell C24 of Figure 12.55. Thus, after discounting all the future cash flows associated with this investment by 12% per year, the investment still generates an NPV of $2,007.

Although the group has been using this type of analysis for many years to make investment decisions, one of Mr. Hunter's investment partners recently read an article in the *Wall Street Journal* about risk analysis and simulation using spreadsheets. As a result, the partner realizes that there is quite a bit of uncertainty associated with many of the economic assumptions shown in Figure 12.55. After explaining the potential problem to Mr. Hunter, the two have decided to apply simulation to this model before making a decision. Because neither of them know how to do simulation, they have asked for your assistance.

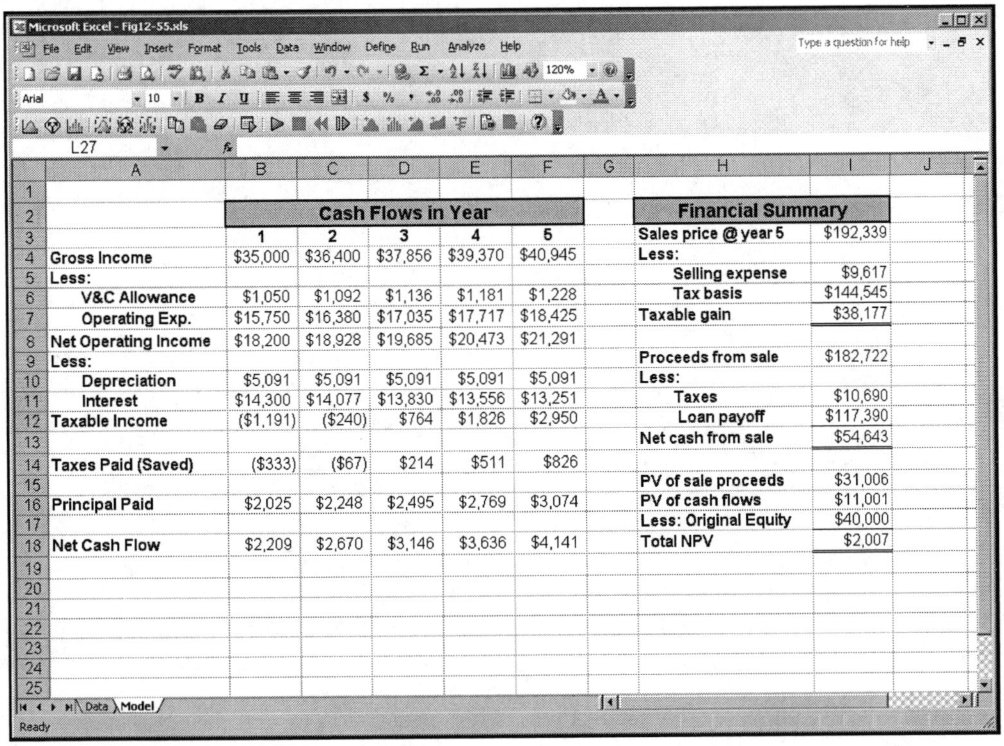

Cash Flows in Year	1	2	3	4	5
Gross Income	$35,000	$36,400	$37,856	$39,370	$40,945
Less:					
V&C Allowance	$1,050	$1,092	$1,136	$1,181	$1,228
Operating Exp.	$15,750	$16,380	$17,035	$17,717	$18,425
Net Operating Income	$18,200	$18,928	$19,685	$20,473	$21,291
Less:					
Depreciation	$5,091	$5,091	$5,091	$5,091	$5,091
Interest	$14,300	$14,077	$13,830	$13,556	$13,251
Taxable Income	($1,191)	($240)	$764	$1,826	$2,950
Taxes Paid (Saved)	($333)	($67)	$214	$511	$826
Principal Paid	$2,025	$2,248	$2,495	$2,769	$3,074
Net Cash Flow	$2,209	$2,670	$3,146	$3,636	$4,141

Financial Summary	
Sales price @ year 5	$192,339
Less:	
Selling expense	$9,617
Tax basis	$144,545
Taxable gain	$38,177
Proceeds from sale	$182,722
Less:	
Taxes	$10,690
Loan payoff	$117,390
Net cash from sale	$54,643
PV of sale proceeds	$31,006
PV of cash flows	$11,001
Less: Original Equity	$40,000
Total NPV	$2,007

FIGURE 12.56

Cash flow and financial summary for the Foxridge Investment Group

To model the uncertainty in this decision problem, Mr. Hunter and his partner have decided that the growth in rental income from one year to the next could vary uniformly from 2% to 6% in years 2 through 5. Similarly, they believe that the V&C allowance in any year could be as low as 1% and as high as 5%, with 3% being the most likely outcome. They think that the operating expenses in each year should be normally distributed with a mean of 45% and standard deviation of 2% but never should be less than 40% and never greater than 50% of gross income. Finally, they believe that the property value growth rate could be as small as 1% or as large as 5%, with 2.5% being the most likely outcome.

a. Revise the spreadsheets shown in Figures 12.55 and 12.56 to reflect the uncertainties outlined.

b. Construct a 95% confidence interval for the average total NPV that the Foxridge Investment Group can expect if they undertake this project. (Use 500 replications.) Interpret this confidence interval.

c. Based on your analysis, what is the probability of this project generating a positive total NPV if the group uses a 12% discount rate?

d. Suppose the investors are willing to buy the property if the expected total NPV is greater than zero. Based on your analysis, should they buy this property?

e. Assume that the investors decide to increase the discount rate to 14% and repeat questions 2, 3, and 4.

f. What discount rate results in a 90% chance of the project generating a positive total NPV?

Chapter 13

Queuing Theory

13.0 Introduction

Sometimes it seems as if we spend most of our lives waiting in lines. We wait in lines at grocery stores, banks, airports, hotels, restaurants, theaters, theme parks, post offices, and traffic lights. At home, we are likely to spend time waiting in an "electronic line" if we use the telephone to order merchandise from mail-order firms, or to call the customer service number of most computer hardware or software companies.

Some reports indicate that Americans spend 37 *billion* hours a year waiting in lines. Much of this time represents a loss of a limited resource (time) that can never be recovered. Add the frustration and irritation that many people experience while waiting in lines, and it is easy to see why businesses should be interested in reducing or eliminating the amount of time their customers spend waiting in lines.

Waiting lines do not always contain people. In a manufacturing company, subassemblies often wait in a line at machining centers to have the next operation performed on them. At a video rental store, returned videos often wait to be placed on shelves so they can be rented again. Electronic messages on the Internet sometimes wait at intermediate computing centers before they are sent to their final destinations. Costs could be reduced, or customer service improved, by reducing the amount of time that the subassemblies, videos, or electronic messages spend waiting in line.

In management science terminology, the term queuing theory represents the body of knowledge dealing with waiting lines. Queuing theory was conceived in the early 1900s when a Danish telephone engineer named A. K. Erlang began studying the congestion and waiting times occurring in the completion of telephone calls. Since then, several quantitative models have been developed to help business people understand waiting lines and make better decisions about how to manage them. This chapter introduces some of these models and discusses other issues involved in queuing theory.

13.1 The Purpose of Queuing Models

Most queuing problems focus on determining the level of service that a company should provide. For example, grocery stores must determine how many cash registers to operate at a given time of day so that customers do not have to wait too long to check out. Banks must determine how many tellers to schedule at various times of day to maintain an acceptable level of service. Companies that lease copying machines must determine the number of technicians to employ so that repairs can be made in a timely manner.

In many queuing problems, management has some control over the level of service provided. In the examples just mentioned, customer waiting times could be kept to a

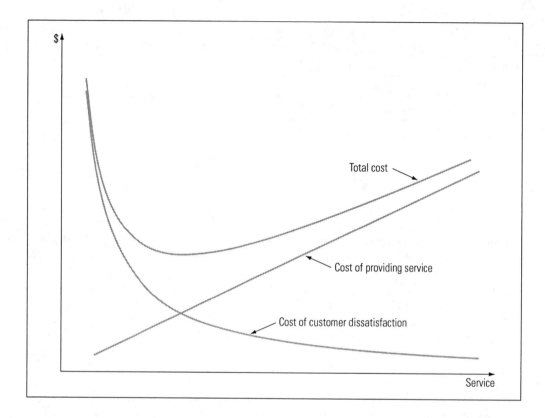

minimum by employing a large number of servers (in the form of cashiers, tellers, and technicians). However, this can be expensive, or actually wasteful, if an excessive number of idle servers is maintained. On the other hand, employing a small number of servers keeps the cost of providing service low, but is likely to result in longer customer waiting times and greater customer dissatisfaction. Thus, a trade-off exists between the cost of providing service and the cost of having dissatisfied customers if service is lacking. The nature of this trade-off is illustrated in Figure 13.1.

Figure 13.1 indicates that as service levels increase, the cost of providing service also increases, but the cost of customer dissatisfaction decreases (as does the length of time customers must wait for service). As service levels decrease, the cost of providing service also decreases, but the cost of customer dissatisfaction increases. The objective in many queuing problems is to find the optimal service level that achieves an acceptable balance between the cost of providing service and customer satisfaction.

13.2 Queuing System Configurations

The queuing systems we encounter in everyday life are configured in a variety of ways. Three typical configurations are illustrated in Figure 13.2.

The first configuration in Figure 13.2 represents a single-queue, single-server system. In this configuration, customers enter the system and wait in line on a first-in, first-out (FIFO) basis until they receive service; then they exit the system. This type of queuing system is employed at most Wendy's and Taco Bell restaurants. You also might encounter this type of queuing system at some automatic teller machines (ATMs).

The second configuration in Figure 13.2 represents a single-queue, multi-server system. Here again, customers enter the system and join a FIFO queue. Upon reaching the

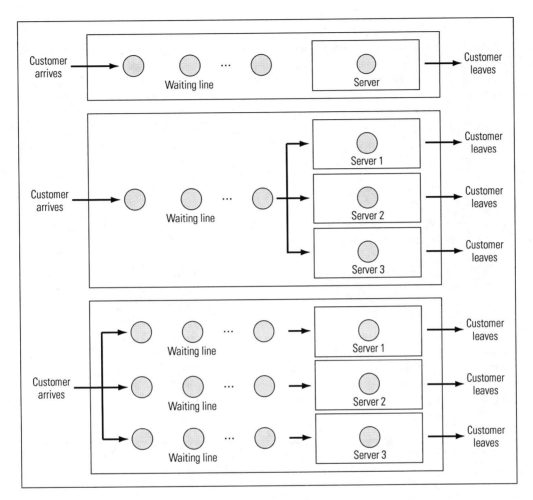

FIGURE 13.2

Examples of different queuing system configurations

front of the line, a customer is serviced by the next available server. The example shows three servers, but there could be more or fewer servers depending on the problem at hand. This type of queuing system is found at most airport check-in counters, post offices, and banks.

The third configuration in Figure 13.2 represents a collection of single-queue, single-server systems. In this type of arrangement, when customers arrive, they must choose one of the queues and then wait in that line to receive service. This type of system is found at most grocery stores and most Burger King and McDonald's restaurants.

This chapter discusses queuing models that can be used to analyze the first two types of configurations shown in Figure 13.2. In some cases, the individual queues in the third configuration in Figure 13.2 can be analyzed as independent, single-queue, single-server systems. Thus, the results presented for the first type of configuration can sometimes be generalized to analyze the third configuration also.

13.3 Characteristics of Queuing Systems

To create and analyze mathematical models of the queuing configurations shown in Figure 13.2, we must make some assumptions about the way in which customers arrive to the system and the amount of time it takes for them to receive service.

13.3.1 ARRIVAL RATE

In most queuing systems, customers (or jobs in a manufacturing environment) arrive in a somewhat random fashion. That is, the number of arrivals that occurs in a given time period represents a random variable. It is often appropriate to model the arrival process in a queuing system as a Poisson random variable. To use the Poisson probability distribution, we must specify a value for the arrival rate, denoted as λ, representing the average number of arrivals per time period. (For a Poisson random variable, the variance of the number of arrivals per time period is also λ.) The probability of x arrivals in a specific time period is represented by:

$$P(x) = \frac{\lambda^x e^{-\lambda}}{x!} \quad \text{for } x = 0, 1, 2, \ldots \qquad \textbf{13.1}$$

where e represents the base of the natural logarithm ($e = 2.71828$) and $x! = (x)(x - 1)(x - 2) \ldots (2)(1)$. ($x!$ is referred to as x factorial and can be calculated using the FACT( ) function in Excel.)

For example, suppose that calls to the customer service hotline of a computer retailer occur at a rate of five per hour and follow a Poisson probability distribution ($\lambda = 5$). The probability distribution associated with the number of calls arriving in a given hour is illustrated in Figure 13.3 (and in the file Fig13-3.xls on your data disk).

In Figure 13.3, the values in column B represent the probabilities associated with each value in column A. For example, the value in cell B5 indicates that a 0.0067 probability exists of 0 calls arriving in a given hour; cell B6 indicates that a 0.0337 probability exists of one call arriving, and so on. The histogram of the probability distribution indicates that, on average, we can expect approximately five calls to arrive in one hour. However,

FIGURE 13.3

Example of a Poisson probability distribution with mean $\lambda = 5$

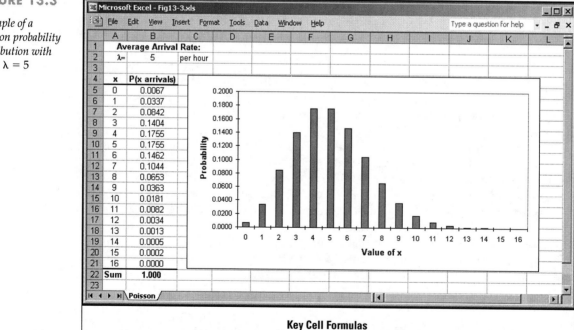

Key Cell Formulas		
Cell	**Formula**	**Copied to**
B5	=($B$2^A5*EXP(-$B$2))/FACT(A5)	B6:B21

because the Poisson distribution is skewed to the right, a significantly larger number of calls (in this case, 13 or more) could arrive in some one-hour time periods.

Figure 13.3 indicates that the probability of six calls occurring in a given hour is 0.1462. However, the six calls probably will not occur all at the same time. Some random amount of time is likely to transpire between arriving calls. This time between arrivals is known as the interarrival time. If the number of arrivals in a given period of time follows a Poisson distribution with mean λ, it can be shown that the interarrival times follow an exponential probability distribution with mean $1/\lambda$.

For example, if calls to the computer retailer's hotline follow a Poisson distribution and occur at an average rate of $\lambda = 5$ per hour, the interarrival times follow an exponential distribution with an average interarrival time of $1/5 = 0.2$ hours. That is, calls occur once every 12 minutes on average (because there are 60 minutes in an hour and 0.2×60 minutes $= 12$ minutes).

The exponential distribution plays a key role in queuing models. It is one of the few probability distributions that exhibits the memoryless (or lack of memory) property. An arrival process is memoryless if the time until the next arrival occurs does not depend on how much time has elapsed since the last arrival. The Russian mathematician Markov was the first to recognize the memoryless property of certain random variables. Therefore, the memoryless property is also sometimes referred to as the Markov or Markovian property.

All the queuing models presented in this chapter assume that arrivals follow a Poisson distribution (or, equivalently, that interarrival times follow an exponential distribution). To use these models, it is important to verify that this assumption is valid for the queuing system being modeled. One way to verify that arrivals can be approximated by the Poisson distribution is to collect data on the number of arrivals occurring per time period for several hours, days, or weeks. The average number of arrivals per time period can be calculated from these data and used as an estimate of λ. A histogram of the actual data can be constructed and compared to a histogram of the actual probabilities expected of a Poisson random variable with mean λ. If the histograms are similar, it is reasonable to assume that the arrival process is approximately Poisson. (Additional goodness-of-fit tests can be found in most texts on queuing and simulation.)

13.3.2 SERVICE RATE

A customer who arrives at a service facility spends some amount of time (possibly 0) waiting in line for service to begin. We refer to this time as queue time. Service time is the amount of time a customer spends at a service facility once the actual performance of service begins. (So service time *does not* include queue time.)

It is often appropriate to model the service times in a queuing system as an exponential random variable. To use the exponential probability distribution for this purpose, we must specify a value for the service rate, denoted by μ, representing the average number of customers (or jobs) that can be served per time period. The average service time per customer is $1/\mu$ time periods (and the variance of the service time per customer is $(1/\mu)^2$ time periods). Because the exponential distribution is continuous, the probability of an exponential random variable equaling any specific value is zero. Thus, probabilities associated with an exponential random variable must be defined in terms of intervals. If the distribution of service times follows an exponential distribution, the probability that the service time T of a given customer will be between t_1 and t_2 time periods is defined by:

$$P(t_1 \leq T \leq t_2) = \int_{t_1}^{t_2} \mu e^{-\mu x} dx = e^{-\mu t_1} - e^{-\mu t_2}, \quad \text{for } t_1 \leq t_2 \qquad \textbf{13.2}$$

FIGURE 13.4

Example of an exponential distribution with μ = 7

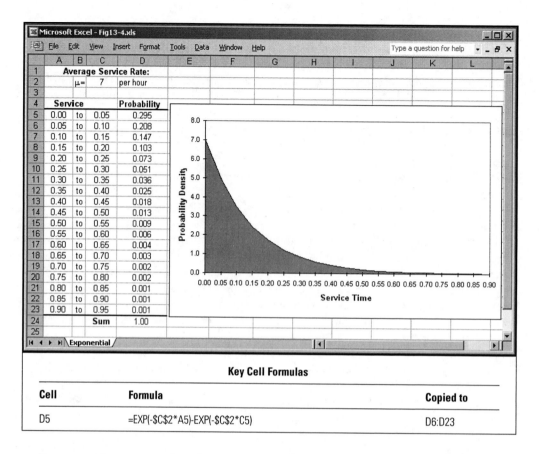

Key Cell Formulas		
Cell	**Formula**	**Copied to**
D5	=EXP(-$C$2*A5)-EXP(-$C$2*C5)	D6:D23

For example, suppose that the operator on the customer service hotline can service calls at a rate of seven per hour, on average, and that the service times follow an exponential distribution ($\mu = 7$). Figure 13.4 (and the file Fig13-4.xls on your data disk) shows the probability of the service time falling within several time intervals.

In Figure 13.4, the value in cell D5 indicates that a 0.295 probability exists that it will take from 0 to 0.05 hours (or 3 minutes) to service any call. Similarly, the value in cell D9 indicates that a 0.073 probability exists that it will take between 0.2 and 0.25 hours (or from 12 to 15 minutes) to service any call.

The data and graph in Figure 13.4 indicate that for exponential distributions, shorter service times have the largest relative probability of occurring. In reality, some minimal amount of time is usually required to provide most services. This might lead us to believe that the exponential distribution would tend to underestimate the actual service time required by most customers. However, the exponential distribution also assumes that some very long service times will occur (though very infrequently). The possibility of these very long (but infrequent) service times provides a balance to the very short (but frequent) service times so that, on average, the exponential distribution provides a reasonably accurate description of the behavior of service times in many real-world problems. But keep in mind that the exponential distribution is not an adequate model of service times in all applications.

One way to verify that the service rate can be modeled using the exponential distribution is to collect data on the service times occurring per time period for several hours, days, or weeks. The average number of customers serviced per time period can be calculated from these data and used as an estimate of the service rate μ. Using actual data, a relative frequency distribution of the service times falling within various intervals can be constructed and compared to the distribution of the actual probabilities expected for each interval for an exponential random variable with a service rate of μ (like the one shown in Figure 13.4). If the distributions are similar, it is reasonable to assume that the distribution of service times is approximately exponential. (Again, additional goodness-of-fit tests can be found in most texts on queuing and simulation.)

13.4 Kendall Notation

Given the variety of queuing models that exist, a system known as Kendall notation was developed to allow the key characteristics of a specific queuing model to be described in an efficient manner. With Kendall notation, simple queuing models can be described by three characteristics in the following general format:

$$1/2/3$$

The first characteristic identifies the nature of the arrival process using the following standard abbreviations:

M = Markovian interarrival times (following an exponential distribution)

D = deterministic interarrival times (not random)

The second characteristic identifies the nature of the service times using the following standard abbreviations:

M = Markovian service times (following an exponential distribution)

G = general service times (following a nonexponential distribution)

D = deterministic service times (not random)

Finally, the third characteristic indicates the number of servers available. So, using Kendall notation, an M/M/1 queue refers to a queuing model in which the time between arrivals follows an exponential distribution, the service times follow an exponential distribution, and there is one server. An M/G/3 queue refers to a model in which the interarrival times are assumed to be exponential, the service times follow some general distribution, and three servers are present.

An expanded version of Kendall notation involves specifying six (rather than three) queue characteristics. A more complete description of this notation can be found in advanced management science or queuing texts.

13.5 Queuing Models

Numerous queuing models are available to evaluate different combinations of arrival distributions, service time distributions, and other queuing characteristics. This chapter discusses only a few of these models. Typical operating characteristics of interest include:

Characteristic	Description
U	Utilization factor, or the percentage of time that all servers are busy
P_0	Probability that there are no units in the system
L_q	Average number of units in line waiting for service
L	Average number of units in the system (in line and being served)
W_q	Average time a unit spends in line waiting for service
W	Average time a unit spends in the system (in line and being served)
P_w	Probability that an arriving unit has to wait for service
P_n	Probability of n units in the system

Information about these operating characteristics can be helpful to managers who need to make decisions about the trade-offs between the costs of providing different levels of service and the associated impact on customers' experiences in the queuing system. Where possible, researchers have derived closed-form equations to calculate various operating characteristics of a particular queuing model. For instance, for the M/M/1 queuing model it can be shown that:

$$W = \frac{1}{\mu - \lambda}$$

$$L = \lambda W$$

$$W_q = W - \frac{1}{\mu}$$

$$L_q = \lambda W_q$$

This chapter does not show the derivation of the equations used to calculate operating characteristics. Rather, it simply states the equations for several common queuing models and shows how they can be used. The equations for the queuing models we will consider are implemented in spreadsheet templates in the file Q.xls on your data disk. Figure 13.5 shows the introduction screen for these templates.

As Figure 13.5 indicates, the templates in this file can be used to analyze four types of queuing models: the M/M/s model, the M/M/s model with finite queue length, the M/M/s model with finite arrival population, and the M/G/1 model.

13.6 The M/M/s Model

The M/M/s model is appropriate for analyzing queuing problems where the following assumptions are met:

- There are *s* servers, where *s* is a positive integer.
- Arrivals follow a Poisson distribution and occur at an average rate of λ per time period.

FIGURE 13.5

Introductory screen for Q.xls queuing template file

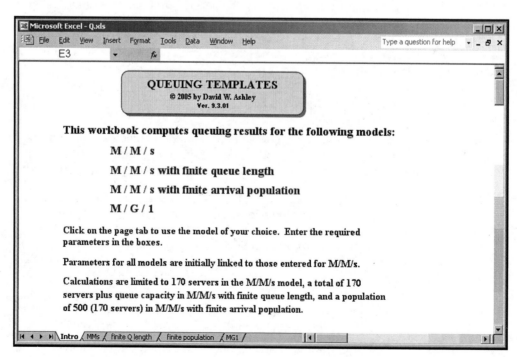

- Each server provides service at an average rate of μ per time period, and actual service times follow an exponential distribution.
- Arrivals wait in a single FIFO queue and are serviced by the first available server.
- $\lambda < s\mu$

The final assumption indicates that the total service capacity of the system, $s\mu$, must be strictly greater than the rate at which arrivals occur λ. If the arrival rate exceeds the system's total service capacity, the system would fill up over time and the queue would become infinitely long. In fact, the queue becomes infinitely long even if the average arrival rate λ is equal to the average service rate $s\mu$. To see why, note that individual arrival times and service times vary in an unpredictable manner (even though their averages may be constant). So there will be times when the servers are idle. This idle time is lost forever and the servers will not be able to make up for this at other times when the demand for service is heavy. (Note that demand is never lost forever but is assumed to wait patiently in the queue.) This causes the servers to fall hopelessly behind if $\lambda \geq s\mu$.

The formulas describing the operating characteristics of the M/M/s model are given in Figure 13.6. Although these formulas might seem somewhat daunting, they are easy to use when implemented in a spreadsheet template.

13.6.1 AN EXAMPLE

The following example illustrates how the M/M/s model might be used.

The customer support hotline for Bitway Computers is currently staffed by a single technician. Calls arrive randomly at a rate of five per hour and follow a Poisson distribution. The technician can service calls at an average rate of seven per hour, but

FIGURE 13.6

Formulas describing the operating characteristics of an M/M/s queue

$$U = \lambda/(s\mu)$$

$$P_0 = \left(\sum_{n=0}^{s-1} \frac{(\lambda/\mu)^n}{n!} + \frac{(\lambda/\mu)^s}{s!} \left(\frac{s\mu}{s\mu - \lambda} \right) \right)^{-1}$$

$$L_q = \frac{P_0(\lambda/\mu)^{s+1}}{(s-1)!(s - \lambda/\mu)^2}$$

$$L = L_q + \frac{\lambda}{\mu}$$

$$W_q = \frac{L_q}{\lambda}$$

$$W = W_q + \frac{1}{\mu}$$

$$P_w = \frac{1}{s!} \left(\frac{\lambda}{\mu} \right)^s \left(\frac{s\mu}{s\mu - \lambda} \right) P_0$$

$$P_n = \begin{cases} \dfrac{(\lambda/\mu)^n}{n!} P_0, \text{ for } n \leq s \\ \dfrac{(\lambda/\mu)^n}{s!s^{(n-s)}} P_0, \text{ for } n > s \end{cases}$$

the actual time required to handle a given call is an exponential random variable. The president of Bitway, Rod Taylor, has received numerous complaints from customers about the length of time they must wait "on hold" for service when calling the hotline. Rod wants to determine the average length of time that customers currently wait before the technician answers their calls. If the average waiting time is more than five minutes, he wants to determine how many technicians would be required to reduce the average waiting time to two minutes or less.

13.6.2 THE CURRENT SITUATION

Because only one technician (or server) currently staffs Bitway's customer service hotline, we can calculate the operating characteristics for the hotline using an M/M/1 queuing model. Figure 13.7 shows the results of this model for Bitway's current configuration.

Cells E2, E3, and E4 contain the values for the arrival rate, service rate, and number of servers in our example problem, respectively. The various operating characteristics of this model are calculated automatically in column F.

The value in cell F12 indicates that a 0.7143 probability exists that callers to Bitway's customer service hotline must wait on hold before receiving service from the technician. The value in cell F10 indicates that the average length of this wait is 0.3571 hours (or approximately 21.42 minutes). The value in cell F11 indicates that, on average, a caller spends a total of 0.5 hours (or 30 minutes) waiting for service and being served under Bitway's current hotline configuration. Thus, it appears that the customer complaints to Bitway's president are justifiable.

13.6.3 ADDING A SERVER

To improve the level of service on the hotline, Bitway could investigate how the operating characteristics of the system would change if two technicians were assigned to

FIGURE 13.7

Results of the M/M/1 model for Bitway's customer service model

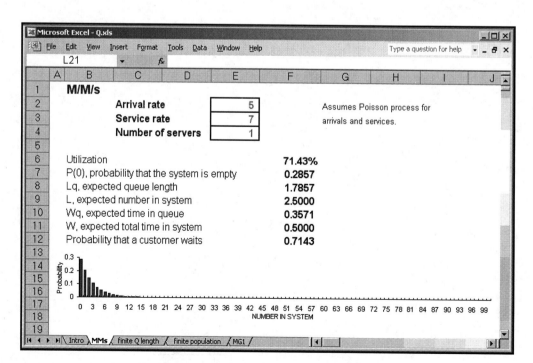

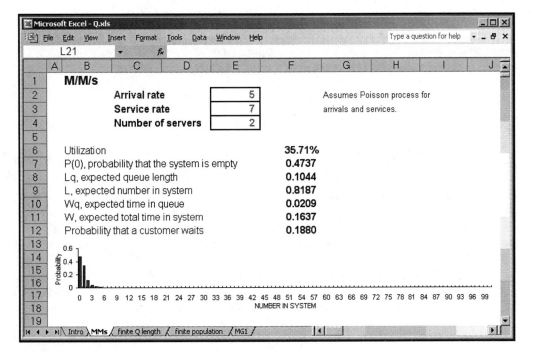

FIGURE 13.8

Results of the M/M/2 model for Bitway's customer service hotline

answer calls. That is, incoming calls could be handled by either one of two equally capable technicians. We can calculate the operating characteristics for this configuration using an M/M/2 queuing model, as shown in Figure 13.8.

The value in cell F12 indicates that, with two servers, the probability that a caller must wait before receiving service drops significantly from 0.7143 to 0.1880. Similarly, cell F10 indicates that the average amount of time a caller must wait before service begins drops to 0.0209 hours (or approximately 1.25 minutes). Thus, it seems that adding a second technician to the customer service hotline would achieve the two-minute average waiting time objective Rod wants.

Although the addition of a second server greatly reduces the average time hotline callers spend waiting for service to begin, it does not reduce the expected *service time*. For the M/M/1 model in Figure 13.7, which includes only one server, the expected total time in the system is 0.5 hours and the expected queue time is 0.3571 hours. This implies that the expected service time is $0.5 - 0.3571 = 0.1429$ hours. For the M/M/2 model in Figure 13.8, which includes two servers, the expected total time in the system is 0.1637 hours and the expected queue time is 0.0209 hours. This implies an expected service time of $0.1637 - 0.0209 = 0.1429$ hours (allowing for a slight rounding error). The M/M/2 model assumes that both servers can provide service at the same rate—in this case, an average of seven calls per hour. Therefore, the average service time per call should be $1/7 = 0.1429$ hours, which is consistent with the observed results.

13.6.4 ECONOMIC ANALYSIS

Bitway undoubtedly will incur some additional costs in going from one to two customer support technicians. This might include the cost of salary and benefits for the additional technician and perhaps an additional telephone line. However, the improved service level provided by the two-server system should reduce the number of customer complaints and perhaps lead to favorable word-of-mouth advertising and increased business for the company. Rod could attempt to quantify these benefits and compare them to the cost of adding a customer support technician. Alternatively, Rod simply might view the addition of the customer support technician as a competitive necessity.

13.7 The M/M/s Model with Finite Queue Length

The results for the M/M/s models in Figures 13.7 and 13.8 assume that the size or capacity of the waiting area is infinite, so that all arrivals to the system join the queue and wait for service. In some situations, however, the size or capacity of the waiting area might be restricted—in other words, there might be a finite queue length. The formulas describing the operating characteristics of an M/M/s queue with a finite queue length of K are summarized in Figure 13.9.

To see how this queuing model might be used, suppose that Bitway's telephone system can keep a maximum of five calls on hold at any point in time. If a new call is made to the hotline when five calls are already in the queue, the new call receives a busy signal. One way to reduce the number of calls encountering busy signals is to increase the number of calls that can be put on hold. However, if a call is answered only to be put on hold for a long time, the caller might find this more annoying than receiving a busy signal. Thus, Rod might want to investigate what effect adding a second technician to answer hotline calls would have on the number of calls receiving busy signals and on the average time callers must wait before receiving service.

FIGURE 13.9

Formulas describing the operating characteristics of an M/M/s queue with a finite queue length of K

$$U = (L - L_q)/s$$

$$P_0 = \left(1 + \sum_{n=1}^{s} \frac{(\lambda/\mu)^n}{n!} + \frac{(\lambda/\mu)^s}{s!} \sum_{n=s+1}^{K} \left(\frac{\lambda}{s\mu}\right)^{n-s}\right)^{-1}$$

$$P_n = \frac{(\lambda/\mu)^n}{n!} P_0, \text{ for } n = 1, 2, \ldots, s$$

$$P_n = \frac{(\lambda/\mu)^n}{s!s^{n-s}} P_0, \text{ for } n = s+1, s+2, \ldots, K$$

$$P_n = 0, \text{ for } n > K$$

$$L_q = \frac{P_0(\lambda/\mu)^s \rho}{s!(1-\rho)^2} (1 - \rho^{K-s} - (K-s)\rho^{K-s}(1-\rho)), \text{ where } \rho = \lambda/(s\mu)$$

$$L = \sum_{n=0}^{s-1} nP_n + L_q + s\left(1 - \sum_{n=0}^{s-1} P_n\right)$$

$$W_q = \frac{L_q}{\lambda(1 - P_K)}$$

$$W = \frac{L}{\lambda(1 - P_K)}$$

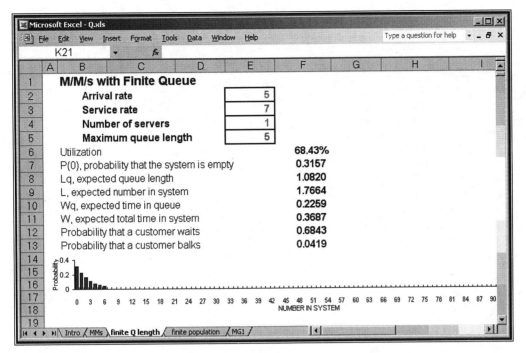

FIGURE 13.10

Results of the M/M/1 model with a finite queue length of five for Bitway's customer service hotline

13.7.1 THE CURRENT SITUATION

Because only one technician (or server) currently staffs Bitway's customer service hotline, we can calculate the current operating characteristics for the hotline using an M/M/1 queuing model with a finite queue length of 5. Figure 13.10 shows the results of this model for Bitway's current configuration.

Cells E2, E3, and E4 contain the values for the arrival rate, service rate, and number of servers in our example problem, respectively. Cell E5 contains the maximum queue length of five.

The value in cell F13 indicates that a 0.0419 probability exists that callers to Bitway's customer service hotline will balk (or, in this case, receive a busy signal). A balk refers to an arrival that does not join the queue because the queue is full or too long. The value in cell F10 indicates that the average length of this wait is 0.2259 hours (or approximately 13.55 minutes). The value in cell F11 indicates that, on average, a caller spends a total of 0.3687 hours (or 22.12 minutes) either waiting for service or being served under Bitway's current hotline configuration.

13.7.2 ADDING A SERVER

To improve the level of service on the hotline, Bitway could investigate how the operating characteristics of the system would change if two technicians were assigned to answer calls. We can calculate the operating characteristics for this configuration using an M/M/2 queuing model with a finite queue length of five, as shown in Figure 13.11.

The value in cell F13 indicates that, with two servers, the probability that a caller receives a busy signal drops to 0.0007. Similarly, cell F10 indicates that the average amount of time a caller must wait before service begins drops to 0.0204 hours (or approximately 1.22 minutes). Thus, it seems that adding a second technician to the customer service hotline would achieve the two-minute average waiting time objective Rod wants and

**FIGURE
13.11**

*Results of the
M/M/2 model with
a finite queue
length of five for
Bitway's customer
service hotline*

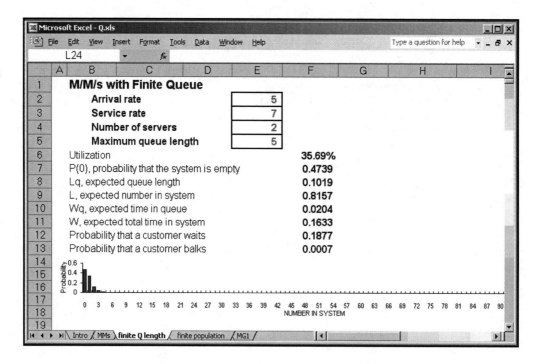

would virtually eliminate any chance of a customer receiving a busy signal. Here again, Rod should consider weighing the costs of adding the additional support technician against the benefits of eliminating the chances of customers receiving busy signals when they call the customer support hotline.

13.8 The M/M/s Model with Finite Population

The previous queuing models assume that the customers (or calls) arriving at the queuing system come from a population of potential customers that is infinite, or extremely large. Under this assumption, the mean arrival rate, λ, remains constant regardless of the number of calls in the system.

In some queuing problems, however, the possible number of arriving customers is finite. In other words, these queuing models have a finite arrival (or calling) population. In such a model, the average arrival rate for the system changes depending on the number of customers in the queue. The M/M/s model for finite arrival populations is appropriate for analyzing queuing problems where the following assumptions are met:

- There are s servers, where s is a positive integer.
- There are N potential customers in the arrival population.
- The arrival pattern of *each customer* follows a Poisson distribution with a mean arrival rate of λ per time period.
- Each server provides service at an average rate of μ per time period, and actual service times follow an exponential distribution.
- Arrivals wait in a single FIFO queue and are serviced by the first available server.

$$P_0 = \left(\sum_{n=0}^{s-1} \frac{N!}{(N-n)!n!} \left(\frac{\lambda}{\mu} \right)^n + \sum_{n=s}^{N} \frac{N!}{(N-n)!s!s^{n-s}} \left(\frac{\lambda}{\mu} \right)^n \right)^{-1}$$

$$P_n = \frac{N!}{(N-n)!n!} \left(\frac{\lambda}{\mu} \right)^n P_0, \text{ if } 0 < n \le s$$

$$P_n = \frac{N!}{(N-n)!s!s^{n-s}} \left(\frac{\lambda}{\mu} \right)^n P_0, \text{ if } s < n \le N$$

$$P_n = 0, \text{ if } n > N$$

$$L_q = \sum_{n=s}^{N} (n-s)P_n$$

$$L = \sum_{n=0}^{s-1} nP_n + L_q + s\left(1 - \sum_{n=0}^{s-1} P_n \right)$$

$$W_q = \frac{L_q}{\lambda(N-L)}$$

$$W = \frac{L}{\lambda(N-L)}$$

Note that the average arrival rate for this model (λ) is defined in terms of the rate at which *each customer* arrives. The formulas describing the operating characteristics for an M/M/s queue with a finite arrival population of size N are summarized in Figure 13.12.

13.8.1 AN EXAMPLE

One of the most common applications for the M/M/s model with a finite arrival population is the machine repair problem, as illustrated in the following example.

The Miller Manufacturing Company owns 10 identical machines that it uses in the production of colored nylon thread for the textile industry. Machine breakdowns occur following a Poisson distribution with an average of 0.01 breakdowns occurring per operating hour per machine. The company loses $100 each hour while a machine is inoperable. The company employs one technician to fix these machines when they break down. Service times to repair the machines are exponentially distributed with an average of eight hours per repair. Thus, service is performed at a rate of 1/8 machines per hour. Management wants to analyze what impact adding another service technician would have on the average length of time required to fix a machine when it breaks down. Service technicians are paid $20 per hour.

13.8.2 THE CURRENT SITUATION

The 10 machines in this problem represent a finite set of objects that can break down. Therefore, the M/M/s model for a finite calling operation is appropriate to use for

**FIGURE
13.13**

*Results of an
M/M/1 model with
a finite population
of 10 machines
for Miller
Manufacturing's
machine repair
problem*

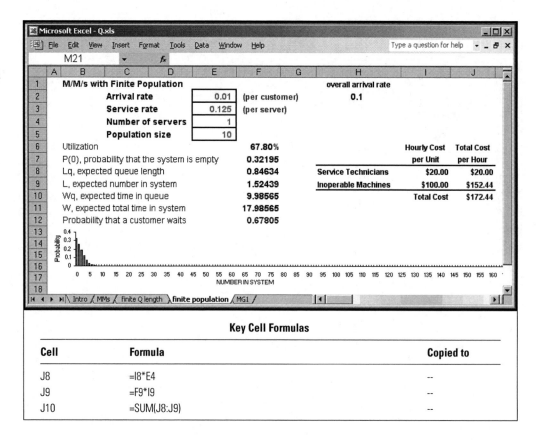

Cell	Formula	Copied to
Key Cell Formulas		
J8	=I8*E4	--
J9	=F9*I9	--
J10	=SUM(J8:J9)	--

analyzing this problem. The current operating characteristics for Miller Manufacturing's machine repair problem are summarized in Figure 13.13.

Because the individual machines break down at a rate of 0.01 per hour, this is the rate at which individual machines "arrive" for repair. Thus, cell E2 contains the value 0.01 to represent the arrival rate per customer (machine). The technician can service broken machines at an average rate of $1/8 = 0.125$ machines per hour, as indicated in cell E3. The number of servers (or technicians) is shown in cell E4. Because there are 10 machines that can break down, cell E5 contains a population size of 10. The spreadsheet calculates the overall arrival rate shown in cell H2. Because there are 10 machines, each with a 0.01 probability of breaking down each hour, the overall arrival rate of broken machines is $10 \times 0.01 = 0.1$, as indicated in cell H2.

The operating characteristics for this system are calculated in cells F6 through F12. According to cell F11, whenever a machine breaks down, it is out of operation for an average of 17.98 hours. Of this total down time, cell F10 indicates that the machine spends approximately 10 hours waiting for service to begin. Cell F9 indicates that approximately 1.524 machines are out of operation at any point in time.

We used columns H through J of the worksheet to calculate the economic consequences of the current situation. There is one server (or service technician) in this problem who is paid $20 per hour. According to cell F9, an average of approximately 1.524 machines are broken in any given hour. Because the company loses $100 each hour a machine is inoperable, cell J9 indicates the company is presently losing about $152.44 per hour due to machine down time. Thus, with a single service technician, the company is incurring costs at the rate of $172.44 per hour.

Software Note

The Q.xls file comes "protected" so that you will not inadvertently write over or delete important formulas in this template. Sometimes, you might want to turn off this protection on a sheet so you can do your own calculations off to the side or format your results (as shown in Figure 13.13). To do this,

1. Click Tools.
2. Click Protection.
3. Select Unprotect Sheet.

If you unprotect a sheet, you should take special care not to alter any of the formulas on the sheet.

13.8.3 ADDING SERVERS

Figure 13.14 shows the expected operation of this system if Miller Manufacturing adds another service technician.

Cell F10 indicates that when a machine breaks down, repairs start, on average, in only 0.82 hours (or approximately 49 minutes), in comparison to the 10-hour waiting time with only one technician. Similarly, cell F9 indicates that with two technicians, an average of only 0.81 machines are out of operation at any point in time. Thus, by adding another repair technician, Miller Manufacturing can keep approximately one more machine in operation at all times. Thus, while the additional service technician increases the total hourly cost to $40, the decrease in the average number of machines in the system saves the company $71.32 per hour (i.e., $152.44 - 81.12 = 71.32$). The net effect is a cost savings of $51.32 as the total hourly cost in cell J10 drops to $121.12.

Figure 13.15 shows the results of adding a third service technician for this problem. Notice that this has the effect of increasing labor costs by $20 per hour over the solution shown in Figure 13.14 while reducing the losses due to idle machines by only $6.36. So, as we go from two to three service technicians, the total hourly cost increases from

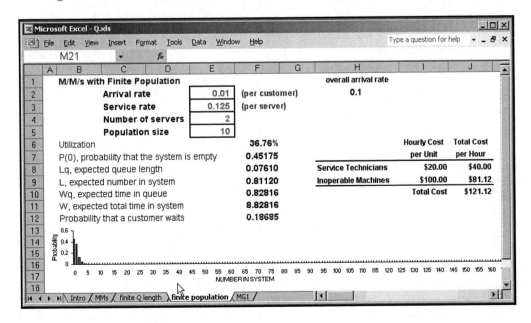

FIGURE 13.14

Results of an M/M/2 model with a finite population of 10 machines for Miller Manufacturing's machine repair problem

FIGURE 13.15

Results of an M/M/3 model with a finite population of 10 machines for Miller Manufacturing's machine repair problem

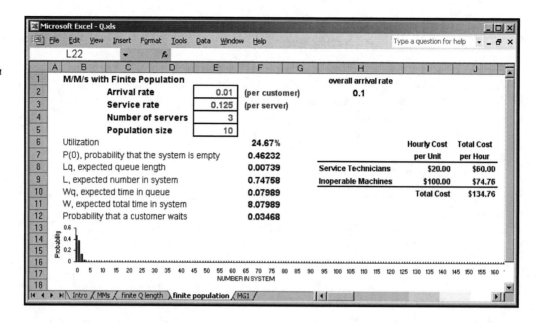

$121.12 to $134.76 per hour. Thus, the optimal solution is for Miller Manufacturing to employ two service technicians because this results in the smallest total hourly cost.

13.9 The M/G/1 Model

All the models presented so far assume that service times follow an exponential distribution. As noted earlier in Figure 13.4, random service times from an exponential distribution can assume *any* positive value. However, in some situations, this assumption is unrealistic. For example, consider the time required to change the oil in a car at an auto service center. This service probably requires *at least* 10 minutes and might require up to 30, 45, or even 60 minutes, depending on the service being performed. The M/G/1 queuing model enables us to analyze queuing problems in which service times cannot be modeled accurately using an exponential distribution. The formulas describing the operating characteristics of an M/G/1 queue are summarized in Figure 13.16.

The M/G/1 queuing model is quite remarkable because it can be used to compute the operating characteristics for *any* one-server queuing system where arrivals follow a Poisson distribution and the mean μ and standard deviation σ of the service times are

FIGURE 13.16

Formulas describing the operating characteristics of an M/G/1 queue

$$P_0 = 1 - \lambda/\mu$$

$$L_q = \frac{\lambda^2\sigma^2 + (\lambda/\mu)^2}{2(1 - \lambda/\mu)}$$

$$L = L_q + \lambda/\mu$$

$$W_q = L_q/\lambda$$

$$W = W_q + 1/\mu$$

$$P_w = \lambda/\mu$$

known. That is, the formulas in Figure 13.16 do not require that service times follow one specific probability distribution. The following example illustrates the use of the M/G/1 queuing model.

> Zippy-Lube is a drive-through automotive oil change business that operates 10 hours a day, 6 days a week. The profit margin on an oil change at Zippy-Lube is $15. Cars arrive randomly at the Zippy-Lube oil change center following a Poisson distribution at an average rate of 3.5 cars per hour. After reviewing the historical data on operations at this business, the owner of Zippy-Lube, Olie Boe, has determined that the average service time per car is 15 minutes (or 0.25 hours) with a standard deviation of 2 minutes (or 0.0333 hours). Olie has the opportunity to purchase a new automated oil dispensing device that costs $5,000. The manufacturer's representative claims this device will reduce the average service time by 3 minutes per car. (Currently, Olie's employees manually open and pour individual cans of oil.) Olie wants to analyze the impact the new automated device would have on his business and determine the payback period for this device.

13.9.1 THE CURRENT SITUATION

We can model Olie's current service facility as an M/G/1 queue. The operating characteristics of this facility are shown in Figure 13.17.

Cell E3 contains the average arrival rate of 3.5 cars per hour. The average service time per car (also in hours) is indicated in cell E4, and the standard deviation of the service time (in hours) is indicated in cell E5. Cell F11 shows that an average of about 3.12 cars wait for service at any given point in time. Cell F14 indicates that, on average, 1.14 hours (or about 68 minutes) elapse between the time a car arrives and leaves the system.

13.9.2 ADDING THE AUTOMATED DISPENSING DEVICE

If Olie purchases the automated oil dispensing device, the average service time per car should drop to 12 minutes (or 0.20 hours). Figure 13.18 shows the impact this would have if the arrival rate remained constant at 3.5 cars per hour.

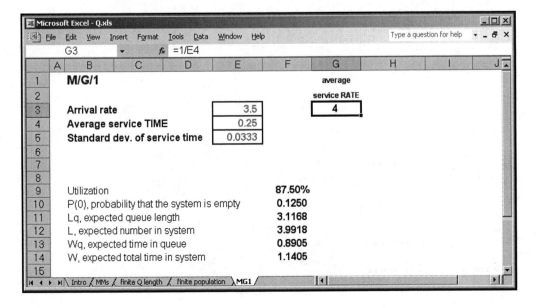

FIGURE 13.17

Results of an M/G/1 model for the original Zippy-Lube problem

FIGURE
13.18

*Results of an
M/G/1 model for
the Zippy-Lube
problem after
purchasing the
automatic oil
dispensing
machine and
assuming an
increase in arrivals*

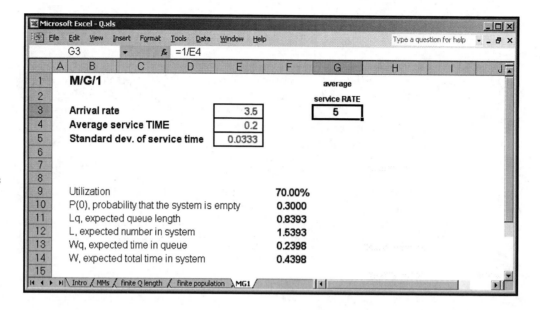

The value in cell F14 indicates that going to the automated oil dispensing device reduces the amount of time a car spends in the system from 1.14 hours to 0.4398 hours (or about 26 minutes). Cell F11 indicates that the expected queue in front of the service bay consists of only 0.8393 cars, on average. Thus, the addition of a new oil dispensing device would improve customer service significantly.

The shorter queue at Zippy-Lube resulting from the acquisition of the automated dispensing device would likely result in an increase in the arrival rate, because customers who previously balked when confronted with a lengthy queue might now consider stopping for service. Thus, Olie might be interested in determining just how much the arrival rate could increase before the average queue length returned to its original level of about 3.12 shown in Figure 13.17. We can use the Goal Seek tool to answer this question. To do this,

1. Click Tools.
2. Click Goal Seek.
3. Fill in the Goal Seek dialog box as shown in Figure 13.19.
4. Click OK.

The results of this Goal Seek analysis are shown in Figure 13.20. Here, we see that if the arrival rate increases to 4.37 cars per hour, the average length of the queue will return to approximately 3.12. Thus, by purchasing the automatic oil dispensing machine, it is reasonable to expect that the average number of cars arriving for service at Zippy-Lube might increase from 3.5 per hour to approximately 4.371.

FIGURE
13.19

*Goal Seek settings
to determine the
arrival rate that
produces an
average queue
length of 3.12 cars*

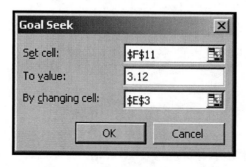

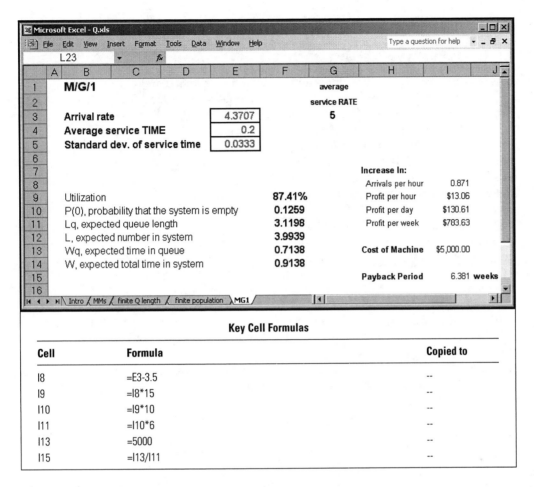

FIGURE 13.20

Results of an M/G/1 model for the Zippy-Lube problem after purchasing the automatic oil dispensing machine and assuming arrival rate will increase

Key Cell Formulas

Cell	Formula	Copied to
I8	=E3-3.5	--
I9	=I8*15	--
I10	=I9*10	--
I11	=I10*6	--
I13	=5000	--
I15	=I13/I11	--

Column I in Figure 13.20 summarizes the financial impact of purchasing the new oil dispensing machine. Because the arrival rate may be expected to increase by approximately 0.871 cars per hour, weekly profits should increase by approximately $783.63 per week. If this increase in profits occurs, the payback period for the new machine will be approximately 6.38 weeks.

13.10 The M/D/1 Model

The M/G/1 model can be used when service times are random with known mean and standard deviation. However, service times might not be random in some queuing systems. For example, in a manufacturing environment, it is not unusual to have a queue of material or subassemblies waiting to be serviced by a certain machine. The machine time required to perform the service might be very predictable—such as exactly 10 seconds of machine time per piece. Similarly, an automatic car wash might spend exactly the same amount of time on each car it services. The M/D/1 model can be used in these types of situations in which the service times are deterministic (not random).

The results for an M/D/1 model can be obtained using the M/G/1 model by setting the standard deviation of the service time to 0 ($\sigma = 0$). Setting $\sigma = 0$ indicates that no variability exists in the service times and, therefore, the service time for each unit is equal to the average service time μ.

13.11 Simulating Queues and the Steady-state Assumption

Queuing theory is one of the oldest and most well-researched areas of management science. Discussions of other types of queuing models can be found in advanced texts on management science and in texts devoted solely to queuing theory. However, keep in mind that the technique of simulation can also be used to analyze virtually any queuing problem you might encounter. Indeed, not all queuing models have closed-form equations to describe their operating characteristics. So, simulation is often the only means available for analyzing complex queuing systems where customers balk (don't join a queue upon arrival), renege (leave a queue before being served), or jockey (switch from one queue to another).

The formulas used in this chapter describe the *steady-state* operations of the various queuing systems presented. At the beginning of each day, most queuing systems start in an "empty and idle" condition and go through a transient period as business activity gradually builds up to reach the normal, or steady-state, level of operation. The queuing models presented describe only the behavior of the system in its steady-state level of operation. A queuing system can have different levels of steady-state operations at different times throughout the day. For example, a restaurant might have one steady-state level of operation for breakfast, and different steady-state levels at lunch and dinner. So, before using the models in this chapter, it is important to identify the arrival rate and service rate for the specific steady-state level of operation that you want to study. If an analysis of the transient phase is needed or if you want to model the operation of the system across different steady-state levels, you should use simulation.

Figure 13.21 (and the file Fig13-21.xls on your data disk) contains a spreadsheet model that simulates the operation of a single server (M/M/1) queue and plots several graphs associated with different operating characteristics of the system. (If you open

FIGURE 13.21

Graph of the average waiting time in the simulation of a single server queuing system

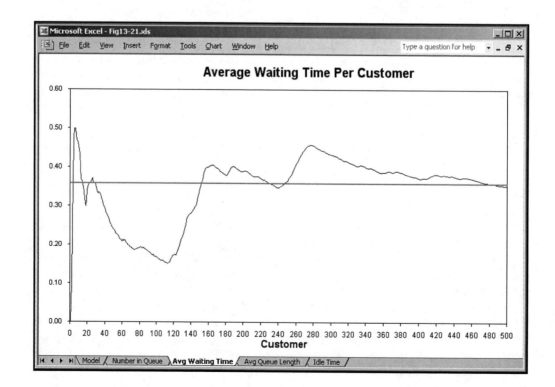

this file, your graph might not match the one in Figure 13.21 because the random numbers used in the simulation will change.) The graph in Figure 13.21 shows a plot of the average waiting time per customer (W_q) for 500 customers. The horizontal line indicates the steady-state value of W_q. Note that several hundred customers are processed in the system in this transient period before the observed average waiting time begins to converge on its steady-state value.

13.12 Summary

Waiting lines, or queues, are a common occurrence in many types of businesses. The study of the operating characteristics of waiting lines is known as queuing theory. Numerous mathematical models are available to represent and study the behavior of different types of queues. These models have different assumptions about the nature of the arrival process to the queuing system, the allowable size and nature of the queuing discipline, and the service process within the system. For many models, closed-form equations have been developed to describe various operating characteristics of the system. When closed-form solutions are not possible, the technique of simulation must be used to analyze the behavior of the system.

13.13 References

Gilliam, R. "An Application of Queueing Theory to Airport Passenger Security Screening." *Interfaces*, vol. 9, 1979.

Gross, D. and C. Harris. *Fundamentals of Queueing Theory*. New York: Wiley, 1985.

Hall, R. *Queueing Methods for Service and Manufacturing*. Englewood Cliffs, NJ: Prentice Hall, 1991.

Kolesar, P. "A Quick and Dirty Response to the Quick and Dirty Crowd: Particularly to Jack Byrd's 'The Value of Queueing Theory'." *Interfaces*, vol. 9, 1979.

Mann, L. "Queue Culture: The Waiting Line as a Social System." *American Journal of Sociology*, vol. 75, 1969.

Quinn, P., et al. "Allocating Telecommunications Resources at LL Bean, Inc." *Interfaces*, vol. 21, 1991.

THE WORLD OF MANAGEMENT SCIENCE

"Wait Watchers" Try to Take Stress Out of Standing in Line

Standing in line—at the bank, the market, the movies—is the time-waster everyone loves to hate. Stand in just one 15-minute line a day, every day, and kiss goodbye to four days of idle time by year's end.

While we've been waiting and grumbling, researchers have been analyzing lines with an eye to making them, if not shorter, at least less stressful.

The field of line analysis—more scientifically known as queuing theory—began in the early 1900s when a Danish telephone engineer devised a mathematical approach to help design phone switches. Researchers found that the principles developed through that system, which helped process calls more efficiently, could be applied to help move people through lines more efficiently.

The concept has spread from the communications and computer industries to other fields, helping modern researchers predict such things as how long customers might wait for a restaurant lunch or how many customers might visit a bank ATM

(Continued)

at noon on Saturday. Now, some researchers have gone beyond a mere mathematical analysis of lines, focusing as well on our psychological reactions.

In one recent study, Richard Larson, a professor of electrical engineering at the Massachusetts Institute of Technology, wanted to determine which of two approaches would be more tolerable to Bank of Boston customers. As Larson's researchers filmed the customers, one group watched an electronic news board while waiting in line; the other group was advised via an electric clock how long the wait would be before each one entered the line. About 300 customers, nearly a third of those filmed, were interviewed after they finished their transactions. The findings, published in the *Sloan Management Review,* an MIT publication circulated to corporate managers, showed that:

- Customers in both lines overestimated their waits by nearly a minute; those who watched the news board overestimated the most. On average, customers thought they had waited 5.1 minutes to see a teller but actually had waited 4.2 minutes.
- Watching the news board did not change customers' perceptions of their waiting time. But it did make the time spent more palatable, customers reported. (After the bank removed the news board, many customers asked that it be reinstalled.)
- The news board also seemed to make customers less fidgety. Without it, they touched their faces and played with their hair. With the news board in view, they stood still with their arms at their sides.
- Customers who were advised of the length of the line via an electronic clock at the entry did not find the experience less stressful than those not told the expected waiting time, much to Larson's surprise. Nor were they more satisfied than the other group with the service. The electronic clock's display of waiting time might backfire, Larson speculates, by making respondents even more aware of time wasted standing in line.
- Customers in the lines with the clock tended to play "beat the clock." They felt they had "won" if they spent less time in line than predicted. The clock also seemed to make more customers balk at joining the line if the predicted delay was lengthy.
- In both lines, customers altered their definition of a "reasonable" wait depending on their time of arrival. They were willing to wait longer during lunch time than during other times of day.

Larson's recent findings bear out a formula published in 1984 by David Maister, a former Harvard Business School faculty member and now a business consultant. When it comes to lines, Maister said, satisfaction is tied to both perception and expectation.

"Nowhere in that [equation] does reality appear," Maister said with a laugh during a telephone interview. Giving a personal example of how perception influences reaction, he said he would wait "40 minutes for a performance by a world-class musician but less than 30 seconds for a hamburger."

Larson, a professional "wait watcher" for 20 years, puts it a bit differently: "When it comes to customer satisfaction, perception is reality."

If those concepts are true, taming customer unrest does not necessarily mean a business must beef up its staff to eliminate lines, Larson and Maister contend. It's much more a matter of "perception management," they say. "People in the service

(Continued)

industries who think they have a line problem may be able to virtually erase customer dissatisfaction and customer complaints not by changing the statistic of the wait but by changing the environment of it," Larson said.

He points to a number of companies already actively wooing waiters. Some companies use a "queue delay guarantee," giving customers free dessert or money if the wait exceeds a preset time period.

Larson predicts customers can expect lines that segment them by personality type. Impatient souls may have the option of paying more to join an automated express line; "people watchers" could opt to wait for less expensive, friendlier human service.

Questions and Problems

1. Consider the three queuing configurations shown in Figure 13.2. For each configuration, describe a situation (besides the examples mentioned in the chapter) in which you have encountered or observed the same type of queuing system.
2. Of the queuing configurations shown in Figure 13.2, which would you prefer to wait in? Explain your response.
3. This chapter implies that customers find waiting in line to be an unpleasant experience. In addition to reducing the length of the wait itself, what other steps could a business take to reduce the frustration that customers experience while waiting? Give specific examples.
4. Describe a situation in which a business might want customers to wait some amount of time before receiving service.
5. The day after a snowstorm, cars arrive at Mel's Auto-Wash at an average rate of 10 per hour according to a Poisson process. The automated car washing process takes exactly 5 minutes from start to finish.
   a. What is the probability that an arriving car will find the car wash empty?
   b. On average, how many cars are waiting for service?
   c. On average, what is the total length of time (from arrival to departure) that cars will spend at the car wash?
6. Tri-Cities Bank has a single drive-in teller window. On Friday mornings, customers arrive at the drive-in window randomly, following a Poisson distribution at an average rate of 30 per hour.
   a. How many customers arrive per minute, on average?
   b. How many customers would you expect to arrive in a 10-minute interval?
   c. Use equation 13.1 to determine the probability of exactly 0, 1, 2, and 3 arrivals in a 10-minute interval. (You can verify your answers using the POISSON( ) function in Excel.)
   d. What is the probability of more than three arrivals occurring in a 10-minute interval?
7. Refer to question 6. Suppose that service at the drive-in window is provided at a rate of 40 customers per hour and follows an exponential distribution.
   a. What is the expected service time per customer?
   b. Use equation 13.2 to determine the probability that a customer's service time is one minute or less. (Verify your answer using the EXPONDIST( ) function in Excel.)

   c. Compute the probabilities that the customer's service time is: between two and five minutes, less than four minutes, and more than three minutes.

8. Refer to questions 6 and 7 and answer the following questions:
   a. What is the probability that the drive-in window is empty?
   b. What is the probability that a customer must wait for service?
   c. On average, how many cars wait for service?
   d. On average, what is the total length of time that a customer spends in the system?
   e. On average, what is the total length of time that a customer spends in the queue?
   f. What service rate would be required to reduce the average total time in the system to two minutes? (*Hint:* You can use Solver or simple what-if analysis to answer this question.)

9. On Friday nights, patients arrive at the emergency room at Mercy Hospital at an average rate of seven per hour, which follows a Poisson distribution. Assume that an emergency-room physician can treat an average of three patients per hour, and that the treatment times follow an exponential distribution. The board of directors for Mercy Hospital wants patients arriving at the emergency room to wait no more than five minutes before seeing a doctor.
   a. How many emergency-room doctors should be scheduled on Friday nights to achieve the hospital's objective?

10. Seabreeze Furniture in Orlando maintains a large central warehouse where it stores items until they are sold or needed by the company's many stores in the central Florida area. A four-person crew works at the warehouse to load or unload trucks that arrive at the warehouse at a rate of one per hour (with exponentially distributed interarrival times). The time that it takes the crew to unload each truck follows an exponential distribution with a mean service rate of 4 trucks per hour. Each worker costs the company $21 per hour in wages and benefits. Seabreeze's management is currently trying to cut costs and is considering reducing the number of workers on this warehouse crew. They believe that three workers could provide a service rate of 3 trucks per hour, two workers a service rate of 2 trucks per hour, and one worker a service rate of 1 truck per hour. The company estimates that it costs $35 for each hour a truck spends at the loading dock (whether it is waiting for service or being loaded or unloaded).
   a. Should Seabreeze ever consider having only one worker on the crew? Explain your answer.
   b. For each possible crew size, determine the expected queue length, expected total time in the system, the probability that a customer waits, and the total hourly cost.
   c. What crew size would you recommend?

11. The Madrid Mist outlet store at Chiswell Mills sells discount luggage and does most of its daily business between 6 pm and 9 pm. During this time, customers arrive at the checkout desk at a rate of one every two minutes following a Poisson distribution. The checkout operation takes an average of three minutes per customer and can be approximated well by an exponential distribution. Madrid Mist's corporate policy is that customers should not have to wait longer than one minute to begin the checkout operation.
   a. What is the average service rate per minute?
   b. What is the average arrival rate per minute?
   c. What would happen if the store operated a single checkout station during the time period in question?
   d. How many checkout stations should the store plan to operate during this time period to stay within the corporate policy on checkout operations?

12. Customers checking out at Food Tiger arrive in a single-line queue served by two cashiers at a rate of eight per hour according to a Poisson distribution. Each cashier processes customers at a rate of eight per hour according to an exponential distribution.
    a. If, on average, customers spend 30 minutes shopping before getting in the checkout line, what is the average time a customer spends in the store?
    b. What is the average number of customers waiting for service in the checkout line?
    c. What is the probability that a customer must wait?
    d. What assumption did you make to answer this question?

13. The manager of the Radford Credit Union (RCU) wants to determine how many part-time tellers to employ to cover the peak demand time in its lobby from 11:00 am to 2:00 pm. RCU currently has three full-time tellers that handle the demand during the rest of the day, but during this peak demand time, customers have been complaining that the wait time for service is too long. The manager at RCU has determined that customers arrive according to a Poisson distribution with an average of 60 arrivals per hour during the peak period. Each teller services customers at a rate of 24 per hour, with service times following an exponential distribution.
    a. On average, how long must customers wait in line before service begins?
    b. Once service begins for a customer, how long does it take to complete the transaction, on average?
    c. If one part-time teller is hired to work during the peak time period, what effect would this have on the average amount of time a customer spends waiting in the queue?
    d. If one part-time teller is hired to work during the peak time period, what effect would this have on the average amount of time it takes to serve a customer?

14. The Westland Title Insurance Company leases one copying machine for $45 per day that is used by all individuals at its office. An average of five persons per hour arrive to use this machine, with each person using it for an average of eight minutes. Assume that the interarrival times and copying times are exponentially distributed.
    a. What is the probability that a person arriving to use the machine will find it idle?
    b. On average, how long will a person have to wait before getting to use the machine?
    c. On average, how many people will be using or waiting to use the copy machine?
    d. Suppose that the people who use the copy machine are paid an average of $9 per hour. On average, how much does the company spend in wages during each eight-hour day paying the people who are using or waiting to use the copy machine?
    e. If the company can lease another copying machine for $45 per day, should they do it?

15. The Orange Blossom Marathon takes place in Orlando, Florida, each December. The organizers of this race are trying to solve a problem that occurs at the finish line each year. Thousands of runners take part in this race. The fastest runners finish the 26-mile course in just over two hours, but the majority of the runners finish about 1 1/2 hours later. After runners enter the finish area, they go through one of four finish chutes where their times and places are recorded. (Each chute has its own queue.) During the time in which the majority of the runners finish the race, the chutes become backlogged and significant delays occur. The race organizers want to determine how many chutes should be added to eliminate this problem. At the time in question, runners arrive at the finish area at a rate of 50 per minute according to a Poisson distribution, and they randomly select one of the four chutes. The time

required to record the necessary information for each finishing runner at any chute is an exponentially distributed random variable with a mean of four seconds.

a. On average, how many runners arrive at each chute per minute?

b. Under the current arrangement with four chutes, what is the expected length of the queue at each chute?

c. Under the current arrangement, what is the average length of time a runner waits before being processed?

d. How many chutes should be added if the race organizers want to reduce the queue time at each chute to an average of five seconds?

16. State University allows students and faculty to access its mainframe computer by modem. The university has 15 modem connections that can be used. When all of the modem connections are in use, the phone system can keep up to 10 callers on hold waiting for a modem connection to become available. If all 15 modem connections are in use and 10 calls are already holding, a new caller receives a busy signal. Calls to the modem pool follow a Poisson distribution and occur at an average rate of 60 per hour. The length of each session with the mainframe is an exponential random variable with a mean of 15 minutes—therefore, each modem services an average of four callers per hour.

a. On average, how many callers are on hold waiting for a modem connection?

b. On average, how long is a caller kept on hold before receiving a modem connection?

c. What is the probability that a caller receives a busy signal?

d. How many modem connections would the university need to add to its modem pool for there to be no more than a 1% chance of a caller receiving a busy signal?

17. During tax season, the IRS hires seasonal workers to help answer the questions of taxpayers who call a special 800 telephone number for tax information. Suppose that calls to this line occur at a rate of 60 per hour and follow a Poisson distribution. The IRS workers manning the phone lines can answer an average of five calls per hour with the actual service times following an exponential distribution. Assume that 10 IRS workers are available and, when they are all busy, the phone system can keep five additional callers on hold.

a. What is the probability that a caller receives a busy signal?

b. What is the probability that a caller is put on hold before receiving service?

c. On average, how long must a caller wait before speaking with an IRS agent?

d. How many additional workers would be required if the IRS wants no more than a 5% chance of a caller receiving a busy signal?

18. Road Rambler sells specialty running shoes and apparel through catalogs and the Web. Customers can phone in orders at any time day or night, seven days a week. During the 4 am to 8 am shift, a single sales rep handles all calls. During this time, calls arrive at a rate of 14 per hour following a Poisson distribution. It takes the sales rep an average of four minutes to process each call. The variability in service times is approximately exponentially distributed. All calls received while the sales rep is busy are placed in a queue.

a. On average, how long (in minutes) must callers wait before talking to the sales rep?

b. On average, how many customers are on hold?

c. What is the probability that the customer will be placed on hold?

d. What is the sales rep's utilization rate?

e. Suppose Road Rambler wants there to be no more than a 10% chance that a customer will be placed on hold. How many sales reps should the company employ?

19. Refer to the previous question. Suppose that Road Rambler's phone system can keep only four calls on hold at any time, the average profit margin of each call is $55, and that sales reps cost the company $12 per hour.
    a. If callers who receive a busy signal take their business elsewhere, how much money is the company losing per hour (on average) if they employ a single sales rep?
    b. What is the net effect on average hourly profits if the company employs two sales reps instead of one?
    c. What is the net effect on average hourly profits if the company employs three sales reps instead of one?
    d. How many sales reps should the company employ if it wants to maximize profit?

20. Several hundred personal computers (PCs) are in use at the corporate headquarters for National Insurance Corporation. The pattern of breakdowns for these PCs follows a Poisson distribution with an average rate of 4.5 breakdowns per five-day work week. The company has a repair technician on staff to repair the PCs. The average time required to repair a PC varies somewhat, but takes an average of one day with a standard deviation of 0.5 days.
    a. What is the average service time in terms of a five-day work week?
    b. What is the standard deviation of the service times in terms of a five-day work week?
    c. On average, how many PCs are either being repaired or waiting to be repaired?
    d. On average, how much time transpires from the time a PC breaks down to the time it is repaired?
    e. Suppose that National Insurance estimates it loses $40 a day in productivity and efficiency for each PC that is out of service. How much should the company be willing to pay to increase service capacity to the point where an average of seven PCs a week could be repaired?

21. Interstate 81 through southwest Virginia is heavily traveled by long-distance truckers. To cut down on accidents, The Virginia State Patrol carries out random inspections of a truck's weight and the condition of its brakes. On Fridays, trucks approach the inspection station at a rate of one every 45 seconds following a Poisson process. The time required to check a truck's weight and brakes follows an exponential distribution with an average inspection time of 5 minutes. The state troopers only pull over trucks when at least one of their three portable inspection units is available.
    a. What is the probability that all three inspection units will be idle at the same time?
    b. What proportion of trucks traveling this section of Interstate 81 will be inspected?
    c. On average, how many trucks will be pulled over for inspection each hour?

22. The drive-thru window at Hokie Burger requires 2.5 minutes on average to process an order with a standard deviation of 3 minutes. Cars arrive at the window at a rate of 20 per hour.
    a. On average, how many cars are waiting to be served?
    b. On average, how long will a car spend in the service process?
    c. Suppose Hokie Burger can install an automated drink-dispensing device that would reduce the standard deviation of the service time to 1 minute. How would your answers to the previous questions change?

23. A manufacturer of engine belts uses multipurpose manufacturing equipment to produce a variety of products. A technician is employed to perform the setup operations needed to change the machines over from one product to the next. The amount of

time required to set up the machines is a random variable that follows an exponential distribution with a mean of 20 minutes. The number of machines requiring a new setup is a Poisson random variable with an average of two machines per hour requiring setup. The technician is responsible for setups on five machines.

a. What percentage of time is the technician idle, or not involved in setting up a machine?

b. What should the technician do during this idle time?

c. On average, how long is a machine out of operation while waiting for the next setup to be completed?

d. If the company hires another equally capable technician to perform setups on these machines, how long on average would a machine be out of operation while waiting for the next setup to be completed?

24. DeColores Paint Company owns ten trucks that it uses to deliver paint and decorating supplies to builders. On average, each truck returns to the company's single loading dock at a rate of three times per eight-hour day (or at a rate of $3/8 = 0.375$ times per hour). The times between arrivals at the dock follow an exponential distribution. The loading dock can service an average of four trucks per hour with actual service times following an exponential distribution.

a. What is the probability that a truck must wait for service to begin?

b. On average, how many trucks wait for service to begin at any point in time?

c. On average, how long must a truck wait before service begins?

d. If the company builds and staffs another loading dock, how would your answers to parts a, b, and c change?

e. The capitalized cost of adding a loading dock is $5.40 per hour. The hourly cost of having a truck idle is $50. What is the optimal number of loading docks that will minimize the sum of dock cost and idle truck cost?

25. Suppose that arrivals to a queuing system with one server follow a Poisson distribution with an average of $\lambda = 5$ per time period, and that service times follow an exponential distribution with an average service rate of $\mu = 6$ per time period.

a. Compute the operating characteristics for this system using the M/M/s model with $s = 1$.

b. Compute the operating characteristics for this system using the M/G/1 model. (Note that the average service time for the exponential random variable is $1/\mu$ and the standard deviation of the service time is also $1/\mu$.)

c. Compare the results obtained from the M/M/1 and M/G/1 models. (They should be the same.) Explain why they are the same.

26. Calls arrive at a rate of 150 per hour to the 800 number for the Land's Beginning mail-order catalog company. The company currently employs 20 operators who are paid $10 per hour in wages and benefits and can each handle an average of six calls per hour. Assume that interarrival times and service times follow the exponential distribution. A maximum of 20 calls can be placed on hold when all the operators are busy. The company estimates that it costs $25 in lost sales whenever a customer calls and receives a busy signal.

a. On average, how many customers are waiting on hold at any point in time?

b. What is the probability that a customer will receive a busy signal?

c. If the number of operators plus the number of calls placed on hold cannot exceed 40, how many operators should the company employ?

d. If the company implements your answer to part c, on average, how many customers will be waiting on hold at any point in time and what is the probability that a customer will receive a busy signal?

May the (Police) Force be with You

"I hope this goes better than last time," thought Craig Rooney as he thought about having to walk into the city council's chambers next week. Craig is the assistant chief of police in Newport, VA, and, each September he has to provide the city council with a report on the effectiveness of the city's police force. This report immediately precedes the council's discussion of the police department's budget. So Craig often feels like a tightrope artist trying to find the right balance in his presentation to both convince the council that the department is being run well and also persuade them to increase the department's budget for new officers.

The city of Newport has a total of 19 police officers assigned to five precincts. Currently, precinct A has three officers assigned to it while the others each have four officers. One of the town council's primary concerns each year is the amount of time it takes for an officer to begin responding when a 911 emergency call is received. Unfortunately, the city's information system does not track this data exactly, but it does keep track of the number of calls received in each precinct each hour and the amount of time that elapses between when officers first begin responding to call and the time they report being available again to respond to other calls (this is also known as the service time for each call).

A student intern from a local university worked for Craig last summer and collected data shown in the file named CallData.xls found on your data disk. One of the sheets in this workbook (named calls per hour) shows the number of 911 calls received during 500 randomly chosen hours of operation in each precinct. Another sheet (named service times) shows the services time required for each of these calls.

The student intern also set up a worksheet (based on the formulas in Figure 13.6) to calculate operating characteristics of an M/M/s queue for each of the Newport's five precincts. Unfortunately, the student intern had to return to school before finishing this project. But Craig believes that with a little work he can use the data collected to figure out appropriate arrival and service rates for each precinct and complete the analysis. More importantly, he feels sure the queuing model will allow him to quickly answer many of the questions he expects the city council to ask.

a. What are the arrival rate of 911 calls and the service rates for each precinct?
b. Does the arrival rate of calls for each precinct appear to follow a Poisson distribution?
c. Does the service rate for each precinct appear to follow an exponential distribution?
d. Using an M/M/s queue, on average, how many minutes must a 911 caller in each precinct wait before a police officer begins responding?
e. Suppose Craig wants to redistribute officers among precincts so as to reduce the maximum amount of time callers in any one precinct have to wait for a police response. What should he do and what effect would this have?
f. How many additional police officers would Newport have to hire for the average response time in each precinct to be less than two minutes?

Call Center Staffing at Vacations Inc.

Vacations Inc. (VI) markets time-share condominiums throughout North America. One way the company generates sales leads is by offering a chance to win a free mini-vacation to anyone who fills out an information card and places it in boxes that VI has distributed at various restaurants and shopping malls. All those who fill out the card and indicate an adequate income level subsequently receive a letter from VI indicating that they have indeed won the mini-vacation. To claim their prize, all the "winner" needs to do is call VI's toll free number. When the "winner" calls the number, they learn that their mini-vacation consists of a free dinner, entertainment, and two-night stay at one of VI's time-share properties; but they must agree to sit through a two hour property tour and sales presentation.

About half the people who call VI's toll free number to claim their prize wind up rejecting the offer after they learn about the two hour property tour. About 40% of those who call accept the mini-vacation and do the property tour but don't buy anything. The remaining 10% of those who call the toll free number accept the mini-vacation and ultimately purchase a time-share. Each mini-vacation that VI awards costs the company about $250. Each sale of a time-share generates a net profit of $7,000 for VI after all commissions and other costs (including the $250 for the buyer's mini-vacation) have been paid.

VI's call center operates from 10 am to 10 pm daily with four sales representatives and receives calls at a rate of 50 per hour following a Poisson distribution. It takes an average of 4 minutes to handle each call with actual times being exponentially distributed. The phone system VI uses can keep up to 10 callers on hold at any time. Assume those who receive a busy signal don't call back.

a. On average, how many customers per hour does each sales person process?
b. What is the expected value of each call to VI's toll free line?
c. Suppose VI pays it phone reps $12 per hour. How many phone reps should it employ if it wants to maximize profit?

CASE 13.3 Bullseye Department Store

Bullseye Department store is a discount retailer of general merchandise in the Southeastern United States. The company owns more than 50 stores in Florida, Georgia, South Carolina, and Tennessee that are serviced by the company's main warehouse near Statesboro, GA. Most of the merchandise received at the warehouse arrives in trucks from ports in Jacksonville, FL and Savannah, GA.

Trucks arrive at the warehouse following a Poisson process with a rate of once every seven minutes. Eight loading docks are available at the warehouse. A single worker mans each dock and can unload a truck in approximately 30 minutes on average. When all the docks are occupied, arriving trucks wait in a queue until one becomes available.

Bullseye has received complaints from some of the trucking firms that deliveries are taking too long at the warehouse. In response, Bullseye is considering several options to try to reduce the time that trucks must spend at the warehouse. One option is to hire an extra worker for each of the loading docks. This is expected to reduce the average time it takes to unload a truck to 18 minutes. It costs approximately $17 per hour in salary and fringe benefits to employ each additional worker.

Alternatively, the company can continue to use a single worker at each loading dock but upgrade the forklift equipment that workers use to unload trucks. The company can replace the existing forklift equipment with a new model that can be leased for $6 per hour and is expected to reduce the average time required to unload a truck to 23 minutes.

Finally, the company can build two new loading docks for a capitalized cost of $6 per hour and hire two additional workers at a rate of $17 per hour to man these locations. Bullseye estimates it costs $60 in goodwill for each hour a truck spends at the warehouse. Which, if any, of the three alternatives would you recommend that Bullseye implement?

Chapter 15

Decision Analysis

15.0 Introduction

The previous chapters in this book describe a variety of modeling techniques that can help managers gain insight and understanding about the decision problems they face. But models do not make decisions—people do. Although the insight and understanding gained by modeling problems can be helpful, decision making often remains a difficult task. The two primary causes for this difficulty are uncertainty regarding the future and conflicting values or objectives.

For example, suppose that when you graduate from college you receive job offers from two companies. One company (company A) is in a relatively new industry that offers potential for spectacular growth—or rapid bankruptcy. The salary offered by this company is somewhat lower than you would like, but would increase rapidly if the company grows. This company is located in the city that is home to your favorite professional sports team and close to your friends and family.

The other job offer is from an established company (company B) that is known for its financial strength and long-term commitment to its employees. It has offered you a starting salary that is 10 percent more than you asked, but you suspect it would take longer for you to advance in this organization. Also, if you work for this company, you would have to move to a distant part of the country that offers few of the cultural and sporting activities that you enjoy.

Which offer would you accept? Or would you reject both offers and continue looking for employment with other companies? For many, this might be a difficult decision. If you accept the job with company A, you might be promoted twice within a year—or you could be unemployed in six months. With company B, you can be reasonably sure of having a secure job for the foreseeable future. But if you accept the job with company B and then company A grows rapidly, you might regret not accepting the position with company A. Thus, the uncertainty associated with the future of company A makes this decision difficult.

To further complicate the decision, company A offers a more desirable location than company B, but the starting salary with company A is lower. How can you assess the trade-offs between starting salary, location, job security, and potential for advancement, to make a good decision? There is no easy answer to this question, but this chapter describes a number of techniques that can help you structure and analyze difficult decision problems in a logical manner.

15.1 Good Decisions Vs. Good Outcomes

The goal of decision analysis is to help individuals make good decisions. But good decisions do not always result in good outcomes. For example, suppose that after carefully considering all the factors involved in the two job offers, you decide to accept the position with company B. After working for this company for nine months, it suddenly announces that, in an effort to cut costs, it is closing the office in which you work and eliminating your job. Did you make a bad decision? Probably not. Unforeseeable circumstances beyond your control caused you to experience a bad outcome, but it would be unfair to say that you made a bad decision. Good decisions sometimes result in bad outcomes.

The techniques for decision analysis presented in this chapter can help you make good decisions, but cannot guarantee that good outcomes always will occur as a result of those decisions. Even when a good decision is made, luck often plays a role in determining whether a good or bad outcome occurs. However, using a structured approach to make decisions should give us enhanced insight and sharper intuition about the decision problems we face. As a result, it is reasonable to expect good outcomes to occur more frequently when using a structured approach to decision making than if we make decisions in a more haphazard manner.

15.2 Characteristics of Decision Problems

Although all decision problems are somewhat different, they share certain characteristics. For example, a decision must involve at least two alternatives for addressing or solving a problem. An alternative is a course of action intended to solve a problem. The job selection example described earlier involves three alternatives: you could accept the offer from company A, accept the offer from company B, or reject both offers and continue searching for a better one.

Alternatives are evaluated on the basis of the value they add to one or more decision criteria. The criteria in a decision problem represent various factors that are important to the decision maker and influenced by the alternatives. For example, the criteria used to evaluate the job offer alternatives might include starting salary, expected salary growth, desirability of job location, opportunity for promotion and career advancement, and so on. The impact of the alternatives on the criteria is of primary importance to the decision maker. Note that not all criteria can be expressed in terms of monetary value, making comparisons of the alternatives more difficult.

Finally, the values assumed by the various decision criteria under each alternative depend on the different states of nature that can occur. The states of nature in a decision problem correspond to future events that are not under the decision maker's control. For example, company A could experience spectacular growth, or it might go bankrupt. Each of these contingencies represents a possible state of nature for the problem. Many other states of nature are possible for the company; for example, it could grow slowly, or not grow at all. Thus, an infinite number of possible states of nature could exist in this, and many other, decision problems. However, in decision analysis, we often use a relatively small, discrete set of representative states of nature to summarize the future events that might occur.

15.3 An Example

The following example illustrates some of the issues and difficulties that arise in decision problems.

FIGURE 15.1

Data for the Magnolia Inns decision problem

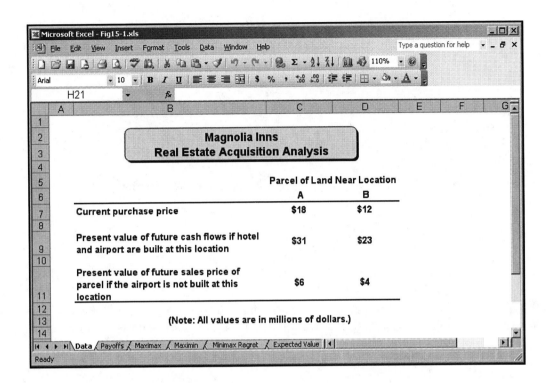

Hartsfield International Airport in Atlanta, Georgia, is one of the busiest airports in the world. During the past 30 years, the airport has expanded again and again to accommodate the increasing number of flights being routed through Atlanta. Analysts project that this increase will continue well into the future. However, commercial development around the airport prevents it from building additional runways to handle the future air-traffic demands. As a solution to this problem, plans are being developed to build another airport outside the city limits. Two possible locations for the new airport have been identified, but a final decision on the new location is not expected to be made for another year.

The Magnolia Inns hotel chain intends to build a new facility near the new airport once its site is determined. Barbara Monroe is responsible for real estate acquisition for the company, and she faces a difficult decision about where to buy land. Currently, land values around the two possible sites for the new airport are increasing as investors speculate that property values will increase greatly in the vicinity of the new airport. The spreadsheet in Figure 15.1 (and in the file Fig15-1.xls on your data disk) summarizes the current price of each parcel of land, the estimated present value of the future cash flows that a hotel would generate at each site if the airport is ultimately located at the site, and the present value of the amount for which the company believes it can resell each parcel if the airport is not built at the site.

The company can buy either site, both sites, or neither site. Barbara must decide which sites, if any, the company should purchase.

15.4 The Payoff Matrix

A common way of analyzing this type of decision problem is to construct a payoff matrix. A payoff matrix is a table that summarizes the final outcome (or payoff) for each decision alternative under each possible state of nature. To construct a payoff matrix, we need to identify each decision alternative and each possible state of nature. The following four decision alternatives are available to the decision maker in our example problem:

15.4.1 DECISION ALTERNATIVES

1. Buy the parcel at location A.
2. Buy the parcel at location B.
3. Buy the parcels at locations A and B.
4. Buy nothing.

Regardless of which parcel or parcels Magnolia Inns decides to purchase, two possible states of nature can occur.

15.4.2 STATES OF NATURE

1. The new airport is built at location A.
2. The new airport is built at location B.

Figure 15.2 shows the payoff matrix for this problem. The rows in this spreadsheet represent the possible decision alternatives, and the columns correspond to the states of nature that might occur. Each value in this table indicates the financial payoff (in millions of dollars) expected for each possible decision under each state of nature.

15.4.3 THE PAYOFF VALUES

The value in cell B5 in Figure 15.2 indicates that if the company buys the parcel of land near location A, and the airport is built in this area, Magnolia Inns can expect to receive a payoff of $13 million. This figure of $13 million is computed from the data shown in Figure 15.1 as:

	Present value of future cash flows if hotel and airport are built at location A	$31,000,000
minus:	Current purchase price of hotel site at location A	−$18,000,000
		$13,000,000

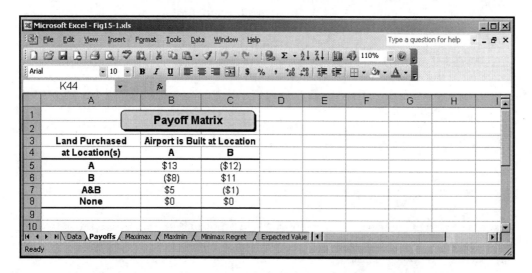

FIGURE 15.2

Payoff matrix for the Magnolia Inns decision problem

The value in cell C5 in Figure 15.2 indicates that if Magnolia Inns buys the parcel of land at location A (for $18 million), and the airport is built at location B, the company would resell the parcel at location A later for only $6 million, incurring a loss of $12 million.

The calculations of the payoffs for the parcel near location B are computed using similar logic. The value in cell C6 in Figure 15.2 indicates that if the company buys the parcel of land near location B, and the airport is built in this area, Magnolia Inns can expect to receive a payoff of $11 million. The value in cell B6 in Figure 15.2 indicates that if Magnolia Inns buys the parcel of land at location B (for $12 million), and the airport is built at location A, the company would resell the parcel at location B later for only $4 million, incurring a loss of $8 million.

Let's now consider the payoffs if the parcels at both locations A and B are purchased. The value in cell B7 in Figure 15.2 indicates that a payoff of $5 million will result if both parcels are purchased and the airport is built at location A. This payoff value is computed as:

	Present value of future cash flows if hotel and airport are built at location A	$31,000,000
plus:	Present value of future sales price for the unused parcel at location B	+$ 4,000,000
minus:	Current purchase price of hotel site at location A	−$18,000,000
minus:	Current purchase price of hotel site at location B	−$12,000,000
		$ 5,000,000

The value in cell C7 indicates that a loss of $1 million will occur if the parcels at both locations A and B are purchased, and the airport is built at location B.

The final alternative available to Magnolia Inns is to not buy either property at this point in time. This alternative guarantees that the company will neither gain nor lose anything, regardless of where the airport is located. Thus, cells B8 and C8 indicate that this alternative has a payoff of $0 regardless of which state of nature occurs.

15.5 Decision Rules

Now that the payoffs for each alternative under each state of nature have been determined, if Barbara knew with certainty where the airport was going to be built, it would be a simple matter for her to select the most desirable alternative. For example, if she knew the airport was going to be built at location A, a maximum payoff of $13 million could be obtained by purchasing the parcel of land at that location. Similarly, if she knew the airport was going to be built at location B, Magnolia Inns could achieve the maximum payoff of $11 million by purchasing the parcel at that location. The problem is that Barbara does not know where the airport is going to be built.

Several decision rules can be used to help a decision maker choose the best alternative. No one of these decision rules works best in all situations and, as you will see, each has some weaknesses. However, these rules help to enhance our insight and sharpen our intuition about decision problems so that we can make more informed decisions.

15.6 Nonprobabilistic Methods

The decision rules we will discuss can be divided into two categories: those that assume that probabilities of occurrence can be assigned to the states of nature in a decision problem (probabilistic methods), and those that do not (nonprobabilistic methods). We will discuss the nonprobabilistic methods first.

15.6.1 THE MAXIMAX DECISION RULE

As shown in Figure 15.2, the largest possible payoff will occur if Magnolia Inns buys the parcel at location A and the airport is built at this location. Thus, if the company optimistically believes that nature will always be "on its side" regardless of the decision it makes, the company should buy the parcel at location A because it leads to the largest possible payoff. This type of reasoning is reflected in the maximax decision rule, which determines the maximum payoff for each alternative and then selects the alternative associated with the largest payoff. Figure 15.3 illustrates the results of the maximax decision rule on our example problem.

Although the alternative suggested by the maximax decision rule enables Magnolia Inns to realize the best possible payoff, it does not guarantee that this payoff will occur. The actual payoff depends on where the airport ultimately is located. If we follow the maximax decision rule and the airport is built at location A, the company would receive $13 million; but if the airport is built at location B, the company would lose $12 million.

In some situations, the maximax decision rule leads to poor decisions. For example, consider the following payoff matrix:

Decision	State of Nature 1	State of Nature 2	MAX	
A	30	−10000	30	← maximum
B	29	29	29	

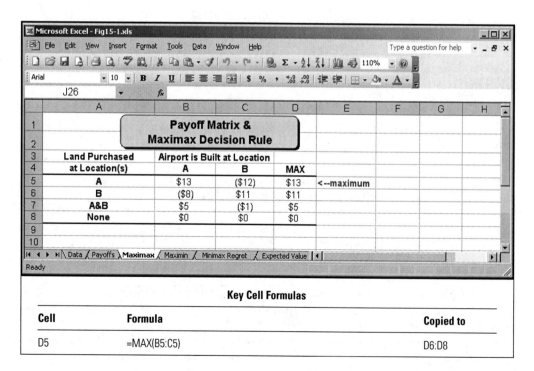

FIGURE 15.3

The maximax decision rule for the Magnolia Inns decision problem

In this problem, alternative A would be selected using the maximax decision rule. However, many decision makers would prefer alternative B because its guaranteed payoff is only slightly less than the maximum possible payoff, and it avoids the potential large loss involved with alternative A if the second state of nature occurs.

15.6.2 THE MAXIMIN DECISION RULE

A more conservative approach to decision making is given by the maximin decision rule, which pessimistically assumes that nature will always be "against us" regardless of the decision we make. This decision rule can be used to hedge against the worst possible outcome of a decision. Figure 15.4 illustrates the effect of the maximin decision rule on our example problem.

To apply the maximin decision rule, we first determine the minimum possible payoff for each alternative and then select the alternative with the largest minimum payoff (or the maximum of the minimum payoffs—hence the term "maximin"). Column D in Figure 15.4 lists the minimum payoff for each alternative. The largest (maximum) value in column D is the payoff of $0 associated with not buying any land. Thus, the maximin decision rule suggests that Magnolia Inns should not buy either parcel because, in the worst case, the other alternatives result in losses whereas this alternative does not.

The maximin decision rule can also lead to poor decision making. For example, consider the following payoff matrix:

	State of Nature			
Decision	1	2	MIN	
A	1000	28	28	
B	29	29	29	← maximum

FIGURE 15.4

The maximin decision rule for the Magnolia Inns decision problem

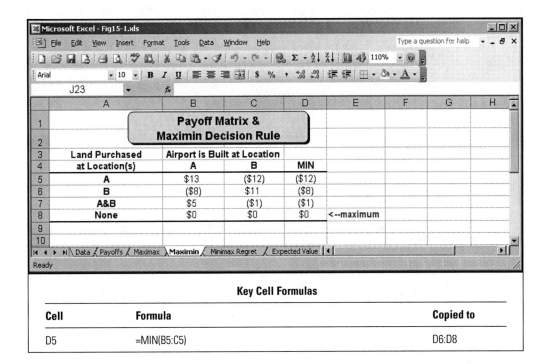

Land Purchased	Airport is Built at Location		
at Location(s)	A	B	MIN
A	$13	($12)	($12)
B	($8)	$11	($8)
A&B	$5	($1)	($1)
None	$0	$0	$0	<--maximum

Key Cell Formulas

Cell	Formula	Copied to
D5	=MIN(B5:C5)	D6:D8

In this problem, alternative B would be selected using the maximin decision rule. However, many decision makers would prefer alternative A because its worst-case payoff is only slightly less than that of alternative B, and it provides the potential for a much larger payoff if the first state of nature occurs.

15.6.3 THE MINIMAX REGRET DECISION RULE

Another way of approaching decision problems involves the concept of regret, or opportunity loss. For example, suppose that Magnolia Inns decides to buy the parcel of land at location A as suggested by the maximax decision rule. If the airport is built at location A, the company will not regret this decision at all because it provides the largest possible payoff under the state of nature that occurred. However, what if the company buys the parcel at location A and the airport is built at location B? In this case, the company would experience a regret, or opportunity loss, of $23 million. If Magnolia Inns had bought the parcel at location B, it would have earned a payoff of $11 million, and the decision to buy the parcel at location A resulted in a loss of $12 million. Thus, there is a difference of $23 million in the payoffs between these two alternatives under this state of nature.

To use the minimax regret decision rule, we first must convert our payoff matrix into a regret matrix that summarizes the possible opportunity losses that could result from each decision alternative under each state of nature. Figure 15.5 shows the regret matrix for our example problem.

The entries in the regret matrix are generated from the payoff matrix as:

Formula for cell B5:   =MAX(Payoffs!B$5:B$8)–Payoffs!B5
(Copy to B5 through C8.)

Each entry in the regret matrix shows the difference between the maximum payoff that can occur under a given state of nature and the payoff that would be realized from

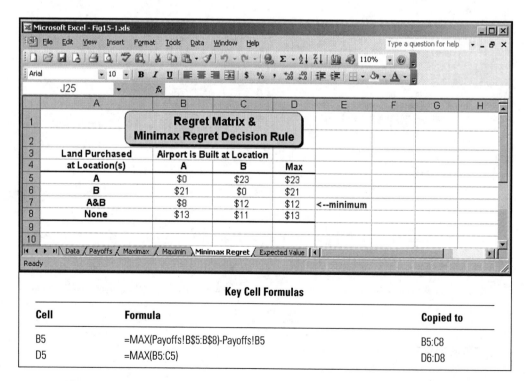

FIGURE 15.5

The maximax regret decision rule for the Magnolia Inns decision problem

Key Cell Formulas

Cell	Formula	Copied to
B5	=MAX(Payoffs!B$5:B$8)-Payoffs!B5	B5:C8
D5	=MAX(B5:C5)	D6:D8

each alternative under the same state of nature. For example, if Magnolia Inns buys the parcel of land at location A and the airport is built at this location, cell B5 indicates that the company experiences 0 regret. However, if the company buys the parcel at location B and the airport is built at location A, the company experiences an opportunity loss (or regret) of $21 million (13 − (−8) = 21).

Column D in Figure 15.5 summarizes the maximum regret that could be experienced with each decision alternative. The minimax regret decision corresponds to the alternative with the smallest (or minimum) maximum regret. As indicated in Figure 15.5, the minimax regret decision in our example problem is to buy the parcels at both sites. The maximum regret that could be experienced by implementing this decision is $12 million, whereas all other decisions could cause a larger regret.

The minimax regret decision rule can lead to peculiar decision making. For example, consider the following payoff matrix:

	State of Nature	
Decision	1	2
A	9	2
B	4	6

The regret matrix and minimax regret decision for this problem are represented by:

	State of Nature			
Decision	1	2	MAX	
A	0	4	4	← minimum
B	5	0	5	

Thus, if the alternatives are given by A and B, the minimax regret decision rule would select alternative A. Now, suppose that we add a new alternative to this decision problem to obtain the following payoff matrix:

	State of Nature	
Decision	1	2
A	9	2
B	4	6
C	3	9

Notice that the payoffs for alternatives A and B have not changed—we simply added a new alternative (C). The regret matrix and minimax regret decision for the revised problem are represented by:

	State of Nature			
Decision	1	2	MAX	
A	0	7	7	
B	5	3	5	← minimum
C	6	0	6	

The minimax regret decision is now given by alternative B. Some decision makers are troubled that the addition of a new alternative, which is not selected as the final decision, can change the relative preferences of the original alternatives. For example, suppose that a person prefers apples to oranges, but would prefer oranges if given the options of apples, oranges, and bananas. This person's reasoning is somewhat inconsistent or incoherent. But such reversals in preferences are a natural consequence of the minimax regret decision rule.

15.7 Probabilistic Methods

Probabilistic decision rules can be used if the states of nature in a decision problem can be assigned probabilities that represent their likelihood of occurrence. For decision problems that occur more than once, it is often possible to estimate these probabilities from historical data. However, many decision problems (such as the Magnolia Inns problem) represent one-time decisions for which historical data for estimating probabilities are unlikely to exist. In these cases, probabilities often are assigned subjectively based on interviews with one or more domain experts. Highly structured interviewing techniques exist to solicit probability estimates that are reasonably accurate and free of the unconscious biases that might affect an expert's opinions. These interviewing techniques are described in several of the references at the end of this chapter. Here, we will focus on the techniques that can be used once appropriate probability estimates have been obtained either from historical data or expert interviews.

15.7.1 EXPECTED MONETARY VALUE

The expected monetary value decision rule selects the decision alternative with the largest expected monetary value (EMV). The EMV of alternative i in a decision problem is defined as:

$$\text{EMV}_i = \sum_j r_{ij} p_j$$

where

r_{ij} = the payoff for alternative i under the jth state of nature

p_j = the probability of the jth state of nature

Figure 15.6 illustrates the EMV decision rule for our example problem. In this case, Magnolia Inns estimates a 40% chance that the airport will be built at location A and a 60% chance that it will be built at location B.

The probabilities for each state of nature are computed in cells B10 and C10, respectively. Using these probabilities, the EMV for each decision alternative is calculated in column D as:

Formula for cell D5:   =SUMPRODUCT(B5:C5,$B$10:$C$10)
(Copy to D6 through D8.)

The largest EMV is associated with the decision to purchase the parcel of land at location B. Thus, this is the decision suggested according to the EMV decision rule.

Let's consider the meaning of the figures in the EMV column in Figure 15.6. For example, the decision to purchase the parcel at location B has an EMV of $3.4 million. What does this figure represent? The payoff table indicates that Magnolia Inns will receive a payoff of $11 million if it buys this land and the airport is built there, or it will lose $8 million if it buys this land and the airport is built at the other location. So, there does not appear to be any way for the company to receive a payoff of $3.4 million if it buys the land at location B. However, imagine that Magnolia Inns faces this same decision not just once, but over and over again (perhaps on a weekly basis). If the company always decides to purchase the land at location B, we would expect it to receive a payoff

FIGURE 15.6

The expected monetary value decision rule for the Magnolia Inns decision problem

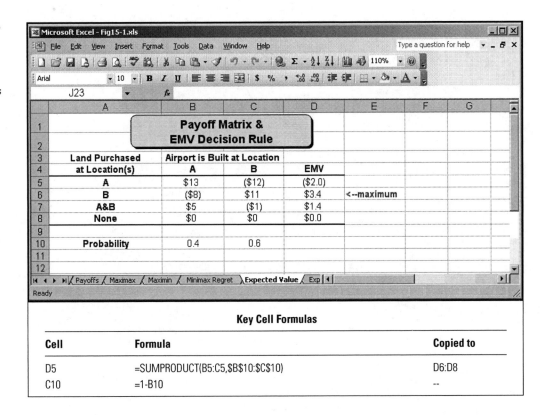

Key Cell Formulas

Cell	Formula	Copied to
D5	=SUMPRODUCT(B5:C5,$B$10:$C$10)	D6:D8
C10	=1-B10	--

of $11 million 60% of the time, and incur a loss of $8 million 40% of the time. Over the long run, then, the decision to purchase land at location B results in an average payoff of $3.4 million.

The EMV for a given decision alternative indicates the average payoff we would receive if we encounter the identical decision problem repeatedly and always select this alternative. Selecting the alternative with the highest EMV makes sense in situations where the identical decision problem will be faced repeatedly and we can "play the averages." However, this decision rule can be very risky in decision problems encountered only once (such as our example problem). For example, consider the following problem:

	State of Nature			
Decision	1	2	EMV	
A	15,000	−5,000	5,000	← maximum
B	5,000	4,000	4,500	
Probability	0.5	0.5		

If we face a decision with these payoffs and probabilities repeatedly and always select decision A, the payoff over the long run would average to $5,000. Because this is larger than decision B's average long-run payoff of $4,500, it would be best to always select decision A. But what if we face this decision problem only once? If we select decision A, we are equally likely to receive $15,000 or lose $5,000. If we select decision B, we are equally likely to receive payoffs of $5,000 or $4,000. In this case, decision A is more risky. Yet this type of risk is ignored completely by the EMV decision rule. Later, we will

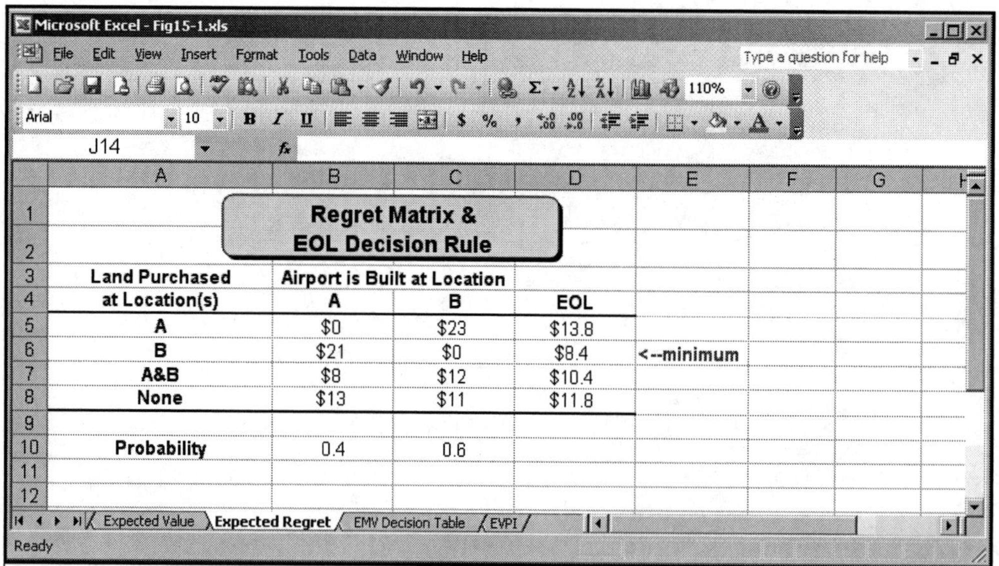

	Regret Matrix & EOL Decision Rule		
Land Purchased	Airport is Built at Location		
at Location(s)	A	B	EOL
A	$0	$23	$13.8
B	$21	$0	$8.4 <--minimum
A&B	$8	$12	$10.4
None	$13	$11	$11.8
Probability	0.4	0.6	

Key Cell Formulas

Cell	Formula	Copied to
B5	=MAX(Payoffs!B$5:B$8)-Payoffs!B5	B5:C8
D5	=SUMPRODUCT(B5:C5,$B$10:$C$10)	D6:D8
C10	=1-B10	--

FIGURE 15.7

The expected regret decision rule for the Magnolia Inns decision problem

discuss a technique—known as the utility theory—that allows us to account for this type of risk in our decision making.

15.7.2 EXPECTED REGRET

We also can use the probability of the states of nature to compute the expected regret, or expected opportunity loss (EOL), for each alternative in a decision problem. Figure 15.7 illustrates this process for our example problem.

The calculations in Figure 15.7 are identical to those used in computing the EMVs, only here we substitute regret values (or opportunity losses) for the payoffs. As shown in Figure 15.7, the decision to purchase the parcel at location B results in the smallest EOL. It is not a coincidence that this same decision also resulted in the largest EMV in Figure 15.6. The decision with the smallest EOL will also have the largest EMV. Thus, the EMV and EOL decision rules always result in the selection of the same decision alternative.

Key Point

The expected monetary value (EMV) and expected opportunity loss (EOL) decision rules always result in the selection of the same decision alternative.

15.7.3 SENSITIVITY ANALYSIS

When using probabilistic decision rules, one should always consider how sensitive the recommended decision is to the estimated probabilities. For instance, the EMV decision rule shown in Figure 15.6 indicates that if there is a 60% probability of the new airport being built at location B, the best decision is to purchase the land at location B. However, what if this probability is 55%? Or 50%? Or 45%? Would it still be best to purchase the land at location B?

We can answer this by building a data table that summarizes the EMVs for each alternative as we vary the probabilities. Figure 15.8 shows how to set up a data table for this problem.

First, in cells A14 through A24, we entered the values from 0 to 1 representing different probabilities for the airport being built at location A. Next, in cells B13 through E13,

FIGURE 15.8

Creating a data table of EMVs for the various alternatives as the probabilities change

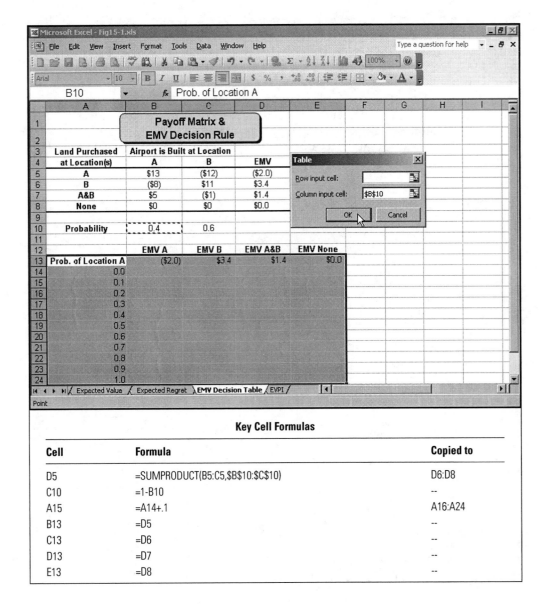

Key Cell Formulas		
Cell	**Formula**	**Copied to**
D5	=SUMPRODUCT(B5:C5,$B$10:$C$10)	D6:D8
C10	=1-B10	--
A15	=A14+.1	A16:A24
B13	=D5	--
C13	=D6	--
D13	=D7	--
E13	=D8	--

we entered formulas that link back to the EMVs for each of the decision alternatives. To finish the data table:

1. Select cells A13 through E24.
2. Click Data, Table. (This causes the Table dialog box shown in Figure 15.8 to appear.)
3. Specify a Column Input Cell of B10 (as shown in Figure 15.8).
4. Click OK.

This causes Excel to plug each of the values in cells A14 through A24 into cell B10, recalculate the spreadsheet, and then record the resulting EMVs for each decision alternative in our table. (Note that the formula in cell C10 makes the probability of the airport being built at location B dependent on the value in cell B10.) The resulting data table is shown in Figure 15.9.

The data table in Figure 15.9 indicates that if the probability of the airport being built at location A is 0.4 or less, then purchasing the land at location B has the highest EMV. However, if the airport is equally likely to be built at either location, then the decision to purchase land at both locations A and B has the highest EMV. If the airport is more likely to be built at location A, then purchasing the land at location A becomes the preferred decision.

The graph of the possible payoffs shown in Figure 15.9 makes it clear that buying the land at both locations A and B is a less risky alternative than buying either location individually. If there is much uncertainty in the probability estimates, the preferred alternative might well be to buy both pieces of property. For probability values between 0.4 and 0.6, the EMV of buying land at both locations A and B is always positive, and varies from \$1.4 million to \$2.6 million. Within this same range of probabilities, a decision to buy at location A individually or location B individually poses a risk of a negative EMV.

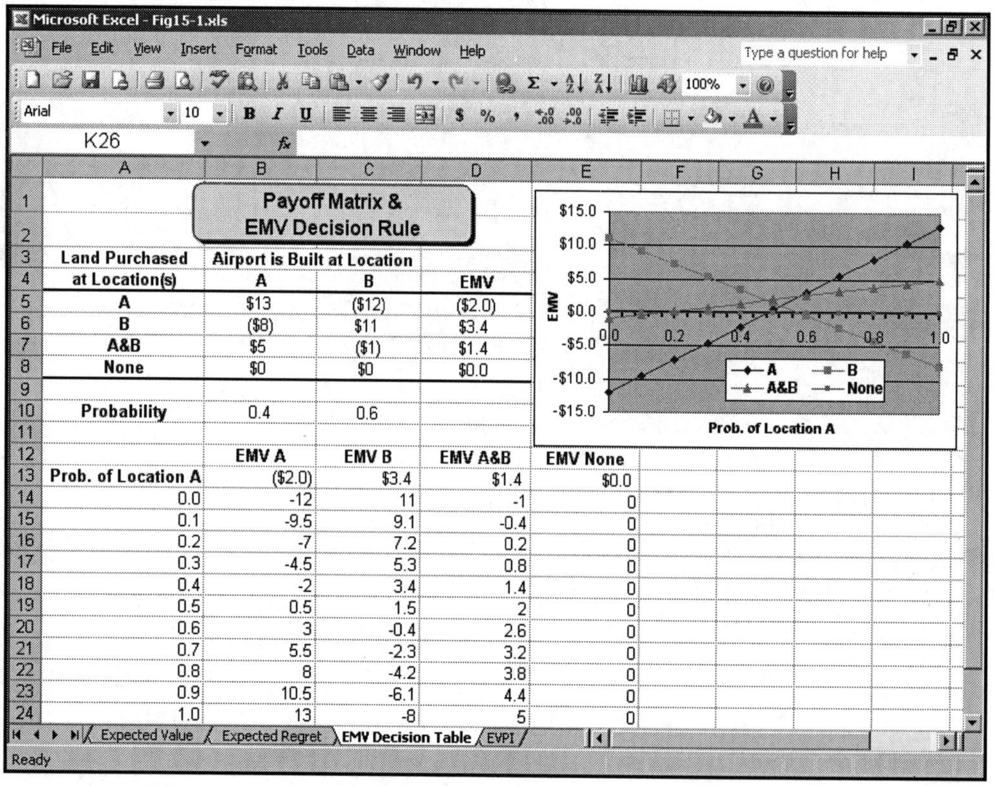

Land Purchased at Location(s)	Airport is Built at Location A	B	EMV
A	$13	($12)	($2.0)
B	($8)	$11	$3.4
A&B	$5	($1)	$1.4
None	$0	$0	$0.0
Probability	0.4	0.6	

Prob. of Location A	EMV A	EMV B	EMV A&B	EMV None
	($2.0)	$3.4	$1.4	$0.0
0.0	-12	11	-1	0
0.1	-9.5	9.1	-0.4	0
0.2	-7	7.2	0.2	0
0.3	-4.5	5.3	0.8	0
0.4	-2	3.4	1.4	0
0.5	0.5	1.5	2	0
0.6	3	-0.4	2.6	0
0.7	5.5	-2.3	3.2	0
0.8	8	-4.2	3.8	0
0.9	10.5	-6.1	4.4	0
1.0	13	-8	5	0

FIGURE 15.9

Data table for the Magnolia Inns decision problem

15.8 The Expected Value of Perfect Information

One of the primary difficulties in decision making is that we usually do not know which state of nature will occur. As we have seen, estimates of the probability of each state of nature can be used to calculate the EMV of various decision alternatives. However, probabilities do not tell us which state of nature will occur—they only indicate the likelihood of the various states of nature.

Suppose that we could hire a consultant who could tell us in advance and with 100% accuracy which state of nature will occur. If our example problem were a repeatable decision problem, 40% of the time the consultant would indicate that the airport will be built at location A, and the company would buy the parcel of land at location A and receive a payoff of $13 million. Similarly, 60% of the time the consultant would indicate that the airport will be built at location B, and the company would buy the parcel at location B and receive a payoff of $11 million. Thus, with advance perfect information about where the airport is going to be built, the average payoff would be:

Expected value *with* perfect information = $0.40 \times \$13 + 0.60 \times \$11 = \$11.8$ (in millions)

So, how much should Magnolia Inns be willing to pay this consultant for such information? From Figure 15.6, we know that *without* the services of this consultant, the best decision identified results in an EMV of $3.4 million. Therefore, the information provided by the consultant would enable the company to make decisions that increase the EMV by $8.4 million ($11.8 − $3.4 = $8.4). Thus, the company should be willing to pay the consultant up to $8.4 million for providing perfect information.

The expected value of perfect information (EVPI) is the expected value obtained with perfect information minus the expected value obtained without perfect information (which is given by the maximum EMV); that is:

$$\begin{matrix} \text{Expected value } of \\ \text{perfect information} \end{matrix} = \begin{matrix} \text{Expected value } with \\ \text{perfect information} \end{matrix} - \text{maximum EMV}$$

Figure 15.10 summarizes the EVPI calculation for our example problem. Cell D6 in Figure 15.10 shows the calculation of the maximum EMV of $3.4 million, which was described earlier in our discussion of the EMV decision rule. The payoffs of the decisions made under each state of nature with perfect information are calculated in cells B12 and C12 as:

Formula for cell B12:   =MAX(B5:B8)

(Copy to C12.)

The expected value *with* perfect information is calculated in cell D12 as:

Formula for cell D12:   =SUMPRODUCT(B12:C12,B10:C10)

Finally, the expected value *of* perfect information is computed in cell D14 as:

Formula for cell D14:   =D12–MAX(D5:D8)

Notice that the $8.4 million EVPI figure in cell D14 is identical to the minimum EOL shown earlier in Figure 15.7. This is *not* just a coincidence. The minimum EOL in a decision problem will always equal the EVPI.

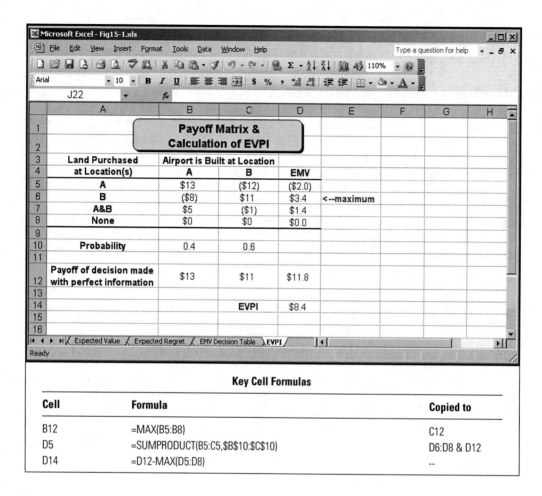

FIGURE 15.10

The expected value of perfect information for the Magnolia Inns decision problem

Key Cell Formulas

Cell	Formula	Copied to
B12	=MAX(B5:B8)	C12
D5	=SUMPRODUCT(B5:C5,$B$10:$C$10)	D6:D8 & D12
D14	=D12-MAX(D5:D8)	--

Key Point

The expected value of perfect information (EVPI) is equivalent to the minimum expected opportunity loss (EOL).

15.9 Decision Trees

Although some decision problems can be represented and analyzed effectively using payoff tables, we can also represent decision problems in a graphical form known as a decision tree. Figure 15.11 shows the decision problem for Magnolia Inns represented in this format.

As shown in Figure 15.11, a decision tree is composed of a collection of nodes (represented by circles and squares) interconnected by branches (represented by lines). A square node is called a decision node because it represents a decision. Branches emanating from a decision node represent the different alternatives for a particular decision. In Figure 15.11, a single decision node (node 0) represents the decision Magnolia Inns faces about where to buy land. The four branches coming out of this decision node

FIGURE 15.11

The decision tree representation of the Magnolia Inns problem

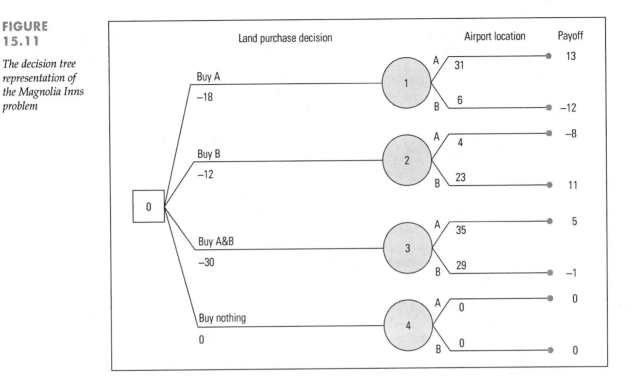

represent the four alternatives under consideration. The cash flow associated with each alternative is also listed. For example, the value –18 below the alternative labeled "Buy A" indicates that if the company purchases the parcel at location A, it must pay $18 million.

The circular nodes in a decision tree are called event nodes because they represent uncertain events. The branches emanating from event nodes (called event branches) correspond to the possible states of nature or the possible outcomes of an uncertain event. Figure 15.11 shows that each decision alternative emanating from node 0 is followed by an uncertain event represented by the event nodes 1, 2, 3, and 4. The branches from each event node represent a possible location of the new airport. In each case, the airport can be built at location A or B. The value next to each branch from the event nodes indicates the cash flow that will occur for that decision/event combination. For example, at node 1, the value 31 next to the first event branch indicates that if the company buys the parcel at location A and the airport is built at this location, a cash flow of $31 million will occur.

The various branches in a decision tree end at the small dots called leaves. Because each leaf corresponds to one way in which the decision problem can terminate, leaves also are referred to as terminal nodes. Each leaf in Figure 15.11 corresponds to an entry in the payoff table in Figure 15.2. The payoff occurring at each leaf is computed by summing the cash flows along the set of branches leading to each leaf. For example, following the uppermost branches through the tree, a payoff of $13 million results if the decision to buy the parcel at location A is followed by the new airport being built at this location (−18 + 31 = 13). You should verify the cash-flow values on each branch and at each leaf before continuing.

15.9.1 ROLLING BACK A DECISION TREE

After computing the payoffs at each leaf, we can apply any of the decision rules described earlier. For example, we could identify the maximum possible payoff for each decision

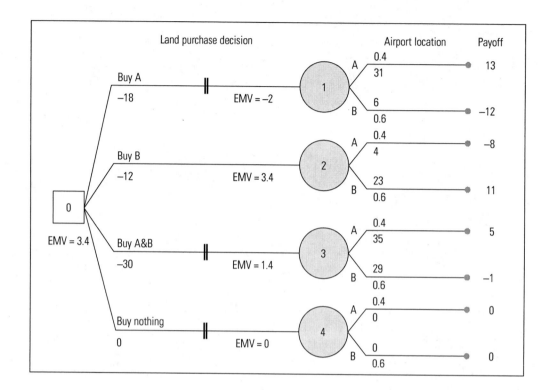

FIGURE
15.12

*Rolling back the
decision tree for
the Magnolia Inns
decision problem*

and apply the maximax decision rule. However, decision trees are used most often to implement the EMV decision rule—that is, to identify the decision with the largest EMV.

We can apply a process known as rolling back to a decision tree to determine the decision with the largest EMV. Figure 15.12 illustrates this process for our example problem.

Because the EMV decision rule is a probabilistic method, Figure 15.12 indicates the probabilities associated with each event branch emanating from each event node (that is, a 0.4 probability exists of the new airport being built at location A, and a 0.6 probability exists of it being built at location B). To roll back this decision tree, we start with the payoffs and work our way from right to left, back through the decision tree, computing the expected values for each node. For example, the event represented by node 1 has a 0.4 probability of resulting in a payoff of \$13 million, and a 0.6 probability of resulting in a loss of \$12 million. Thus, the EMV at node 1 is calculated as:

$$\text{EMV at node } 1 = 0.4 \times 13 + 0.6 \times -12 = -2.0$$

The expected value calculations for the remaining event nodes in Figure 15.12 are summarized as:

$$\text{EMV at node } 2 = 0.4 \times -8 + 0.6 \times 11 = 3.4$$
$$\text{EMV at node } 3 = 0.4 \times 5 + 0.6 \times -1 = 1.4$$
$$\text{EMV at node } 4 = 0.4 \times 0 + 0.6 \times 0 = 0.0$$

The EMV for a decision node is computed in a different way. For example, at node 0, we face a decision among four alternatives that lead to events with expected values of −2, 3.4, 1.4, and 0, respectively. At a decision node, we always select the alternative that leads to the best EMV. Thus, the EMV at node 0 is 3.4, which corresponds to the EMV resulting from the decision to buy land at location B. The optimal alternative at a decision node is sometimes indicated by "pruning" the suboptimal branches. The pruned

FIGURE
15.13

*Alternative
decision tree
representation of
the Magnolia Inns
decision problem*

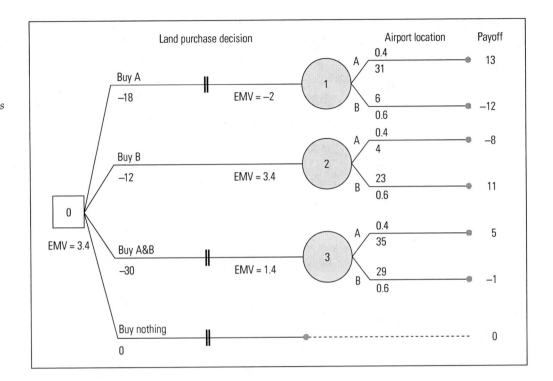

branches in Figure 15.12 are indicated by the double vertical lines (‖) shown on the sub-optimal alternatives emanating from node 0.

The relationship between the decision tree in Figure 15.12 and the payoff table in Figure 15.2 should now be clear. However, you might wonder if it is necessary to include event node 4 in the tree shown in Figure 15.12. If Magnolia Inns decides not to buy either property, the payoff it receives does not depend on where the airport ultimately is built—regardless of where the airport is built, the company will receive a payoff of 0.

Figure 15.13 shows an alternative, and perhaps more efficient, way of representing this problem as a decision tree in which it is clear that the decision not to purchase either parcel leads to a definite payoff of 0.

15.10 Using TreePlan

A spreadsheet add-in called TreePlan can help us create and analyze decision trees in Excel. We will use TreePlan to implement the decision tree shown in Figure 15.13 in Excel.

To attach the TreePlan add-in, choose the Open command from the File menu and open the file named treeplan.xla provided on your data disk. To create a decision tree using TreePlan, open a new workbook, then invoke TreePlan by choosing the DecisionTree command from the Tools menu (or by pressing [Ctrl][t]). In response, TreePlan displays the dialog box shown in Figure 15.14.

If you click the New Tree button, TreePlan creates a tree diagram with one initial decision node and two decision branches. As shown in Figure 15.15, this initial tree diagram is inserted in the spreadsheet near the cell that is active when TreePlan is invoked. Also note that TreePlan uses the vertical lines shown in cells F3 and F8 to denote the leaves (or terminal nodes) in a decision problem.

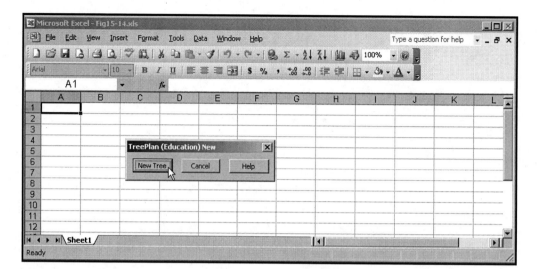

FIGURE
15.14

*Initial TreePlan
dialog box*

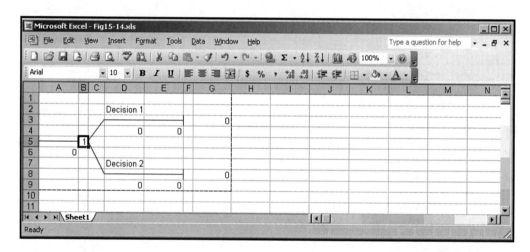

FIGURE
15.15

*Initial decision tree
created by
TreePlan*

TreePlan automatically labels the branches in the tree as Decision 1 and Decision 2. Later, we will change these labels to describe more accurately the decisions in our example problem. First, we will add two more decision branches to the initial tree shown in Figure 15.14.

15.10.1 ADDING BRANCHES

To add a new decision branch to our tree:

1. Click the decision node (cell B5).
2. Press [Ctrl][t] to invoke TreePlan.

The dialog box shown in Figure 15.16 appears. Because we selected a decision node before invoking TreePlan, this dialog box displays the options for working on a selected decision node. Different dialog boxes appear if we select an event node or terminal node and then invoke TreePlan. It is important to understand that TreePlan is context-sensitive— that is, the dialog box that appears when you invoke TreePlan depends on which cell is selected when TreePlan is invoked.

To add a branch to the currently selected decision node, click the Add branch option, and then click OK. A third branch is added to the tree, as shown in Figure 15.17.

FIGURE 15.16

TreePlan Decision dialog box

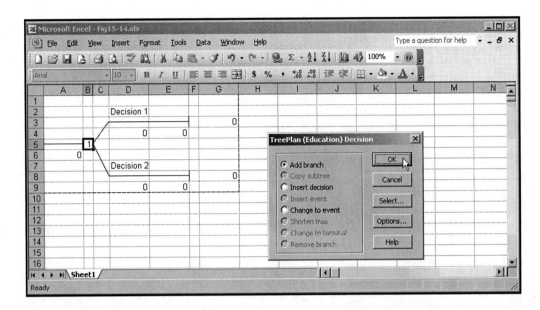

FIGURE 15.17

Modified tree with three decision branches

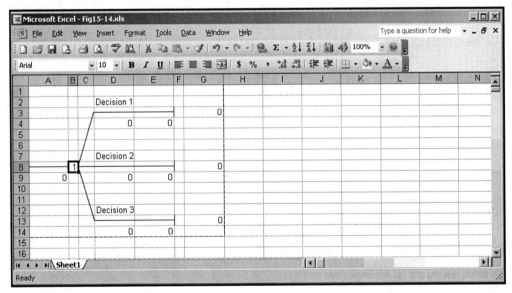

To add the fourth decision branch to the tree, we can follow the same procedure:

1. Click the decision node (cell B8).
2. Press [Ctrl][t] to invoke TreePlan.
3. Click Add branch.
4. Click OK.

The four decision branches for this problem appear as shown in Figure 15.18. Notice that we changed the label on each branch to reflect the decision alternatives for Magnolia Inns.

15.10.2 ADDING EVENT NODES

Each of the first three decision branches in Figure 15.13 leads to an event node with two event branches. Thus, we need to add similar event nodes to the decision tree shown in Figure 15.18. To add an event node:

1. Select the terminal node for the branch labeled Buy A (cell F3).
2. Press [Ctrl][t] to invoke TreePlan.

Because we selected a terminal node before invoking TreePlan, the TreePlan Terminal dialog box appears as shown in Figure 15.19.

This dialog box displays the options for working on a terminal node. In this case, we want to change the selected terminal node into an event node with two branches, as shown in Figure 15.19. The resulting spreadsheet is shown in Figure 15.20.

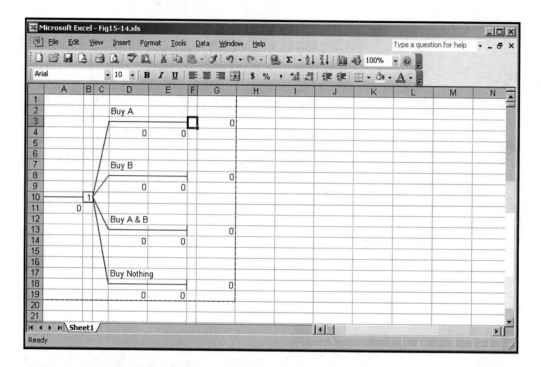

FIGURE 15.18

Modified tree with four decision branches labeled for the Magnolia Inns decision problem

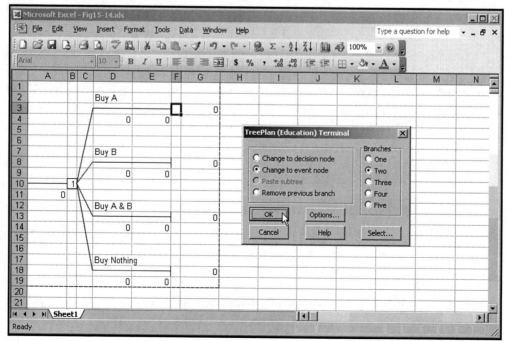

FIGURE 15.19

TreePlan Terminal dialog box

FIGURE 15.20

Modified tree with an event node

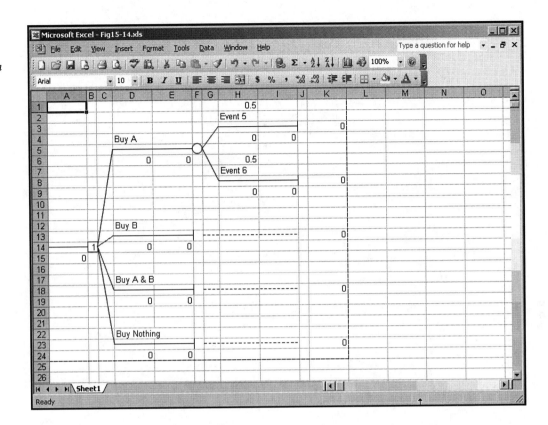

In Figure 15.20, an event node with two event branches now follows the decision to purchase the parcel at location A. TreePlan automatically labels these branches as Event 5 and Event 6, but we can change the labels to whatever we want. The cells immediately above each event branch label (cells H1 and H6) are reserved to represent the probability of each event. By default, TreePlan assumes that the events have equal probability (0.5), but we can change these values to whatever is appropriate for our particular problem.

In Figure 15.21, we changed the labels and probabilities of the event branches to correspond to the events occurring in the Magnolia Inns problem. The procedure used to create the event node for the Buy A decision could be repeated to create event nodes for the decisions corresponding to Buy B and Buy A & B. However, because all of the event nodes are identical in this problem, we can simply copy the existing event node.

You might be tempted to copy and paste the existing event node using the standard Excel commands—but if you use the standard Excel commands, TreePlan cannot update the tree settings properly. As indicated in Figure 15.21, TreePlan provides a built-in option that allows you to copy a section, or subtree, of a decision tree to another part of the tree. It is important to copy subtrees using this command so that TreePlan can update the appropriate formulas in the spreadsheet. To create a copy of the event node:

1. Select the event node you want to copy (cell F5).
2. Press [Ctrl][t] to invoke TreePlan.
3. Click Copy subtree.
4. Click OK.

This creates a copy of the selected event node on the Clipboard. As shown in Figure 15.22, to paste a copy of this subtree into the decision tree:

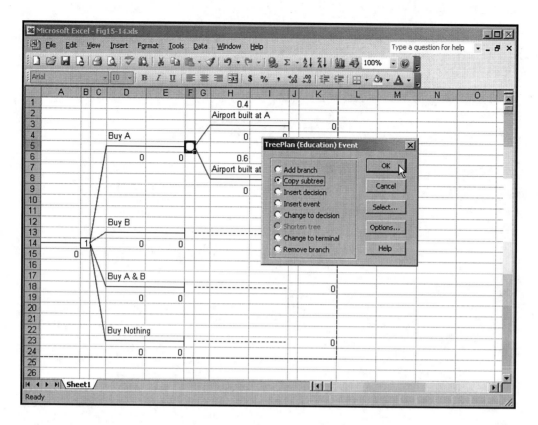

FIGURE
15.21

*Using TreePlan to
copy a subtree*

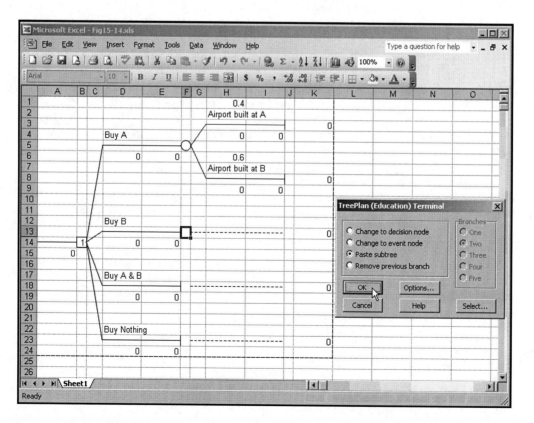

FIGURE
15.22

*Using TreePlan to
paste the copied
subtree*

FIGURE 15.23

Decision tree with three event nodes

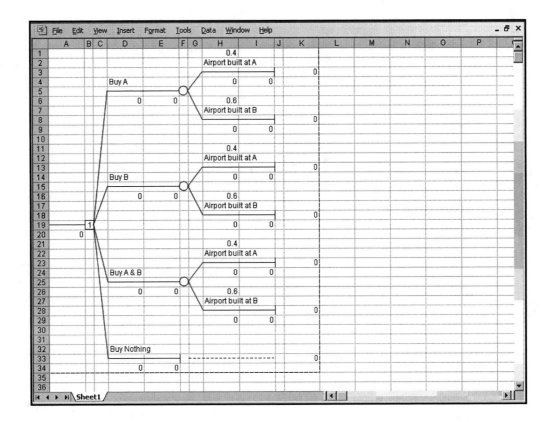

1. Select the target cell location (cell F13).
2. Press [Ctrl][t] to invoke TreePlan.
3. Click Paste subtree.
4. Click OK.

We can repeat this copy-and-paste procedure to create the third event node needed for the decision to buy the parcels at both locations A and B. Figure 15.23 shows the resulting spreadsheet.

15.10.3 ADDING THE CASH FLOWS

To complete the decision tree, we need to add the cash flows that are associated with each decision and event. TreePlan reserves the first cell below each branch to represent the partial cash flow associated with that branch. For example, in Figure 15.24 (and in the file Fig15-24.xls on your data disk), cell D6 represents the partial cash flow that occurs if Magnolia Inns buys the parcel at location A, and cell H4 represents the partial cash flow that occurs if the company buys the parcel at location A *and* the airport is built at that location. The remaining partial cash flows for each decision are entered in the appropriate cells in Figure 15.24 in a similar manner.

15.10.4 DETERMINING THE PAYOFFS AND EMVs

Next to each terminal node, TreePlan automatically created a formula that sums the payoffs along the branches leading to that node. For example, cell K3 in Figure 15.24 contains the formula =SUM(H4,D6). Thus, when we enter or change the partial cash flows for the branches in the decision tree, the payoffs are updated automatically.

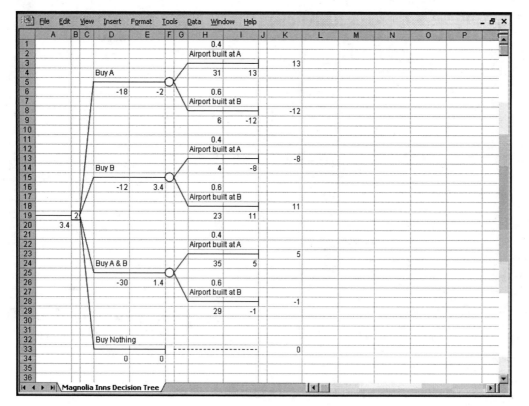

Immediately below and to the left of each node, TreePlan created formulas that compute the EMV at each node in the same way as described earlier in our discussion of rolling back a decision tree. Thus, cell A20 in Figure 15.24 indicates that the largest EMV at the decision node is $3.4 million. The value 2 in the decision node (cell B19) indicates that this maximum EMV is obtained by selecting the second decision alternative (that is, by purchasing the parcel at location B).

15.10.5 OTHER FEATURES

The preceding discussion of TreePlan was intended to give you an overview of how TreePlan operates, its capabilities, and some of its options. Most of the other TreePlan options are self-explanatory, and you can obtain descriptions of them by clicking the Help button available in all the TreePlan dialog boxes. The Select and Options buttons available in all the TreePlan dialog boxes presented earlier lead, respectively, to the two dialog boxes shown in Figure 15.25.

At times, we might want to select all the instances of a certain type of element in a decision tree. For example, we might want to select all the partial cash flows and display them in a currency format, or we might want to hide all the EMV values. The TreePlan Select dialog box shown in Figure 15.25 is designed to simplify this process. By selecting an option in this dialog box, all the elements of the type chosen will be selected automatically in the spreadsheet, enabling us to format them all at the same time.

The TreePlan Options dialog box serves two purposes. By default, TreePlan assumes that we want to analyze the decision tree using expected values. However, another technique (described later) uses exponential utility functions in place of expected values.

FIGURE
15.25

*TreePlan Select
and TreePlan
Options dialog
boxes*

TreePlan (Education) Select   ☒

┌─Cells─────────────┐ ┌─Objects───────────┐ ┌─Columns───────────┐
○ Branch names   ⊙ Decision nodes   ○ Nodes
○ Partial cash flows ○ Event nodes   ○ Diagonals
○ Probabilities   ○ Terminal nodes   ○ Left branches
○ Rollback EVs/CEs   ○ Branch lines   ○ Right branches
○ Rollback EUs   ○ Diagonal lines   ○ Terminal values
○ Terminal values   ○ Connectors

[OK]   [Options...]   [Cancel]   [Help]

TreePlan (Education) Options   ☒

┌─Certainty Equivalents──────────────┐
⊙ Use Expected Values
○ Use Exponential Utility Function

┌─Decision Node EV/CE Choices────────┐
⊙ Maximize (profits)
○ Minimize (costs)

[OK]   [Cancel]   [Select...]   [Help]

Thus, this dialog box provides options for selecting whether TreePlan should use expected values or exponential utility functions. Also by default, TreePlan assumes that the EMVs that it calculates represent profit values, and that we want to identify the decision with the largest EMV. However, in some decision trees, the expected values could represent costs that we want to minimize. Thus, this dialog box provides options for maximizing profits or minimizing costs.

About TreePlan

TreePlan is a *shareware* product. The developer of this package, Dr. Michael Middleton, graciously allows it to be distributed with this textbook at no charge to you. If you like this software package and plan to use it for more than 30 days, you are expected to pay a nominal registration fee. Details on registration are available near the end of the TreePlan help file, which you can access by clicking the Help button in any TreePlan dialog box or on the Web at http://www.treeplan.com.

15.11 Multistage Decision Problems

To this point, our discussion of decision analysis has considered only single-stage decision problems—that is, problems in which a single decision must be made. However, most decisions that we face lead to other decisions. As a simple example, consider the decision of whether to go out to dinner. If you decide to go out to dinner, you must then decide how much to spend, where to go, and how to get there. Thus, before you actually decide to go out to dinner, you'll probably consider the other issues and decisions that must be made if you choose that alternative. These types of problems are called multistage decision problems. The following example illustrates how a multistage decision problem can be modeled and analyzed using a decision tree.

The Occupational Safety and Health Administration (OSHA) has recently announced that it will award an $85,000 research grant to the person or company submitting the best proposal for using wireless communications technology to enhance safety in the coal-mining industry. Steve Hinton, the owner of COM-TECH, a small communications research firm located just outside of Raleigh, North Carolina, is considering whether or not to apply for this grant. Steve estimates that he would spend approximately $5,000 preparing his grant proposal and that he has about a 50-50 chance of actually receiving the grant. If he is awarded the grant, he then would need to decide whether to use microwave, cellular, or infrared communications technology. He has some experience in all three areas, but would need to acquire some new equipment depending on which technology is used. The cost of the equipment needed for each technology is summarized as:

Technology	Equipment Cost
Microwave	$4,000
Cellular	$5,000
Infrared	$4,000

In addition to the equipment costs, Steve knows that he will spend money in research and development (R&D) to carry out the research proposal, but he does not know exactly what the R&D costs will be. For simplicity, Steve estimates the following best-case and worst-case R&D costs associated with using each technology, and he assigns probabilities to each outcome based on his degree of expertise in each area.

	Possible R&D Costs			
	Best Case		Worst Case	
	Cost	Prob.	Cost	Prob.
Microwave	$30,000	0.4	$60,000	0.6
Cellular	$40,000	0.8	$70,000	0.2
Infrared	$40,000	0.9	$80,000	0.1

Steve needs to synthesize all the factors in this problem to decide whether or not to submit a grant proposal to OSHA.

15.11.1 A MULTISTAGE DECISION TREE

The immediate decision in this example problem is whether or not to submit a grant proposal. To make this decision, Steve also must consider the technology selection decision that he will face if he receives the grant. So, this is a multistage decision problem. Figure 15.26 (and the file Fig15-26.xls on your data disk) shows the decision tree representation of this problem where, for clarity, we have temporarily hidden the rollback EMVs at each event and decision node in the tree.

FIGURE 15.26

Multistage decision tree for COM-TECH's grant proposal problem

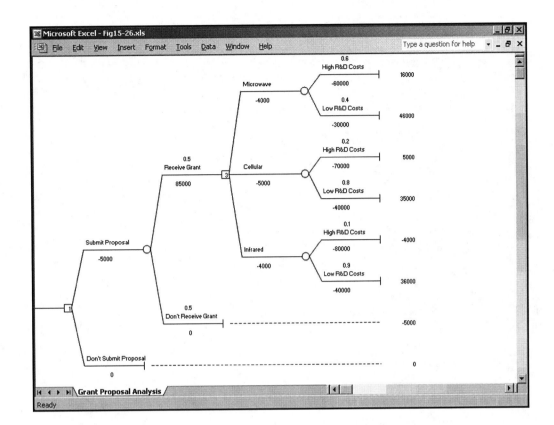

This decision tree clearly shows that the first decision Steve faces is whether or not to submit a proposal, and that submitting the proposal will cost $5,000. If a proposal is submitted, we then encounter an event node showing a 0.5 probability of receiving the grant (and a payoff of $85,000), and a 0.5 probability of not receiving the grant (leading to a net loss of $5,000). If the grant is received, we then encounter a decision about which technology to pursue. Each of the three technology options has an event node representing the best-case (lowest) and worst-case (highest) R&D costs that might be incurred. The final (terminal) payoffs associated with each set of decisions and outcomes are listed next to each terminal node. For example, if Steve submits a proposal, receives the grant, employs cellular technology, and encounters low R&D costs, he will receive a net payoff of $35,000.

In Figure 15.26, note that the probabilities on the branches at any event node always must sum to 1 because these branches represent all the events that could occur. The R&D costs that actually would occur using a given technology could assume an infinite number of values. Some might argue that these costs could be modeled more accurately by some continuous random variable. However, our aim is to estimate the expected value of this random variable. Most decision makers probably would find it easier to assign subjective probabilities to a small, discrete set of representative outcomes for a variable such as R&D costs rather than try to identify an appropriate probability distribution for this variable.

Figure 15.27 (and the file Fig15-27.xls on your data disk) shows the completed decision tree for our example problem, including the EMV at each node. According to this decision tree, Steve should submit a proposal because the expected value of this decision is $13,500 and the expected value of not submitting a proposal is $0. The decision tree also indicates that if Steve receives the grant, he should pursue the infrared

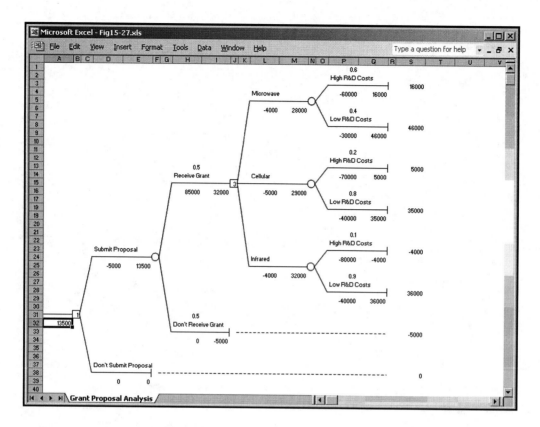

FIGURE
15.27

*Multistage
decision tree with
EMVs for COM-
TECH's grant
proposal problem*

communications technology because the expected value of this decision ($32,000) is larger than the expected values for the other technologies.

15.11.2 DEVELOPING A RISK PROFILE

When using decision trees to analyze one-time decision problems, it is particularly helpful to develop a risk profile to make the sure that the decision maker understands all the possible outcomes that might occur. A *risk profile* is a graph or tree that shows the chances associated with possible outcomes. Figure 15.28 shows the risk profile associated with not submitting the proposal, and that of the optimal EMV decision-making strategy (submitting the proposal and using infrared technology) identified from Figure 15.27.

From Figure 15.28, it is clear that if the proposal is not submitted, the payoff will be $0. If the proposal is submitted, there is a 0.50 chance of not receiving the grant and incurring a loss of $5,000. If the proposal is submitted, there is a 0.05 chance (0.5 × 0.1 = 0.05) of receiving the grant but incurring high R&D costs with the infrared technology and suffering a $4,000 loss. Finally, if the proposal is submitted, there is a 0.45 chance (0.5 × 0.9 = 0.45) of enjoying small R&D costs with the infrared technology and making a $36,000 profit.

A risk profile is an effective tool for breaking an EMV into its component parts and communicating information about the actual outcomes that can occur as the result of various decisions. By looking at Figure 15.28, a decision maker could reasonably decide that the risks (or chances) of losing money if a proposal is submitted are not worth the potential benefit to be gained if the proposal is accepted and low R&D costs occur. These risks would not be apparent if the decision maker was provided only with information about the EMV of each decision.

FIGURE 15.28

A risk profile for the alternatives of submitting or not submitting the proposal

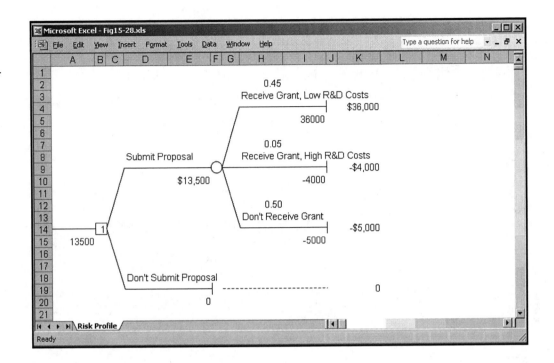

15.12 Sensitivity Analysis

Before implementing the decision to submit a grant proposal as suggested by the previous analysis, Steve would be wise to consider how sensitive the recommended decision is to changes in values in the decision tree. For example, Steve estimated that a 50-50 chance exists that he will receive the grant if he submits a proposal. But what if that probability assessment is wrong? What if only a 30%, 20%, or 10% chance exists of receiving the grant? Should he still submit the proposal?

Using a decision tree implemented in a spreadsheet, it is fairly easy to determine how much any of the values in the decision tree can change before the indicated decision would change. For example, Figure 15.29 shows how we can use Solver to determine how small the probability of receiving the grant would need to be before it would no longer be wise to submit the grant proposal (according to the EMV decision rule).

In this spreadsheet, we are using cell H13 (the probability of receiving the grant) as both our set cell and our variable cell. In cell H31, we entered the following formula to compute the probability of not receiving the grant:

Formula for cell H31:   =1–H13

Minimizing the value in cell H13 while constraining the value of B31 to equal 1 determines the probability of receiving the grant that makes the EMV of submitting the grant equal to zero. The resulting probability (*i.e.*, approximately 0.1351) gives the decision maker some idea of how sensitive the decision is to changes in the value of cell H13.

If the EMV of submitting the grant is zero, most decision makers probably would not want to submit the grant proposal. Indeed, even with an EMV of $13,500 (as shown in Figure 15.28), some decision makers still would not want to submit the grant proposal because there is still a risk that the proposal would be turned down and a $5,000 loss incurred. As mentioned earlier, the EMV decision rule is best applied when we face a

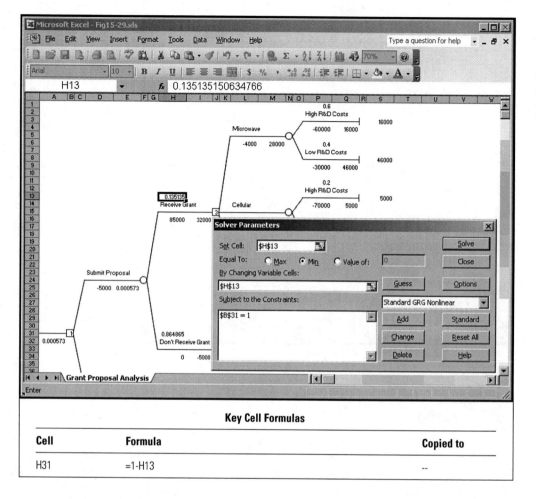

FIGURE
15.29

*Using Solver to
determine the
sensitivity of a
decision to changes
in probabilities*

Key Cell Formulas

Cell	Formula	Copied to
H31	=1-H13	--

decision that will be made repeatedly and the results of bad outcomes can be balanced or averaged with good outcomes.

15.12.1 SPIDER CHARTS AND TORNADO CHARTS

As shown in the previous section, Solver can be used to determine the amount by which almost any value in a decision tree can be changed before a recommended decision (based of EMV) would change. However, given the number of probability and financial estimates used as inputs to a decision tree, it is often helpful to use spider charts and/or tornado charts to identify the inputs that, if changed, have the greatest impact on the EMV. This helps to identify the areas where sensitivity analysis is most important and prioritize where time and resources should be applied in refining probability and financial estimates represented in the decision tree.

The Crystal Ball software package (discussed in Chapter 12) includes a Tornado Chart tool that assists in creating spider charts and tornado charts. (The Tornado Chart tool is found under the Run, Tools menu when Crystal Ball is loaded in Excel.) This tool allows you to specify an output cell of interest and up to 256 input cells that are believed to affect the value of the output cell. It then incrementally changes the value of each input cell from its base case value (while holding the other input cells constant) within a user specified percentage range (e.g., ± 20%) and records the effect of each change on the output cell's value.

FIGURE 15.30

Tornado chart of R&D costs for COM-TECH's decision problem

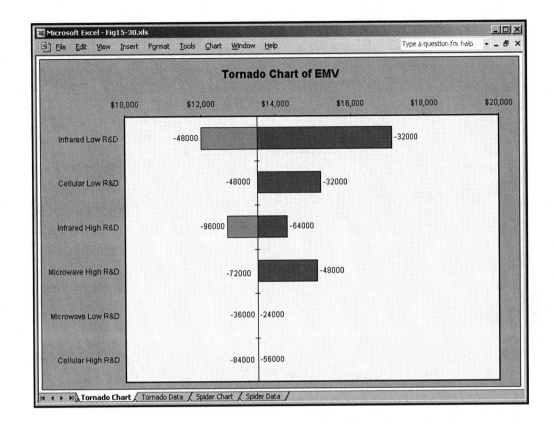

As an example, suppose we are interested in examining the sensitivity of the EMV shown in cell A32 in Figure 15.29 to changes in the high and low R&D costs estimated for the microwave, cellular, and infrared technologies as given in cells P4, P9, P14, P19, P24, and P29. Crystal Ball's Tornado Chart tool was used to create the tornado chart and spider charts shown (after some cosmetic adjustment) in Figures 15.30 and 15.31, respectively.

The tornado chart in Figure 15.30 summarizes the impact on the decision tree's EMV of each input cell being set at +20% and −20% of its original (base case) value. The input cell with the largest impact on the EMV's range is shown first, the input cell with the next largest impact is shown second, and so on. At the top of the tornado chart we readily see that the low R&D cost estimate for the infrared technology has the largest impact on the EMV as it is adjusted from −20% to +20% of its original value (of −$40,000). At the bottom end of the tornado chart we see that the low R&D cost estimate for microwave technology and the high R&D cost estimate for cellular have no impact on the EMV if they are adjusted from −20% to +20% of their original values. Thus, the tornado chart quickly gives us a good sense for which R&D cost estimates (if wrong) have the most direct impact on the EMV and the associated recommended decision.

The spider chart in Figure 15.31 conveys the same information as the tornado chart but with a bit more detail. Again we see that changes in the low R&D cost estimate for infrared technology produces the greatest amount of change in the EMV. However, notice there is an inflection point on the associated line in the graph when this cost is increased by 10%. That is, after the low R&D cost estimate is increased by 10%, additional increases in this estimated cost no longer produce changes in the EMV. This often indicates that the recommended decision has changed at (or around) that point. (You can verify this manually by increasing the estimated R&D cost in cell P29 from −$40,000 to −$44,000 and observing that the recommended technology then changes from infrared to cellular).

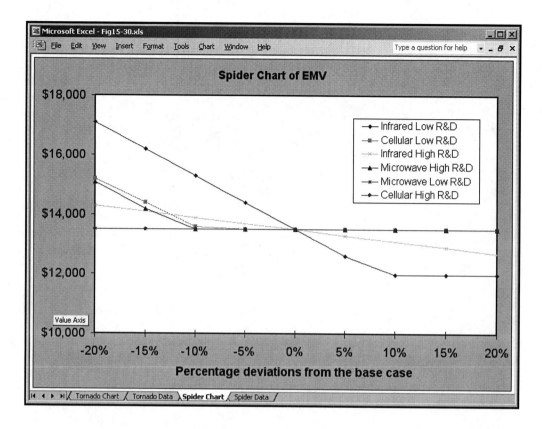

**FIGURE
15.31**

*Spider chart of
R&D costs for
COM-TECH's
decision problem*

Thus, the spider chart also gives us a good sense for which R&D cost estimates (if wrong) have the most direct impact on the EMV, and provides additional clues as to when the recommended decision might change. However, because the spider chart is constructed using discrete percentage changes from the base case values (discrete steps of 5% in this example), the exact point at which the recommended decision changes cannot always be inferred from the chart, and the use of Solver may be warranted.

> ## Creating a Tornado Charts & Spider Charts
>
> To create a tornado chart or spider chart like the ones shown in Figure 15.30 and Figure 31:
>
> 1. Load the Crystal Ball add-in as described in Chapter 12.
> 2. Click the Run, Tools menu.
> 3. Click Tornado Chart.
>
> Crystal Ball's Chart Wizard first prompts you to enter the target cell (or output cell) you want to track. On the next dialog, you can use the "Add Range" button to identify the various input cells you want to consider in the analysis. On the next dialog, you make several selections concerning how the charts should be constructed. After Crystal Ball creates the basic charts, you can customize them in many ways. Double-clicking a chart element displays a dialog box with options for modifying the appearance of the element.

15.12.2 STRATEGY TABLES

A *strategy table* is another sensitivity analysis technique that allows a decision maker to analyze how the optimal decision strategy changes in response to two simultaneous changes in probability estimates. For example, the optimal strategy in Figure 15.27 is to submit the proposal and use infrared technology. However, suppose that there is uncertainty about the probability of receiving the grant and the probability of encountering high R&D costs while carrying out the research proposal. Specifically, suppose that the decision maker wants to see how the optimal strategy changes as the probability of receiving the grant varies from 0.0 to 1.0 and the probability of encountering high infrared R&D costs varies from 0.0 to 0.5. As shown in Figure 15.32, a two-way data table can be used to analyze this situation.

In Figure 15.32, cells W12 through W22 represent different probabilities of receiving the grant. Using the Data Table command, we will instruct Excel to plug each of these values into cell H13, representing the probability of receiving the grant. The following formula was entered in cell H31 to calculate the complementary probability of not receiving the grant.

$$\text{Formula for cell H31:} \qquad =1-H13$$

FIGURE 15.32

Setting up a strategy table for the COM-TECH decision problem

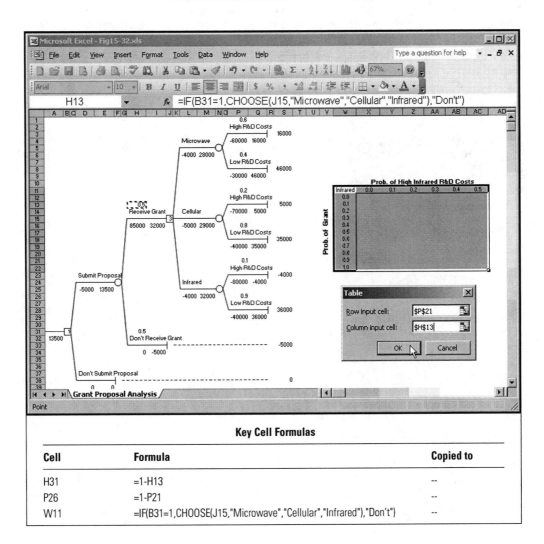

Key Cell Formulas

Cell	Formula	Copied to
H31	=1-H13	--
P26	=1-P21	--
W11	=IF(B31=1,CHOOSE(J15,"Microwave","Cellular","Infrared"),"Don't")	--

Cells X11 through AC11 represent different probabilities of encountering high R&D costs. Using the Data Table command, we will instruct Excel to plug each of these values into cell P21, representing the probability of receiving the grant. The following formula was entered in cell P26 to calculate the complementary probability of not receiving the grant.

Formula for cell P26: $=1-P21$

As these different probabilities are changed, the spreadsheet will be recalculated and the value returned by the formula in cell W11 will be recorded in the appropriate cell in the data table.

Formula for cell W11:   =IF(B31=1,CHOOSE
(J15,"Microwave","Cellular","Infrared"),"Don't")

This formula first inspects the value of cell B31; which equals 1 if the EMV of submitting the proposal is positive. Thus, if B31 is equal to 1, the formula then returns (chooses) the label "Microwave," "Cellular," or "Infrared" depending on whether the value in cell J15 is one, two, or three, respectively. Otherwise, the previous formula returns the label "Don't" indicating that the proposal should not be submitted. The results of executing the Data Table command are shown in Figure 15.33.

Figure 15.33 summarizes the optimal strategy for the various probability combinations. For instance, if the probability of receiving the grant is 0.10 or less, the company should not submit a proposal. Note that cell Y17 corresponds to the base case solution shown earlier in Figure 15.27. The strategy table makes it clear that this solution is relatively insensitive to changes in the probability of receiving the grant. However, if the probability of encountering high infrared R&D costs increases, the preferred strategy

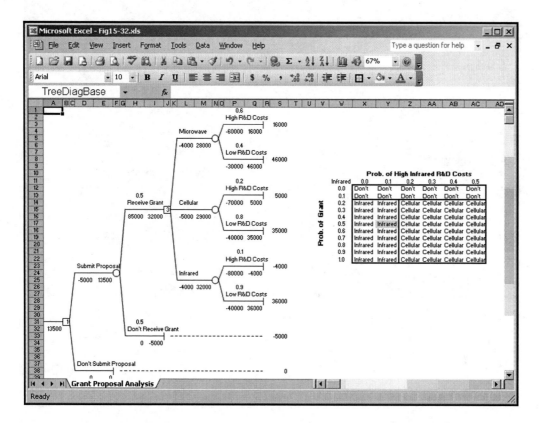

FIGURE 15.33

Completed strategy table for the COM-TECH decision problem

quickly switches to the cellular technology alternative. Thus, the decision maker might want to give closer attention to the risks of encountering high infrared R&D costs before implementing this strategy.

15.13 Using Sample Information in Decision Making

In many decision problems, we have the opportunity to obtain additional information about the decision before we actually make the decision. For example, in the Magnolia Inns decision problem, the company could have hired a consultant to study the economic, environmental, and political issues surrounding the site selection process, and to predict which site would be selected for the new airport by the planning council. This information might help Magnolia Inns make a better (or more informed) decision. The potential for using this type of additional sample information in decision making raises several interesting issues that are illustrated using the following example.

Colonial Motors (CM) is trying to determine what size of manufacturing plant to build for a new car it is developing. Only two plant sizes are under consideration: large and small. The cost of constructing a large plant is $25 million and the cost of constructing a small plant is $15 million. CM believes that a 70% chance exists that the demand for this new car will be high and a 30% chance exists that it will be low. The following table summarizes the payoffs (in millions of dollars) that the company expects to receive for each factory size and demand combination (not counting the cost of the factory).

	Demand	
Factory Size	High	Low
Large	$175	$ 95
Small	$125	$105

A decision tree for this problem is shown in Figure 15.34 (and in the file Fig15-34.xls on your data disk). The decision tree indicates that the optimal decision is to build the large plant and that this alternative has an EMV of $126 million.

FIGURE
15.34

Decision tree for the CM plant size problem

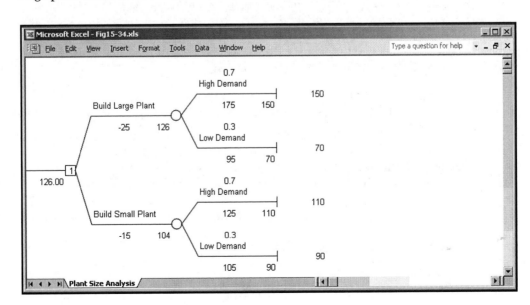

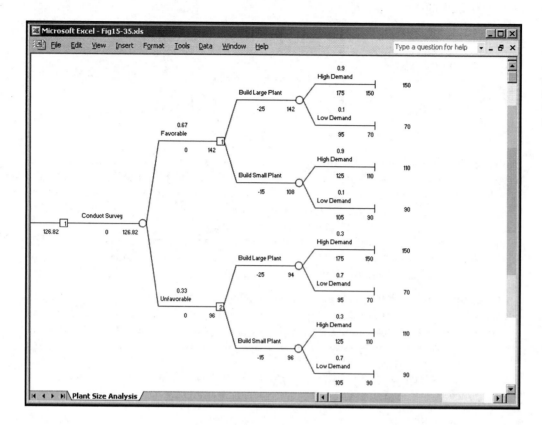

Now suppose that before making the plant size decision, CM conducts a survey to assess consumer attitudes about the new car. For simplicity, we will assume that the results of this survey indicate either a favorable or unfavorable attitude about the new car. A revised decision tree for this problem is shown in Figure 15.35 (and in the file Fig15-35.xls on your data disk).

The decision tree in Figure 15.35 begins with a decision node with a single branch representing the decision to conduct the market survey. For now, assume that this survey can be done at no cost. An event node follows, corresponding to the outcome of the market survey, which can indicate either favorable or unfavorable attitudes about the new car. We assume that CM believes that the probability of a favorable response is 0.67 and the probability of an unfavorable response is 0.33.

15.13.1 CONDITIONAL PROBABILITIES

After the survey results are known, the decision nodes in the tree indicate that a decision must be made about whether to build a large plant or a small plant. Following each decision branch, event nodes occur with branches representing the market demands for the car that could occur. Four event nodes represent the market demand that might occur for this car. However, the probabilities that we assign to the branches of these nodes are likely to differ depending on the results of the market survey.

Earlier, we indicated that CM believed a 0.70 probability exists that demand for the new car will be high, expressed mathematically as:

$$P(\text{high demand}) = 0.7$$

In this formula P(A) = X is read, "the probability of A is X." If the market survey indicates that consumers have a favorable impression of the new car, this will raise expectations that demand will be high for the car. Thus, given a favorable survey response, we might increase the probability assessment for a high-market demand to 0.90. This is expressed mathematically as the following *conditional* probability:

$$P(\text{high demand} \mid \text{favorable response}) = 0.90$$

In this formula P(A | B) = X is read, "the probability of A given B is X."

As noted earlier, the probabilities on the branches at any event node always must sum to 1. If the favorable survey response increases the probability assessment of a high demand occurring, it must decrease the probability assessment of a low demand given this survey result. Thus, the probability of a low demand given a favorable response on the survey is:

$$
\begin{aligned}
P(\text{low demand} \mid \text{favorable response}) &= 1 - P(\text{high demand} \mid \text{favorable response}) \\
&= 1 - 0.90 = 0.10
\end{aligned}
$$

These conditional probabilities are shown in Figure 15.35 on the first four event branches representing high and low demands given a favorable survey response.

If the market survey indicates that consumers have an unfavorable response to the new car, this will lower expectations for high-market demand. Thus, given an unfavorable survey response, we might reduce the probability assessment of a high-market demand to 0.30:

$$P(\text{high demand} \mid \text{unfavorable response}) = 0.30$$

We must also revise the probability assessment for a low-market demand given an unfavorable market response as:

$$
\begin{aligned}
P(\text{low demand} \mid \text{unfavorable response}) &= 1 - P(\text{high demand} \mid \text{unfavorable response}) \\
&= 1 - 0.3 = 0.70
\end{aligned}
$$

These conditional probabilities are shown on the last four demand branches in Figure 15.35. Later, we will discuss a more objective method for determining these types of conditional probabilities.

15.13.2 THE EXPECTED VALUE OF SAMPLE INFORMATION

The additional information made available by the market survey allows us to make more precise estimates of the probabilities associated with the uncertain market demand. This, in turn, allows us to make more precise decisions. For example, Figure 15.35 indicates that if the survey results are favorable, CM should build a large plant; and if the survey results are unfavorable, it should build a small plant. The expected value of this decision-making strategy is $126.82 million, assuming that the survey can be done at no cost—which is unlikely. So, how much should CM be willing to pay to perform this survey? The answer to this question is provided by the expected value of sample information (EVSI), which is defined as:

$$
EVSI = \begin{pmatrix} \text{Expected value of the best} \\ \text{decision with sample infor-} \\ \text{mation (obtained at no cost)} \end{pmatrix} - \begin{pmatrix} \text{Expected value of the best} \\ \text{decision without sample} \\ \text{information} \end{pmatrix}
$$

The EVSI represents the *maximum* amount we should be willing to pay to obtain sample information. From Figure 15.35, we know that the expected value of the best decision *with* sample information for our example problem is $126.82 million. From Figure 15.34, we know that the expected value of the best decision *without* sample information is $126 million. So for our example problem, the EVSI is determined as:

$$\text{EVSI} = \$126.82 \text{ million} - \$126 \text{ million} = \$0.82 \text{ million}$$

Thus, CM should be willing to spend up to $820,000 to perform the market survey.

15.14 Computing Conditional Probabilities

In our example problem, we assumed that the values of the conditional probabilities were assigned subjectively by the decision makers at CM. However, a company often has data available from which it can compute these probabilities. We will illustrate this process for the CM example. To simplify our notation, we will use the following abbreviations:

H	=	high demand
L	=	low demand
F	=	favorable response
U	=	unfavorable response

To complete the decision tree in Figure 15.35, we determined values for the following six probabilities:

- $P(F)$
- $P(U)$
- $P(H \mid F)$
- $P(L \mid F)$
- $P(H \mid U)$
- $P(L \mid U)$

Assuming that CM has been in the auto business for some time, it undoubtedly has performed other market surveys before introducing other new models. Some of these models probably achieved high consumer demand, whereas others achieved only low demand. Thus, CM can use historical data to construct the joint probability table shown at the top of Figure 15.36 (and in the file Fig15-36.xls on your data disk).

The value in cell B4 indicates that of all the new car models CM developed and performed market surveys on, 60% received a favorable survey response and subsequently enjoyed high demand. This is expressed mathematically as:

$$P(F \cap H) = 0.60$$

In this formula $P(A \cap B) = X$ is read, "the probability of A *and* B is X." Similarly, in the joint probability table we see that:

$$P(F \cap L) = 0.067$$
$$P(U \cap H) = 0.10$$
$$P(U \cap L) = 0.233$$

The column totals in cells B6 and C6 represent, respectively, the estimated probabilities of high and low demands as:

$$P(H) = 0.70$$
$$P(L) = 0.30$$

FIGURE
15.36

*The calculation of
conditional
probabilities for the
CM decision
problem*

The row totals in cells D4 and D5 represent, respectively, the estimated probabilities of a favorable and unfavorable response. These values correspond to the first two of the six probability values listed earlier; that is:

$$P(F) = 0.667$$
$$P(U) = 0.333$$

With these values, we are now ready to compute the necessary conditional probabilities. One general definition of a conditional probability is:

$$P(A \mid B) = \frac{P(A \cap B)}{P(B)}$$

We can use this definition, along with the values in the joint probability table, to compute the conditional probabilities required for Figure 15.35 as:

$$P(H \mid F) = \frac{P(H \cap F)}{P(F)} = \frac{0.60}{0.667} = 0.90$$

$$P(L \mid F) = \frac{P(L \cap F)}{P(F)} = \frac{0.067}{0.667} = 0.10$$

$$P(H \mid U) = \frac{P(H \cap U)}{P(U)} = \frac{0.10}{0.333} = 0.30$$

$$P(L \mid U) = \frac{P(L \cap U)}{P(U)} = \frac{0.233}{0.333} = 0.70$$

We can calculate these conditional probabilities of the demand levels for a given survey response in the spreadsheet. This is done in the second table in Figure 15.36 using the following formula:

Formula for cell B12:   =B4/$D4

(Copy to B12 through C13.)

Although not required for Figure 15.35, we also can compute the conditional probabilities of the survey responses for a given level of demand as:

$$P(F \mid H) = \frac{P(H \cap F)}{P(H)} = \frac{0.60}{0.70} = 0.857$$

$$P(U \mid H) = \frac{P(H \cap U)}{P(H)} = \frac{0.10}{0.70} = 0.143$$

$$P(F \mid L) = \frac{P(L \cap F)}{P(L)} = \frac{0.067}{0.30} = 0.223$$

$$P(U \mid L) = \frac{P(L \cap U)}{P(L)} = \frac{0.233}{0.30} = 0.777$$

The third table in Figure 15.36 calculates conditional probabilities of the survey responses for a given level of demand using the following formula:

Formula for cell B19:   =B4/B$6

(Copy to B20 through C20.)

15.14.1 BAYES'S THEOREM

Bayes's Theorem provides another definition of conditional probability that is sometimes useful. This definition is:

$$P(A \mid B) = \frac{P(B \mid A)P(A)}{P(B \mid A)P(A) + P(B \mid \bar{A})P(\bar{A})}$$

In this formula, A and B represent any two events, and $\bar{A}$ is the complement of A. To see how this formula might be used, suppose that we want to determine $P(H \mid F)$ but we do not have access to the joint probability table in Figure 15.36. According to Bayes's Theorem, we know that:

$$P(H \mid F) = \frac{P(F \mid H)P(H)}{P(F \mid H)P(H) + P(F \mid L)P(L)}$$

If we know the values for the various quantities on the RHS of this equation, we can compute $P(H \mid F)$ as in the following example:

$$P(H \mid F) = \frac{P(F \mid H)P(H)}{P(F \mid H)P(H) + P(F \mid L)P(L)} = \frac{(0.857)(0.70)}{(0.857)(0.70) + (0.223)(0.30)} = 0.90$$

This result is consistent with the value of $P(H \mid F)$ shown in cell B12 in Figure 15.36.

15.15 Utility Theory

Although the EMV decision rule is widely used, sometimes the decision alternative with the highest EMV is not the most desirable or most preferred alternative by the decision maker. For example, suppose that we could buy either of the two companies listed in the following payoff table for exactly the same price:

	State of Nature			
Company	1	2	EMV	
A	150,000	−30,000	60,000	← maximum
B	70,000	40,000	55,000	
Probability	0.5	0.5		

The payoff values listed in this table represent the annual profits expected from this business. Thus, in any year, a 50% chance exists that company A will generate a profit of $150,000 and a 50% chance that it will generate a loss of $30,000. On the other hand, in each year, a 50% chance exists that company B will generate a profit of $70,000 and a 50% chance that it will generate a profit of $40,000.

According to the EMV decision rule, we should buy company A because it has the highest EMV. However, company A represents a far more risky investment than company B. Although company A would generate the highest EMV over the long run, we might not have the financial resources to withstand the potential losses of $30,000 per year that could occur in the short run with this alternative. With company B, we can be sure of making at least $40,000 each year. Although company B's EMV over the long run might not be as great as that of company A, for many decision makers, this is more than offset by the increased peace of mind associated with company B's relatively stable profit level. However, other decision makers might be willing to accept the greater risk associated with company A in hopes of achieving the higher potential payoffs this alternative provides.

As this example illustrates, the EMVs of different decision alternatives do not necessarily reflect the relative attractiveness of the alternatives to a particular decision maker. Utility theory provides a way to incorporate the decision maker's attitudes and preferences toward risk and return in the decision-analysis process so that the most desirable decision alternative is identified.

15.15.1 UTILITY FUNCTIONS

Utility theory assumes that every decision maker uses a utility function that translates each of the possible payoffs in a decision problem into a nonmonetary measure known as a utility. The utility of a payoff represents the total worth, value, or desirability of the outcome of a decision alternative to the decision maker. For convenience, we will begin by representing utilities on a scale from 0 to 1, where 0 represents the least value and 1 represents the most.

Different decision makers have different attitudes and preferences toward risk and return. Those who are "risk neutral" tend to make decisions using the maximum EMV decision rule. However, some decision makers are risk avoiders (or "risk averse"), and others look for risk (or are "risk seekers"). The utility functions typically associated with these three types of decision makers are shown in Figure 15.37.

Figure 15.37 illustrates how the same monetary payoff might produce different levels of utility for three different decision makers. A "risk averse" decision maker assigns the largest relative utility to any payoff but has a diminishing marginal utility for increased

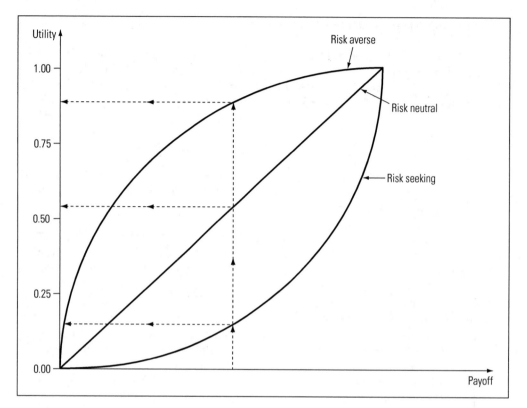

FIGURE 15.37

Three common types of utility functions

payoffs (that is, every additional dollar in payoff results in smaller increases in utility). The "risk seeking" decision maker assigns the smallest utility to any payoff but has an increasing marginal utility for increased payoffs (that is, every additional dollar in pay-off results in larger increases in utility). The "risk neutral" decision maker (who follows the EMV decision rule) falls in between these two extremes and has a constant marginal utility for increased payoffs (that is, every additional dollar in payoff results in the same amount of increase in utility). The utility curves in Figure 15.37 are not the only ones that can occur. In general, utility curves can assume virtually any form depending on the preferences of the decision maker.

15.15.2 CONSTRUCTING UTILITY FUNCTIONS

Assuming that decision makers use utility functions (perhaps at a subconscious level) to make decisions, how can we determine what a given decision maker's utility function looks like? One approach involves assigning a utility value of 0 to the worst outcome in a decision problem and a utility value of 1 to the best outcome. All other payoffs are assigned utility values between 0 and 1. (Although it is convenient to use endpoint values of 0 and 1, we can use any values provided that the utility value assigned to the worst payoff is less than the utility value assigned to the best payoff.)

We will let $U(x)$ represent the utility associated with a payoff of $x. Thus, for the decision about whether to buy company A or B, described earlier, we have:

$$U(-30,000) = 0$$
$$U(150,000) = 1$$

Now suppose that we want to find the utility associated with the payoff of $70,000 in our example. To do this, we must identify the probability p at which the decision maker is indifferent between the following two alternatives:

Alternative 1.   Receive $70,000 with certainty.

Alternative 2.   Receive $150,000 with probability p and lose $30,000 with probability $(1 - p)$

If $p = 0$, most decision makers would choose alternative 1 because they would prefer to receive a payoff of $70,000 rather than lose $30,000. On the other hand, if $p = 1$, most decision makers would choose alternative 2 because they would prefer to receive a payoff of $150,000 rather than $70,000. So as p increases from 0 to 1, it reaches a point—p^*—at which the decision maker is indifferent between the two alternatives. That is, if $p < p^*$, the decision maker prefers alternative 1, and if $p > p^*$, the decision maker prefers alternative 2. The point of indifference, p^*, varies from one decision maker to another, depending on his attitude toward risk and according to his ability to sustain a loss of $30,000.

In our example, suppose that the decision maker is indifferent between alternative 1 and 2 when $p = 0.8$ (so that $p^* = 0.8$). The utility of the $70,000 payoff for this decision maker is computed as:

$$U(70,000) = U(150,000)\, p^* + U(-30,000)(1 - p^*) = 1\, p^* + 0(1 - p^*) = p^* = 0.8$$

Notice that when $p = 0.8$, the expected value of alternative 2 is:

$$\$150,000 \times 0.8 - \$30,000 \times 0.2 = \$114,000$$

Because the decision maker is indifferent between a risky decision (alternative 2) that has an EMV of $114,000 and a nonrisky decision (alternative 1) that has a certain payoff of $70,000, this decision maker is "risk averse." That is, the decision maker is willing to accept only $70,000 to avoid the risk associated with a decision that has an EMV of $114,000.

The term certainty equivalent refers to the amount of money that is equivalent in a decision maker's mind to a situation that involves uncertainty. For example, $70,000 is the decision maker's certainty equivalent for the uncertain situation represented by alternative 2 when $p = 0.8$. A closely related term, risk premium, refers to the EMV that a decision maker is willing to give up (or pay) to avoid a risky decision. In our example, the risk premium is $114,000 - $70,000 = $44,000; that is:

$$\text{Risk premium} = \left(\begin{array}{c} \text{EMV of an} \\ \text{uncertain situation} \end{array} \right) - \left(\begin{array}{c} \text{certainty equivalent of} \\ \text{the same uncertain situation} \end{array} \right)$$

To find the utility associated with the $40,000 payoff in our example, we must identify the probability p at which the decision maker is indifferent between the following two alternatives:

Alternative 1.   Receive $40,000 with certainty.

Alternative 2.   Receive $150,000 with probability p and lose $30,000 with probability $(1 - p)$.

Because we reduced the payoff amount listed in alternative 1 from its earlier value of $70,000, we expect that the value of p at which the decision maker is indifferent also would be reduced. In this case, suppose that the decision maker is indifferent between the two alternatives when $p = 0.65$ (so that $p^* = 0.65$). The utility associated with a payoff of $40,000 is:

$$U(40,000) = U(150,000) \, p^* + U(-30,000)(1 - p^*) = 1 \, p^* + 0(1 - p^*) = p^* = 0.65$$

Again, the utility associated with the amount given in alternative 1 is equivalent to the decision maker's indifference point p^*. This is not a coincidence.

Key Point

When utilities are expressed on a scale from 0 to 1, the probability p^* at which the decision maker is indifferent between alternatives 1 and 2 always corresponds to the decision maker's utility for the amount listed in alternative 1.

Notice that when $p = 0.65$, the expected value of alternative 2 is:

$$\$150,000 \times 0.65 - \$30,000 \times 0.35 = \$87,000$$

Again, this is "risk averse" behavior because the decision maker is willing to accept only $40,000 (or pay a risk premium of $47,000) to avoid the risk associated with a decision that has an EMV of $87,000.

For our example, the utilities associated with payoffs of –$30,000, $40,000, $70,000, and $150,000 are 0.0, 0.65, 0.80, and 1.0, respectively. If we plot these values on a graph and connect the points with straight lines, we can estimate the shape of the decision maker's utility function for this decision problem, as shown in Figure 15.38. Note that the shape of this utility function is consistent with the general shape of the utility function for a "risk averse" decision maker given in Figure 15.37.

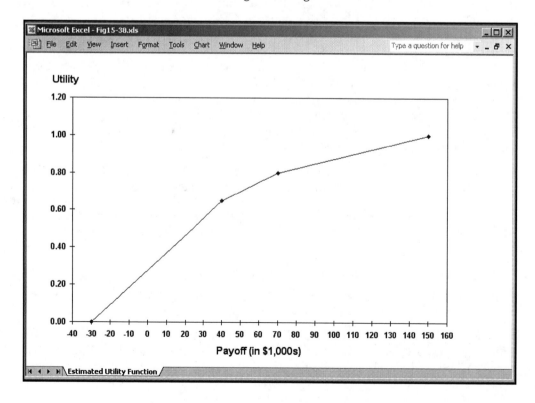

FIGURE 15.38

An estimated utility function for the example problem

15.15.3 USING UTILITIES TO MAKE DECISIONS

After determining the utility value of each possible monetary payoff, we can apply the standard tools of decision analysis to determine the alternative that provides the highest expected utility. We do so using utility values in place of monetary values in payoff tables or decision trees. For our current example, we substitute the appropriate utilities in the payoff table and compute the expected utility for each decision alternative as:

	State of Nature			
Company	**1**	**2**	**Expected Utility**	
A	1.00	0.00	0.500	
B	0.80	0.65	0.725	← maximum
Probability	0.5	0.5		

In this case, the decision to purchase company B provides the greatest expected level of utility to this decision maker—even though our earlier analysis indicated that its EMV of $55,000 is less than company A's EMV of $60,000. Thus, by using utilities, decision makers can identify the alternative that is most attractive given their personal attitudes about risk and return.

15.15.4 THE EXPONENTIAL UTILITY FUNCTION

In a complicated decision problem with numerous possible payoff values, it might be difficult and time-consuming for a decision maker to determine the different values for p^* that are required to determine the utility for each payoff. However, if the decision maker is "risk averse," the exponential utility function can be used as an approximation of the decision maker's actual utility function. The general form of the exponential utility function is:

$$U(x) = 1 - e^{-x/R}$$

In this formula, e is the base of the natural logarithm ($e = 2.718281\ldots$) and R is a parameter that controls the shape of the utility function according to a decision maker's risk tolerance. Figure 15.39 shows examples of the graph of this function for several values of R. Note that as R increases, the shape of the utility curve becomes flatter (or less "risk averse"). Also note that as x becomes large, $U(x)$ approaches 1; when $x = 0$, then $U(x) = 0$; and if x is less than 0, then $U(x) < 0$.

To use the exponential utility function, we must determine a reasonable value for the risk tolerance parameter R. One method for doing so involves determining the maximum value of Y for which the decision maker is willing to participate in a game of chance with the following possible outcomes:

Win $Y with probability 0.5

Lose $Y/2 with probability 0.5

The maximum value of Y for which the decision maker would accept this gamble should give us a reasonable estimate of R. Note that a decision maker willing to accept this gamble only at very small values of Y is "risk averse," whereas a decision maker willing to play for larger values of Y is less "risk averse." This corresponds with the relationship between the utility curves and values of R shown in Figure 15.39. (As a rule of thumb, anecdotal evidence suggests that many firms exhibit risk tolerances of approximately one-sixth of equity or 125% of net yearly income.)

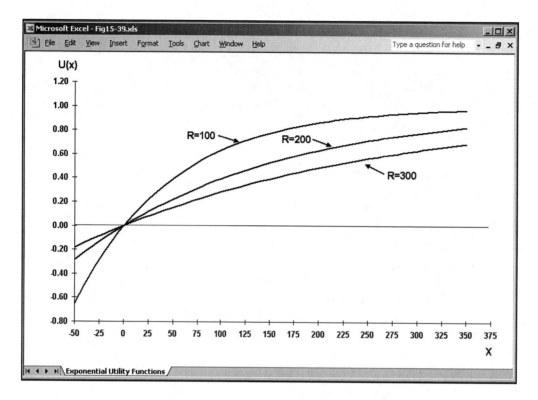

**FIGURE
15.39**

*Examples of the
exponential utility
function*

15.15.5 INCORPORATING UTILITIES IN TREEPLAN

The TreePlan add-in provides a simple way to use the exponential utility function to model "risk averse" decision preferences in a decision tree. We will illustrate this using the decision tree developed earlier for Magnolia Inns, where Barbara needs to decide which parcel of land to purchase. The decision tree developed for this problem is shown in Figure 15.40 (and in the file Fig15-40.xls on your data disk).

To use the exponential utility function, we first construct a decision tree in the usual way. We then determine the risk tolerance value of R for the decision maker using the technique described earlier. Because Barbara is making this decision on behalf of Magnolia Inns, it is important that she provide an estimated value of R based on the acceptable risk levels of the corporation—not her own personal risk tolerance level.

In this case, let's assume that $4 million is the maximum value of Y for which Barbara believes Magnolia Inns is willing to gamble winning $Y with probability 0.5 and losing $Y/2 with probability 0.5. Therefore, $R = Y = 4$. (Note that the value of R should be expressed in the same units as the payoffs in the decision tree.)

TreePlan requires that we enter the value of R in a cell named "RT" (short for Risk Tolerance). (This cell must be outside of the rectangular region containing the decision tree.) Cell D36 in Figure 15.36 serves this purpose. To assign the name "RT" to this cell:

1. Click cell D36.
2. Click the Insert menu.
3. Click Name.
4. Click Define.
5. Type RT.
6. Click OK.

**FIGURE
15.40**

*Decision tree for
the Magnolia Inns
land purchase
problem*

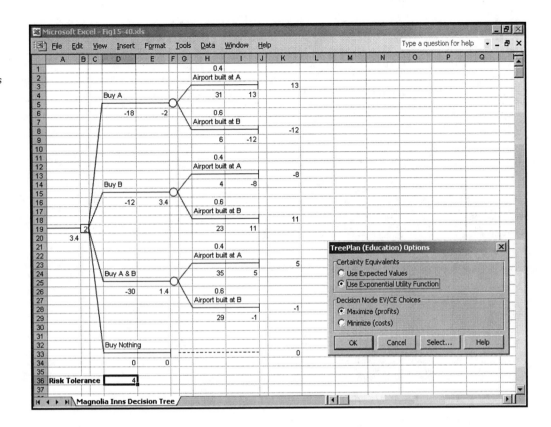

We can now instruct TreePlan to use an exponential utility function to determine the optimal decision. To do this:

1. Click cell D3.
2. Press [Ctrl][t] to invoke TreePlan.
3. Click the Options button.
4. Click Use Exponential Utility Function.
5. Click OK.

TreePlan automatically converts the decision tree so that the rollback operation is performed using expected utilities rather than EMVs. The resulting tree is shown in Figure 15.41. The certainty equivalent at each node appears in the cell directly below and to the left of each node (previously the location of the EMVs). The expected utility at each node appears immediately below the certainty equivalents. According to this tree, the decision to buy the parcels at locations A and B provides the highest expected utility for Magnolia Inns.

Here again, it might be useful to create a strategy table to show how the recommended decision might change if we had used a different risk tolerance value and/or different probabilities. Figure 15.42 (and file Fig15-42.xls on your data disk) shows a completed strategy table for the problem.

15.16 Multicriteria Decision Making

A decision maker often uses more than one criterion or objective to evaluate the alternatives in a decision problem. Sometimes, these criteria conflict with one another. For example, consider again the criteria of risk and return. Most decision makers desire high

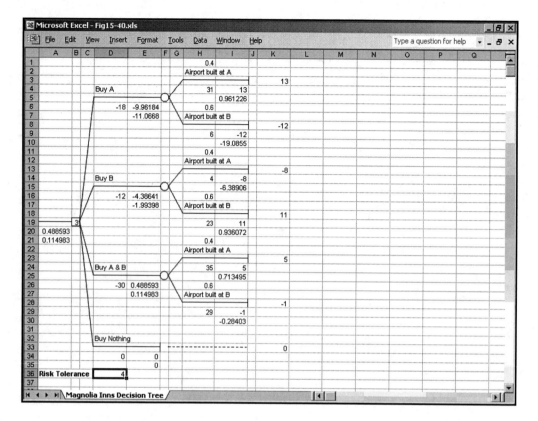

FIGURE
15.41

*Analysis of the
Magnolia Inns
decision tree using
an exponential
utility function*

levels of return and low levels of risk. But high returns usually are accompanied by high risks, and low levels of return are associated with low risk levels. In making investment decisions, a decision maker must assess the trade-offs between risk and return to identify the decision that achieves the most satisfying balance of these two criteria. As we have seen, utility theory represents one approach to assessing the trade-offs between the criteria of risk and return.

Many other types of decision problems involve multiple conflicting criteria. For example, in choosing between two or more different job offers, you must evaluate the alternatives on the basis of starting salary, opportunity for advancement, job security, location, and so on. If you purchase a video camcorder, you must evaluate a number of different models based on the manufacturer's reputation, price, warranty, size, weight, zoom capability, lighting requirements, and a host of other features. If you must decide whom to hire to fill a vacancy in your organization, you will likely have to evaluate a number of candidates on the basis of education, experience, references, and personality. This section presents two techniques that can be used in decision problems that involve multiple criteria.

15.17 The Multicriteria Scoring Model

The multicriteria scoring model is a simple procedure in which we score (or rate) each alternative in a decision problem based on each criterion. The score for alternative j on criterion i is denoted by S_{ij}. Weights (denoted by w_i) are assigned to each criterion

FIGURE 15.42

Strategy table for the Magnolia Inns decision problem using expected utility

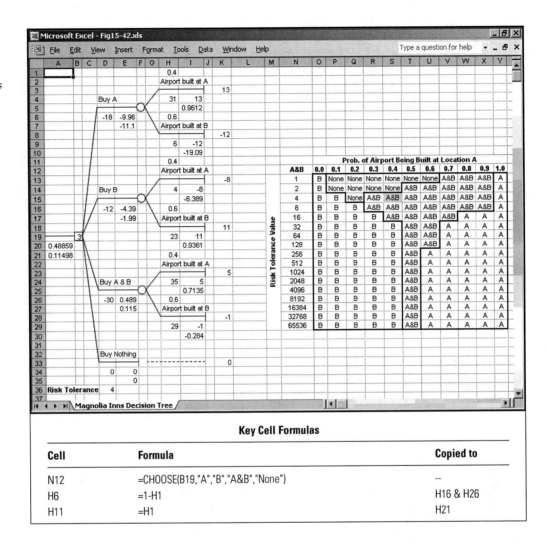

Key Cell Formulas		
Cell	**Formula**	**Copied to**
N12	=CHOOSE(B19,"A","B","A&B","None")	--
H6	=1-H1	H16 & H26
H11	=H1	H21

indicating its relative importance to the decision maker. For each alternative, we then compute a weighted average score as:

$$\text{Weighted average score for alternative } j = \sum_i w_i s_{ij}$$

We then select the alternative with the largest weighted average score.

The beginning of this chapter described a situation that many students face when they graduate from college—choosing between two job offers. The spreadsheet in Figure 15.43 (and in the file Fig15-43.xls on your data disk) illustrates how we might use a multicriteria scoring model to help in this problem.

In choosing between two (or more) job offers, we would evaluate criteria for each alternative, such as the starting salary, potential for career development, job security, location of the job, and perhaps other factors. The idea in a scoring model is to assign a value from 0 to 1 to each decision alternative that reflects its relative worth on each criterion. These values can be thought of as subjective assessments of the utility that each alternative provides on the various criteria.

In Figure 15.43, scores for each criterion were entered in cells C6 through D9. These scores indicate that the starting salary offered by company B provides the greatest value, but the salary offered by company A is not much worse. (Note that these scores do not necessarily mean that the starting salary offered by company B was the highest.

FIGURE
15.43

A multicriteria
scoring model

	Microsoft Excel - Fig15-43.xls							
	A	**B**	**C**	**D**	**E**	**F**	**G**	**H**	**I**
1								
2			**Job Selection**					
3			**Multi-Criteria Scoring**					
4			Raw Score For					
5		Criterion	Company A	Company B				
6		Starting Salary	0.85	0.90				
7		Career Potential	0.95	0.70				
8		Job Security	0.60	0.95				
9		Location	0.90	0.70				
10		Score	0.825	0.813				
11								
12								
13			Weighted Score For		Criterion			
14		Criterion	Company A	Company B	Weights			
15		Starting Salary	0.085	0.090	0.10			
16		Career Potential	0.285	0.210	0.30			
17		Job Security	0.240	0.380	0.40			
18		Location	0.180	0.140	0.20			
19		Weighted Score	0.790	0.820	1.00			
20								

▶ ▶ Data / Radar Chart - Raw Scores / Radar Chart - Weighted Scores /

Key Cell Formulas

Cell	Formula	Copied to
C10	=AVERAGE(C6:C9)	D10
C15	=C6*$E15	C15:D18
C19	=SUM(C15:C18)	D19:E19

These scores reflect the *value* of the salaries to the decision maker, taking into account such factors as the cost of living in the different locations.) The remaining scores in the table indicate that company A provides the greatest potential for career advancement and is in the most attractive location, but provides considerably less job security than that offered by company B. The average scores associated with each job offer are calculated in cells C10 and D10 as follows:

Formula for cell C10:   =AVERAGE(C6:C9)

(Copy to D10.)

Notice that the offer from company A has a higher average score than that of company B. However, this implicitly assumes that all the criteria are of equal importance to the decision maker—which often is not the case.

Next, the decision maker specifies weights that indicate the relative importance of each criterion. Again, this is done subjectively. Hypothetical weights for each criterion in this example are shown in cells E15 through E18 in Figure 15.43. Note that these weights must sum to 1. The weighted scores for each criterion and alternative are calculated in cells C15 through D18 as:

Formula for cell C15:   =C6*$E15

(Copy to C15 to D18.)

We can then sum these values to calculate the weighted average score for each alternative as:

Formula for cell C19:   =SUM(C15:C18)

(Copy to E19.)

FIGURE
15.44

*Radar chart of the
raw scores*

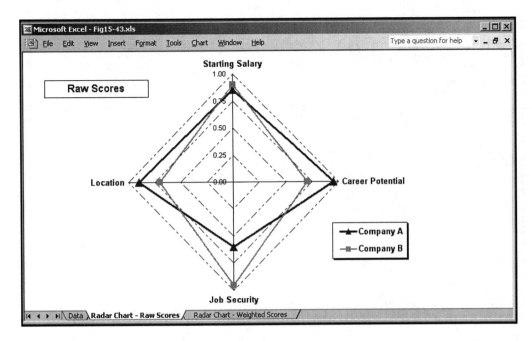

In this case, the total weighted average scores for company A and B are 0.79 and 0.82, respectively. Thus, when the importance of each criterion is accounted for via weights, the model indicates that the decision maker should accept the job with company B because it has the largest weighted average score.

Radar charts provide an effective way of summarizing numerous alternatives graphically in a multicriteria scoring model. Figure 15.44 shows the raw scores associated with each of the alternatives in our job selection example. A glance at this chart makes it clear that the offers from both companies offer very similar values in terms of salary. Company A is somewhat more desirable in terms of career potential and location, and company B is quite a bit more desirable in terms of job security.

Figure 15.45 shows another radar chart of the weighted scores for each of the alternatives. Using the weighted scores, the radar chart tends to accentuate the differences on criteria that were heavily weighted. For instance, here the offers from the two companies are very similar in terms of salary and location and are most different with respect to career potential and job security. The radar chart's ability to graphically portray the differences in the alternatives can be quite helpful—particularly for decision makers who do not relate well to tables of numbers.

Creating a Radar Chart

To create a radar chart like the one shown in Figure 15.45:

1. Select cells B14 through D18.
2. Click the Insert menu.
3. Click Chart.
4. Click Radar.

Excel's Chart Wizard then prompts you to make a number of selections concerning how the chart should be labeled and formatted. After Excel creates a basic chart, you can customize it in many ways. Double-clicking a chart element displays a dialog box with options for modifying the appearance of the element.

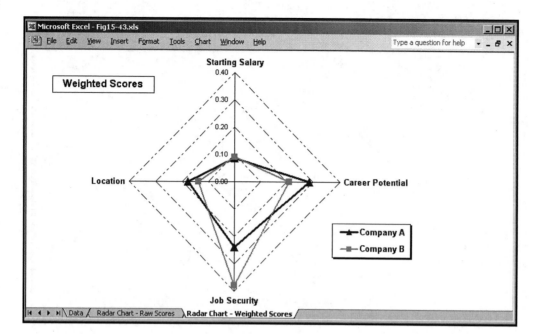

FIGURE 15.45

Radar chart of the weighted scores

15.18 The Analytic Hierarchy Process

Sometimes, a decision maker finds it difficult to subjectively determine the criterion scores and weights needed in the multicriteria scoring model. In this case, the analytic hierarchy process (AHP) can be helpful. AHP provides a more structured approach for determining the scores and weights for the multicriteria scoring model described earlier. This can be especially helpful in focusing attention and discussion on the important aspects of a problem in group decision making environments. However, there is not universal acceptance as to the validity of AHP. As with any structured decision making process, the recommendations of AHP should not be followed blindly but carefully considered and evaluated by the decision maker(s).

To illustrate AHP, suppose that a company wants to purchase a new payroll and personnel records information system and is considering three systems, identified as X, Y, and Z. The systems differ with respect to three key criteria: price, user support, and ease of use.

15.18.1 PAIRWISE COMPARISONS

The first step in AHP is to create a pairwise comparison matrix for each alternative on each criterion. We will illustrate the details of this process for the price criterion. The values shown in Figure 15.46 are used in AHP to describe the decision maker's preferences between two alternatives on a given criterion.

To create a pairwise comparison matrix for the price criterion, we must perform pairwise comparisons of the prices of systems X, Y, and Z using the values shown in Figure 15.46. Let P_{ij} denote the extent to which we prefer alternative i to alternative j on a given criterion. For example, suppose that when comparing system X to Y, the decision maker strongly prefers the price of X. In this case, $P_{XY} = 5$. Similarly, suppose that when comparing system X to Z, the decision maker very strongly prefers the price of X, and when comparing Y to Z, the decision maker moderately prefers the price of Y. In this case, $P_{XZ} = 7$ and $P_{YZ} = 3$. We used the values of these pairwise comparisons to create the pairwise comparison matrix shown in Figure 15.47.

FIGURE 15.46

Scale for pairwise comparisons in AHP

Value	Preference
1	Equally Preferred
2	Equally to Moderately Preferred
3	Moderately Preferred
4	Moderately to Strongly Preferred
5	Strongly Preferred
6	Strongly to Very Strongly Preferred
7	Very Strongly Preferred
8	Very Strongly to Extremely Preferred
9	Extremely Preferred

FIGURE 15.47

Pairwise comparisons of the price criterion for the three systems

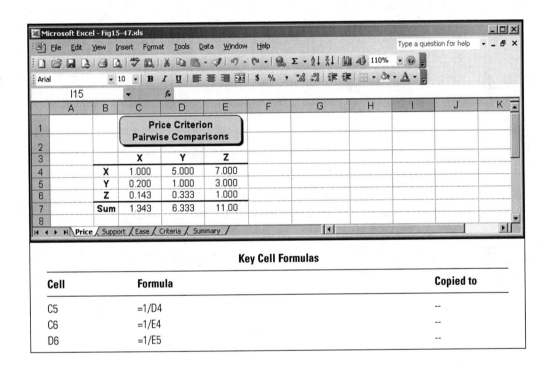

Key Cell Formulas

Cell	Formula	Copied to
C5	=1/D4	--
C6	=1/E4	--
D6	=1/E5	--

The values of P_{XY}, P_{XZ}, and P_{YZ} are shown in cells D4, E4, and E5 in Figure 15.47. We entered the value 1 along the main diagonal in Figure 15.47 to indicate that if an alternative is compared against itself, the decision maker should equally prefer either alternative (because they are the same).

The entries in cells C5, C6, and D6 correspond to P_{YX}, P_{ZX}, and P_{ZY}, respectively. To determine these values, we could obtain the decision maker's preferences between Y and X, Z and X, and Z and Y. However, if we already know the decision maker's preference between X and Y (P_{XY}), we can conclude that the decision maker's preference between Y and X (P_{YX}) is the reciprocal of the preference between X and Y; that is, $P_{YX} = 1/P_{XY}$. So, in general, we have:

$$P_{ji} = \frac{1}{P_{ij}}$$

Thus, the values in cells C5, C6, and D6 are computed as:

Formula for cell C5:   =1/D4

Formula for cell C6:   =1/E4

Formula for cell D6:   =1/E5

15.18.2 NORMALIZING THE COMPARISONS

The next step in AHP is to normalize the matrix of pairwise comparisons. To do this, we first calculate the sum of each column in the pairwise comparison matrix. We then divide each entry in the matrix by its column sum. Figure 15.48 shows the resulting normalized matrix.

We will use the average of each row in the normalized matrix as the score for each alternative on the criterion under consideration. For example, cells F11, F12, and F13 indicate that the average scores on the price criterion for X, Y, and Z are 0.724, 0.193, and 0.083, respectively. These scores indicate the relative desirability of the three alternatives to the decision maker with respect to price. The score for X indicates that this is by far the most attractive alternative with respect to price, and alternative Y is somewhat more attractive than Z. Note that these scores reflect the preferences expressed by the decision maker in the pairwise comparison matrix.

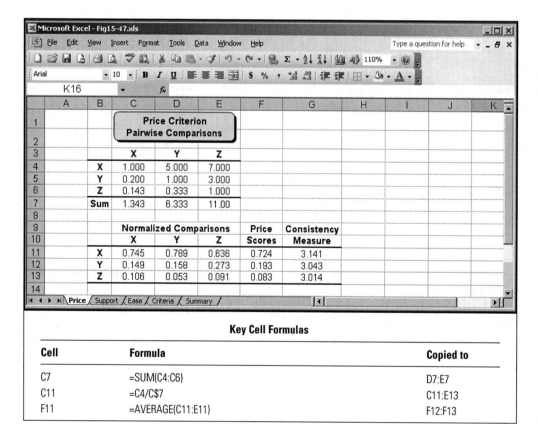

FIGURE 15.48

Price scores obtained from the normalized comparison matrix

15.18.3 CONSISTENCY

In applying AHP, the decision maker should be consistent in the preference ratings given in the pairwise comparison matrix. For example, if the decision maker strongly prefers the price of X to that of Y, and strongly prefers the price of Y to that of Z, it would be inconsistent for the decision maker to indicate indifference (or equal preference) regarding the price of X and Z. Thus, before using the scores derived from the normalized comparison matrix, the preferences indicated in the original pairwise comparison matrix should be checked for consistency.

A consistency measure for each alternative is obtained as:

$$\text{Consistency measure for X} = \frac{0.724 \times 1 + 0.193 \times 5 + 0.083 \times 7}{0.724} = 3.141$$

$$\text{Consistency measure for Y} = \frac{0.724 \times 0.2 + 0.193 \times 1 + 0.083 \times 3}{0.193} = 3.043$$

$$\text{Consistency measure for Z} = \frac{0.724 \times 0.143 + 0.193 \times 0.333 \times 0.083 \times 1}{0.083} = 3.014$$

The numerator in each of these calculations multiplies the scores obtained from the normalized matrix by the preferences given in one of the rows of the original pairwise comparison matrix. The products are summed and then divided by the score for the alternative in question. These consistency measures are shown in Figure 15.49 in cells G11 through G13.

FIGURE 15.49

Checking the consistency of the pairwise comparisons

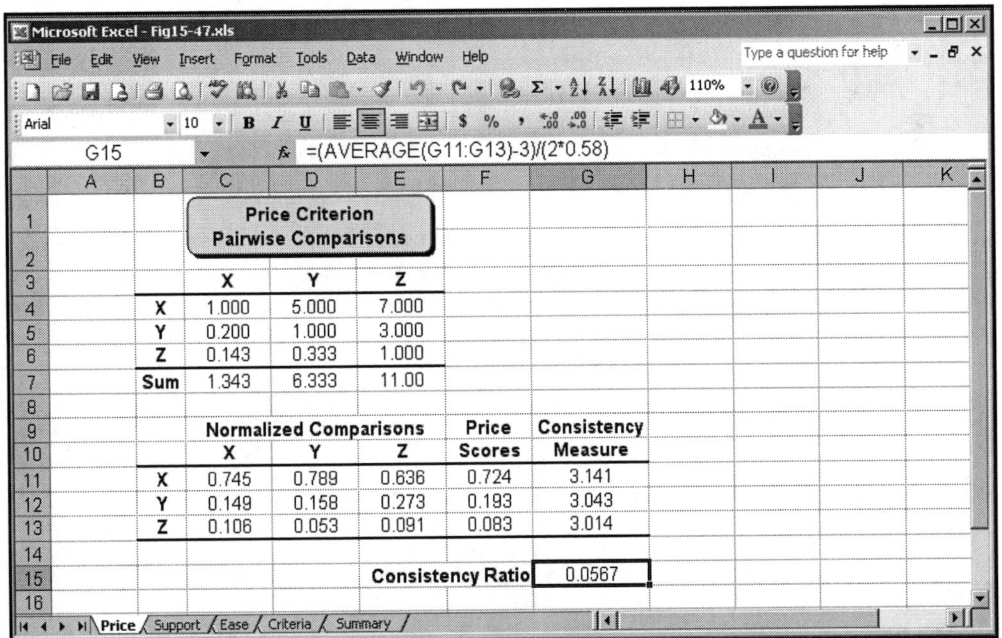
Microsoft Excel - Fig15-47.xls

G15 =(AVERAGE(G11:G13)-3)/(2*0.58)

Price Criterion Pairwise Comparisons

	X	Y	Z		
X	1.000	5.000	7.000		
Y	0.200	1.000	3.000		
Z	0.143	0.333	1.000		
Sum	1.343	6.333	11.00		
	Normalized Comparisons			**Price**	**Consistency**
	X	Y	Z	**Scores**	**Measure**
X	0.745	0.789	0.636	0.724	3.141
Y	0.149	0.158	0.273	0.193	3.043
Z	0.106	0.053	0.091	0.083	3.014
				Consistency Ratio	0.0567

Price / Support / Ease / Criteria / Summary

Key Cell Formulas

Cell	Formula	Copied to
G11	=MMULT(C4:E4,$F$11:$F$13)/F11	G12:G13
G15	=(AVERAGE(G11:G13)-3)/(2*0.58)	--

n	RI
2	0.00
3	0.58
4	0.90
5	1.12
6	1.24
7	1.32
8	1.41

FIGURE 15.50

Values of RI for use in AHP

If the decision maker is perfectly consistent in stating preferences, each consistency measure will equal the number of alternatives in the problem (which, in this case, is three). So, there appears to be some amount of inconsistency in the preferences given in the pairwise comparison matrix. This is not unusual. It is difficult for a decision maker to be perfectly consistent in stating preferences between a large number of pairwise comparisons. Provided that the amount of inconsistency is not excessive, the scores obtained from the normalized matrix will be reasonably accurate. To determine whether the inconsistency is excessive, we compute the following quantities:

$$\text{Consistency Index (CI)} = \frac{\lambda - n}{n - 1}$$

$$\text{Consistency Ratio (CR)} = \frac{CI}{RI}$$

where:

λ = the average consistency measure for all alternatives

n = the number of alternatives

RI = the appropriate random index from Figure 15.50

If the pairwise comparison matrix is perfectly consistent, then $\lambda = n$ and the consistency ratio is 0. The values of RI in Figure 15.50 give the average value of CI if all the entries in the pairwise comparison matrix were chosen at random, given that all the diagonal entries equal 1 and $P_{ij} = 1/P_{ji}$. If CR $\leq$ 0.10, the degree of consistency in the pairwise comparison matrix is satisfactory. However, if CR > 0.10, serious inconsistencies might exist and AHP might not yield meaningful results. The value for CR shown in cell G15 in Figure 15.49 indicates that the pairwise comparison matrix for the price criterion is reasonably consistent. Therefore, we can assume that the scores for the price criterion obtained from the normalized matrix are reasonably accurate.

15.18.4 OBTAINING SCORES FOR THE REMAINING CRITERIA

We can repeat the process for obtaining the price criterion scores to obtain scores for the user support and ease-of-use criteria. Hypothetical results for these criteria are shown in Figures 15.51 and 15.52, respectively.

We can create these two spreadsheets easily by copying the spreadsheet for the price criterion (shown in Figure 15.49) and having the decision maker fill in the pairwise comparison matrices with preferences related to the user support and ease-of-use criteria. Notice that the preferences given in Figures 15.51 and 15.52 appear to be consistent.

FIGURE 15.51

Spreadsheet used to calculate scores for the user support criterion

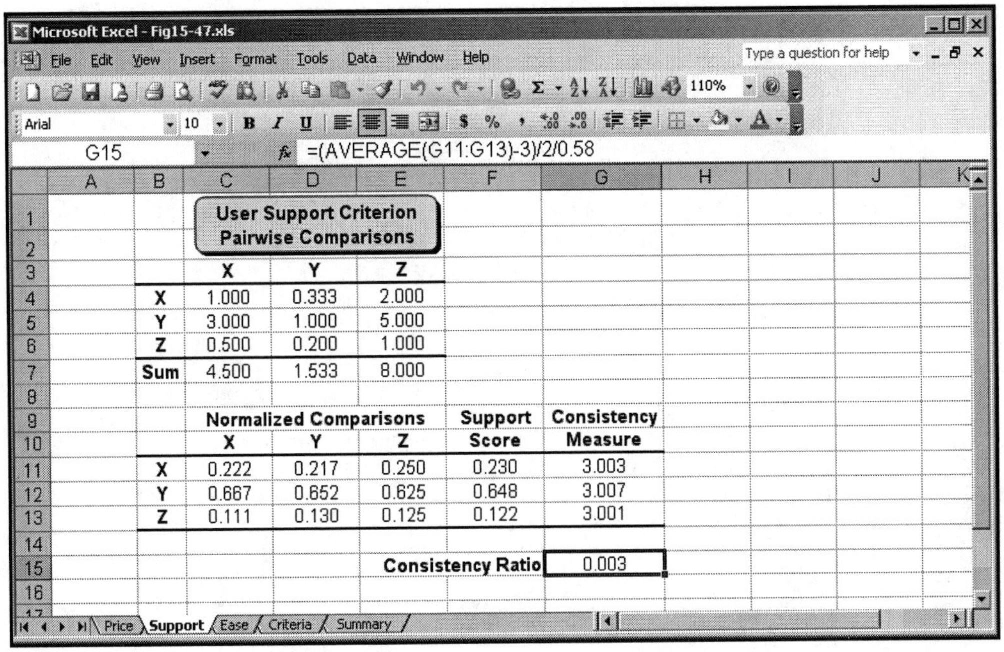

Microsoft Excel - Fig15-47.xls

G15 =(AVERAGE(G11:G13)-3)/2/0.58

User Support Criterion Pairwise Comparisons

	X	Y	Z
X	1.000	0.333	2.000
Y	3.000	1.000	5.000
Z	0.500	0.200	1.000
Sum	4.500	1.533	8.000

	Normalized Comparisons X	Y	Z	Support Score	Consistency Measure
X	0.222	0.217	0.250	0.230	3.003
Y	0.667	0.652	0.625	0.648	3.007
Z	0.111	0.130	0.125	0.122	3.001
				Consistency Ratio	0.003

FIGURE 15.52

Spreadsheet used to calculate scores for the ease-of-use criterion

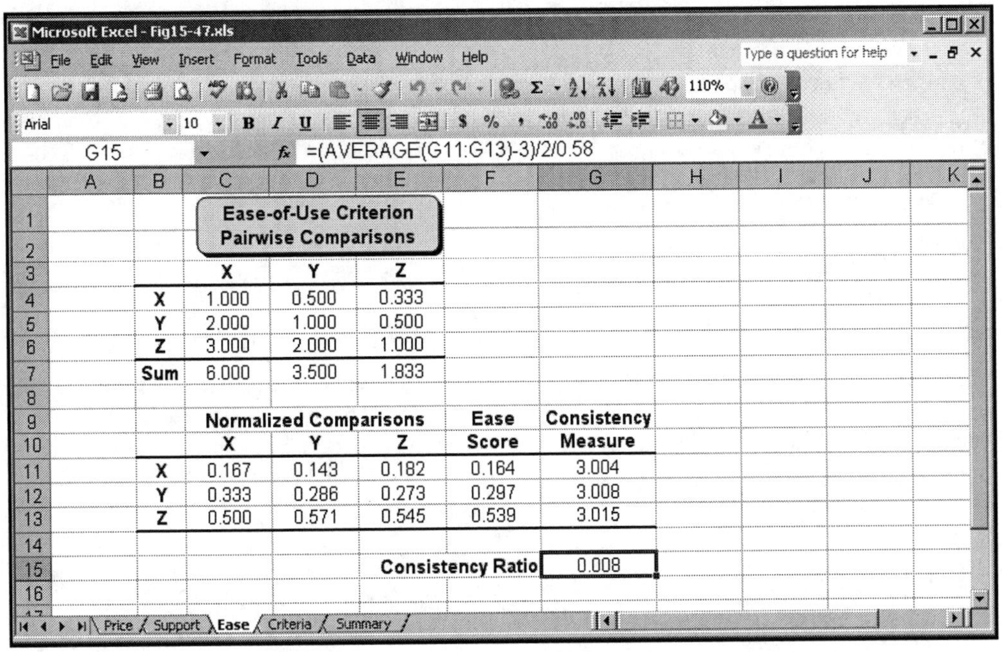

Microsoft Excel - Fig15-47.xls

G15 =(AVERAGE(G11:G13)-3)/2/0.58

Ease-of-Use Criterion Pairwise Comparisons

	X	Y	Z
X	1.000	0.500	0.333
Y	2.000	1.000	0.500
Z	3.000	2.000	1.000
Sum	6.000	3.500	1.833

	Normalized Comparisons X	Y	Z	Ease Score	Consistency Measure
X	0.167	0.143	0.182	0.164	3.004
Y	0.333	0.286	0.273	0.297	3.008
Z	0.500	0.571	0.545	0.539	3.015
				Consistency Ratio	0.008

15.18.5 OBTAINING CRITERION WEIGHTS

The scores shown in Figures 15.49, 15.51, and 15.52 indicate how the alternatives compare with respect to the price, user support, and ease-of-use criteria. Before we can use these values in a scoring model, we also must determine weights that indicate the relative importance of the three criteria to the decision maker. The pairwise comparison

FIGURE
15.53

*Spreadsheet used
to determine the
criterion weights*

process used earlier to generate scores for the alternative on each criteria also can be used to generate criterion weights.

The pairwise comparison matrix in Figure 15.53 shows the decision maker's preferences for the three criteria. The values in cells C5 and C6 indicate that the decision maker finds user support and ease of use to be more important (or more preferred) than price, and cell D6 indicates that ease of use is somewhat more important than user support. These relative preferences are reflected in the criterion weights shown in cells F11 through F13.

15.18.6 IMPLEMENTING THE SCORING MODEL

We now have all the elements required to analyze this decision problem using a scoring model. Thus, the last step in AHP is to calculate the weighted average scores for each decision alternative. The weighted average scores are shown in cells C8 through E8 in Figure 15.54. According to these scores, alternative Y should be selected.

15.19 Summary

This chapter presented a number of techniques for analyzing a variety of decision problems. First, it discussed how a payoff table can be used to summarize the alternatives in a single-stage decision problem. Then, a number of nonprobabilistic and probabilistic decision rules were presented. No one decision rule works best in all situations, but together, the rules help to highlight different aspects of a problem and can help develop and sharpen a decision maker's insight and intuition about a problem so that better decisions can be made. When probabilities of occurrence can be estimated for the alternatives in a problem, the EMV decision rule is the most commonly used technique.

FIGURE 15.54

Final scoring model for selecting the information system

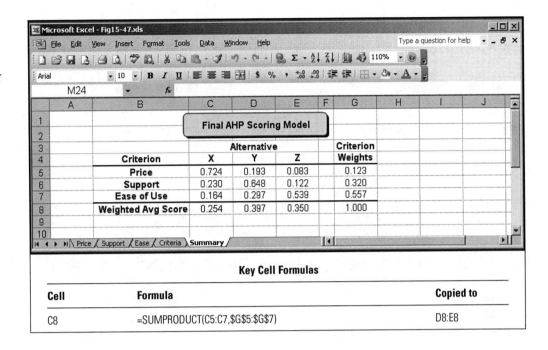

Key Cell Formulas

Cell	Formula	Copied to
C8	=SUMPRODUCT(C5:C7,$G$5:$G$7)	D8:E8

Decision trees are particularly helpful in expressing multistage decision problems in which a series of decisions must be considered. Each terminal node in a decision tree is associated with the net payoff that results from each possible sequence of decisions. A rollback technique determines the alternative that results in the highest EMV. Because different decision makers derive different levels of value from the same monetary payoff, the chapter also discussed how utility theory can be applied to decision problems to account for these differences.

Finally, the chapter discussed two procedures for dealing with decision problems that involve multiple conflicting decision criteria. The multicriteria scoring model requires the decision maker to assign a score for each alternative on each criterion. Weights are then assigned to represent the relative importance of the criteria, and a weighted average score is computed for each alternative. The alternative with the highest score is the recommended alternative. AHP provides a structured approach to determining the scores and weights used in a multicriteria scoring model if the decision maker has difficulty specifying these values.

15.20 References

Bodin, L. and S. Gass. "On Teaching the Analytic Hierarchy Process." *Computers & Operations Research*, vol. 30, pp. 1487–1497, 2003.

Clemen, R. *Making Hard Decisions: An Introduction to Decision Analysis.* Duxbury Press, 1997.

Corner and Kirkwood. "Decision Analysis Applications in the Operations Research Literature 1970–1989." *Operations Research*, vol. 39, no. 2, 1991.

Coyle, R. *Decision Analysis.* London: Nelson, 1972.

Hastie, R. and R. Dawes. *Rational Choice in an Uncertain World: The Psychology of Judgment and Decision Making.* Thousand Oaks, CA: Sage Publications, Inc., 2001.

Heian, B. and J. Gale. "Mortgage Selection Using a Decision-Tree Approach: An Extension." *Interfaces*, vol. 18, July–August 1988.

Howard, R.A., "Decision Analysis: Practice and Promise." *Management Science*, vol. 34, pp. 679–695, 1988.

Keeney, R. and H. Raiffa. *Decision With Multiple Objectives.* New York: Wiley, 1976.

Keeney, R. *Value-Focused Thinking.* Cambridge, MA: Harvard University Press, 1992.

Merkhofer, M.W. "Quantifying Judgmental Uncertainty: Methodology, Experiences & Insights." *IEEE Transactions on Systems, Man, and Cybernetics,* vol. 17, pp. 741–752, 1987.

Skinner, D. *Introduction to Decision Analysis: A Practitioner's Guide to Improving Decision Quality.* Gainesville, FL: Probabilistic Publishing, 2001.

Wenstop, F., and A. Carlsen. "Ranking Hydroelectric Power Projects with Multicriteria Decision Analysis." *Interfaces,* vol. 18, no. 4, 1988.

Zahedi, F. "The Analytic Hierarchy Process—A Survey of the Method and Its Applications." *Interfaces,* vol. 16, no. 4, 1986.

THE WORLD OF MANAGEMENT SCIENCE

Decision Theory Helps Hallmark Trim Discards

Many items distributed by Hallmark Cards, Incorporated, can be sold only during a single season. Leftovers, or discards, then must be disposed of outside normal dealer channels. For example, table items such as napkins can be used in the company's cafeteria, donated to charity, or sold without the brand name to volume discounters. Other items have no salvage value at all.

A product manager deciding the size of a production run or quantity to purchase from a supplier faces two risks. First is the consequence of choosing a quantity that is larger than the eventual demand for the product. Products that have been paid for must be discarded, and the salvage value (if any) might not make up for the cost. The second risk is that the quantity might be less than demand, in which case revenues are lost.

A substantial increase in the dollar volume of discards prompted Hallmark management to initiate a training program for product managers and inventory controllers. They were taught to use product cost and selling price together with a probability distribution of demand to make order quantity decisions. The format for conducting the analysis was a payoff matrix in which rows represented order quantities and columns represented demand levels. Each cell in the payoff matrix contained a computed contribution to profit.

Salvage values and shortage costs were not included in the values of the payoff matrix cells. Instead, sensitivity analysis provided ranges of values within which the order quantity was still optimal.

Although some probability distributions could be estimated from sales data for previous years, sometimes it was necessary to use subjective probabilities. This was especially true for special promotions that had no relevant product history. For this reason, product managers were trained in specifying subjective probabilities. Although direct assessment of a cumulative distribution function would have tied into the order quantity decision more efficiently, it turned out that the managers became more adept at estimating a discrete probability function.

Enough managers adopted the payoff matrix technique, with positive results, that the training program has been continued and expanded within the company.

Source: F. Hutton Barron. "Payoff Matrices Pay Off at Hallmark." *Interfaces,* vol. 15, no. 4, August 1985, pp. 20–25.

Questions and Problems

1. This chapter presented the problem of having to decide between two job offers. The decision maker could accept the job with company A, accept the job with company B, or reject both offers and hope for a better one. What other alternatives can you think of for this problem?
2. Give an example of a national business, political, or military leader who made a good decision that resulted in a bad outcome, or a bad decision that resulted in a good outcome.
3. Consider the following payoff matrix:

	State of Nature		
Decision	1	2	3
A	50	75	35
B	40	50	60
C	40	35	30

   Should a decision maker ever select decision alternative C? Explain your answer.
4. Brenda Kelley runs a specialty ski clothing shop outside of Boone, North Carolina. She must place her order for ski parkas well in advance of ski season because the manufacturer produces them in the summer months. Brenda needs to determine whether to place a large, medium, or small order for parkas. The number sold will depend largely on whether the area receives a heavy, normal, or light amount of snow during the ski season. The following table summarizes the payoffs Brenda expects to receive under each scenario.

	Amount of Snow		
Size of Order	Heavy	Normal	Light
Large	10	7	3
Medium	8	8	6
Small	4	4	4

Payoffs (in $1000s)

   Brenda estimates the probability of heavy, normal, and light snowfalls as 0.25, 0.6, and 0.15, respectively.
   a. What decision should be made according to the maximax decision rule?
   b. What decision should be made according to the maximin decision rule?
   c. What decision should be made according to the minimax regret decision rule?
   d. What decision should be made according to the EMV decision rule?
   e. What decision should be made according to the EOL decision rule?
5. One of Philip Mahn's investments is going to mature, and he wants to determine how to invest the proceeds of $30,000. Philip is considering two new investments: a stock mutual fund and a one-year certificate of deposit (CD). The CD is guaranteed to pay an 8% return. Philip estimates the return on the stock mutual fund as 16%, 9%, or −2%, depending on whether market conditions are good, average, or poor, respectively. Philip estimates the probability of a good, average, and poor market to be 0.1, 0.85, and 0.05, respectively.
   a. Construct a payoff matrix for this problem.
   b. What decision should be made according to the maximax decision rule?
   c. What decision should be made according to the maximin decision rule?
   d. What decision should be made according to the minimax regret decision rule?

e. What decision should be made according to the EMV decision rule?
f. What decision should be made according to the EOL decision rule?
g. How much should Philip be willing to pay to obtain a market forecast that is 100% accurate?

6. A car dealer is offering the following three two-year leasing options:

Plan	Fixed Monthly Payment	Additional Cost Per Mile
I	$200	$0.095 per mile.
II	$300	$0.061 for the first 6,000 miles; $0.050 thereafter.
III	$170	$0.000 for the first 6,000 miles; $0.14 per mile thereafter.

Assume that a customer expects to drive between 15,000 to 35,000 miles during the next two years according to the following probability distribution:

$$P(\text{driving 15,000 miles}) = 0.1$$

$$P(\text{driving 20,000 miles}) = 0.2$$

$$P(\text{driving 25,000 miles}) = 0.2$$

$$P(\text{driving 30,000 miles}) = 0.3$$

$$P(\text{driving 35,000 miles}) = 0.2$$

a. Construct a payoff matrix for this problem.
b. What decision should be made according to the maximax decision rule? (Keep in mind that the "payoffs" here are costs, where less is better.)
c. What decision should be made according to the maximin decision rule?
d. What decision should be made according to the minimax regret decision rule?
e. What decision should be made according to the EMV decision rule?
f. What decision should be made according to the EOL decision rule?

7. The Fish House (TFH) in Norfolk, Virginia, sells fresh fish and seafood. TFH receives daily shipments of farm-raised trout from a nearby supplier. Each trout costs $2.45 and is sold for $3.95. To maintain its reputation for freshness, at the end of the day TFH sells any leftover trout to a local pet food manufacturer for $1.25 each. The owner of TFH wants to determine how many trout to order each day. Historically, the daily demand for trout is:

Demand	10	11	12	13	14	15	16	17	18	19	20
Probability	0.02	0.06	0.09	0.11	0.13	0.15	0.18	0.11	0.07	0.05	0.03

a. Construct a payoff matrix for this problem.
b. What decision should be made according to the maximax decision rule?
c. What decision should be made according to the maximin decision rule?
d. What decision should be made according to the minimax regret decision rule?
e. What decision should be made according to the EMV decision rule?
f. What decision should be made according to the EOL decision rule?
g. How much should the owner of TFH be willing to pay to obtain a demand forecast that is 100% accurate?
h. Which decision rule would you recommend that TFH use in this case? Why?
i. Suppose that TFH receives a quantity discount that reduces the price to $2.25 per trout if it purchases 15 or more. How many trout would you recommend that TFH order each day in this case?

8. Bob Farrell, owner of Farrell Motors, is trying to decide whether to buy an insurance policy to cover hail damage on his inventory of more than 200 cars and trucks. Thunderstorms occur frequently, sometimes producing golfball-sized hailstones that can damage automobiles severely. Bob estimates the potential damage from hail in the next year as:

Hail Damage (in $1000s)	0	15	30	45	60	75	90	105
Probability	0.25	0.08	0.10	0.12	0.15	0.12	0.10	0.08

Bob is considering the following three alternatives for dealing with this risk:
- Bob can buy an insurance policy for $47,000 that would cover 100% of any losses that occur.
- Bob can buy an insurance policy for $25,000 that would cover all losses in excess of $35,000.
- Bob can choose to self-insure, in which case he will not have to pay any insurance premium but will pay for any losses that occur.
  a. Construct a payoff matrix for this problem.
  b. What decision should be made according to the maximax decision rule?
  c. What decision should be made according to the maximin decision rule?
  d. What decision should be made according to the minimax regret decision rule?
  e. What decision should be made according to the EMV decision rule?
  f. What decision should be made according to the EOL decision rule?

9. Morley Properties is planning to build a condominium development on St. Simons Island, Georgia. The company is trying to decide between building a small, medium, or large development. The payoffs received for each size of development will depend on the market demand for condominiums in the area, which could be low, medium, or high. The payoff matrix for this decision problem is:

	Market Demand		
Size of Development	Low	Medium	High
Small	400	400	400
Medium	200	500	500
Large	−400	300	800

(Payoffs in $1000s)

The owner of the company estimates a 21.75% chance that market demand will be low, a 35.5% chance that it will be medium, and a 42.75% chance that it will be high.
  a. What decision should be made according to the maximax decision rule?
  b. What decision should be made according to the maximin decision rule?
  c. What decision should be made according to the minimax regret decision rule?
  d. What decision should be made according to the EMV decision rule?
  e. What decision should be made according to the EOL decision rule?

10. Refer to the previous question. Morley Properties can hire a consultant to predict the most likely level of demand for this project. This consultant has done many similar studies and has provided Morley Properties with the following joint probability table summarizing the accuracy of the results:

	Actual Demand		
Forecasted Demand	Low	Medium	High
Low	0.1600	0.0300	0.0100
Medium	0.0350	0.2800	0.0350
High	0.0225	0.0450	0.3825

The sum of the entries on the main diagonal of this table indicates that the consultant's forecast is correct about 82.25% of the time, overall.

a. Construct the conditional probability table showing the probabilities of the various actual demands given each of the forecasted demands.

b. What is the EMV of the optimal decision without the consultant's assistance?

c. Construct a decision tree that Morley Properties would use to analyze the decision problem if the consultant is hired at a cost of $0.

d. What is the EMV of the optimal decision with the consultant's free assistance?

e. What is the maximum price that Morley Properties should be willing to pay to the consultant?

11. Refer to question 9. Suppose that the utility function for the owner of Morley Properties can be approximated by the exponential utility function:

$$U(x) = 1 - e^{-x/R}$$

where the risk tolerance value $R = 100$ (in $1000s).

a. Convert the payoff matrix to utility values.

b. What decision provides the owner of the company with the largest expected utility?

12. Refer to question 10. Suppose that the consultant's fee is $5,000 and the utility function for the owner of Morley Properties can be approximated by the exponential utility function:

$$U(x) = 1 - e^{-x/R}$$

where the risk tolerance value $R = 100$ (in $1000s).

a. What expected level of utility is realized if Morley Properties hires the consultant?

b. What expected level of utility is realized if Morley Properties does not hire the consultant?

c. Based on this analysis, should Morley Properties hire the consultant?

13. The Tall Oaks Wood Products Company is considering purchasing timberland for $5 million that would provide a future source of timber supply for the company's operations over the next 10 years. Alternatively, for $5 million the company could also buy timber as needed on the open market for an estimated $5 million. The future cash flows from using the timber are estimated to have a present value of $6 million regardless of whether the company buys the timberland today or waits to purchase its timber as needed over the next 10 years. This means that there is a $1 million net present value (NPV) of either buying the timberland now or buying the timber as needed. In other words, from a financial standpoint, the two alternative timber acquisition strategies would be equal. Now suppose that the company believes there is only a 60% chance that the environmental regulations affecting timber supply will remain unchanged. Furthermore, the company believes that there is a 30% chance that these regulations will become stricter during the next 10 years and only a 10% chance that these regulations will be relaxed. A reduction in timber supply should cause an increase in both the present value of future cash flows from using the timber due to higher sales prices and an increase in the present value of the cost of purchasing the timber as needed. (Of course, the change in selling price and buying cost may not be equal.) Should regulations become stricter, the company believes the NPV from buying the timberland now would increase to $1.5 million while in NPV of buying the timber as needed would decrease to -0.50 million. Increases in the timber supply should have the opposite effects. Thus, should regulations become less strict, the company believes the NPV from buying the timberland now would decrease to -0.5 million while the NPV of buying the timber as needed would increase to $1.50 million.

   a. Construct a payoff matrix for this problem.
   b. What decision should be made according to the maximax decision rule?
   c. What decision should be made according to the maximin decision rule?
   d. What decision should be made according to the minimax regret decision rule?
   e. What decision should be made according to the EMV decision rule?
   f. What decision should be made according to the EOL decision rule?
   g. Construct a decision tree for this problem.
14. MicroProducts, Incorporated (MPI) manufactures printed circuit boards for a major PC manufacturer. Before a board is sent to the customer, three key components must be tested. These components can be tested in any order. If any of the components fail, the entire board must be scrapped. The costs of testing the three components are provided in the following table, along with the probability of each component failing the test:

Component	Cost of Test	Probability of Failure
X	$1.75	0.125
Y	$2.00	0.075
Z	$2.40	0.140

   a. Create a decision tree for this problem that could be used to determine the order in which the components should be tested to minimize the expected cost of performing the tests.
   b. In which order should the components be tested?
   c. What is the expected cost of performing the tests in this sequence?
15. Refer to the previous question. A manufacturing engineer for MPI collected the following data on the failure rates of components X, Y, and Z in a random sample of 1,000 circuit boards:

X	Y	Z	Number of Boards
p	p	p	710
p	f	p	45
p	p	f	110
p	f	f	10
f	p	p	95
f	f	p	10
f	p	f	10
f	f	f	10
		Total:	1000

(p=pass, f=fail)

For example, the first row in this table indicates that components X, Y, and Z all passed their inspections in 710 out of the 1,000 boards checked. The second row indicates that 45 boards passed inspection on components X and Z, but failed on component Y. The remaining rows can be interpreted similarly.
   a. Using this data, compute conditional probabilities for the decision tree you developed in question 13. (Note that $P(A \mid B) = P(A \cap B)/P(B)$ and $P(A \mid B \cap C) = P(A \cap B \cap C)/ P(B \cap C)$.)
   b. According to the revised probabilities, in which order should the components be tested?
   c. What is the expected cost of performing the tests in this sequence?
16. Bill and Ted are going to the beach with hopes of having an excellent adventure. Before going, they read a report by the world's leading authority on tiger shark behavior indicating that when a tiger shark is in the vicinity of swimmers at the

beach, there is a 0.20 probability of the shark biting a swimmer. Shortly after arriving at the beach and getting in the water, Bill and Ted spot the unmistakable dorsal fin of a tiger shark on the surface of the water in the vicinity of where they are swimming. Bill says to Ted, "Dude, let's get out of the water, there's a 0.20 probability someone is going to get bitten by that shark." Ted replies to Bill, "You are *way* wrong, man! That probability *could* be zero. Chill out and enjoy the surf, dude."

   a. Show that Ted is correct about the probability. (*Hint:* Consider that $P(A) = P(A \cap B) + P(A \cap \bar{B})$.

   b. Suppose Bill and Ted decide to stay in the water and are bitten by the shark. Was staying in the water a good decision? Was the outcome of the decision good or bad?

   c. Suppose Bill and Ted decide to stay in the water and are not bitten by the shark. Was staying in the water a good decision? Was the outcome of the decision good or bad?

17. The Banisco Corporation is negotiating a contract to borrow $300,000 to be repaid in a lump sum at the end of nine years. Interest payments will be made on the loan at the end of each year. The company is considering the following three financing arrangements:

   • The company can borrow the money using a fixed rate loan (FRL) that requires interest payments of 9% per year.

   • The company can borrow the money using an adjustable rate loan (ARL) that requires interest payments of 6% at the end of each of the first five years. At the beginning of the sixth year, the interest rate on the loan could change to 7%, 9%, or 11% with probabilities of 0.1, 0.25, and 0.65, respectively.

   • The company can borrow the money using an ARL that requires interest payments of 4% at the end of each of the first three years. At the beginning of the fourth year, the interest rate on the loan could change to 6%, 8%, or 10% with probabilities of 0.05, 0.30, and 0.65, respectively. At the beginning of the seventh year, the interest rate could decrease by 1 percentage point with a probability of 0.1, increase by 1 percentage point with a probability of 0.2, or increase by 3 percentage points with a probability of 0.7.

   a. Create a decision tree for this problem, computing the total interest paid under each possible scenario.

   b. Which decision should the company make if it wants to minimize its expected total interest payments?

18. Refer to the previous question. The present value (PV) of a future cash-flow value (FV) is defined as:

$$PV = \frac{FV}{(1 + r)^n}$$

where n is the number of years into the future in which the cash flow occurs and r is the discount rate. Suppose that the discount rate for Banisco is 10% ($r = 0.1$).

   a. Create a decision tree for this problem, computing the PV of the total interest paid under each possible scenario.

   b. Which decision should the company make if it wants to minimize the expected PV of its total interest payments?

19. Southern Gas Company (SGC) is preparing to make a bid for oil and gas leasing right in a newly opened drilling area in the Gulf of Mexico. SGC is trying to decide whether to place a high bid of $16 million or a low bid of $7 million. SGC expects to be bidding against its major competitor, Northern Gas Company (NGC) and predicts NGC to place a bid of $10 million with probability 0.4 or a bid of $6 million with probability 0.6. Geological data collected at the drilling site indicates a 0.15 probability of the reserves at the site being large, a 0.35 probability of being average, and a 0.50 probability of being unusable. A large or average reserve would most

likely represent a net asset value of $120 million or $28 million, respectively, after all drilling and extraction costs are paid. The company that wins the bid will drill an exploration well at the site for a cost of $5 million.

a. Develop a decision tree for this problem.
b. What is the optimal decision according to the EMV criterion?
c. Create a sensitivity table showing how the optimal decision would change if the probability of the NGC bidding $10 million varies from 0% to 100% in steps of 10%.
d. Create a sensitivity table showing how the optimal decision would change if the net asset value of a large reserve varies from $100 million to $140 million in $5 million increments and the net asset value of an average reserve varies from $20 million to $36 million in increments of $2 million.

20. Bulloch County never has allowed liquor to be sold in restaurants. However, in three months, county residents are scheduled to vote on a referendum to allow liquor to be sold by the drink. Currently, polls indicate a 60% chance that the referendum will be passed by voters. Phil Jackson is a local real estate speculator who is eyeing a closed restaurant building that is scheduled to be sold at a sealed bid auction. Phil estimates that if he bids $1.25 million, there is a 25% chance he will obtain the property; if he bids $1.45 million, there is a 45% chance he will obtain the property; and if he bids $1.85 million, there is an 85% chance he will obtain the property. If he acquires the property and the referendum passes, Phil believes he could then sell the restaurant for $2.2 million. However, if the referendum fails, he believes he could sell the property for only $1.15 million.

a. Develop a decision tree for this problem.
b. What is the optimal decision according to the EMV criterion?
c. Create a sensitivity table showing how the optimal decision might change if the probability of the referendum passing varies from 0% to 100% in steps of 10%.
d. To which financial estimate in the decision tree is the EMV most sensitive?

21. Medical studies have shown that 10 out of 100 adults have heart disease. When a person with heart disease is given an EKG test, a 0.9 probability exists that the test will indicate the presence of heart disease. When a person without heart disease is given an EKG test, a 0.95 probability exists that the test will indicate that the person does not have heart disease. Suppose that a person arrives at an emergency room complaining of chest pains. An EKG is given that indicates that the person has heart disease. What is the probability that the person actually has heart disease?

22. The Mobile Oil company has recently acquired oil rights to a new potential source of natural oil in Alaska. The current market value of these rights is $90,000. However, if there is natural oil at the site, it is estimated to be worth $800,000; however, the company would have to pay $100,000 in drilling costs to extract the oil. The company believes there is a 0.25 probability that the proposed drilling site actually would hit the natural oil reserve. Alternatively, the company can pay $30,000 to first carry out a seismic survey at the proposed drilling site. Historically, if the seismic survey produces a favorable result, there is a 0.50 chance of hitting oil at the drilling site. However, if the seismic survey produces an unfavorable result, there is only a 0.14285 probability of hitting oil. The probability of a favorable seismic survey when oil is present at the drilling site is 0.6. The probability of an unfavorable seismic survey when no oil is present is 0.80.

a. What is the probability of a favorable seismic survey?
b. What is the probability of an unfavorable seismic survey?
c. Construct a decision tree for this problem.
d. What is the optimal decision strategy using the EMV criterion?
e. To which financial estimate in the decision tree is the EMV most sensitive?

23. Johnstone & Johnstone (J&J) has developed a new type of hand lotion with a distinctive fragrance. Before distributing it nationally, J&J will test market the new product. The joint probability of a successful test market and high sales upon national distribution is 0.5. The joint probability of a successful test market and low sales nationally is 0.1. The joint probabilities of an unsuccessful test market and either high or low sales are both 0.2.
    a. Use this data to construct a joint probability table.
    b. What is the marginal probability of a successful test market?
    c. What is the conditional probability of high sales given a successful test market?
    d. What is the conditional probability of a successful test market given that the product is destined for high sales nationally?

24. Eagle Credit Union (ECU) has experienced a 10% default rate with its commercial loan customers (i.e., 90% of commercial loan customers pay back their loans). ECU has developed a statistical test to assist in predicting which commercial loan customers will default. The test assigns either a rating of "Approve" or "Reject" to each loan applicant. When applied to recent commercial loan customers who paid their loans, the test gave an "Approve" rating in 80% of the cases examined. When applied to recent commercial loan customers who defaulted, it gave a "Reject" rating in 70% of the cases examined.
    a. Use this data to construct a joint probability table.
    b. What is the conditional probability of a "Reject" rating given that the customer defaulted?
    c. What is the conditional probability of an "Approve" rating given that the customer defaulted?
    d. Suppose a new customer receives a "Reject" rating. If that customer gets the loan anyway, what is the probability of default?

25. From industry statistics, a credit card company knows that 0.8 of its potential card holders are good credit risks and 0.2 are bad credit risks. The company uses discriminant analysis to screen credit card applicants and determine which ones should receive credit cards. The company awards credit cards to 70% of those who apply. The company has found that of those awarded credit cards, 95% turn out to be good credit risks. What is the probability that an applicant who is a bad credit risk will be denied a credit card?

26. Thom DeBusk, an architect, is considering buying, restoring, and reselling a home in the Draper-Preston historic district of Blacksburg, VA. The cost of the home is $240,000 and Thom believes it can be sold for $450,000 after being restored. Thom expects that he can sell the house as soon as the restoration is completed. He expects to pay $1500 a month in finance charges from the time he purchases the house until it is sold. Thom has developed two sets of plans for the restoration. Plan A will cost $125,000 and will require three months to complete. This plan does not require changes to the front of the house. Plan B is expected to cost $85,000 and require four months of work. This plan does involve changes to the front of the house—which will require the approval of the town's historic preservation committee. Thom expects the approval process for plan B to take two months and cost about $5,000. Thom thinks there is a 40% chance that the historic preservation committee will approve this design. Thom plans to buy the home immediately but cannot decide what he should do next. He could proceed immediately with restoration plan A or he could start immediately with restoration plan B. Of course, if he starts immediately with plan B, he will not know for two months whether the historic preservation committee approves of this plan. If they do not approve it, he will have to start over and implement plan A instead. Starting over with plan A would cost an additional $20,000 over plan A's normal cost and would add an additional month to plan

A's normal completion schedule. Alternatively, Thom can hold off implementing either plan until he knows the outcome of the historic planning committee's decision.
   a.   Create a decision tree for this problem.
   b.   What set of decisions should Thom make if he follows the maximum EMV criterion?

27. Suppose that you are given the following two alternatives:

> Alternative 1: Receive $200 with certainty.
> Alternative 2: Receive $1,000 with probability p or
> lose $250 with probability $1 - p$.

   a.   At what value of p would you be indifferent between these two alternatives?
   b.   Given your response to part a, would you be classified as risk averse, risk neutral, or risk seeking?
   c.   Suppose that alternative 2 changed so that you would receive $1,000 with probability p or lose $0 with probability $(1 - p)$. At what value of p would you now be indifferent between these alternatives?
   d.   Given your response to part c, would you be classified as risk averse, risk neutral, or risk seeking?

28. Rusty Reiker is looking for a location to build a new restaurant. He has narrowed the options down to three possible locations. The following table summarizes how he rates each location on the criteria that are most important to his business.

Criterion	Location 1	Location 2	Location 3
Price	0.9	0.7	0.4
Accessibility	0.6	0.7	0.8
Traffic Growth	0.9	0.8	0.7
Competition	0.4	0.5	0.8

Upon reflection, Rusty decides that the weights he would assign to each criterion are as follows: Price 20%, Accessibility 30%, Traffic Growth 20%, and Competition 30%.
   a.   Create a multicriteria scoring model for this problem.
   b.   Create a radar chart showing the weighted scores for each location on each of the criteria.
   c.   According to this model, which location should Rusty purchase?

29. Hiro Tanaka is going to purchase a new car and has narrowed the decision down to three different sedans. The following table summarizes how he rates each sedan on the criteria that are most important to him.

Criterion	Sedan 1	Sedan 2	Sedan 3
Economy	0.9	0.7	0.4
Safety	0.6	0.7	0.8
Reliability	0.9	0.8	0.7
Style	0.4	0.5	0.8
Comfort	0.5	0.8	0.9

Upon reflection, Hiro decides that the weights he would assign to each criterion are as follows: Economy 30%, Safety 15%, Reliability 15%, Style 15%, and Comfort 25%.
   a.   Create a multicriteria scoring model for this problem.
   b.   Create a radar chart showing the weighted scores for each car on each of the criteria.
   c.   According to this model, which car should Hiro purchase?
   d.   Suppose Hiro is uncertain about the weights he assigned to the comfort and safety criteria. If he is willing to trade comfort for safety, how would the solution change?
   e.   Suppose Hiro is uncertain about the weights he assigned to the economy and safety criteria. If he is willing to trade economy for safety, how would the solution change?

30. The president of Pegasus Corporation is trying to decide which of three candidates (denoted as candidates A, B, and C) to hire as the firm's new vice president of Marketing. The primary criteria the president is considering are each candidate's leadership ability, interpersonal skills, and administrative ability. After carefully considering their qualifications, the president used AHP to create the following pairwise comparison matrices for the three candidates on the various criteria:

Leadership Ability

	A	B	C
A	1	3	4
B	1/3	1	2
C	1/4	1/2	1

Interpersonal Skills

	A	B	C
A	1	1/2	3
B	2	1	8
C	1/3	1/8	1

Administrative Ability

	A	B	C
A	1	1/5	1/8
B	5	1	1/3
C	8	3	1

Next, the president of Pegasus considered the relative importance of the three criteria. This resulted in the following pairwise comparison matrix:

	Criteria		
	Leadership Ability	Interpersonal Skills	Administrative Ability
Leadership Ability	1	1/3	1/4
Interpersonal Skills	3	1	1/2
Administrative Ability	4	2	1

a. Use AHP to compute scores for each candidate on each of the three criteria, and to compute weights for each of the criteria.
b. Was the president consistent in making pairwise comparisons?
c. Compute the weighted average score for each candidate. Which candidate should be selected according to your results?

31. Kathy Jones is planning to buy a new minivan but, after narrowing her choices down to three models (X, Y, and Z) within her price range, she is having difficulty deciding which one to buy. Kathy has compared each model against the others on the basis of four criteria: price, safety, economy, and comfort. Her comparisons are summarized as:

Price

	X	Y	Z
X	1	1/4	3
Y	4	1	7
Z	1/3	1/7	1

Safety

	X	Y	Z
X	1	1/2	3
Y	2	1	8
Z	1/3	1/8	1

	Economy				Comfort		
	X	**Y**	**Z**		**X**	**Y**	**Z**
X	1	1/3	1/6	X	1	1/4	1/8
Y	3	1	1/3	Y	4	1	1/3
Z	6	3	1	Z	8	3	1

Kathy wants to incorporate all of these criteria into her final decision, but not all of the criteria are equally important. The following matrix summarizes Kathy's comparisons of the importance of the criteria:

	Criteria			
	Price	**Safety**	**Economy**	**Comfort**
Price	1	1/7	1/2	1/5
Safety	7	1	4	2
Economy	2	1/4	1	1/2
Comfort	5	1/2	2	1

   a. Use AHP to compute scores for each minivan on each of the four criteria, and to compute weights for each of the criteria.

   b. Was Kathy consistent in making pairwise comparisons?

   c. Compute the weighted average score for each minivan. Based on this analysis, which minivan should Kathy buy?

32. Identify a consumer electronics product that you want to purchase (for example, a TV, VCR, camcorder, personal computer, and so on). Identify at least three models of this product that you would consider purchasing. Identify at least three criteria on which these models differ (for example, price, quality, warranty, options).

   a. Create a multicriteria scoring model and radar charts for this decision problem. Using this model, which product would you choose?

   b. Use AHP to determine scores for each model on each of the criteria and to determine weights for the criteria. Which model should you choose according to the AHP results?

CASE 15.1   Hang on or Give Up?

Success or failure as a farmer depends in large part of the uncertainties of the weather during the growing seasons. Consider the following quote from a recent news article:

"... In a summer plagued by drought and heat, many Southern crops are withering in the fields, taking farmers' profits down with them. Some farmers are fighting to break even. But others have had to give up hope that this year's crop will survive to harvest. 'Farmers must decide if they're going to continue to nurture that crop or give up and plow it under,' said George Shumaker, an Extension Service economist with the University of Georgia College of Agricultural and Environmental Sciences. Making that decision takes courage and careful calculation."

Assume that you are a farmer facing the (above) decision of whether or not to plow under your crops. Suppose you already have invested $50 per acre in seed, water, fertilizer, and labor. You estimate that it will require another $15 per acre to produce and harvest a marketable crop. If the weather remains favorable, you estimate that your crop will bring a market price of $26 per acre. However, if the weather becomes unfavorable, you estimate that your crop will bring a market price of $12 per acre. Currently, the weather forecasters are predicting favorable weather conditions with a probability of 0.70. The owner of the farm next to yours (who is growing the same product and has made the same $50 per acre investment) has just decided to plow his fields under because the additional $15 per acre to produce a marketable crop would just be "throwing good money after bad."

a. Develop a decision tree for your decision problem.
b. What is the EMV of harvesting and bringing the crop to market?
c. Would you bring this crop to market or plow it under like your neighbor?
d. By how much would the probability of favorable weather have to change before your answer to the question in part c would change?
e. By how much would the $15 per acre cost of bringing the crop to market have to change before your answer to the question in part c would change?
f. What other factors might you want to consider in making this decision?

Should Larry Junior Go to Court or Settle?

(Inspired from a paper titled "Sex, Lies, and the Hillblom Estate: A Decision Analysis" by Steven Lippman and Kevin McCardle.)

In the mid-1990s, DHL was the world's largest shipping company, with $5.7 billion in revenue and 60,000 employees. Larry Hillblom was the "H" in DHL and founder of the company. DHL started on a shoestring budget in 1969 with a business plan to deliver shipping documents by air courier to ports of call days before cargo ships arrived, so that vessels could be unloaded quickly upon arrival and be on their way. The company grew into an international air courier, making Hillblom a millionaire before he turned 30. While not as famous in the U.S. as Federal Express, overseas DHL is so ubiquitous that its name is synonymous with next-day-air shipping in the same manner that the word "Coke" is used to mean "soft drink."

To avoid U.S. income taxes, Hillblom moved from the San Francisco Bay area to Saipan, a tropical tax haven a thousand miles off the southeast coast of Japan. He became a Micronesian kingpin, launching dozens of businesses and financing land development projects in the Philippines, Hawaii, and Vietnam. He owned European castles and hotels, a Chinese jet, an airline called Continental Micronesia and, in addition to his mansion in Saipan, maintained residences in Manila, Hawaii, and Half Moon Bay. His hobbies included high-end stereo equipment, boats, airplanes, fancy cars and, reportedly, illicit relationships with young Asian girls.

On May 21, 1995, Hillblom and two business associates took off for Saipan in Hillblom's twin-engine seaplane from nearby Pagan Island for a short business trip. Bad weather turned the travelers back and, soon thereafter, dispatchers lost track of the plane. The next morning a search party located parts of the plane and the sodden bodies of Hillblom's companions. Hillblom's body was never found.

Larry Hillblom never married and had no legitimate children. Unfortunately for the Hillblom estate, his will did not contain a clause disinheriting any illegitimate children. Under the prevailing laws, he could have written his children out of the will, but because he didn't, anyone who could prove to be his child would be entitled to an inheritance. Shortly after Hillblom's death, one such child, Larry Junior (age 12), filed suit claiming a share of the estate. (Months after Hillblom's death, several young women emerged from Vietnam, the Philippines, and the Islands of Micronesia claiming that Hillblom had taken up with them briefly and left them with children. See http://dna-view.com/sfstory.htm for additional sordid details.)

Several possible impediments stood in the way of Larry Junior's claim to the Hillblom estate. First, Larry Junior and his attorneys must await the outcome of a proposed law (known as the Hillblom Law) written under serious financial pressure from attorneys for the Hillblom estate. If passed by the legislature and signed by the governor, the proposed law would retroactively invalidate the claims of illegitimate heirs not specifically mentioned in a will. Larry Junior's advisers estimate a 0.60 probability of the proposed law passing. If the law passes, Larry Junior's attorneys plan to challenge its constitutionality and assign a 0.7 probability to this challenge being successful.

If the Hillblom Law does not pass (or passes and is later deemed unconstitutional) Larry Junior will still have to present evidence that he is the son of the deceased Larry Hillblom. Such claims of paternity are routinely proven or disproven using DNA matching. However, Hillblom disappeared without leaving a physical trace. (Twelve gallons of muriatic acid were delivered to Hillblom's house shortly after his death, and by the time Larry Junior's attorneys got there, the house was antiseptically clean.) However, during facial reconstruction surgery following another plane crash that Larry Hillblom had been in and survived, a mole was removed from his face. That mole could be used for DNA testing if Larry Junior's attorneys can gain access to it. But the mole is in possession of a medical center that is the primary beneficiary of the estate under the contested will. Without DNA evidence, the case cannot go forward. Larry Junior's attorney's estimate a 0.8 probability of being able to obtain appropriate DNA evidence in one way or another. If they are able to obtain a DNA sample, the attorneys estimate a 0.7 probability of it proving a biological relation between Larry Junior and the decedent.

If DNA proof of Larry Junior's claimed parentage is established, his attorneys believe the Hillblom estate will offer a settlement of approximately $40 million to avoid going to court. If this settlement offer is rejected, Larry Junior's legal team faces an uncertain outcome in court. His attorneys believe there is a 0.20 chance that their claim could be dismissed by the court (in which case Larry Junior would receive $0). However, even if they are successful in court, the amount of the award to Larry Junior would depend on how many other illegitimate children make successful claims against the estate. Larry Junior's advisors estimate a 0.04 probability that he would win $338 million, a 0.16 probability that he would receive $68 million, a 0.40 probability that he would receive $34 million, and a 0.20 probability that he would receive $17 million.

While vehemently denying that Larry Junior was Mr. Hillblom's son, in early 1996 (and prior to the outcome of the Hillblom Law) the trustees of the Hillblom estate offered Larry Junior a settlement worth approximately $12 million if he would relinquish all his claims to the Hillblom estate. So Larry Junior and his attorneys face a difficult decision. Do they accept the estate's settlement offer or hope the Hillblom Law doesn't pass and that DNA evidence will establish Larry Junior's rightful claim to the Hillblom estate?

a. Create a decision tree for this problem.
b. What decision should Larry Junior make according to the EMV criterion?
c. What is the minimum settlement offer Larry Junior should accept according to the EMV criterion?
d. What would you do if you were Larry Junior?
e. If you were advising Larry Junior, what other issues might you want to consider in making this decision?

The Spreadsheet Wars

Contributed by Jack Yurkiewicz, Lubin School of Business, Pace University, New York.

Sam Ellis is worried. As president and CEO of Forward Software, Sam introduced a new spreadsheet product, Cinco, to the market last year. Forward Software has been developing and marketing high-quality software packages for more than five years, but these products are mostly computer software language interpreters, similar to Pascal, FORTRAN, and C. These products received excellent critical reviews, and because of Forward's aggressive pricing and marketing, the company quickly captured a major share of that software market. Buoyed by its wide acceptance, last year Forward decided to enter the applications arena for the IBM and compatible audience, leading off with Cinco and following up with a word-processing application, Fast.

The spreadsheet market is dominated by Focus Software, whose product—Focus A-B-C—has an 80% market share. Focus A-B-C was released in 1981, shortly after the IBM personal computer (PC) was introduced, and the two products had an immediate symbiotic effect. The spreadsheet was a major advance over what was available at the time, but required the extra 16-bit processing power that the IBM PC offered. IBM, on the other hand, needed an application that would make its PC a "must buy." Sales of Focus A-B-C and the IBM PC took off as a result of their near-simultaneous release.

At the time of its release, Focus A-B-C was a superb product, but it did have flaws. For example, because the software was copy-protected, it could be installed on a hard disk, but the original floppy disk had to be inserted each time before the software could run. Many users found this step an annoyance. Another problem with A-B-C was printing graphs. To print a graph, users had to exit the software and load a new program, called Printgraf, which then would print the graph. Finally, the product had a list price of $495, and the best discounted price available was approximately $300.

However, Focus A-B-C had a unique menu system that was intuitive and easy to use. Pressing the slash key (/) displayed the menu system at the top of the spreadsheet. The menu allowed the user to make choices and provided a one-line explanation of each menu option. Compared to the cryptic commands or keystrokes users had to enter in other products, the Focus A-B-C menu system was a model of simplicity and clarity. Millions of users became accustomed to the menu system and hailed its use.

Another advantage of Focus A-B-C was its ability to let users write their own macros. Literally a program, a macro allowed a user to automate spreadsheet tasks and then run them with a keystroke or two.

In 1985, a small company named Discount Software introduced its own spreadsheet to the market. Called VIP Scheduler, the product looked and worked exactly the same as Focus A-B-C. Pressing the slash key displayed the identical menu as found in Focus A-B-C, and the product could read any macros developed with Focus A-B-C. VIP Scheduler was designed to look and work exactly like Focus A-B-C so that users would not have to learn a new system and could start productive work immediately. VIP Scheduler also offered two advantages over Focus A-B-C: its list price was $99, and the software was not copy-protected. Sales for VIP Scheduler were strong, but many consumers, perhaps feeling safer with the Focus name, did not buy the product, even though critical reviews were positive. VIP Scheduler did find a receptive market in academia.

When Forward released its first spreadsheet product, Cinco, it was hailed by critics as a better all-around product than Focus A-B-C. It had better graphics, allowed users to print graphs from within Cinco, and was 100% compatible with Focus A-B-C. Cinco had its own menu system, which was as flexible as the Focus A-B-C system, but the menus and options were arranged more intuitively. For users who did not want to invest the time to learn a new menu system, Cinco could emulate the Focus A-B-C menu system. Both menus were activated by pressing the slash key, and users could specify easily which menu system they wanted. All macros written for Focus A-B-C ran perfectly on Cinco, provided that the Focus A-B-C menu system was being used. Because of favorable reviews and aggressive marketing by Forward, Cinco quickly gained market share.

In a move that surprised the industry, Focus recently sued Discount Software, publisher of VIP Scheduler, for copyright infringement. Focus claimed that its menu system was an original work, and that VIP Scheduler, by incorporating that menu system in its product, had violated copyright laws. Focus claimed that the look and feel of its menu system could not be used in another product without permission. Sam is certain that Focus initiated this lawsuit because Cinco has made such dramatic progress in gaining a share of the spreadsheet market. Sam also is sure that Focus's target is not really VIP Scheduler, because it has such a small market share, but Cinco.

After discussions with Forward's attorneys, Sam thinks that if he makes a quiet overture to Focus to settle out of court, Focus would be amenable to such a proposal. This would stave off potential negative publicity if Focus wins its suit against Discount Software and then follows up with a lawsuit against Forward. Based on projections of Cinco's sales, Forward's attorneys think that Focus could ask for $5, $8, or even $15 million in damages. Sam believes that the probability of Focus agreeing to $5 million is 50%, $8 million is 30%, and $15 million is 20%.

Sam knows that settling now means an immediate loss of income, in the amount of one of the three estimates given, plus an admission of defeat and guilt for Forward. On the other hand, Sam could wait for the outcome of the Focus versus Discount Software unit. Forward's attorneys believe that Focus has a 40% chance of winning its lawsuit against Discount Software. With a win, Focus would have its legal precedent to sue Forward. It is by no means certain that Focus would institute a lawsuit against Forward because Forward is a much larger company than Discount Software and could afford a vigorous legal defense. Also the case against Forward is not as clear–cut, because Cinco has its own menu system as the primary mode of operation and offers the Focus A-B-C menu system for those who want to use it. VIP Scheduler provides only the Focus A-B-C menu system. However, Forward's attorneys believe there is an 80% chance that Focus would initiate a lawsuit against Forward if Focus wins its suit against Discount Software.

Sam believes that even if Focus sues Forward, he could still try to settle the case out of court at that time or decide to go to trial. An attempt to settle out of court at that time would be more expensive for Forward because Focus would feel secure that it would win its case against Forward, already having won its lawsuit against Discount Software. Thus, Forward's attorneys think that Focus would settle for no less than $7 million, possibly asking for $10 million or even $12 million. The respective probabilities that Focus would settle for these amounts ($7, $10, and $12 million) are estimated to be 30%, 40%, and 30%. Also, Forward would have to pay its attorneys roughly $1 million to go through the settling process.

However, if Focus sues Forward and Forward decides to go to trial instead of initiating settlement proceedings, Forward could lose the case. Forward's attorneys estimate there is an 80% chance that Forward would lose the trial, resulting in a judgment of either $10 million, $12 million, or $18 million against Forward, with probabilities of 10%, 20%, and 70%, respectively. The attorneys also estimate that their fees for a trial could reach $1.5 million.

Use decision analysis to determine what Sam's optimal strategy should be. Create the decision tree for this problem, including all costs and probabilities, and find the optimal decision strategy and expected cost for that strategy. Consider Sam to be "risk neutral" in this analysis.